Lecture Notes in Computer Science 1378
Edited by G. Goos, J. Hartmanis and J. van Leeuwen

Springer
Berlin
Heidelberg
New York
Barcelona
Budapest
Hong Kong
London
Milan
Paris
Santa Clara
Singapore
Tokyo

Maurice Nivat (Ed.)

Foundations of Software Science and Computation Structures

First International Conference, FoSSaCS'98
Held as Part of the Joint European Conferences on Theory and Practice of Software, ETAPS'98
Lisbon, Portugal, March 28 – April 4, 1998
Proceedings

Springer

Series Editors

Gerhard Goos, Karlsruhe University, Germany
Juris Hartmanis, Cornell University, NY, USA
Jan van Leeuwen, Utrecht University, The Netherlands

Volume Editor

Maurice Nivat
LITP, Université Paris 7
2, Place Jussieu, F-75251 Paris Cedex 05, France
E-mail: Maurice.Nivat@litp.liafa.jussieu.fr

Cataloging-in-Publication data applied for

Die Deutsche Bibliothek - CIP-Einheitsaufnahme

Foundations of software science and computation structures : first international conference ; proceedings / FoSSaCS '98, held as part of the Joint European Conferences on Theory and Practice of Software, ETAPS '98, Lisbon, Portugal, March 28 - April 4, 1998. Maurice Nivat (ed.). - Berlin ; Heidelberg ; New York ; Barcelona ; Budapest ; Hong Kong ; London Milan ; Paris ; Santa Clara ; Singapore ; Tokyo : Springer, 1998
(Lecture notes in computer science ; Vol. 1378)
ISBN 3-540-64300-1

CR Subject Classification (1991): F.3. F.4.2, F.1.1, D.3.3-4, D.2.1

ISSN 0302-9743
ISBN 3-540-64300-1 Springer-Verlag Berlin Heidelberg New York

Typesetting: Camera-ready by author
SPIN 10631968 06/3142 – 5 4 3 2 1 0 Printed on acid-free paper

Foreword

The European conference situation in the general area of software science has long been considered unsatisfactory. A fairly large number of small and medium-sized conferences and workshops take place on an irregular basis, competing for high-quality contributions and for enough attendees to make them financially viable. Discussions aiming at a consolidation have been underway since at least 1992, with concrete planning beginning in summer 1994 and culminating in a public meeting at TAPSOFT'95 in Aarhus.

On the basis of a broad consensus, it was decided to establish a single annual federated spring conference in the slot that was then occupied by TAPSOFT and CAAP/ESOP/CC, comprising a number of existing and new conferences and covering a spectrum from theory to practice. ETAPS'98, the first instance of the European Joint Conferences on Theory and Practice of Software, is taking place this year in Lisbon. It comprises five conferences (FoSSaCS, FASE, ESOP, CC, TACAS), four workshops (ACoS, VISUAL, WADT, CMCS), seven invited lectures, and nine tutorials.

The events that comprise ETAPS address various aspects of the system development process, including specification, design, implementation, analysis and improvement. The languages, methodologies and tools which support these activities are all well within its scope. Different blends of theory and practice are represented, with an inclination towards theory with a practical motivation on one hand and soundly-based practice on the other. Many of the issues involved in software design apply to systems in general, including hardware systems, and the emphasis on software is not intended to be exclusive.

ETAPS is a natural development from its predecessors. It is a loose confederation in which each event retains its own identity, with a separate programme committee and independent proceedings. Its format is open-ended, allowing it to grow and evolve as time goes by. Contributed talks and system demonstrations are in synchronized parallel sessions, with invited lectures in plenary sessions. Two of the invited lectures are reserved for "unifying" talks on topics of interest to the whole range of ETAPS attendees. The aim of cramming all this activity into a single one-week meeting is to create a strong magnet for academic and industrial researchers working on topics within its scope, giving them the opportunity to learn about research in related areas, and thereby to foster new and existing links between work in areas that have hitherto been addressed in separate meetings.

ETAPS'98 has been superbly organized by José Luis Fiadeiro and his team at the Department of Informatics of the University of Lisbon. The ETAPS steering committee has put considerable energy into planning for ETAPS'98 and its successors. Its current membership is:

André Arnold (Bordeaux), Egidio Astesiano (Genova), Jan Bergstra (Amsterdam), Ed Brinksma (Enschede), Rance Cleaveland (Raleigh), Pierpaolo Degano (Pisa), Hartmut Ehrig (Berlin), José Fiadeiro (Lisbon), Jean-Pierre Finance (Nancy), Marie-Claude Gaudel (Paris), Tibor

Gyimothy (Szeged), Chris Hankin (London), Stefan Jähnichen (Berlin), Uwe Kastens (Paderborn), Paul Klint (Amsterdam), Kai Koskimies (Tampere), Tom Maibaum (London), Hanne Riis Nielson (Aarhus), Fernando Orejas (Barcelona), Don Sannella (Edinburgh, chair), Bernhard Steffen (Dortmund), Doaitse Swierstra (Utrecht), Wolfgang Thomas (Kiel)

Other people were influential in the early stages of planning, including Peter Mosses (Aarhus) and Reinhard Wilhelm (Saarbrücken). ETAPS'98 has received generous sponsorship from:

Portugal Telecom
TAP Air Portugal
the Luso-American Development Foundation
the British Council
the EU programme "Training and Mobility of Researchers"
the University of Lisbon
the European Association for Theoretical Computer Science
the European Association for Programming Languages and Systems
the Gulbenkian Foundation

I would like to express my sincere gratitude to all of these people and organizations, and to José in particular, as well as to Springer-Verlag for agreeing to publish the ETAPS proceedings.

Edinburgh, January 1998

Donald Sannella
ETAPS Steering Committee chairman

Preface

The conference FoSSaCS, Foundations of Software Science and Computation Structures was not created ex nihilo: For 20 years the same group of people has been organizing a conference called CAAP, Colloque sur les Arbres en Algèbre et en Programmation, whose french acronym is explained by the fact that it was created in France at Lille and held more frequently in France than in any other country. The last CAAP took place in Lille in April 1997.

The fact that FoSSaCS appears as part of ETAPS, linked to conferences dedicated to more applied aspects of computer science is not new either: Every two years, CAAP used to join with the conference TAPSOFT, a conference on programming, to form a series of joint conferences which were initiated in Berlin and ended last year also in Lille. The reorganization which led to the new name FoSSaCS and the inclusion of FoSSaCS into ETAPS has been discussed at length by many people including a majority of past organizers and PC chairmen of the former CAAP. The idea which was eventually shared by all is that while remaining a conference for theorists and, say, mathematically trained and minded people, FoSSaCS should focus on the part of theoretical computer science that aims at modeling and understanding phenonema linked with the design and validation of software and descibes and studies structures useful to run actual and effective computations.

Our hope is that not only theoretical computer scientists find some interest in the present collection of 19 papers but also more applied ones. We hope that since participants to the various components of ETAPS will be gathered for one week in Lisbon, some who came for other conferences will listen to talks presented in FoSSaCS and some FoSSaCS participants will listen to talks in the other conferences.

Personally, as chairman of the pogram committee of FoSSaCS 1998, I would like to thank the PC members for agreeing to stand in the committee, for their evaluation work, and for helping to select these contributions from the 44 submitted papers. The discussion which led to this choice, which was also a discussion on what FoSSaCS should be and what kind of theories and formalisms are useful to software researchers and engineers, was a courteous, vigorous, and enriching one where each participant made use of good purely scientific arguments. Among the members of the PC, I wish to mention the special role played by André Arnold and Wolfgang Thomas who are also the 2 theoreticians in the steering committee of ETAPS.

January 1998 Maurice Nivat

Table of Contents

Generalizing Domain Theory
Michael Mislove 1

A Cook's Tour of Equational Axiomatizations for Prefix Iteration
Luca Aceto, Wan Fokkink, and Anna Ingólfsdóttir 20

The WHILE Hierarchy of Program Schemes Is Infinite
Can Adam Albayrak and Thomas Noll 35

Analysis of a Guard Condition in Type Theory
Roberto M. Amadio and Solange Coupet-Grimal 48

An Event Structure Semantics of P/T Contextual Nets: Asymmetric Event Structures
Paolo Baldan, Andrea Corradini, and Ugo Montanari 63

Pumping Lemmas for Timed Automata
Danièle Beauquier 81

Asynchronous Observations of Processes
Michele Boreale, Rocco De Nicola, and Rosario Pugliese 95

Minor Searching, Normal Forms of Graph Relabelling: Two Applications Based on Enumerations by Graph Relabelling
Anne Bottreau and Yves Métivier 110

Partial Metrics and Co-continuous Valuations
Michael A. Bukatin and Svetlana Yu. Shorina 125

Mobile Ambients
Luca Cardelli and Andrew D. Gordon 140

Rational Term Rewriting
Andrea Corradini and Fabio Gadducci 156

The Appearance of Big Integers in Exact Real Arithmetic Based on Linear Fractional Transformations
Reinhold Heckmann 172

Net Refinement by Pullback Rewriting
Renate Klempien-Hinrichs 189

On Piecewise Testable, Starfree, and Recognizable Picture Languages
Oliver Matz 203

Functor Categories and Two-Level Languages
Eugenio Moggi 211

Deciding Properties for Message Sequence Charts
Anca Muscholl, Doron Peled, and Zhendong Su 226

The Church-Rosser Languages Are the Deterministic Variants of the Growing Context-Sensitive Languages
Gundula Niemann and Friedrich Otto 243

Deterministic Rational Transducers and Random Sequences
Sylvain Porrot, Max Dauchet, Bruno Durand, and Nikolai K. Vereshchagin 258

Resource Based Models for Asynchrony
Julian Rathke 273

Author Index 289

Generalizing Domain Theory

Michael Mislove*

Tulane University, New Orleans, LA 70118, USA
e-mail: `mwm@math.tulane.edu`
WWW home page: `http://www.math.tulane.edu/mislove.html`

Abstract. Domain theory began in an attempt to provide mathematical models for high-level programming languages, an area where it has proved to be particularly useful. It is perhaps the most widely-used method for devising semantic models for such languages. This paper is a survey of some generalizations of domain theory that have arisen in efforts to solve related problems. In each case, a description is given of the problem and of the solution generalizing domain theory it inspired. The problems range from the relation of domain theory to other approaches for providing semantic models, particularly in process algebra, to issues surrounding the notion of a computational model, an approach inspired by the recent work of Abbas Edalat.

1 The Basics – How Domain Theory Began

This section is a brief outline of some of the "basic ingredients" of domain theory and the applications that inspired them.

1.1 *In the beginning...*

Domain theory began in an attempt by DANA SCOTT to find mathematical models for high-level programming languages. Upon his arrival in Oxford in the mid 1960s, Scott found CHRISTOPHER STRACHEY and his colleagues at the Programming Research Group using the untyped lambda calculus of Church and Curry as a model for programming, something Scott found disturbing because he regarded it as a "formal and unmotivated" notation (cf. [11]). He thus set out to find alternative models for Strachey and his colleagues to use. Because programs can call other programs, and indeed, can even call themselves, Scott was led to consider objects X in some category or other which satisfy the property that they contain a copy of their space of selfmaps in the category. Of course, Cantor's Lemma implies the only such objects in the category of sets and functions are *degenerate* (i.e., they consist of a single point), and so no such objects can be found there. But the reals have only as many continuous selfmaps as there are real numbers (because of their having a dense, countable subset on which all continuous selfmaps are completely determined), so it is potentially

* This work partially supported by the US Office of Naval Research

possible to find such objects X among topological spaces. While attempting to find appropriate models of partially defined maps, Scott realized there had to be T_0 spaces isomorphic to their space of continuous selfmaps, and he then constructed such an object in the category of algebraic lattices and so-called *Scott continuous* maps.

In the years since Scott constructed the first model of the untyped lambda calculus, the nature of the construction has become much better understood, and it now is realized that very little of the machinery that is available in the category of algebraic lattices and Scott continuous maps actually is necessary for the construction. In fact, it now is understood that only *directed complete partial orders* are needed to carry out the construction. Remarkably, despite this much better understanding, the only known models of the calculus are within the category of such partial orders and Scott continuous functions. We now describe this setting.

1.2 Directed Complete Partial Orders

Let's switch gears for a moment, and consider what we need to model a recursive process. If we are working within some language – let's not worry about typing issues – and we are confronted with a term $\mathbf{rec}\, x.f(x)$, then the operational rule which allows us to understand this process is given by

$$\mathbf{rec}\, x.f(x) \mapsto f[(\mathbf{rec}\, x.f(x))/x].$$

This *unwinding* of recursion allows us to deduce that the recursive process $\mathbf{rec}\, x.f(x)$ actually should be a *fixed point* for the body of the recursion. In any case, if we are to model programs as functions, then the unwinding rule tells us the functions we are interested in must have fixed points. In fact, it would be nice if those fixed points were *canonical* in some sense, so that their choice is not arbitrary. This is what domain theory offers us.

To begin, a *partial order* (or *poset*) is a non-empty set P equipped with a reflexive, symmetric and transitive relation, usually denoted $\sqsubseteq$. A simple example is to take any non-empty set X and equip it with the *discrete order*, where $x \sqsubseteq y \Leftrightarrow x = y$. A subset $D \subseteq P$ of such a set is *directed* if every finite subset of D has an upper bound *in* D. In our example, the only directed subsets are the singleton sets. Finally, a partial order P is *directed complete* if every directed subset has a least upper bound in P. These are called *dcpos*. Clearly, discrete orders satisfy this condition, since the only directed subsets are singleton sets. A directed complete partial order which has a least element $\perp$ (i.e., one which is below all other elements) is sometimes called a *cpo*.

What is important about cpos is that monotone[1] selfmaps have *least fixed points*:

Theorem 1 (Tarski). *A monotone mapping $f: P \to P$ of a cpo has a least fixed point, namely,*

$$\mathrm{FIX}\, f = \sqcup_{\alpha \in \mathrm{Ord}} f^{\alpha}(\perp). \qquad \square$$

[1] A map $f: P \to Q$ is *monotone* if $x \sqsubseteq y \implies f(x) \sqsubseteq f(y)$.

(Here, Ord stands for the class of ordinals.) Thus, a good place to seek models for recursion is within the category of cpos and monotone mappings. But, if we require our functions to preserve sups of directed sets, we can do better.

Definition 1. *A mapping $f: P \to Q$ between dcpos is* Scott continuous *if f is monotone*[2] *and f preserves sups of directed sets:*

$$(\forall D \subseteq P \text{ directed})\ f(\sqcup D) = \sqcup f(D).$$

Corollary 1 (Scott). *A Scott continuous selfmap $f: P \to P$ on a cpo has its least fixed point given by*

$$\mathrm{FIX}\, f = \sqcup_{n \in \mathbf{N}} f^n(\bot).$$ □

The category of directed complete partial orders and Scott continuous maps has many desirable properties – it is Cartesian closed, for example. We denote the family of continuous maps between (d)cpos P and Q by $[P \to Q]$; this space becomes a dcpo when endowed with the *pointwise order*, in which

$$f \sqsubseteq g \quad \Leftrightarrow \quad f(x) \sqsubseteq g(x)\ (\forall x \in P).$$

The full subcategory whose objects are cpos also is Cartesian closed, and it is within these categories where one can find ample support for constructing denotational models of programming languages. We even can conclude more here. Since the least fixed point of a monotone or continuous selfmap always exists, assigning it as the meaning of a recursive process is in some sense canonical. In fact,

Theorem 2. *The least fixed point operator* $\mathrm{Y}: [P \to P] \to P$ *by* $\mathrm{Y} f = \mathrm{FIX}\, f$ *is continuous.* □

The implication here is that one has continuous fixed point operators of all orders, so modeling recursion at higher types can be done in the same way it is at the start. There is even a *transfer principle* available; it tells us that "fixed points are preserved" by certain operators:

Proposition 1. *Let $f: P \to P$ and $g: Q \to Q$ be continuous selfmaps of cpos P and Q, and let $h: P \to Q$ also be a continuous strict*[3] *map satisfying $g \circ h = h \circ f$. Then* $\mathrm{FIX}\, g = h(\mathrm{FIX}\, f)$. □

The categories DCPO and CPO of directed complete partial orders (with least element in the second case) and Scott continuous maps thus enjoy several appealing properties. In addition to Cartesian closure, they also are closed under (arbitrary) products and direct sums. In addition, there is a closely-related adjunction. If $\mathsf{CPO}_!$ denotes the category of cpos and strict Scott continuous maps, then the forgetful functor into DCPO has the *lift functor* as left adjoint; this functor adds a (new) least element to a dcpo P and extends a continuous mapping to the lifted domains to be strict.

[2] This hypothesis is simply to guarantee that the image of a directed set in P is directed in Q.

[3] By *strict*, we mean h takes the least element of P to the least element of Q.

1.3 The Myhill-Sheperdson Theorem

The results described so far make an appealing, if somewhat abstract case for using domain theory to build models for programming languages – well, at least for modeling recursion. We now describe a result which puts more substance to this claim.

Perhaps the most natural place to start to model programs is over the natural numbers. In order to invoke a domain-theoretic setting, we can endow N with the discrete order, and clearly we have a dcpo. Our interest is in using domain theory to model computable functions. Functions on N are mappings $f: \mathbb{N} \to \mathbb{N}$, so we want to ***start*** with the cpo $[\mathbb{N} \to \mathbb{N}]$. This is not quite right, either. Church's thesis says the ***partial recursives*** are the computable functions, and so we should consider partial mappings $f: \mathbb{N} \rightharpoonup \mathbb{N}$. Now, the family of such mappings – $[\mathbb{N} \rightharpoonup \mathbb{N}]$ – is a cpo under the *extensional ordering:*

$$f \sqsubseteq g \quad \Leftrightarrow \quad \mathrm{dom}\, f \subseteq \mathrm{dom}\, g \;\&\; g|_{\mathrm{dom}\, f} = f.$$

Here, a directed family of partial mappings has for its supremum the union of the family. Two convenient facts are that any function from N to itself is monotone – even continuous – with respect to the discrete order, and the extensional order on the space of mappings between two discretely ordered sets is in fact the pointwise order. Thus, the partial mappings on N with the extensional order are just the partial mappings endowed with the pointwise order from the discrete order on N.

But how do we distinguish the partial recursives from arbitrary partial self-maps of N? A simple and *very* well-worn example shows how. Consider the factorial function

$$\mathrm{Fac}(n) = \begin{cases} 1 & \text{if } n = 0, \\ n \cdot \mathrm{Fac}(n-1) & \text{otherwise.} \end{cases}$$

This leads us to define a ***functional*** $F: [\mathbb{N} \rightharpoonup \mathbb{N}] \to [\mathbb{N} \rightharpoonup \mathbb{N}]$ by

$$F(f)(m) = \begin{cases} 1 & \text{if } m = 0 \\ m \cdot f(m-1) & \text{if } m > 0 \;\&\; f(m-1) \text{ defined.} \end{cases}$$

It is easy to show that this functional is continuous (it only needs to preserve increasing unions of partial functions), and that its least fixed point is the factorial. What is harder is the fact that the effective structure (in the sense of recursion theory) on N can be extended to one on $[\mathbb{N} \rightharpoonup \mathbb{N}] \to [\mathbb{N} \rightharpoonup \mathbb{N}]$ (using ideas from the next section – see [26] for details), and F can be shown to be effective with respect to this structure. This means F's restriction to the partial recursives leaves them invariant; i.e., $F(g)$ is partial recursive if g is. If we let $[\mathbb{N} \rightharpoonup \mathbb{N}]_k$ denote the computable mappings on the natural numbers (i.e., the partial recursives), the following says every partial recursive arises exactly in this way:

Theorem 3 (Myhill-Sheperdson). *The effective operators on* $[\mathbb{N} \rightharpoonup \mathbb{N}]_k$ *are exactly the restrictions of the the effective continuous functionals* $G: [\mathbb{N} \rightharpoonup \mathbb{N}] \to [\mathbb{N} \rightharpoonup \mathbb{N}]$ *to* $[\mathbb{N} \rightharpoonup \mathbb{N}]_k$. □

1.4 Algebraicity and Continuity

A second component of domain theory – apart from the ease with which one can model recursion – is that of *approximation*. The idea is illustrated by the Myhill-Sheperdson Theorem. For any continuous functional $G: [\mathbb{N} \rightharpoonup \mathbb{N}] \to [\mathbb{N} \rightharpoonup \mathbb{N}]$, the least fixed point $\mathrm{FIX}\, G = \sqcup_{n \in \mathbb{N}} G^n(\emptyset)$, since $\emptyset$ is the least partial function. In the case of G is effective, $G^n(\emptyset)$ is a finite function. The finite functions play a special role in $[\mathbb{N} \rightharpoonup \mathbb{N}]$: they are the *compact* elements.

Definition 2. *An element $k \in P$ in a dcpo is* compact *if $k \sqsubseteq \sqcup D$ implies $(\exists d \in D)\, k \sqsubseteq d$ for all directed subsets $D \subseteq P$. The set of compact elements of P is denoted $K(P)$, and, for each $x \in P$ the set of compact elements below x is denoted $K(x)$.*

Lastly, P is algebraic *if $K(x)$ is directed and $x = \sqcup K(x)$ for every $x \in P$.*

Since any partial mapping $f: \mathbb{N} \rightharpoonup \mathbb{N}$ satisfies

$$f = \sqcup\{f|_X \mid X \subseteq \mathrm{dom}\, f \text{ finite}\},$$

$[\mathbb{N} \rightharpoonup \mathbb{N}]$ is algebraic.

The compact elements of an algebraic dcpo completely determine the dcpo, since each element of the dcpo is the directed supremum of the compact elements below it. This association can be made more precise. Indeed, if we call a subset $I \subseteq Q$ of a partially ordered set an *ideal* if $I = \downarrow I$ is a lower set which also is directed, then we have the association $x \mapsto K(x): P \to \mathrm{Idl}K(P)$ which sends each element of P to the ideal of compact elements below it. This association is an isomorphism, where the inverse mapping simply sends an ideal to its supremum (which exists because P is a dcpo). Hence, $P \simeq \mathrm{Idl}K(P)$ for each algebraic dcpo P. This gives rise to an adjunction between the category ALG of algebraic dcpos and Scott continuous maps and the category POS of posets and monotone mappings. The right adjoint is the forgetful functor from ALG to POS, and the left adjoint is the ideal functor, which sends a partially ordered set to its family of ideals ordered under inclusion. One of the important consequences of this adjunction is that each continuous mapping $f: P \to Q$ between algebraic dcpos is completely determined by the restriction of f to the compact elements of P, and, conversely, each monotone mapping $f: K(P) \to Q$ from the compact elements of P to any dcpo Q extends to a unique continuous map from P to Q.

All of this has an important extension. The motivating example is the unit interval, which has 0 as its only compact element. Yet there is a clear notion of approximation here: if $x < y$, then for a directed set to have its supremum above y, some element of the directed set must be above x.

Definition 3. *The elements $x, y \in P$ in a dcpo satisfy $x \ll y$ (read "x is* relatively compact in *y") if $y \sqsubseteq \sqcup D$ implies there is some $d \in D$ with $x \sqsubseteq d$, for all directed subsets D of P. The set of elements relatively compact in y is denoted $\Downarrow y$, and the dcpo P is called* continuous *if $\Downarrow y$ is directed and $y = \sqcup \Downarrow y$ or all $y \in P$.*

An adjunction similar to the one between **ALG** and **POS** is available for continuous dcpos. It involves the notion of an *abstract basis* originally due to SMYTH [21].

Definition 4. *An* abstract basis *is a non-empty set X equipped with a transitive relation $\prec$ which satisfies the* interpolation property*:*

$$(\forall y \in X)(\forall M \subseteq X \text{ finite})\; M \prec y \quad \Rightarrow \quad (\exists x \in X)\; M \prec x \prec y.$$

A function $f\colon X \to Y$ between abstract bases is ideal *if $x \prec y$ in X implies that $\{z \in Y \mid z \prec f(x)\} \subseteq \{z \in Q \mid z \prec f(y)\}$.*

For example, in any continuous dcpo P, the pair $(P, \ll)$ is an abstract basis. Any abstract basis satisfies the property that the family of ideals (defined just as in the partially ordered set case) is a continuous dcpo under the inclusion order. The notion of an ideal mapping is designed precisely to capture those functions between abstract bases which extend to continuous mappings between their ideal completions. The following result generalizes the situation for algebraic domains.

Theorem 4 ([17]). *The functor which associates to a continuous dcpo P the abstract basis $(P, \ll)$ and to a continuous mapping $f\colon P \to Q$ the ideal mapping $f(I) = \{y \in Q \mid (\exists z \in I)\, y \ll f(z)\}$ is right adjoint to the ideal functor which associates to an abstract basis its ideal completion and to an ideal mapping the associated continuous mapping on the space of ideals.* □

Notes: This completes our rather cursory outline of domain theory. We have left out far more than we have included, but our intention is to provide only the barest of introductions to motivate the generalizations that we describe below.

We have not made specific reference to any result. Except for the last results on continuous dcpos (which can be found in [2] for the most part), most of this is folklore now, and can be found in many places. Again, [2] is an excellent source for referencing most of these results. The last theorem, however, appears only in [17]. A survey of a number of the ideas presented here can be found in [18].

2 Continuous Posets

A rather successful approach to modeling concurrent computation was devised by the members of the Programming Research Group at Oxford using the language CSP. We briefly outline this approach below, with an eye toward finding the relationship between the CSP models and more standard ones from domain theory. In endeavoring to understand this relationship, it became clear that one of the fundamental principles of domain theory had to be relaxed in order to describe the CSP models in purely domain-theoretic terms. That fundamental property of dcpos is that they are *directed complete*: all directed subsets have least upper bounds. This property is crucial in assuring that all continuous self-maps have (least) fixed points. But it turns out that describing the CSP models in domain-theoretic terms requires relaxing this condition in order to relate the models to the world of domains. The model we focus on for this discussion is the *failures model* for CSP, which we now describe.

2.1 CSP and the Failures Model

CSP is a process algebra for reasoning about concurrent processes. It was originally devised by C. A. R. HOARE and the first, definitive model for the language was presented in [3]. This is the so-called *failures model*, which models a process in terms of the communication events it can participate in (the *traces* of the process) together with the events it may refuse to participate in after a given trace (the so-called *refusals*). A syntax for CSP suitable for our purposes is given by the following BNF-like production rules:

$$P ::= STOP \mid SKIP \mid a \to P \mid P \setminus a \mid P;P \mid P_A\|_B P \mid P\Box P \mid P \sqcap P \mid x \mid \mu x.P$$

In this syntax, *STOP* denotes immediate abnormal termination, while *SKIP* denotes immediate normal termination. The actions a range over a set Σ of atomic actions which denote communication events between processes; $a \to P$ is a process which first wishes to participate in the action a and then to act like process P. $P \setminus a$ is the process P with all occurrences of the action a hidden from the environment (but they still occur, and as soon as they are offered). $P;P$ is the sequential composition of the two component processes; $P_A\|_B P$ is the process which has the two components synchronize on all actions in $A \cap B$ $(A, B \subseteq \Sigma)$, but either branch is free to perform actions not in the intersection whenever it wishes. $P\Box P$ is the *external choice* of the two processes, in which the environment is allowed to decide which branch will be chosen on the first action only, while $P \sqcap P$ is the *internal choice* of the branches, in which the machine decides. The term x denotes a process variable, and the last term is recursion.

The failures model for CSP as presented, e.g., in [3] gives a model for this language based of pairs (s, X), where $s \in \Sigma^* \cup \Sigma^* \surd$ is a finite sequence of actions, possibly ending in the normal termination event $\surd \notin \Sigma$, and $X \subseteq \Sigma$ is a set of *refusals* – events which the process may refuse to participate in after execution of s. The second component is needed in the model in order to distinguish internal and external choice. The failures model $\mathcal{FM}$ interprets each process as a set of such pairs, and the sets F that qualify to represent a process in CSP must satisfy the following conditions:

1. $\emptyset \neq F$.
2. $(s, X) \in F$ and t a prefix of s imply $(t, \emptyset) \in F$.
3. $(s, X) \in F$ and $Y \subseteq X$ imply $(s, Y) \in F$.
4. $(s, X) \in F$ and $(s\langle c\rangle, \emptyset) \notin F$ for all $c \in Y \subseteq A$ finite imply $(s, X \cup Y) \in F$.

The sets satisfying these conditions are called the *failures model* for CSP; it is shown in [3] that they form a complete inf-semilattice. This structure is used as the basis for showing this family of sets can be endowed with operations corresponding to each of the CSP operators. This allows an interpretation of CSP in the set of subsets of $(\Sigma^* \cup \Sigma^* \surd) \times \mathcal{P}(\Sigma)$ satisfying 1) – 4) – i.e., it provides the ingredients to show the family $\mathcal{FM}$ is a denotational model for CSP.

The order on the failures model is *reverse containment* on sets. So, the smaller the set, the higher it is in the order. Because the inf-operation is used to model nondeterminism, the order on the model is the order of nondeterminism – the higher a set, the more deterministic the process it represents. In fact, the maximal elements of the model are the deterministic processes. These have the property that they cannot be refined by any other process.

The order on the model also is used to model recursion, just as in the case of cpos. All the operators from CSP are modeled by operations on the model that are continuous with respect to reverse inclusion, and so Scott's corollary to Tarski's Theorem implies that each of the recursive processes can be modeled as the least fixed point of a continuous operator on the model.

2.2 The Failures Model as Closed Sets

All of the above indicates that the failures model is a cpo (the least element of the model is the set $CHAOS = \{(s, X) \mid s \in \Sigma^* \cup \Sigma^*\surd \;\&\; X \subseteq \Sigma\}$). But the construction is far from "standard", and it is unclear what relationship this model has to languages other than CSP. The work in [15] resulted from an effort to better understand this relationship. The analysis relies on a closer scrutiny of the properties that define failures sets.

The first three conditions imply that the sets F that qualify as process meanings are lower sets from some related partial order, and it was this idea that led to a realization that the conditions listed actually describe certain closed sets from a partial order. By *closed*, we mean closed with respect to the Scott topology, which we now define. But notice that we relax the situation somewhat, and consider *any* partial order, not just ones that are directed complete. This is because the partial order that gives rise to the failures model is not directed complete.

Definition 5. *Let P be a partially ordered set. A subset $U \subseteq P$ is Scott open if*

1. $U = \uparrow U = \{y \in P \mid (\exists x \in U)\; x \sqsubseteq y\}$ *is an upper set in P, and*
2. $\sqcup D \in U \implies D \cap U \neq \emptyset$ *for all directed subsets D of P.*

It is routine to show that the Scott open sets on any partial order are closed under finite intersections and arbitrary unions, so they do indeed form a topology. This topology is always T_0, which means distinct points can be separated by some open set (containing exactly one of them), but the topology is Hausdorff if and only if the partial order is the discrete order. What is more, the functions we defined earlier as being Scott continuous are in fact exactly those that are continuous with respect to this topology.

The Scott closed sets are those whose complements are Scott open, and since we have a description of the latter, we can derive the following characterization of the former.

Proposition 2. *$X \subseteq P$ is Scott closed if and only if*

1. $X = \downarrow X$ *is a lower set in P, and*

2. $D \subseteq X$ directed implies $\sqcup D \in X$. □

Notice that a corollary of this result is that the closure of a point $x \in P$ is $\downarrow x$, the principal lower set x defines. This is what makes Scott-closed sets an appealing model for concurrent computation – in the traces setting, they naturally include the history of a process since they are lower sets.

As with any topological space, the family of Scott closed sets forms a complete Brouwerian lattice under containment (cf. [11]). But in the case of an algebraic or continuous poset[4], we can say a lot more. Indeed, in this case, the family of Scott-closed sets forms a completely distributive, hence continuous lattice. If the underlying poset P is algebraic, then the family of Scott-closed sets is in fact completely distributive and algebraic, which in turn imply it forms a *complete ring of sets.* Finally, the relation $X \ll Y$ on the family of Scott-closed sets is completely determined by that of P, and the compact elements in the Scott-closed sets are exactly the closed sets generated by finite sets of compact elements of P.

In particular, the family of non-empty Scott-closed subsets of a continuous (resp., algebraic) dcpo is a continuous (resp., algebraic) dcpo semilattice (under union) whose relative compactness relation $\ll$ is completely determined by that of the underlying poset. Moreover, in the case P is algebraic, this family is an algebraic dcpo under *reverse* containment as well, and the compact elements here are the sets of the form $P \setminus (\uparrow F)$ as $F \subseteq K(P)$ ranges over the non-empty finite sets of compact elements of P.

What all this has to do with CSP and the failures model is explained by the following:

Example 1. Consider the set $P_F = \{(s, X) \mid s \in \Sigma^* \cup \Sigma^*\surd \;\&\; X \subseteq \Sigma\}$. We define a partial order of P_F by

$$(s, X) \sqsubseteq (t, Y) \iff (s < t \;\&\; X = \emptyset) \vee (s = t \;\&\; X \subseteq Y).$$

It is routine to show this is a partial order, and it also is easy to see that the pairs (s, X) with X finite are compact in this order. Hence P_F is an algebraic poset.

Theorem 5 ([15]). *The failures model consists of Scott-closed sets from the algebraic poset P_F, and this family is closed in the family of all Scott-closed sets under filtered intersections. Each of the operators from CSP gives rise to an operation on all the Scott-closed sets that is continuous with respect to usual containment, and all but the hiding operator give rise to operations that are continuous with respect reverse containment.* □

The point to note here is that it is the hiding operator that "causes all the problems" with the failures model. More to the point, the approach adopted with

[4] By a *continuous poset* we mean a partial order P in which $\Downarrow y$ is directed and $y = \sqcup \Downarrow y$ for all $y \in P$; P is an *algebraic poset* if $K(y)$ is directed and $y = \sqcup K(y)$ for all $y \in P$. The point is that we no longer require P to be directed complete.

the failures model was to use the order of nondeterminism to model a certain type of partial correctness – namely, that deadlock or divergence is catastrophic. That decision required a model in which all the operators are continuous with respect to reverse set containment, and since hiding is the only operation which doesn't satisfy this property on all Scott-closed sets, it is the reason for the condition 4) in the definition of the sets that comprise the model. In other words, if one were to seek a model for CSP without hiding, then all the Scott closed sets of the poset P_F could be used.

3 Local Cpos

From the outset, computation has viewed sequential composition as the "most primitive" operation. When the issue of modeling concurrent computation arose, the reaction was to devise models for nondeterminism using subset-like constructions, and then to model parallel composition in terms of sequential composition and nondeterministic choice. As described in [12], three distinct models for nondeterministic choice emerged in domain theory – the so-called *power domains*. These three constructs were first defined in terms of ideal completions of three distinct orders that can be defined on the finite subsets of the set $K(P)$ of compact elements of the underlying domain P. This works for any algebraic dcpo, but more restrictive domains allow for alternative descriptions of these constructions. As described in [22], *coherent domains* (i.e., those algebraic cpos for which the intersection of any finite family of Scott compact upper sets is again compact in the Scott topology) allow the three power domains to be described in completely topological terms:

- The *lower power domain* is the family of non-empty Scott-closed subsets of the underlying domain equipped with the usual order, and with union as the nondeterministic choice operation. This family is the free sup-semilatiice cpo over P.
- the *upper power domain* is the family of non-empty Scott compact upper sets from P, again with union as the operation, but this time under the reverse containment order. This family is the free inf-semilattice cpo over P.
- the *convex power domain* is the family of non-empty order-convex subsets $X = \uparrow X \cap \downarrow X$ of P whose lower set $\downarrow X$ is Scott closed and whose upper set $\uparrow X$ is Scott compact. The operation is the convex hull of the union:

  $$(X,Y) \mapsto \downarrow(X \cup Y) \cap \uparrow(X \cup Y),$$

  and the order is the *Egli-Milner order*:

  $$X \sqsubseteq Y \;\Leftrightarrow\; X \subseteq \downarrow Y \;\&\; Y \subseteq \uparrow X.$$

  This family is the free semilattice cpo over P.

Each of these constructions produces a coherent domain from an underlying coherent domain; these are the more-or-less standard constructions for modeling nondeterministic choice within domain theory. Each construct allows operations (such as sequential composition) defined on the underlying domain P to be extended to the power domain. But, these extended operations all distribute over the nondeterministic choice operation, and so modeling *bisimulation* requires the additional step of solving a *domain equation* defined in terms of the convex power domain (cf. [1]).

All of the above applies to bounded nondeterminism, but *unbounded* nondeterminism also is useful, especially for specification. For example, consider a process-algebraic setting in which one wants to specify a process that can participate in any finite number of a given action, say a, but which is not supposed to participate in infinitely many a's. This requires distinguishing the process $\sqcap_{n \in \mathbf{N}} (a^n \to STOP)$ from the process $(\sqcap_{n \in \mathbf{N}} (a^n \to STOP)) \sqcap a^\infty$. But, these two processes must be identified in any of the models described above, and so we have to generalize domain theory and power domains in order to allow these processes to be distinguished.

In [24], an approach to modeling unbounded nondeterminism in CSP was presented. This approach added a new component to the meaning of each process – the *infinite traces* that a process could execute. By actually listing these traces, it became possible to distinguish a process that could execute an infinite trace from one which couldn't. But the resulting model was no longer a dcpo. Moreover, some selfmaps of the model no longer were continuous, and some of those that were didn't have any fixed points, let alone least ones. The point is that the new model was not a dcpo. The question then became how to make sure all the processes that could be meanings of recursive CSP processes in this setting actually had well-defined meanings. In other words, the question became one of how to assure that the recursive terms from CSP had meanings given by least fixed points in this new model.

The solution that was found was quite inventive. It amounted to using the fact that the model $\mathcal{U}$ for unbounded nondeterminism naturally contained a model for CSP with bounded nondeterminism – i.e., a copy of the failures-divergences model $\mathcal{FD}$ [4]. This was obtained by sending each CSP process to its meaning in $\mathcal{FD}$ together with those infinite traces that the process could execute, and this gave an embedding of $\mathcal{FD}$ within $\mathcal{U}$ "at the top": any element of $\mathcal{U}$ is the infimum of those elements in $\mathcal{FD}$ that are above it. This provided a cpo "at the top" of $\mathcal{U}$, which in turn proved crucial for deriving the results that were needed to show that $\mathcal{U}$ actually could serve as a model for unbounded nondeterminism in CSP.

The heart of the proof presented in [24] amounts to showing that each of the operations on $\mathcal{U}$ from CSP has a corresponding operation on $\mathcal{FD}$ from CSP with bounded nondeterminism that "dominates" it in the pointwise order. In terms of selfmaps of the model, the dominating operation leaves $\mathcal{FD}$ invariant (as it sits in $\mathcal{U}$). As a result, each term from CSP with bounded nondeterminism has a least fixed point on this submodel, and this fixed point is a *pre-fixed point* for any corresponding term on $\mathcal{U}$ that is dominated by the original term from CSP. But a pre-fixed point for a monotone mapping is all that is necessary to assure the mapping has a least fixed point ***provided each element of the model satisfies the property that its lower set is a cpo.*** This indeed is the case, and this is how it is shown that each term from CSP with unbounded nondeterminism actually has a least fixed point on $\mathcal{U}$. We now present a more general description of these results that also is more precise.

Inspired by the work in [24] and by related work in [25] on unbounded nondeterminism for Timed CSP, an effort was made to find an underlying mathematical principle for the results that were obtained in these two papers. The resulting principle turned out to be remarkably simple. It hinged on two main ideas:

- the notion of a *local cpo*, and
- a *dominated fixed point theorem.*

Definition 6. *A partial order P is a* local cpo *if $\downarrow x$ is a cpo for each $x \in P$.*

Clearly any cpo is a local cpo, but there are local cpos which are not directed complete. For example, consider $(\mathbb{N}, \leq)$ the natural numbers in the usual order – the lower set of each point is finite, but $\mathbb{N}$ has no upper bound. This is not exactly the example we have in mind for modeling unbounded nondeterminism, however.

The dominated fixed point theorem can then be stated as follows:

Theorem 6 (Dominated Fixed Point Theorem [19]). *Let P be a local cpo and E a space for which there is a mapping $\iota: E \to P$. Suppose that $f: P \to P$ is monotone and satisfies the property that there is some mapping $F: E \to E$ with $f \circ \iota \sqsubseteq \iota \circ F$. If F has a fixed point in E, then f has a least fixed point in P.* □

The proof of this result is straightforward. One only has to note that a fixed point $x = F(x)$ for F satisfies $\iota(x)$ is a *pre-fixed point* for f: $f(\iota(x)) \sqsubseteq \iota(F(x)) = \iota(x)$ by the hypothesis of the Theorem. Thus, $f: \downarrow x \to \downarrow x$, and this set is a cpo as P is a local cpo. Hence f has a least fixed point by Tarski's Theorem.

In [19] it is shown how this result provides the common mathematical underpinning for the models for unbounded nondeterminism in Timed and untimed CSP. In the former case, the space E is one of the metric space models for Timed CSP with bounded nondeterminism devised by REED and ROSCOE [23], and in the later, the space E is the failures-divergences model for untimed CSP with bounded nondeterminism. One result of [19] was the internalization of the fixed point theory for recursive process meanings in each model; in the first approach devised by Roscoe for untimed CSP, an operational model for unbounded nondeterminism and a congruence theorem were used to justify the existence of meanings for each recursive process; of course, this still is needed to validate that the fixed point meanings defined in the model are the operationally correct ones. Another result of [19] was the realization that the work done in [24] to show that each process meaning in the model is the infimum of meanings in that lie in the subspace E (which is a cpo) is not needed. It is enough to know that each mapping for which a least fixed point is required has a dominating mapping on E in the sense of the Dominated Fixed Point Theorem.

As outlined above, for coherent domains, the three power domains are each describable in topological terms. But more generally, they can be defined for any algebraic dcpo in terms of the family of non-empty finite subsets of the set of compact elements of the underlying dcpo. For example, the lower power domain is the ideal completion of the family of non-empty subsets of $K(P)$ under the quasiorder $F \sqsubseteq G \Leftrightarrow F \subseteq \downarrow G$. Similarly, the upper power domain is the ideal completion of the same family, but endowed with the quasiorder $F \sqsubseteq G \Leftrightarrow G \subseteq \uparrow F$. In both of these cases, union defines a monotone operation which extends to the ideal completions to define the meaning of nondeterministic choice. Finally, the convex power domain is the ideal completion of the same family, this time ordered by the common refinement of these two quasiorders.

In [16], an attempt was made to develop a general theory for modeling unbounded nondeterminism in a domain-theoretic setting based on the results just described. In fact, the goal of that work was to devise analogues for each of the power domains for unbounded nondeterminism. The point of departure was the assumption that the underlying model for sequential composition – P – embeds in the model for unbounded nondeterminism so that elements of P are "free" with respect to unbounded nondeterminism. More precisely, the underlying assumption is that $a \not\sqsubseteq \sqcap X$ if $a \notin \downarrow X$ for *any* subset $X \subseteq P$. This assumption is what is required if one wants to distinguish processes such as $\sqcap_{n \in \mathbf{N}} (a^n \to STOP)$ from $(\sqcap_{n \in \mathbf{N}} (a^n \to STOP)) \sqcap a^\infty$. We now describe the results obtained.

First, it was found that *there is no analogue to the lower power domain.* The reason is that the order of nondeterminism ($x \sqsubseteq y \Leftrightarrow x \sqcap y = x$) corresponds to the order used to model recursion as least fixed points in any analogue to the lower power domain, so any element that dominates all of the terms $a^n \to STOP$ also must dominate a^∞.

On the other hand, it was shown that there is an analogue to the upper power domain. This is possible because, in the setting of the upper power domain, the order of nondeterminism is opposite to the order of recursion. The model in question is defined simply as the family of all non-empty upper sets $\{X \mid \emptyset \neq X = \uparrow X \subseteq P\}$ of the underlying domain P with union as the operation. It was shown in [16] that one could construct a Cartesian closed category of local cpos and monotone mappings having least fixed points (via the Dominated Fixed Point Theorem) which is closed under this construction of an ***unbounded upper power space***. By the way, this is the abstract analogue of the model devised to model unbounded nondeterminism for untimed and Timed CSP.

Finally, an open question is whether there is an analogue for the convex power domain in this setting. In [16] an example is provided which shows that the analogue for the upper power space just described will not work: it is shown there that the family of all non-empty order-convex subsets of the underlying domain P is not a local cpo in general. (Unfortunately, more is claimed there – that there is no such model – but that claim remains unsettled.) It would be nice to know if this family can be completed into a local cpo which then could serve as the desired model for unbounded nondeterminism.

Readers familiar with PLOTKIN's work on countable nondeterminism [20] may wonder about the relationship between that work and what has been described here from [16]. Plotkin's approach was to weaken the continuity properties of the maps under consideration – instead of being continuous, they are only $\aleph_1$-continuous (so that they preserve sups of directed sets of less than $\aleph_1$-cardinality). Plotkin shows there is a free object supporting countable sums within the category of $\aleph_1$-complete objects and $\aleph_1$-continuous maps. This is not at odds with our results, since we studied objects which are not assumed to be directed complete for any cardinality of directed subsets, and the maps we consider are only monotone, and do not satisfy any stronger continuity properties. Our approach is justified by the work in [24, 25] which shows that these hypotheses are as strong as can be invoked, at least in the CSP setting.

4 Computational Models

So far the generalizations we have described have been inspired by work in process algebra. In this section, we focus on another area of application of domain theory – models of computation. In the early and mid1990s, ABBAS EDALAT began producing a number of striking applications of domain theory to areas of mathematics and computation. These began with an application showing how domain theory could provide a simpler approach to modeling fractals and iterated functions systems [5], even providing new algorithms for computing these objects. There followed applications to neural networks [6], and then to integration [7]. This last was notable because it showed how domain theory could be used to devise a new approach to Riemann integration in which the focus shifted from varying the function being integrated to varying measures which approximate Riemann measure, thus allowing domain theory to define the integral. Most recently, Edalat has continued his work by developing real PCF, which contains a real numbers datatype, along with efficient algorithms for exact computations in this datatype using continued fractions [10].

In all of this work, an emerging theme has been modeling topological spaces in domain theory, thus allowing the approximation theory of domains to be applied to problems in this setting. A focal point then becomes the question of which topological spaces admit computational (i.e., domain-theoretic) models. The precise statement is:

Which topological spaces can be embedded as the set of maximal elements in a domain?

An initial answer was provided by LAWSON [13] who showed that any Polish space (complete, separable metric space) can be so represented. Shortly thereafter, EDALAT and HECKMANN [9] produced the *formal ball model* which shows that any metric space can be embedded as the space of maximal elements in a continuous poset. The model is the family of all pairs $\{(x,r) \mid x \in X \ \& \ r \geq 0\}$ under the order $(x,r) \sqsubseteq (y,s) \iff d(x,y) \leq r - s$. Moreover, they show that the model is a continuous poset whose completion (as described in Section 2) has the completion of the metric space as its space of maximal elements. Both of these results focus on domains which satisfy the property that the Scott topology is *weak at the top* [8], and indeed under this assumption, the maximal elements of the underlying domain form a separable metric space.

We now outline some results that are due to KEYE MARTIN, a PhD student at Tulane, which provide an alternative approach to these and related results. They all will be contained in [14].

To begin, Martin begins with the notion of a *measurement* on a domain.

Definition 7. *Let P be a continuous poset. A* measurement *on P is a Scott-continuous mapping $\mu: P \to ([0,\infty), \geq)$ satisfying*

1. $\mu^{-1}(0) = \mathrm{MAX}(P)$, and
2. μ induces the Scott topology near the top of P:

$$(\forall x \in \mathrm{MAX}(P))(\forall U \subseteq P \text{ open})\ x \in U \ \Rightarrow\ (\exists \epsilon > 0)\ \downarrow\! x \cap \mu^{-1}([0,\epsilon)) \subseteq U.$$

Numerous examples are available here, including:

1. The space $\mathbb{IR}$ of compact intervals of real numbers, ordered by reverse inclusion, and with length as the measurement.
2. The family LIST(A) of lists over a set A, again with length of the list as the measurement.

In both of these cases – and in most others – the measurement actually induces the Scott topology on the whole domain, not just near the top.

Theorem 7 (Martin [14]). *Let (P,μ) be a continuous poset with a measurement, and suppose that μ satisfies:*

$$(\forall x,y \in P)\ x \uparrow y\ \Rightarrow\ (\exists z \in P)\ z \sqsubseteq x,y\ \&\ \mu(z) \leq 2 \cdot \max\{\mu(x),\mu(y)\}.$$

Then MAX(P) *is metrizable.* □

Notice that the result makes no mention of the weak topology – it holds for any continuous poset with measurement.

The converse of this result follows from Edalat's and Heckmann's result about the formal ball model [9], since that model has a measurement, the function $(x,r) \mapsto r$.

4.1 Modeling Algorithms

The inspiration for Martin's results was the intuition that two of the most common algorithms had something domain-theoretic in common. Those algorithms are:

1. The *bisection algorithm* which seeks a root for a continuous selfmap $f: \mathbb{R} \to \mathbb{R}$ on an interval $[a,b] \subseteq \mathbb{R}$. It proceeds by testing whether the function changes sign, first on the left half of the interval and then on the right, and recursively subdivides the interval. The algorithm can be viewed as a partial mapping $\mathrm{split}_f: \mathbb{IR} \rightharpoonup \mathbb{IR}$. Note that split_f is not monotone, let alone continuous.

2. Any of the searching algorithms on LIST(A), the domain of lists over a set A. Here again, these algorithms give rise to partial selfmaps of LIST(A) that are not generally monotone.

These examples inspired the following:

Definition 8. *Let P be a continuous poset. A partial mapping $f: P \rightharpoonup P$ is a* splitting *if $x \sqsubseteq f(x)$ $(\forall x \in \mathrm{dom}(f))$.*

Theorem 8 (Martin [14]). *Let $f: P \to P$ be a partial selfmap on a continuous dcpo P with measurement μ. If $\mu \circ f: P \rightharpoonup [0, \infty)$ is continuous, and if f is a splitting, then $\sqcup_{n \in \mathbb{N}} f^n(x)$ is a fixed point for f $(\forall x \in \mathrm{dom}(f))$.* □

A corollary of this result is that any continuous selfmap $f: \mathbb{R} \to \mathbb{R}$ has a root on any interval $[a, b]$ for which $\mathrm{split}_f([a, b]) \subseteq [a, b]$. Similarly, many of the familiar searching algorithms can be built up from splittings on the domain of lists to which the same result can be applied to do correctness proofs. Thus, the theory of continuous posets with measurements and splittings provides a common environment to model both the "discrete" algorithms from searching and the continuous algorithms such as the bisection algorithm.

4.2 Derivatives and Rates of Convergence

Since the setting of continuous posets with measurements includes the interval domain $\mathbb{IR}$, we can use this setting to generalize some results from numerical analysis.

Definition 9. *Let $f: P \rightharpoonup P$ be a partial mapping on a continuous poset P with measurement μ. If $p \in \mathrm{MAX}(P) \setminus K(P)$, then we define the* derivative of f at p *by*

$$\frac{\mathrm{d}f}{\mathrm{d}\mu}(p) = \lim_{x \to p} \frac{\mu(f(x)) - \mu(f(p))}{\mu(x) - \mu(p)}.$$

For example, for a continuous selfmap $f: \mathbb{R} \to \mathbb{R}$, if f changes sign on the interval $[a, b]$, then the above definition says that split_f has derivative $\frac{1}{2}$ at $[a, b]$, in keeping with the fact that the mapping splits the interval in half on each iteration.

The following shows this definition is sensible.

Theorem 9 (Martin [14]). *If $f: \mathbb{R} \to \mathbb{R}$ is differentiable at x, then*

$$\frac{\mathrm{d}F}{\mathrm{d}\mu}(\{p\}) = |f'(p)|,$$

where $F: \mathbb{IR} \rightharpoonup \mathbb{IR}$ is $F([a, b]) = f([a, b])$ and $\mu([a, b]) = b - a$. Conversely, if f is locally monotone and F has a derivative at $\{p\}$, then so does f and the above equation holds. □

This result shows that the following theorem generalizes results from numerical analysis.

Proposition 3 (Martin [14]). *Let $f: P \rightharpoonup P$ be a partial mapping on a continuous poset P with measurement μ. Suppose that* $\lim_{n>0} f^n(x) = r \in \mathrm{MAX}(P)$ *is a fixed point for f. Then* $\lim_{n>0} \dfrac{\mu(f^{n+1}(x))}{\mu(f^n(x))} = \dfrac{\mathrm{d}f}{\mathrm{d}\mu}(r)$. □

We also can use $\dfrac{\mathrm{d}f}{\mathrm{d}\mu}(r)$ to give an estimate of how fast $f^n(x)$ converges to a fixed point $r \in \mathrm{MAX}(P)$. If $\lim_n \mu(f^n(x)) = 0$, then for any given $\epsilon > 0$ there is some n for which $\mu(f^m(r)) < \epsilon$, for $m \geq n$. Now $\dfrac{\mathrm{d}f}{\mathrm{d}\mu}(r)$ can be used to give an estimate for the number of iterations of f for which this inequality actually holds – i.e., it provides an estimate for the number of iterations required to obtain the answer to within "ϵ accuracy."

5 Summary

We have given three generalizations of domain theory along with outlines of the problems that inspired those generalizations. The applications range from process algebra to models of computation, and include novel ideas that generalize some of the basic tenets of the original theory. Namely, they include

- Relaxing the assumption that the objects under study are directed complete, but retain the structure of continuity. The result is a theory that helps explain how the models for CSP relate to standard domain-theoretic constructions, and also makes clear that the hiding operator from CSP is the one operation that requires using a subfamily of the poset of non-empty Scott closed sets.
- Relaxing the condition of directed completeness and continuity to consider local cpos and monotone maps. The theory developed provides a general setting for modeling unbounded nondeterminism, and includes using cpos "at the top" of such objects to generate (least) fixed point theorems to assure that process meanings are well-defined.
- Considering continuous posets and mapping which are not monotone in order to model examples from computation, but which include the notion of a measurement. The theory provides a rich setting for devising computational models that encompass both the continuous approach =and the discrete approach represented by list searching algorithms. In this setting, it also is possible to generalize standard results from numerical analysis.

We believe these applications only serve to scratch the surface in terms of the potential applications for domain theory, and indeed many existing results are not mentioned here. This rather cursory survey is meant only to pique the reader's interest, and to provide some examples which we believe make a convincing case that domain theory is a rich theory whose potential applications range far from the setting that inspired it.

References

1. Abramsky, S. A domain equation for bisimulation. Information and Computation **92** (1991), 161–218.
2. Abramsky, S., Jung, A. Domain Theory. in: Handbook of Computer Science and Logic, Volume **3** (1994), Clarendon Press
3. Brookes, S. D., Hoare, C. A. R., Roscoe, A. W. A theory of communicating sequential processes. Journal ACM **31** (1984), 560–599.
4. Brookes, S. D., Roscoe, A. W. An improved failures model for communicating processes. Lecture Notes in Computer Science **197** (1985) 281–305.
5. Edalat, A. Dynamical systems, measures and fractals via domain theory. Information and Computation **120** (1995), 32–48.
6. Edalat, A. Domain theory in learning processes. Electronic Notes in Theoretical Computer Science **1** (1995), URL: `http://www.elsevier.com/locate/entcs/volume1.html`.
7. Edalat, A. Domain theory and integration. Theoretical Computer Science **151** (1995), 163–193.
8. Edalat, A. When Scott is weak at the top. Mathematical Structures in Computer Science, to appear.
9. Edalat, A., Heckmann, R. A computational model for metric spaces. Theoretical Computer Science, to appear.
10. Edalat, A., Potts, P. A new representation for exact real numbers. Electronic Notes in Theoretical Computer Science **6** (1997), URL: `http://www.elsevier.com/locate/entcs/volume6.html`.
11. Gierz, G., Hofmann, K. H., Keimel, K., Lawson, J., Mislove, M., Scott, D. "A Compendium of Continuous Lattices." Springer-Verlag, Berlin, Heidelberg, New York (1980) 326pp.
12. Hennessy, M., Plotkin. G. Full abstraction for a simple parallel programming language. Lecture Notes in Computer Science **74** (1979) Springer-Verlag.
13. Lawson, J. Spaces of maximal points, Mathematical Structures in Computer Science, to appear.
14. Martin, K. Ph.D. thesis, Tulane University, in preparation.
15. Mislove, M. Algebraic posets, algebraic cpo's and models of concurrency. in: Topology and Category Theory in Computer Science. G. M. Reed, A. W. Roscoe and R. Wachter, editors, Clarendon Press (1991), 75–111.
16. Mislove. M. Denotational models for unbounded nondeterminism. Electronic Notes in Theoretical Computer Science **1** (1995), URL: `http://www.elsevier.com/locate/entcs/volume1.html`
17. Mislove, M. Using duality to solve domain equations. Electronic Notes in Theoretical Computer Science **6** (1997), URL: `http://www.elsevier.nl/locate/entcs/volume6.html`.
18. Mislove, M. Topology, domain theory and theoretical computer science. Topology and Its Applications, to appear.
19. Mislove. M., Roscoe, A. W., Schneider, S. A. Fixed points without completeness. Theoretical Computer Science **138** (1995), 273–314.
20. Plotkin, G. D. A powerdomain for countable nondeterminism. Lecture Notes in Computer Science **140** (1982).
21. Smyth, M. Effectively given domains. Theoretical Computer Science **5** (1977) 257–274.

22. Smyth, M. Power domains and predicate transformers: a topological view. Lecture Notes in Computer Science **154** (1983) Springer-Verlag, 662–675.
23. Reed, G. M., Roscoe, A. W. Metric spaces as models for real-time concurrency. Lecture Notes in Mathematics **298** (1988), 331–343.
24. Roscoe, A. W., Barrett, G. Unbounded nondeterminism in CSP. Lecture Notes in Computer Science **442** (1990).
25. Schneider, S. A. An operational semantics for timed CSP. Information and Computation **116** (1995).
26. Stoltenberg-Hansen, A., Lindström, I., Griffor, E. B. "Mathematical Theory of Domains." Cambridge Tracts in Theoretical Computer Science **22** (1994), Cambridge University Press, 349pp.

A Cook's Tour of Equational Axiomatizations for Prefix Iteration

Luca Aceto[1]*, Wan Fokkink[2]** and Anna Ingólfsdóttir[3]***

[1] BRICS (Basic Research in Computer Science), Department of Computer Science, Aalborg University, Fredrik Bajers Vej 7-E, DK-9220 Aalborg Ø, Denmark.
[2] Department of Computer Science, University of Wales Swansea, Singleton Park, Swansea SA2 8PP, Wales.
[3] Dipartimento di Sistemi ed Informatica, Università di Firenze, Via Lombroso 6/17, 50134 Firenze, Italy.

Abstract. Prefix iteration is a variation on the original binary version of the Kleene star operation P^*Q, obtained by restricting the first argument to be an atomic action, and yields simple iterative behaviours that can be equationally characterized by means of finite collections of axioms. In this paper, we present axiomatic characterizations for a significant fragment of the notions of equivalence and preorder in van Glabbeek's linear-time/branching-time spectrum over Milner's basic CCS extended with prefix iteration. More precisely, we consider ready simulation, simulation, readiness, trace and language semantics, and provide complete (in)equational axiomatizations for each of these notions over BCCS with prefix iteration. All of the axiom systems we present are finite, if so is the set of atomic actions under consideration.

1 Introduction

Equationally based proof systems play an important role in both the practice and the theory of process algebras. From the point of view of practice, these proof systems can be used to perform system verifications in a purely syntactic way, and form the basis of axiomatic verification tools like, e.g., PAM [10]. From the theoretical point of view, complete axiomatizations of behavioural equivalences capture the essence of different notions of semantics for processes in terms of a basic collection of identities, and this often allows one to compare semantics which may have been defined in very different styles and frameworks. Some researchers also measure the naturalness of a process semantics by using the existence of a finite complete axiomatization for it over, say, finite behaviours as an acid test.

* Partially supported by the Human Capital and Mobility project EXPRESS. Email: `luca@cs.auc.dk`. Fax: +45 9815 9889.
** Email: `W.J.Fokkink@swansea.ac.uk`. Fax: +44 1792 295708.
*** Supported by a grant from the Danish National Research Foundation. Email: `annai@dsi2.ing.unifi.it`. Fax: +39 55 4796730.

An excellent example of the unifying role played by equational axiomatizations of process semantics may be found in [7]. *Ibidem* van Glabbeek presents the so-called linear time/branching time spectrum, i.e., the lattice of all the known behavioural equivalences over labelled transition systems ordered by inclusion. The different identifications made by these semantic equivalences over finite synchronization trees are beautifully characterized by the author of *op. cit.* in terms of a few simple axioms. This permits an illuminating comparison of these semantics within a uniform axiomatic framework. However, despite the complete inference systems for bisimulation-based equivalences over regular processes presented in, e.g., [11, 8] and years of intense research, little is still known on the topic of effective complete axiomatizations of the notions of semantics studied in [7] over iterative processes.

In this study, we shall present a contribution to this line of research by investigating a significant fragment of the notions of equivalence and preorder from [7] over Milner's basic CCS (henceforth referred to as BCCS) [12] extended with prefix iteration. Prefix iteration [6] is a variation on the original binary version of the Kleene star operation P^*Q [9], obtained by restricting the first argument to be an atomic action, and yields simple iterative behaviours that can be equationally characterized by means of finite collections of axioms. Furthermore, prefix iteration combines better with the action prefixing operator of CCS than the more general binary Kleene star. A significant advantage of iteration over recursion, as a means to express infinite processes, is that it does not involve a parametric process definition, because the development of process theory is easier if parameterization does not have to be taken as primitive (see, e.g., Milner [13, page 212]).

Our study of equational axiomatizations for BCCS with prefix iteration has so far yielded complete equational axiomatizations for all the main notions of bisimulation equivalence [6, 1]. In this paper, we continue this research programme by studying axiomatic characterizations for more abstract semantics over this language than those based on variations of bisimulation. More precisely, we consider ready simulation, simulation, readiness, trace and language semantics, and provide complete (in)equational axiomatizations for each of these notions over BCCS with prefix iteration. All of the axiom systems we present are finite, if so is the set of atomic actions under consideration. Although the high level structure of the proofs of our main results follows standard lines in the literature on process theory, the actual details of the arguments are, however, rather subtle (cf., e.g., the proof of Thm. 4.6). To our mind, this shows how the analysis of the collection of valid identities for the semantics considered in this paper already becomes difficult even in the presence of very simple iterative behaviours, like those that can be expressed using prefix iteration.

The paper is organized as follows. After a brief review of the basic notions from process theory needed in the remainder of the paper (Sect. 2), we present the language BCCS with prefix iteration and its labelled transition system semantics (Sect. 3). Sect. 4 is devoted to a guided tour of our completeness results. The paper concludes with a mention of further results that will be presented in a full account of this work, and a discussion of ongoing research (Sect. 5).

2 Preliminaries

In this section we present the basic notions from process theory that will be needed in the remainder of this study.

2.1 Labelled Transitions Systems

A *labelled transition system* is a triple $(\mathsf{Proc}, \mathsf{Lab}, \{\stackrel{\ell}{\to} \mid \ell \in \mathsf{Lab}\})$, where:

- Proc is a set of *states*, ranged over by s, possibly subscripted or superscripted;
- Lab is a set of *labels*, ranged over by ℓ, possibly subscripted;
- $\stackrel{\ell}{\to} \subseteq \mathsf{Proc} \times \mathsf{Proc}$ is a *transition relation*, for every $\ell \in \mathsf{Lab}$. As usual, we shall use the more suggestive notation $s \stackrel{\ell}{\to} s'$ in lieu of $(s, s') \in \stackrel{\ell}{\to}$, and write $s \stackrel{\ell}{\not\to}$ iff $s \stackrel{\ell}{\to} s'$ for no state s'.

All the labelled transition systems we shall consider in this paper will have a special label $\checkmark$ in their label set—used to represent successful termination—, and will enjoy the following property: if $s \stackrel{\checkmark}{\to} s'$, then $s' \stackrel{\ell}{\not\to}$ for every label ℓ.

For $n \geq 0$ and $\varsigma = \ell_1 \ldots \ell_n \in \mathsf{Lab}^*$, we write $s \stackrel{\varsigma}{\to} s'$ iff there exist states $s_0, \ldots, s_n$ such that $s = s_0 \stackrel{\ell_1}{\to} s_1 \stackrel{\ell_2}{\to} \cdots s_{n-1} \stackrel{\ell_n}{\to} s_n = s'$. In that case, we say that ς is a *trace* (of length n) of the state s. For a state $s \in \mathsf{Proc}$ we define:

$$\mathsf{initials}(s) \triangleq \left\{\ell \in \mathsf{Lab} \mid \exists s' : s \stackrel{\ell}{\to} s'\right\} .$$

2.2 From Ready Simulation to Language Equivalence

Labelled transition systems describe the operational behaviour of processes in great detail. In order to abstract from irrelevant information on the way processes compute, a wealth of notions of behavioural equivalence or approximation have been studied in the literature on process theory. A systematic investigation of these notions is presented in [7], where van Glabbeek studies the so-called linear time/branching time spectrum, i.e., the lattice of all the known behavioural equivalences over labelled transition systems ordered by inclusion. In this study, we shall investigate a significant fragment of the notions of equivalence and preorder from [7]. These we now proceed to present for the sake of completeness.

Definition 2.1 (Simulation, Ready Simulation and Bisimulation).

- A binary relation $\mathcal{R}$ on states is a *simulation* iff whenever $s_1 \mathcal{R} s_2$ and ℓ is a label:
  - if $s_1 \stackrel{\ell}{\to} s_1'$, then there is a transition $s_2 \stackrel{\ell}{\to} s_2'$ such that $s_1' \mathcal{R} s_2'$.

- A binary relation $\mathcal{R}$ on states is a *ready simulation* iff it is a simulation with the property that, whenever $s_1 \mathcal{R} s_2$ and ℓ is a label:
  - if $s_1 \stackrel{\ell}{\nrightarrow}$, then $s_2 \stackrel{\ell}{\nrightarrow}$.
- A *bisimulation* is a symmetric simulation.

Two states s and s' are *bisimilar*, written $s \leftrightarroweq s'$, iff there is a bisimulation that relates them. Henceforth the relation $\leftrightarroweq$ will be referred to as *bisimulation equivalence*. We write $s \precsim_S s'$ (resp. $s \precsim_{RS} s'$) iff there is a simulation (resp. a ready simulation) $\mathcal{R}$ with $s \mathcal{R} s'$.

Bisimulation equivalence [14] relates two states in a labelled transition system precisely when they have the same branching structure. Simulation (see, e.g., [14]) and ready simulation [3] relax this requirement to different degrees. The following notion, which is based on a version of decorated traces, is induced by yet another way of abstracting from the full branching structure of processes.

Definition 2.2 (Readiness Semantics). For a state s we define:

$$readies(s) \triangleq \left\{(\varsigma, X) \mid \varsigma \in \mathsf{Lab}^*, X \subseteq \mathsf{Lab} \text{ and } \exists s' : s \stackrel{\varsigma}{\to} s' \text{ and } \mathsf{initials}(s') = X\right\}$$

For states s, s' we write $s \precsim_R s'$ iff $readies(s)$ is included in $readies(s')$.

The classical notion of language equivalence for finite state automata may be readily defined over labelled transition systems. To this end, it is sufficient to consider the states from which a $\checkmark$-labelled transition is possible as accept states.

Definition 2.3 (Language and Trace Semantics).

- We say that a sequence of labels ς is accepted by a state s iff $s \stackrel{\varsigma\checkmark}{\to} s'$ for some state s'. For states s, s' we write $s \precsim_L s'$ iff every sequence accepted by s is also accepted by s'.
- For states s, s' we write $s \precsim_T s'$ iff the set of traces of s is included in that of s'.

For $\Theta \in \{S, RS, L, R, T\}$, the relation $\precsim_\Theta$ is a preorder over states of an arbitrary labelled transition system; its kernel will be denoted by $\simeq_\Theta$.

3 BCCS with Prefix Iteration

We begin by presenting the language of Basic CCS (henceforth often abbreviated to BCCS) with prefix iteration [6], together with its operational semantics.

3.1 The Syntax

We assume a non-empty alphabet Act of atomic actions, with typical elements a, b, c. The language BCCS^{p*} of Basic CCS with prefix iteration is given by the following BNF grammar:

$$P ::= \mathbf{0} \mid \mathbf{1} \mid a.P \mid P + P \mid a^*P \ .$$

We shall use P, Q, R, S, T to range over BCCS^{p*}. In writing terms over the above syntax, we shall always assume that the operator $a.\_$ binds stronger than $+$. We shall use the symbol $\equiv$ to stand for syntactic equality of terms. The expression $P[+Q]$ will be used to denote the fact that Q is an optional summand. The size of a term is the number of operators occurring in it.

Remark 3.1. The reader might have noticed that the syntax for the language BCCS^{p*} presented above includes two distinguished constants, viz. $\mathbf{0}$ and $\mathbf{1}$. Intuitively, the term $\mathbf{0}$ will stand for a deadlocked process, whereas $\mathbf{1}$ will stand for a process that can only terminate immediately with success. Our choice of notation is in keeping with a standard one for regular expressions, cf., e.g., [5].

3.2 Operational Semantics

Let $\checkmark$ be a distinguished symbol not contained in Act. We shall use $\checkmark$ to stand for the action performed by a process as it reports its successful termination. The meta-variable ξ will range over the set $\mathrm{Act} \cup \{\checkmark\}$. The operational semantics for the language BCCS^{p*} is given by the labelled transition system

$$\left(\mathrm{BCCS}^{p*}, \mathrm{Act} \cup \{\checkmark\}, \left\{\stackrel{\xi}{\to} \mid \xi \in \mathrm{Act} \cup \{\checkmark\}\right\}\right)$$

where the transition relations $\stackrel{\xi}{\to}$ are the least binary relations over BCCS^{p*} satisfying the rules in Table 1. Intuitively, a transition $P \stackrel{a}{\to} Q$ means that the system represented by the term P can perform the action a, thereby evolving into Q. On the other hand, $P \stackrel{\checkmark}{\to} Q$ means that P can terminate immediately with success; the reader will immediately realize that, in that case, $Q \equiv \mathbf{0}$.

With the above definitions, the language BCCS^{p*} inherits all the notions of equivalence and preorder over processes defined in Sect. 2.2. The following result is standard.

Proposition 3.2. *For $\Theta \in \{RS, S, L, R, T\}$, the relations $\sqsubseteq_\Theta$ and $\simeq_\Theta$ are preserved by the operators in the signature of* BCCS^{p*}. *The same holds for bisimulation equivalence.*

4 Equational Axiomatizations

The study of equational axiomatizations of behavioural equivalences and preorders over BCCS^{p*} was initiated in the paper [6]. In *op. cit.* it is shown that

$$\frac{}{a.P \xrightarrow{a} P} \qquad \frac{}{\mathbf{1} \xrightarrow{\surd} \mathbf{0}}$$

$$\frac{P \xrightarrow{\xi} P'}{P + Q \xrightarrow{\xi} P'} \qquad \frac{Q \xrightarrow{\xi} Q'}{P + Q \xrightarrow{\xi} Q'}$$

$$\frac{}{a^*P \xrightarrow{a} a^*P} \qquad \frac{P \xrightarrow{\xi} P'}{a^*P \xrightarrow{\xi} P'}$$

Table 1. Transition Rules

the axiom system in Table 2 completely axiomatizes bisimulation equivalence over the language of **1**-free BCCS^{p*} terms. Our aim in the remainder of this study will be to extend this result to the semantics in the linear-time/branching-time spectrum discussed in Sect. 2.2.

A1	$x + y = y + x$
A2	$(x + y) + z = x + (y + z)$
A3	$x + x = x$
A4	$x + \mathbf{0} = x$
PA1	$a.(a^*x) + x = a^*x$
PA2	$a^*(a^*x) = a^*x$

Table 2. The axiom system $\mathcal{F}$

For an axiom system $\mathcal{T}$, we write $\mathcal{T} \vdash P \leq Q$ iff the inequation $P \leq Q$ is provable from the axioms in $\mathcal{T}$ using the rules of inequational logic. An equation $P = Q$ will be used as a short-hand for the pair of inequations $P \leq Q$ and $Q \leq P$. Whenever we write an inequation of the form $P[+\mathbf{1}] \leq Q[+\mathbf{1}]$, we mean that if the **1** summand appears on the left-hand side of the inequation, then it also appears on the right-hand side. $P =_{\mathrm{AC}} Q$ denotes that P and Q are equal modulo associativity and commutativity of +, i.e., that A1,A2 $\vdash P = Q$. For a collection of (in)equations X over the signature of BCCS^{p*}, we write $P \overset{(\mathrm{X})}{\leq} Q$ as a short-hand for A1,A2,X $\vdash P \leq Q$. For $I = \{i_1, \ldots, i_n\}$ a finite index set, we write $\sum_{i \in I} P_i$ for $P_{i_1} + \cdots + P_{i_n}$. By convention, $\sum_{i \in \emptyset} P_i$ stands for $\mathbf{0}$.

Henceforth process terms will be considered modulo associativity and commutativity of the +-operation, i.e., modulo axioms A1–2.

We begin the technical developments by noting that the proof of the completeness of the axiom system $\mathcal{F}$ with respect to bisimulation equivalence over the language of **1**-free BCCS^{p*} terms applies *mutatis mutandis* to the whole of the language BCCS^{p*}.

Proposition 4.1. *For every $P, Q \in$ BCCS^{p*}, $P \leftrightarrow Q$ iff $\mathcal{F} \vdash P = Q$.*

The collection of possible transitions of each process term P is finite, say $\{P \stackrel{a_i}{\to} P_i \mid i = 1, ..., m\} \cup \left\{P \stackrel{\checkmark}{\to} \mathbf{0} \mid j = 1, \ldots, n\right\}$. We call the term

$$\exp(P) \triangleq \sum_{i=1}^{m} a_i.P_i + \sum_{j=1}^{n} \mathbf{1}$$

the *expansion* of P. The terms a_iP_i and $\mathbf{1}$ will be referred to as the *summands* of P. A straightforward structural induction on terms, using axiom PA1, yields:

Lemma 4.2. *Each process term is provably equal to its expansion.*

We aim at identifying a subset of process terms of a special form, which will be convenient in the proof of the completeness results to follow. Following a long-established tradition in the literature on process theory, we shall refer to these terms as *normal forms*. The set of normal forms we are after is the smallest subset of BCCS^{p*} including process terms having one of the following two forms:

$$\sum_{i\in I} a_i.P_i[+\mathbf{1}] \quad \text{or} \quad a^*(\sum_{i\in I} a_i.P_i[+\mathbf{1}]),$$

where the terms P_i are themselves normal forms, and I is a finite index set. (Recall that the empty sum represents $\mathbf{0}$, and the notation $[+\mathbf{1}]$ stands for optional inclusion of $\mathbf{1}$ as a summand.)

Lemma 4.3. *Each term in* BCCS^{p*} *can be proven equal to a normal form using equations* A3, A4 *and* PA1.

4.1 Ready Simulation

We begin our tour of equational axiomatizations for prefix iteration by presenting a complete axiom system for the ready simulation preorder (cf. Defn. 2.1 for the definition of this relation). The axiom system $\mathcal{E}_{RS}$ consists of the laws for bisimulation equivalence (cf. Table 2) and of the inequations RS1–2 below:

RS1	$a.x$	$\leq$	$a.x + a.y$
RS2	a^*x	$\leq$	$a^*(x + a.y)$.

Theorem 4.4. *For every $P, Q \in$ BCCS^{p*}, $P \sqsubseteq_{RS} Q$ iff $\mathcal{E}_{RS} \vdash P \leq Q$.*

Proof. We leave it to the reader to check the soundness of the axiom system $\mathcal{E}_{RS}$, and concentrate on its completeness. In view of Lem. 4.3, it is sufficient to show that if $P \lesssim_{RS} Q$ holds for normal forms P and Q, then $\mathcal{E}_{RS} \vdash P \leq Q$. This we now proceed to prove by induction on the sum of the sizes of P and Q.

We proceed by a case analysis on the form the normal forms P and Q may take.

- CASE: $P =_{AC} \sum_{i\in I} a_i.P_i[+\mathbf{1}]$ and $Q =_{AC} \sum_{j\in J} b_j.Q_j[+\mathbf{1}]$.
  As $P \lesssim_{RS} Q$, we infer that:
  1. for every i there exists an index j_i such that $a_i = b_{j_i}$ and $P_i \lesssim_{RS} Q_{j_i}$,
  2. $\mathbf{1}$ is a summand of P iff it is a summand of Q, and
  3. the collections of actions $\{a_i \mid i \in I\}$ and $\{b_j \mid j \in J\}$ are equal.

  The induction hypothesis and substitutivity yield that, for every $i \in I$,
  $$\mathcal{E}_{RS} \vdash a_i.P_i \leq b_{j_i}.Q_{j_i} \ .$$
  Again using substitutivity, we obtain that
  $$\mathcal{E}_{RS} \vdash P \leq \sum_i b_{j_i}.Q_{j_i}[+\mathbf{1}] \ .$$
  Note now that, for every index j that is not contained in the set $\{j_i \mid i \in I\}$, there is an index j_l ($l \in I$) such that $b_j = b_{j_l}$. We can therefore apply axiom RS1 as necessary to infer that
  $$\mathcal{E}_{RS} \vdash \sum_i b_{j_i}.Q_{j_i}[+\mathbf{1}] \leq Q \ .$$
  The provability of the inequation $P \leq Q$ from the axiom system $\mathcal{E}_{RS}$ now follows immediately by transitivity.
- CASE: $P =_{AC} \sum_{i\in I} a_i.P_i[+\mathbf{1}]$ and $Q =_{AC} b^*(\sum_{j\in J} b_j.Q_j[+\mathbf{1}])$.
  To deal with this case, begin by applying PA1 to Q to obtain the equality
  $$Q = b.Q + \sum_{j\in J} b_j.Q_j[+\mathbf{1}] \ .$$
  We can now reason as in the first case of the proof to derive that
  $$P \leq b.Q + \sum_{j\in J} b_j.Q_j[+\mathbf{1}] \ .$$
  Transitivity now yields the inequation $P \leq Q$.
- CASE: $P =_{AC} a^*(\sum_i a_i.P_i[+\mathbf{1}])$ and $Q =_{AC} \sum_j b_j.Q_j[+\mathbf{1}]$.
  Apply PA1 to P, and reason as in the previous case.
- CASE: $P =_{AC} a^*(\sum_i a_i.P_i[+\mathbf{1}])$ and $Q =_{AC} b^*(\sum_j b_j.Q_j[+\mathbf{1}])$.
  As $P \lesssim_{RS} Q$, we infer that:
  1. there exists a Q' such that $Q \xrightarrow{a} Q'$ and $P \lesssim_{RS} Q'$,
  2. for every i there exists a $Q(i)$ such that $Q \xrightarrow{a_i} Q(i)$ and $P_i \lesssim_{RS} Q(i)$,

3. **1** is a summand of P iff it is a summand of Q, and
4. the collections of actions $\{a_i \mid i \in I\} \cup \{a\}$ and $\{b_j \mid j \in J\} \cup \{b\}$ are equal.

Because of the form Q takes, Q' and every $Q(i)$ is either Q itself or one of the Q_j's. Therefore we may apply the inductive hypothesis to each of the inequivalences $P_i \precapprox_{RS} Q(i)$ and substitutivity to infer that

$$\mathcal{E}_{RS} \vdash \sum_i a_i.P_i \leq \sum_i a_i.Q(i) \ . \tag{1}$$

We proceed with the proof by considering the following two sub-cases:

A. There is an index j such that $a = b_j$ and $P \precapprox_{RS} Q_j$;
B. For no index j with $a = b_j$ it holds that $P \precapprox_{RS} Q_j$.

We consider these two cases in turn.

A. Assume that there is an index j such that $a = b_j$ and $P \precapprox_{RS} Q_j$. In this case, we may apply the inductive hypothesis to derive that

$$\mathcal{E}_{RS} \vdash P \leq Q_j \ . \tag{2}$$

We can now finish the proof of the inequation $P \leq Q$ from the axiom system $\mathcal{E}_{RS}$ as follows:

$$\begin{aligned} P &\overset{\text{(PA1)}}{=} a.P + \sum_i a_i.P_i[+\mathbf{1}] \\ &\overset{(1),(2)}{\leq} b_j.Q_j + \sum_i a_i.Q(i)[+\mathbf{1}] \\ &\overset{\text{(RS1)}}{\leq} b_j.Q_j + \sum_i a_i.Q(i) + \exp(Q)[+\mathbf{1}] \\ &\overset{\text{(A3),(PA1)}}{=} Q \ . \end{aligned}$$

B. Assume that for no index j with $a = b_j$ it holds that $P \precapprox_{RS} Q_j$. In this case, we infer that $a = b$. We can now reason as follows:

$$\begin{aligned} P \equiv a^*(\sum_i a_i.P_i[+\mathbf{1}]) &\overset{(1)}{\leq} a^*(\sum_i a_i.Q(i)[+\mathbf{1}]) \\ &\overset{\text{(RS1),(RS2)}}{\leq} a^*(\sum_i a_i.Q(i) + a.Q + \sum_j b_j.Q_j[+\mathbf{1}]) \\ &\overset{\text{(A3),(PA1)}}{\leq} a^*Q \\ &\overset{\text{(PA2)}}{=} Q \ . \end{aligned}$$

This completes the proof of the theorem.

4.2 Simulation

The axiom system $\mathcal{E}_S$ consists of the laws for bisimulation equivalence in Table 2 and of the axiom

$$\text{S} \quad x \leq x + y \;.$$

Inequation S is well-known to characterize the simulation preorder over finite synchronization trees. Unlike in the case of ready simulation, no extra law is needed to deal with prefix iteration explicitly.

Theorem 4.5. *For every $P, Q \in \mathrm{BCCS}^{p*}$, $P \precsim_S Q$ iff $\mathcal{E}_S \vdash P \leq Q$.*

4.3 Readiness

In this section we present a complete axiom system for prefix iteration with respect to the readiness preorder. The axiom system $\mathcal{E}_R$ consists of the collection of laws for ready simulation and of those listed below:

$$\begin{array}{llcl} \text{R1} & a.(b.x + b.y + v) & \leq & a.(b.x + v) + a.(b.y + w) \\ \text{R2} & a.a^*(b.x + b.y + v) & \leq & a.a^*(b.x + v) + a.a^*(b.y + w) \\ \text{R3} & a^*(b.x + b.y + v + a.(b.y + w)) & = & a^*(b.x + v + a.(b.y + w)) + b.y \end{array}$$

Theorem 4.6. *For every $P, Q \in \mathrm{BCCS}^{p*}$, $P \precsim_R Q$ iff $\mathcal{E}_R \vdash P \leq Q$.*

We focus on the completeness of $\mathcal{E}_R$, and leave soundness to the reader. Before proving this completeness theorem, we introduce some auxiliary definitions and results.

Definition 4.7. A term P is *saturated* if for each pair of derivations $P \xrightarrow{a} Q \xrightarrow{b} Q'$ and $P \xrightarrow{a} R$ with $b \in \mathsf{initials}(R)$ we have $R \xrightarrow{b} R'$ with $Q' \precsim_R R'$.

The following lemma stems from [2].

Lemma 4.8. *If $P \precsim_R Q$ and $P \xrightarrow{a} P'$ and Q is saturated, then $Q \xrightarrow{a} Q'$ with $P' \precsim_R Q'$.*

Definition 4.9. A normal form P is *strongly saturated* if:

1. P is saturated;
2. if $P =_{\mathrm{AC}} \sum_{i \in I} a_i.P_i[+1]$, then the term P_i is strongly saturated, for every $i \in I$.

Axioms R1–R3 play a crucial role in the proof of the following key result.

Lemma 4.10. *Each term is provably equal, by the axioms in $\mathcal{E}_R$, to a strongly saturated normal form, in which each subterm of the form a^*R occurs in the context $a.\_$.*

Finally we are in a position to prove Thm. 4.6.

Proof. Suppose that $P \precsim_R Q$; we prove that $\mathcal{E}_R \vdash P \leq Q$. By Lem. 4.10 it is not hard to see that it suffices to establish the claim under the following assumptions:

1. P and Q are normal forms;
2. Q is strongly saturated;
3. proper subterms of P and Q of the form a^*R occur in the context $a.\_$;
4. if $P =_{\mathrm{AC}} a^*R$ and $Q =_{\mathrm{AC}} b^*S$, then $a = b$.

(In fact, according to Lem. 4.10, the last two conditions could be replaced by the stronger condition that *all* subterms of P and Q of the form a^*R occur in the context $a.\_$. However, we shall need the weaker formulation above to be able to satisfy the induction hypothesis.) We derive the desired inequality $P \leq Q$ from $\mathcal{E}_R$ by induction with respect to the following lexicographic ordering on pairs of process terms: $(P, Q) < (R, S)$ if

- either $size(P) < size(R)$;
- or $size(P) = size(R)$ and $size(Q) < size(S)$.

The next two cases distinguish the possible syntactic forms of P.

- CASE 1: $P =_{\mathrm{AC}} \sum_{i\in I} a_i.P_i[+1]$.
  Since $P \precsim_R Q$, $P \xrightarrow{a_i} P_i$ and Q is saturated, Lem. 4.8 implies that for each $i \in I$ we have $Q \xrightarrow{a_i} Q_i$ for some Q_i such that $P_i \precsim_R Q_i$. According to Lem. 4.10, $\mathcal{E}_R \vdash Q_i = R_i$, with R_i a strongly saturated normal form, in which each subterm of the form c^*S occurs in the context $c.\_$. Moreover, each P_i is a normal form, in which all proper subterms of the form c^*S occur in the context $c.\_$, with $size(P_i) < size(P)$. Hence, we can apply induction to $P_i \precsim_R R_i$ to derive $\mathcal{E}_R \vdash P_i \leq R_i$. Therefore, for each $i \in I$,

  $$\mathcal{E}_R \vdash a_i.P_i \leq a_i.R_i = a_i.Q_i\ . \tag{3}$$

  By substitutivity, we have that

  $$P =_{\mathrm{AC}} \sum_{i\in I} a_i.P_i[+1] \overset{(3)}{\leq} \sum_{i\in I} a_i.Q_i[+1]\ . \tag{4}$$

  Since $P \precsim_R Q$ implies $\mathsf{initials}(P) = \mathsf{initials}(Q)$, it follows that $\mathsf{initials}(Q) \setminus \{\checkmark\}$ is equal to $\{a_i \mid i \in I\}$. Furthermore, $P \precsim_R Q$ implies that P has a summand $\mathbf{1}$ if and only if $Q \xrightarrow{\checkmark} \mathbf{0}$. Hence,

  $$\sum_{i\in I} a_i.Q_i[+1] \overset{(\mathrm{RS1})}{\leq} \mathsf{exp}(Q) \overset{(\mathrm{Lem.4.2})}{=} Q$$

  which together with equation (4) yields $\mathcal{E}_R \vdash P \leq Q$.
- CASE 2: $P =_{\mathrm{AC}} a^*(\sum_{i\in I} a_i.P_i[+1])$.
  The next two cases distinguish the possible syntactic forms of Q.

- CASE 2.1: $Q =_{\text{AC}} \sum_{j\in J} b_j.Q_j[+1]$.
Suppose that $P \overset{c}{\to} P'$. Since $P \precsim_R Q$ and Q is saturated, Lem. 4.8 implies that there is a $j \in J$ such that $c = b_j$ and $P' \precsim_R Q_j$. Both P' and Q_j are normal forms, and since Q is strongly saturated, by Defn. 4.9(2) Q_j is strongly saturated too. Furthermore, if $P' =_{\text{AC}} d^*R$ and $Q_j =_{\text{AC}} e^*S$, then $c = d$ and $b_j = e$, owing to property 3 of P and Q, and so $d = c = b_j = e$. Moreover, it is easy to see that property 3 of P and Q implies that the same property holds for P' and Q_j. Finally, $size(P') \leq size(P)$ and $size(Q_j) < size(Q)$. Hence, we can apply induction to $P' \precsim_R Q_j$ to derive $\mathcal{E}_R \vdash P' \leq Q_j$. Substitutivity now yields

$$\mathcal{E}_R \vdash c.P' \leq b_j.Q_j \ . \tag{5}$$

Hence,

$$P \overset{\text{(Lem.4.2)}}{=} \exp(P) \overset{(5)}{\leq} \sum_{j\in J_0} b_j.Q_j[+1] \tag{6}$$

for some $J_0 \subseteq J$. It is easy to see that $P \precsim_R Q$ implies $\mathsf{initials}(Q) \setminus \{\checkmark\} = \mathsf{initials}(P) \setminus \{\checkmark\} = \{b_j \mid j \in J_0\}$. Moreover, $P \overset{\checkmark}{\to} \mathbf{0}$ if and only if Q has a summand $\mathbf{1}$. Hence,

$$\sum_{j\in J_0} b_j.Q_j[+1] \overset{\text{(RS1)}}{\leq} \sum_{j\in J} b_j.Q_j[+1] =_{\text{AC}} Q \ .$$

Together with equation (6) this yields $\mathcal{E}_R \vdash P \leq Q$.
- CASE 2.2: $Q =_{\text{AC}} a^*(\sum_{j\in J} b_j.Q_j[+1])$.
Since $P \precsim_R Q$ and $P \overset{a_i}{\to} P_i$ and Q is saturated, Lem. 4.8 implies that for each $i \in I$

  1. either $a_i = a$ and $P_i \precsim_R Q$,
  2. or there is a j such that $a_i = b_j$ and $P_i \precsim_R Q_j$.

Clearly, each P_i is a normal form in which all proper subterms of the form c^*S occur in the context $c.\_$, and with $size(P_i) < size(P)$.
In the first case, applying induction to $P_i \precsim_R Q$, we infer that $\mathcal{E}_R \vdash P_i \leq Q$. Therefore, by substitutivity,

$$\mathcal{E}_R \vdash a_i.P_i \leq a.Q \ . \tag{7}$$

In the second case, Lem. 4.10 implies $\mathcal{E}_R \vdash Q_j = R_j$, with R_j a strongly saturated normal form, in which each subterm of the form c^*S occurs in the context $c.\_$. Then by induction $P_i \precsim_R R_j$ implies $\mathcal{E}_R \vdash P_i \leq R_j$. It follows, by substitutivity, that

$$\mathcal{E}_R \vdash a_i.P_i \leq a_i.R_j = b_j.Q_j \ . \tag{8}$$

Hence, for some $J_0 \subseteq J$:

$$P \overset{\text{(RS2)}}{\leq} a^*(a.Q + \sum_{i \in I} a_i.P_i[+1]) \overset{(8),(7)}{\leq} a^*(a.Q + \sum_{j \in J_0} b_j.Q_j[+1]) \ . \qquad (9)$$

It is easy to see that $P \sqsubseteq_R Q$ implies that initials$(Q) \setminus \{\checkmark\} = \{b_j \mid j \in J_0\} \cup \{a\}$, and that $P \overset{\checkmark}{\to} \mathbf{0}$ if and only if $Q \overset{\checkmark}{\to} \mathbf{0}$. Hence

$$a^*(a.Q + \sum_{j \in J_0} b_j.Q_j[+1]) \overset{\text{(RS1)}}{\leq} a^*(a.Q + \sum_{j \in J} b_j.Q_j[+1]) \overset{\text{(PA1),(PA2)}}{=} Q \ .$$

Together with equation (9) this yields $\mathcal{E}_R \vdash P \leq Q$.

The proof is now complete.

4.4 Traces

The axiom system $\mathcal{E}_T$ consists of the laws for bisimulation equivalence in Table 2 and of

T1	$a.(x+y)$	$=$	$a.x + a.y$
T2	$a^*(x+y)$	$=$	$a^*x + a^*y$
T3	$a^*(a.x)$	$=$	$a.(a^*x)$.

Axiom T1 is a well-known equation used to characterize trace equivalence over finite synchronization trees, and axiom T2 is the adaptation of this equation to the case of prefix iteration. Finally, T3 is, to the best of our knowledge, a new axiom.

Theorem 4.11. *For every $P, Q \in \mathrm{BCCS}^{p*}$,*

1. *$P \simeq_T Q$ iff $\mathcal{E}_T \vdash P = Q$;*
2. *$P \sqsubseteq_T Q$ iff $\mathcal{E}_T \cup \{(\mathrm{S})\} \vdash P \leq Q$.*

4.5 Language Semantics

The axiom system $\mathcal{E}_L$ consists of the laws for bisimulation equivalence in Table 2, T1–3 and the equations

L1	$a.\mathbf{0}$	$=$	$\mathbf{0}$
L2	$a^*\mathbf{0}$	$=$	$\mathbf{0}$.

Axiom L1 is an adaptation to action prefixing of a well-known equation from regular algebra, and axiom L2 is the generalization of this equation to the case of prefix iteration.

Theorem 4.12. *For every $P, Q \in \mathrm{BCCS}^{p*}$,*

1. *$P \simeq_L Q$ iff $\mathcal{E}_L \vdash P = Q$;*
2. *$P \sqsubseteq_L Q$ iff $\mathcal{E}_L \cup (\mathrm{S}) \vdash P \leq Q$.*

Proof. We leave it to the reader to check the soundness of the axiom system $\mathcal{E}_L \cup (\mathrm{S})$, and concentrate on the completeness results.

1. Assume that $P \simeq_L Q$. We shall prove that $\mathcal{E}_L \vdash P = Q$. A simple term rewriting analysis (which is omitted here) shows that each process term is provably equal to a term which is either $\mathbf{0}$-free, or of the form $\mathbf{0}$.
   Suppose that two terms P and Q are language equivalent. We distinguish two cases.
   - CASE 1: $P \equiv \mathbf{0}$. Then clearly also $Q \equiv \mathbf{0}$, so $P \equiv \mathbf{0} \equiv Q$.
   - CASE 2: P is $\mathbf{0}$-free. Then clearly Q is also $\mathbf{0}$-free. Since P and Q are $\mathbf{0}$-free and language equivalent, it is not hard to see that they are also trace equivalent. So, according to Thm. 4.11, the equation $P = Q$ can be derived from $\mathcal{E}_T$, which is included in $\mathcal{E}_L$.
2. Note that, for every $P, Q \in \mathrm{BCCS}^{p*}$, the following holds:

$$P \lesssim_L Q \text{ iff } P + Q \simeq_L Q \ .$$

   Thus the completeness of the axiom system $\mathcal{E}_L \cup \{(\mathrm{S})\}$ with respect to $\lesssim_T$ is an immediate consequence of the first statement of the theorem.

5 Further Work

The completeness results presented in this paper deal with a significant fragment of the notions of semantics discussed in [7]. To our mind, the most important omission is a complete proof system for failures semantics [4] over BCCS with prefix iteration. We conjecture that a complete axiomatization for the failure preorder can be obtained by adding the laws

$$\begin{array}{rcl}
a.(x+y) & \leq & a.x + a.(y+z) \\
a.a^*(x+y) & \leq & a.a^*x + a.a^*(y+z) \\
a.a^*x & \leq & a^*a.(x+y) \\
a^*(x+y+a.(y+z)) & \leq & a^*(x+a.(y+z)) + y \\
a^*x & \leq & a^*(x+a.y)
\end{array}$$

to those for bisimulation equivalence (cf. Table 2), and we are currently working on the details of such a proof. The crux of the argument is a proof to the effect that the suggested inequations are sufficient to convexly saturate each process term, in the sense of [2]. We have also obtained irredundancy results for the axioms systems for ready simulation, simulation, trace and language equivalence. These will be presented in the full version of this paper, together with a characterization of the expressive power of BCCS with prefix iteration.

Acknowledgements: The research reported in this paper originates from a question posed by Rocco De Nicola. We thank the anonymous referees for their comments.

References

1. L. ACETO, W. J. FOKKINK, R. J. VAN GLABBEEK, AND A. INGÓLFSDÓTTIR, *Axiomatizing prefix iteration with silent steps*, Information and Computation, 127 (1996), pp. 26–40.
2. J. BERGSTRA, J. W. KLOP, AND E.-R. OLDEROG, *Readies and failures in the algebra of communicating processes*, SIAM J. Comput., 17 (1988), pp. 1134–1177.
3. B. BLOOM, S. ISTRAIL, AND A. R. MEYER, *Bisimulation can't be traced*, J. Assoc. Comput. Mach., 42 (1995), pp. 232–268.
4. S. BROOKES, C. HOARE, AND A. ROSCOE, *A theory of communicating sequential processes*, J. Assoc. Comput. Mach., 31 (1984), pp. 560–599.
5. J. H. CONWAY, *Regular Algebra and Finite Machines*, Mathematics Series (R. Brown and J. De Wet eds.), Chapman and Hall, London, United Kingdom, 1971.
6. W. J. FOKKINK, *A complete equational axiomatization for prefix iteration*, Inf. Process. Lett., 52 (1994), pp. 333–337.
7. R. J. V. GLABBEEK, *The linear time – branching time spectrum*, in Proceedings CONCUR 90, Amsterdam, J. Baeten and J. Klop, eds., vol. 458 of Lecture Notes in Computer Science, Springer-Verlag, 1990, pp. 278–297.
8. ——, *A complete axiomatization for branching bisimulation congruence of finite-state behaviours*, in Mathematical Foundations of Computer Science 1993, Gdansk, Poland, A. Borzyszkowski and S. Sokołowski, eds., vol. 711 of Lecture Notes in Computer Science, Springer-Verlag, 1993, pp. 473–484. Available by anonymous ftp from `Boole.stanford.edu`.
9. S. KLEENE, *Representation of events in nerve nets and finite automata*, in Automata Studies, C. Shannon and J. McCarthy, eds., Princeton University Press, 1956, pp. 3–41.
10. H. LIN, *An interactive proof tool for process algebras*, in 9th Annual Symposium on Theoretical Aspects of Computer Science, vol. 577 of Lecture Notes in Computer Science, Cachan, France, 13–15 Feb. 1992, Springer, pp. 617–618.
11. R. MILNER, *A complete inference system for a class of regular behaviours*, J. Comput. System Sci., 28 (1984), pp. 439–466.
12. ——, *Communication and Concurrency*, Prentice-Hall International, Englewood Cliffs, 1989.
13. ——, *The polyadic π-calculus: a tutorial*, in Proceedings Marktoberdorf Summer School '91, Logic and Algebra of Specification, NATO ASI Series F94, Springer-Verlag, 1993, pp. 203–246.
14. D. PARK, *Concurrency and automata on infinite sequences*, in 5th GI Conference, Karlsruhe, Germany, P. Deussen, ed., vol. 104 of Lecture Notes in Computer Science, Springer-Verlag, 1981, pp. 167–183.

The WHILE Hierarchy of Program Schemes Is Infinite

Can Adam Albayrak and Thomas Noll

RWTH Aachen
Ahornstr. 55, 52056 Aachen, Germany
e-mail: albayrak@informatik.rwth-aachen.de and noll@informatik.rwth-aachen.de
fax: +49 241 8888 217

Abstract. We exhibit a sequence S_n ($n \geq 0$) of WHILE program schemes, i. e., WHILE programs without interpretation, with the property that the WHILE nesting depth of S_n is n, and prove that any WHILE program scheme which is scheme equivalent to S_n, i. e., equivalent for all interpretations over arbitrary domains, has WHILE nesting depth at least n. This shows that the WHILE nesting depth imposes a strict hierarchy (the WHILE hierarchy) when programs are compared with respect to scheme equivalence and contrasts with Kleene's classical result that every program is equivalent to a program of WHILE nesting depth 1 (when interpreted over a fixed domain with arithmetic on non–negative integers). Our proof is based on results from formal language theory; in particular, we make use of the notion of star height of regular languages.

1 Introduction

When comparing programming languages, one often has a vague impression of one language being more powerful than another. However, a basic result of the theory of computability is that even simple models of computation like Turing machines, WHILE programs (with arithmetic), and partial recursive functions are universal in the following sense: They describe exactly the class of computable functions, according to Church's thesis. The proof uses encodings of functions by non–negative integers with the help of zero and successor function. Thus, if the programming language under consideration supports arithmetic on non–negative integers, then it is capable of simulating any effective control structure.

A compiler implementing a programming language could in principle adopt this method. In general, such languages do not only specify computations over non–negative integers but they handle data types like floating–point numbers, character strings, and trees as well. Additionally, modern programming languages allow recursion as means for the description of algorithms. In principle, these extended capabilities could be implemented (1) by embedding them in the setting of non–negative integers using appropriate encodings, (2) by simulating their behavior as a computable function, and (3) by translating the result back into the original context. However, it is clear that this approach is of purely theoretical interest; there is no hope for achieving good efficiency in this way. Instead these concepts are implemented directly: for example recursion is usually translated into iterative algorithms using a run–time stack.

Thus a comparison of the computational power of programming languages requires the distinction between the control structures of a program and other aspects like the semantic domains involved in the computations. Therefore we use the approach to decompose a program into a *program scheme* and an *interpretation* (which comprises the semantic domain). We study only the scheme part as an abstraction of the family of all programs represented by this scheme. In this generalized approach, two schemes are considered to be *equivalent* iff the concrete programs obtained by addition of an interpretation are equivalent for all interpretations. It is well–known that the schematic concept of "recursion" is more powerful than that of "iteration" [12], that "recursion" equals "iteration + stack" [2], and that "iteration" equals "while + Boolean variables" [1].

Unfortunately the question of scheme equivalence is undecidable in the general case [11]. The reason is not, as one might expect, the "large number" of interpretations which one has to apply for deciding scheme equivalence — it suffices to consider *free interpretations* (or *Herbrand interpretations*) only. Instead, the undecidability is caused by the structure of the state space of the program, more precisely the state space has too many components. If we abstract from the state space we obtain *simple* or *monadic schemes* for which the question of scheme equivalence becomes decidable in most cases.

In this paper we consider the class of Dijkstra schemes which are inductively built up from atomic statements by means of sequential composition, branching instructions, and WHILE loops. A characterization of scheme equivalence via regular languages is exploited: the star height of the regular language associated with a Dijkstra scheme yields a lower bound for the WHILE nesting depth required. We exhibit a sequence S_n ($n \geq 0$) of Dijkstra schemes with the property that the WHILE nesting depth of S_n is n, and prove (via the correspondence to regular languages) that any Dijkstra scheme which is equivalent to S_n has WHILE nesting depth at least n. This shows that the WHILE nesting depth of Dijkstra schemes imposes a strict hierarchy with respect to the computational power of the corresponding class of programs – the WHILE hierarchy. It contrasts with Kleene's classical result [10] that every program is equivalent to a program of WHILE nesting depth 1 (beside some fixed number of other loops) when interpreted over a fixed domain with arithmetic on non–negative integers.

2 Dijkstra schemes

Here we introduce the class of Dijkstra schemes. The only construction elements for Dijkstra schemes are sequential composition, branching, and conditional iteration. Thus, Dijkstra schemes can be regarded as WHILE *programs without interpretations.*

Let Ω, Π be non–empty, finite, and disjoint sets of unary *function symbols* and unary *predicate symbols.* (Ω, Π) is called a *signature.* The set $\mathbf{BExp}(\Pi)$ of *Boolean expressions over* Π is the smallest set which contains Π and which is closed under the Boolean operations (i. e. $\wedge$, $\vee$ and $\neg$). The class $\mathbf{Dij}(\Omega, \Pi)$ of *Dijkstra schemes over* Ω *and* Π is the smallest set which, for every $S, S_1, S_2 \in \mathbf{Dij}(\Omega, \Pi)$ and $b \in \mathbf{BExp}(\Pi)$, satisfies the following conditions:

- $\Omega \subseteq \mathbf{Dij}(\Omega, \Pi)$
- $(S_1; S_2) \in \mathbf{Dij}(\Omega, \Pi)$
- **if** b **then** S_1 **else** S_2 **fi** $\in \mathbf{Dij}(\Omega, \Pi)$
- **while** b **do** S **done** $\in \mathbf{Dij}(\Omega, \Pi)$.

We allow to omit braces.

Example 1. Let $\Omega := \{f, g, h\}$ and $\Pi := \{p\}$. Then

$$\begin{array}{l} f; \\ \textbf{while } p \textbf{ do} \\ \qquad (g; h) \\ \textbf{done} \end{array}$$

is a Dijkstra scheme.

A (Ω, Π)*–interpretation*, or *interpretation* for short, is a pair $\mathcal{A} := \langle A; \alpha \rangle$ where A is a non–empty set, the *domain* of the interpretation, and α is a mapping which assigns a predicate $\alpha(p) : A \to \{0, 1\}$ to every symbol $p \in \Pi$ and a total function $\alpha(f) : A \to A$ to every symbol $f \in \Omega$. Instead of $\alpha(f)$ we write $f_{\mathcal{A}}$. The class of all (Ω, Π)–interpretations is denoted by $\mathbf{Int}(\Omega, \Pi)$.

A pair $(S, \mathcal{A})$ consisting of a Dijkstra scheme $S \in \mathbf{Dij}(\Omega, \Pi)$ and an interpretation $\mathcal{A} \in \mathbf{Int}(\Omega, \Pi)$ is called a *Dijkstra program.* The *semantics* of $(S, \mathcal{A})$ is the (partial) mapping $[\![S]\!]_{\mathcal{A}} : A \to A$, given as follows:

$$[\![S]\!]_{\mathcal{A}}(a) := \begin{cases} f_{\mathcal{A}}(a) & \text{, if } S \in \Omega \\ [\![S_2]\!]_{\mathcal{A}}([\![S_1]\!]_{\mathcal{A}}(a)) & \text{, if } S = (S_1; S_2) \\ [\![S_1]\!]_{\mathcal{A}}(a) & \text{, if } S = \textbf{if } b \textbf{ then } S_1 \textbf{ else } S_2 \textbf{ fi} \text{ and } [\![b]\!]_{\mathcal{A}}(a) = 1 \\ [\![S_2]\!]_{\mathcal{A}}(a) & \text{, if } S = \textbf{if } b \textbf{ then } S_1 \textbf{ else } S_2 \textbf{ fi} \text{ and } [\![b]\!]_{\mathcal{A}}(a) = 0 \\ [\![S']\!]^k_{\mathcal{A}}(a) & \text{, if } S = \textbf{while } b \textbf{ do } S' \textbf{ done} \\ & \quad \text{and the WHILE } \textit{condition} \text{ holds} \\ \textit{undefined} & \text{else} \end{cases}$$

where $[\![b]\!]_{\mathcal{A}}(a)$ is the truth value of b on input a which is induced by the interpretation $\mathcal{A}$ and where the WHILE *condition* depending on b, S and a is given by

$$\forall i \in \{0, \ldots, k-1\} : [\![b]\!]_{\mathcal{A}}([\![S']\!]^i_{\mathcal{A}}(a)) = 1 \text{ and } [\![b]\!]_{\mathcal{A}}([\![S']\!]^k_{\mathcal{A}}(a)) = 0 \, .$$

As usual $[\![b]\!]_{\mathcal{A}}([\![S']\!]^i_{\mathcal{A}}(a)) = 1$ means that the *ith iteration* $[\![S']\!]^i_{\mathcal{A}}$ of the mapping $[\![S']\!]_{\mathcal{A}}$ applied to a is defined and that the results satisfies condition b.

Example 2. Let S the Dijkstra scheme in Example 1 and $\mathcal{A} := \langle \mathbf{N}^2; \alpha \rangle$ ($\mathbf{N}$ is the set of all non–negative integers) with $f_{\mathcal{A}}(m,n) := (m,1)$, $g_{\mathcal{A}}(m,n) := (m, m \cdot n)$, $h_{\mathcal{A}}(m,n) := (\max\{0, m-1\}, n)$ and $p_{\mathcal{A}}(m,n) = 1 \iff m \neq 0$. Then $[\![S]\!]_{\mathcal{A}}$ computes the factorial function, more precisely $[\![S]\!]_{\mathcal{A}}(m,n) = (0, m!)$.

As mentioned in the introduction we define:

Two Dijkstra schemes $S_1, S_2 \in \mathbf{Dij}(\Omega, \Pi)$ are *(strongly) equivalent* iff the equation

$$[\![S_1]\!]_{\mathcal{A}} = [\![S_2]\!]_{\mathcal{A}}$$

is valid for all interpretations $\mathcal{A} \in \mathbf{Int}(\Omega, \Pi)$. We write $S_1 \sim S_2$ iff S_1 and S_2 are equivalent.

Hence *scheme equivalence* comprises *program equivalence* which expresses that, under a fixed interpretation, both programs compute the same function.

3 Characterization of Dijkstra scheme equivalence

Now we give a characterization of scheme equivalence in terms of formal languages. The language L_S which we associate with a given Dijkstra scheme S is a regular language capturing the full computation potential of S. To simulate the behaviour of S under arbitrary interpretations, we especially record the decisions which have been taken in the Boolean conditions. The languages we define use Boolean vectors for this protocol; a word of this language consists of function symbols and Boolean vectors in alternation. The central point is the representation of scheme composition by a *conditional product* [9] of the corresponding languages. It allows two computations to be concatenated only if their adjacent Boolean vectors coincide.

For a set Ω of unary function symbols and a set $\Pi = \{p_1, \ldots, p_n\}$ of predicate symbols with n elements let

$$\mathbf{B} := \{0,1\}^n$$

be the set of all Boolean vectors of length n. We associate with each Boolean expression $b \in \mathbf{BExp}(\Pi)$ a set of Boolean vectors $L_b \subseteq \mathbf{B}$ by induction: for $p_i \in \Pi$ let

$$L_{p_i} := \{(x_1, \ldots, x_{i-1}, 1, x_{i+1}, \ldots, x_n) \mid x_1, \ldots, x_{i-1}, x_{i+1}, \ldots, x_n \in \{0,1\}\},$$

and $L_{b_1 \wedge b_2} := L_{b_1} \cap L_{b_2}$, $L_{b_1 \vee b_2} := L_{b_1} \cup L_{b_2}$, and $L_{\neg b} := \mathbf{B} \setminus L_b$. Now we are ready to specify the *Dijkstra scheme language* L_S of an arbitrary scheme

$S \in \mathbf{Dij}(\Omega, \Pi)$. It is given by the following inductive definition:

$$L_f := \mathbf{B} \cdot \{f\} \cdot \mathbf{B}$$
$$L_{(S_1;S_2)} := L_{S_1} \circ L_{S_2}$$
$$L_{\textbf{if } b \textbf{ then } S_1 \textbf{ else } S_2 \textbf{ fi}} := (L_b \circ L_{S_1}) \cup ((\mathbf{B} \setminus L_b) \circ L_{S_2})$$
$$L_{\textbf{while } b \textbf{ do } S \textbf{ done}} := \left(\bigcup_{i \in \mathbf{N}} (L_b \circ L_S)^i \right) \circ (\mathbf{B} \setminus L_b)$$

where $L_1 \circ L_2$ is the *conditional product* defined by

$$L_1 \circ L_2 := \{w\beta v \mid \beta \in \mathbf{B},\ w \in (\mathbf{B}\Omega)^*,\ v \in (\Omega\mathbf{B})^*,\ w\beta \in L_1 \text{ and } \beta v \in L_2\}$$

and $L^0 := \mathbf{B}$ and $L^{i+1} := L^i \circ L$ for every $i \in \mathbf{N}$. The class of all Dijkstra scheme languages over Ω and Π is denoted by $\mathcal{L}_{\mathbf{Dij}}(\Omega, \Pi)$.

Example 3. Let S be the Dijkstra scheme in Example 1, and let $B := (0+1)$. Then L_S is the language denoted by the regular expression

$$Bf(1gBh)^*0\,.$$

Proposition 4. ***(Characterization of Dijkstra scheme equivalence)*** *For any two Dijkstra schemes $S_1, S_2 \in \mathbf{Dij}(\Omega, \Pi)$ the following condition holds:*

$$S_1 \sim S_2 \quad \Longleftrightarrow \quad L_{S_1} = L_{S_2}\,.$$

Proof. It is well-known that every Dijkstra scheme is translatable into an equivalent *Ianov scheme*, which can be considered as an uninterpreted (monadic) flowchart (see [7], [6], [8], and [13] for further details). For this class of schemes, I. I. Ianov gave a language-theoretic description of equivalence by assigning to every scheme a deterministic finite automaton whose recognized language characterizes the scheme equivalence. The combination of both techniques yields our proof: by induction on the syntactic structure of $S \in \mathbf{Dij}(\Omega, \Pi)$ it is possible to show that the language associated with the equivalent Ianov scheme $\mathbf{trans}(S)$ and the language L_S assigned to S coincide. □

Example 5. Let S once again be the Dijkstra scheme in Example 1 and S' be the Dijkstra scheme

```
f;
if (¬p) then
  while p do (g; h) done
else
  (g; h);
  while p do (g; h) done
fi
```

Let $B := (0+1)$. Then the Dijkstra scheme language $L_{S'}$ is the language denoted by the regular expression

$$(Bf0) \; + \; (Bf1gBh(1gBh)^*0)\,.$$

Since it is the same language as the Dijkstra scheme language for S we can deduce by Proposition 4 that S and S' are equivalent.

4 The star height of regular languages

In order to prove the main theorem we use the concept of *star height of regular languages*. After presenting some known facts concerning the star height, we show that there exists an infinite family of regular languages $(L_n)_{n \in \mathbb{N}}$ such that every language L_n of this family has star height n. This knowledge will be exploited in the next section.

We use $\emptyset$ to denote the empty language, ε to denote the language which consists of the empty word and $L(\alpha)$ for the language denoted by the regular expression α. The set of all regular expressions over a finite alphabet Σ is denoted by $\mathbf{RE}(\Sigma)$.

The star height of a *regular expression* is the maximal number of nested stars which appear in this expression, and the star height of a *regular language* is the minimal star height of all regular expressions denoting this language, more formally one defines for a finite alphabet Σ

- $\mathbf{sh}(\emptyset) = \mathbf{sh}(\varepsilon) = \mathbf{sh}(a) = 0$ for all symbols $a \in \Sigma$
- $\mathbf{sh}(\alpha\beta) = \mathbf{sh}(\alpha + \beta) = \max\{\mathbf{sh}(\alpha), \mathbf{sh}(\beta)\}$ for $\alpha, \beta \in \mathbf{RE}(\Sigma)$
- $\mathbf{sh}(\alpha^*) = \mathbf{sh}(\alpha) + 1$ for $\alpha \in \mathbf{RE}(\Sigma)$,

and for a regular language $L \subseteq \Sigma^*$

$$\mathbf{sh}(L) := \min\{\mathbf{sh}(\alpha) \mid \alpha \in \mathbf{RE}(\Sigma) \text{ and } L(\alpha) = L\}$$

is called the *star height of L*.

Example 6. **(Star height** [3]**)** Let $\Sigma := \{a, b\}$. The regular expression

$$(ba^*b)^*$$

has star height 2 but the language $L((ba^*b)^*)$ denoted by this regular expression has at most star height 1, because

$$L(\varepsilon + b(a + bb)^*b) = L((ba^*b)^*)$$

and $\mathbf{sh}(\varepsilon + b(a + bb)^*b) = 1$. Furthermore it is easy to show that a regular language is finite iff it has zero star height. So we get $\mathbf{sh}(L((ba^*b)^*)) = 1$.

In 1963 L. C. Eggan has raised up the question whether there are languages of arbitrary star height over a two letter alphabet [5]. F. Dejean and M. P. Schützenberger gave a positive answer to this question by showing that for every $n \in \mathbb{N} \setminus \{0\}$ the language L_n over the alphabet $\{a, b\}$ which is recognized by the deterministic finite automaton $\mathcal{A}_n$

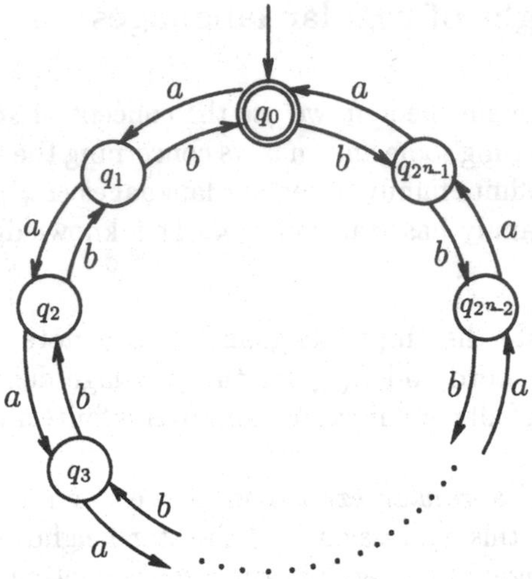

with 2^n states has star height n. We pick up the technique which has been used in [4] for showing that in a special subclass of regular languages, the class $\mathcal{L}_{\mathbf{Dij}}(\Omega, \Pi)$ of all Dijkstra scheme languages, there also exist languages of arbitrary star height.

The following well–known lemma, which we need in the next section, is easy to prove.

Lemma 7. ***(Star height of homomorphic images)*** *Let Σ be a finite alphabet and $h : \Sigma^* \to \Sigma^*$ be a homomorphism on Σ^*. Then for every regular language $L \subseteq \Sigma^*$:*

$$\mathbf{sh}(h(L)) \leq \mathbf{sh}(L)\,.$$

The next lemma presents the regular language family by which we are going to establish the connection to Dijkstra schemes.

Lemma 8. ***(Star height of a certain family of regular languages)*** *Let $(\alpha_n)_{n \in \mathbf{N}}$ be a family of regular expressions over the alphabet $\Sigma := \{f, g\}$, defined inductively by*

$$\begin{aligned} \alpha_0 &:= \varepsilon \\ \alpha_1 &:= (fg)^* \\ \alpha_{n+1} &:= (f^{2^n} \alpha_n f g g^{2^n} \alpha_n f g)^* \quad \textit{(for } n \in \mathbf{N} \setminus \{0\}\textit{)}\,. \end{aligned} \tag{1}$$

Then for all $n \in \mathbf{N}$ it holds that

$$\mathbf{sh}(L(\alpha_n)) = n\,.$$

Proof. To identify the star height of a language given by a regular expression, one has to prove the nonexistence of equivalent expressions of lower star height. Here we are forced to give a proof for every parameter $n \in \mathbf{N}$. The technique applied in [4] (cf. also [14] for a similar approach) can be used to obtain this result. Here we only sketch the proof. For every $n \in \mathbf{N} \setminus \{0\}$, let $\mathcal{K}_n$ be a class of regular languages which satisfies the following three conditions (a), (b), and (c):

(a) For every language L in $\mathcal{K}_n$

$$\exists z \forall w \in L : |w|_f - |w|_g = z\,,$$

where $|w|_f$ and $|w|_g$ denote the number of occurrences of f and g, respectively, in the word w.

(b) For $m, n \in \mathbf{N} \setminus \{0\}$ let $w_{(n,m)} \in \{f, g\}^*$ be given by

$$\begin{aligned} w_{(1,m)} &:= fg \\ w_{(n+1,m)} &:= f^{2^n} \left(w_{(n,m)}\right)^m fgg^{2^n} \left(w_{(n,m)}\right)^m fg\,. \end{aligned}$$

For every $n \in \mathbf{N} \setminus \{0\}$, the *n–subword index set of a language L* is

$$\mathbf{T}_n^L := \{m \in \mathbf{N} \setminus \{0\} \mid (w_{(n,m)})^m \text{ is a subword of a word in } L\}\,.$$

The cardinality of this set, which is called *n–subword index of L*, must be infinite for each L in $\mathcal{K}_n$:

$$|\mathbf{T}_n^L| = \infty\,,$$

i. e. there are (for every index n of $\mathcal{K}_n$) infinitely many subwords of the form $(w_{(n,m)})^m$ in L.

(c) Every element $L \in \mathcal{K}_n$ is minimal with respect to the star height among all languages which satisfy the conditions (a) and (b), i. e. for all regular languages L' over $\{f, g\}$ which also fulfil conditions (a) and (b) it holds that

$$\mathbf{sh}(L) \leq \mathbf{sh}(L')\,.$$

Thus all languages in $\mathcal{K}_n$ have the same star height.

It is easy to see that, for every $n \in \mathbf{N} \setminus \{0\}$, $L(\alpha_n)$ (cf. (1)) has properties (a) and (b). Hence, $\mathbf{sh}(L) \leq n$ for every $L \in \mathcal{K}_n$. The proof of the reverse inequation is shown by induction on n. For the case where $n = 1$ this follows from the fact that every infinite regular language has a star height of at least 1. For the inductive step we consider a decomposition of $L \in \mathcal{K}_{n+1}$ in a finite union of expressions of the form

$$\gamma_0^* \gamma_1 \gamma_2^* \gamma_3 \cdots \gamma_{2k-1} \gamma_{2k}^*$$

with $\mathbf{sh}(\gamma_i) < \mathbf{sh}(L)$ and verify that there is an index i_0 such that γ_{i_0} meets (a) and (b) for the parameter n. With the inductive assumption we conclude $\mathbf{sh}(L) \geq n + 1$. □

5 Nested WHILE loops in Dijkstra schemes

We now consider Dijkstra schemes with nested WHILE loops. We want to know whether it is possible to restrict the number of nested WHILE loops if we do not use coding mechanisms like in recursion theory, and if we do not require any special data structures.

We will show that such a limit does not exist in general. To this aim we exploit our characterization of Dijkstra scheme equivalence by formal languages and the star height property of regular languages. According to our preliminary definitions, the proof must be founded on a fixed finite signature of function and predicate symbols. Before studying this situation we consider the simpler case where the set of predicate symbols may become arbitrarily large. In this case it suffices to consider the *value language* $\mathbf{val}(S)$ of a Dijkstra scheme S to establish the connection to formal language theory. It collects all execution paths of S, represented by the sequence of function symbols as they are applied, and is defined as the homomorphic image of the Dijkstra scheme language L_S under the homomorphism which erases all Boolean vectors.

Proposition 9. ***(Value language of a Dijkstra scheme)*** *Let Ω be a set of unary function symbols and $R \subseteq \Omega^*$ be an arbitrary non–empty regular language over Ω. Then there exist*

- *a set Π_R of predicate symbols*
- *and a Dijkstra scheme $S_R \in \mathbf{Dij}(\Omega, \Pi_R)$*

such that $\mathbf{val}(S_R) = R$.

Proof. The proof is an easy induction on the set $\mathbf{RE}(\Omega)$ of all regular expressions over Ω, where for the inductive step we assume that the sets of predicate symbols of the constituent schemes are disjoint and where we obtain one of the schemes

- **if** p **then** S_{R_1} **else** S_{R_2} **fi** with a new predicate symbol p for the case "$R_1 \cup R_2$"
- $(S_{R_1}; S_{R_2})$ for "$R_1 \cdot R_2$"
- **while** p **do** S_{R_1} **done** with a new predicate symbol p for the case "R_1^*".

□

Note that the WHILE nesting depth of the resulting scheme coincides with the star height of the regular expression representing R.

Corollary 10. ***(Star height of Dijkstra scheme languages with infinite signatures)*** *Let Ω be a set of function symbols with at least two elements and Π be an arbitrary large set of predicate symbols. Then for every $n \in \mathbf{N}$ there exists a Dijkstra scheme $S_n \in \mathbf{Dij}(\Omega, \Pi)$ such that*

$$\mathbf{sh}(L_{S_n}) = n\,,$$

i. e. the star height of Dijkstra scheme languages over infinite signatures is unbounded.

Proof. We use the following result, cited in Section 4: In the class of regular languages over an alphabet with at least two elements there exists, for every number $n \in \mathbf{N}$, a regular language L_n such that $\mathbf{sh}(L_n) = n$. Let $n \in \mathbf{N}$, and let α be a regular expression with $L(\alpha) = L_n$ and $\mathbf{sh}(\alpha) = n$. According to Proposition 9, there exists (a set Π of predicate symbols and) a Dijkstra schema S with $\mathbf{val}(S) = L_n$, constructed inductively on the structure of α. Because its value language $\mathbf{val}(S)$ is a homomorphic image of the scheme language L_S, Lemma 7 yields

$$\mathbf{sh}(L_S) \geq \mathbf{sh}(\mathbf{val}(S)) = n\,. \tag{2}$$

As mentioned above, since S has been built up according to α, it contains at most n nested WHILE loops. On the other hand, only WHILE loops yield a contribution to the star height of the scheme language L_S. Thus we obtain

$$\mathbf{sh}(L_S) \leq n$$

and hence, by (2),

$$\mathbf{sh}(L_S) = n\,.$$

The question arises whether it is really necessary to introduce new predicate symbols, as in the proof of Theorem 9. If it was possible to reuse them, then our proof could be based on a fixed signature. The following example illustrates the difficulties.

Example 11. Let $\Pi := \{p\}$ and $\Omega := \{f, g, h\}$. We consider the Dijkstra schemes S_1 and S_2 over this signature where

$$S_1 := \textbf{if } p \textbf{ then } f \textbf{ else } g \textbf{ fi}$$

and

$$S_2 := h\,.$$

Then we get $L_{S_1} = \{1f0, 1f1, 0g0, 0g1\}$ and $L_{S_1} = \{0h0, 0h1, 1h0, 1h1\}$ and therefore $\mathbf{val}(S_1) = \{f, g\}$ and $\mathbf{val}(S_2) = \{h\}$.

If in the case "$R_1 \cup R_2$" of the above construction we would not introduce a new predicate symbol then we would obtain the Dijkstra scheme

$$S = \textbf{if } p \textbf{ then } (\textbf{if } p \textbf{ then } f \textbf{ else } g \textbf{ fi}) \textbf{ else } h \textbf{ fi}\,,$$

which has the scheme language $L_S = \{1f0, 1f1, 0h0, 0h1\}$ and thus the value language $\mathbf{val}(S) = \{f, h\}$. But then

$$\mathbf{val}(S) = \{f, h\} \neq \{f, g, h\} = \mathbf{val}(S_1) \cup \mathbf{val}(S_2)\,.$$

The reason for this is simply that g becomes never applied in any interpretation because of the repeated use of the predicate symbol p — S is not *free*.

Now we present our proof of the hierarchy result with a fixed signature. We assume that we have at least one predicate symbol p and at least two function symbols. In the discussion at the end of the paper we will explain why we cannot extend our proof technique to signatures where we have one function symbol only.

The set of predicate symbols which we need in the proof of Theorem 9 must contain at least as many symbols as the number of occurrences of $+$ and * in the regular expression where we start from. To restrict the number of predicate symbols we should sparingly use the symbol $+$, and we should reuse predicate symbols. The above example shows that such a reuse can at best be accomplished by employing *free Dijkstra schemes*, i. e. Dijkstra schemes where between two condition evaluations a computation (function application) must take place. This can be achieved by appending function symbols after WHILE loops.

An appropriate family $(S_n)_{n\in\mathbf{N}}$ of Dijkstra schemes over $\Omega = \{f,g\}$ and $\Pi := \{p\}$ is given as follows. For every $n \in \mathbf{N}$, let

$$f^{2^n} := \underbrace{f;\ldots;f}_{2^n \text{ times}}$$

(g^{2^n} analogously). Then $(S_n)_{n\in\mathbf{N}}$ is defined as

$$\begin{aligned} S_0 &:= \textbf{while } (p \wedge \neg p) \textbf{ do } f; g \textbf{ done} \\ S_1 &:= \textbf{while } p \textbf{ do } f;\ g \textbf{ done}; \\ S_{n+1} &:= \textbf{while } p \textbf{ do} \\ &\qquad\qquad f^{2^n};\ S_n;\ f;\ g;\ g^{2^n};\ S_n;\ f;\ g; \\ &\quad\ \ \textbf{done}; \end{aligned} \tag{3}$$

(where $n \geq 1$). Now the following theorem holds:

Theorem 12. ***(Star height of Dijkstra scheme languages over a fixed signature)*** *Let $\Omega := \{f,g\}$ and $\Pi := \{p\}$. For $n \in \mathbf{N}$ let $S_n \in \mathbf{Dij}(\Omega,\Pi)$ be the Dijkstra schemes defined in (3). The Dijkstra scheme language L_{S_n} has the following property:*

$$\mathbf{sh}(L_{S_n}) = n\,.$$

Proof. An easy induction over $n \in \mathbf{N}$ shows for the value language $\mathbf{val}(S_n)$:

$$\mathbf{val}(S_n) = L(\alpha_n)\,,$$

where α_n is the regular expression defined in Lemma 8. According to Proposition 8 we get $\mathbf{sh}(\mathbf{val}(S_n)) = n$ (for every $n \in \mathbf{N}$). As in the proof of Corollary 10, Lemma 7 on the star height of homomorphic images and the observation that only WHILE loops can contribute to the star height of a Dijkstra scheme language yield

$$n \stackrel{(8)}{=} \mathbf{sh}(\mathbf{val}(S_n)) \stackrel{(7)}{\leq} \mathbf{sh}(L_{S_n}) \leq n\,,$$

which implies that $\mathbf{sh}(L_{S_n}) = n$. □

From this theorem we can deduce a corollary which shows clearly the effect of the different notions of equivalence (program equivalence, scheme equivalence) and of the encodings by means of special data structures. While from the standpoint of recursion theory the number of nested loops can be bounded, such a limit does not exist from the standpoint of program scheme theory (because otherwise there would exist a limit on the star height of Dijkstra scheme languages). We express the main result of this section:

Corollary 13. ***(The WHILE Hierarchy of Dijkstra schemes)*** *The hierarchy of nested* WHILE *loops in Dijkstra schemes is strict, i. e. for every $n \in \mathbb{N}$ there exists a Dijkstra scheme S_{n+1} such that S_{n+1} uses $n+1$ nested* WHILE *loops and S_{n+1} cannot be equivalent to any Dijkstra scheme with less than $n+1$ nested* WHILE *loops.*

6 Conclusion and Discussion

Conclusion: By combining two well-known techniques we characterized the equivalence of Dijkstra schemes which respect to the inductive structure of the class of Dijkstra schemes. We have shown, by considering the star height of Dijkstra scheme languages, that the renounce of coding mechanism and special data structures leads to an infinite hierarchy concerning the number of nested WHILE loops.

Discussion: Unfortunately Theorem 12 does not express anything about minimal signatures, i. e. signatures with one predicate symbol and one function symbol only. Since value languages of a Dijkstra scheme over such a signature are regular languages over a one-letter alphabet, the star height of the value language can only be 0 or 1. So the technique we used in our proof can not be extended to such a signature, because the inequality

$$\mathbf{sh}(\mathbf{val}(S_n)) \leq \mathbf{sh}(L_{S_n})$$

degenerates to $0 \leq \mathbf{sh}(L_{S_n})$ or $1 \leq \mathbf{sh}(L_{S_n})$, respectively. Thus the question is still open in this setting. Since it suffices to identify languages of arbitrary star height in the homomorphic images of the scheme languages, a possible approach might be a homomorphism which erases the function symbols instead of the Boolean vectors, yielding a regular language over the two-letter alphabet of truth values.

Acknowledgements: We would like to thank Klaus Indermark for the premise of this work, as well as Markus Mohnen and Thomas Wilke for the effort of reading a draft version of this paper.

References

1. Corrado Böhm and Giuseppe Jacopini. Flow diagrams, Turing machines and languages with only two formation rules. *Communications of the ACM*, 9(5):366–371, 1966.

2. Steven Brown, David Gries, and Thomas Szymanski. Program schemes with pushdown stores. *SIAM Journal on Computing*, 1:242–268, 1972.
3. Rina S. Cohen and Janusz A. Brzozowski. General properties of star heigt of regular events. *Journal of Computer and System Sciences*, 4:260–280, 1970.
4. F. Dejean and M. P. Schützenberger. On a question of Eggan. *Information and Control*, 9:23–25, 1966.
5. L. C. Eggan. Transition graphs and the star-height of regular events. *The Michigan Mathematical Journal*, 10:385–397, 1963.
6. Iu. I. Ianov. On matrix program schemes. *Communications of the ACM*, 12(1):3–6, 1958.
7. Iu. I. Ianov. On the equivalence and transformation of program schemes. *Communications of the ACM*, 10(1):8–12, 1958.
8. Iu. I. Ianov. The logical schemes of algorithms. *Problems of Cybernetics*, 1:82–140, 1960.
9. Klaus Indermark. On a class of schematic languages. In R. Aguilar, editor, *Formal Languages and Programming, Proceedings of a Seminar Organized by UAM-IBM Scientific Center*, pages 1–13, 1975.
10. S. C. Kleene. General recursive functions of natural numbers. *Mathematische Annalen*, 112:727–742, 1936.
11. D. C. Luckham, D. M. R. Park, and M. S. Paterson. On formalised computer programs. *Journal of Computer and System Sciences*, 4(3):220–249, 1970.
12. Michael S. Paterson and Carl E. Hewitt. Comparative schematology. Technical Report AI memo 201, MIT AI Lab, Publications Office, 545 Technology Sq. Cambridge, MA 02139, 1970.
13. Joseph D. Rutledge. On Ianov's program schemata. *Journal of the ACM*, 11(1):1–9, 1964.
14. Arto Salomaa. *Jewels of formal language theory*. Computer Science Press, 1981.

Analysis of a Guard Condition in Type Theory (Extended Abstract)

Roberto M. Amadio Solange Coupet-Grimal

Université de Provence, Marseille *

Abstract. We present a realizability interpretation of co-inductive types based on partial equivalence relations (per's). We extract from the per's interpretation sound rules to type recursive definitions. These recursive definitions are needed to introduce 'infinite' and 'total' objects of co-inductive type such as an infinite stream, a digital transducer, or a non-terminating process. We show that the proposed type system subsumes those studied by Coquand and Gimenez while still enjoying the basic syntactic properties of subject reduction and strong normalization with respect to a confluent rewriting system first put forward by Gimenez.

1 Introduction

Coquand proposes in [4] an approach to the representation of infinite objects such as streams and processes in a predicative type theory extended with *co-inductive types*. Related analyses on the role of co-inductive types (or definitions) in logical systems can be found in [14, 11] for the system F, [16] for the system HOL, and [20] for Beeson's Elementary theory of Operations and Numbers. Two important features of Coquand's approach are that: (1) Co-inductive types, and related constructors and destructors, are added to the theory, rather than being represented by second order types and related λ-terms, as in [7, 17]. (2) Recursive definitions of infinite objects are restricted so that consideration of *partial elements* is *not* needed. Thus this work differs from work on the representation of infinite structures in lazy programming languages like Haskell (see, e.g., [21]).

In his thesis [8], Gimenez has carried on a realization of Coquand's programme in the framework of the calculus of constructions [5]. More precisely, he studies a calculus of constructions extended with a type of streams (i.e., finite and infinite lists), and proves subject reduction and strong normalization for a related confluent rewriting system. He also applies co-inductive types to the representation and mechanical verification of concurrent systems by relying on the Coq system [3] extended with co-inductive types (another case study can be found in [6]). In this system, processes can be *directly represented* in the logic as elements of a certain type. This approach differs sharply from those where, say,

* CMI, 39 rue Joliot-Curie F-13453, Marseille, France. *amadio@gyptis.univ-mrs.fr.* The first author was partially supported by *CTI-CNET 95-1B-182*, *Action Incitative INRIA*, *IFCPAR 1502-1*, *WG Confer*, and *HCM Express*. A preliminary version of this paper (including proofs) can be found in [1].

processes are represented at a syntactic level as elements of an *inductively defined* type (see, e.g., [15]). Clearly the representation based on co-inductive types is more direct because recursion is built-in. This may be a decisive advantage when carrying on *formal proofs*. Therefore, the issue is whether this representation is *flexible* enough, that is whether we can type enough objects and whether we can reason about their equality. These questions are solid motivations for our work.

The introduction of infinite 'total' objects relies on recursive definitions which are intuitively 'guarded' in a sense frequently arising in formal languages [18]. An instance of the new typing rule in this approach is:

$$\frac{\Gamma, x : \sigma \vdash M : \sigma \quad M \downarrow x \quad \sigma \text{ co-inductive type}}{\Gamma \vdash \mathsf{fix}\; x.M : \sigma} \,. \tag{1}$$

This allows for the introduction of 'infinite objects' in a 'co-inductive type', by means of a 'guarded' (recursive) definition. Of course, one would like to have notions of co-inductive type and of guarded definition which are as liberal as possible and that are supported by an intuitive, i.e., *semantic*, interpretation.

In Coquand's proposal, the predicate $M \downarrow x$ is defined by a straightforward analysis of the syntactic structure of the term. This is a syntactic approximation of the main issue, that is to know when the recursive definition $\mathsf{fix}\; x.M$ determines a unique total object. To answer this question we interpret co-inductive types in the category of per's (partial equivalence relations), a category of *total* computations, and we find that the guard predicate $M \downarrow x$ has a semantic analogy which can be stated as follows:

$$\forall \alpha \left((d,e) \in \mathcal{F}^{\alpha}_{\sigma} \;\Rightarrow\; ([\![M]\!][d/x], [\![M]\!][e/x]) \in \mathcal{F}^{\alpha+1}_{\sigma} \right) \tag{2}$$

where $\mathcal{F}_\sigma$ is a monotonic function on per's associated to the co-inductive type σ, and $\mathcal{F}^{\alpha}_{\sigma}$ is its αth iteration, for α ordinal. We propose to represent condition (2) in the syntax by introducing some extra-notation. With the side conditions of rule (1), we introduce two types $\breve{\sigma}$ and $\breve{\sigma}^+$ which are interpreted respectively by $\mathcal{F}^{\alpha}_{\sigma}$ and $\mathcal{F}^{\alpha+1}_{\sigma}$. We can then replace the guard condition $M \downarrow x$ by the typing judgment $x : \breve{\sigma} \vdash M : \breve{\sigma}^+$ whose interpretation is basically condition (2). The revised typing system also includes: (1) *Subtyping* rules which relate a co-inductive type σ to its approximations $\breve{\sigma}$ and $\breve{\sigma}^+$, so that we will have: $\sigma \leq \breve{\sigma}^+ \leq \breve{\sigma}$. (2) Rules which *overload* the constructors of the co-inductive type, e.g., if $f : \sigma \to \sigma$ is a unary constructor over σ, then f will also have the type $\breve{\sigma} \to \breve{\sigma}^+$ (to be understood as $\forall \alpha \;\; x \in \mathcal{F}^{\alpha}_{\sigma} \;\Rightarrow\; f(x) \in \mathcal{F}^{\alpha+1}_{\sigma}$). The types $\sigma \to \sigma$ and $\breve{\sigma} \to \breve{\sigma}^+$ will be incomparable with respect to the subtyping relation.

The idea of expressing the guard condition via approximating types, subtyping, and overloading can be traced back to Gimenez's system. Our contribution here is to provide a semantic framework which:

(1) Justifies and provides an intuition for the typing rules. In particular, we will see how it is possible to understand semantically Gimenez's system.

(2) Suggests new typing rules and simplifications of existing ones. In particular, we propose: (i) a rule to type nested recursive definitions, and (ii) a way to type recursive definitions without labelling types.

(3) Can be readily adapted to prove strong normalization with respect to the confluent reduction relation introduced by Gimenez.

2 A simply typed calculus

We will carry on our study in a simply typed λ-calculus extended with co-inductive types.[2] Let F be a countable set of *constructors*. We let $\mathsf{f}_1, \mathsf{f}_2, \ldots$ range over F. Let tv be the set of type variables $t, s, \ldots$ The language of *raw* types is given by the following (informal) grammar:

$$\tau ::= tv \mid (\tau \to \tau') \mid \nu tv.(\mathsf{f}_1 : \tau_1 \to tv \ldots \mathsf{f}_k : \tau_k \to tv) \tag{3}$$

where $\tau_i \to tv$ stands for $\tau_{i,1} \to \cdots \to \tau_{i,n_i} \to tv$ ($\to$ associates to the right), and all f_i are distinct. Intuitively, a type of the shape $\nu t.(\mathsf{f}_1 : \tau_1 \to t \ldots \mathsf{f}_k : \tau_k \to t)$ is well-formed if the type variable t occurs positively in the well-formed types $\tau_{i,j}$, for $i = 1 \ldots k$, $j = 1 \ldots n_i$. Note that the type variable t is bound by ν and it can be renamed. We call types of this shape co-inductive types, the symbols $\mathsf{f}_1 \ldots \mathsf{f}_k$ represent the constructors of the type. We will denote co-inductive types with the letters $\sigma, \sigma', \sigma_1, \ldots$, and unless specified otherwise, we will suppose that they have the generic form in (3). A precise definition of the well-formed types is given as follows.

Definition 1 types. If τ is a raw type and s is a type variable then the predicates $wf(\tau)$ (well-formed), $pos(s,\tau)$ (positive occurrence only), and $neg(s,\tau)$ (negative occurrence only) are the least predicates which satisfy the following conditions.

(1) If $t \in tv$ then $wf(t)$, $pos(s,t)$, and $neg(s,t)$ provided $t \neq s$.

(2) If $wf(\tau)$ and $wf(\tau')$ then $wf(\tau \to \tau')$. Moreover, $pos(s, \tau \to \tau')$ if $pos(s,\tau')$ and $neg(s,\tau)$, and $neg(s,\tau \to \tau')$ if $neg(s,\tau')$ and $pos(s,\tau)$.

(3) If $\sigma = \nu t.(\mathsf{f}_1 : \tau_1 \to t \ldots \mathsf{f}_k : \tau_k \to t)$ and $t \neq s$ (otherwise rename t) then $wf(\sigma)$ provided $wf(\tau_{i,j})$ and $pos(t, \tau_{i,j})$ for $i = 1 \ldots k$, $j = 1 \ldots n_i$. Moreover, $pos(s,\sigma)$ if $pos(s,\tau_{i,j})$ for $i = 1 \ldots k$, $j = 1 \ldots n_i$, and $neg(s,\sigma)$ if $neg(s,\tau_{i,j})$ for $i = 1 \ldots k$, $j = 1 \ldots n_i$.

Example 1. Here are a few examples of well-formed co-inductive types where we suppose that the type τ is not bound by ν.

(1) Infinite streams over τ: $\nu s.(\mathsf{cons} : \tau \to (s \to s))$.

(2) Input-output processes over τ: $\nu p.(\mathsf{nil} : p, ! : \tau \to p \to p, ? : (\tau \to p) \to p)$.

(3) An involution: $\nu t.(\mathsf{inv} : ((t \to \tau) \to \tau) \to t)$.

Definition 1 allows mutually recursive definitions. For instance, we can define processes over streams over processes ...:

$$\sigma = \nu t.(\mathsf{nil} : t, ! : \sigma' \to t \to t, ? : (\sigma' \to t) \to t) \quad \sigma' = \nu s.(\mathsf{cons} : t \to s \to s) .$$

[2] Per's interpretations support other relevant extensions of the type theory, including second-order types (see, e.g., [13]) and inductive types (see, e.g., [12]). As expected, an inductive type, e.g., $\mu t.(\mathsf{nil} : t, \mathsf{cons} : o \to t \to t)$ is interpreted as the *least fixpoint* of the operator $\mathcal{F}$ described in section 3. It follows that there is a natural subtyping relation between the inductive type and the corresponding co-inductive type $\nu t.(\mathsf{nil} : t, \mathsf{cons} : o \to t \to t)$.

These mutually recursive definitions lead to some complication in the typing of constructors. For instance, the type of cons should be $[\sigma/t](t \to \sigma' \to \sigma')$, and moreover we have to make sure that all occurrences of a cons have the same type (after unfolding). To make our analysis clearer, we prefer to gloss over these technical issues by taking a stronger definition of positivity. Thus, in the case (3) of definition 1, we say $pos(s,\sigma)$ (or $neg(s,\sigma)$) if s does not occur free in σ. In this way a type variable which is free in a co-inductive type cannot be bound by a ν.

Let v be the set of term variables $x, y, \ldots$ A context Γ is a possibly empty list $x_1 : \tau_1 \ldots x_n : \tau_n$ where all x_i are distinct. Raw terms are defined by the following grammar:

$$M ::= v \mid (\lambda v.M) \mid (MM) \mid \mathsf{f}^\sigma \mid \mathsf{case}^\sigma \mid (\mathsf{fix}\ v.M)\ . \tag{4}$$

We denote with $FV(M)$ the set of variables occurring free in the term M. The typing rules are defined as follows:

$$\frac{x : \tau \in \Gamma}{\Gamma \vdash x : \tau} \qquad \frac{\Gamma, x : \tau \vdash M : \tau'}{\Gamma \vdash \lambda x.M : \tau \to \tau'} \qquad \frac{\Gamma \vdash M : \tau' \to \tau \quad \Gamma \vdash N : \tau'}{\Gamma \vdash MN : \tau}$$

$$\text{Assuming:}\ \begin{array}{l} \sigma = \nu t.(\mathsf{f}_1 : \tau_1 \to t \ldots \mathsf{f}_k : \tau_k \to t) \\ \tau' \to \sigma = \tau'_1 \to \ldots \tau'_m \to \sigma \quad (m \geq 0) \end{array}$$

$$\frac{}{\Gamma \vdash \mathsf{f}_i^\sigma : [\sigma/t]\tau_{i,1} \to \cdots [\sigma/t]\tau_{i,n_i} \to \sigma}$$

$$\frac{}{\Gamma \vdash \mathsf{case}^\sigma : \sigma \to ([\sigma/t]\tau_1 \to \tau) \to \cdots ([\sigma/t]\tau_k \to \tau) \to \tau}$$

$$\frac{\Gamma, x : \tau' \to \sigma \vdash M : \tau' \to \sigma \quad M \downarrow x}{\Gamma \vdash \mathsf{fix}\ x.M : \tau' \to \sigma}$$

The guard predicate '$M \downarrow x$' is left unspecified. Intuitively, this predicate has to guarantee that a recursive definition does determine a unique 'total' object. Before trying a formal definition, we will consider a few examples of recursive definitions, where we use the notation $\mathsf{let}\ x = M\ \mathsf{in}\ N$ for $(\lambda x.M)N$, and let application associate to the left.

Example 2. Let o be a basic type of numerals with constants $0 : o$ and $suc : o \to o$. Let us first consider the type of infinite streams of numerals, with destructors head and tail:

$$\sigma_1 = \nu t.(\mathsf{cons} : o \to (t \to t))$$
$$hd = \lambda x.\mathsf{case}^{\sigma_1}\ x(\lambda n.\lambda y.n) \qquad tl = \lambda x.\mathsf{case}^{\sigma_1}\ x(\lambda n.\lambda y.y)\ .$$

(1) We can introduce an infinite list of 0's as follows: $\mathsf{fix}\ x.\mathsf{cons}^{\sigma_1} 0 x$.

(2) We can also define a function which adds 1 to every element of a stream:

$$\mathsf{fix}\ add1.\lambda x.\mathsf{case}^{\sigma_1}\ x(\lambda n.\lambda x'.\mathsf{cons}^{\sigma_1}(suc\ n)(add1\ x'))\ .$$

(3) Certain recursive definitions should not type, e.g., fix $x.\mathsf{cons}^{\sigma_1}0(tl\ x)$. The equation does not determine a stream, as all streams of the form $\mathsf{cons}^{\sigma_1}0z'$ give a solution.

(4) The function db doubles every element in the stream:

$$\mathsf{fix}\ db.\lambda x.\mathsf{let}\ n = (hd\ x)\ \mathsf{in}\ \mathsf{cons}^{\sigma_1}n(\mathsf{cons}^{\sigma_1}n\ db(tl\ x))\ .$$

(5) Next we work over the type σ_2 of finite and infinite streams. The function C concatenates two streams.

$$\sigma_2 = \nu t.(\mathsf{nil} : t, \mathsf{cons} : o \to t \to t)$$
$$C \equiv \mathsf{fix}\ conc.\lambda x.\lambda y.\mathsf{case}^{\sigma_2}\ x\ y\ \lambda n.\lambda x'.(\mathsf{cons}^{\sigma_2}n(conc\ x'\ y))\ .$$

(6) Finally, we consider the type σ_3 of infinite binary trees whose nodes may have two colours, and the following recursive definition:

$$\sigma_3 = \nu t.(\mathsf{bin}_1 : t \to t \to t, \mathsf{bin}_2 : t \to t \to t)$$
$$(\mathsf{fix}\ x.\mathsf{bin}_1^{\sigma_3}\ x\ (\mathsf{fix}\ y.\mathsf{bin}_2^{\sigma_3}\ x\ y))\ .$$

We recall next Coquand's definition [4] of the guard predicate in the case the type theory includes just one co-inductive type, say $\sigma = \nu t.(\mathsf{nil} : t, \mathsf{cons} : o \to t \to t)$.

Definition 2. Supposing $\Gamma, x : \tau' \to \sigma \vdash M : \tau' \to \sigma$, we write $M \downarrow x$ if the judgment $\Gamma, x : \tau' \to \sigma \vdash M \downarrow_1^{\tau' \to \sigma} x$ can be derived by the following rules, where n ranges over $\{0, 1\}$. The intuition is that 'x is guarded by at least a constructor in M'. For the sake of readability, we omit in the premisses the conditions that $x : \tau' \to \sigma \in \Gamma$ and the terms have the right type.

$$\frac{x \notin FV(M)}{\Gamma \vdash M \downarrow_n^{\tau} x} \qquad \frac{\Gamma, y : \tau \vdash M \downarrow_n^{\tau \to \sigma} x \quad y \neq x}{\Gamma \vdash \lambda y.M \downarrow_n^{\tau \to \tau \to \sigma} x}$$

$$\frac{x \notin FV(M_1) \quad \Gamma \vdash M_2 \downarrow_0^{\sigma} x}{\Gamma \vdash \mathsf{cons}^{\sigma} M_1 M_2 \downarrow_1^{\sigma} x} \qquad \frac{x \notin FV(M_1) \quad \Gamma \vdash M_2 \downarrow_0^{\sigma} x}{\Gamma \vdash \mathsf{cons}^{\sigma} M_1 M_2 \downarrow_0^{\sigma} x}$$

$$\frac{x \notin FV(N) \quad \Gamma \vdash M_1 \downarrow_n^{\sigma} x \quad \Gamma \vdash M_2 \downarrow_n^{o \to \sigma \to \sigma} x}{\Gamma \vdash \mathsf{case}^{\sigma} N M_1 M_2 \downarrow_n^{\sigma} x} \qquad \frac{x \notin FV(M_j) \quad j = 1 \ldots m}{x M_1 \ldots M_m \downarrow_0^{\sigma} x}\ .$$

Coquand's definition is quite restrictive. In particular: (i) it is unable to traverse β-redexes as in example 2(4), and (ii) it does not cope with nested recursive definitions as in example 2(6). We present in the next section a simple semantic framework which clarifies the typing issues and suggests a guard condition more powerful than the one above.

3 Interpretation

In this section we present an interpretation of the calculus in the well-known category of partial equivalence relations (per's) over a λ-model (cf., e.g., [19]). Let $(D, \cdot, k, s, \epsilon)$ be a $\lambda\beta$-model (cf. [2]). We often write de for $d \cdot e$. We denote with $A, B, \ldots$ binary relations over D. We write $d\,A\,e$ for $(d, e) \in A$ and we set: $[d]_A = \{e \in D \mid d\,A\,e\}$, $|A| = \{d \in D \mid d\,A\,d\}$, and $[A] = \{[d]_A \mid d \in |A|\}$.

Definition 3 partial equivalence relations. Let D be a λ-model. The category of per's over D ($\mathbf{per}_D$) is defined as follows:

$$\begin{array}{ll}\mathbf{per}_D & = \{A \mid A \subseteq D \times D \text{ and } A \text{ is symmetric and transitive}\} \\ \mathbf{per}_D[A, B] & = \{f : [A] \to [B] \mid \exists \phi \in D \ (\phi \Vdash f)\} \\ \phi \Vdash f : [A] \to [B] \text{ iff } & \forall d \in D \ (d \in |A| \Rightarrow \phi d \in f([d]_A)) \,.\end{array}$$

We will use the λ-notation to denote elements of the λ-model D. E.g., $\lambda x.x \Vdash f$ stands for $[\![\lambda x.x]\!]^D \Vdash f$. The category $\mathbf{per}_D$ has a rich structure, in particular it has finite products, finite sums, and exponents, whose construction is recalled below.

$$\begin{array}{c} d\, A_1 \times \ldots \times A_n\, e \ \text{ iff } \ \forall i \in \{1 \ldots n\} \ (p_i d)\, A_i\, (p_i e) \ \text{ where:} \\ p_i = \lambda u.u(\lambda x_1 \ldots \lambda x_n.x_i) \quad p_i \Vdash \pi_i : [\Pi_{i=1\ldots n} A_i] \to [A_i] \\ \phi_i \Vdash f_i : [C] \to [A_i] \ \Rightarrow \ \lambda d.\lambda u.u(\phi_1 d) \ldots (\phi_n d) \Vdash \langle f_1 \ldots f_n \rangle : [C] \to [\Pi_{i=1\ldots n} A_i] \end{array}$$

$$\begin{array}{c} d\, A_1 + \ldots + A_n\, e \ \text{ iff } \exists i \in \{1 \ldots n\} \ (d = (j_i d'),\ (e = j_i e') \text{ and } d'\, A_i\, e') \text{ where:} \\ j_i = \lambda u.\lambda y_1 \ldots \lambda y_n.y_i u \quad j_i \Vdash in_i : [A_i] \to [\Sigma_{i=1\ldots n} A_i] \\ \phi_i \Vdash f_i : [A_i] \to [C] \ \Rightarrow \ \lambda d.d\phi_1 \ldots \phi_n \Vdash [f_1 \ldots f_n] : [\Sigma_{i=1\ldots n} A_i] \to [C] \end{array}$$

$$\begin{array}{c} d\, A \to B\, e \ \text{ iff } \ \forall d', e' \ (d'\, A\, e' \ \Rightarrow \ (dd')\, B\, (ee')) \ \text{ where:} \\ \lambda d.(p_1 d)(p_2 d) \Vdash ev : [B^A \times A] \to B \\ \phi \Vdash f : [C \times A] \to [B] \ \Rightarrow \ \lambda d.\lambda d'.\phi(\lambda u.(ud)d') \Vdash \Lambda(f) : [C] \to [B^A] \,. \end{array}$$

As degenerate cases of empty product and empty sum we get terminal and initial objects:

$$1 = D \times D \quad \lambda x.x \Vdash f : [A] \to 1 \quad 0 = \emptyset \quad \lambda x.x \Vdash f : [0] \to [A] \,.$$

We denote with $\eta : tv \to \mathbf{per}_D$ type environments. The interpretation of type variables and higher types is then given as follows:

$$[\![t]\!]_\eta = \eta(t) \quad [\![\tau \to \tau']\!]_\eta = [\![\tau]\!]_\eta \to [\![\tau']\!]_\eta \,.$$

As for co-inductive types, given a type $\sigma = \nu t.(\mathsf{f}_1 : \tau_1 \to t \ldots \mathsf{f}_k : \tau_k \to t)$, and a type environment η, we define a function $\mathcal{F}_{\sigma,\eta}$ on $\mathbf{per}_D$ as follows:

$$\mathcal{F}_{\sigma,\eta}(A) = \Sigma_{i=1\ldots k}(\Pi_{j=1\ldots n_i} [\![\tau_{i,j}]\!]_{\eta[A/t]}) \,. \tag{5}$$

We then observe that $\mathbf{per}_D$ is a complete lattice with respect to set-inclusion, and that thanks to the positivity condition in the definition of co-inductive type, $\mathcal{F}_{\sigma,\eta}$ is monotonic on $\mathbf{per}_D$. Therefore we can define (*gfp* stands for greatest fixpoint):

$$[\![\sigma]\!]_\eta = \bigcup \{A \mid A \subseteq \mathcal{F}_{\sigma,\eta}(A)\} \ \ (= gfp(\mathcal{F}_{\sigma,\eta})) \,. \tag{6}$$

In general, if f is a monotonic function over a poset with greatest element $\top$ and glb's, we define the iteration f^α, for α ordinal as follows:

$$f^0 = \top \quad f^{\alpha+1} = f(f^\alpha) \quad f^\lambda = \bigwedge\nolimits_{\alpha<\lambda} f^\alpha \quad (\lambda \text{ limit ordinal}) \,.$$

With this notation, we have $gfp(\mathcal{F}_{\sigma,\eta}) = \mathcal{F}^{\alpha}_{\sigma,\eta}$ for some ordinal α.

Since $\mathbf{per}_D$ is a CCC there is a canonical interpretation of the simply typed λ-calculus. The interpretation of constructors and case is driven by equation (5). Note that to validate the typing rules it is enough to know that the interpretation of a co-inductive type is *a* fixpoint of the related functional defined by equation (5) (as a matter of fact, these rules are sound also for *inductive* types). The interpretation of fix is more problematic (and represents the original contribution of this section as far as semantics is concerned). We proceed as follows:

- We define an erasure function *er* from the terms in the language to (pure) untyped λ-terms, and we interpret the untyped λ-terms in the λ-model D. This interpretation, is always well-defined as the λ-model accommodates arbitrary recursive definitions.
- We see what it takes for the interpretation of (the erasure of) a fixpoint to be in the corresponding type interpretation, and we derive a suitable guard condition which is expressed by additional typing rules in a suitably enriched language.
- We prove *soundness* of the interpretation with respect to the enriched typing system.

Definition 4 erasure. We define an erasure function from terms to (pure) untyped λ-terms, by induction on the structure of the term (assuming $\sigma = \nu t.(\mathsf{f}_1 : \tau_1 \to t \ldots \mathsf{f}_k : \tau_k \to t)$).

$$er(x) = x \quad er(\lambda x.M) = \lambda x.er(M) \quad er(MN) = er(M)er(N)$$

$$er(\mathsf{f}_i{}^{\sigma}) = \lambda x_1 \ldots \lambda x_{n_i}.\lambda y_1 \ldots \lambda y_k.y_i(\lambda u.ux_1 \ldots x_{n_i})$$

$$er(\mathsf{case}^{\sigma}) = \lambda x.\lambda y_1 \ldots \lambda y_k.xU(y_1)\ldots U(y_k) \text{ with } U(y_i) = \lambda u.y_i(p_1 u)\ldots(p_{n_i}u)$$

$$er(\mathsf{fix}\ x.M) = Y(\lambda x.er(M)) \text{ with } Y = \lambda f.(\lambda x.f(xx))(\lambda x.f(xx)) .$$

If $n_i = 0$ then we have $er(\mathsf{f}_i{}^{\sigma}) = \lambda y_1 \ldots \lambda y_k.y_i(\lambda u.u)$ and $U(y_i) = \lambda u.y_i$. If $k = 1$ then the definitions simplify to $er(\mathsf{f}_1{}^{\sigma}) = \lambda x_1 \ldots \lambda x_{n_1}.\lambda u.ux_1 \ldots x_{n_1}$ and $er(\mathsf{case}^{\sigma}) = \lambda x.\lambda y_1.y_1(p_1 x)\ldots(p_{n_1}x)$.

The erasures of $\mathsf{f}_i{}^{\sigma}$ and case^{σ} are designed to fit the per interpretation of co-inductive types, in particular they rely on the definition of sum and product in $\mathbf{per}_D$.

We sketch with an informal notation an instance of our semantic analysis. We write $\models P : \tau$ if $[\![P]\!]^D \in |[\![\tau]\!]|$. The typing rule for recursive definitions is sound if we can establish:

$$\models Y(\lambda x.er(M)) : \sigma . \tag{7}$$

Given the iterative definitions of the interpretation of the co-inductive type σ, we can try to prove:

$$\forall \alpha \text{ ordinal } \models Y(\lambda x.er(M)) : \mathcal{F}^{\alpha}_{\sigma} \tag{8}$$

by induction on the ordinal α. The case $\alpha = 0$ is trivial since $\mathcal{F}^{\alpha}_{\sigma} = 1$, and the case α limit ordinal follows by an exchange of universal quantifications. For the case $\alpha = \alpha' + 1$, it would be enough to know:

$$\forall \alpha \ (\models Y(\lambda x.er(M)) : \mathcal{F}^{\alpha}_{\sigma} \ \Rightarrow \ \models Y(\lambda x.er(M)) : \mathcal{F}^{\alpha+1}_{\sigma}) \ . \tag{9}$$

Since $Y(\lambda x.er(M)) = [Y(\lambda x.er(M))/x]M$, property (9) is implied by the following property:

$$\forall \alpha, P \ (\models P : \mathcal{F}^{\alpha}_{\sigma} \ \Rightarrow \ \models [P/x]er(M) : \mathcal{F}^{\alpha+1}_{\sigma}) \ . \tag{10}$$

In order to represent this condition in the syntax, we parameterize the type interpretation on an ordinal α, and we introduce types $\breve{\sigma}$ and $\breve{\sigma}^{+}$ so that $[\![\breve{\sigma}]\!]^{\alpha} = \mathcal{F}^{\alpha}_{\sigma}$, and $[\![\breve{\sigma}^{+}]\!]^{\alpha} = \mathcal{F}^{\alpha+1}_{\sigma}$. Property (10) is then expressed by the judgment $x : \breve{\sigma} \vdash M : \breve{\sigma}^{+}$.

Let T be the set of types specified in definition 1. We define the set T' as the least set such that: (i) $T \subseteq T'$, (ii) if $\sigma \in T$ is a co-inductive type then $\breve{\sigma} \in T'$ and $\breve{\sigma}^{+} \in T'$, and (iii) if $\tau \in T'$ and $\tau' \in T'$ then $\tau \to \tau' \in T'$. We also define the set T^{+} as the set of types in T' such that all types of the form $\breve{\sigma}$ and $\breve{\sigma}^{+}$ appear in positive position (the interpretation of these types is going to be anti-monotonic in the ordinal). If Γ is a context then $T(\Gamma) = \{\tau \mid x : \tau \in \Gamma\}$.

The revised typing system contains the typing rules presented in section 2 (applied with the enriched set of types) but for the rule for fix which is replaced by the rules displayed below. Of course, all the rules are applied on the enriched set of types, and under the hypothesis that all types are well-formed.

$$\text{Assuming:} \quad \begin{array}{l} \sigma = \nu t.(\mathsf{f}_1 : \tau_1 \to t \ldots \mathsf{f}_k : \tau_k \to t) \\ \tau' \to \sigma = \tau'_1 \to \ldots \tau'_m \to \sigma \ \ (m \geq 0) \end{array}$$

$$\frac{\begin{array}{c} T(\Gamma) \cup \{\tau'_1 \ldots \tau'_m\} \subseteq T \\ \Gamma, x : \tau' \to \sigma \vdash M : \tau' \to \sigma \\ \Gamma, x : \tau' \to \breve{\sigma} \vdash M : \tau' \to \breve{\sigma}^{+} \end{array}}{\Gamma \vdash \mathsf{fix}\ x.M : \tau' \to \sigma} \qquad \frac{\begin{array}{c} T(\Gamma) \cup \{\tau'_1 \ldots \tau'_m\} \subseteq T^{+} \\ \Gamma, x : \tau' \to \breve{\sigma} \vdash M : \tau' \to \breve{\sigma}^{+} \end{array}}{\Gamma \vdash \mathsf{fix}\ x.M : \tau' \to \breve{\sigma}^{+}}$$

$$\frac{}{\Gamma \vdash \mathsf{f}_i^{\sigma} : [\breve{\sigma}/t]\tau_{i,1} \to \cdots \to [\breve{\sigma}/t]\tau_{i,n_i} \to \breve{\sigma}^{+}} \qquad \frac{\Gamma \vdash M : \tau \quad \tau \leq \tau'}{\Gamma \vdash M : \tau'}$$

$$\frac{}{\Gamma \vdash \mathsf{case}^{\sigma} : \breve{\sigma}^{+} \to ([\breve{\sigma}/t]\tau_1 \to \tau) \to \cdots ([\breve{\sigma}/t]\tau_k \to \tau) \to \tau}$$

$$\frac{}{\tau \leq \tau} \quad \frac{}{\sigma \leq \breve{\sigma}^{+}} \quad \frac{}{\sigma \leq \breve{\sigma}} \quad \frac{}{\breve{\sigma}^{+} \leq \breve{\sigma}} \quad \frac{\tau_2 \leq \tau_1 \quad \tau'_1 \leq \tau'_2}{\tau_1 \to \tau'_1 \leq \tau_2 \to \tau'_2}$$

We give some motivation and intuition for these rules. In the first rule, the condition $M \downarrow x$ is replaced by the typing judgment $\Gamma, x : \tau \to \breve{\sigma} \vdash M : \tau \to \breve{\sigma}^{+}$. The second rule for fix is used to type nested fixpoints as in example 2(6). In the rules for fix, the side conditions $T(\Gamma) \cup \{\tau'_1 \ldots \tau'_k\} \subseteq T$ and $T(\Gamma) \cup \{\tau'_1 \ldots \tau'_k\} \subseteq T^{+}$ guarantee independence and anti-monotonicity, respectively, of the type interpretation with respect to the ordinal parameter.

The additional rule for the constructors f_i is needed to introduce terms of type $\breve{\sigma}^+$. Note that in this way we *overload* the constructors f_i by giving them two related types (but incomparable with respect to subtyping). There is also a related rule which overloads the destructor case.

The following rules just state the *subtyping* relations between σ, $\breve{\sigma}$, and $\breve{\sigma}^+$, and the way this relation is lifted higher-order. The obvious transitivity rule for the subtyping relation $\leq$ can be derived. Types with the relation $\leq$ form a quite simple partial order. In particular, if $R = \leq \cup \leq^{-1}$ then $\{\tau' \mid \tau R^* \tau'\}$ is finite. We state some basic properties of the typing system.

Lemma 5. (1) *Exchange. If $\Gamma, x : \tau_1, y : \tau_2, \Gamma' \vdash M : \tau$ then $\Gamma, y : \tau_2, x : \tau_1, \Gamma' \vdash M : \tau$ (with a proof of the same depth).*

(2) *Remove. If $\Gamma, x : \tau' \vdash M : \tau$ and $x \notin FV(M)$, then $\Gamma \vdash M : \tau$.*

(3) *Weakening (restricted). If $\Gamma \vdash M : \tau$, x fresh, and either $\tau' \in T$ or* fix *does not occur in M then $\Gamma, x : \tau' \vdash M : \tau$.*

(4) *Transitivity. If $\vdash \tau \leq \tau'$ and $\vdash \tau' \leq \tau''$ then $\vdash \tau \leq \tau''$.*

(5) *Substitution. If $\Gamma, x : \tau' \vdash M : \tau$ and $\Gamma \vdash N : \tau'$ then $\Gamma \vdash [N/x]M : \tau$.*

The terms typable using Coquand's guard condition, are strictly contained in the terms typable in the proposed typing system (as a matter of fact, all examples in 2 (but (3) of course) can be typed). This is a consequence of the following lemma.

Lemma 6. (1) *If $\Gamma, x : \tau \to \sigma \vdash M : \tau$, $x \notin FV(M)$, and M has no occurrence of* fix*, then $\Gamma, x : \tau \to \breve{\sigma} \vdash M : \tau$.*

(2) *If $\Gamma, x : \tau \to \sigma \vdash M \downarrow_0^{\tau' \to \sigma} x$ then $\Gamma, x : \tau \to \breve{\sigma} \vdash M : \tau' \to \breve{\sigma}$.*

(3) *If $\Gamma, x : \tau \to \sigma \vdash M \downarrow_1^{\tau' \to \sigma} x$ then $\Gamma, x : \tau \to \breve{\sigma} \vdash M : \tau' \to \breve{\sigma}^+$.*

We parameterize the type interpretation on an ordinal α, and we define for $\sigma = \nu t.(f_1 : \tau_1 \to t \ldots f_k : \tau_k \to t)$:

$$
\begin{array}{llll}
[\![t]\!]^\alpha_\eta = \eta(t) & [\![\tau \to \tau']\!]^\alpha_\eta = [\![\tau]\!]^\alpha_\eta \to [\![\tau']\!]^\alpha_\eta \\
[\![\sigma]\!]^\alpha_\eta = gfp(\mathcal{F}_{\sigma,\eta,\alpha}) & \mathcal{F}_{\sigma,\eta,\alpha}(A) = \Sigma_{i=1\ldots k}(\Pi_{j=1\ldots n_i}[\![\sigma]\!]^\alpha_{\eta[A/t]}) \\
[\![\breve{\sigma}]\!]^\alpha_\eta = \mathcal{F}^\alpha_{\sigma,\eta,\alpha} & [\![\breve{\sigma}^+]\!]^\alpha_\eta = \mathcal{F}^{\alpha+1}_{\sigma,\eta,\alpha} .
\end{array}
$$

Remark. If $\tau \in T$ then $[\![\tau]\!]^\alpha_\eta$ does not depend on α. In particular, if $\breve{\sigma} \in T'$ or $\breve{\sigma}^+ \in T'$ then $\sigma \in T$ and therefore $\mathcal{F}_{\sigma,\eta,\alpha} = \mathcal{F}_{\sigma,\eta}$. If $\tau \in T^+$ and $\alpha \leq \alpha'$ then $[\![\tau]\!]^\alpha_\eta \supseteq [\![\tau]\!]^{\alpha'}_\eta$, since the types of the shape $\breve{\sigma}$ and $\breve{\sigma}^+$ occur in positive position.

Let us now consider the soundness of the typing rules. If P is a pure λ-term, we write $x_1 : \tau_1 \ldots x_n : \tau_n \models P : \tau$ if

$$\forall \alpha, \eta \ ((\forall i \in \{1 \ldots n\} \ d_i \, [\![\tau_i]\!]^\alpha_\eta \, d'_i) \ \Rightarrow \ ([\![P]\!][\mathrm{d}/\mathrm{x}] \, [\![\tau]\!]^\alpha_\eta \, [\![P]\!][\mathrm{d}'/\mathrm{x}])).$$

Proposition 7 soundness. *If $\Gamma \vdash M : \tau$ then $\Gamma \models er(M) : \tau$.*

It follows from proposition 7 that: $\vdash M : \tau \Rightarrow [er(M)] \in |[\![\tau]\!]|$. This result justifies the interpretation of a typed term as the equivalence class of its erasure (it is straightforward to adapt this interpretation to take into account contexts and environments). Thus, if $\vdash M : \tau$, then we set $[\![M]\!] = [[\![er(M)]\!]]_{[\tau]}$.

Clearly, there is a trade-off between power and simplicity/decidability of the type system. Our contribution here is to offer a framework in which this trade-off can be studied, and to extract from it *one possible* type system. We will see in section 4 that this 'experimental' type system has some desirable syntactic properties, and we will discuss its relationships with Gimenez's system. We hint here, by example, to limits and possible extensions of the system.

(1) The following two definitions 'make sense' but are not typable. Here we work with the type of infinite streams $\sigma = \nu t.(\mathsf{cons} : o \to t \to t)$:

- If x is a stream of numerals we denote with x_i its ith element. We define a function F such that $F(x)_i = (suc^{(2^i)} x_i)$, for $i \in \omega$:

$$F \equiv \mathsf{fix}\ f.\lambda x.\mathsf{cons}^{\sigma}(suc(hd\ x))(f(f(tl\ x))) \,. \tag{11}$$

- A 'constant' definition which determines the infinite stream of 0's.

$$\mathsf{fix}\ x.\mathsf{case}^{\sigma}\ x(\lambda n.\lambda y.(\mathsf{fix}\ x'.\mathsf{cons}^{\sigma}\ 0\ x')) \,.$$

(2) We can *soundly* generalize the two rules for fix as follows:

$$\frac{\begin{array}{c} T(\Gamma) \cup \{\tau_1' \ldots \tau_m'\} \subseteq T \quad pos(t,\tau_i') \\ \Gamma, x : [\sigma/t](\tau' \to t) \vdash M : [\sigma/t](\tau' \to t) \\ \Gamma, x : [\breve{\sigma}/t](\tau' \to t) \vdash M : [\breve{\sigma}^+/t](\tau' \to t) \end{array}}{\Gamma \vdash \mathsf{fix}\ x.M : [\sigma/t](\tau' \to t)} \quad \frac{\begin{array}{c} T(\Gamma) \cup \{\tau_1' \ldots \tau_m'\} \subseteq T^+ \quad pos(t,\tau_i') \\ \Gamma, [\breve{\sigma}/t](\tau' \to t) \vdash M : [\breve{\sigma}^+/t](\tau' \to t) \end{array}}{\Gamma \vdash \mathsf{fix}\ x.M : [\tilde{\sigma}/t](\tau' \to t)} \tag{12}$$

where $\tilde{\sigma} \in \{\breve{\sigma}, \breve{\sigma}^+\}$. These rules are particularly powerful and will be analysed in a forthcoming paper. For instance, they can be used to type: the representation of a sequential circuit as a function over streams of booleans (we found the rules trying this example), the example (11) above, and a tail append function.

(3) One may consider the extension of the type system with a finite or infinite hierarchy of approximating types, say: $\sigma \leq \cdots \leq \breve{\sigma}^{+++} \leq \breve{\sigma}^{++} \leq \breve{\sigma}^{+} \leq \breve{\sigma}$.

Next we turn to equations. We say that an equation $M = N : \tau$ is *valid* in the per interpretation, if

$$\forall \Gamma \ (\Gamma \vdash M : \tau \text{ and } \Gamma \vdash N : \tau \ \Rightarrow \ \Gamma \models M = N : \tau)$$

where $x_1 : \tau_1 \ldots x_n : \tau_n \models M = N : \tau$, if

$$\forall \alpha, \eta \ ((\forall i \in \{1 \ldots n\} \ d_i [\![\tau_i]\!]^{\alpha}_{\eta} d_i') \ \Rightarrow \ [\![er(M)]\!][\mathrm{d}/\mathrm{x}]\, [\![\tau]\!]^{\alpha}_{\eta}\, [\![er(N)]\!][\mathrm{d}'/\mathrm{x}]) \,.$$

Reasoning at the level of erasures, it is easy to derive some valid equations.

Proposition 8 valid equations. *The following equations are valid in the per interpretation:*

$$(\beta)\ (\lambda x.M)N = [N/x]M : \tau \qquad (\eta)\ \lambda x.(Mx) = M : \tau \to \tau' \quad x \notin FV(M)$$

$$(\mathsf{case})\ (\mathsf{case}^{\sigma}\ (\mathsf{f}_i^{\sigma} M_1 \ldots M_{n_i})\mathrm{N}) = N_i M_1 \ldots M_{n_i} : \tau$$

$$(\mathsf{case}_{\eta})\ (\mathsf{case}^{\sigma}\ x\ \mathsf{f}_1^{\sigma} \ldots \mathsf{f}_k^{\sigma}) = x : \sigma \quad (\mathsf{fix})\ \mathsf{fix}\ x.M = [\mathsf{fix}\ x.M/x]M : \tau \to \sigma \,.$$

The following proposition introduces an important principle to prove the equality of terms of co-inductive type.

Proposition 9 unique fixed point. *Suppose* $\Gamma \vdash N : \tau \to \sigma$, $\Gamma \vdash N' : \tau \to \sigma$, $\Gamma, x : \tau \to \breve{\sigma} \vdash M : \tau \to \breve{\sigma}^{+}$, *and* $T(\Gamma) \cup \{\tau\} \subseteq T$. *Then* $\Gamma \models [N/x]M = N : \tau \to \sigma$ *and* $\Gamma \models [N'/x]M = N' : \tau \to \sigma$ *implies* $\Gamma \models N = N' : \tau \to \sigma$.

Proposition 9 resembles Banach's theorem: contractive functions have a unique fixed point (in our case, 'contractive' is replaced by 'guarded'). Combining with unfolding (fix), one can then prove equivalences such as (cf. [18]):

$$\mathsf{fix}\ x.\mathsf{cons}\ n\ (\mathsf{cons}\ n\ x) = \mathsf{fix}\ x.\mathsf{cons}\ n\ x\ .$$

An interesting question is whether the interpretation identifies as many *closed* terms of co-inductive type as possible. We consider this question for the type of streams of numerals $\sigma = \nu t.(\mathsf{cons} : o \to t \to t)$ (cf. example 2) and leave the generalization to a following paper. Suppose that for M, N closed terms of type o we have:

$$M = N : o \ \text{ iff } \ [\![M]\!] = [\![N]\!]$$

where the left equality denotes conversion. We define a *simulation* relation $\sim^{\omega}$ over the closed terms of type o, say Λ^0_σ as $\sim^{\omega} = \bigcap_{n<\omega} \sim^n$, where:

$$\sim^0 = \Lambda^0_\sigma \times \Lambda^0_\sigma \quad \sim^{n+1} = \{(M,N) \mid (hdM = hdN \text{ and } (tlM, tlN) \in \sim^n)\}\ . \quad (13)$$

Equivalently, we can characterize $\sim^{\omega}$ as:

$$M \sim^{\omega} N \ \text{ iff } \ \forall n \in \omega \ \ hd(tl^n M) = hd(tl^n N)\ .$$

Clearly $\sim^{\omega}$ is the largest (sensible) equivalence we can expect on Λ^0_σ. We can show that this equivalence is precisely that induced by the per's interpretation.

Proposition 10. *Let* $M, N \in \Lambda^0_\sigma$. *Then* $M \sim^{\omega} N$ *iff* $[\![M]\!] = [\![N]\!]$.

4 Reduction

It is easy to see that the equality induced by the per's interpretation on co-inductive types is in general undecidable (E.g., let the nth element of a stream witness the termination of a Turing machine after n steps). In the presence of dependent types (like in the Calculus of Constructions), it is imperative to have a theory of conversion which is decidable. Thus the approach is to: (i) Consider a weaker (but decidable) notion of conversion on terms, and (ii) Define in the logical system a notion of term equivalence which captures the intended meaning, e.g., using a notion of simulation as in (13). A standard way to achieve decidability for an equational theory is to exhibit a rewriting system which is confluent and terminating. In order to achieve termination, the unfolding of fixpoints has to be restricted somehow. Gimenez has proposed a solution in which fix is *unfolded only under a* case. Intuitively, fix is considered as an additional constructor which can be simplified only when it meets the corresponding destructor.[3] In the following we will simplify the matter by ignoring the extensional rules:

$$\begin{array}{ll} (\lambda x.M)N & \rightarrow [N/x]M \\ \mathsf{case}^{\sigma}\ (\mathsf{f}_i^{\sigma}\mathrm{M})\mathrm{N} & \rightarrow N_i\mathrm{M} \\ \mathsf{case}^{\sigma}\ ((\mathsf{fix}\ x.M)\mathrm{M})\mathrm{N} \rightarrow \mathsf{case}^{\sigma}\ (([\mathsf{fix}\ x.M/x]M)\mathrm{M})\mathrm{N}\ . \end{array}$$

We also denote with $\rightarrow$ the compatible closure of the rules above. It is easily seen that the resulting rewriting system is locally confluent. Subject reduction is stated as follows.

Proposition 11. *If $\Gamma \vdash M : \tau$ and $M \rightarrow M'$ then $\Gamma \vdash M' : \tau$.*

The strong normalization proof is based on an interpretation of types as reducibility candidates. We outline the construction (which is quite similar to the one for per's) by assuming that there is just one ground type o and one co-inductive type $\sigma = \nu t.(\mathsf{cons} : o \rightarrow t \rightarrow t)$. Let SN be the set of strongly normalizing terms. We say that a term is *not neutral* if it has the shape (we omit the type labels on cons and case):

$$\lambda x.M,\ \mathsf{cons}\mathrm{M},\ (\mathsf{fix}\ x.M)\mathrm{M},\ \mathsf{case},\ \mathsf{case}(\mathsf{cons}M_1M_2),\ \mathsf{case}((\mathsf{fix}\ x.M)\mathrm{M})\ .$$

We note a fundamental property of neutral terms.

Lemma 12. *If M is neutral, then for any term N, MN and* case*MN are neutral, and they are not redexes.*

Therefore a reduction of MN (or caseMN) is either a reduction of M or a reduction of N. Following closely [10], we define the collection of reducibility candidates.

Definition 13. The set of terms X belongs to the collection RC of reducibility candidates if: (C_1) $X \subseteq SN$. (C_2) If $M \in X$ and $M \rightarrow M'$ then $M' \in X$. (C_3) If M is neutral and $\forall M'(M \rightarrow M' \Rightarrow M' \in X)$ then $M \in X$.

The following are standard properties of reducibility candidates (but for (P_5) and (P_6) which *mutatis mutandis* appear in [8]):

Proposition 14. *The set RC enjoys the following properties:*

(P_1) *$SN \in RC$.*

(P_2) *If $X \in RC$ then $x \in X$. Hence $X \neq \emptyset$.*

(P_3) *If $X, Y \in RC$ then $X \rightarrow Y = \{M \mid \forall N \in X\ (MN \in Y)\} \in RC$.*

(P_4) *If $\forall i \in I\ X_i \in RC$ then $\bigcap_{i \in I} X_i \in RC$.*

(P_5) *If $X \in RC$ then*

$$\mathcal{N}(X) = \{M \mid \forall Y \in RC\ \forall P \in SN \rightarrow X \rightarrow Y\ \mathsf{case}\ MP \in Y\} \in RC\ .$$

(P_6) *If $X \subseteq X'$ then $\mathcal{N}(X) \subseteq \mathcal{N}(X')$.*

[3] Another possible approach, is to stop unfolding under a constructor. However this leads to a non-confluent system (exactly as in a 'weak' λ-calculus where reduction stops at λ's).

We can then define the type interpretation which is (again) parameterized on an ordinal α (of course, we take $\mathcal{N}^0 = SN$):

$$[o]^\alpha = SN \quad [\tau \to \tau']^\alpha = [\tau]^\alpha \to [\tau']^\alpha$$

$$[\sigma]^\alpha = gfp(\mathcal{N}) \quad [\breve{\sigma}]^\alpha = \mathcal{N}^\alpha \quad [\breve{\sigma}^+]^\alpha = \mathcal{N}^{\alpha+1}.$$

We define $x_1 : \tau_1 \dots x_n : \tau_n \models_{RC} M : \tau$ if $\forall \alpha$ $((\forall i \in \{1 \dots n\}\ P_i \in [\tau_i]^\alpha) \Rightarrow [P_1/x_1 \dots P_n/x_n]M \in [\tau]^\alpha)$. We can then state the following result from which strong normalization immediately follows by taking $P_i \equiv x_i$.

Proposition 15 strong normalization. *If* $\Gamma \vdash M : \tau$ *then* $\Gamma \models_{RC} M : \tau$.

Remark. From these results, we can conclude that it is always better to normalize the body M of a recursive definition fix $x.M$, before checking the guard condition, e.g., consider: $M \equiv (\lambda z.\text{case } z(\lambda n.\lambda z'.z'))(\text{cons } n \text{ (cons } n\ x))$. This term *cannot* be typed, but if M' is the normal form of M then fix $x.M'$ can be typed.

In his thesis, Gimenez has studied an extension of the calculus of constructions with the co-inductive type of finite and infinite streams (cf. example 2(5)). In the Coq system, the user can actually introduce other co-inductive types. Among the examples of co-inductive type considered in this paper, the type in example 1(3) is the only one which is rejected. The reason is that Coq relies on a stricter notion of positivity to avoid some consistency problems which arise at higher-order types [9]. It should be noted that Coq implementation of co-inductive types was developed *before* the type theory was settled, and cannot be considered as a faithful implementation of it.

We sketch a semantic reconstruction of Gimenez's system. In the interpretation studied in section 3, all approximating types are assigned the *same* ordinal. We might consider a more liberal system in which *different* ordinals can be assigned to different approximating types. However, to express the guard condition, we still need a linguistic mechanism to say in which cases the ordinal assignment really has to be the *same*. Following this intuition, we label the approximating types with the intention to assign an ordinal to each label. As before, we restrict our attention to the type of infinite streams, say σ with constructor cons : $o \to \sigma \to \sigma$. The collection of types is then defined as follows:

$$\tau ::= o \mid \sigma \mid \sigma^x \mid \sigma^{x+1} \mid (\tau \to \tau) . \tag{14}$$

Roughly, we replace the type $\breve{\sigma}$ with the types σ^x and the type $\breve{\sigma}^+$ with the types σ^{x+1}, where x is a label which we take for convenience as ranging over the set of term variables $x, y, \dots$ (any other infinite set would do). More precisely, if h denotes an assignment from variables to ordinals then we define a type interpretation parametric in h.

$$[o]_h = O \text{ (for some chosen } per\ O) \qquad [\tau \to \tau']_h = [\tau]_h \to [\tau']_h$$
$$[\sigma]_h = gfp(\mathcal{F}) \qquad \mathcal{F}(A) = O \times A$$
$$[\sigma^x]_h = \mathcal{F}^{h(x)} \qquad [\sigma^{x+1}]_h = \mathcal{F}^{h(x)+1}.$$

If P is a pure λ-term, we write $x_1 : \tau_1 \ldots x_n : \tau_n \models P : \tau$ if

$$\forall h \; ((\forall i \in \{1 \ldots n\} \; d_i \, [\![\tau_i]\!]_h \, d'_i) \;\; \Rightarrow \;\; ([\![P]\!][\mathrm{d}/\mathrm{x}] \, [\![\tau]\!]_h \, [\![P]\!][\mathrm{d}'/\mathrm{x}])) \; .$$

We now turn to syntax. Let $var(\tau)$ be the set of variables which occur in the type τ. If Γ is a context, we also define $var(\Gamma) = \bigcup\{var(\tau) \mid x : \tau \in \Gamma\}$. If x is a variable, we define $T^+(x)$ as the set of types such that all subtypes of the form σ^x or σ^{x+1} occur in positive position. Following the interpretation above, the typing rules for, e.g., fix can be formulated as follows, where $\tau' \to \sigma^u \equiv \tau'_1 \to \cdots \to \tau'_m \to \sigma^u$, $m \geq 0$, u can be a label or nothing.

$$\frac{\begin{array}{c} x \notin var(\Gamma) \cup \bigcup\{var(\tau'_i) \mid i = 1 \ldots m\} \\ \Gamma, x : \tau' \to \sigma \vdash M : \tau' \to \sigma \\ \Gamma, x : \tau' \to \sigma^x \vdash M : \tau' \to \sigma^{x+1} \end{array}}{\Gamma \vdash \mathsf{fix}\, x.M : \tau' \to \sigma} \qquad \frac{\begin{array}{c} T(\Gamma) \cup \{\tau'_i \mid i = 1 \ldots m\} \subseteq T^+(y) \\ \Gamma, x : \tau' \to \sigma^y \vdash M : \tau' \to \sigma^{y+1} \end{array}}{\Gamma \vdash \mathsf{fix}\, x.M : \tau' \to \sigma^{y+1}} \; .$$

Soundness can be proved as for proposition 7. When Gimenez's system is considered in a simply-typed framework, the following differences appear with respect to the system with labelled types (ignoring some minor notational conventions): (1) Gimenez's typing system is presented in a 'Church' style. More precisely, the variables bound by λ and fix carry a type, and this type is used to constraint (in the usual way) the application of the related typing rules. (2) The subtyping rule for functional types $\tau \to \tau'$ is missing. (3) The second rule for typing recursive definitions is missing.

Obviously these differences imply that one can give *less* types to a term in Gimenez's system than in our system. To be fair, one has to notice that the presentation as a Church system and the absence of subtyping at higher-types is essentially justified by the complexity of the calculus of constructions, and by the desire to avoid too many complications at once. On the other hand, the lack of the second rule for fix is, in our opinion, a genuine difference, which moreover has an impact in practice, as the rule is needed to type nested recursive definitions as that of example 2(6) and can be further generalized as shown in (12). A question which should be raised is whether the system with type labels is better *in practice* than the simpler system without type labels. So far, we could not find any 'natural' example suggesting a positive answer.

Acknowledgement The first author would like to thank Eduardo Gimenez for providing the simply typed formulation of his system and explaining its motivations, and Alexandra Bac for a number of discussions on the type system presented here.

References

1. R. Amadio and S. Coupet-Grimal. Analysis of a guard condition in type theory (preliminary report). Technical Report TR 1997.245. Also appeared as RR-INRIA 3300, Université de Provence (LIM), 1997. Available at *http://protis.univ-mrs.fr/~amadio*.

2. H. Barendregt. *The lambda calculus; its syntax and semantics.* North-Holland, 1984.
3. Coq-project. The Coq proof assistant reference manual. Available at *http://pauillac.inria.fr/coq*, 1996.
4. T. Coquand. Infinite objects in type theory. In *Types for proofs and programs, Springer Lect. Notes in Comp. Sci. 806*, 1993.
5. T. Coquand and G. Huet. A calculus of constructions. *Information and Computation*, 76:95–120, 1988.
6. S. Coupet-Grimal and L. Jakubiec. Coq and hardware verification: a case study. In *Proc. TPHOL, Springer Lect. Notes in Comp. Sci. 1125*, 1996.
7. H. Geuvers. Inductive and coinductive types with iteration and recursion. In *Proc. of Workshop on types for proofs and programs, Nordström et al. (eds.)*, pages 193–217, 1992. Available electronically.
8. E. Gimenez. *Un calcul de constructions infinies et son application à la vérification de systèmes communicants.* PhD thesis, ENS Lyon, 1996.
9. E. Gimenez. Personal communication. October 1997.
10. J.-Y. Girard, Y. Lafont, and P. Taylor. *Proofs and Types.* Cambridge University Press, 1989.
11. F. Leclerc and C. Paulin-Morhing. Programming with streams in Coq. A case study: the sieve of Eratosthenes. In *Proc. TYPES, Springer Lect. Notes in Comp. Sci. 806*, 1993.
12. R. Loader. Equational theories for inductive types. *Annals of Pure and Applied Logic*, 84:175–218, 1997.
13. G. Longo and E. Moggi. Constructive natural deduction and its modest interpretation. *Mathematical Structures in Computer Science*, 1:215–254, 1992.
14. N. Mendler. Recursive types and type constraints in second-order lambda calculus. In *Proc. IEEE Logic in Comp. Sci.*, 1987.
15. M. Nesi. A formalization of the process algebra CCS in higher order logic. Technical Report 278, Computer Laboratory, University of Cambridge, December 1992.
16. L. Paulson. Mechanizing coinduction and corecursion in higher-order logic. *J. of Logic and Computation*, 7(2):175–204, 1997.
17. C. Raffalli. *L'arithmétique fonctionnelle du second ordre avec point fixes.* PhD thesis, Université Paris VII, 1994.
18. A. Salomaa. Two complete systems for the algebra of complete events. *Journal of the ACM*, 13-1, 1966.
19. D. Scott. Data types as lattices. *SIAM J. of Computing*, 5:522–587, 1976.
20. M. Tatsuta. Realizability interpretation of coinductive definitions and program synthesis with streams. *Theoretical Computer Science*, 122:119–136, 1994.
21. S. Thompson. *Haskell. The craft of functional programming.* Addison-Wesley, 1996.

An Event Structure Semantics for P/T Contextual Nets: Asymmetric Event Structures*

Paolo Baldan[1], Andrea Corradini[1], and Ugo Montanari[2**]

[1] *Dipartimento di Informatica - University of Pisa*
Corso Italia, 40, 56125 Pisa, Italy

[2] *Computer Science Laboratory - SRI International*
333 Ravenswood Ave. Menlo Park, CA 94025 USA

E-mail: {baldan, andrea, ugo}@di.unipi.it

Abstract. We propose an event based semantics for *contextual nets*, i.e. an extension of Place/Transition Petri nets where transitions can also have *context* conditions, modelling resources that can be read without being consumed. The result is a generalization of Winskel's work on safe nets: the event based semantics is given at categorical level via a chain of coreflections leading from the category **WS-CN** of weakly safe contextual nets to the category **Dom** of finitary prime algebraic domains. A fundamental rôle is played by the notion of *asymmetric event structures* that generalize Winskel's prime event structures, following an idea similar to that of "possible flow" introduced by Pinna and Poignè. Asymmetric event structures have the usual causal relation of traditional prime event structures, but replace the symmetric conflict with a relation modelling *asymmetric conflict* or *weak causality*. Such relation allows one to represent the new kind of dependency between events arising in contextual nets, as well as the usual symmetric conflict. Moreover it is used in a non-trivial way in the definition of the ordering of configurations, which is different from the standard set-inclusion.

1 Introduction

Contextual nets, as introduced in [14], extend classical Petri nets, a formalism for the specification of the behaviour of concurrent systems, with the possibility of handling contexts: in a contextual net transitions can have not only preconditions and postconditions, but also *context* conditions, that, intuitively, specify something which is necessary for the transition to be fired, but is not affected by the firing of the transition. In other words, a context can be thought of as an item which is *read but not consumed* by the transition, in the same way as preconditions can be considered as being read and consumed and postconditions

* Research partly supported by the EC TMR Network GETGRATS (General Theory of Graph Transformation Systems) and by the EC Esprit WG APPLIGRAPH (Applications of Graph Transformation).

** On leave from University of Pisa, Computer Science Department.

being simply written. Consistently with this view, the same token can be used as context by many transitions at the same time and with multiplicity greater than one by the same transition. Context conditions of [14] are also called *test arcs* in [5], *activator arcs* in [10] or *read arcs* in [18,19].

The possibility of faithfully representing the "reading of resources" allows contextual nets to model a lot of concrete situations more naturally than classical nets. In recent years they have been used to model concurrent access to shared data (e.g. reading in a database) [17,7], to provide a concurrent semantics to concurrent constraint (CC) programs [13], to model priorities [9], to specify a net semantics for the π-calculus [3]. Moreover they have been studied for their connections with another powerful formalism for the representation of concurrent computations, namely graph grammars [14,6].

In this paper we consider *marked contextual P/T nets* (shortly *c-nets*), that following the lines suggested in [14] for C/E systems, add contexts to classical P/T nets. The problem of giving a truly concurrent semantics based on (deterministic) processes has been faced by various authors (see, e.g., [9,14,4,19]). Each process of a c-net records the events occurring in a *single* computation of the net and the relations existing between such events.

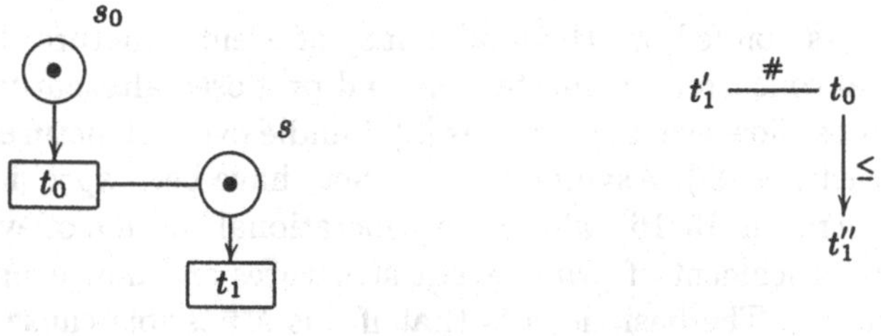

Fig. 1. A simple contextual net and a prime event structure representing its behaviour.

Here we provide (weakly safe) c-nets with a truly concurrent event structure semantics following another classical approach. Generalizing Winskel's construction for safe nets [20], we associate to each c-net an event structure that describes *all* the possible behaviours of the net. Recall that *prime event structures (PES)* are a simple event based model of (concurrent) computations in which events are considered as atomic, indivisible and instantaneous steps, which can appear only once in a computation. An event can occur only after some other events (its causes) have taken place and the execution of an event can inhibit the execution of other events. This is formalized via two binary relations: *causality*, modelled by a partial order relation and *conflict*, modeled by a symmetric and irreflexive relation, hereditary w.r.t. causality. When working with c-nets the main critical point is represented by the fact that the presence of context conditions leads to *asymmetric conflicts* or *weak dependencies* between events. To understand this basic concept, consider two transitions t_0 and t_1 such that the same place s is a context for t_0 and a precondition for t_1. Following [14], such a situation is represented pictorially as in Fig. 1.(a), i.e., non-directed arcs are used to represent context conditions. The possible firing sequences are t_0, t_1 and $t_0; t_1$, while $t_1; t_0$ is not allowed. This situation cannot be modelled in a direct way within a traditional prime event structure: t_0 and t_1 are neither in conflict nor concurrent nor causal dependent. Simply, as for a traditional conflict, the firing of t_1 prevents t_0 to be executed, so that t_0 can never follow t_1 in a computation. But the converse is not true, since t_0 *can* fire before t_1. This situation can be naturally interpreted as an *asymmetric conflict* between the two transitions. Equivalently, since t_0 precedes t_1 in any computation where both are fired, in such computations, t_0 acts as a cause of t_1. However, differently from a true cause, t_0 is not necessary for t_1 to be fired. Therefore we can also think of the relation between the two transitions as a *weak* form of *causal dependency*.

A reasonable way to encode this situation in a PES is to represent the firing of t_1 with two distinct mutually exclusive events (as shown in Fig. 1.(b)): t_1', representing the execution of t_1 that prevents t_0, thus mutually exclusive with t_0, and t_1'', representing the execution of t_1 after t_0 (caused by t_0). This encoding can be unsatisfactory since it leads to a "duplication" of events (e.g., see [1]). The events of the prime event structure associated to a system would not represent the elementary actions of the system, but the possible histories of such actions.

Several authors pointed out the inadequacy of event structures for faithfully modeling general concurrent computations and proposed alternative definitions of event structures (flow event structures [2], bundle event structures [11], prioritized event structures [8]). Asymmetric conflicts have been specifically treated by Pinna and Poigné in [15, 16], where the "operational" notion of event automaton suggests an enrichment of prime event structures and flow event structures with *possible causes*. The basic idea is that if e is a possible cause of e' then e can precede e' or it can be ignored, but the execution of e never follows e'. This is formalized by introducing an explicit subset of possible events in prime event structures or adding a "possible flow relation" in flow event structures. Similar ideas are developed, under a different perspective, in [8], where PES are enriched with a partial order relation modeling priorities between events.

In order to provide a more direct, event based representation of c-nets we introduce a new kind of event structure, called *asymmetric event structure (aES)*. Despite of some differences in the definition and in the related notions, aES's can be seen as a generalization of event structures with possible events and of prioritized event structures. Besides of the usual causal relation ($\leq$) of a traditional prime event structure, an aES has a relation $\nearrow$, that allows us to specify the new situation analyzed above simply as $t_0 \nearrow t_1$. As just remarked, the same relation has two natural interpretations: it can be thought of as an asymmetric version of conflict or as a weak form of causality. We decided to call it *asymmetric conflict*, but the reader should keep in mind both views, since in some situations it will be preferable to refer to the *weak causality* interpretation. *Configurations* of an aES are then introduced and the set of configurations of an aES, ordered in a suitable way using the asymmetric conflict relation, turns out to be a finitary prime algebraic domain. We prove that such a construction extends to a functor from the category **aES** of asymmetric event structures to the category **Dom** of finitary prime algebraic domain, that establishes a coreflection between **aES** and **Dom**. Recalling that **Dom** is equivalent to the category **PES** of prime event structures we can recover a semantics in terms of traditional prime event structures.

The seminal work by Winskel presents an adjunction between event structures and a subclass of P/T nets, namely *safe* nets. Such a result is extended in [12] to the wider category of *weakly safe* nets, i.e. P/T nets in which the initial marking is a set and transitions can generate at most one token in each post-condition. Similarly, we restrict here to a (full) subcategory of contextual nets, called *weakly safe* c-nets and we show how, given a weakly-safe c-net N, an *unfolding* construction allows us to obtain an occurrence c-net $\mathcal{U}_a(N)$. i.e. an "acyclic c-net" that describes in a static way the behaviour of N, by expressing possible events and the dependency relations between them. The unfolding operation can be extended to a functor $\mathcal{U}_a$ from **WS-CN** to the category **O-CN** of occurrence c-net, that is right adjoint of the inclusion functor $\mathfrak{I}_O$: **O-CN** → **WS-CN**.

Transitions of an occurrence c-net are related by causal dependency and asymmetric conflict, while mutual exclusion is a derived relation. Thus, the semantics of weakly safe c-nets given in terms of occurrence c-nets can be naturally abstracted to an aES semantics. Again this construction extends, at categorical level, to a coreflection from **aES** to **O-CN**.

Finally we exploit the coreflection between **aES** and **Dom**, to complete the chain of coreflections from **WS-CN** to **Dom**.

2 Asymmetric event structures

We stressed in the introduction that PES's (and in general Winskel's event structures) are too poor to model in a direct way the behaviour of models of computation allowing context sensitive firing of events, such as string, term and graph rewriting, and contextual nets. The fact that an event to be fired requires the presence of some resources that are not "consumed", but just read, leads to a new kind of dependency between events that can be seen as an asymmetric version of conflict or a weak form of causality. Technically speaking, the problem is essentially the axiom of event structures (see [20]) stating that the enabling relation $\vdash$ is "monotone" w.r.t. set inclusion:

$$A \vdash e \wedge A \subseteq B \wedge B \textit{ consistent} \quad \Rightarrow \quad B \vdash e.$$

As a consequence the computational order between configurations is set inclusion, the idea being that if $A \subseteq B$ are finite configurations then starting from A we can reach B by performing the events in $B - A$. This means that the conflict is symmetric, i.e. it cannot be the case that the execution of an event e_1 prevents e_0 to be executed but e_0 can precede e_1 in a computation.

To faithfully represent the dependencies existing between events in such models, avoiding the unpleasant phenomenon of duplication of events (see Fig. 1), we generalize prime event structures by replacing the usual symmetric conflict relation with a new binary relation $\nearrow$, called *asymmetric conflict*. If $e_0 \nearrow e_1$ then the firing of e_1 inhibits e_0: the execution of e_0 may precede the execution of e_1 or e_0 can be ignored, but e_0 cannot follow e_1. By using the terminology of Pinna and Poigné [16], we can say that e_0 is a "possible" cause of e_1. Nicely, the symmetric binary conflict can be represented easily with cycles of asymmetric conflict. Therefore symmetric conflict will be a derived relation.

We first introduce some basic notations. Let $r \subseteq X \times X$ be a binary relation and let $Y \subseteq X$. Then r_Y denotes the restriction of r to $Y \times Y$, i.e. $r \cap (Y \times Y)$, r^+ denotes the transitive closure of r and r^* denotes the reflexive and transitive closure of r. We say that r is *well-founded* if it has no infinite descending chains, i.e. $\langle e_i \rangle_{i \in \mathbb{N}}$ with $e_{i+1} \, r \, e_i$, $e_i \neq e_{i+1}$, for all $i \in \mathbb{N}$. The relation r is *acyclic* if it has no "cycles" $e_0 \, r \, e_1 \, r \, \ldots \, r \, e_n \, r \, e_0$, with $e_i \in X$. In particular, if r is well-founded it has no (non-trivial) cycles. The powerset of X is denoted by $\mathbf{2}^X$, while $\mathbf{2}^X_{fin}$ denotes the set of finite subsets of X.

Definition 1 (asymmetric event structure). An *asymmetric event structure* (*aES*) is a tuple $G = \langle E, \leq, \nearrow \rangle$, where E is a set of *events* and $\leq$, $\nearrow$ are binary relations on E called *causality relation* and *asymmetric conflict* respectively, s.t.:

1. the relation $\leq$ is a partial order and $\lfloor e \rfloor = \{e' \in E : e' \leq e\}$ is finite for all $e \in E$;
2. the relation $\nearrow$ satisfies for all $e, e' \in E$:
   (a) $e < e' \quad \Rightarrow \quad e \nearrow e'$;[1]
   (b) $\nearrow_{\lfloor e \rfloor}$ is acyclic;[2]

If $e \nearrow e'$, accordingly to the double interpretation of $\nearrow$, we say that e *is prevented* by e' or e *weakly causes* e'. Moreover we say that e *is strictly prevented* by e' (or e *strictly weakly causes* e'), written $e \rightsquigarrow e'$, if $e \nearrow e'$ and $\neg(e < e')$.

The definition can be easily understood by giving a more formal account of the ideas presented at the beginning of the section. Let *Fired*(e) denote the fact that the event e has been fired in a computation and let *prec*(e, e') denote that e precedes e' in the computation. Then

$$e < e' \quad \stackrel{def}{\equiv} \quad \mathit{Fired}(e') \Rightarrow \mathit{Fired}(e) \land \mathit{prec}(e, e')$$

$$e \nearrow e' \quad \stackrel{def}{\equiv} \quad \mathit{Fired}(e) \land \mathit{Fired}(e') \Rightarrow \mathit{prec}(e, e')$$

Therefore $<$ represents a global order of execution, while $\nearrow$ determines an order of execution only locally, in each configuration (computation). Thus it is natural to impose $\nearrow$ to be an extension of $<$. Moreover if a set of events forms an asymmetric conflict cycle $e_0 \nearrow e_1 \nearrow \ldots \nearrow e_n \nearrow e_0$, then such events cannot appear

[1] With $e < e'$ we mean $e \leq e$ and $e \neq e'$.

[2] Equivalently, we can require $(\nearrow_{\lfloor e \rfloor})^+$ irreflexive. This implies that, in particular, $\nearrow$ is irreflexive.

in the same computation, otherwise the execution of each event should precede the execution of the event itself. This explains why we require the acyclicity of $\nearrow$, restricted to the causes $\lfloor e \rfloor$ of an event e. Otherwise not all causes of e can be executed in the same computation and thus e itself cannot be executed. The informal interpretation makes also clear that $\nearrow$ is *not* in general transitive. If $e \nearrow e' \nearrow e''$ it is not true that e must precede e'' when both fire. This holds only in a computation where also e' fires.

The fact that a set of n events in a weak-causality cycle can never occur in the same computation can be naturally interpreted as a form of n-ary conflict. More formally, it is useful to associate to each aES an explicit conflict relation (on sets of events) defined in the following way:

Definition 2 (induced conflict relation). Let $G = \langle E, \leq, \nearrow \rangle$ be an aES. The *conflict* relation $\#^a \subseteq \mathbf{2}^E_{fin}$ associated to G is defined as:

$$\frac{e_0 \nearrow e_1 \nearrow \ldots \nearrow e_n \nearrow e_0}{\#^a\{e_0, e_1, \ldots, e_n\}} \qquad \frac{\#^a(A \cup \{e\}) \quad e \leq e'}{\#^a(A \cup \{e'\})}$$

where A denotes a generic finite subset of E. The superscript a in $\#^a$ reminds that this relation is induced by asymmetric conflict. Sometimes we use the infix notation for the "binary version" of the conflict, i.e. we write $e\#^a e'$ for $\#^a\{e, e'\}$.

It is worth noticing that the binary version of the conflict relation $\#^a$, satisfies all the properties of the conflict relation of traditional PES's, i.e. it is irreflexive, symmetric and hereditary w.r.t. the causal dependency relation.

The notion of aES morphism is a quite natural extension of that of PES morphism. Intuitively, it is a (possibly partial) mapping of events that "preserves computations".

Definition 3 (category aES). Let $G_0 = \langle E_0, \leq_0, \nearrow_0 \rangle$ and $G_1 = \langle E_1, \leq_1, \nearrow_1 \rangle$ be two aES. An *aES-morphism* $f : G_0 \to G_1$ is a partial function $f : E_0 \to E_1$ such that:

1. for all $e_0 \in E_0$, if $f(e_0)$ is defined then $\lfloor f(e_0) \rfloor \subseteq f(\lfloor e_0 \rfloor)$;
2. for all $e_0, e_0' \in E_0$
   (a) $(f(e_0) = f(e_0')) \wedge (e_0 \neq e_0') \quad \Rightarrow \quad e_0 \#_0^a e_0'$;
   (b) $f(e_0) \nearrow_1 f(e_0') \quad \Rightarrow \quad (e_0 \nearrow_0 e_0') \vee (e_0 \#_0^a e_0')$.

We denote with **aES** the category of asymmetric event structures and aES morphisms.

It can be shown that aES morphisms are closed under composition and thus category **aES** is well-defined. Moreover, analogously to what happens for PES's, one can prove that aES morphisms reflect the (n-ary derived) conflict relation.

Lemma 4 (prime and asymmetric event structures). *Let $ES = \langle E, \leq, \# \rangle$ be a prime event structure. Then $G = \langle E, \leq, < \cup \# \rangle$ is and aES, where the* *asymmetric conflict relation is defined as the union of the "strict" causality and conflict relations.*

Moreover, if $f : ES_0 \rightarrow ES_1$ is an event structure morphism then f is an aES-morphism between the corresponding aES's G_0 and G_1, and if $g : G_0 \rightarrow G_1$ is an aES morphism then it is also a PES morphism between the original PES's.

By the lemma, there is a full embedding functor $\mathfrak{J}$: **PES** $\rightarrow$ **aES** defined on objects as $\mathfrak{J}(\langle E, \leq, \# \rangle) = \langle E, \leq, < \cup \# \rangle$ and on arrows as $\mathfrak{J}(f : ES_0 \rightarrow ES_1) = f$.

A configuration of an event structure is a set of events representing a possible computation of the system modelled by the event structure. The presence of the asymmetric conflict relation makes such definition slightly more involved w.r.t. the traditional one.

Definition 5 (configuration). Let $G = \langle E, \leq, \nearrow \rangle$ be an aES. A *configuration* of G is a set of events $C \subseteq E$ such that

1. $\nearrow_C$ is well-founded;
2. $\{e' \in C : e' \nearrow e\}$ is finite for all $e \in C$;
3. C is left-closed w.r.t. $\leq$, i.e. for all $e \in C$, $e' \in E$, $e' \leq e$ implies $e' \in C$.

The set of all configurations of G is denoted by $Conf(G)$.

Condition 1 first ensures that in C there are no $\nearrow$ cycles, and thus excludes the possibility of having in C a subset of events in conflict (formally, for any $A \subseteq_{fin} C$, we have $\neg(\#^a A)$). Moreover it guarantees that $\nearrow$ has no infinite descending chain in C, that, together with Condition 2, implies that the set $\{e' \in C : e'(\nearrow_C)^+ e\}$ is finite for each event e in C; thus each event has to be preceded only by finitely many other events of the configuration. Finally Condition 3 requires that all the causes of each event are present.

If a set of events A satisfies only the first two properties of Definition 5 it is called *consistent* and we write $co(S)$. Notice that, unlike for traditional event structures, consistency is not a finitary property.[3] For instance, let $A = \{e_i : i \in \mathbb{N}\} \subseteq E$ be a set of events such that all e_i's are distinct and $e_{i+1} \nearrow e_i$ for all $i \in \mathbb{N}$. Then A is not consistent, but each finite subset of A is.

A remarkable difference w.r.t. to the classical approach is that the order on configurations is not simply set-inclusion, since a configuration C cannot be extended with an event inhibited by some of the events already present in C.

Definition 6 (extension). Let $G = \langle E, \leq, \nearrow \rangle$ be an aES and let $A, A' \subseteq E$ be sets of events. We say that A' *extends* A and we write $A \sqsubseteq A'$, if

1. $A \subseteq A'$;
2. $\neg(e' \nearrow e)$ for all $e \in A, e' \in A' - A$.

[3] A property Q on the subsets of a set X is *finitary* if given any $Y \subseteq X$, from $Q(Z)$ for all finite subsets $Z \subseteq Y$ it follows $Q(Y)$.

An important result is the fact that the set $Conf(G)$ of configurations of an aES endowed with the extension relation is a finitary prime algebraic domain, i.e. a coherent, prime algebraic, finitary partial order, in the following simply referred to as ***domain***. Therefore asymmetric event structures, as well as prime [20] and flow [1] event structures, provide a concrete presentation of prime algebraic domains.

The proof of such result is technically involved and will appear in the full paper: only a sketch is presented here. The fact that $\langle Conf(G), \sqsubseteq \rangle$ is a partial order immediately follows from the definition. Moreover for pairwise compatible sets of configurations the least upper bound and the greatest lower bound are given by union and intersection.

Interestingly, the primes of the domain of configurations turn out to be the possible histories of the various events. We call ***history*** of an event e in a configuration C the set of events of C that ***must*** be executed before e (together with e itself). Recall that in a prime event structure an event e uniquely determines its history, that is the set $\lfloor e \rfloor$ of its causes, independently from the configuration at hand. In the case of asymmetric event structures, instead, an event e may have different histories. In fact, given a configuration C, the set of events that must precede e is $C[\![e]\!] = \{e' \in C : e' (\nearrow_C)^* e\}$, and clearly, such a set depends on the configuration C. The set of all possible histories of an event e, namely $\{C[\![e]\!] : C \in Conf(G)\}$ is denoted by $Hist(e)$.

Theorem 7. *Let G be an aES. Then $\langle Conf(G), \sqsubseteq \rangle$ is a (finitary prime algebraic) domain. The primes of $Conf(G)$ are the possible histories of events in G, i.e. the configurations in $\bigcup_{e \in E} Hist(e)$.*

Winskel in his seminal work [20] proved the equivalence between the category **PES** of prime event structures and the category **Dom** of domains and additive, stable, immediate precedence-preserving functions.

$$\mathbf{PES} \underset{\mathcal{L}}{\overset{\mathcal{P}}{\rightleftarrows}} \mathbf{Dom} \quad (\sim)$$

The functor $\mathcal{L}$ associates to each PES the domain of its configurations, while the functor $\mathcal{P}$ associates to each domain a PES having its prime elements as events.

We want now to generalize this result to our framework by showing the existence of a coreflection between **aES** and **Dom**. One can prove that aES morphisms preserve configurations and that the natural function between the domains of configurations induced by an aES morphism is a domain morphism. These results, together with Theorem 7, ensure that the functor $\mathcal{L}_a$ leading from the category **aES** of asymmetric event structures to the category **Dom** of finitary prime algebraic domains is well-defined. The functor $\mathcal{P}_a$ performing the backward step is obtained simply by embedding in **aES** the Winskel's construction.

Definition 8. Let $\mathcal{L}_a : \mathbf{aES} \to \mathbf{Dom}$ be the functor defined as:
- $\mathcal{L}_a(G) = \langle Conf(G), \sqsubseteq \rangle$, for any **aES**-object G;

- $\mathcal{L}_a(f) = f^* : \mathcal{L}_a(G_0) \to \mathcal{L}_a(G_1)$, for any **aES**-morphism $f : G_0 \to G_1$.[4]
The functor $\mathcal{P}_a$: **Dom** $\to$ **aES** is defined as $\mathcal{J} \circ \mathcal{P}$.

The proof of the following main result will appear in the full paper.

Theorem 9. *The functor $\mathcal{P}_a$ is left adjoint of $\mathcal{L}_a$. The counit of the adjunction $\epsilon : \mathcal{P}_a \circ \mathcal{L}_a \dot{\to} 1$ is defined by $\epsilon_G(C) = e$, if $C \in Hist(e)$.*

3 Contextual nets

We introduce here *marked contextual P/T nets (c-nets)*, that, following the lines suggested in [14] for C/E systems, add contexts to classical P/T nets. We first recall some notation for multisets. Let A be a set; a *multiset* of A is a function $m : A \to \mathbb{N}$. Such a multiset will be denoted sometimes as a formal sum $m = \sum_{a \in A} n_a \cdot a$, where $n_a = m(a)$. The set of multisets of A is denoted as μA. The usual operations and relations on multisets of A are used. As an example, multiset union is denoted by $+$ and defined as $(m + m')(a) = m(a) + m'(a)$; multiset difference $(m - m')$ is defined as $(m - m')(a) = m(a) - m'(a)$ if $m(a) \geq m'(a)$ and $(m - m')(a) = 0$ otherwise. We write $m \leq m'$ if $m(a) \leq m'(a)$ for all $a \in A$. If m is a multiset of A, we denote by $[\![m]\!]$ the multiset $\sum_{\{a \in A | m(a) > 0\}} 1 \cdot a$, obtained by changing all non-zero coefficients of m to 1. Sometimes we will confuse the multisets $[\![m]\!]$ with the corresponding subsets $\{a \in A : m(a) > 0\}$ of A, and use on them the usual set operations and relations. A *multirelation* $f : A \to B$ is a multiset of $A \times B$. It induces in an obvious way a function $\mu f : \mu A \to \mu B$, defined as $\mu f(\sum_{a \in A} n_a \cdot a) = \sum_{b \in B} \sum_{a \in A} (n_a \cdot f(a, b)) \cdot b$. If the multirelation f satisfies $f(a, b) \leq 1$ for all $a \in A$ and $b \in B$ then we sometimes confuse it with the corresponding set-relation and write $f(a, b)$ for $f(a, b) = 1$.

Definition 10 (c-net). A *(marked) contextual Petri net* (*c-net*) is a tuple $N = \langle S, T, F, C, m \rangle$, where

- S is a set of *places*;
- T is a set of *transitions*;
- $F = \langle F_{pre}, F_{post} \rangle$ is a pair of multirelations from T to S;
- C is a multirelation from T to S, called the *context relation*;
- m is a multiset of S, called the *initial marking*.

We assume, without loss of generality, that $S \cap T = \emptyset$. Moreover, we require that for each transition $t \in T$, there exists a place $s \in S$ such that $F_{pre}(t, s) > 0$.[5]

Let N be a c-net. As usual, the functions from μT to μS induced by the multirelations F_{pre} and F_{post} are denoted by ${}^\bullet(\,)$ and $(\,)^\bullet$, respectively. If $A \in \mu T$ is a multiset of transitions, ${}^\bullet A$ is called its *pre-set*, while $A^\bullet$ is called its *post-set*. Moreover, by $\underline{A}$ we denote the *context* of A, defined as $\underline{A} = \mu C(A)$.

[4] With f^* we denote the natural extension of the function f to the powerset of E_0 (i.e., $f^*(A) = \{f(a) : a \in A\}$, for $A \subseteq E_0$).

[5] This is a weak version of the condition of *T-restrictness* that requires also $F_{post}(t, s) > 0$, for some $s \in S$.

The same notation is used to denote the functions from S to $\mathbf{2}^T$ defined as, for $s \in S$, ${}^{\bullet}s = \{t \in T : F_{post}(t,s) > 0\}$, $s^{\bullet} = \{t \in T : F_{pre}(t,s) > 0\}$, $\underline{s} = \{t \in T : C(t,s) > 0\}$.

In the following when considering a c-net N, we implicitly assume that $N = \langle S, T, F, C, m\rangle$. Moreover superscripts and subscripts on the nets names carry over the names of the involved sets, functions and relations. For instance $N_i = \langle S_i, T_i, F_i, C_i, m_i\rangle$.

For a finite multiset of transitions A to be enabled by a marking M, it is sufficient that M contains the pre-set of A and at least one *additional* token in each place of the context of A. This corresponds to the intuition that a token in a place can be used as context by many transitions at the same time and with multiplicity greater than one by the same transition.

Definition 11 (token game). Let N be a c-net and let M be a *marking* of N, that is a multiset $M \in \mu S$. Given a finite multiset $A \in \mu T$, we say that A is *enabled* by M if ${}^{\bullet}A + [\![\underline{A}]\!] \leq M$.[6] The *transition relation* between markings is defined as

$$M\,[A\rangle\, M' \qquad \text{iff} \qquad A \text{ is enabled by } M \text{ and } M' = M - {}^{\bullet}A + A^{\bullet}.$$

We call $M\,[A\rangle\, M'$ a *step*. A *simple step* or *firing* is a step involving just one transition. A marking M is called *reachable* if there exists a finite *step sequence* $m\,[A_0\rangle\, M_1\,[A_1\rangle\, M_2 \ldots [A_n\rangle\, M$, starting from the initial marking and leading to M.

A c-net morphism is a partial mapping between transitions that "preserves" pre- and post-sets, and also contexts in a weak sense.

Definition 12 (c-net morphism). Let N_0 and N_1 be c-nets. A *c-net morphism* $h : N_0 \to N_1$ is a pair $h = \langle h_T, h_S\rangle$, where $h_T : T_0 \to T_1$ is a partial function and $h_S : S_0 \to S_1$ is a multirelation such that (1) $\mu h_S(m_0) = m_1$ and, for each $A \in \mu T$, (2) $\mu h_S({}^{\bullet}A) = {}^{\bullet}\mu h_T(A)$, (3) $\mu h_S(A^{\bullet}) = \mu h_T(A)^{\bullet}$ and (4) $[\![\underline{\mu h_T(A)}]\!] \leq \mu h_S(\underline{A}) \leq \underline{\mu h_T(A)}$.
We denote by **CN** the category having c-nets as objects and c-net morphisms as arrows.

Conditions (1)-(3) are standard, but condition (4), regarding contexts, deserves some comments. It can be explained by recalling that, since in our model a single token can be used as context with multiplicity greater than one, the firing of a transition t can use as context any multiset X satisfying $[\![\underline{t}]\!] \leq X \leq \underline{t}$. Given any multiset of tokens that can be used as context in a firing of a transition,

[6] Other approaches (e.g. [9, 18]) allow for the concurrent firing of transitions that use the same token as context and precondition. For instance, in [9] the formal condition for a multiset A of transitions to be enabled by a marking M is ${}^{\bullet}A \leq M$ and $\underline{A} \leq M$. We do not admit such steps, the idea being that two concurrent transitions should be allowed to fire also in any order.

its image should be a set of tokens that can be used as context by the image of the transition. This can be formalized by requiring that $\lfloor \underline{\mu h_T(A)} \rfloor \leq \mu h_S(X) \leq \underline{\mu h_T(A)}$ for any $X \in \mu S_0$ such that $\lfloor \underline{A} \rfloor \leq X \leq \underline{A}$, which is equivalent to the above condition (4).

The basic result to prove (to check that the definition of morphism is "meaningful") is that the token game is preserved by c-net morphisms.

Theorem 13 (morphisms preserve the token game). *Let N_0 and N_1 be c-nets, and let $h = \langle h_T, h_S \rangle : N_0 \to N_1$ be a c-net morphism. Then for each $M, M' \in \mu S$ and $A \in \mu T$*

$$M\,[A\rangle\, M' \quad \Rightarrow \quad \mu h_S(M)\,[\mu h_T(A)\rangle\, \mu h_S(M').$$

Therefore c-net morphisms preserve reachable markings, i.e. if M_0 is a reachable marking in N_0 then $\mu h_S(M_0)$ is reachable in N_1.

The seminal work by Winskel [20] presents a coreflection between event structures and a subclass of P/T nets, namely *safe* nets. In [12] it is shown that essentially the same constructions work for the larger category of "weakly safe nets" as well (while the generalization to the whole category of P/T nets requires some original technical machinery and allows one to obtain a proper adjunction rather than a coreflection). In the next sections we will relate by a coreflection event structures and "weakly safe c-nets".

Definition 14 (weakly safe c-nets). A *weakly safe* c-net is a c-net N such that the initial marking m is a set and F_{post} is a relation (i.e. $t^{\bullet}$ is a set for all $t \in T$). We denote by **WS-CN** the full subcategory of **CN** having weakly safe c-nets as objects.

A weakly safe c-net is called *safe* if also F_{pre} and C are relations (i.e., ${}^{\bullet}t$ and $\underline{t}$ are sets for all $t \in T$) and each reachable marking is a set.

4 Occurrence c-nets and the unfolding construction

Occurrence c-nets are intended to represent, via an unfolding construction, the behaviour of general c-nets in a static way, by expressing the events (firing of transitions) which can appear in a computation and the dependency relations between them. Occurrence c-nets will be defined as safe c-nets such that the dependency relations between transitions satisfy suitable acyclicity and well-foundedness requirements. While for traditional occurrence nets one has to take into account the causal dependency and the conflict relations, by the presence of contexts, we have to consider an asymmetric conflict (or weak dependency) relation as well. Interestingly, the conflict relation turns out to be a derived (from asymmetric conflict) relation.

Causal dependency is defined as for traditional nets, with an additional clause stating that transition t causes t' if it generates a token in a context place of t'.

Definition 15 (causal dependency). Let N be a safe c-net. The *causal dependency relation* $<_N$ is the transitive closure of the relation $\prec$ defined by:

1. if $s \in {}^{\bullet}t$ then $s \prec t$;
2. if $s \in t^{\bullet}$ then $t \prec s$;
3. if $t^{\bullet} \cap \underline{t'} \neq \emptyset$ then $t \prec t'$.

Given a place or transition $x \in S \cup T$, we denote with $\lfloor x \rfloor$ the set of *causes* of x, defined as $\lfloor x \rfloor = \{t \in T : t \leq_N x\} \subseteq T$, where $\leq_N$ is the reflexive closure of $<_N$.

Definition 16 (asymmetric conflict). Let N be a safe c-net. The ***strict asymmetric conflict relation*** $\leadsto_N$ is defined as

$$t \leadsto_N t' \quad \text{iff} \quad \underline{t} \cap {}^{\bullet}t' \neq \emptyset \text{ or } (t \neq t' \wedge {}^{\bullet}t \cap {}^{\bullet}t' \neq \emptyset).$$

The ***asymmetric conflict relation*** $\nearrow_N$ is the union of the strict asymmetric conflict and causal dependency relations:

$$t \nearrow_N t' \quad \text{iff} \quad t <_N t' \text{ or } t \leadsto_N t'.$$

In our informal interpretation, $t \nearrow_N t'$ if t must precede t' in each computation in which both fire or, equivalently, t' prevents t to be fired:

$$t \nearrow t' \quad \stackrel{def}{\equiv} \quad Fired(t) \wedge Fired(t') \Rightarrow prec(t, t') \qquad (\dagger)$$

As noticed in the introduction, this is surely the case when the same place s appears as context for t and as precondition for t'. But (†) is trivially true (with t and t' in interchangeable roles) when t and t' have a common precondition, since they never fire in the same computation. This is apparently a little tricky but corresponds to the clear intuition that a (usual) symmetric (direct) conflict leads to asymmetric conflict in both directions. Finally, since, as noticed for the general model of aES, (†) is weaker than the condition that expresses causality, the condition (†) is satisfied when t causes (in the usual sense) t'.[7] For technical reasons it is convenient to distinguish the first two cases from the last one.

The c-net in Fig. 2 shows that, as expected, the relation $\nearrow_N$ is not transitive. In fact we have $t_1 \nearrow_N t_3 \nearrow_N t_2 \nearrow_N t_1$, but, for instance, it is not true that $t_1 \nearrow_N t_2$.

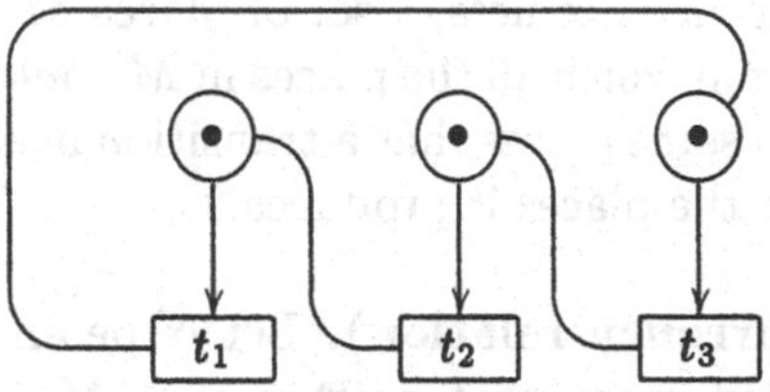

Fig. 2. An occurrence c-net with a cycle of asymmetric conflict.

An occurrence c-net is a safe c-net that exhibits an acyclic behaviour and such that each transition in it can be fired.

[7] This is the origin of the weak causality interpretation of $\nearrow$.

Definition 17 (occurrence c-nets). An *occurrence c-net* is a safe c-net N such that

- each place $s \in S$ is in the post-set of at most one transition, i.e. $|{}^\bullet s| \leq 1$;
- the *causal relation* $<_N$ is irreflexive and its reflexive closure $\leq_N$ is a partial order, such that $\lfloor t \rfloor$ is finite for any $t \in T$;
- the *initial marking* m is the set of minimal places w.r.t. $\leq_N$, i.e., $m = \{s \in S : {}^\bullet s = \emptyset\}$;
- $(\nearrow_N)_{\lfloor t \rfloor}$ is acyclic[8] for all transitions $t \in T$.

The full subcategory of **WS-CN** having occurrence c-nets as objects is denoted by **O-CN**.

The last condition corresponds to the requirement of irreflexivity for the conflict relation in ordinary occurrence nets. In fact, if a transition t has a $\nearrow_N$ cycle in its causes then it can never fire, since in an occurrence c-net N, the order in which transitions appear in a firing sequence must be compatible with the transitive closure of the (restriction to the transitions in the sequence of the) asymmetric conflict relation.

As anticipated, the asymmetric conflict relation induces a symmetric conflict relation (on sets of transitions) defined in the following way:

Definition 18 (conflict). Let N be a c-net. The *conflict* relation $\# \subseteq \mathbf{2}^T_{fin}$ associated to N is defined as:

$$\frac{t_0 \nearrow t_1 \nearrow \ldots \nearrow t_n \nearrow t_0}{\#\{t_0, t_1, \ldots, t_n\}} \qquad\qquad \frac{\#(A \cup \{t\}) \quad t \leq t'}{\#(A \cup \{t'\})}$$

where A denotes a generic finite subset of T. As for aES's, we use the infix notation $t\#t'$ for $\#\{t, t'\}$.

For instance, referring to Fig. 2, we have $\#\{t_1, t_2, t_3\}$, but not $\#\{t_i, t_j\}$ for any $i, j \in \{1, 2, 3\}$.

As for traditional occurrence nets, a set of places M is concurrent if there is some reachable marking in which all the places in M contain a token. However for the presence of contexts some places that a transition needs to be fired (contexts) can be concurrent with the places it produces.

Definition 19 (concurrency relation). Let N be an occurrence c-net. A set of places $M \subseteq S$ is called *concurrent*, written *conc*(M), if

1. $\forall s, s' \in M.\ \neg(s < s')$;
2. $\lfloor M \rfloor$ is finite, where $\lfloor M \rfloor = \bigcup\{\lfloor s \rfloor : s \in M\}$;
3. $\nearrow_{\lfloor M \rfloor}$ is acyclic (and thus well-founded, since $\lfloor M \rfloor$ is finite).

[8] We can equivalently require $((\nearrow_N)_{\lfloor t \rfloor})^+$ to be irreflexive. In particular this implies $\nearrow_N$ irreflexive.

It can be shown that, indeed, the concurrent sets of places of an occurrence c-net coincide with the (subsets of) reachable markings. In particular, for each transition t in an occurrence c-net, since $conc({}^{\bullet}t + \underline{t})$, there is a reachable marking $M \supseteq {}^{\bullet}t + \underline{t}$, in which t is enabled.

It is possible to prove that c-net morphisms preserve the concurrency relation. Moreover, they preserve the "amount of concurrency" also on transitions. More precisely, they reflect causal dependency and conflicts, while asymmetric conflict is reflected or becomes conflict. These results are fundamental for establishing a connection between occurrence c-nets and aES's.

Theorem 20. *Let N_0 and N_1 be c-nets and let $h : N_0 \to N_1$ be a morphism. Then, for all $t_0, t_0' \in T_0$*

1. $\lfloor h_T(t_0) \rfloor \subseteq h_T(\lfloor t_0 \rfloor)$;
2. $(h_T(t_0) = h_T(t_0')) \wedge (t_0 \neq t_0') \quad \Rightarrow \quad t_0 \#_0 t_0'$;
3. $h_T(t_0) \nearrow_1 h_T(t_0') \quad \Rightarrow \quad (t_0 \nearrow_0 t_0') \vee (t_0 \#_0 t_0')$;
4. $\# h_T(A) \quad \Rightarrow \quad \# A$.

Given a weakly-safe c-net N, an *unfolding* construction allows us to obtain an occurrence c-net $\mathcal{U}_a(N)$ that describes the behaviour of N. As for traditional nets, each transition in $\mathcal{U}_a(N)$ represents an instance of a precise firing of a transition in N, and places in $\mathcal{U}_a(N)$ represent occurrences of tokens in the places of N. The unfolding operation can be extended to a functor $\mathcal{U}_a$: **WS-CN** $\to$ **O-CN** that is right adjoint of the inclusion functor $\mathfrak{I}_O$: **O-CN** $\to$ **WS-CN** and thus establishes a coreflection between **WS-CN** and **O-CN**.

Definition 21 (unfolding). Let $N = \langle S, T, F, C, m \rangle$ be a weakly safe c-net. The unfolding $\mathcal{U}_a(N) = \langle S', T', F', C', m' \rangle$ of the net N and the *folding morphism* $f_N : \mathcal{U}_a(N) \to N$ are the unique occurrence c-net and c-net morphism satisfying the following equations.

$$
\begin{aligned}
m' &= \{\langle \emptyset, s \rangle : s \in m\} \\
S' &= m' \cup \{\langle t', s \rangle : t' = \langle M_p, M_c, t \rangle \in T' \ \wedge \ s \in t^{\bullet}\} \\
T' &= \{\langle M_p, M_c, t \rangle : M_p, M_c \subseteq S' \ \wedge \ M_p \cap M_c = \emptyset \ \wedge \ conc(M_p \cup M_c) \ \wedge \\
&\qquad t \in T \ \wedge \ \mu f_S(M_p) = {}^{\bullet}t \ \wedge \ [\![\underline{t}]\!] \leq \mu f_S(M_c) \leq \underline{t}\}
\end{aligned}
$$

$$
\begin{array}{lll}
F'_{pre}(t', s') & \text{iff} & t' = \langle M_p, M_c, t \rangle \ \wedge \ s' \in M_p \quad (t \in T) \\
C'(t', s') & \text{iff} & t' = \langle M_p, M_c, t \rangle \ \wedge \ s' \in M_c \quad (t \in T) \\
F'_{post}(t', s') & \text{iff} & s' = \langle t', s \rangle \quad (s \in S) \\
f_T(t') = t & \text{iff} & t' = \langle M_p, M_c, t \rangle \\
f_S(s', s) & \text{iff} & s' = \langle x, s \rangle \quad (x \in T' \cup \{\emptyset\})
\end{array}
$$

The unfolding can be effectively constructed by giving an inductive definition. Uniqueness follows from the fact that to each item in a occurrence c-net we can associate a finite depth.

Places and transitions in the unfolding of a c-net represent respectively tokens and firing of transitions in the original net. Each place in the unfolding is a pair recording the "history" of the token and the corresponding place in the original net. Each transition is a triple recording the precondition and context used in the firing, and the corresponding transition in the original net. A new place with empty history $\langle \emptyset, s \rangle$ is generated for each place s in the initial marking. Moreover a new transition $t' = \langle M_p, M_c, t \rangle$ is inserted in the unfolding whenever we can find a concurrent set of places (precondition M_p and context M_c) that corresponds, in the original net, to a marking that enables t. For each place s in the post-set of such t, a new place $\langle t', s \rangle$ is generated, belonging to the post-set of t'. The folding morphism f maps each place (transition) of the unfolding to the corresponding place (transition) in the original net.

We can now state the main result of this section, establishing a coreflection between weakly safe c-nets and occurrence c-nets.

Theorem 22. *The unfolding construction extends to a functor* $\mathcal{U}_a$: **WS-CN** $\rightarrow$ **O-CN** *which is right adjoint to the obvious inclusion functor* $\mathcal{I}_O$: **O-CN** $\rightarrow$ **WS-CN** *and thus establishes a coreflection between* **WS-CN** *and* **O-CN**.

The component at an object N *in* **WS-CN** *of the counit of the adjunction,* $f : \mathcal{I}_O \circ \mathcal{U}_a \dot{\rightarrow} 1$, *is the folding morphism* $f_N : \mathcal{U}_a(N) \rightarrow N$.

5 Occurrence c-nets and asymmetric event structures

We now show that the semantics of weakly safe c-nets given in terms of occurrence c-nets can be related with event structures and prime algebraic domains semantics. First we show that there exists a coreflection from **aES** to **O-CN** and thus aES's represent a suitable model for giving event based semantics to c-nets. Given an occurrence c-net we obtain an aES simply forgetting the places, but remembering the dependency relations that they induce between transitions, namely causality and asymmetric conflict. In the same way a morphism between occurrence c-nets naturally restricts to a morphism between the corresponding aES's.

Definition 23. Let $\mathcal{E}_a$: **O-CN** $\rightarrow$ **aES** be the functor defined as:

- $\mathcal{E}_a(N) = \langle T, \leq_N, \nearrow_N \rangle$, for each occurrence c-net N;
- $\mathcal{E}_a(h : N_0 \rightarrow N_1) = h_T$, for each morphism $h : N_0 \rightarrow N_1$.

Notice that the induced conflict relation $\#^a$ in the aES $\mathcal{E}_a(N)$, given by Definition 2, is the restriction to transitions of the induced conflict relation in the net N, given by Definition 18. Therefore in the following we will confuse the two relations and simply write $\#$.

An aES can be identified with a canonical occurrence c-net, via a free construction that mimics Winskel's: for each set of events related in a certain way by causal dependency or asymmetric conflict relations we generate a unique place that induces such kind of relation on the events.

Definition 24. Let $G = \langle E, \leq, \nearrow \rangle$ be an aES. Then $\mathcal{N}_a(G)$ is the net $N = \langle S, T, F, C, m \rangle$ defined as follows:

$$- \; m = \left\{ \langle \emptyset, A, B \rangle : \begin{array}{l} A, B \subseteq E, \; \forall a \in A. \; \forall b \in B. \; a \nearrow b \; \vee \; a\#b, \\ \forall b, b' \in B. \; b \neq b' \Rightarrow b\#b' \end{array} \right\};$$

$$- \; S = m \cup \left\{ \langle e, A, B \rangle : \begin{array}{l} A, B \subseteq E, \; e \in E, \; \forall x \in A \cup B. \; e < x, \\ \forall a \in A. \; \forall b \in B. \; a \nearrow b \; \vee \; a\#b, \\ \forall b, b' \in B. \; b \neq b' \Rightarrow b\#b' \end{array} \right\};$$

- $T = E$;
- $F = \langle F_{pre}, F_{post} \rangle$, with
  $F_{pre} = \{(e, s) : s = \langle x, A, B \rangle \in S, \; e \in B\}$,
  $F_{post} = \{(e, s) : s = \langle e, A, B \rangle \in S\}$;
- $C = \{(e, s) : s = \langle x, A, B \rangle \in S, \; e \in A\}$.

The generation process extends to a functor $\mathcal{N}_a$: **aES** $\rightarrow$ **O-CN**

The only unexpected thing for the reader could be the fact that we insert a place that gives rise to asymmetric conflicts between the transitions of B and A, but we require only that all the transition of B are in asymmetric conflict *or in conflict* with all the transitions in A. Therefore we add asymmetric conflicts between events that are in conflict. Abstracting from the formal details, this becomes very natural since, being $\#$ the symmetric conflict relation, we can think that conceptually $t\#t'$ implies $t \nearrow t'$.

The next proposition relates the causal dependency and asymmetric conflict relations of an aES with the corresponding relations of the c-net $\mathcal{N}_a(G)$. In particular it is useful in proving that $\mathcal{N}_a(G)$ is indeed an occurrence c-net.

Proposition 25. *Let $G = \langle E, \leq, \nearrow \rangle$ be an aES and let $\mathcal{N}_a(G)$ be the net $N = \langle S, T, F, C, m \rangle$. Then for all $e, e' \in E$:*

1. $e <_N e'$ *iff* $e < e'$;
2. $e \nearrow_N e'$ *iff* $e \nearrow e'$ *or* $e\#e'$.

Let $G = \langle E, \leq, \nearrow \rangle$ be an aES. By Proposition 25, $\mathcal{E}_a(\mathcal{N}_a(G)) = \langle E, \leq, \nearrow \cup \# \rangle$. Therefore the identity on events $\eta_G : G \rightarrow \mathcal{E}_a(\mathcal{N}_a(G))$, defined by $\eta_G(e) = e$, for all $e \in E$, is an aES morphism. Moreover $\eta_G^{-1} : \mathcal{E}_a(\mathcal{N}_a(G)) \rightarrow G$, again defined as identity on events is clearly a morphism, and η_G and η_G^{-1} are one the inverse of the other. Therefore η_G is an isomorphism. We are now able to state the main result of this section.

Theorem 26. *The functor $\mathcal{N}_a$:* **aES** $\rightarrow$ **O-CN** *is left adjoint to $\mathcal{E}_a$:* **O-CN** $\rightarrow$ **aES** *and it establishes a coreflection from* **aES** *to* **O-CN**. *The unit of the the coreflection is $\eta : 1 \rightarrow \mathcal{N}_a \circ \mathcal{E}_a$.*

Such a result completes the chain of coreflections leading from **WS-CN** to **Dom**. Therefore, as claimed at the beginning, we provide weakly safe c-nets with a truly concurrent semantics, by associating to each weakly safe c-net a finitary prime algebraic domain. The construction works at categorical level and establishes a coreflection between the corresponding categories.

Finally, notice that, as an easy extension, Winskel's coreflection between **PES** and **Dom** can be used to provide weakly safe c-nets with a traditional event structure semantics. The PES semantics is obtained from the aES semantics by introducing an event for each possible different history of events in the aES. This reflects the idea of duplication of events discussed in the introduction.

6 Conclusions and future work

We presented a truly concurrent event-based semantics for (weakly safe) P/T contextual nets. The semantics is given at categorical level via a coreflection between the categories **WS-CN** of weakly safe c-nets and **Dom** of finitary prime algebraic domains (or equivalently **PES** of prime event structures). Such a coreflection factorizes through the following chain of coreflections:

$$\mathbf{WS\text{-}CN} \underset{\mathcal{U}_a}{\overset{\mathcal{I}_O}{\rightleftarrows}} \mathbf{O\text{-}CN} \underset{\mathcal{E}_a}{\overset{\mathcal{N}_a}{\rightleftarrows}} \mathbf{aES} \underset{\mathcal{L}_a}{\overset{\mathcal{P}_a}{\rightleftarrows}} \mathbf{Dom}$$

It is worth noticing that such a construction associates to a safe c-net without context places (thus essentially a traditional safe net), the same domain produced by Winskel's construction and therefore can be considered as a consistent extension of Winskel's result. The use of finitary prime algebraic domains, widely accepted as standard semantics models for concurrency, makes our result satisfactory. Moreover the existence of a coreflection provides an abstract semantics (the domain associated to each c-net) and a standard choice in each class of equivalent c-nets (the c-net obtained by embedding the semantics into the category of nets), defined by a universal property. This is one of the more pleasant semantic frameworks one can desire.

An immediate future work should be the generalization of these results to general P/T c-nets, based on a suitable extension of the notions of decorated occurrence net and family morphism introduced in [12] to give unfolding semantics to traditional P/T nets. Moreover, notions and results on c-nets can be seen as a first step towards the definition of an unfolding semantics for graph grammars. We think that the work on c-nets could be a guide for the introduction of the notions of non-deterministic occurrence graph grammar and graph grammar unfolding that are still lacking or not consolidated.

Apart from the application to c-nets analyzed in this paper, asymmetric event structures seem to be rather promising in the semantic treatment of models of computation, such as string, term and graph rewriting, allowing context sensitive firing of events. Therefore, as suggested in [16], it would be interesting to investigate the possibility of developing a general theory of event structures with asymmetric conflict (or weak causality) similar to that in [20].

References

1. G. Boudol. Flow Event Structures and Flow Nets. In *Semantics of System of Concurrent Processes*, volume 469 of *LNCS*, pages 62–95. Springer Verlag, 1990.

2. G. Boudol and I. Castellani. Permutation of transitions: an event structure semantics for CCS and SCCS. In *Linear Time, Branching Time and Partial Order Semantics in Logics and Models for Concurrency*, volume 354 of *LNCS*, pages 411–427. Springer Verlag, 1988.
3. N. Busi and R. Gorrieri. A Petri Nets Semantics for π-calculus. In *Proceedings CONCUR'95*, volume 962 of *LNCS*, pages 145–159. Springer Verlag, 1995.
4. N. Busi and G. M. Pinna. Non Sequential Semantics for Contextual P/T Nets. In *Application and Theory of Petri Nets*, volume 1091 of *LNCS*, pages 113–132. Springer Verlag, 1996.
5. S. Christensen and N. D. Hansen. Coloured Petri nets extended with place capacities, test arcs and inhibitor arcs. In M. Ajmone-Marsan, editor, *Applications and Theory of Petri Nets*, volume 691 of *LNCS*, pages 186–205. Springer Verlag, 1993.
6. A. Corradini. Concurrent Graph and Term Graph Rewriting. In U. Montanari and V. Sassone, editors, *Proceedings CONCUR'96*, volume 1119 of *LNCS*, pages 438–464. Springer Verlag, 1996.
7. N. De Francesco, U. Montanari, and G. Ristori. Modeling Concurrent Accesses to Shared Data via Petri Nets. In *Programming Concepts, Methods and Calculi, IFIP Transactions A-56*, pages 403–422. North Holland, 1994.
8. P. Degano, R. Gorrieri, and S. Vigna. On Relating Some Models for Concurrency. In M. C. Gaudel and J. P. Jouannaud, editors, *4th Conference on Theory and Practice of Software Development*, volume 668 of *LNCS*, pages 15–30. Springer-Verlag, 1993.
9. R. Janicki and M Koutny. Invariant semantics of nets with inhibitor arcs. In *Proceedings CONCUR '91*, volume 527 of *LNCS*. Springer Verlag, 1991.
10. R. Janicki and M. Koutny. Semantics of inhibitor nets. *Information and Computation*, 123:1–16, 1995.
11. R. Langerak. Bundle Event Structures: A Non-Interleaving Semantics for Lotos. In *5th Intl. Conf. on Formal Description Techniques (FORTE'92)*, pages 331–346. North-Holland, 1992.
12. J. Meseguer, U. Montanari, and V. Sassone. On the semantics of Petri nets. In *Proceedings CONCUR '92*, volume 630 of *LNCS*, pages 286–301. Springer Verlag, 1992.
13. U. Montanari and F. Rossi. Contextual occurrence nets and concurrent constraint programming. In H.-J. Schneider and H. Ehrig, editors, *Proceedings of the Dagstuhl Seminar 9301 on Graph Transformations in Computer Science*, volume 776 of *LNCS*. Springer Verlag, 1994.
14. U. Montanari and F. Rossi. Contextual nets. *Acta Informatica*, 32, 1995.
15. G. M. Pinna and A. Poigné. On the nature of events. In *Mathematical Foundations of Computer Science*, volume 629 of *LNCS*, pages 430–441. Springer Verlag, 1992.
16. G. M. Pinna and A. Poigné. On the nature of events: another perspective in concurrency. *Theoretical Computer Science*, 138:425–454, 1995.
17. G. Ristori. *Modelling Systems with Shared Resources via Petri Nets*. PhD thesis, Università di Pisa, 1994.
18. W. Vogler. Efficiency of asynchronous systems and read arcs in Petri nets. Technical Report 352, Institüt für Mathematik, Augsburg University, 1996.
19. W. Vogler. Partial Order Semantics and Read Arcs. In *Mathematical Foundations of Computer Science*, volume 1295 of *LNCS*, pages 508–518. Springer Verlag, 1997.
20. G. Winskel. Event Structures. In *Petri Nets: Applications and Relationships to Other Models of Concurrency*, volume 255 of *LNCS*, pages 325–392. Springer Verlag, 1987.

Pumping Lemmas for Timed Automata

Danièle Beauquier[1]

Abstract. We remark that languages recognized by timed automata in the general case do not satisfy classical Pumping Lemma (PL) well known in the theory of finite automata. In this paper we prove two weaker versions of Pumping Lemma for timed words : a general one (DPL) where iterations preserve the duration of timed word, and another more restricted one, (LPL) when iterations preserve the length of timed word.

1 Introduction

An automata-theoretic approach to verification of timing requirements of real-time systems has been extensively developped in recent years using timed automata [1], among recent papers we mention [2, 3] which influenced our work. A timed automaton is a finite automaton with a finite set of real valued clocks. The clocks can be reset to zero within the transitions of the automaton and keep track of the time elapsed since the last reset. Some constraints on the clocks are attached both to locations (analogous to states of usual finite automata) and transitions of the automaton.

Timed automata recognize finite or infinite timed words which are right-continuous discrete-valued functions having letters as values. Several papers study timed automata from the perspective of formal languages theory [1, 4]. Closure properties and some decision problems for deterministic and nondeterministic timed automata have been considered. In [4] a version of Kleene theorem for timed automata has been elaborated. The authors prove that it is necessary to include intersection in the operations which define regular expressions. In this paper we are interested in another classic feature of regular languages, namely in properties of iterations usually called Pumping Lemmas. We prove that the general version of Pumping Lemma does not hold for timed automata, giving a counter-example. This negative result underlines the fact that the introduction of dense time provides to languages recognized by timed automata a more complicated structure. Nevertheless we establish a weak version of Pumping Lemma

---

[1] *Address: University Paris-12, Dept. of Informatics, 61, Av. du Gén. de Gaulle, 94010 Créteil, France.*
E-mail: *beauquier@univ-paris12.fr*

(DPL) where the iteration preserves the duration of the timed word. The part of this result concerning a positive iteration can be found also in [5] (this was pointed out by referees). The dual version (LPL) where the iteration preserves the length of the timed word is proved for a sub-family of timed automata, the strict timed automata.
The paper is organized as follows : in section 2 we recall the definition of timed automata and timed words recognized by timed automata. Section 3 contains a series of lemmas concerning the iteration properties of runs of timed automata which are used in the last section. The last section studies different versions of Pumping Lemma and their status with respect to regular languages.

2 Timed Automata: Definitions

2.1 Timed words

Let Σ be a finite alphabet, and $\boldsymbol{R}_{\geq 0}$ be the set of non negative reals. A *(finite) timed word* is a right-continuous piecewise-constant function $\xi : [0, k) \to \Sigma$ for some $k \in \boldsymbol{R}_{\geq 0}$ such that ξ has a finite number of discontinuities. If k is equal to 0, ξ is the empty word denoted by ϵ. Here we slightly deviate from the definition given in [4], because the right-continuity of timed words seems to better reflect the semantics of the runs of timed automata.
Every timed word ξ can be written (in many ways) $a_1^{r_1}a_2^{r_2}\dots a_n^{r_n}$, where $a_i \in \Sigma$, $r_i \in \boldsymbol{R}_+$ and $\sum r_i = k$ if $\xi(t) = a_i$ for $t \in [r_{i-1}, r_i)$. If we impose $a_i \neq a_{i+1}$, then the representation of ξ is unique and the *length* of ξ denoted by $|\xi|$ is equal to n and its *duration* denoted by $d(\xi)$ is equal to k. Length and duration of ϵ are equal to zero. We denote by $T(\Sigma)$ the set of all finite timed words over the alphabet Σ.
For every $\xi_1, \xi_2 \in T(\Sigma)$ with respective durations k_1 and k_2 their *concatenation* $\xi_1\xi_2$ is the timed word ξ with duration $k_1 + k_2$ such that for $t \in [0, k_1)$, $\xi(t) = \xi_1(t)$, and for $t \in [k_1, k_1 + k_2)$ $\xi(t) = \xi_2(t - t_1)$. Clearly, $|\xi_1\xi_2| \leq |\xi_1| + |\xi_2|$ and $d(\xi_1\xi_2) = d(\xi_1) + d(\xi_2)$.
For $u = a_1^{r_1}a_2^{r_2}\dots, a_n^{r_n}$ and a positive integer p, denote by $u^{\frac{1}{p}}$ the timed word $a_1^{\frac{r_1}{p}}a_2^{\frac{r_2}{p}}\dots a_n^{\frac{r_n}{p}}$. We have $|u^{\frac{1}{p}}| = |u|$ and $d(u^{\frac{1}{p}}) = \frac{1}{p}d(u)$. Note that $(u^{\frac{1}{p}})^p = u$ iff u is of the form a^r for some $a \in \Sigma$.
A *timed language* over the alphabet Σ is a subset of the set of timed words $T(\Sigma)$.

2.2 Timed automata

Timed automata were introduced by R. Alur and D. Dill [1].
A timed automaton consists of a finite number of locations supplied with clocks and constraints in terms of equalities and inequalities involving clocks. The edges of the automaton now depend on time, and this makes the automaton more powerful than the classical one.
The *clocks* of an automaton constitute a finite set of identifiers. Given a set C of clocks, the set of *clock constraints*, denoted by *guard*(C), is the set of formulas of the form:

- *true*, *false*, $c \sim n$ where $c \in C$, $n \in \boldsymbol{N}$ and $\sim \in \{>, <, =\}$,
- $f_1 \wedge f_2$, $f_1 \vee f_2$ where f_1 and f_2 are formulas in $guard(C)$.

A *timed automaton* over Σ is a tuple $\mathcal{A} = (S, \lambda, \mu, s_{init}, F, C, E)$ where:

- S is a finite set of *locations*,
- C is a finite set of clocks,
- $\lambda : S \rightarrow \Sigma$ is an *output* function,
- $\mu : S \rightarrow guard(C)$, assigns to each location a guard called *invariant* of the location,
- $s_{init} \in S$ is the *initial* location,
- $F \subseteq S$ is a set of *final* locations,
- $E \subseteq S \times guard(C) \times 2^C \times S$ gives the set of *edges* between locations labeled by sets of clocks and formulas.

Let (s, s', ϕ, δ) be an edge from s to s'. The set $\phi \subset C$ gives the set of clocks to be reset and δ is a clock constraint in $guard(C)$ to be satisfied when following this edge.
A *clock assignment* for a set of clocks C is a function ν from C to R, i. e. $\nu \in \boldsymbol{R}^C$.
A *state* of the system is a triple of the form $\langle s, \nu, t\rangle$, where $s \in S$, $\nu \in \boldsymbol{R}^C$, and $t \in \boldsymbol{R}_{\geq 0}$.
By $\nu + t$, where $t \in \boldsymbol{R}$, we denote the clock assignment which assigns to every clock c the value $\nu(c) + t$. In the same way if A is a state $\langle s, \nu, \tau\rangle$, $A + t$ denotes the state $\langle s, \nu + t, \tau + t\rangle$.
Let ν be a clock assignment. For $X \subset C$, we denote by $\langle X\rangle\nu$ the clock assignment which assigns 0 to each c in X and agrees with ν over the rest of the clocks.
A *transition* is a pair of states $\sigma = (\langle s, \nu, t\rangle, \langle s', \nu', t'\rangle)$ of the automaton $\mathcal{A}$, with an edge $(s, s', \phi, \delta) \in E$ such that

- $\nu + t' - t$ satisfies δ,
- for all $\tau \in [0, t' - t)$, $\nu + \tau$ satisfies $\mu(s)$,
- $\nu' = \langle\phi\rangle(\nu + t' - t)$ and ν' satisfies $\mu(s')$.

The value $t' - t$ is called the *delay* of the transition.

Now let us define a *finite run* of a timed automaton simply called a run below.
A *finite run* ρ is a pair of sequences $(\mathcal{S}(\rho), \mathcal{E}(\rho))$ such that $\mathcal{S}(\rho)$ is a sequence of states $(\langle s_i, \nu_i, t_i\rangle)_{0 \leq i \leq n}$ and $\mathcal{E}(\rho)$ is a sequence of edges $(s_{i-1}, s_i, a_i, \phi_i, \delta_i)_{0 < i \leq n}$ satisfying the following requirement:
for every $i = 1, \ldots, n$
the pair $(\langle s_{i-1}, \nu_{i-1}, t_{i-1}\rangle, \langle s_i, \nu_i, t_i\rangle)$ with the edge $(s_{i-1}, s_i, \phi_i, \delta_i)$ is a transition.
The *length* of the run ρ is equal to n and its *duration* denoted by $d(\rho)$ is equal to $t_n - t_0$.
The *trace* of the run ρ is the timed word $\lambda(s_0)^{t_1 - t_0}\lambda(s_1)^{t_2 - t_1} \ldots, \lambda(s_{n-1})^{t_n - t_{n-1}}$.
Note that the duration of ρ is equal to the duration of its trace but the length of ρ can be treater than the length of its trace.

When the edges are irrelevant, we represent a run as $(\langle s_i, \nu_i, t_i\rangle)_{0 \leq i \leq n}$.
A run $(\langle s_i, \nu_i, t_i\rangle)_{0 \leq i \leq n}$ is an *accepting run* if $s_0 = s_{init}$, $t_0 = 0$, $\nu_0(c) = 0$ for every clock c and $s_n \in F$.

A finite timed word over the alphabet Σ is *recognized* or *accepted* by the automaton $\mathcal{A}$ if it is the trace of an accepting run of $\mathcal{A}$. The set of finite timed words recognized by the automaton $\mathcal{A}$ is denoted by $L(\mathcal{A})$.

Example. The language accepted by the automaton of Figure 1 where s_2 is the

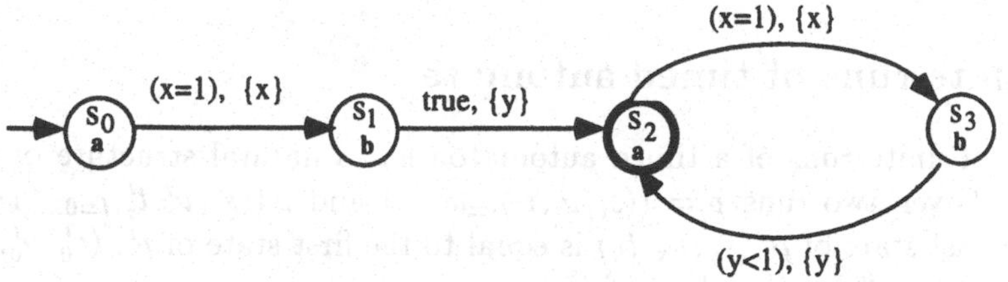

Fig. 1. A timed automaton

final location is:

$$\{a^{r_0}b^{q_0}a^{r_1}b^{q_1}\dots a^{r_n}b^{q_n} \mid n > 0,\ r_0 = 1,\ q_0 < 1,\ \text{for } i = 1,\dots,n\ q_{i-1} + r_i = 1 \text{ and } r_i + q_i < 1\} \cup \{a^{r_0}b^{q_0} \mid r_0 = 1, q_0 > 0\}.$$

Here the function μ is the constant "true". A sample word accepted by the automaton is:

$$a^1 b^{0.7} a^{0.3} b^{0.2} a^{0.8} b^{0.1}.$$

Every timed word accepted by this automaton has the property that the sequence (q_i) of exponents of the letter b is strictly decreasing.

Two finite runs ρ_1 and ρ_2 are *equivalent* if they have the same extremities, i. e. their first and last states are respectively equal: $\mathcal{S}(\rho_1)(0) = \mathcal{S}(\rho_2)(0)$ and $\mathcal{S}(\rho_1)(k) = \mathcal{S}(\rho_2)(l)$ where k and l are the lengths of respectively ρ_1 and ρ_2. Clearly, two equivalent runs have the same duration.

2.3 Clock regions

The set of states of a timed automaton is infinite. The set of *clock regions* is a finite set obtained as a quotient of an equivalence relation among the clock assignments. More details about this notion of region is in [1]. Let K_0 be the greatest constant appearing in the clock constraints of the automaton. Remind that clock constants are natural numbers. For clock assignments ν and ν' in $\boldsymbol{R}^C$ we say that $\nu \equiv \nu'$ iff the following conditions are met:

- For each clock $x \in C$ either $\lfloor \nu_x \rfloor$ and $\lfloor \nu'_x \rfloor$ are the same, or both are greater than K_0,

- For every pair of clocks $x, y \in C$ such that $\nu(x) \leq K_0$ and $\nu(y) \leq K_0$
  1. $fract(\nu(x)) \geq fract(\nu(y))$ iff $fract(\nu'(x)) \geq fract(\nu'(y))$
  2. $fract(\nu(x)) = 0$ iff $fract(\nu'(x)) = 0$.

The relation $\equiv$ is an equivalence relation, and $[\nu]$ will denote the equivalence class of $\boldsymbol{R}^C$ to which ν belongs. A *clock region* is such an equivalence class. There are only finitely many such regions. Note that $\nu \equiv \nu'$ does not necessarily imply $\nu + t \equiv \nu' + t$.

3 Finite runs of timed automata

The set of finite runs of a timed automaton has a natural structure of *partial* monoïd. Given two runs $\rho = (\langle s_i, \nu_i, t_i\rangle_{i=0,\dots,k})$ and $\rho'(\langle s'_i, \nu'_i, t'_i\rangle_{i=0,\dots,k'})$ such that the last state of ρ, $\langle s_k, \nu_k, t_k\rangle$ is equal to the first state of ρ', $\langle s'_0, \nu'_0, t'_0\rangle$ we define the run $\rho'' = \rho\rho'$ to be as follows:
$\rho'' = (\langle s''_i, \nu''_i, t''_i\rangle_{i=0,\dots,k+k'})$ where $\langle s''_i, \nu''_i, t''_i\rangle = \langle s_i, \nu_i, t_i\rangle$ for $i = 0, \dots, k$ and $\langle s''_{k+i}, \nu''_{k+i}, t''_{k+i}\rangle = \langle s'_i, \nu'_i, t'_i\rangle$ for $i = 1, \dots, k'$.
Note that it is a partial law. In particular if ρ is a run with positive length, ρ^2 is never defined because unlike [1, 4] we add the absolute time in the states of the timed automaton.
A finite run $\rho = (\langle s_i, \nu_i, t_i\rangle_{i=0,\dots,k})$ is a *pseudo-cycle* if $s_k = s_0$ and $[\nu_k] = [\nu_0]$.
The main notion in this part is the notion of *conjugation*.
Two runs $\rho = (\langle s_i, \nu_i, t_i\rangle_{i=0,\dots,k})$ and $\rho' = (\langle s_i, \nu'_i, t'_i\rangle_{i=0,\dots,k})$ of length $k > 0$ are *conjugate* if
$\mathcal{E}(\rho) = \mathcal{E}(\rho')$, $[\nu_i] = [\nu'_i]$ for $i = 0, \dots, k$, and $t'_i - t'_{i-1} = t_i - t_{i-1}$ for $i = 1, \dots, k$.
Let n be a positive integer and $\rho = (\langle s_i, \nu_i, t_i\rangle_{i=0,\dots,k})$ and $\rho' = (\langle s_i, \nu'_i, t'_i\rangle_{i=0,\dots,k})$ be two runs. The run ρ' is a $\frac{1}{n}$*-conjugate* of the run ρ if
$\mathcal{E}(\rho) = \mathcal{E}(\rho')$, $[\nu_i] = [\nu'_i]$ for $i = 0, \dots, k$, and $t'_i - t'_{i-1} = \frac{t_i - t_{i-1}}{n}$ for $i = 1, \dots, k$.
If $n = 1$ ρ' is called simply a *conjugate* of ρ.
From the definition of a $\frac{1}{n}$-conjugate we can deduce:

Lemma 1 *(1) If $\bar{\rho}$ is a $\frac{1}{n}$-conjugate of ρ, then $d(\rho) = \frac{1}{n}d(\bar{\rho})$.*
(2) Given a run ρ with first state $\langle s_0, \nu_0, t_0\rangle$, and a clock assignment ν'_0, there is at most one $\frac{1}{n}$-conjugate of ρ with its first state equal to $\langle s_0, \nu'_0, t_0\rangle$.
(3) Two $\frac{1}{n}$-conjugates of a run ρ have the same trace.

Given a finite run ρ there exists at most one run which can be written $\rho_1\rho_2\dots\rho_n$, where for $i = 1, \dots, n$ ρ_i is a $\frac{1}{n}$-conjugate of ρ and ρ_1 has the same first state as ρ. This unique run, when it exists is denoted by $\rho^{[n]}$ and called the *n-iteration* of ρ. It satisfies the following property:

Lemma 2 *If $\rho^{[n]}$ exists for some $n > 1$, then*
(1) $d(\rho^{[n]}) = d(\rho)$ and $|\rho^{[n]}| = n|\rho|$,
(2) ρ is a pseudo-cycle.

Proof. (1) is clear from the definition of a $1/n$-conjugate.
To prove (2) note that the last state of ρ_1 is equal to the first state of ρ_2, and so it implies that ρ is a pseudo-cycle.
□

We say that a clock c *crosses an integer value* during the run $\rho = (\langle s_i, \nu_i, t_i \rangle)_{i \leq n}$ if there is a transition $(\langle s_i, \nu_i, t_i \rangle, \langle s_{i+1}, \nu_{i+1}, t_{i+1} \rangle)$ and some $t \in [0, t_{i+1} - t_i]$ such that $\nu_i(c) + t$ is a positive integer.
Clearly we have:

Lemma 3 *If a finite run is such that no clock crosses an integer value during it, the value of the delay of any transition of the run is strictly less than 1.*

Let X be a subset of clocks. Two states $A = \langle s, \nu, t \rangle$ and $A' = \langle s, \nu', t' \rangle$ are X-*equal* if they satisfy :

if $c \in X$ then $\nu(c) = \nu'(c)$, and if $c \notin X$ then $\nu(c)$ and $\nu'(c)$ are both strictly less than 1 and $\nu(c) = 0 \Leftrightarrow \nu'(c) = 0$.

Transitions where clocks do not cross an integer value have the following basic property:

Lemma 4 *Let $\mathcal{A}$ be a timed automaton, X be a subset of clocks, and $A = \langle s, \nu, t \rangle$, $A' = \langle s, \nu', t' \rangle$ be two X-equal states of $\mathcal{A}$. Suppose there exists a transition from state A to some state B with edge e and delay τ where the clocks do not cross an integer value. Suppose at last that for $c \notin X$ we have $\nu'(c) + \tau < 1$, then there exists a transition from A' to some state B' with the same edge e and the same delay, moreover B and B' are X-equal.*

Proof. Let us consider the transition from state A to state $B = \langle s_1, \langle \phi \rangle \nu, t + \tau \rangle$ with edge $e = (s, s_1, \phi, \delta)$.
For an atomic proposition $c \sim n$ where $\sim \in \{>, <, =\}$ and $n \in \boldsymbol{N}$ consider two cases : c belongs to X or not.
• Case 1: $c \in X$.
For every $\tau' \in [0, \tau]$, $(\nu' + \tau')(c) = (\nu + \tau')(c)$. So $(\nu + \tau')(c)$ satisfies $c \sim n$ iff $(\nu' + \tau')(c)$ satisfies $c \sim n$.
• Case 2: $c \notin X$.
For every $\tau' \in [0, \tau]$, $(\nu + \tau')(c)$ is strictly less than 1 because in the transition the clocks do not cross an integer value and $(\nu' + \tau')(c)$ is also strictly less than 1. So $(\nu' + \tau')(c)$ satisfies $c \sim n$ iff $\nu + \tau'$ satisfies $c \sim n$.
At last, for the same reasons, $\langle \phi \rangle (\nu + \tau)$ and $\langle \phi \rangle (\nu' + \tau)$ satisfy exactly the same set of atomic propositions.
So there is a transition with the edge e, the same delay τ, from A' to $B' = \langle s_1, \langle \phi \rangle (\nu' + \tau), t' + \tau \rangle$. Clearly, B and B' are X-equal.
□

By induction on the length of a run we can deduce the following lemma:

Lemma 5 *Let $\mathcal{A}$ be a timed automaton, X be a subset of clocks, and $A = \langle s, \nu, t \rangle$, $A' = \langle s, \nu', t' \rangle$ be two X-equal states of $\mathcal{A}$. Suppose there exists a run ρ from A with duration τ where the clocks do not cross an integer value. Suppose* *at last that for $c \notin X$ $\nu'(c) + \tau < 1$, then there exists a run ρ' conjugate of ρ starting from A'. Moreover the terminal states of ρ and ρ' are X-equal.*

The *reset* of a finite run $(\langle s_i, \nu_i, t_i \rangle)_{i \leq k}$ is the set of clocks which are reset to 0 during the run, i. e. the union of sets ϕ_i where $\mathcal{E}(\rho) = (s_{i-1}, s_i, \phi_i, \delta_i)_{0<i\leq k}$. It is denoted by $reset(\rho)$.

Lemma 6 *If a pseudo-cycle ρ is such that no clock crosses an integer value, then $\rho^{[n]}$ exists for every positive integer n.*

Proof. Let R be equal to $reset(\rho)$. First we prove that there exists a $\frac{1}{n}$-conjugate ρ_1 of ρ starting in the same state as ρ. Let $\rho = (A_0, A_1, \ldots, A_p)$, $\mathcal{E}(\rho) = (e_1, \ldots, e_p)$ and denote by t_i the delay of transition (A_{i-1}, A_i).
We prove that there is a transition from state $A_0 = \langle s, \nu, t \rangle$ using edge $e_1 = (s, s', \phi_1, \delta_1)$ with delay t_1/n, to state $A'_1 = \langle s', \langle \phi_1 \rangle(\nu + t_1/n), t + t_1/n \rangle$.
Let $c > k$ be an atomic proposition and consider a value $\tau \in [0, t_1]$. Then $A_0 + \tau$ satisfies $c > k$ iff $A_0 + \tau/n$ satisfies $c > k$, because c cannot cross an integer value during the run. The same for an atomic proposition $c < k$. And a constraint $c = k$ is never satisfied neither by $A_0 + \tau$ nor by $A_0 + \tau/n$. At last for the same reason $\langle \phi_1 \rangle(\nu + t_1/n)$ and $\langle \phi_1 \rangle(\nu + t_1)$ satisfy the same atomic propositions. So there is a transition from A_0 with delay t_1/n, using edge e_1, and arriving in A'_1. Moreover we have $[A'_1] = [A_1]$. Indeed, clocks in ϕ_1 are equal to 0 in both A_1 and A'_1. Let c, c' two clocks not in ϕ_1. If $fract(\nu(c) + t_1) \leq fract(\nu(c') + t_1)$ then $fract(\nu(c) + t_1/n) \leq fract(\nu(c') + t_1/n)$ and $fract(c)$ is non zero in both A_1 and A'_1. So we have $[A'_1] = [A_1]$.

Suppose we have proved there exists a run $(A_0, A'_1, \ldots, A'_i)$, with some edges $(e_1, \ldots, e_i)$ and delays $t_1/n, \ldots, t_i/n$ such that $[A'_j] = [A_j]$ for $j = 1, \ldots, i$. Let c be a clock, and denote by c_i its value in A_i and by c'_i its value in A'_i. Let $\tau \in [0, t_{i+1}]$.
• If $c \notin R$ or if c has not still been reset to zero between A_0 and A_i, then $c_i = c_0 + \sum_{j=1,\ldots,i} t_j$ and $c'_i = c_0 + \sum_{j=1,\ldots,i} t_j/n$. States $A_i + \tau$ and $A'_i + \tau/n$ satisfy the same atomic propositions concerning the clock c again because c cannot cross an integer value during the run.
• If $c \in R$ and c has been reset to zero between A_0 and A_i then the values of c in $A_i + \tau$ and in $A'_i + \tau/n$ are strictly less than 1, thus $A_i + \tau$ and $A'_i + \tau/n$ satisfy the same constraints relative to c.
At last, let ϕ_{i+1} be the reset of the edge e_{i+1}. The same arguments prove that $\langle \phi_{i+1} \rangle(A_i + t_{i+1})$ and $\langle \phi_{i+1} \rangle(A'_i + t_{i+1}/n)$ satisfy the same atomic propositions. So there is a transition from A'_i with edge e_{i+1} and delay $\frac{t_{i+1}}{n}$ and $[A'_i] = [A_i]$.
We have proved by induction the existence of a $1/n$-conjugate ρ_1 of ρ starting in the same state as ρ.
Suppose we have defined $\rho_1, \ldots, \rho_i$ some $1/n$-conjugates of ρ such that the product $\rho_1 \ldots, \rho_i$ exists, with $i < n$. Let T be the duration of ρ. Consider the state Y_i which is the last state of ρ_i. Let c be a clock, and denote by c_i its value in Y_i. If $c \notin R$, then $c_i = c_0 + \frac{iT}{n}$ and if $c \in R$ then its values in Y_i and in A_0 are less than

1. So we can repeat the same reasoning and prove that there is a $1/n$-conjugate of ρ, ρ_{i+1} starting in Y_i. Actually, since ρ is a pseudo-cycle we have $[A_0] = [A_p]$, and on other hand $[Y_i] = [A_p]$ so $[Y_i] = [A_0]$. And the lemma is proved.
□

Note that in general $\rho^{[n]}$ is not equivalent to ρ. We need some synchronization to get two equivalent runs. It is done in the lemma below.

Lemma 7 *Let ρ be a run with duration strictly less than 1 such that $\rho = \rho_1\beta\rho_2$ where ρ_1, ρ_2 are pseudo-cycles with the same reset. Suppose that no clock crosses an integer value during the run ρ, then for every positive integer n there exists a conjugate $\overline{\beta\rho_2}$ of $\beta\rho_2$ such that the run $\rho_1^{[n]}\overline{\beta\rho_2}$ exists and is equivalent to ρ.*

Proof. If $n = 1$ nothing to prove. Suppose $n > 1$.
Let ρ be a run such that $\rho = \rho_1\beta\rho_2$ where ρ_1 and ρ_2 are pseudo-cycles and $reset(\rho_1) = reset(\rho_2) = X$. Suppose that ρ_1 starts in A and finishes in A', and ρ_2 starts in B and finishes in B'. The run ρ_1 satisfies the hypothesis of Lemma 6. So $\rho_1^{[n]}$ exists and finishes in some state Y. Observe that if $A' =< s_{A'}, \nu_{A'}, t_{A'} >$, and $Y =< s_Y, \nu_Y, t_Y >$ then $s_Y = s_{A'}$, $t_Y = t_{A'}$ and states A' and Y are $\overline{X}$-equal, where $\overline{X}$ is the complement of X. Moreover, we have $\nu_Y(c) \leq \nu_{A'}(c)$ for every clock c.
Denote by τ the duration of the run $\beta\rho_2$. Since ρ has a duration strictly less than 1 we can guarantee that for every clock $c \in X$ we have $\nu_Y(c)+\tau \leq \nu_{A'}(c)+\tau < 1$. On the other hand, the run $\beta\rho_2$ is such that no clock crosses an integer value, so applying Lemma 5, we prove that there exists a run $\beta'\rho_2'$, conjugate of $\beta\rho_2$, starting in Y and arriving in some state B''. We claim that $B'' = B'$. Actually the clocks reset during ρ_2 are also reset during ρ_2' and have the same value in B' and in B'', because the two runs are conjugate and then the delays are the same. The clocks not reset during ρ_2 were not reset during ρ_1 so they have the same value in Y and in A' and then also in B' and B''. And we can conclude that $\rho_1^{[n]}\overline{\beta\rho_2}$ exists and is equivalent to ρ.
□

Lemma 8 *Let ρ be a run where no clock crosses an integer value, with duration strictly less than 1, and such that $\rho = \rho_1\beta\rho_2 x\gamma\rho_3$ where ρ_1, ρ_2 and ρ_3 are pseudo-cycles with the same reset and $|x| = 1$. There exists a transition x' and a conjugate $\overline{\gamma\rho_3}$ of $\gamma\rho_3$ such that $\rho_1\beta x'\overline{\gamma\rho_3}$ exists and is equivalent to ρ.*

Proof. Suppose that ρ contains three disjoint successive pseudo-cycles ρ_1, ρ_2, ρ_3 with the same reset. The pseudo-cycle ρ_1 begins in A and finishes in A', ρ_2 begins in B and finishes in B', ρ_3 begins in C and finishes in C'.
Let t be the duration of ρ from B to B' and B_1' be the successor of B' in ρ. The transition (B', B_1') has a delay t_0, and corresponds to some edge $e = (s, s_1, \phi, \delta)$. Let $B = (s, \nu_B, t_B), B' = (s, \nu_{B'}, t_{B'}), B_1' = (s_1, \nu_{B_1'}, t_{B_1'})$.
Then $t_{B'} - t_B = t$ and $t_{B_1'} - t_{B'} = t_0$.
We will prove that from B there is a possible transition using the edge e, with

a delay equal to $t+t_0$, to some state B_1'', R-equal to B_1', with R being equal to the complement of $reset(\rho_2)$. We have to verify three conditions.
(1) For every $\tau \in [0, t+t_0)$, $\nu_B + \tau$ satisfies $\mu(s_B)$
(2) $\nu_B + t + t_0$ satisfies δ
(3) $\langle\phi\rangle(\nu_B + t + t_0)$ satisfies $\mu(s_1)$.
Condition (1) :
Due to the fact that the clocks do not cross an integer value during the run and the run has a duration less than 1, for every clock c there is a unique interval $[k, k+1)$, with $k \in N$ to which the value of the clock belongs during the whole run ρ. Let c be a clock, and $\tau \in [0, t+t_0)$. If $c \in reset(\rho_2) = reset(\rho_1)$ then $(\nu_B + \tau)(c)$ is less than 1 as $\nu_B(c)$. If $c \notin reset(\rho_2)$, then $\nu_{B'}(c) = \nu_B(c) + t$ and $\nu_B(c), \nu_{B'}(c), \nu_{B'}(c) + t_0$ belong to the same interval $[k, k+1)$ and $(\nu_B + \tau)(c)$ belongs to this interval. Since ν_B satisfies $\mu(s_B)$ then $\nu_B + \tau$ satisfies also $\mu(s_B)$.
Condition (2) :
The clocks which do not belong to $reset(\rho_2)$ have the same value in $\nu_B + t + t_0$ and in $\nu_{B'} + t_0$. The clocks which belong to $reset(\rho_2) = reset(\rho_1)$ have a value less than 1 in $\nu_B + t + t_0$ and in $\nu_{B'} + t_0$. Since $\nu_{B'} + t_0$ satisfies δ, $\nu_B + t + t_0$ satisfies also δ.
Condition (3) :
In the same way, since $\langle\phi\rangle(\nu_{B'} + t_0)$ satisfies $\mu(s_1)$ then $\langle\phi\rangle(\nu_B + t + t_0)$ satisfies also $\mu(s_1)$. So there is a transition x' from $B = \langle s, \nu_B, t_B\rangle$ to $B_1'' = \langle s_1, \langle\phi\rangle(\nu_B + t + t_0), t_{B_1''}\rangle$.
And $t_{B_1''} = t_B + t + t_0 = t'_B + t_0 = t_{B_1'}$.
The main point is that B_1' and B_1'' are R-equal where R is the complement of $reset(\rho_2)$. Indeed
- if $c \in \phi$ then $\nu_{B_1'}(c)$ and $\nu_{B_1''}(c)$ are both equal to 0,
- if $c \notin \phi$ and $c \notin reset(\rho_2)$ then $\nu_{B_1'}(c) = \nu_{B'}(c) + t_0 = \nu_B(c) + t + t_0 = \nu_{B_1''}(c)$,
- if $c \notin \phi$ and $c \in reset(\rho_2)$ then $\nu_{B_1'}(c)$ and $\nu_{B_1''}(c)$ are both strictly less than 1.
Let τ be the duration of $\gamma\rho_3$. For every clock $c \in reset(\rho_1)$, we have $\nu_B(c) + t + t_0 + \tau < 1$ since the duration of ρ is strictly less than 1. So $\nu_B(c) + t + t_0 + \tau = \nu_{B_1''}(c) + \tau < 1$ for $c \in reset(\rho_1$, and we can apply Lemma 5 to states B_1' and B_1''. There is a run $\gamma'\rho_3'$ starting in B_1'', conjugate of $\gamma\rho_3$, arriving in some state C''. Now we prove that $C'' = C'$.
Let $C' = \langle s_{C'}, \nu_{C'}, t_{C'}\rangle$ and $C'' = \langle s_{C''}, \nu_{C''}, t_{C''}\rangle$.
Sure, $s_{C''} = s_{C'} = s$ and $t_{C''} = t_{C'}$. Compare the values of the clocks in C' and C'', that is $\nu_{C'}$ and $\nu_{C''}$.
• The clocks which are reset to 0 in $\gamma'\rho_3'$ between B_1'' and C'' are the same as the clocks reset during the run $\gamma\rho_3$ between B_1' and C', and since the durations of the transitions are the same, these clocks have the same value in C' and C''.
• The clocks not reset between B_1' and C' in $\gamma\rho_3$ (and so between B_1'' and C'' in $\gamma'\rho_3'$) have never been reset between B and B_1' in $\rho_2 x$ neither between B and B_1'' in x'. So their values are the same in B_1' and B_1'', and then remain the same in C' and C''.
□

Let $\mathcal{A}$ be a timed automaton, C be its set of clocks, m be the number of regions of $\mathcal{A}$ and K_0 be the constant equal to $(2\,2^{|C|}+1)(|S|m+1)$.

Proposition 1 *If a run ρ with duration strictly less than 1 has a length greater than or equal to $(|C|+1)K_0$, then ρ can be written $\alpha\rho_1\beta\rho_2 x\gamma\rho_3\eta$ with $|x|=1$ such that:*
(1) there exists some transition x' and some conjugate $\gamma'\rho_3'$ of $\gamma\rho_3$ with the timed word $\alpha\rho_1\beta x'\gamma'\rho_3'\eta$ equivalent to ρ
(2) for every positive integer n there is a conjugate $\overline{x\gamma\rho_3}$ of $x\gamma\rho_3$ such that $\alpha\rho_1\beta\rho_2^{[n]}\overline{x\gamma\rho_3}\eta$ is equivalent to ρ.

Proof. There are at most $|C|$ moments during this run when a clock can cross an integer value because the duration of the run is less than 1, thus a clock can cross an integer part only once. So since ρ has a length more than $(|C|+1)K_0$, there is a finite run ρ', part of ρ with length at least $K_0=(2\,2^{|C|}+1)(|S|m+1)$ where no clock crosses an integer value. This run ρ' contains $(2\,2^{|C|}+1)$ disjoint parts which are pseudo-cycles because every run of length $|S|m$ contains a pseudo-cycle. And among these pseudo-cycles at least three have the same reset. The factor $|S|m+1$ in K_0 instead of $|S|m$ ensures that the pseudo-cycles are not only disjoint but are separated by at least one transition, what justifies the existence of transition x. Then we apply Lemmas 7 and 8.
□

4 Pumping Lemmas

Here we discuss some versions of "Pumping Lemma" for a given language $L \subset S(\Sigma)$, as a natural extension of the classical one [6]. There are two versions according to considering "large words" with respect to their duration or to their length. For timed words the classical Pumping Lemma could be stated as follows:
Pumping Lemma Property (PL) *There exists a constant $K>0$ such that for every timed word $u \in L$ with length (respectively duration) more than K, there exist timed words v, w, z, $w \neq \epsilon$ which satisfy:*

$$u = vwz \text{ and for every integer } n \geq 0,\ vw^n z \in L.$$

Proposition 2 *There is a timed automaton $\mathcal{A}$ such that $L(\mathcal{A})$ does not satisfy* **(PL)**.

Proof. Consider the automaton of Figure 1. Suppose it satisfies Pumping Lemma Property (PL) for the "duration" version. Let K be a constant for which the property holds. There exists a timed word u in $L(\mathcal{A})$ with $d(u)>K$. We can choose u of the form $a^{r_0}b^{q_0}a^{r_1}b^{q_1}\ldots, a^{r_p}b^{q_p}$ with $p>0$. By our assumption there are words v, w, z such that $u=vwz$ and $vw^n z \in L$ for every integer $n \geq 0$. Several cases are to be considered for w.
If $w=a^r$, $r>0$, there exists an integer n such that $nr>1$. So $uw^n z$ does not belong to $L(\mathcal{A})$. The same if $w=b^r$, $r>0$.

If w contains both letters a and b, then w^2 cannot be a factor of a word in $L(\mathcal{A})$ because the sequence of exponents of the letter b is not decreasing. Thus $vw^2z \notin L(\mathcal{A})$. And $L(\mathcal{A})$ does not satisfy **(PL)** for the "duration" version.
A similar reasoning can be done if $|u| > K$. Thus $L(\mathcal{A})$ does not satisfy the Pumping Lemma Property (PL) for the "length" version.
□

In [4] it is proved that the family of languages recognized by timed automata satisfies some Kleene property. In their regular expressions the authors include the intersection. It is not surprising, because a classical Kleene theorem without intersection in regular expressions would imply easily the Pumping Lemma (PL) for languages recognized by timed automata.
Nevertheless using properties established in section 3 we can elaborate some weak versions which will hold. There is a first version when an iteration can be done increasing the duration of the timed word but conserving its length. We prove that for a sub-family of timed automata, the strict automata, some Pumping Lemma holds.
A timed automaton on an alphabet Σ is *strict* if two adjacent locations have different labellings by λ. Strict timed automata are less expressive as it is proved by the following example. The timed language recognized by the automaton of Figure 2 is

$$\{a^r \mid r \in (2, +\infty) \cup \{1\} - \{3\}\}$$

If a strict automaton recognizes such a language it has a single location and it is easy to prove that no such a strict automaton exists.

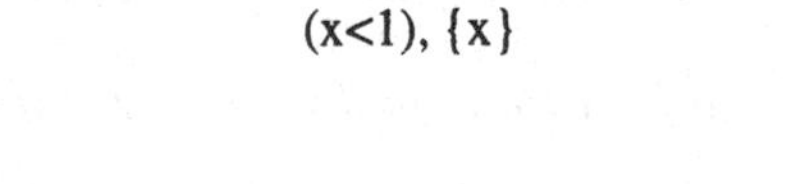

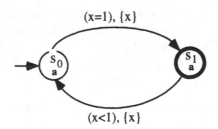

Fig. 2. A counter-example

Lemma 9 *If a timed word u is accepted by a strict timed automaton then the lengths of the runs which accept u are equal and equal to the length of u.*

Proof. Due to the fact that the automaton is strict, the length of a run is exactly the length of the word it recognizes.
□

We give first a Pumping Lemma (**LPL**) which holds for languages recognized by strict timed automata. In this version, the iteration increases the duration of the word but conserves its length.

Proposition 3 Pumping Lemma (LPL) *Let L be a language recognized by a strict timed automaton $\mathcal{A}$. There exists a constant $K > 0$ such that for every timed word $u \in L$ with duration $d(u) > K|u|$, there exist $v, w \in T(\Sigma)$, $a \in \Sigma$, $r > K$ such that $u = va^r w$ with $r > K$ and $va^{r'} w \in L$ for every $r' > K$.*

Proof. Denote by K the greatest integer appearing in the guards and the invariants of the automaton $\mathcal{A}$. Let u be a word recognized by $\mathcal{A}$ such that $d(u) > K|u|$, u can be written $a_1^{r_1} a_2^{r_2} \ldots, a_p^{r_p}$, where $a_i \in \Sigma$, $r_i \in \mathbf{R}_+$, $a_i \neq a_{i+1}$, and every run which accepts u has length equal to p. There exists some $i \in \{1, \ldots, p\}$ such that $r_i > K$. Let ρ be an accepting run which recognizes the word u, it can be written as $\rho_1 x \rho_2$ where x is some transition with delay r_i from a state $A = \langle s, \nu, t \rangle$ to some state $\langle s', \nu', t + r_i \rangle$, with an edge $e = (s, s', \phi, \delta)$ and $\mu(s) = a_i$. The main point is that K is the greatest integer appearing in the guards and the invariants of the automaton $\mathcal{A}$. For this reason there is a possible transition x' from A using the edge e and with a delay r' for every $r' > K$. Let B' be the end of this transition. Every clock c has either a value zero in both B and B' (if $c \in \delta$), or a value greater than K in both B and B'. Due to this fact, there exists a conjugate ρ_2' of ρ_2 starting in B' and since $\rho_1 x \rho_2$ was an accepting run, $\rho_1 x' \rho_2'$ is also an accepting run, and thus $va^{r'} w \in L$ for every $r' > K$.
□

One can formulate another version of Pumping Lemma, when an iteration can be done in a way that increases (in general) the length of the timed word but conserves its duration.

Proposition 4 Pumping Lemma (DPL) *Let L be a language recognizable by a timed automaton $\mathcal{A}$. There exists a constant $K > 0$ such that the following properties hold. For every word $u \in L$ with length greater than $(\lfloor d(u) \rfloor + 1)K$ there exist $v_1, v_2, v_3 \in T(\Sigma)$, $v_2 \neq \epsilon$, $a \in \Sigma$ and a real $r > 0$ such that:*
(1) $u = v_1 v_2 a^r v_3$
(2) $v_1 (v_2^{\frac{1}{n}})^n a^r v_3 \in L$ *for every positive integer n*
(3) $v_1 a^{r + d(v_2)} v_3 \in L$.

Proof. Let $K = (|C| + 1)K_0$ be the constant of Proposition 1. Consider a run ρ of the automaton $\mathcal{A}$ which accepts u. The length of ρ is at least $(\lfloor d(u) \rfloor + 1)K$, and its duration is $d(u)$. Thus, there is a finite part ρ' of ρ of length K and with duration strictly less than 1. Then we apply to this run ρ' Proposition 1. The run ρ' can be written $\alpha \rho_1 \beta \rho_2 x \gamma \rho_3 \eta$. So ρ is some $\alpha' \alpha \rho_1 \beta \rho_2 x \gamma \rho_3 \eta \eta'$. And ρ recognizes a timed word $v_1 v_2 a^r v_3$ where :
- v_1 is the trace of $\alpha' \alpha \rho_1 \beta$
- v_2 is the trace of ρ_2
- a^r is the trace of x

– v_3 is the trace of $\gamma\rho_3\eta\eta'$.
Now, there is some $\alpha\rho_1\beta\rho_2 x'\gamma'\rho_3'\eta$ which is equivalent to ρ' so $\alpha'\alpha\rho_1\beta\rho_2 x'\gamma'\rho_3'\eta\eta'$ is equivalent to ρ and recognizes the word $v_1 a^{r+d(\rho_2)} v_3$. Recall that the delay of transition x' is equal to the delay of x plus the duration of ρ_2. So $v_1 a^{r+d(v_2)} v_3 \in L$.
In the same way, there is a conjugate $\overline{x\gamma\rho_3}$ of $x\gamma\rho_3$ such that for every positive integer n $\alpha\rho_1\beta\rho_2^{[n]}\overline{x\gamma\rho_3}\eta$ is equivalent to ρ'. Therefore $\alpha'\alpha\rho_1\beta\rho_2^{[n]}\overline{x\gamma\rho_3}\eta\eta'$ is equivalent to ρ and recognizes $v_1(v_2^{\frac{1}{n}})^n a^r v_3$, and $v_1(v_2^{\frac{1}{n}})^n a^r v_3 \in L$.
□

Remarks

In part (3) of Proposition 4 we cannot claim that $v_1 a^r v_3$ belongs to $L(\mathcal{A})$. That is we cannot suppress directly the factor v_2, we have to increase at the same time the exponent of a.
Part (2) of Proposition 4 claims that if a timed word u is large enough compared to its duration, then some factor v_2 of u can be replaced by $(v_2^{\frac{1}{n}})^n$.

Example
We give here an example of application of this Pumping Lemma, to prove that some language cannot be recognized by a timed automaton.
Consider the timed language

$$L = \{a^{r_0} b^{r_1} a^{r_2} b^{r_3} \ldots a^{r_{2n}} b^{r_{2n+1}} | r_0 > r_1 > \ldots > r_{2n+1}, n \geq 0\}$$

Suppose that L is recognized by some timed automaton, and let K be the constant of Proposition 4 for this timed automaton.
There exist in L words with an arbitrarily great length and simultaneously an arbitrarily small duration. So there is a timed word u in L such that $|u| > K(\lfloor d(u) \rfloor + 1)$. By Proposition 4, u can be written $u = v_1 v_2 x^r v_3$, $x \in \{a, b\}$, $v_2 \neq \epsilon$, and $v_1 x^{r+d(v_2)} v_3 \in L$, $v_1(v_2^{\frac{1}{n}})^n x^r v_3 \in L$. But clearly $v_1 x^{r+d(v_2)} v_3 \notin L$ neither $v_1(v_2^{\frac{1}{n}})^n x^r v_3$ if $n \neq 1$. Therefore L cannot be recognized by a timed automaton. Note that this property cannot be used considering the untimed language associated to L which is $(ab)^+$ and so is a regular language.

Conclusion
We have proved that languages recognized by timed automata do not satisfy classical Pumping Lemma Property, but only weaker versions. This result can be used to prove that a language is not recognizable by a timed automaton by proving that the language does not satisfy this weak Pumping Lemma. We have used also this result to prove that model-checking is decidable for a class of problems formulated in a rather high-level language [7].

Acknowledgments I thank the anonymous referees for their numerous and sound remarks.

References

1. R. Alur and D. Dill. A theory of timed automata. *Theoretical Computer Science*, 126:183–235, 1994.
2. A. Henzinger and O. Kupferman. From quantity to quality. In *Hybrid and Real-Time Systems Proceeding of HART'97*, pages 48–62. Springer Verlag, 1997. Lect. Notes in Comput. Sci., vol. 1201.
3. F. Wang. Parametric timing analysis for real-time systems. *Information and Computation*, 130:131–150, 1996.
4. E. Asarin, P. Caspi, and O. Maler. A kleene theorem for timed automata. In *IEEE Computer Society, LICS'97*, pages 160–171, 1997.
5. T. Wilke. *Automaten und Logiken fur zeitabhangige Systeme*. Ph.d. thesis, Kiel University, 1994.
6. J. E. Hopcroft and J.D. Ullman. *Introduction to Automata Theory, Languages and Computation*. Addison-Wesley, 1979.
7. D. Beauquier and A. Slissenko. Decidable model checking for a class of timed automata specified in first order logic. Technical Report 97-11, University Paris-12, Department of Informatics, 1997.

Asynchronous Observations of Processes*

Michele Boreale[1] Rocco De Nicola[2] Rosario Pugliese[2]

[1]Dipartimento di Scienze dell'Informazione, Università di Roma "La Sapienza"
[2]Dipartimento di Sistemi e Informatica, Università di Firenze

Abstract. We study may and must testing–based preorders in an asynchronous setting. In particular, we provide some full abstraction theorems that offer alternative characterizations of these preorders in terms of context closure w.r.t. basic observables and in terms of traces and acceptance sets. These characterizations throw light on the asymmetry between input and output actions in asynchronous interactions and on the difference between synchrony and asynchrony.

1 Introduction

Distributed systems can seldom rely on a global clock, and little assumptions can be made about their relative speed; as a consequence, it is natural to adopt for them an *asynchronous* communication mechanism. This calls for non–blocking sending primitives that do not oblige producers and consumers to synchronize when exchanging messages, but allow the sender of a message to continue with its task while the message travels to destination. Therefore, for describing distributed systems, a model based on a paradigm that imposes a neat distinction between input and output primitives, in the style of [1] and [17], appears to be a natural choice. In spite of these considerations, the most studied concurrency models in the process algebra community (e.g. [18, 3, 14, 20]) are based on *synchronous* communications and model process interaction as the execution of simultaneous "complementary actions".

Only recently, variants of process algebras based on asynchronous communications have been studied. Two main approaches have been followed to this purpose. They differ in the way (non–blocking) output actions are modelled. These actions are rendered either as *state transformers* or as *processes* themselves. The asynchronous variants of ACP [9] and CSP [16] follow the first approach and introduce explicit buffers in correspondence of output channels. This makes outputs non–blocking and immediately executable; their executions make messages available for consumption. The asynchronous variants of π-calculus [15, 6, 12, 2] and CCS [21, 11, 8] follow the second approach and model outputs by creating new concurrent processes. This amounts to modelling an output prefix $\overline{a}.P$ as a parallel composition $\overline{a} \mid P$.

* Work partially supported by EEC: HCM project EXPRESS, and by CNR: project "Specifica ad alto livello e verifica formale di sistemi digitali". The third author has been supported by a scholarship from CNR — Comitato Scienza e Tecnologie dell'Informazione.

The problem of specifying the abstract behaviour of asynchronous processes, i.e. of defining "good" observational semantics, has not yet been investigated in depth. Only few observational semantics have been considered. The maximal congruence induced by completed trace equivalence has been studied in [9] for asynchronous ACP. Bisimulation [18] for asynchronous π-calculus has been investigated in [15, 12, 2].

A natural alternative is represented by the *testing* framework of [10, 13]. Testing offers a uniform mechanism to define sensible behavioural equivalences on different process algebras, as it relies on little more than a notion of reduction relation ($\stackrel{\tau}{\longrightarrow}$). Moreover, testing has the advantage of identifying only those processes that cannot be differentiated by running observers in parallel with them. No new operator is introduced, as both the parallel composition operator and the observers are taken from the process description language under investigation. The testing approach has been partially followed in [22], where *synchronous* processes and observers are connected via input/output queues. This permits asynchronously testing synchronous processes.

In this paper we investigate the testing theory for a variety of asynchronous process algebras. For the sake of simplicity, the basic theory will be developed for an asynchronous version of CCS [18] (ACCS); we will then see how the obtained results can be extended with little effort to an asynchronous variant of π-calculus and to an asynchronous version of CCS with non–injective relabelling. The latter leads to a significantly different theory.

We shall study both the *may* and the *must* testing preorders. While natural, these preorders rely on a universal quantification over the set of all observers that makes reasoning about processes extremely difficult. This calls for alternative, observers–independent characterizations that permit a full appreciation of the impact of an asynchronous semantics over the considered languages. For each preorder, we will offer two characterizations: one in terms of the traces/acceptances of processes, the other in terms of the context–closure w.r.t. some *basic observables*, in the same spirit as [5].

As far as basic observables are concerned, we will see that, differently from the synchronous case, the only important actions are the output ones. In particular, for capturing the may preorder, we will need, as basic observables, tests about the possibility of processes to perform specific output actions. For capturing the must preorder, we will need, as basic observables, tests about the guarantee that processes offer of performing specific output actions.

The other alternative characterizations for the may preorder will be based on sequences of visible actions (*traces*), while that for the must preorder will rely on pairs ⟨trace, acceptance set⟩ in the same spirit as [13] and [7]. However, the usual trace containment for may is not adequate anymore, and the notion of acceptance–set for must is more complicate. We have for both may and must preorders equalities like $a.\overline{a} = \mathbf{0}$. The underlying reason is that, since no behaviour can causally depend upon outputs, observers cannot fully determine the occurrence of process *input* actions. As a consequence, both for may and for must, the set of traces will have to be factored via the preorder induced by the three laws below, whose intuition is that whenever a trace s performed by some process is "acceptable" for the environment, then any $s' \preceq s$ is acceptable as well:

- (*deletion*) $\epsilon \preceq a$: process inputs cannot be forced;
- (*postponement*) $sa \preceq as$: observations of process inputs can be delayed;
- (*annihilation*) $\epsilon \preceq a\overline{a}$: buffers are not observable.

The extension of the alternative characterizations to the π-calculus is relatively straightforward and vindicates the stability of the approach. The extension to a process description language with non–injective relabelling shows that this operator enables external observers to get more precise information about inputs of asynchronous systems.

The rest of the paper is organized as follows. Section 2 introduces Asynchronous CCS and the testing preorders. Section 3 presents the alternative characterizations based on traces and acceptance–sets, while the next section presents those based on basic observables. The extensions to π-calculus and to CCS with general relabelling are sketched in Section 5. Some concluding remarks are reported in Section 6. Due to space limitations, many proofs will be omitted.

2 Asynchronous CCS

In this section we present syntax, and operational and testing semantics of asynchronous CCS (ACCS, for short). It differs from standard CCS because only guarded choices are used and output guards are not allowed. The absence of output guards "forces" the asynchrony; it is not possible to have processes that causally depends on output actions.

2.1 Syntax

We let $\mathcal{N}$, ranged over by $a, b, \ldots$, be an infinite set of *names* and $\overline{\mathcal{N}} = \{\overline{a} \mid a \in \mathcal{N}\}$, ranged over by $\overline{a}, \overline{b}, \ldots$, be the set of *co-names*. $\mathcal{N}$ and $\overline{\mathcal{N}}$ are disjoint and are in bijection via the *complementation* function $(\bar{\cdot})$; we define: $\overline{(\overline{a})} = a$. We let $\mathcal{L} = \mathcal{N} \cup \overline{\mathcal{N}}$ be the set of *visible actions*, and let $l, l', \ldots$ range over it. We let $\mathcal{L}_\tau = \mathcal{L} \cup \{\tau\}$ for a distinct action τ, be the set of all *actions* or *labels*, ranged over by μ. We shall use $A, B, L, \ldots$, to range over subsets of $\mathcal{L}$, M to range over multisets of $\mathcal{L}$ and s to range over $\mathcal{L}^*$. We define $\overline{L} = \{\overline{l} \mid l \in L\}$ and similarly for M and s. We let $\mathcal{X}$, ranged over by $X, Y, \ldots$, be a countable set of *process variables*.

Definition 1. The set of *ACCS terms* is generated by the grammar:

$$E ::= \overline{a} \;\mid\; \textstyle\sum_{i \in I} g_i.E_i \;\mid E_1 \mid E_2 \;\mid E\backslash L \;\mid E\{f\} \;\mid X \;\mid recX.E$$

where $g_i \in \mathcal{N} \cup \{\tau\}$, I is finite and $f : \mathcal{N} \to \mathcal{N}$, called *relabelling function*, is injective and such that $\{l \mid f(l) \neq l\}$ is finite. We extend f to $\mathcal{L}$ by letting $\forall \overline{a} \in \overline{\mathcal{N}} : f(\overline{a}) = \overline{f(a)}$. We let $\mathcal{P}$, ranged over by P, Q, etc., denote the set of *closed* and *guarded* terms or *processes* (i.e. those terms where every occurrence of any agent variable X lies within the scope of some $recX.\_$ and $\sum$ operators).

Notation. In the sequel, $\sum_{i\in\{1,2\}} g_i.E_i$ will be abbreviated as $g_1.E_1 + g_2.E_2$, $\sum_{i\in\emptyset} g_i.E_i$ will be abbreviated as $\mathbf{0}$; we will also write g for $g.\mathbf{0}$. $\Pi_{i\in I} E_i$ represents the parallel composition of the terms E_i. We write $\_\{l'_1/l_1, \ldots, l'_n/l_n\}$ for the relabelling operator $\_\{f\}$ where $f(l) = l'_i$ if $l = l_i$, $i \in \{1, \ldots, n\}$, and $f(l) = l$ otherwise. As usual, we write $E[F/X]$ for the term obtained by replacing each occurrence of X in E by F (with possibly renaming of bound process variables).

Throughout the paper, we will use the *structural congruence* relation over ACCS processes, $\equiv$, as defined in, e.g., [19] (the unique change with respect to [19] is the addition of some obvious distribution laws for injective relabelling).

2.2 Operational Semantics

The labelled transition system $(\mathcal{P}, \mathcal{L}_\tau, \xrightarrow{\mu})$, which characterizes the operational semantics of the language, is given by the rules in Figure 1.

$$\textbf{AR1}\ \sum_{i\in I} g_i.P_i \xrightarrow{g_j} P_j \quad j\in I \qquad \textbf{AR2}\ \overline{a} \xrightarrow{\overline{a}} \mathbf{0}$$

$$\textbf{AR3}\ \frac{P \xrightarrow{\mu} P'}{P\{f\} \xrightarrow{f(\mu)} P'\{f\}} \qquad \textbf{AR4}\ \frac{P \xrightarrow{\mu} P'}{P\backslash L \xrightarrow{\mu} P'\backslash L} \quad \text{if } \mu \notin L \cup \overline{L}$$

$$\textbf{AR5}\ \frac{P \xrightarrow{\mu} P'}{P\,|\,Q \xrightarrow{\mu} P'\,|\,Q} \qquad \textbf{AR6}\ \frac{P[recX.P/X] \xrightarrow{\mu} P'}{recX.P \xrightarrow{\mu} P'}$$

$$\textbf{AR7}\ \frac{P \xrightarrow{l} P', \quad Q \xrightarrow{\overline{l}} Q}{P\,|\,Q \xrightarrow{\tau} P'\,|\,Q'}$$

Fig. 1. Operational semantics of ACCS (symmetric of rule **AR5** omitted)

As usual, we use $\Longrightarrow$ or $\stackrel{\epsilon}{\Longrightarrow}$ to denote the reflexive and transitive closure of $\xrightarrow{\tau}$ and use $\stackrel{s}{\Longrightarrow}$ (resp. $\xrightarrow{s}$) for $\Longrightarrow \xrightarrow{l} \stackrel{s'}{\Longrightarrow}$ (resp. $\xrightarrow{l} \xrightarrow{s'}$) when $s = ls'$. Moreover, we write $P \stackrel{s}{\Longrightarrow}$ for $\exists P' : P \stackrel{s}{\Longrightarrow} P'$ ($P \xrightarrow{s}$ and $P \xrightarrow{\tau}$ will be used similarly). We will call *sort* of P the set $sort(P) = \{l \in \mathcal{L} \mid \exists s \in \mathcal{L}^* : P \stackrel{sl}{\Longrightarrow}\}$, *input* (resp. *output*) *successors* of P the set $In(P) = \{l \in \mathcal{N} \mid P \stackrel{l}{\Longrightarrow}\}$ ($Out(P) = \{l \in \overline{\mathcal{N}} \mid P \stackrel{l}{\Longrightarrow}\}$), *successors* of P the set $S(P) = In(P) \cup Out(P)$ and *language* generated by P the set $L(P) = \{s \in \mathcal{L}^* \mid P \stackrel{s}{\Longrightarrow}\}$. We say that a process P is *stable* if $P \stackrel{\tau}{\not\longrightarrow}$.

From now onward, we adopt the following convention: an action declared *fresh* in a statement is assumed different from any other name and co-name mentioned in the statement. Note that, since for all relabelling operators f we have that $\{l \mid f(l) \neq l\}$ is finite, every ACCS process has a finite sort.

The following lemma implies that behaviours do not causally depend on the execution of output actions.

Lemma 2. For any process P and $\overline{a} \in \overline{\mathcal{N}}$, $P \xrightarrow{\overline{a}} Q$ implies $P \equiv Q \,|\, \overline{a}$.

2.3 Testing Semantics

We are now ready to instantiate the general framework of testing equivalences [10, 13] on ACCS.

Definition 3. *Observers* are ACCS processes that can also perform a distinct *success action* ω. $\mathcal{O}$ denotes the set of all the ACCS observers. A *computation* from a process P and an observer O is sequence of transitions

$$P \mid O = P_0 \mid O_0 \xrightarrow{\tau} P_1 \mid O_1 \xrightarrow{\tau} P_2 \mid O_2 \cdots P_k \mid O_k \xrightarrow{\tau} \cdots$$

which is either infinite or such that the last $P_k \mid O_k$ is stable. The computation is *successful* iff there exists some $n \geq 0$ such that $O_n \xrightarrow{\omega}$.

Definition 4. For every process P and observer O, we say

- $P\ \underline{may}\ O$ iff there exists a successful computation from $P \mid O$;
- $P\ \underline{must}\ O$ iff each computation from $P \mid O$ is successful.

Definition 5. We define the following preorders over processes:

- $P \mathrel{\underset{\sim}{\sqsubset}_m} Q$ iff for every observer $O \in \mathcal{O}$, $P\ \underline{may}\ O$ implies $Q\ \underline{may}\ O$;
- $P \mathrel{\underset{\sim}{\sqsubset}_M} Q$ iff for every observer $O \in \mathcal{O}$, $P\ \underline{must}\ O$ implies $Q\ \underline{must}\ O$.

We will use $\simeq$ to denote the equivalence obtained as the kernel of a preorder $\underset{\sim}{\sqsubset}$ (i.e. $\simeq = \underset{\sim}{\sqsubset} \cap \underset{\sim}{\sqsubset}^{-1}$).

3 Alternative Characterizations of Testing Semantics

The adaptation of the testing framework to an asynchronous setting discussed in the previous section is straightforward, but, like in the synchronous case, universal quantification on observers makes it difficult to work with the operational definitions of the two preorders. This calls for alternative characterizations that will make it easier to reason about processes. These characterizations will be given in terms of the traces and of the acceptance sets of processes.

3.1 A trace ordering

The following ordering over sequences of actions will be used for defining the alternative characterizations of the testing preorders.

Definition 6. Let $\preceq$ be the least preorder over $\mathcal{L}^*$ preserved under trace composition and satisfying the laws in Figure 2.

TO1	$\epsilon \preceq a$	TO2	$la \preceq al$	TO3	$\epsilon \preceq a\bar{a}$

Fig. 2. Trace Ordering Laws

The intuition behind the three laws in Figure 2 is that, whenever a process interacts with its environment by performing a sequence of actions s, an interaction is possible also if the process performs any $s' \preceq s$. To put it differently, if the environment offers $\overline{s}$, then it also offers any $\overline{s'}$ s.t. $s' \preceq s$.

More specifically, law T01 (*deletion*) says that process inputs cannot be forced to take place. For example, we have $\bar{b}c \preceq a\bar{b}c$: if the environment offers the sequence $\bar{a}b\bar{c}$, then it also offers $b\bar{c}$, as there can be no causal dependence of $b\bar{c}$ upon the output $\bar{a}$. Law T02 (*postponement*) says that observations of process inputs can be delayed. For example, we have that $\bar{b}ac \preceq a\bar{b}c$. Indeed, if the environment offers $\bar{a}b\bar{c}$ then it also offers $b\bar{a}\bar{c}$. Finally, law T03 (*annihilation*) allows the environment to internally consume pairs of complementary actions, e.g. $\bar{b} \preceq a\bar{a}\bar{b}$. Indeed, if the environment offers $\bar{a}ab$ it can internally consume $\bar{a}$ and a and offer b.

Definition 7. Given $s \in \mathcal{L}^*$, we let $\{\!\mid s \mid\!\}$ denote the multiset of actions occurring in s, and $\{\!\mid s \mid\!\}_i$ (resp. $\{\!\mid s \mid\!\}_o$) denote the multiset of input (resp. output) actions in s. We let $s \ominus s'$ denote the multiset of input actions $(\{\!\mid s \mid\!\}_i \backslash \{\!\mid s' \mid\!\}_i) \backslash \overline{(\{\!\mid s \mid\!\}_o \backslash \{\!\mid s' \mid\!\}_o)}$, where $\backslash$ denotes difference between multisets.

Intuitively, if $s' \preceq s$ then $s \ominus s'$ is the multiset of input actions of s which have actually been deleted (law T01), and not annihilated (law T03), in s'. For instance, if $s = ab\bar{a}c$ and $s' = b$ then $s \ominus s' = \{\!\mid c \mid\!\}$.

Notation. If M is a multiset of actions, we will write $\Pi\, M$ for denoting $\Pi_{l \in M} l$, the parallel composition of all actions in M. We shall write "$P \stackrel{M}{\Longrightarrow} P'$" if $P \stackrel{s}{\Longrightarrow} P'$ for some sequentialization s of the actions in M. When M is a multiset of input actions, with a slight abuse of notation, we will sometimes denote by M also the trace obtained by arbitrarily ordering the elements of M (remember that we work modulo law T02). We shall write "$P \stackrel{s}{\Longrightarrow} P'$ l-free" if there exists a sequence of transitions $P = P_0 \stackrel{\mu_1}{\longrightarrow} P_1 \stackrel{\mu_2}{\longrightarrow} \cdots \stackrel{\mu_n}{\longrightarrow} P_n = P'$ such that $P_i \stackrel{l}{\not\longrightarrow}$ for $0 \le i \le n$ and s is obtained from $\mu_1 \cdots \mu_n$ by erasing the τ's.

The following is the crucial lemma for the preorder $\preceq$. Its proof relies on Lemma 2 and proceeds by induction on the number of times the laws in Figure 2 are used.

Lemma 8. Let P be a process and l an action and assume $s' \preceq s$. If $P \stackrel{\overline{s}}{\Longrightarrow} P'$ l-free then there exists P'' such that $P \stackrel{\overline{s'}}{\Longrightarrow} P''$ l-free and $P'' \equiv P' \mid \Pi\, \overline{s \ominus s'}$.[2]

3.2 The may case

By relying on the trace ordering $\preceq$, we can now define a new preorder that will be proved to be an alternative characterization of the may preorder $\underset{\sim m}{\sqsubset}$.

[2] We remind the reader that $\equiv$ denotes structural congruence.

Definition 9. For processes P and Q, we write $P \ll_m Q$ iff whenever $P \stackrel{s}{\Longrightarrow}$ then there exists s' such that $s' \preceq s$ and $Q \stackrel{s'}{\Longrightarrow}$.

The difference with respect to the synchronous case (see, e.g., [10, 13]) is that we require a weaker condition than trace inclusion by taking advantage of a preorder over single traces. We define below a special class of observers.

Definition 10. Let $s \in \mathcal{L}^*$. The observers $t(s)$ are defined inductively as follows: $t(\epsilon) \stackrel{\mathrm{def}}{=} \omega$, $t(\overline{a}s') \stackrel{\mathrm{def}}{=} a.t(s')$ and $t(as') \stackrel{\mathrm{def}}{=} \overline{a} \mid t(s')$.

The following property can be easily proved relying on Lemma 8.

Proposition 11. For every process P and $s \in \mathcal{L}^*$, $P\, \underline{may}\, t(s)$ iff there exists $s' \in L(P)$ such that $s' \preceq s$.

Theorem 12. For all processes P and Q, $P \sqsubseteq_m Q$ iff $P \ll_m Q$.

PROOF: 'Only if' part. Suppose that $P \sqsubseteq_m Q$ and that $s \in L(P)$. We must show that there exists $s' \in L(Q)$ such that $s' \preceq s$. The hypothesis $s \in L(P)$ implies that $P\, \underline{may}\, t(s)$. Since $P \sqsubseteq_m Q$, we infer that $Q\, \underline{may}\, t(s)$. The thesis follows from Proposition 11.

'If' part. Suppose that $P \ll_m Q$ and that $P\, \underline{may}\, O$ for an observer O. Then there exists a successful computation with an initial sequence of transitions $P \mid O \Longrightarrow P' \mid O'$ where $O' \stackrel{\omega}{\longrightarrow}$. This sequence of transitions may be unzipped into two sequences $P \stackrel{s}{\Longrightarrow} P'$ and $O \stackrel{\overline{s}}{\Longrightarrow} O'$. The hypothesis $P \ll_m Q$ implies that there exist s' and Q' such that $s' \preceq s$ and $Q \stackrel{s'}{\longrightarrow} Q'$. By Lemma 8, there exists an observer O'' such that $O \stackrel{\overline{s'}}{\Longrightarrow} O''$ and $O'' \equiv O' \mid \overline{\Pi\, s \ominus s'}$. Now, $O' \stackrel{\omega}{\longrightarrow}$ implies $O'' \stackrel{\omega}{\longrightarrow}$. Hence, the sequence of transitions $Q \mid O \Longrightarrow Q' \mid O''$ can be extended to a successful computation and the thesis is proved. □

By relying on the alternative characterization $\ll_m$ one can easily prove that $\sqsubseteq_m$ is a pre–congruence.

Examples. We show some examples of pairs of processes related by the preorder. All of the relationships can be proven by using the alternative characterization of the preorder $\ll_m$.

- Since $L(P) \subseteq L(Q)$ implies $P \sqsubseteq_m Q$, all of the relationships for the synchronous may preorder do hold in our setting.
- Since $\epsilon \in L(P)$ for each process P, from T01 and T03 in Figure 2, we get $a \simeq_m \mathbf{0}$ and $a.\overline{a} \simeq_m \mathbf{0}$. In particular, from $a \simeq_m \mathbf{0}$ we get $a \simeq_m b$ and $a.b \simeq_m b.a$ which imply that all processes containing only input actions are equivalent to $\mathbf{0}$.
- An interesting law is the $a.(\overline{a}|b) \simeq_m b$. More generally, we have $a.(\overline{a}|G) \sqsubseteq_m G$, where G is an input guarded summation $\sum_{i \in I} a_i.P_i$ (in fact, $a.\overline{a} \simeq_m \mathbf{0}$ is just a consequence of this law). Guardedness of G is essential: $\overline{b} \sqsubseteq_m a.(\overline{a} \mid \overline{b})$ does not hold (consider the observer $b.\omega$).

3.3 The must case

Definition 13.

- Let P be a process and $s \in \mathcal{L}^*$. We write $P \downarrow$, and say that P *converges*, if and only if there is no infinite sequence of internal transitions $P \xrightarrow{\tau} P_1 \xrightarrow{\tau} P_2 \xrightarrow{\tau} \cdots$ starting from P. We write $P \downarrow s$, and say that P *converges along* s if and only if whenever s' is a prefix of s and $P \stackrel{s'}{\Longrightarrow} P'$ then P' converges. We write $P \uparrow s$, and say that P *diverges along* s if it is not the case that $P \downarrow s$.
- Let P be a process and $s \in \mathcal{L}^*$. The set of processes $P\,\underline{after}\,s$ is defined by:
$$P\,\underline{after}\,s \stackrel{\text{def}}{=} \{(P' \mid \Pi\ \overline{s \ominus s'}) : s' \preceq s \text{ and } P \stackrel{s'}{\Longrightarrow} P'\}.$$
- Let X be a set of processes and $L \subseteq_{\text{fin}} \overline{\mathcal{N}}$. We write $X\ \underline{must}\ L$ if and only if for each $P \in X$ there exists $\overline{a} \in L$ s.t. $P \stackrel{\overline{a}}{\Longrightarrow}$.

In the sequel, given a set of traces $T \subseteq \mathcal{L}^*$, we will let $P \downarrow T$ stand for $P \downarrow s$ for each $s \in T$. Furthermore, we define $\widehat{s} \stackrel{\text{def}}{=} \{s' : s' \preceq s\}$.

Definition 14. We set $P \ll_M Q$ iff for each $s \in \mathcal{L}^*$ s.t. $P \downarrow \widehat{s}$ it holds that:

- $Q \downarrow \widehat{s}$, and
- for each $L \subseteq_{\text{fin}} \overline{\mathcal{N}}$: $(P\,\underline{after}\,s)\ \underline{must}\ L$ implies $(Q\,\underline{after}\,s)\ \underline{must}\ L$.

Note that the above definition is formally similar to that for the synchronous case [10, 13]. The difference lies in the definition of the set $P\,\underline{after}\,s$: the latter can be seen as the set of possible states that P can reach after an interaction triggered by the environment offering $\overline{s}$. In an asynchronous setting, output actions can be freely performed by the environment, without any involvement of the process under consideration. In the definition of $P\,\underline{after}\,s$, these particular output actions represent the "difference" between the behaviour of the environment, $\overline{s}$, and the actual behaviour of the process, s', that is, $\Pi\ \overline{s \ominus s'}$.

Lemma 15. Let P be any process.

1. If P is stable then $In(P) \cap Out(P) = \emptyset$.
2. If P is stable then there exist P' and a unique multiset $M \subseteq_{\text{fin}} \overline{\mathcal{N}}$ s.t. $P \equiv P' \mid \Pi\ M$ and $Out(P') = \emptyset$.
3. If $P \stackrel{\overline{a}}{\Longrightarrow} P'$ then $S(P') \cup \{\overline{a}\} \subseteq S(P)$.

When P is stable, we will use $\mathsf{O}(P)$ to denote the unique multiset M implicitly defined by part 2 of the above lemma.

Theorem 16. If $P \ll_M Q$ then $P \sqsubsetapprox_M Q$.

PROOF: Let O be any observer and suppose that $Q\ \underline{m\!\!/ust}\ O$: we show that $P\ \underline{m\!\!/ust}\ O$ as well. We make a case analysis on why $Q\ \underline{m\!\!/ust}\ O$. All cases can be easily reduced to the case of a finite unsuccessful computation, i.e. a sequence of transitions $Q \mid O \Longrightarrow Q' \mid O'$ such that, for some s: $Q \stackrel{s}{\Longrightarrow} Q'$, $O \stackrel{\overline{s}}{\Longrightarrow} O'$ ω–free and $Q' \mid O'$ is stable. Furthermore, we suppose that $P \downarrow \widehat{s}$ and $Q \downarrow \widehat{s}$.

From the fact that $Q' \mid O'$ is stable and from Lemma 15(1), we deduce that:

$$(i)\ Out(Q') \cap \overline{In(O')} = \emptyset$$
$$(ii)\ In(Q') \cap \overline{Out(O')} = \emptyset$$
$$(iii)\ In(O') \cap \overline{Out(O')} = \emptyset\ .$$

We show now how to build an unsuccessful computation for $P \mid O$. Let us define the set of output actions $L \stackrel{\text{def}}{=} \overline{In(O')}$ and the multiset of input actions $M \stackrel{\text{def}}{=} \mathsf{O}(O')$ (note that, since O' is stable, this multiset is well defined in virtue of Lemma 15(2)). First, we show that

$$(Q\ \underline{after}\ sM)\ \underline{m\!\!/ust}\ L\,. \tag{1}$$

Indeed, since $s \preceq sM$ and $Q \stackrel{s}{\Longrightarrow} Q'$, we have that $Q' \mid \Pi\ \overline{M} \in (Q\ \underline{after}\ sM)$; furthermore, we have that $Q' | \Pi\ \overline{M} \stackrel{\tau}{\not\longrightarrow}$ (from (ii) and $Q' \stackrel{\tau}{\not\longrightarrow}$), that $Out(Q') \cap L = \emptyset$ (from (i)) and that $\overline{M} \cap L = \emptyset$ (from (iii)). From these facts, it follows that $Out(Q' \mid \Pi\ \overline{M}) \cap L = \emptyset$. This proves (1).

Now, from (1) and definition of $\ll_M$ it follows that $(P\ \underline{after}\ sM)\ \underline{m\!\!/ust}\ L$, which means that there are P' and $s' \preceq sM$ such that:

$$P \stackrel{s'}{\Longrightarrow} P' \text{ and } Out(P' \mid \Pi\ \overline{sM \ominus s'}) \cap L = \emptyset\ . \tag{2}$$

Now, since O' is stable, from Lemma 15(2), it follows that there exists O'' such that $O' \equiv O'' \mid \Pi\ \overline{M}$ and $Out(O'') = \emptyset$. Hence $O' \stackrel{\overline{M}}{\longrightarrow} \equiv O''$ and therefore $O \stackrel{\overline{sM}}{\Longrightarrow} \equiv O''$ ω–free. Since $s' \preceq sM$, from Lemma 8 it then follows that there is O_1 such that $O \stackrel{\overline{s'}}{\Longrightarrow} O_1 \equiv O'' \mid \Pi\ \overline{sM \ominus s'}$ ω–free. Combining these transitions of O with $P \stackrel{s'}{\Longrightarrow} P'$ in (2), we get:

$$P \mid O \Longrightarrow P' \mid O_1 \equiv P' \mid O'' \mid \Pi\ \overline{sM \ominus s'} \quad \omega\text{–free.} \tag{3}$$

To prove that (3) leads to an unsuccessful computation, it suffices to show that $P' | O'' | \Pi\ \overline{sM \ominus s'} \stackrel{\omega}{\not\Longrightarrow}$. The latter is a consequence of the following three facts:

1. $Out(P' | \Pi\ \overline{sM \ominus s'}) \cap \overline{In(O'')} = \emptyset$. This derives from (2) and from $In(O'') \subseteq In(O') = \overline{L}$ (Lemma 15(3) applied to $O' \stackrel{\overline{M}}{\longrightarrow} \equiv O''$);
2. $Out(O'') = \emptyset$;
3. $O'' \stackrel{\omega}{\not\Longrightarrow}$ (Lemma 15(3) applied to $O' \stackrel{\overline{M}}{\longrightarrow} \equiv O''$). □

For proving the converse of the above theorem, we will use two families of observers: the first can be used to test for convergence along sequences of a given set $\widehat{s}$, and the second to test that a given pair (s, L) is an "acceptance" pair.

Definition 17. Let $s \in \mathcal{L}^*$ and $L \subseteq_{\text{fin}} \mathcal{N}$. The observers $c(s)$ and $a(s, L)$ are defined by induction on s as follows:

$$\begin{array}{llll} c(s): & c(\epsilon) = \tau.\omega & a(s,L): & a(\epsilon, L) = \sum_{\overline{a} \in L} a.\omega \\ & c(bs') = \overline{b} \mid c(s') & & a(bs', L) = \overline{b} \mid a(s', L) \\ & c(\overline{b}s') = \tau.\omega + b.c(s') & & a(\overline{b}s', L) = \tau.\omega + b.a(s', L)\,. \end{array}$$

Lemma 18. Let P be a process, $s \in \mathcal{L}^*$ and $L \subseteq_{\text{fin}} \overline{\mathcal{N}}$. We have:

1. $P\, \underline{must}\, c(s)$ if and only if $P \downarrow \widehat{s}$.
2. Suppose that $P \downarrow \widehat{s}$. Then $P\, \underline{must}\, a(s, L)$ if and only if $(P\, \underline{after}\, s)\, \underline{must}\, L$.

PROOF: An easy application of Lemma 8. □

Theorem 19. $P \sqsubseteq_M Q$ implies $P \ll_M Q$.

PROOF: An easy consequence of Lemma 18. □

By relying on $\ll_M$, it is straightforward to show that $\sqsubseteq_M$ is a pre–congruence.

Examples. We give below some meaningful examples of processes that are related (or unrelated) according to the preorder. All the examples are checked relying on the alternative characterization provided by $\ll_M$. In the examples, we shall also refer to the asynchronous bisimilarity[3] of [2].

- The process $\mathbf{0}$ represents the top element for the family of terms built using only input actions: $a \sqsubseteq_M \mathbf{0}$, but $\mathbf{0} \not\sqsubseteq_M a$; thus $a{+}b \sqsubseteq_M a$, but $a \not\sqsubseteq_M a{+}b$.
- Input prefixes can be distributed over summation, i.e. $a.(b{+}c) \simeq_M a.b{+}a.c$. This is in sharp contrast with the asynchronous bisimilarity.
- Sequences of inputs can absorb their own prefixes, as in $a.b{+}a \simeq_M a.b$ This law was also present in [9], but is not valid for asynchronous bisimilarity.
- Like in [2], we have $a.\overline{a} \simeq_M \mathbf{0}$. This is an instance of the more general law $a.(\overline{a} \mid G){+}G \simeq_M G$, where G is any guarded summation $\sum_{i \in I} g_i.P_i$. Unlike [2], however, the law does not hold for infinite behaviours: $recX.(a.(\overline{a} \mid X)) \not\simeq_M \mathbf{0}$. This is due to the sensitivity of must to divergence: when put in parallel with $\overline{a}$, $recX.(a.(\overline{a} \mid X))$ diverges, while $\mathbf{0}$ does not.

As shown in the examples above, must equivalence and asynchronous bisimilarity are in general incomparable, due to the sensitivity of must to divergence. They are comparable if we consider only *strongly convergent* processes, i.e. those processes P such that $P \downarrow s$ for each s. The crux is given by the following characterization of $\approx$:

Proposition 20. $P \approx Q$ if and only if whenever $P \stackrel{s}{\Longrightarrow} P'$ then there is $s' \preceq s$ s.t. $Q \stackrel{s'}{\Longrightarrow} Q'$ and $P' \approx Q' \mid \Pi\, \overline{s \ominus s'}$, and vice–versa for Q and P.

Corollary 21. Let P and Q be strongly convergent processes. Then $P \approx Q$ implies $P \sqsubseteq_M Q$.

[3] We remind the reader that asynchronous bisimilarity is defined as the maximal equivalence relation $\approx$ s.t. whenever $P \approx Q$ and $P \stackrel{\mu}{\longrightarrow} P'$ then:

(a) if $\mu = \tau$ then there is Q' such that $Q \Longrightarrow Q'$ and $P' \approx Q'$,

(b) if $\mu = \overline{a}$ then there is Q' such that $Q \stackrel{\overline{a}}{\Longrightarrow} Q'$ and $P' \approx Q'$, and

(c) if $\mu = a$ then there is Q' such that either (i) $Q \stackrel{a}{\Longrightarrow} Q'$ and $P' \approx Q'$, or (ii) $Q \Longrightarrow Q'$ and $P' \approx Q' \mid \overline{a}$.

4 Basic Observables for Asynchronous Processes

Following [5], we introduce a characterization of the asynchronous may and must preorders in terms of the pre–congruence induced by *basic observables*. The difference with the synchronous case is that here only output actions are important.

Definition 22. A *context* is a term C with one free occurrence of a process variable, usually denoted by $\_$. We write $C[P]$ instead of $C[P/\_]$.

The context *closure* $\mathcal{R}^c$ of a given binary relation $\mathcal{R}$ over processes, is defined as: $P\,\mathcal{R}^c\,Q$ iff for each context C, $C[P]\,\mathcal{R}\,C[Q]$. $\mathcal{R}^c$ enjoys two important properties: (a) $(\mathcal{R}^c)^c = \mathcal{R}^c$, and (b) $\mathcal{R} \subseteq \mathcal{R}'$ implies $\mathcal{R}^c \subseteq \mathcal{R}'^c$. In the following, we will write $\not\mathcal{R}$ for the complement of $\mathcal{R}$.

4.1 The may case

Definition 23. Let P be a process and $\overline{a} \in \overline{\mathcal{N}}$. We define the following *observation predicate* over processes: $P\surd\overline{a}$ (P *offers* $\overline{a}$) iff $P \overset{\overline{a}}{\Longrightarrow}$.

The observation preorder induced by $\surd$ is defined as follows: $P \preceq_{\surd} Q$ iff for each $\overline{a} \in \overline{\mathcal{N}}$: $P\surd\overline{a}$ implies $Q\surd\overline{a}$.

Of course, the observation preorder is very coarse; a more refined relation can be obtained by closing it under all ACCS contexts. The *contextual preorder* of $\preceq_{\surd}$ is just its context closure $\preceq^c_{\surd}$; the latter is another characterization of $\sqsubseteq_m$ (with $\sim$ under $\sqsubseteq$).

Theorem 24. For all processes P and Q, $P \underset{\sim}{\sqsubset}_m Q$ iff $P \preceq^c_{\surd} Q$.

PROOF: We use the alternative characterization $\ll_m$ of $\underset{\sim}{\sqsubset}_m$.

'Only if' part. From the definition, it is easily seen that $\ll_m$ is contained in $\preceq_{\surd}$ (note that for each $\overline{a} \in \overline{\mathcal{N}}$, $s \preceq \overline{a}$ implies $s = \overline{a}$). From this fact, by closing under contexts and recalling that $\preceq^c_{\surd}$ is a pre–congruence the thesis follows.

'If' part. Here, we show that $\preceq^c_{\surd}$ is contained in $\ll_m$. From this fact and recalling that $\preceq^c_{\surd}$ is a pre–congruence the thesis will follow. Assume that $P \preceq^c_{\surd} Q$ and that $s \in L(P)$, for some $s \in \mathcal{L}^*$. We have to show that there exists $s' \in L(Q)$ such that $s' \preceq s$. Now, let $t'(s)$ be the process defined like the observer $t(s)$ in Definition 10, but with a fresh, standard action $\overline{c}$ in place of ω. The following fact, where R is any process where neither c nor $\overline{c}$ occur, is straightforward to prove by relying on Lemma 8: $(t'(s) \mid R)\surd\overline{c}$ iff there exists $s' \in L(R)$ such that $s' \preceq s$. The thesis is an immediate consequence of this fact. □

4.2 The must case

We introduce below the *guarantee* predicate, $P\,!\,l$; informally, this predicate checks whether P will always be able to offer a communication on l; however, differently from [5], we here only consider output actions.

Definition 25. Let P be a process and $\overline{a} \in \overline{\mathcal{N}}$. We write $P\,!\,\overline{a}$ (P *guarantees* $\overline{a}$) if and only if whenever $P \Longrightarrow P'$ then $P' \stackrel{\overline{a}}{\Longrightarrow}$.

The *observation preorder* induced by $\downarrow$ and $!$ is defined as: $P \,{}_{\downarrow}\!\preceq_{!}\, Q$ if and only if for each $\overline{a}$: ($P\downarrow$ and $P\,!\,\overline{a}$) implies ($Q\downarrow$ and $Q\,!\,\overline{a}$).

Theorem 26. $P \sqsubseteq_{M} Q$ if and only if $P \,{}_{\downarrow}\!\preceq_{!}^{c}\, Q$.

PROOF: We use the characterization of the must preorder in terms of $\ll_{M}$.

'If' part. First, note that $P\,!\,\overline{a}$ if and only if $(P\,\underline{after}\,\epsilon)\ \underline{must}\ \{\overline{a}\}$. Hence, by definition, $\ll_{M}$ is included in ${}_{\downarrow}\!\preceq_{!}$. The thesis then follows by closing under contexts and recalling that $\sqsubseteq_{M}$ is a pre–congruence.

'Only if' part. Fix any s and L and suppose that $P\downarrow\widehat{s}$ and $(P\,\underline{after}\,s)\ \underline{must}\ L$. We have to show that $Q\downarrow\widehat{s}$ and $(Q\,\underline{after}\,s)\ \underline{must}\ L$. Now, let $c'(s)$ and $a'(s,L)$ be the observers defined like in Definition 17, but with a fresh, standard action $\overline{c}$ in place of ω. The following two facts, where R is any process where neither c nor $\overline{c}$ occur, are straightforward to prove relying on Lemma 8:

- $R\downarrow\widehat{s}$ if and only if $R\,|\,c'(s)\downarrow$.
- Suppose that $R\downarrow\widehat{s}$. Then $R\,|\,a'(s,L)\downarrow$ and furthermore $(R\,\underline{after}\,s)\ \underline{must}\ L$ if and only if $R\,|\,a'(s,L)\,!\,\overline{c}$.

Then $Q\downarrow\widehat{s}$ and $(Q\,\underline{after}\,s)\ \underline{must}\ L$ follow from the definition of ${}_{\downarrow}\!\preceq_{!}^{c}$ and from the above two facts. □

5 Dealing with Richer Languages

In this section we discuss the extensions of our theory to the asynchronous variant of π-calculus [15, 6, 12, 2] and to a version of asynchronous CCS of Section 2 with possibly non–injective relabelling.

5.1 π-calculus

For the sake of simplicity, we confine ourselves to the may preorder. The must preorder requires a more complex notational machinery but also leads to results similar to those for ACCS.

A countable set $\mathcal{N}$ of *names* is ranged over by $a, b, \ldots$. Processes are ranged over by P, Q and R. The syntax of asynchronous π–calculus contains the operators for output action, input–guarded summation, restriction, parallel composition, matching and replication:

$$P ::= \overline{a}b \mid \sum_{i \in I} a_i(b).P_i \mid \nu\, a P \mid P_1 \mid P_2 \mid [a = b]P \mid !P.$$

Free names and *bound names* of a process P, written $\mathrm{fn}(P)$ and $\mathrm{bn}(P)$ respectively, arise as expected; the *names* of P, written $\mathrm{n}(P)$ are $\mathrm{fn}(P) \cup \mathrm{bn}(P)$. Due to lack of space, we omit the definition of operational semantics (see, e.g., [2]). Recall that transition labels (actions), ranged over by μ, can be of four forms: τ (interaction), ab (input), $\overline{a}b$ (output) or $\overline{a}(b)$ (bound output). Functions $\mathrm{bn}(\cdot)$, $\mathrm{fn}(\cdot)$ and $\mathrm{n}(\cdot)$ are extended to actions as expected: in particular, $\mathrm{bn}(\mu) = b$ if $\mu = \overline{a}(b)$ and $\mathrm{bn}(\mu) = \emptyset$ otherwise.

In the sequel, we will write $P \overset{a(b)}{\longrightarrow} P'$ if $P \overset{ab}{\longrightarrow} P'$ and $b \notin \mathrm{fn}(P)$. The new kind of action $a(b)$ is called *bound input*; we extend $\mathrm{bn}(\cdot)$ to bound inputs by letting $\mathrm{bn}(a(b)) = \{b\}$. Below, we shall use $\mathcal{L}_\pi$ to denote the set of all visible π-calculus actions, including bound inputs, and let θ range over it. Given a trace $s \in \mathcal{L}_\pi^*$, we say that s is *normal* if, whenever $s = s'.\theta.s''$ (the dot . stands for trace composition), for some s', θ and s'', then $\mathrm{bn}(\theta)$ does not occur in s' and $\mathrm{bn}(\theta)$ is different from any other bound name occurring in s' and s''. The set of normal traces over $\mathcal{L}_\pi$ is denoted by $\mathcal{T}$ and ranged over by s. From now on, we shall work with normal traces only. Functions $\mathrm{bn}(\cdot)$ and $\mathrm{fn}(\cdot)$ are extended to $\mathcal{T}$ as expected. A complementation function on $\mathcal{T}$ is defined by setting $\overline{a(b)} \overset{\mathrm{def}}{=} \overline{a}(b)$, $\overline{ab} \overset{\mathrm{def}}{=} \overline{a}b$, $\overline{\overline{a}b} \overset{\mathrm{def}}{=} ab$ and $\overline{\overline{a}(b)} \overset{\mathrm{def}}{=} a(b)$; please notice that $\overline{\overline{s}} = s$.

P1	$\epsilon \preceq \theta$	if θ is an input action
P2	$s.\theta \preceq \theta.s$	if θ is an input action and $\mathrm{bn}(\theta) \cap \mathrm{bn}(s) = \emptyset$
P3	$\epsilon \preceq \theta.\overline{a}b$	if $\theta = ab$ or $\theta = a(b)$
P4	$\overline{a}c.(s\{c/b\}) \preceq \overline{a}(b).s$	

Fig. 3. Rules for the preorder $\preceq$ over $\mathcal{T}$

The definition of $\ll_m$ remains formally unchanged, but the relation $\preceq$ is now the least preorder over $\mathcal{T}$ closed under composition and generated by the rules in Figure 3. Rules P1, P2, P3 are the natural extensions to asynchronous π-calculus of the rules for ACCS. Here, some extra attention has to be paid to bound names: in the environment, an output declaring a new name (bound output) cannot be postponed after those actions which use the new name (side condition of P2). For an example, consider actions $\overline{a}(b)$ and $b(c)$ of $\nu\, b\,(\overline{a}b|b(c).P)$. Rule P4 is specific to π-calculus; it is due to the impossibility for observers to fully discriminate between free and bound outputs. Informally, rule P4 states that if $\overline{a}(c).s$ is "acceptable" for an observer (i.e. leads to success), then $\overline{a}b.(s\{b/y\})$ would be acceptable as well. Rule P4 would not hold if we extended the language with the *mismatching* operator $[a \neq b]P$, considered e.g. in [4]. It is worthwhile to note that ruling out matching from the language would not change the discriminating power of observers. The effect of the test $[a = b]O$ can be simulated by the parallel composition $\overline{a} \mid b.O$.

5.2 ACCS with General Relabelling

A consequence of the presence of non–injective relabelling functions, is that observers and contexts become more discriminating. For instance, they lead to $a.\bar{a} \not\sqsubseteq_{M} \mathbf{0}$ and $a.\bar{a} \not\sqsubseteq_{m} \mathbf{0}$. These can be proved by considering the observer $(\bar{b} \mid a.\omega)\{a/b\}$. We also have $\mathbf{0} \not\sqsubseteq_{M} a.\bar{a}$, that can be proved by considering the observer $(\bar{b} \mid (\tau.\omega + a))\{a/b\}$. Therefore, the general laws $a.(\bar{a} \mid G_1) \simeq_{m} G_1$, where $G_1 = \sum_{i \in I} a_i.P_i$, and $a.(\bar{a} \mid G_2) + G_2 \simeq_{M} G_2$, where $G_2 = \sum_{i \in I} g_i.P_i$, are not sound anymore. By means of general relabelling, observers are able to distinguish between the messages they emit and those emitted by the observed processes.

The trace preorder is now defined as the least preorder over $\mathcal{L}^*$ closed under trace composition and satisfying the laws T01 and T02 in Figure 2. Notice that if $s' \preceq s$ then $\{\!|\, s \,|\!\}_o = \{\!|\, s' \,|\!\}_o$, therefore now we have $s \ominus s' = \{\!|\, s \,|\!\}_i \setminus \{\!|\, s' \,|\!\}_i$. The definition of $\ll_{m}$ remains formally unchanged.

Let us now consider the must preorder. In the following we shall write $s' \sim s$ iff $s' \preceq s$ and $\{\!|\, s' \,|\!\} = \{\!|\, s \,|\!\}$, and for M finite multiset of $\mathcal{L}$ and $L \subseteq_{\text{fin}} \mathcal{L}$ we shall write $M \setminus L$ for the multiset $\{\!|\, l \in M \mid l \notin L \,|\!\}$. The alternative characterization of the $\sqsubseteq_{M}$ preorder is now the following.

Definition 27. We set $P \ll_{M} Q$ iff for each $s \in \mathcal{L}^*$ s.t. $P \downarrow \hat{s}$ it holds that:

a) $Q \downarrow \hat{s}$, and
b) for each $s' \in \hat{s}$, for each $L \subseteq_{\text{fin}} \mathcal{N}$:
$$(P\,\underline{after}\,s'(s \ominus s'))\ \underline{must}\,L \text{ implies } (Q\,\underline{after}\,s'(s \ominus s'))\ \underline{must}\,L,$$

where for any process R, $s \in \mathcal{L}^*$ and M multiset of $\mathcal{N}$, we define $R\,\underline{after}\,sM$ as
$$\{P' : R \stackrel{s'}{\Longrightarrow} P', s' \preceq sM, s' \sim s(s' \ominus s), In(P') \cap (M \setminus (s' \ominus s)) = \emptyset\}.$$

6 Conclusions

We have examined the impact of the testing framework as proposed in [10, 13] on asynchronous CCS. In particular, we have given three equivalent characterizations of asynchronous testing observational semantics. The first one is given in terms of observers and successful computations, the second relies on sets of traces and acceptances, the third one is defined in terms of basic observables and context closures. We have discussed generalizations of the results to asynchronous π-calculus and to ACCS with non–injective relabelling.

The above mentioned characterizations provide a good starting point for understanding asynchronous semantics and for relating testing semantics to other approaches. The picture would have been more complete with an equational characterization of our semantics; this will be the topic of a forthcoming paper.

Acknowledgments. Three anonymous referees provided valuable suggestions. We are grateful to the Dipartimento di Scienze dell'Informazione of Università di Roma "La Sapienza" and to Istituto di Elaborazione dell'Informazione in Pisa for making our collaboration possible.

References

1. G.Agha. *Actors: a model of concurrent computation in Distributed Systems.* Mit-Press, Boston, 1986.
2. R.M. Amadio, I. Castellani, D. Sangiorgi. On Bisimulations for the Asynchronous π–calculus. *CONCUR'96, LNCS* 1119, pp.147-162, Springer, 1996.
3. J. Bergstra, J.W. Klop. Process Algebra for Synchronous Communication. *Information and Control*, 60:109-137, 1984.
4. M. Boreale, R. De Nicola. Testing Equivalence for Mobile Systems. *Information and Computation*, 120: 279-303, 1995.
5. M. Boreale, R. De Nicola, R. Pugliese. Basic Observables for Processes. *ICALP'97, LNCS* 1256, pp.482-492, Springer, 1997.
6. G. Boudol. Asynchrony in the π–calculus (note). Rapport de Recherche 1702, INRIA Sophia–Antipolis, 1992.
7. S.D. Brookes, C.A.R. Hoare, A.W. Roscoe. A theory of communicating sequential processes. *Journal of the ACM*, 31(3):560-599, 1984.
8. N. Busi, R. Gorrieri, G-L. Zavattaro. A process algebraic view of Linda coordination primitives. Technical Report UBLCS-97-05, University of Bologna, 1997.
9. F.S. de Boer, J.W. Klop, C. Palamidessi. Asynchronous Communication in Process Algebra. *LICS'92*, IEEE Computer Society Press, pp. 137-147, 1992.
10. R. De Nicola, M.C.B. Hennessy. Testing Equivalence for Processes. *Theoretical Computers Science*, 34:83-133, 1984.
11. R. De Nicola, R. Pugliese. A Process Algebra based on Linda. *COORDINATION'96, LNCS* 1061, pp.160-178, Springer, 1996.
12. M. Hansen, H. Huttel, J. Kleist. Bisimulations for Asynchronous Mobile Processes. In Proc. of the Tblisi Symposium on Language, Logic, and Computation, 1995.
13. M.C.B. Hennessy. *Algebraic Theory of Processes.* The MIT Press, 1988.
14. C.A.R. Hoare. *Communicating Sequential Processes.* Prentice-Hall Int., 1985.
15. K. Honda, M. Tokoro. An Object Calculus for Asynchronous Communication. *ECOOP'91, LNCS* 512, pp.133-147, Springer, 1991.
16. H. Jifeng, M.B. Josephs, C.A.R. Hoare. A Theory of Synchrony and Asynchrony. *Proc. of the IFIP Working Conf. on Programming Concepts and Methods*, pp.446-465, 1990.
17. N.A. Lynch, M.R. Tuttle. Hierarchical correctness proofs for distributed algorithms. *In* 6th *ACM Symposium on Principles of Distributed Computing*, pp.137–151, 1987.
18. R. Milner. *Communication and Concurrency.* Prentice Hall International, 1989.
19. R. Milner. The Polyadic π-calculus: A Tutorial. Technical Report, University of Edinburgh, 1991.
20. R. Milner, J. Parrow, D. Walker. A calculus of mobile processes, (Part I and II). *Information and Computation*, 100:1-77, 1992.
21. R. Pugliese. A Process Calculus with Asynchronous Communications. 5th Italian Conference on Theoretical Computer Science, (A. De Santis, ed.), pp.295-310, World Scientific, 1996.
22. J. Tretmans. A formal approach to conformance testing. Ph.D. Thesis, University of Twente, 1992.

Minor Searching, Normal Forms of Graph Relabelling: Two Applications Based on Enumerations by Graph Relabelling*

Anne Bottreau and Yves Métivier**

LaBRI, Université Bordeaux I, ENSERB
351 cours de la Libération 33405 Talence cedex FRANCE
{bottreau,metivier}@labri.u-bordeaux.fr, fax:(+33) 05 56 84 66 69

Abstract: *This paper deals with graph relabelling introduced in [LMS95]. Our first result concerns the open problem of searching a graph as a minor in a graph with a distinguished vertex, by means of graph relabellings. We give and prove a graph rewriting system which answers to this problem. Secondly we define and study normal forms of graph relabellings. We prove that any graph rewriting system can be simulated by a system in k-normal form (with an integer k depending on the original system). Proofs for both results are linked by the enumeration systems they used.*

Key-words: *Local computations, graph relabelling, enumerations, paths, minor, normal form of graph rewritings.*

Introduction

Graph rewriting systems have been introduced in [LMS95] as a suitable tool for expressing distributed algorithms on a network of communicating processors. In that model a network is considered as a labelled graph whose vertices stand for processors and edges stand for communication links. Vertex labels hold for the states of processors and edge labels for the states of communication links. A computation in a network then corresponds to a sequence of labels transformations leading to a final labelled graph. A computation step on a labelled graph consists in relabelling a connected subgraph, using a graph rewriting rule.

Given a vertex in the graph, the computation of its new state depends on its current state and on the states of its neighbours. In that way graph rewritings are an example of local computations.

Among models related to our model there are the local computations defined by Rosensthiel and al. [RFH72], Angluin [Ang80], and more recently by Yamashita and Kameda [YK96a,YK96b]. In [RFH72] a synchronous model is considered, where vertices represent identical deterministic finite automata. The basic computation step is to compute the next state of each processor according to its state and the states of its neighbours. In [Ang80] an asynchronous model is considered. A computation step means that two adjacent vertices exchange their labels and then compute new ones. In [YK96a,YK96b] an asynchronous model is studied where a basic computation step means that a processor either changes its state and then sends a message or receives a message. Our model is an asynchronous model too.

Limitations of our formalism have been discussed in [LMZ95] and [BM96]. Some graph properties have been proved to be unrecognizable by local computations.

On the other side, graph rewriting power has been studied in [LM93,LMS95]. It has more particularly concerned the definition of different classes of graph rewriting systems. Moreover authors dealed with graphs with a distinguished vertex (also called 1-graphs in [Cou90]), showing that graph rewriting were powerful on this kind of graph.

In [CM94], it has been proved that we can not decide whether or not a fixed graph is included as a minor in a given graph by means of local computations. This problem remained open for 1-graphs. In this paper we prove that searching a minor can be done by graph rewritings on 1-graphs

* This work has been supported by the EC TMR Network GETGRATS (General theory of Graph Transformation) through the University of Bordeaux.

** Member of the Institut universitaire de France.

(Theorem 1) : given a graph H, there is a graph rewriting system with priority which verifies if H is a minor of G where G is a 1-graph. We describe a system with a finite number of rules and labels depending on H. Rules number is given by a polynomial function of the edges number and the vertices number of H whereas the labels number is given by an exponential function in the number of vertices of H.

Given a positive integer k we define that a rewriting system is in k-normal form if each rule only rewrites a path of length bounded by $k-1$. In this paper we prove that graph rewriting systems with priority can be normalized in k-normal form, for a convenient integer k depending on the original system.

From any graph rewriting system $\mathcal{R}$ we use systems of enumeration so as to obtain a graph rewriting system with priority in k-normal form which has the same behaviour as $\mathcal{R}$ (Theorem 2).

The paper is organized as follows. The first section reviews the definitions related to graph rewriting. In the second part we present systems of enumeration (m-enumeration and enumeration of simple paths). The third part is devoted to the subgraph and minor searchings. Finally, in Section 4, we present the notion of k-normal form and we explain our method for the normalization of graph rewriting system.

1 Graph rewriting

All graphs considered in this paper are finite, undirected and simple (i.e. without multiple edges and self-loops). A graph G denoted $(V(G), E(G))$ is defined by a finite vertex-set and a finite edge-set. An edge with end-points v and v' is denoted $\{v, v'\}$. If v is a vertex of a graph G, the degree of v is denoted $deg_G(v)$ and the neighbourhood of v in G is denoted $N_G(v)$. The subscript G is omitted when there is no ambiguity.

1.1 Labelled graphs

Our work deals with labelled graph over an alphabet usually denoted L. A *labelled graph* over L is a couple (G, λ) where G is a connected graph, and λ is a mapping of $V(G) \cup E(G)$ in L. This function is called the *labelling function* of the graph.

Two labelled graphs are isomorphic if the underlying graphs are isomorphic and if the labellings are preserved.

An injection Θ of $V(G)$ in $V(G')$ is an *occurrence* of (G, λ) in (G', λ') if, for any vertices x and y of $V(G)$:

$$\begin{aligned}&\{x,y\} \in E(G) \implies \{\Theta(x), \Theta(y)\} \in E(G'),\\&\lambda(x) = \lambda'(\Theta(x)),\\&\lambda(\{x,y\}) = \lambda'(\{\Theta(x), \Theta(y)\}).\end{aligned}$$

The graph $(\Theta(G), \lambda')$ having $\Theta(V(G))$ as vertex-set and $\{\{\Theta(x), \Theta(y)\}/\{x,y\} \in E(G)\}$ as edge-set is a subgraph of (G', λ').

If the graph $(\Theta(G), \lambda')$ is an induced subgraph of (G', λ'), Θ is an *induced occurrence* of (G, λ) in (G', λ').

Let Θ be an occurrence of (G, λ) in (H, ν) and Θ' an occurrence of (G', λ') in (H, ν), Θ and Θ' are disjoint if the corresponding subgraph are disjoint, which is denoted $\Theta \cap \Theta' = \emptyset$.

1.2 Graph rewriting system

A rewriting rule r is a couple $\{(G_r, \lambda_r), (G_r, \lambda'_r)\}$ of two connected labelled graphs having the same underlying graph. Formally we define such a rule as a triplet :

Definition 1 A graph rewriting rule r *is a triplet* $(G_r, \lambda_r, \lambda'_r)$ *where* G_r *is a connected graph,* λ_r *the initial labelling function and* λ'_r *the final labelling function.*

A rewriting rule r is applicable to a labelled graph (G, λ) if there exists an occurrence (G_1, l_1) of (G_r, λ_r) in (G, λ). This will be denoted by $(G, \lambda) \xrightarrow[r]{} (G, \lambda')$ with λ' equal to λ except on G_1 where it's equal to λ'_r.

Definition 2 A graph rewriting system $\mathcal{R}$ (GRS for short) is a triplet $\mathcal{R} = (L, I, P)$ where $L = L_v \cup L_e$ is a set of labels, $I = I_v \cup I_e$ is the set of initial labels, ($I_v \subseteq L_v$ and $I_e \subseteq L_e$), and P the set of graph rewriting rules.

If a rule r of a graph rewriting system $\mathcal{R}$ can be applied onto a labelled graph (G, λ), then we write $(G, \lambda) \xrightarrow[\mathcal{R}]{} (G, \lambda')$ where λ' is equal to λ except on the rewritten part of the graph.

Consider a *GRS* $\mathcal{R} = (L, I, P)$, a labelled graph (G, λ_0) where λ_0 is a labelling function over I.

Definition 3 A rewriting sequence of length n, coming from (G, λ_0) by means of $\mathcal{R}$ is defined as the sequence of labelled graphs $(G, \lambda_i)_{0 \leq i \leq n}$ where $\forall i, i < n$, $(G, \lambda_i) \xrightarrow[\mathcal{R}]{} (G, \lambda_{i+1})$.

Our notion of rewriting sequence corresponds to a notion of *sequential* computation. We can define a distributed way of computing by saying that two consecutive relabelling steps concerning non-overlapping occurrencies may be applied in any order. Then they may be applied *concurrently*. Our notion of relabelling sequence may be regarded as a *serialization* [Maz87] of some distributed computation. This model is clearly asynchronous : several relabelling steps may be done at the same time but we do not demand all of them to be done.

Definition 4 Given a rewriting sequence $(G, \lambda_i)_{0 \leq i \leq n}$ and x in $V(G) \cup E(G)$, the history of x linked to the rewriting sequence $(G, \lambda_i)_{0 \leq i \leq n}$ is the word $h_n(x)$ defined by:

$$h_n(x) = \lambda_{i_0}(x)\lambda_{i_1}(x) \cdots \lambda_{i_j}(x).$$

with $i_0 = 0$,
$i_0 < i_1 < \cdots < i_j \leq n$
$\forall k \in \{1, \cdots, n\}$, $k \in \{i_0, \cdots, i_j\}$ *iff x belongs to the rewritten occurrence in the rewriting step* $(G, \lambda_{k-1}) \xrightarrow[\mathcal{R}]{} (G, \lambda_k)$

Given a graph rewriting system $\mathcal{R}$, the reflexive and transitive closure of $\mathcal{R}$ is denoted $\xrightarrow[\mathcal{R}]{*}$.

Definition 5 An irreductible graph with respect to a *GRS* $\mathcal{R}$ *is a labelled graph to which no rule is applicable.*

Given a labelled graph (G, λ) over I, we denote $Irred_{\mathcal{R}}((G, \lambda))$ the set of irreductible graphs coming from (G, λ):
$Irred_{\mathcal{R}}((G, \lambda)) = \{(G, \lambda') \,/\, (G, \lambda) \xrightarrow[\mathcal{R}]{*} (G, \lambda')$ and (G, λ') irreductible with respect to $\mathcal{R}\}$.

Definition 6 A GRS $\mathcal{R} = (L, I, P)$ is called noetherian *if there doesn't exist any infinite rewriting sequence coming from a graph labelled over I.*

A graph rewriting system where the set of rules is given with a partial order is called a *graph rewriting system with priority* (*PGRS* for short).

The partial order defined on the set of rules is denoted $<$, the applicability of the rules of such a system is defined in the following way.

Let $\mathcal{R}$ be a *PGRS*, r a rule of this system, and (G, λ) a labelled graph. The rule r is applicable to an occurrence Θ of (G_r, λ_r) in (G, λ) if there doesn't exist in (G, λ) any occurrence Θ' of $(G_{r'}, \lambda_{r'})$ with $r' > r$ which overlaps Θ.

Example 1 Let us consider the following *PGRS* with two rules.

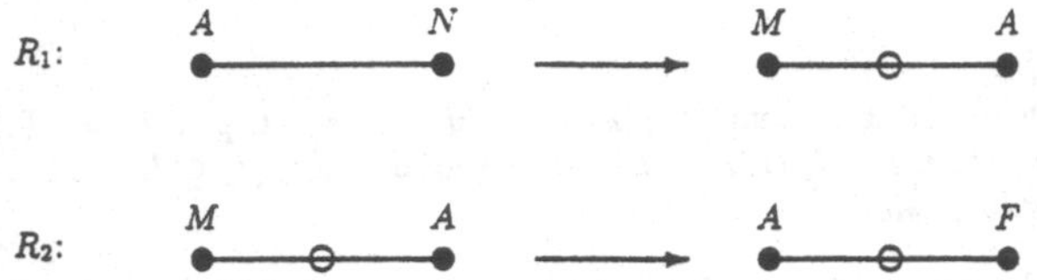

With, $R_1 > R_2$.

The order defined on the set of rules has the following meaning : the rule R_2 is applicable to an occurrence Θ if and only if there is no occurrence for R_1 overlapping Θ.

This system labels vertices and edges in order to form a spanning tree.

A graph rewriting rule with forbidden contexts is a pair $(r, \mathcal{H}_r)$ where r is a rewriting rule $(G_r, \lambda_r, \lambda'_r)$ and $\mathcal{H}_r$ is a finite family of pairs $\{((G_i, \lambda_i), \Theta_i)\}_{i \in I_r}$ with (G_i, λ_i) a labelled graph (called forbidden context) and Θ_i an occurrence of (G_r, λ_r) in (G_i, λ_i). The forbidden contexts of such a rule are used as follows :

Let $(r, \mathcal{H}_r)$ be a graph rewriting rule with fobidden contexts, let Θ be an occurrence of (G_r, λ_r) in a graph (G, λ). The rule $(r, \mathcal{H}_r)$ is applicable to Θ if there doesn't exist, for no i, an occurrence Φ_i of (G_i, λ_i) such that $\Phi_i \Theta_i = \Theta$.

Such rules define *graph rewriting system with forbidden contexts* (*FCGRS* for short).

2 Some enumeration's problems solved by graph rewriting systems

Several graph rewriting systems exist for the computation of a spanning tree on a labelled graph with a distinguished vertex. Such a computation is done thanks to labelling. A set of edges is labelled so that it forms a spanning tree of the graph in which the root is the distinguished vertex. Given such a labelled graph, there exists a graph rewriting system with priority which allows depth-first traversals of the tree. Such a *PGRS* has been introduced in [LMS95].

In this section we recall a well-known *PGRS* for the enumeration of m-tuples of vertices and we introduce a new *PGRS* for the enumeration of simple paths. These graph rewriting systems use a *PGRS* for the computation of a spanning tree which we call $\mathcal{R}_{span}$ and a *PGRS* for the traversal of a tree which we call $\mathcal{R}_{trav}$.

2.1 m-enumeration

In [LMS95], it was proved that enumerating all the m-tuples of vertices of a labelled graph can be done by means of a graph rewriting system. Without going into further details, we recall how this system runs.

We consider labelled graphs with a distinguished vertex. Firstly, $\mathcal{R}_{span}$ is used on such a labelled graph in order to obtain a spanning tree (by labelling). This enumeration uses m traversals of the spanning tree in order to obtain a m-tuple $(x_1, x_2, \cdots, x_m)$. Then, given a m-tuple $(x_1, x_2, \cdots, x_m)$, a new traversal is started so as to obtain a new m-tuple $(x_1, x_2, \cdots, y)$ with $y \neq x_m$. This process is repeated until we can't find any vertex y for this last position. Then we start new traversals by changing the two last vertices of the m-tuple, and so on until there is no vertex to be the first vertex of a m-tuple.

Thus this graph rewriting system is based on the system $\mathcal{R}_{trav}$. The labels of the enumeration system are made up of three components :

- a label issued from the traversal system.
- a label of the set $\{Search, Return, Reset, Stop\}$ with the following meaning :
  - **Search** : a vertex is searched.
  - **Return** : a vertex has been found.
  - **Reset** : the current m-tuple is modified.
  - **Stop** : the enumeration is done.
- a m-tuple of labels such that the label in position i gives an information about the position of the vertex in the current m-tuple. There are three different values :
  - **0** : the vertex is not the ith vertex of the current m-tuple.
  - **1** : the vertex is the ith vertex of the current m-tuple.
  - $\overline{1}$: the vertex was the ith vertex of all the m-tuple having the same first $i-1^{th}$ components.

The system has a finite number of rules ($\#rules_{enum} = O(m)$) and a finite number of labels ($\#labels_{enum} = O(m * 2^m)$).

2.2 Enumeration of simple paths

In a connected labelled graph, we consider the simple paths coming from a source vertex to a target vertex. Our aim is to enumerate all these simple paths by means of graph rewritings. To this end, we encode a graph rewriting system which labels these paths one by one. Each path is encoded by labels on its vertices and edges. We consider that the source vertex is labelled *Search* and the target vertex is labelled *Ending*.

Description

We work on a connected labelled graph G. We denote by I the *Search*-labelled vertex of G. We denote by J the *Ending*-labelled vertex. At the beginning, no edge is labelled.

We start on I. We mark a simple path from I to J, by labelling the edges and the vertices used in the path (the labels are E_{IJ} and V_{IJ}). When we have a path, backtracking is used in order to change the last edge and to look for a new path. So we keep the same prefix of the path, we just change the last edge. We go on until we have tried all the possibilities from the vertex I.

Let us now describe a graph rewriting system encoding this algorithm.

Let $Y \in \{Ending, \epsilon\}$ where ϵ design the empty word that is to say "no label".

Graph rewriting system with priority $\mathcal{R}_{enum,\mathcal{P}}(I, J)$ ▼

The first rule allows the traversal to go on. We label the vertex and the edge which we put in the path we are building.

R_{E1}:

(1)

If we reach the Ending-labelled vertex, then we have found a simple path coming from I :

R_{E2}:

(1)

As we have a simple path, we use the backtracking in order to search another path. We label this edge with $\overline{E}_{IJ}$ so that we won't use it in a new path with the same prefix.

R_{E3}:

(1)

If there are no unlabelled edges incident to the Search-labelled vertex, then there are no paths with this prefix anymore. We have to change this prefix :

$$R_{E4}: \qquad \overset{Search}{\bullet} \qquad \longrightarrow \qquad \overset{Clean}{\bullet} \qquad (0)$$

We erase the labels $\overline{E}_{IJ}$ from the edges incident to the Clean-labelled vertex :

$$R_{E5}: \qquad \overset{Clean}{\bullet} \underset{\overline{E}_{IJ}}{\relbar\joinrel\relbar} \overset{Y}{\bullet} \qquad \longrightarrow \qquad \overset{Clean}{\bullet} \relbar\joinrel\relbar \overset{Y}{\bullet} \qquad (2)$$

When the cleaning mode is done, we start a backtrack :

$$R_{E6}: \qquad \overset{Clean}{\bullet} \qquad \longrightarrow \qquad \overset{Back}{\bullet} \qquad (1)$$

We go back from the vertex labelled Back (the edge labelled E_{IJ} and incident to the Back-labelled vertex changes its label). Then we start a new search of path :

$$R_{E7}: \qquad \overset{V_{IJ}}{\bullet} \underset{E_{IJ}}{\relbar\joinrel\relbar} \overset{Back}{\bullet} \qquad \longrightarrow \qquad \overset{Search}{\bullet} \underset{\overline{E_{IJ}}}{\relbar\joinrel\relbar} \bullet \qquad (1)$$

When we can no longer backtrack, the enumeration is done.

$$R_{E8}: \qquad \overset{Back}{\bullet} \qquad \longrightarrow \qquad \overset{End}{\bullet} \qquad (0)$$

Invariants and properties

Let G be a connected graph. The initial labelling function of G λ_0 is defined by :

$$\lambda_0(I) = Search$$
$$\lambda_0(J) = Ending$$
$$\forall x \in V(G) \cup E(G) \setminus \{I_0\} \cup \{J\}, \ \lambda_0(x) = \epsilon.$$

Let L be the set of labels :

$$L = \{Search, Found, Ending, Clean, Back, End\}.$$

We say that L is the set of active labels.
Let A be the set of labels of the whole system :

$$A = \{\epsilon, V_{IJ}, E_{IJ}, \overline{E}_{IJ}\} \cup L.$$

From now on we consider a connected graph G with an initial labelling function λ_0 (as we defined it before). We consider a rewriting sequence $(G_i)_{i \geq 0}$[1] obtained by the application of $\mathcal{R}_{enum,\mathcal{P}}$ on (G, λ_0).

In order to prove the ending and the validity of our system, we give some properties of $\mathcal{R}_{enum,\mathcal{P}}$.
The easy proofs of the four following invariants will be omitted.

---

[1] G_i stands for (G, λ_i).

Invariant 1 $\forall i \geq 0$, *there exists only one vertex* x *in* G_i *such that* $\lambda_i(x) \in L \setminus \{Ending\}$.

We denote this vertex x_L.

Each unlabelled edge can not receive E_{IJ} as a label if its end-points are labelled V_{IJ} (R_{E1}).

Invariant 2 $\forall i \geq 0$, *the set of edges labelled* E_{IJ} *in* G_i *forms a simple path from* I *to* x_L.

We denote this simple path $C_i(x_L)$.

Invariant 3 $\forall i \geq 0$, *any vertex* x *labelled* V_{IJ} *by* λ_i *is on the path* $C_i(x_L)$.

Invariant 4 $\forall i \geq 0$, *let* a *be an edge of* G *such that* $\lambda_i(a) = \overline{E}_{IJ}$. *The edge* a *is incident to only one vertex of* $C_i(x_L)$.

We denote this vertex by $\overline{x}_a$ and we denote by $\overline{C}_i(a)$ the prefix of $C_i(x_L)$ from I to $\overline{x}_a$.

Let P be a simple path, e be an edge incident to an end-point of P, $(P.e)$ denotes the path obtained by extending P by the edge e.

Invariant 5 *Let* $i \geq 0$, *let* a *be an edge of* G *with* $\lambda_i(a) = \overline{E}_{IJ}$. $\forall k \geq i$, *one of the following propositions is true :*

(i) $\lambda_k(a) = \overline{E}_{IJ}$;
(ii) $\lambda_k(a) \neq \overline{E}_{IJ}$, *and there is a vertex* x *of* $\overline{C}_i(a)$ *such that* $\lambda_k(x) \in \{Clean, Back, End\}$;
(iii) $\lambda_k(a) \neq \overline{E}_{IJ}$, $\overline{C}_i(a)$ *is no longer a prefix of* $C_k(x_L)$ *and there is an edge* b *of* G *such that* $\lambda_k(b) = \overline{E}_{IJ}$ *and such that* $(\overline{C}_k(b).b)$ *is a prefix of* $\overline{C}_i(a)$.

Proof Proof is rather technical and not detailed there. We use an induction on k, starting with $k = i$. □

Consider a vertex x, labelled *Search* after i steps of rewriting, then the vertices, which are labelled V_{IJ}, are not concerned by the rewritings until x is not labelled *Back*. The history of x, $h_i(x)$, concerning the sequence of rewriting of length i, is the prefix of all the histories of x concerning any sequence of length j, for $j > i$. We denote $h_j(x) = h_i(x)m_{i,j}(x)$, and we state that :

Property 1 *Let* $x \in V(G)$ *and* $i \geq 0$ *such that* $h_i(x)$ *is ending by Search. For any vertex* x' *of* $V(G)$ *which has a history* $h_i(x')$ *ending by* V_{IJ}, *and for all* j, $j > i$, *such that* $m_{i,j}(x)$ *doesn't contain Back, the vertex* x' *keeps the same history :* $h_j(x') = h_i(x')$.

We denote by $S(G_i, x)$ the subgraph of G_i induced by the vertices labelled ϵ or *Ending* which are connected to x by simple paths made of unlabelled edges. This connected subgraph contains x.

Lemma 1 *For any vertex* x *of* G, *for any positive integer* i *such that* $\lambda_i(x) = Search$, *there is* j, $j > i$, *such that the three following propositions are true :*

i) $\lambda_j(x) = Clean$ *and* $m_{i,j}(x)$ *doesn't contain Back.*
ii) *The subgraphs* $S(G_i, x)$ *and* $S(G_j, x)$ *are isomorphic.*
iii) *The rewriting sequence from* G_i *to* G_j *allowed to enumerate all the simple paths of* $S(G_j, x)$ *starting at* x *and finishing on the vertex labelled Ending if this vertex is in the subgraph.*

Proof By induction on the number of edges of G. □

Proposition 1 *The graph rewriting system* $\mathcal{R}_{enum,\mathcal{P}}$ *is noetherian for any connected graph* G *given with an initial labelling function* λ_0 *as it has been previously defined.*

Proof Consider a connected graph G, with an initial labelling function λ_0 such that :

$$\exists x \in V(G), \lambda_0(x) = Search.$$

Lemma 1 is applicable to G with x and the initial labelling : $\exists j > 0$ such that $\lambda_j(x) = Clean$, $m_{0,j}(x)$ doesn't contain *Back*, and such that the subgraphs $S(G_0, x)$ and $S(G_j, x)$ are equal. On G_j, we can apply the rule R_{E6}, R_{E7} and then R_{E8}, and we have after these two steps of rewriting : $\lambda_{j+2}(x) = End$, and $\forall y \in (V(G) \setminus \{x\}) \cup E(G), \lambda_{j+2}(y) = \epsilon$. Eventually, no more rules are applicable to G_{j+2}. □

Proposition 2 *On any connected graph G given with an initial labelling function λ_0 such that one vertex is Search-labelled and another one is Ending-labelled, the system $\mathcal{R}_{enum,\mathcal{P}}$ enumerates all the simple paths having these two singular vertices as end-points.*

Proof The proof directly comes from the Lemma 1 applied to the graph G with the labelling function λ_0. □

Our system $\mathcal{R}_{enum,\mathcal{P}}$ has a constant number of rules and a constant number of labels.

3 Subgraph and minor searching

In the previous section we introduced two systems encoding two different kinds of enumeration. Our purpose is now to present a first application of these two systems :

The m-enumeration is used so as to verify if a connected labelled graph contains a connected labelled graph H as a subgraph.

The enumeration of simple paths is used in order to verify if a connected labelled graph contains a connected labelled graph H as a minor.

3.1 Subgraph searching

We consider a connected labelled graph H with m vertices. We know that we are able to enumerate all the m-tuples of vertices of any graph G with an appropriate labelling function, thanks to a graph rewriting system with priority. Given a m-tuple of vertices of G, it's rather easy to associate each vertex to a vertex of H. Thus, we just have to check if this mapping is a good one.

Our graph rewriting system works into two parts of computation :

First part It consists in enumerating all the m-tuples of vertices of G. So, we use the *PGRS* defined in [LMS95] $\mathcal{R}_{enum}$. When a m-tuple is found (we use a label $Found_m$ when we find the last vertex of the m-tuple), the second part has to start. If we can't find H as subgraph thanks to this m-tuple, then we have to change it i.e. to resume the m-enumeration. If the end of the m-enumeration is reached, then H isn't a subgraph of G.

Second part It consists in checking that the mapping of the vertex-set $V(H)$ into the m-tuple of G is an isomorphism between H and a subgraph of G having the m-tuple as vertex-set. Let us describe how we solve this problem by means of a graph rewriting system $\mathcal{R}_{const}$.
First, we use a graph traversal to label the jth vertex of the m-tuple with the degree of the jth vertex of H. Then, using another graph traversal, we just have to check if for any edge $\{i, j\}$ in H there is in G an edge linking the jth and ith vertices of the m-tuple. Then we use another graph traversal in order to verify if every edges have been found (partial subgraph) and if there isn't any other edge between vertices of the m-tuple (induced subgraph). Thus at the end of such a traversal, either the last vertex of the m-tuple is labelled *Fail* or the root of the spanning tree is labelled *Win*. In the first case, the m-enumeration has to resume. In the second case, the rewriting has to be stopped.

These parts are realized by means of graph rewriting systems with priority. Our general system, called $\mathcal{R}_{subgraph}$, is the result of the composition of $\mathcal{R}_{enum}$ [LMS95] (with a weak modification), and $\mathcal{R}_{const}$ introduced and proved in [Bot97].

For the sake of brevity we shan't give this system in details. For such a composition we use couples of labels. The first component concerns the m-enumeration. The second component concerns the subgraph's checking. We consider that such a system works on a labelled graph with a distinguished vertex (with a labelling function issued from $\mathcal{R}_{span}$).

In order to prove the termination and the validity of $\mathcal{R}_{subgraph}$, we use the fact that each part is noetherian and valid. Moreover the rules used in this system are very simple (the left-hand-side are isomorphic to a single vertex or a single edge). Therefore we state that :

Proposition 3 *Given a connected labelled graph H, the graph rewriting system with priority $\mathcal{R}_{subgraph}$ allows to check on any connected labelled graph with a distinguished vertex if H is one of its subgraph (partial or induced).*

Our graph rewriting system $\mathcal{R}_{subgraph}$ has a finite number of rules depending of the number of rules of $\mathcal{R}_{enum}$ and linearly depending on m^2 where m is the vertices number of H : $\#rules_{subgraph} = O(m^2)$. The number of labels depends (linearly) on $\#labels_{enum}$ and m : $\#labels_{subgraph} = \#labels_{enum} = O(m * 2^m)$.

3.2 Minor searching

Thanks to the notion of model defined in [RS95], we are able to prove the following equivalence :

Lemma 2 *Given two connected graphs H and G, the following statements are equivalent :*

- *H is a minor of G ;*
- *There exists a model Φ from H onto G defined by :*
  - *for any edge e of H, $\Phi(e)$ is an edge of G;*
  - *for any vertex u of H, $\Phi(u)$ is a connected partial subgraph of G (non empty).*

  The model Φ has the following properties :

  1) *for any u and v of $V(H)$, the intersection of $\Phi(u)$ by $\Phi(v)$ is empty;*
  2) *for any $e \in E(H)$, for any $u \in V(H)$, the edge $\Phi(e)$ doesn't belong to the partial subgraph $\Phi(u)$;*
  3) *Let $e = \{u, v\}$ be an edge of H, then $\Phi(e)$ has an end-point in $V(\Phi(u))$ and the other in $V(\Phi(v))$.*
- *There exists an injection γ from $V(H)$ to $V(G)$ such that for any edge $\{u, v\}$ of H, there is a simple path in G between $\gamma(u)$ and $\gamma(v)$, denoted $P(\gamma(u), \gamma(v))$. Moreover these paths are said to be valid i.e. they verify the following properties :*
  1) *For any edges $\{a, b\}$ and $\{c, d\}$ of H, with disjoint end-points, the paths $P(\gamma(a), \gamma(b))$ and $P(\gamma(c), \gamma(d))$ are vertex-disjoint.*
  2) *For any edge $\{a, b\} \in E(H)$, the path $P(\gamma(a), \gamma(b))$ has at least one edge that is disjoint from any other path $P(\gamma(c), \gamma(d))$ for $\{c, d\} \in E(H)$. Such kind of edge is called own edge.*

We present a graph rewriting system based on the fact that a minor of graph can be defined thanks to particular simple paths. Such simple paths (as defined in our lemma 2) will now be called *valid simple paths.*

Explanations The connected labelled graph H is known. We assume that we perfectly know its vertex-set $\mathcal{V}$ and its edge-set $\mathcal{E}$. Let m be the number of vertices of H. We assume that $\mathcal{V} = \{1, 2, 3, \cdots, m\}$. The edges are denoted $\{i, j\}$ with $i < j$. Thus an order is defined on $\mathcal{E}$: $\{i, j\} < \{l, k\}$ iff $(i, j) <_2 (l, k)$ (i.e $i < l$ or $i = l$ and $j < k$). We denote by $succ(i, j)$ the successor of $\{i, j\}$ and $pred(i, j)$ the predecessor of $\{i, j\}$ according to $<$. We consider that $succ(i, j) = \{i, j\}$ if it is the greatest edge in $\mathcal{E}$ (denoted $max(i, j)$), $pred(i, j) = \{i, j\}$ if it is the smallest one (denoted $min(i, j)$).

The whole system consists of a part of m-enumeration and a part of research of valid paths linking vertices of the m-tuple. We explain the algorithm we used for the second part.

The computation starts on a graph G with a m-tuple $(x_1, x_2, \cdots, x_m)$. For any edge $\{i,j\}$ of H, we mark in G a valid simple path between the vertices x_i and x_j (starting with the smallest edge). The construction of valid paths is made with the enumeration of simple paths (with a checking of validity) and also backtracking. At the end of this computation, we have two possibilities. If we have found all the valid simple paths, then H is a minor of G. If we haven't succeeded with the current m-tuple, then it means that we have to change the m-tuple i.e. to resume the m-enumeration. If the m-enumeration is done, then H isn't minor of G.

Valid paths We are able to mark simple paths thanks to the system $\mathcal{R}_{enum,\mathcal{P}}$. In order to mark a simple path concerning the jth and ith vertices of the m-tuple, we use this previous system with parameter (I, J). We have to check that :

- For any couple of vertices (L, K) disjoint from (I, J), any vertex labelled V_{LK} mustn't be labelled V_{IJ} by $\mathcal{R}_{enum,\mathcal{P}}(I, J)$. It must be the same for the edges.
- Given a path from I to J, there is at least one edge uniquely labelled with E_{IJ}.

The first condition is easy to realize, we just have to change the two first rules to prevent the labelling. The second one is done by means of a traversal of the simple path in order to check that this path contains at least one own edge, and that all the other valid paths are still valid.

The new graph rewriting system obtained is denoted $\mathcal{R}_{EV}(i,j)$ for the edge $\{i,j\}$. Such a system is made up of traversals based on a spanning tree.

Sum up The graph rewriting system $\mathcal{R}_{minor}$ consists of the following systems with the following priorities :

$$\mathcal{R}_{enum} > \mathcal{R}_{init} > \mathcal{R}_{EV}(i,j)_{min} > \cdots > \mathcal{R}_{EV}(i,j)_{max}.$$

With,

- $\mathcal{R}_{enum}$, enumeration of m-tuples in G ;
- $\mathcal{R}_{init}$, beginning of the second part ;
- $\mathcal{R}_{EV}(i,j)$, system of enumeration of valid simple path between the vertices i and j in the current m-tuple. These system are made by the system of enumeration of simple paths, a part for the checking of validity, and optionally a part for acknowledgment sending (for $\{i,j\}$ different from the minimal edge) and cleaning (if $\{i,j\}$ is the minimal edge).

We show on the following example how we use acknowledgment in order to compute valid simple paths according to the order $<$.

Example 2 Consider the following graphs H and G. The graph H has three vertices and three edges : $\{1,2\} < \{1,3\} < \{2,3\}$. The graph G has a distinguished vertex called v, which is the root of a spanning tree (denoted $T(G)$) computed by a graph rewriting system.

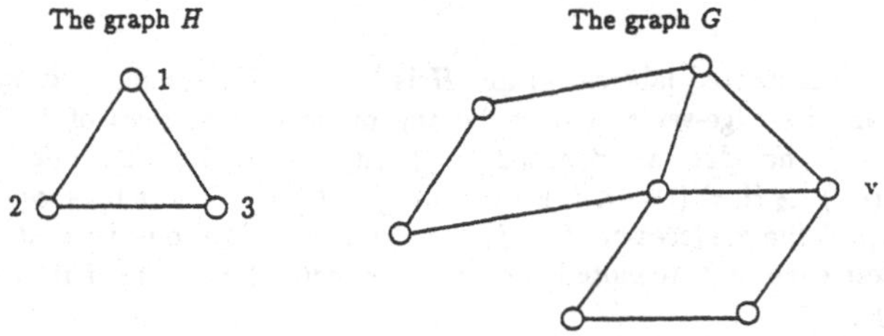

Given a 3-tuple of vertices labelled on G, we start the construction of valid simple paths for the three edges of H. Firstly, a traversal of the spanning tree is used to label the vertex 1 and 2 by the list of *Search* labels.

This part is done by the rules of the system $\mathcal{R}_{init}$.

The spanning tree $T(G)$ rooted in v.

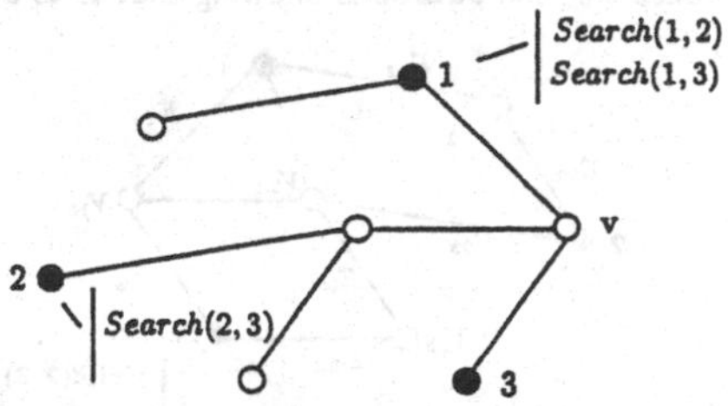

The smallest edge of H related to < is the edge $\{1, 2\}$. Computations start now by the labelling of a valid simple path for this edge, thanks to a system $\mathcal{R}_{EV}(1, 2)$. As this is the smallest edge, we haven't to wait for an acknowledgment.

The following picture shows a computation leading to a valid path : the vertex 2 receives a label of success $Valid(1, 2)$.

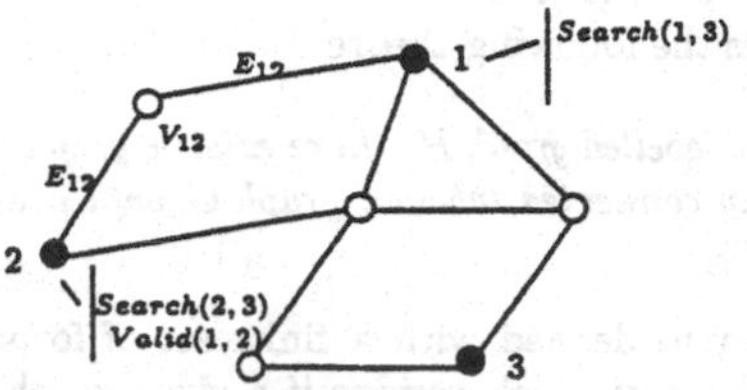

As a valid path has been found, an acknowledgment is sent to the vertex 1, smallest end-point of the next edge. A traversal of the spanning tree is used.

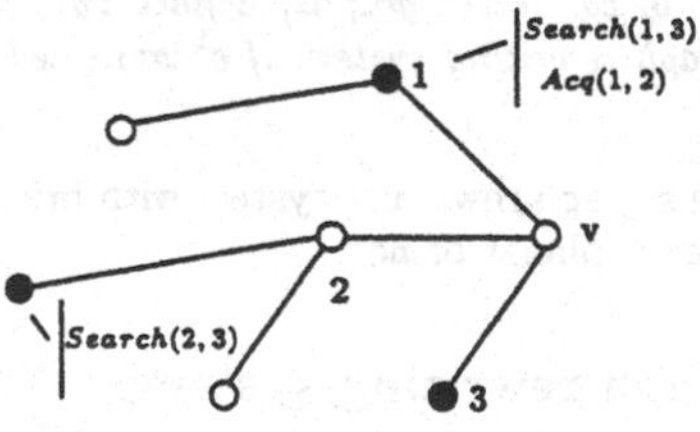

The vertex 1 has got labels $Search(1, 3)$ and $Acq(1, 2)$: rules of $\mathcal{R}_{EV}(1, 3)$ are thus applicable and the enumeration of valid simple paths for this couple of vertices can start.

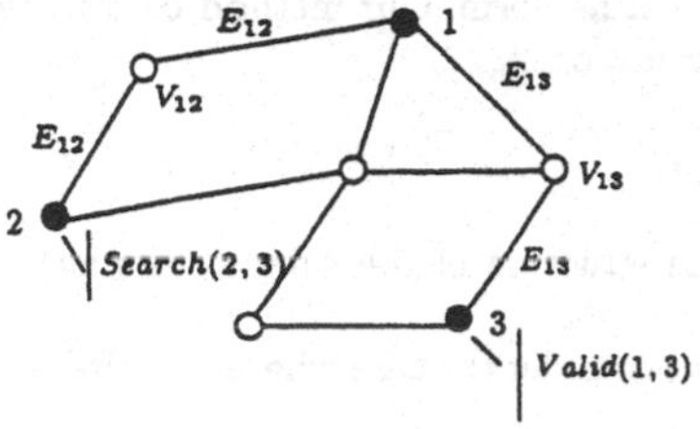

In this example, a valid simple path has been found for the couple $(1,3)$. Thus, an acknowledgment is sent to the vertex 2 (smallest end-point of the next edge). This is done by a traversal. The rules of $\mathcal{R}_{EV}(2,3)$ become applicable to the graph because of this acknowledgment. If a valid simple path is found for this couple, then the computation stops (i.e. no more rules are applicable) : H is a minor of G. In the case where no valid simple path exists, the enumeration of valid simple path is resumed for the previous couple $(1,3)$, and so on.

The last picture gives us successful computations showing that H is a minor of G.

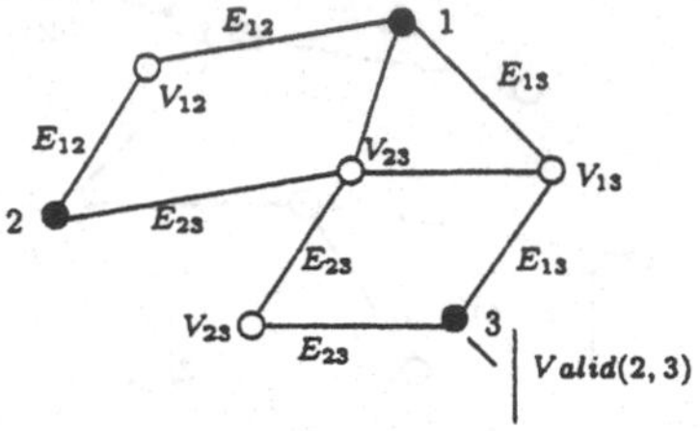

Details about this graph rewriting system can be found in [Bot97]. We recall that h denotes the number of edges of H. The number of rules of $\mathcal{R}_{minor}$ is a linear function of $\#rules_{enum}$, m and h^2 : $\#rules_{minor} = O(h^2 + m)$. The number of labels is a linear function of $\#labels_{enum}$, h and h^2 : $\#labels_{minor} = O(m * 2^m + h^2)$.

The system $\mathcal{R}_{minor}$ satisfies the following theorem :

Theorem 1 *Given a connected labelled graph H, there exists a graph rewriting system with priority which allows to check onto any connected labelled graph G with a distinguished vertex if H is a minor of G.*

Thus, given a family of graphs defined with a finite set of forbidden minors, there exists a graph rewriting system with priority which verifies if a given graph with a distinguished vertex belongs to the family. The forbidden minors must be known. We just have to compose a set of systems $\mathcal{R}_{minor}$ corresponding to the forbidden minors.

Corollary 1 *Let $\mathcal{F}$ be a family of connected graphs, defined by a finite set of forbidden minors. We can check by means of a graph rewriting system if a connected graph G with a distinguished vertex belongs to $\mathcal{F}$.*

Therefore we are able to give a graph rewriting system with priority which verifies if a labelled graph with a distinguished vertex is planar or not.

4 Normal forms for graph rewriting systems

In this part we introduce different kinds of normal forms for graph rewritings and more particularly the k-normal form of graph rewriting. Then we prove that for any graph rewriting system there exists a *PGRS* in k-normal form equivalent to the original system : any *GRS* can be normalized according to the k-normal form. Our method consists in building the *PGRS* in k-normal form using systems of enumeration.

4.1 Definitions

We are interested in the structure of the subgraphs which are rewritten by the rules of our systems.

As a first normal form we consider the case where the left-hand sides of the rules are isomorphic to a vertex or an edge :

***Definition 7** A graph rewriting system has a* 2-normal form *if each rule rewrites one vertex or one edge and the two incident vertices.*

Most of our graph rewriting systems are in 2-normal form. The computation of a spanning tree, the traversal of a tree, and of course the subgraph searching can be done thanks to graph rewriting systems in 2-normal form.

We can also consider that the left-hand sides are equal to simple paths of bounded length.

***Definition 8** A graph rewriting system has a* k-normal form *if each rule rewrites a simple path of length bounded by* $k-1$.

4.2 Simulation of a *FCGRS* by a *PGRS* in k-normal form

We want to prove that any *GRS* without normal form can be simulated by a *GRS* in 2-normal or k-normal form. To this end, we use the method introduced in [LMS95] to simulate any *FCGRS* by a *PGRS*. In a first part we recall this method, and then we provide our application.

Method for the simulation of a *FCGRS* by a *PGRS*

This method is made up of three steps.

I The first part concerns the partition of the initial graph into subgraphs of k-bounded diameter where k is the maximal diameter of the graphs in the rules of the *FCGRS*. This part is called the k-election. The k-election problem (introduced in [LMS95]) can be explained as follows. Each vertex of the graph stands for a *town*. We want to organize the graph by delimiting *countries*, each country having one *capital*. In each country the distance between town and the capital must at most be k. Moreover, the distance between two different capitals in the graph must be at least $k+1$. This part is done by a *PGRS* in $(2k+1)$-normal form.

II The second part consists in supervising the activity of the capitals. If a capital is active, it means that we can simulate on its country the application of a rule of the system. This part is done by a *PGRS* in $k+1$-normal form.

III The third part consists in simulating the application of the rules on a country having an active capital. This part is called the **local simulation**. We have to adapt this local simulation to our problem.

Application to the k-normal form

We are able to realize a local simulation by a *PGRS* in 2-normal form.
We consider we are working on a country with an active capital.

1. Using a tree traversal, towns are activated one by one ($\mathcal{R}_{trav}$).
2. Given an active town, we construct a spanning tree of the ball of center the active town and of radius k ($\mathcal{R}_{span}(k)$ with orientation from the root to the leaves).
3. For each rule r with forbidden context, we make a system $\mathcal{R}_r$ so as to test the applicability of r on the ball of radius k. We now explain this part of the simulation :
   (a) We look for a subgraph isomorphic to (G_r, λ_r) in the ball of center this town and of radius k. We can do that by means of $\mathcal{R}_{subgraph}$. Then in G, some vertices have label $(1_i, x)$ and some edges have label (p, x) where x is a symbol holding for the label issued from λ_r. These vertices and edges form a subgraph isomorphic to (G_r, λ_r). The values of i are in $\{1, \cdots, |V(G_r)|\}$.
   (b) Then, given an occurrence of (G_r, λ_r), we search all the forbidden contexts using one *PGRS* $\mathcal{R}_{subgraph}$ by context.
   (c) If we find such a forbidden context, then we resume the searching of another occurrence.

(d) If there aren't any forbidden contexts, then we have to apply the rule r by changing the labels of the edges and then of the vertices. In this way we will realize a rewriting in 2-normal form. Let us now introduce the system $\mathcal{R}_{norme}$ in 2-normal form. We consider we are working on a connected graph having a labelled spanning tree (one vertex is labelled *Edge*, the others N_0). Some vertices and edges have labels coming from λ_r (as explained before). A first traversal is done in order to change the label for the edges (p, x), a second traversal deals with the vertices. The symbol x' means the label issued from λ'_r.

─────────────────── *System* $\mathcal{R}_{norme}$ ─────────────────── ▼

We walk on a branch of the tree (by using edges of the tree).

$$R_1: \qquad \overset{Edge}{\bullet}\!\!-\!\!-\!\!\overset{N_0}{\circ}\!\!-\!\!-\!\!\bullet \qquad \longrightarrow \qquad \overset{W}{\bullet}\!\!-\!\!-\!\!\circ\!\!-\!\!-\!\!\overset{Edge}{\bullet} \qquad (3)$$

If we meet a vertex labelled 1_l, then we change the labels of all the edges incident to this vertex. Edges could be edges of the spanning tree, we don't specify it in our rule.

$$k > l, \; R_2(l, k): \qquad \underset{1_l \quad\; p,x \;\quad 1_k}{\overset{Edge \qquad\quad X}{\bullet\!\!-\!\!-\!\!\bullet}} \qquad \longrightarrow \qquad \underset{1_l \quad\; p,x' \;\quad 1_k}{\overset{Edge \qquad\quad X}{\bullet\!\!-\!\!-\!\!\bullet}} \qquad (2)$$

When we reach a leaf or when there is nothing else to do, then we come back in the tree.

$$R_3: \qquad \overset{W \qquad Edge}{\bullet\!\!-\!\!\circ\!\!-\!\!\bullet} \qquad \longrightarrow \qquad \overset{Edge \qquad N_1}{\bullet\!\!-\!\!\circ\!\!-\!\!\bullet} \qquad (1)$$

When we are on the root of the tree, then we start a new traversal in order to rewrite the vertices.

$$R_4: \qquad \overset{Edge}{\bullet} \qquad \longrightarrow \qquad \overset{Vertex}{\bullet} \qquad (0)$$

We advance on a branch of the tree.

$$R_5: \qquad \overset{Vertex \qquad N_1}{\bullet\!\!-\!\!\circ\!\!-\!\!\bullet} \qquad \longrightarrow \qquad \overset{W \qquad Vertex}{\bullet\!\!-\!\!\circ\!\!-\!\!\bullet} \qquad (3)$$

When we reach a vertex which is an image of a vertex of $V(G_r)$, then we change its label.

$$R_6: \qquad \underset{1_i, x}{\overset{Vertex}{\bullet}} \qquad \longrightarrow \qquad \underset{1_i, x'}{\overset{Vertex}{\bullet}} \qquad (2)$$

The traversal goes on by going back to the root.

$$R_7: \qquad \overset{W \qquad Vertex}{\bullet\!\!-\!\!\circ\!\!-\!\!\bullet} \qquad \longrightarrow \qquad \overset{Vertex \qquad N_0}{\bullet\!\!-\!\!\circ\!\!-\!\!\bullet} \qquad (1)$$

When we reach the root, then the computation is done.

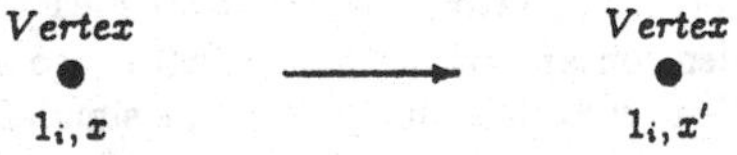

R_4:

(0)

This graph rewriting system comes from the traversal of a tree. A system for tree traversals has been proved to be noetherian and valid in [LMS95]. Thus our system is noetherian and valid because we are sure to reach all the vertices and the edges we have to rewrite.

For our simulation we use graph rewriting systems in $k+1$-normal form and systems in 2-normal form. The k-election problem and the computation of a spanning tree of a ball of radius k are realized by graph rewriting systems in $k+1$-normal form (in respect of our notation).

Proposition 4 *Any graph rewriting system with forbidden context can be simulated by a graph rewriting system with priority which is in $k+1$-normal form.*

Moreover any graph rewriting system with priority can be moved into a graph rewriting system with forbidden context as it is explained in [LMS95]. Thus,

Theorem 2 *Any graph rewriting system (with priority or forbidden context) can be normalized into a graph rewriting system with priority in k-normal form with a convenient integer k.*

References

[Ang80] D. Angluin. Local and global properties in networks of processors. In 12th *STOC*, pages 82–93, 1980.

[BM96] A. Bottreau and Y. Métivier. Kronecker product and local computation in graphs. In *CAAP'96*, volume 1059 of *Lect. Notes in Comp. Sci.*, pages 2–16, 1996.

[Bot97] A. Bottreau. *Réécritures de graphe et calculs distribués*. PhD thesis, Université Bordeaux I, LaBRI, juin 1997.

[CM94] B. Courcelle and Y. Métivier. Coverings and minors : Application to local computations in graphs. *Europ. J. Combinatorics*, 15:127–138, 1994.

[Cou90] B. Courcelle. The monadic second order logic of graphs i. recognizable sets of finite graphs. *Inform. and Comput.*, 85:12–75, 1990.

[LM92] I. Litovsky and Y. Métivier. Computing trees with graph rewriting systems with priorities. *Tree Automata and Languages*, pages 115–139, 1992.

[LM93] I. Litovsky and Y. Métivier. Computing with graph rewriting systems with priorities. *Theoretical Computer Science*, 115:191–224, 1993.

[LMS95] I. Litovský, Y. Métivier, and E. Sopena. Different local controls for graph relabelling systems. *Mathematical Systems Theory*, 28:41–65, 1995.

[LMZ95] I. Litovsky, Y. Métivier, and W. Zielonka. On the recognition of families of graphs with local computations. *Information and computation*, 115(1):110–119, 1995.

[Maz87] A. Mazurkiewicz. *Petri nets, applications and relationship to other models of concurrency*, volume 255, chapter Trace Theory, pages 279–324. W. Brauer et al., 1987.

[RFH72] P. Rosensthiel, J.R. Fiksel, and A. Holliger. Intelligent graphs : networks of finite automata capable of solving graph problems. In *Graph Theory and Computing*, pages 219–265. Academic Press, 1972.

[RS95] N. Robertson and P.D. Seymour. Graph minors xiii. the disjoint paths problem. *Journal of combinatorial theory, Series B*, 63:65–110, 1995.

[YK96a] M. Yamashita and T. Kameda. Computing on anonymous networks: Part i - characterizing the solvable cases. *IEEE Transactions on parallel and distributed systems*, 7(1):69–89, 1996.

[YK96b] M. Yamashita and T. Kameda. Computing on anonymous networks: Part ii - decision and membership problems. *IEEE Transactions on parallel and distributed systems*, 7(1):90–96, 1996.

Partial Metrics and Co-continuous Valuations*

Michael A. Bukatin[1] and Svetlana Yu. Shorina[2]

[1] Department of Computer Science, Brandeis University, Waltham, MA 02254, USA; **bukatin@cs.brandeis.edu**; *http://www.cs.brandeis.edu/~bukatin/papers.html*
[2] Faculty of Mechanics and Mathematics, Moscow State University, Moscow, Russia; **sveta@cpm.ru**

Abstract. The existence of deep connections between partial metrics and valuations is well known in domain theory. However, the treatment of non-algebraic continuous Scott domains has been not quite satisfactory so far.

In this paper we return to the continuous normalized valuations μ on the systems of open sets and introduce notions of *co-continuity* ($\{U_i, i \in I\}$ is a filtered system of open sets $\Rightarrow \mu(\mathrm{Int}(\bigcap_{i\in I} U_i)) = \inf_{i\in I} \mu(U_i)$) and *strong non-degeneracy* ($U \subset V$ are open sets $\Rightarrow \mu(U) < \mu(V)$) for such valuations. We call the resulting class of valuations CC-valuations. The first central result of this paper is a construction of CC-valuations for Scott topologies on all continuous dcpo's with countable bases. This is a surprising result because neither co-continuous, nor strongly non-degenerate valuations are usually possible for ordinary Hausdorff topologies.

Another central result is a new construction of partial metrics. Given a continuous Scott domain A and a CC-valuation μ on the system of Scott open subsets of A, we construct a continuous partial metric on A yielding the Scott topology as $u(x, y) = \mu(A \setminus (C_x \cap C_y)) - \mu(I_x \cap I_y)$, where $C_x = \{y \in A \mid y \sqsubseteq x\}$ and $I_x = \{y \in A \mid \{x, y\}$ is unbounded$\}$. This construction covers important cases based on the real line and allows to obtain an induced metric on $Total(A)$ without the unpleasant restrictions known from earlier work.

1 Introduction

Recently the theory of *partial metrics* introduced by Matthews [14] undergoes active development and is used in various applications from computational description of metric spaces [9] to the analysis of parallel computation [13]. The relationship between partial metrics and *valuations* was first noticed by O'Neill in [15].

In [3] Bukatin and Scott generalized this relationship by considering valuations on powersets of bases, instead of valuations on the domains themselves, as in [15]. They also explained the computational intuition of partial metrics by generalizing them to *relaxed metrics*, which take values in the *interval numbers*.

* Supported by **Applied Continuity in Computations Project**.

Partial metrics can be considered as taking values in the *upper bounds* of those interval numbers. However it is often desirable to remove the most restrictive axioms of partial metrics, like *small self-distances*, $u(x,x) \leq u(x,y)$, and strong *Vickers-Matthews triangle inequality*, $u(x,z) \leq u(x,y)+u(y,z)-u(y,y)$. Thus [3] only requires symmetry and the ordinary triangle inequality for the upper bounds of relaxed metrics.

However, it can be shown (see Section 6) that if the upper bounds $u(x,y)$ of relaxed metrics are based on the idea that common information, or more precisely, *measure of common information* about x and y, brings *negative contribution* to $u(x,y)$ — e.g. in the normalized world we can consider $u(x,y) = 1 - \mu(Info(x) \cap Info(y))$ — then all axioms of partial metrics should hold for u. In fact, it makes sense to introduce both positive and negative information, and to define $u(x,y) = 1 - \mu(Info(x) \cap Info(y)) - \mu(Neginfo(x) \cap Neginfo(y))$, then defining meaningful lower bounds $l(x,y) = \mu(Info(x) \cap Neginfo(y)) + \mu(Info(y) \cap Neginfo(x))$ and obtaining an induced metric on $Total(A)$.

This is, essentially, the approach of Section 5 of [3], where $Info(x)$ and $Neginfo(x)$ can be understood as subsets of a domain basis. However, there was a number of remaining *open problems*. In particular, while [3] builds partial metrics on all continuous Scott domains with countable bases, the reliance of [3] on finite weights of non-compact basic elements does not allow to obtain some natural partial metrics on real-line based domains, and also introduces some unpleasant restrictions on domains which should be satisfied in order to obtain an induced classical metric on $Total(A)$.

1.1 Co-continuous Valuations

This paper rectifies these particular open problems by defining partial metrics via *valuations on the systems of Scott open sets* of domains. The theory of valuations on open sets underwent a considerable development recently (see [5, 11, 18, 2] and references therein). However we have found that we need a special condition of *co-continuity* for our valuations — for a filtered system of open sets $\{U_i, i \in I\}$, $\mu(\text{Int}(\bigcap_{i \in I} U_i)) = \inf_{i \in I}(\mu(U_i))$. We need this condition to ensure Scott continuity of our partial metrics.

The paper starts as follows. In Section 2 we remind the necessary definitions of domain theory. Section 3 defines various properties of valuations and introduces the class of *CC-valuations* — continuous, normalized, strongly non-degenerate, co-continuous valuations. Section 4 builds a CC-valuation on the system of Scott open sets of every continuous dcpo with a countable basis. This is the first central result of this paper.

It seems that the notion of co-continuity of valuations and this result for the case of continuous Scott domains with countable bases are both new and belong to us. The generalization of this result to continuous dcpo's with countable bases belongs to Klaus Keimel [12]. He worked directly with *completely distributive lattices* of Scott open sets of continuous dcpo's and used the results about completely distributive lattices obtained by Raney in the fifties (see Exercise 2.30

on page 204 of [8]). Here we present a proof which can be considered a simplification of both our original proof and the proof obtained by Keimel. This proof also works for all continuous dcpo's with countable bases. A part of this proof, as predicted by Keimel, can be considered as a special case of Raney's results mentioned above. However, our construction is very simple and self-contained.

Keimel also pointed out in [12] that our results are quite surprising, because both co-continuity and *strong non-degeneracy*, $U \subset V$ are open sets $\Rightarrow \mu(U) < \mu(V)$, seem contradictory, as neither of them can hold for the system of open sets of the ordinary Hausdorff topology on $[0, 1]$. However, if we replace the system of open sets of this Hausdorff topology with the system of open intervals, both conditions would hold. We believe that the reason behind our results is that the Scott topology is coarse enough for its system of open sets to exhibit behaviors similar to the behaviors of typical *bases of open sets* of Hausdorff topologies.

1.2 Application to Partial Metrics

Section 5 discusses partial and relaxed metrics and their properties. Section 6 describes an approach to partial and relaxed metrics where the upper bounds $u(x, y)$ are based on the idea of common information about x and y bringing negative contribution to $u(x, y)$. We formalize this approach introducing the notion of μ*Info*-structure. However, we feel that this formalization can be further improved.

In particular, Section 6 presents the second central result of this paper — given a CC-valuation on the system of Scott open sets of any continuous Scott domain (no assumptions about the cardinality of the basis are needed here), we build a Scott continuous relaxed metric $\langle l, u \rangle : A \times A \to \mathbf{R}^I$, such that $u : A \times A \to \mathbf{R}^-$ is a partial metric, the relaxed metric topology coincides with the Scott topology, and if $x, y \in Total(A)$, $l(x, y) = u(x, y)$ and the resulting classical metric $Total(A) \times Total(A) \to \mathbf{R}$ defines a subspace topology on $Total(A)$. Here $\mathbf{R}^I$ is the domain of interval numbers, $\mathbf{R}^-$ is the domain of upper bounds, and $Total(A)$ is the set of maximal elements of A.

Section 7 discusses various examples and possibilities to weaken the strong non-degeneracy condition — to find a sufficiently general weaker condition is an open problem.

A more detailed presentation can be found in [4].

2 Continuous Scott Domains

Recall that a non-empty partially ordered set (poset), $(S, \sqsubseteq)$, is *directed* if $\forall x, y \in S.\ \exists z \in S.\ x \sqsubseteq z, y \sqsubseteq z$. A poset, $(A, \sqsubseteq)$, is a *dcpo* if it has a least element, $\perp$, and for any directed $S \subseteq A$, the least upper bound $\sqcup S$ of S exists in A. A set $U \subseteq A$ is *Scott open* if $\forall x, y \in A.\ x \in U, x \sqsubseteq y \Rightarrow y \in U$ and for any directed poset $S \subseteq A$, $\sqcup S \in U \Rightarrow \exists s \in S.\ s \in U$. The Scott open subsets of a dcpo form the *Scott topology*.

Consider dcpo's $(A, \sqsubseteq_A)$ and $(B, \sqsubseteq_B)$ with the respective Scott topologies. $f : A \to B$ is (Scott) continuous iff it is monotonic ($x \sqsubseteq_A y \Rightarrow f(x) \sqsubseteq_B f(y)$) and for any directed poset $S \subseteq A$, $f(\sqcup_A S) = \sqcup_B \{f(s) \mid s \in S\}$.

We define continuous Scott domains in the spirit of [10]. Consider a dcpo $(A, \sqsubseteq)$. We say that $x \ll y$ (x is *way below* y) if for any directed set $S \subseteq A$, $y \sqsubseteq \sqcup S \Rightarrow \exists s \in S.\ x \sqsubseteq s$. An element x, such that $x \ll x$, is called *compact*. We say that A is *bounded complete* if $\forall B \subseteq A.\ (\exists a \in A.\ \forall b \in B. b \sqsubseteq a) \Rightarrow \sqcup_A B$ exists.

Consider a set $K \subseteq A$. Notice that $\perp_A \in K$. We say that a dcpo A is a *continuous dcpo* with *basis* K, if for any $a \in A$, the set $K_a = \{k \in K \mid k \ll a\}$ is directed and $a = \sqcup K_a$. We call elements of K *basic* elements. A continuous, bounded complete dcpo is called a *continuous Scott domain*.

3 CC-valuations

Consider a topological space $(X, \mathcal{O})$, where $\mathcal{O}$ consists of all open subsets of X. The following notions of the theory of valuations can be considered standard (for the most available presentation in a regular journal see [5]; the fundamental text in the theory of valuations on Scott opens sets is [11]).

Definition 3.1. A function $\mu : \mathcal{O} \to [0, +\infty]$ is called *valuation* if

1. $\forall U, V \in \mathcal{O}.\ U \subseteq V \Rightarrow \mu(U) \leq \mu(V)$;
2. $\forall U, V \in \mathcal{O}.\ \mu(U) + \mu(V) = \mu(U \cap V) + \mu(U \cup V)$;
3. $\mu(\emptyset) = 0$.

Definition 3.2. A valuation μ is *bounded* if $\mu(X) < +\infty$. A valuation μ is *normalized* if $\mu(X) = 1$.

Remark: If a valuation μ is bounded and $\mu(X) \neq 0$, then it is always easy to replace it with a normalized valuation $\mu'(U) = \mu(U)/\mu(X)$.

Definition 3.3. Define a *directed system of open sets*, $\mathcal{U} = \{U_i, i \in I\}$, as satisfying the following condition: for any finite number of open sets $U_{i_1}, U_{i_2}, \cdots, U_{i_n} \in \mathcal{U}$ there is $U_i, i \in I$, such that $U_{i_1} \subseteq U_i, \cdots, U_{i_n} \subseteq U_i$.

Definition 3.4. A valuation μ is called *continuous* when for any directed system of open sets $\mu(\bigcup_{i \in I} U_i) = \sup_{i \in I} \mu(U_i)$.

We introduce two new properties of valuations.

Definition 3.5. A valuation $\mu : \mathcal{O} \to [0, +\infty]$ is *strongly non-degenerate* if $\forall U, V \in \mathcal{O}.\ U \subset V \Rightarrow \mu(U) < \mu(V)$.[3]

This is, obviously, a very strong requirement, and we will see later that it might be reasonable to look for weaker non-degeneracy conditions.

Consider a decreasing sequence of open sets $U_1 \supseteq U_2 \supseteq \ldots$, or, more generally, a *filtered system of open sets* $\mathcal{U} = \{U_i, i \in I\}$, meaning that for any finite system of open sets $U_{i_1}, \cdots U_{i_n} \in \mathcal{U}$ there is $U_i, i \in I$, such that $U_i \subseteq$

[3] We use $U \subset V$ as an equivalent of $U \subseteq V$ & $U \neq V$.

$U_{i_1}, \cdots, U_i \subseteq U_{i_n}$. Consider the interior of the intersection of these sets. It is easy to see that for a valuation μ

$$\mu(\mathrm{Int}(\bigcap_{i\in I} U_i)) \leq \inf_{i\in I} \mu(U_i).$$

Definition 3.6. A valuation μ is called *co-continuous* if for any filtered system of open sets $\{U_i, i \in I\}$

$$\mu(\mathrm{Int}(\bigcap_{i\in I} U_i)) = \inf_{i\in I} \mu(U_i).$$

Definition 3.7. A continuous, normalized, strongly non-degenerate, co-continuous valuation μ is called a *CC-valuation*.

Informally speaking, the strong non-degeneracy provides for non-zero contributions of compact elements and reasonable "pieces of space". The co-continuity provides for single non-compact elements and borders $B \setminus \mathrm{Int}(B)$ of "reasonable" sets $B \subseteq A$ to have zero measures.

"Reasonable" sets here are Alexandrov open (i.e. upwardly closed) sets. Thus, it is possible to consider co-continuity as a method of dealing with non-discreteness of Scott topology. We follow here the remarkable definition of a discrete topology given by Alexandrov: a topology is discrete if an intersection of arbitrary family of open sets is open (e.g. see [1]). Of course, if one assumes the T_1 separation axiom, then the Alexandrov's definition implies that all sets are open — the trivial (and more standard) version of the definition. In this sense, Alexandrov topology of upwardly closed sets is discrete, but Scott topology is not.

We should also notice that since our valuations are bounded, they can be extended onto closed sets via formula $\mu(C) = \mu(A) - \mu(A \setminus C)$, and all definitions of this section can be expressed in the dual form.

A bounded valuation μ can be uniquely extended to an additive measure defined on the ring of sets generated from the open sets by operations $\cap$, $\cup$, $\setminus$ [16]. The issues of σ-additivity are not in the scope of this text (interested readers are referred to [11, 2]). We deal with the specific infinite systems of sets we need, and mainly focus on quite orthogonal conditions given to us by co-continuity of μ.

3.1 Example: Valuations Based on Weights of Basic Elements

This example essentially reproduces a construction in [3]. Consider a continuous dcpo A with a countable basis K. Assign a converging system of weights to basic elements: $w(k) > 0$, $\sum_{k\in K} w(k) = 1$. Define $\mu(U) = \sum_{k\in U} w(k)$. It is easy to see that μ is a continuous, normalized, strongly non-degenerate valuation.

However, μ is co-continuous if and only if all basic elements are compact (which is possible only if A is algebraic). This is proved in [4] using the following observations.

First, observe that arbitrary intersections of Alexandrov open (i.e. upwardly closed) sets are Alexandrov open. Also it is a well-known fact that $\{y \mid x \ll y\}$ is Scott open in a continuous dcpo.

Lemma 3.1 (Border Lemma) *Consider an Alexandrov open set $B \subseteq A$. Then its interior in the Scott topology,* $\mathrm{Int}(B) = \{y \in A \mid \exists x \in B. x \ll y\}$. *Correspondingly, the border of B in the Scott topology,* $B \setminus \mathrm{Int}(B) = \{y \in B \mid \neg(\exists x \in B. x \ll y)\}$

3.2 A Vertical Segment of Real Line

Consider the segment $[0, 1]$, $\sqsubseteq = \leq$. Define $\mu((x, 1]) = 1 - x$. Unfortunately, to ensure strong non-degeneracy we have to define $\mu([0, 1]) = 1 + \epsilon$, $\epsilon > 0$. This is the first hint that strong non-degeneracy is too strong in many cases. In order to obtain a normalized valuation we have to consider $\mu'(U) = \mu(U)/(1+\epsilon)$. The resulting μ' is a CC-valuation.

4 Constructing CC-valuations

In this section we build a CC-valuation for all continuous dcpo's with countable bases. The construction generalizes the one of Subsection 3.1. We are still going to assign weights, $w(k) > 0$, to compact elements. For non-compact basic elements we proceed as follows. We focus our attention on the pairs of non-compact basic elements, (k', k''), which do not have any compact elements between them, and call such elements *continuously connected*. We observe, that for every such pair we can construct a special kind of vertical chain, which "behaves like a vertical segment $[0, 1]$ of real line". We call such chain a *stick*. We assign weights, $v(k', k'') > 0$, to sticks as well, in such a way that the sum of all $w(k)$ and all $v(k', k'')$ is 1.

As in Subsection 3.1, compact elements k contribute $w(k)$ to $\mu(U)$, if $k \in U$. An intersection of the stick, associated with a continuously connected pair (k', k''), with an open set U "behaves as either $(q, 1]$ or $[q, 1]$", where $q \in [0, 1]$. Such stick contributes $(1 - q) \cdot v(k', k'')$ to $\mu(U)$. The resulting μ is the desired CC-valuation.

It is possible to associate a complete lattice homomorphism from the lattice of Scott open sets to $[0, 1]$ with every compact element and with every stick defined by basic continuously connected elements, k' and k''. Then, as suggested by Keimel [12], all these homomorphisms together can be thought of as an injective complete lattice homomorphism to $[0, 1]^J$. From this point of view, our construction of μ is the same as in [12].

Thus the discourse in this section yields the proof of the following:

Theorem 4.1 *For any continuous dcpo A with a countable basis, there is a CC-valuation μ on the system of its Scott open sets.*

4.1 Continuous Connectivity and Sticks

Definition 4.1. Two elements $x \ll y$ are called *continuously connected* if the set $\{k \in A | k \text{ is compact}, x \ll k \ll y\}$ is empty.

Remark: This implies that x and y are not compact.

Lemma 4.1 *If $x \ll y$ are continuously connected, then $\{z \,|\, x \ll z \ll y\}$ has cardinality of at least continuum.*

Proof. We use the well-known theorem on intermediate values that $x \ll y \Rightarrow \exists z \in A \; x \ll z \ll y$ (see [10]). Applying this theorem again and again we build a countable system of elements between x and y as follows, using rational numbers as indices for intermediate elements:

$$x \ll a_{1/2} \ll y, \quad x \ll a_{1/4} \ll a_{1/2} \ll a_{3/4} \ll y, \ldots$$

All these elements are non-compact and hence non-equal. Now consider a directed set $\{a_i \,|\, i \leq r\}$, where r is a real number, $0 < r < 1$. Introduce $b_r = \sqcup\{a_i \,|\, i \leq r\}$. We prove that if $r < s$ then $b_r \ll b_s$, and also that $x \ll b_r \ll b_s \ll y$, thus obtaining the required cardinality. Indeed it is easy to find such n and numbers q_1, q_2, q_3, q_4, that

$$x \ll a_{q_1/2^n} \sqsubseteq b_r \sqsubseteq a_{q_2/2^n} \ll a_{q_3/2^n} \sqsubseteq b_s \ll a_{q_4/2^n} \ll y$$

□

Definition 4.2. We call the set of continuum different non-compact elements $\{a_r \,|\, r \in (0, 1)\}$ between continuously connected $x \ll y$, built in the proof above, such that $x \ll a_r \ll a_q \ll z \Leftrightarrow r < q$ a (vertical) *stick*.

4.2 Proof of Theorem 4.1

Consider a continuous dcpo A with a countable basis K. As discussed earlier, with every compact $k \in K$ we associate weight $w(k) > 0$, and with every continuously connected pair (k', k''), $k', k'' \in K$, we associate weight $v(k', k'') > 0$ and a stick $\{a_r^{k',k''} \,|\, r \in (0, 1)\}$. Since K is countable, we can require $\sum w(k) + \sum v(k', k'') = 1$.

Whenever we have an upwardly closed (i.e. Alexandrov open) set U, for any stick $\{a_r^{k',k''} \,|\, r \in (0, 1)\}$ there is a number $q_U^{k',k''} \in [0, 1]$, such that $r < q_U^{k',k''} \Rightarrow a_r^{k',k''} \notin U$ and $q_U^{k',k''} < r \Rightarrow a_r^{k',k''} \in U$. In particular, for a Scott open set U define

$$\mu(U) = \sum_{k \in U \text{is compact}} w(k) + \sum_{k', k'' \in K \text{are continuously connected}} (1 - q_U^{k',k''}) \cdot v(k', k'')$$

It is easy to show that μ is a normalized valuation. The rest follows from the following Lemmas.

Lemma 4.2 *μ is continuous.*

Lemma 4.3 *μ is strongly non-degenerate.*

Proof. Let U and V be Scott open subsets of A and $U \subset V$. Let us prove that $V \setminus U$ contains either a compact element or a stick between basic elements. Take $x \in V \setminus U$. If x is compact, then we are fine. Assume that x is not compact. We know that $x = \sqcup K_x$, $K_x = \{k \in K \mid k \ll x\}$ is directed set. Since V is open $\exists k \in K_x.\ k \in V$. Since $k \sqsubseteq x$ and $x \notin U$, $k \in V \setminus U$. If there is k' – compact, such that $k \ll k' \ll x$, we are fine, since $k' \in V \setminus U$. Otherwise, since any basis includes all compact elements, k and x are continuously connected.

Now, as in the theorem of intermediate values $x = \sqcup \widetilde{K}_x$, $\widetilde{K}_x = \{k' \in K \mid \exists k'' \in K.\ k' \ll k'' \ll x\}$ is directed set, thus $\exists k' k''.\ k \sqsubseteq k' \ll k'' \ll x$, thus (k, k'') yields the desired stick.

If $k \in V \setminus U$ and k is compact, then $\mu(V) - \mu(U) \geq w(k) > 0$. If the stick formed by (k, k') is in $V \setminus U$, then $\mu(V) - \mu(U) \geq v(k, k') > 0$.

□

Lemma 4.4 *μ is co-continuous.*

Proof. Recall the development in Subsection 3.1. Consider a filtered system of open sets $\{U_i,\ i \in I\}$. By Lemma 3.1 for $B = \bigcap_{i \in I} U_i$, $B \setminus \mathrm{Int}(B) = \{y \in B \mid \neg(\exists x \in B.\ x \ll y)\}$. Notice that $B \setminus \mathrm{Int}(B)$, in particular, does not contain compact elements. Another important point is that for any stick, $q_B^{k',k''} = q_{\mathrm{Int}(B)}^{k',k''}$.

The further development is essentially dual to the omitted proof of Lemma 4.2. We need to show that for any $\epsilon > 0$, there is such $U_i, i \in I$, that $\mu(U_i) - \mu(\mathrm{Int}(B)) < \epsilon$.

Take enough (a finite number) of compact elements, $k_1, \ldots, k_n$, and continuously connected pairs of basic elements, $(k_1', k_1''), \ldots, (k_m', k_m'')$, so that $w(k_1) + \ldots + w(k_n) + v(k_1', k_1'') + \ldots + v(k_m', k_m'') > 1 - \epsilon/2$. For each $k_j \notin \mathrm{Int}(B)$, take $U_{i_j}, i_j \in I$, such that $k_j \notin U_{i_j}$. For each (k_j', k_j''), such that $q_{\mathrm{Int}(B)}^{k_j',k_j''} > 0$, take $U_{i_j'}, i_j' \in I$, such that $q_{\mathrm{Int}(B)}^{k_j',k_j''} - q_{U_{i_j'}}^{k_j',k_j''} < \epsilon/(2m)$. A lower bound of these U_{i_j} and $U_{i_j'}$ is the desired U_i.

□

It should be noted that Bob Flagg suggested and Klaus Keimel showed that Lemma 5.3 of [7] can be adapted to obtain a dual proof of existence of CC-valuations (see [6] for one presentation of this). Klaus Keimel also noted that one can consider all pairs k, k' of basic elements, such that $k \ll k'$, instead of considering just continuously connected pairs and compact elements.

5 Partial and Relaxed Metrics on Domains

The motivations behind the notion of relaxed metric, its computational meaning and its relationships with partial metrics [14] were explained in [3]. Here we focus on the definitions and basic properties, revisit the issue of specific axioms of partial metrics, and list the relevant open problems.

The distance domain consists of pairs $\langle a, b\rangle$ (also denoted as $[a, b]$) of non-negative reals ($+\infty$ included), such that $a \leq b$. We denote this domain as R^I. $[a, b] \sqsubseteq_{R^I} [c, d]$ iff $a \leq c$ and $d \leq b$.

We can also think about R^I as a subset of $R^+ \times R^-$, where $\sqsubseteq_{R^+} = \leq$, $\sqsubseteq_{R^-} = \geq$, and both R^+ and R^- consist of non-negative reals and $+\infty$. We call R^+ a *domain of lower bounds*, and R^- a *domain of upper bounds*. Thus a distance function $\rho : A \times A \to R^I$ can be thought of as a pair of distance functions $\langle l, u\rangle$, $l : A \times A \to R^+$, $u : A \times A \to R^-$.

Definition 5.1. A symmetric function $u : A \times A \to R^-$ is called a *relaxed metric* when it satisfies the triangle inequality. A symmetric function $\rho : A \times A \to R^I$ is called a *relaxed metric* when its upper part u is a relaxed metric.

An *open ball* with a center $x \in A$ and a real radius ϵ is defined as $B_{x,\epsilon} = \{y \in A \mid u(x, y) < \epsilon\}$. Notice that only upper bounds are used in this definition — the ball only includes those points y, about which we are *sure* that they are not too far from x.

We should formulate the notion of a relaxed metric open set more carefully than for ordinary metrics, because it is now possible to have a ball of a non-zero positive radius, which does not contain its own center.

Definition 5.2. A subset U of A is *relaxed metric open* if for any point $x \in U$, there is an $\epsilon > u(x, x)$ such that $B_{x,\epsilon} \subseteq U$.

It is easy to show that for a continuous relaxed metric on a dcpo all relaxed metric open sets are Scott open and form a topology.

5.1 Partial Metrics

The distances p with $p(x, x) \neq 0$ were first introduced by Matthews [14, 13]. They are known as *partial metrics* and obey the following axioms:

1. $x = y$ iff $p(x, x) = p(x, y) = p(y, y)$.
2. $p(x, x) \leq p(x, y)$.
3. $p(x, y) = p(y, x)$.
4. $p(x, z) \leq p(x, y) + p(y, z) - p(y, y)$.

Whenever partial metrics are used to describe a partially ordered domain, a stronger form of the first two axioms is used: If $x \sqsubseteq y$ then $p(x, x) = p(x, y)$, otherwise $p(x, x) < p(x, y)$. We include the stronger form in the definition of partial metrics for the purposes of this paper.

Section 8.1 of [3] discusses the issue of whether axioms $u(x, x) \leq u(x, y)$ and $u(x, z) \leq u(x, y) + u(y, z) - u(y, y)$ should hold for the upper bounds of relaxed metrics. In particular, the approach in this paper is based on $u(x, y) = 1 - \mu(\text{Common information between } x \text{ and } y)$ and thus, as will be explained in details in the next section, the axioms of partial metrics hold. Further discussion of the utilitarian value of these axioms can be found in [4].

6 Partial and Relaxed Metrics via Information

6.1 μ*Info*-structures

Some of the earlier known constructions of partial metrics can be understood via the mechanism of *common information* between elements x and y bringing negative contribution to $u(x, y)$ (see [3, Section 8]). This can be further formalized as follows. Assume that there is a set $\mathcal{I}$ representing information about elements of a dcpo A. We choose a ring, $\mathcal{M}(\mathcal{I})$, of admissible subsets of $\mathcal{I}$ and introduce a measure-like structure, μ, on $\mathcal{M}(\mathcal{I})$. We associate a set, $Info(x) \in \mathcal{M}(\mathcal{I})$, with every $x \in A$, and call $Info(x)$ a set of (positive) information about x. We also would like to consider negative information about x, $Neginfo(x) \in \mathcal{M}(\mathcal{I})$, — intuitively speaking, this is information which cannot become true about x, when x is arbitrarily increased.

Definition 6.1. Given a dcpo A, the tuple of $(A, \mathcal{I}, \mathcal{M}(\mathcal{I}), \mu, Info, Neginfo)$ is called a μ*Info-structure* on A, if $\mathcal{M}(\mathcal{I}) \subseteq \mathcal{P}(\mathcal{I})$ — a ring of subsets closed with respect to $\cap, \cup, \setminus$ and including $\emptyset$ and $\mathcal{I}$, $\mu : \mathcal{M}(\mathcal{I}) \to [0, 1]$, $Info : A \to \mathcal{M}(\mathcal{I})$, and $Neginfo : A \to \mathcal{M}(\mathcal{I})$, and the following axioms are satisfied:

1. **(VALUATION AXIOMS)**
   (a) $\mu(\mathcal{I}) = 1$, $\mu(\emptyset) = 0$;
   (b) $U \subseteq V \Rightarrow \mu(U) \leq \mu(V)$;
   (c) $\mu(U) + \mu(V) = \mu(U \cap V) + \mu(U \cup V)$;
2. **(*Info* AXIOMS)**
   (a) $x \sqsubseteq y \Leftrightarrow Info(x) \subseteq Info(y)$;
   (b) $x \sqsubset y \Rightarrow Info(x) \subset Info(y)$;
3. **(*Neginfo* AXIOMS)**
   (a) $Info(x) \cap Neginfo(x) = \emptyset$;
   (b) $x \sqsubseteq y \Rightarrow Neginfo(x) \subseteq Neginfo(y)$;
4. **(STRONG RESPECT FOR TOTALITY)**
   $x \in Total(A) \Rightarrow Info(x) \cup Neginfo(x) = \mathcal{I}$;
5. **(CONTINUITY OF INDUCED RELAXED METRIC)**
   if B is a directed subset of A and $y \in A$, then
   (a) $\mu(Info(\sqcup B) \cap Info(y)) = sup_{x \in B}(\mu(Info(x) \cap Info(y)))$,
   (b) $\mu(Info(\sqcup B) \cap Neginfo(y)) = sup_{x \in B}(\mu(Info(x) \cap Neginfo(y)))$,
   (c) $\mu(Neginfo(\sqcup B) \cap Info(y)) = sup_{x \in B}(\mu(Neginfo(x) \cap Info(y)))$,
   (d) $\mu(Neginfo(\sqcup B) \cap Neginfo(y)) = sup_{x \in B}(\mu(Neginfo(x) \cap Neginfo(y)))$;
6. **(SCOTT OPEN SETS ARE RELAXED METRIC OPEN)**
   for any (basic) Scott open set $U \subseteq A$ and $x \in U$, there is an $\epsilon > 0$, such that $\forall y \in A.\ \mu(Info(x)) - \mu(Info(x) \cap Info(y)) < \epsilon \Rightarrow y \in U$.

In terms of lattice theory, μ is a (normalized) valuation on a lattice $\mathcal{M}(\mathcal{I})$. The consideration of unbounded measures is beyond the scope of this paper, and $\mu(\mathcal{I}) = 1$ is assumed for convenience. Axioms relating $\sqsubseteq$ and *Info* are in the spirit of information systems [17], although we are not considering any inference structure over $\mathcal{I}$ in this paper.

The requirements for negative information are relatively weak, because it is quite natural to have $\forall x \in A.\ Neginfo(x) = \emptyset$ if A has a top element.

The axiom that for $x \in Total(A)$, $Info(x) \cup Neginfo(x) = \mathcal{I}$, is desirable because indeed, if some $i \in \mathcal{I}$ does not belong to $Info(x)$ and x can not be further increased, then by our intuition behind $Neginfo(x)$, i should belong to $Neginfo(x)$. However, this axiom might be too strong and will be further discussed later.

The last two axioms are not quite satisfactory — they almost immediately imply the properties, after which they are named, but they are complicated and might be difficult to establish. We hope, that these axioms will be replaced by something more tractable in the future. One of the obstacles seems to be the fact in some valuable approaches (in particular, in this paper) it is not correct that $x_1 \sqsubseteq x_2 \sqsubseteq \cdots$ implies that $Info(\sqcup_{i\in\mathbf{N}} x_i) = \bigcup_{i\in\mathbf{N}} Info(x_i)$.

The nature of these set-theoretical representations, $\mathcal{I}$, of domains may vary: one can consider sets of tokens of information systems, powersets of domain bases, or powersets of domains themselves, custom-made sets for specific domains, etc. The approach via powersets of domain bases (see [3]) can be thought of as a partial case of the approach via powersets of domains themselves adopted in the present paper.

6.2 Partial and Relaxed Metrics via $\mu Info$-structures

Define the (upper estimate of the) distance between x and y from A as $u : A \times A \to \mathbf{R}^-$:

$$u(x, y) = 1 - \mu(Info(x) \cap Info(y)) - \mu(Neginfo(x) \cap Neginfo(y)).$$

I.e. the more information x and y have in common the smaller is the distance between them. However a partially defined element might not have too much information at all, so its self-distance $u(x, x) = 1 - \mu(Info(x)) - \mu(Neginfo(x))$ might be large.

It is possible to find information which will never belong to $Info(x) \cap Info(y)$ or $Neginfo(x) \cap Neginfo(y)$ even when x and y are arbitrarily increased. In particular, $Info(x) \cap Neginfo(y)$ and $Info(y) \cap Neginfo(x)$ represent such information. Then we can introduce the lower estimate of the distance $l : A \times A \to \mathbf{R}^+$:

$$l(x, y) = \mu(Info(x) \cap Neginfo(y)) + \mu(Info(y) \cap Neginfo(x)).$$

The proof of Lemma 9 of [3] is directly applicable and yields $l(x, y) \leq u(x, y)$. Thus we can form an **induced relaxed metric**, $\rho : A \times A \to R^I$, $\rho = \langle l, u \rangle$, with a meaningful lower bound.

The following theorem is proved in [4] without using the **strong respect for totality** axiom.

Theorem 6.1 *Function u is a partial metric. Function ρ is a continuous relaxed metric. The relaxed metric topology coincides with the Scott topology.*

Due to the axiom $\forall x \in Total(A).\ Info(x) \cup Neginfo(x) = \mathcal{I}$, the proof of Lemma 10 of [3] would go through, yielding

$$x, y \in Total(A) \Rightarrow l(x, y) = u(x, y)$$

and allowing to obtain the following theorem (cf. Theorem 8 of [3]).

Theorem 6.2 *For all x and y from $Total(A)$, $l(x, y) = u(x, y)$. Consider $d : Total(A) \times Total(A) \to \mathbf{R}$, $d(x, y) = l(x, y) = u(x, y)$. Then $(Total(A), d)$ is a metric space, and its metric topology is the subspace topology induced by the Scott topology on A.*

However, in [3] $x \in Total(A) \Rightarrow Info(x) \cup Neginfo(x) = \mathcal{I}$ holds under an awkward condition, the regularity of the basis. While bases of algebraic Scott domains and of continuous lattices can be made regular, there are important continuous Scott domains, which cannot be given regular bases. In particular, in $\mathbf{R}^I$ no element, except for $\perp$, satisfies the condition of regularity, hence a regular basis cannot be provided for $\mathbf{R}^I$.

The achievement of the construction to be described in Section 6.4 is that by removing the reliance on the weights of non-compact basic elements, it eliminates the regularity requirement and implies $x \in Total(A) \Rightarrow Info(x) \cup Neginfo(x) = \mathcal{I}$ for all continuous Scott domains equipped with a CC-valuation (which is built above for all continuous Scott domains with countable bases) where $Info(x)$ and $Neginfo(x)$ are as described below in the Subsection 6.4.

However, it still might be fruitful to consider replacing the axiom $\forall x \in Total(A).\ Info(x) \cup Neginfo(x) = \mathcal{I}$ by something like $\forall x \in Total(A).\ \mu(\mathcal{I} \setminus (Info(x) \cup Neginfo(x))) = 0$.

6.3 A Previously Known Construction

Here we recall a construction from [3] based on a generally non-co-continuous valuation of Subsection 3.1. We will reformulate it in our terms of $\mu Info$-structures. In [3] it was natural to think that $\mathcal{I} = K$. Here we reformulate that construction in terms of $\mathcal{I} = A$, thus abandoning the condition $x \in Total(A) \Rightarrow Info(x) \cup Neginfo(x) = \mathcal{I}$ altogether.

Define $I_x = \{y \in A \mid \{x, y\} \text{ is unbounded}\}$, $P_x = \{y \in A \mid y \ll x\}$ (cf. $I_x = \{k \in K \mid \{k, x\} \text{ is unbounded}\}$, $K_x = \{k \in K \mid k \ll x\}$ in [3]).

Define $Info(x) = P_x$, $Neginfo(x) = I_x$. Consider a valuation μ of Subsection 3.1: for any $S \subset \mathcal{I} = A$, $\mu(S) = \sum_{k \in S \cap K} w(k)$. μ is a continuous strongly non-degenerate valuation, but it is not co-continuous unless K consists only of compact elements.

Because of this we cannot replace the inconvenient definition of $Info(x) = P_x$ by $Info(x) = C_x = \{y \in A \mid y \sqsubseteq x\}$ (which would restore the condition $x \in Total(A) \Rightarrow Info(x) \cup Neginfo(x) = A$) as $\mu(C_k)$ would not be equal to $\sup_{k' \ll k} \mu(C_{k'})$ if k is a non-compact basic element, leading to the non-continuity of the partial metric $u(x, y)$.

Also the reliance on countable systems of finite weights excludes such natural partial metrics as metric $u : \mathbf{R}^-_{[0,1]} \times \mathbf{R}^-_{[0,1]} \to \mathbf{R}^-$, where $\mathbf{R}^-_{[0,1]}$ is the set $[0, 1]$ equipped with the dual partial order $\sqsubseteq = \geq$, and $u(x, y) = max(x, y)$. We rectify all these problems in the next Subsection.

6.4 Partial and Relaxed Metrics via CC-valuations

Assume that there is a CC-valuation $\mu(U)$ on Scott open sets of a domain A. Then it uniquely extends to an additive measure μ on the ring of sets generated by the system of open sets. Define $\mathcal{I} = A$, $Info(x) = C_x$, $Neginfo(x) = I_x$. It is easy to see that valuation, *Info*, and *Neginfo* axioms of μ*Info*-structure hold. We have $x \in Total(A) \Rightarrow C_x \cup I_x = A$. Thus we only need to establish the axioms of **continuity of induced relaxed metrics** and **Scott open sets are relaxed metric open** in order to prove theorems 6.1 and 6.2 for our induced relaxed metric $(u(x, y) = 1 - \mu(C_x \cap C_y) - \mu(I_x \cap I_y),\ l(x, y) = \mu(C_x \cap I_y) + \mu(C_y \cap I_x))$. These axioms are established by the Lemmas below.

You will also see that for such bare-bones partial metrics, as $u(x, y) = 1 - \mu(C_x \cap C_y)$, which are nevertheless quite sufficient for topological purposes and for domains with $\top$, only *co-continuity* matters, continuity is not important.

Observe also that since the construction in Section 3.1 does form a CC-valuation for algebraic Scott domains with bases of compact elements, the construction in [3] can be considered as a partial case of our current construction if the basis does not contain non-compact elements.

Lemma 6.1 *Assume that μ is a co-continuous valuation and B is a directed subset of A. Then $\mu(C_{\sqcup B} \cap Q) = \sup_{x \in B}(\mu(C_x \cap Q))$, where Q is a closed or open subset of A.*

Remark: Note that continuity of μ is not required here.

Lemma 6.2 *Assume that μ is a continuous valuation and B is a directed subset of A. Then $\mu(I_{\sqcup B} \cap Q) = \sup_{x \in B}(\mu(I_x \cap Q))$, where Q is an open or closed subset of A.*

Remark: Co-continuity is not needed here.

Lemma 6.3 *Assume that μ is a strongly non-degenerate valuation. Then the μInfo-structure axiom* **Scott open sets are relaxed metric open** *holds.*

Remark: Neither continuity, nor co-continuity required, and even the strong non-degeneracy condition can probably be made weaker (see the next Section).

7 Examples and Non-degeneracy Issues

In this section we show some examples of "nice" partial metrics, based on valuations for vertical and interval domains of real numbers. Some of these valuations are strongly non-degenerate, while others are not, yet all examples are quite natural.

Consider the example from Subsection 3.2. The partial metric, based on the strongly non-degenerate valuation μ' of that example would be $u'(x,y) = (1 - \min(x,y))/(1+\epsilon)$, if $x, y > 0$, and $u'(x,y) = 1$, if x or y equals to 0. However, another nice valuation, μ'', can be defined on the basis of μ of Subsection 3.2: $\mu''((x,1]) = \mu((x,1]) = 1 - x$, $\mu''([0,1]) = 1$. μ'' is not strongly non-degenerate, however it yields the nice partial metric $u''(x,y) = 1 - \min(x,y)$, yielding the Scott topology.

Now we consider several valuations and distances on the domain of interval numbers located within the segment $[0,1]$. This domain can be thought of as a triangle of pairs $\langle x, y\rangle$, $0 \leq x \leq y \leq 1$. Various valuations can either be concentrated on $0 < x \leq y < 1$, or on $x = 0, 0 \leq y \leq 1$ and $y = 1, 0 \leq x \leq 1$, or, to insure non-degeneracy, on both of these areas with an extra weight at $\langle 0, 1\rangle$.

Among all these measures, the classical partial metric $u([x,y],[x',y']) = \max(y,y') - \min(x,x')$ results from the valuation accumulated at $x = 0, 0 \leq y \leq 1$, and $y = 1, 0 \leq x \leq 1$, namely $\mu(U) = (Length(\{x = 0, 0 \leq y \leq 1\} \cap U) + Length(\{y = 1, 0 \leq x \leq 1\} \cap U))/2$. Partial metrics generated by strongly non-degenerate valuations contain quadratic expressions.

It is our current feeling, that instead of trying to formalize weaker non-degeneracy conditions, it is fruitful to build a $\mu Info$-structure based on $\mathcal{I} = [0,1] + [0,1]$ in situations like this.

8 Conclusion

We introduced notions of co-continuous valuations and CC-valuations, and built CC-valuations for all continuous dcpo's with countable bases. Given such a valuation, we presented a new construction of partial and relaxed metrics for all continuous Scott domains, improving a construction known before.

The key open problem is to learn to construct not just topologically correct, but canonical measures and relaxed metrics for higher-order functional domains and reflexive domains, and also to learn how to compute these measures and metrics quickly.

Acknowledgements

The authors benefited from discussions with Michael Alekhnovich, Reinhold Heckmann, Klaus Keimel, Harry Mairson, Simon O'Neill, Joshua Scott and from the detailed remarks made by the referees. They thank Gordon Plotkin for helpful references. They are especially thankful to Abbas Edalat for his suggestion to think about continuous valuations instead of measures in this context, and to Alexander Artemyev for his help in organizing this joint research effort.

References

1. Aleksandrov P.S. *Combinatory Topology*, vol.1. Graylock Press, Rochester, NY, 1956, p.28.
2. Alvarez M., Edalat A., Saheb-Djahromi N. *An extension result for continuous valuations*, 1997, available via URL
`http://theory.doc.ic.ac.uk/people/Edalat/extensionofvaluations.ps.Z`
3. Bukatin M.A., Scott J.S. Towards computing distances between programs via Scott domains. In S. Adian, A. Nerode, eds., Logical Foundations of Computer Science, *Lecture Notes in Computer Science*, **1234**, 33–43, Springer, 1997.
4. Bukatin M.A., Shorina S.Yu. *Partial Metrics and Co-continuous Valuations (Extended Version)*, Unpublished notes, 1997, available via one of the URLs
`http://www.cs.brandeis.edu/~bukatin/ccval_draft.{dvi,ps.gz}`
5. Edalat A. Domain theory and integration. *Theoretical Computer Science*, **151** (1995), 163–193.
6. Flagg R. *Constructing CC-Valuations*, Unpublished notes, 1997. Available via URL `http://macweb.acs.usm.maine.edu/math/archive/flagg/biCts.ps`
7. Flagg R., Kopperman R. Continuity spaces: Reconciling domains and metric spaces. *Theoretical Computer Science*, **177** (1997), 111–138.
8. Gierz G., Hofmann K., Keimel K., Lawson J., Mislove M., Scott D. *A Compendium of Continuous Lattices*, Springer, 1980.
9. Heckmann R. Approximation of metric spaces by partial metric spaces. To appear in *Applied Categorical Structures*, 1997.
10. Hoofman R. Continuous information systems. *Information and Computation*, **105** (1993), 42–71.
11. Jones C. *Probabilistic Non-determinism*, PhD Thesis, University of Edinburgh, 1989. Available via URL
`http://www.dcs.ed.ac.uk/lfcsreps/EXPORT/90/ECS-LFCS-90-105/index.html`
12. Keimel K. *Bi-continuous Valuations*, to appear in the Proceedings of the Third Workshop on Computation and Approximation, University of Birmingham, Sept. 1997. Available via URL
`http://theory.doc.ic.ac.uk/forum/comprox/data/talk.3.1.6.ps.gz`
13. Matthews S.G. An extensional treatment of lazy data flow deadlock. *Theoretical Computer Science*, **151** (1995), 195–205.
14. Matthews S.G. Partial metric topology. In S. Andima et al., eds., Proc. 8th Summer Conference on General Topology and Applications, *Annals of the New York Academy of Sciences*, **728**, 183–197, New York, 1994.
15. O'Neill S.J. Partial metrics, valuations and domain theory. In S. Andima et al., eds., Proc. 11th Summer Conference on General Topology and Applications, *Annals of the New York Academy of Sciences*, **806**, 304–315, New York, 1997.
16. Pettis B.J. On the extension of measures. *Annals of Mathematics*, **54** (1951), 186-197.
17. Scott D.S. Domains for denotational semantics. In M. Nielsen, E. M. Schmidt, eds., Automata, Languages, and Programming, *Lecture Notes in Computer Science*, **140**, 577–613, Springer, 1982.
18. Tix R. *Stetige Bewertungen auf topologischen Räumen*, (Continuous Valuations on Topological Spaces, in German), Diploma Thesis, Darmstadt Institute of Technology, 1995. Available via URL
`http://www.mathematik.th-darmstadt.de/ags/ag14/papers/papers.html`

Mobile Ambients

Luca Cardelli[*] Andrew D. Gordon[*]

Digital Equipment Corporation
Systems Research Center

University of Cambridge
Computer Laboratory

Abstract
We introduce a calculus describing the movement of processes and devices, including movement through administrative domains.

1 Introduction

There are two distinct areas of work in mobility: *mobile computing*, concerning computation that is carried out in mobile devices (laptops, personal digital assistants, etc.), and *mobile computation*, concerning mobile code that moves between devices (applets, agents, etc.). We aim to describe all these aspects of mobility within a single framework that encompasses mobile *agents*, the *ambients* where agents interact and the mobility of the ambients themselves.

The inspiration for this work comes from the potential for mobile computation over the World-Wide Web. The geographic distribution of the Web naturally calls for mobility of computation, as a way of flexibly managing latency and bandwidth. Because of recent advances in networking and language technology, the basic tenets of mobile computation are now technologically realizable. The high-level software architecture potential, however, is still largely unexplored.

The main difficulty with mobile computation on the Web is not in mobility per se, but in the handling of *administrative domains*. In the early days of the Internet one could rely on a flat name space given by IP addresses; knowing the IP address of a computer would very likely allow one to talk to that computer in some way. This is no longer the case: firewalls partition the Internet into administrative domains that are isolated from each other except for rigidly controlled pathways. System administrators enforce policies about what can move through firewalls and how.

Mobility requires more than the traditional notion of authorization to run or to access information in certain domains: it involves the authorization to enter or exit certain domains. In particular, as far as mobile computation is concerned, it is not realistic to imagine that an agent can migrate from any point A to any point B on the Internet. Rather, an agent must first exit its administrative domain (obtaining permission to do so), enter someone else's administrative domain (again, obtaining permission to do so) and then enter a protected area of some machine where it is allowed to run (after obtaining permission to do so). Access to information is controlled at many levels, thus multiple levels of authorization may be involved. Among these levels we have: local computer, local area network, regional area network, wide-area intranet and internet. Mobile programs must be equipped to navigate this hierarchy of administrative domains, at every

[*] Current affiliation: Microsoft Research.

step obtaining authorization to move further. Similarly, laptops must be equipped to access resources depending on their location in the administrative hierarchy. Therefore, at the most fundamental level we need to capture notions of locations, of mobility and of authorization to move.

With these motivations, we adopt a paradigm of mobility where computational ambients are hierarchically structured, where agents are confined to ambients and where ambients move under the control of agents. A novelty of this approach is in allowing the movement of self-contained nested environments that include data and live computation, as opposed to the more common techniques that move single agents or individual objects. Our goal is to make mobile computation scale-up to widely distributed, intermittently connected and well administered computational environments.

This paper is organized as follows. In the rest of Section 1 we introduce our basic concepts and we compare them to previous and current work. In Section 2 we describe a calculus based exclusively on mobility primitives, and we use it to represent basic notions such as numerals and Turing machines, and to code a firewall-crossing protocol. In Section 3 we extend our calculus with local communication, and we show how we can represent more general communication mechanisms as well as the π-calculus.

1.1 Ambients

Ambients have the following main characteristics.

An ambient is a *bounded* placed where computation happens. The interesting property here is the existence of a boundary around an ambient. If we want to move computations easily we must be able to determine what should move; a boundary determines what is inside and what is outside an ambient. Examples of ambients, in this sense, are: a web page (bounded by a file), a virtual address space (bounded by an addressing range), a Unix file system (bounded within a physical volume), a single data object (bounded by "self") and a laptop (bounded by its case and data ports). Non-examples are: threads (where the boundary of what is "reachable" is difficult to determine) and logically related collections of objects. We can already see that a boundary implies some flexible addressing scheme that can denote entities across the boundary; examples are symbolic links, Uniform Resource Locators and Remote Procedure Call proxies. Flexible addressing is what enables, or at least facilitates, mobility. It is also, of course, a cause of problems when the addressing links are "broken".

An ambient can be nested within other ambients. As we discussed, administrative domains are (often) organized hierarchically. If we want to move a running application from work to home, the application must be removed from an enclosing (work) ambient and inserted into another enclosing (home) ambient. A laptop may need a removal pass to leave a workplace, and a government pass to leave or enter a country.

An ambient can be moved as a whole. If we move a laptop to a different network, all the address spaces and file systems within it move accordingly. If we move an agent from one computer to another, its local data moves accordingly.

Each ambient has a name that is used to control access to the ambient. A name is something that can be created and passed around, and from which access capabilities can be extracted. In a realistic situation the true name of an ambient would be guarded very closely, and only specific capabilities would be handed out.

1.2 Technical Context: Systems

Many software systems have explored and are exploring notions of mobility.

Obliq [5] attacks the problems of distribution and mobility for intranet computing. Obliq works well for its intended application, but is not really suitable for computation and mobility over the Web (like other distributed paradigms based on the remote procedure call model) because of the fragility of network proxies over the Web.

Our ambient model is partially inspired by Telescript [16], but is almost dual to it. In Telescript, agents move whereas places stay put. Ambients, instead, move whereas agents are confined to ambients. A Telescript agent, however, is itself a little ambient, since it contains a "suitcase" of data. Some nesting of places is allowed in Telescript.

Java [11] provides a working framework for mobile computation, as well as a widely available infrastructure on which to base more ambitious mobility efforts.

Linda [6] is a "coordination language" where multiple processes interact in a common space (called a tuple space) by exchanging tokens asynchronously. Distributed versions of Linda exist that use multiple tuple spaces and allow remote operations. A dialect of Linda [7] allows nested tuple spaces, but not mobility of the tuple spaces.

1.3 Technical Context: Formalisms

Many existing calculi have provided inspiration for our work.

The π-calculus [15] is a process calculus where channels can "move" along other channels. The movement of processes is represented as the movement of channels that refer to processes. Therefore, there is no clear indication that processes themselves move. For example, if a channel crosses a firewall (that is, if it is communicated to a process meant to represent a firewall), there is no clear sense in which the process has also crossed the firewall. In fact, the channel may cross several independent firewalls, but a process could not be in all those places at once. Nonetheless, many fundamental π-calculus concepts and techniques underlie our work.

The spi calculus [1] extends the π-calculus with cryptographic primitives. The need for such extensions does not seem to arise immediately within our ambient calculus. Some of the motivations for the spi calculus extension are already covered by the notion of encapsulation within an ambient. However, we do not know yet how extensively we can use our ambient primitives for cryptographic purposes.

The Chemical Abstract Machine [3] is a semantic framework, rather than a specific formalism. Its basic notions of reaction in a solution and of membranes that isolate subsolutions, closely resemble ambient notions. However, membranes are not meant to provide strong protection, and there is no concern for mobility of subsolutions. Still, we adopt a "chemical style" in presenting our calculus.

The join-calculus [9] is a reformulation of the π-calculus with a more explicit notion of places of interaction; this greatly helps in building distributed implementations of channel mechanisms. The distributed join-calculus [10] adds a notion of named locations, with essentially the same aims as ours, and a notion of distributed failure. Locations in the distributed join-calculus form a tree, and subtrees can migrate from one part of the tree to another. A main difference with our ambients is that movement may happen directly from any active location to any other known location.

LLinda [8] is a formalization of Linda using process calculi techniques. As in distributed versions of Linda, LLinda has multiple distributed tuple spaces. Multiple tuple spaces are very similar in spirit to multiple ambients, but Linda's tuple spaces do not nest, and there are no restrictions about accessing a tuple space from another one.

Finally, a growing body of literature is concentrating on the idea of adding discrete locations to a process calculus and considering failure of those locations [2, 10]. Our notion of locality is built into our basic calculus. It is induced by a non-trivial and dynamic topology of locations, in the sense that a location that is "far" from the current one can only be reached through multiple individual moves. Failure of a location can be represented as becoming forever unreachable.

2 Mobility

We begin by describing a minimal calculus of ambients that includes only mobility primitives. Still, we shall see that this calculus is quite expressive. In Section 3 we then add communication primitives.

2.1 Mobility Primitives

The syntax of the calculus is defined in the following table. The main syntactic categories are processes (including ambients and agents that execute actions) and capabilities.

Mobility Primitives

$P,Q ::=$	processes	n	names
$(\nu n)P$	restriction		
$\mathbf{0}$	inactivity	$M ::=$	capabilities
$P \mid Q$	composition	*in* n	can enter n
$!P$	replication	*out* n	can exit n
$n[P]$	ambient	*open* n	can open n
$M.P$	action		

Syntactic conventions

$(\nu n)P \mid Q =$	$((\nu n)P) \mid Q$	$(\nu n_1 ... n_m)P$	$\triangleq (\nu n_1)...(\nu n_m)P$	
$!P \mid Q \quad =$	$(!P) \mid Q$	$n[]$	$\triangleq n[\mathbf{0}]$	
$M.P \mid Q \ =$	$(M.P) \mid Q$	M	$\triangleq M.\mathbf{0}$	(where appropriate)

The first four process primitives (restriction, inactivity, composition and replication) have the same meaning as in the π-calculus (see Section 2.3), namely: restriction is used to introduce new names and limit their scope; $\mathbf{0}$ has no behavior; $P \mid Q$ is the parallel composition of P and Q; and $!P$ is an unbounded number of parallel replicas of P. The main difference with respect to the π-calculus is that names are used to name ambients instead of channels. To these standard primitives we add ambients, $n[P]$, and the exercise of capabilities, $M.P$. Next we discuss these new primitives in detail.

2.2 Explanations

We begin by introducing the semantics of ambients informally. A reduction relation $P \longrightarrow Q$ describes the evolution of a process P into a new process Q.

Ambients

An ambient is written $n[P]$, where n is the name of the ambient, and P is the process running inside the ambient. In $n[P]$, it is understood that P is actively running, and that P can be the parallel composition of several processes. We emphasize that P is running even when the surrounding ambient is moving. Running while moving may or may not be realistic, depending on the nature of the ambient and of the communication medium through which the ambient moves, but it is consistent to think in those terms. We express the fact that P is running by a rule that says that any reduction of P becomes a reduction of $n[P]$:

$$P \longrightarrow Q \;\Rightarrow\; n[P] \longrightarrow n[Q]$$

In general, an ambient exhibits a tree structure induced by the nesting of ambient brackets. Each node of this tree structure may contain a collection of (non-ambient) processes running in parallel, in addition to subambients. We say that these processes are running in the ambient, in contrast to the ones running in subambients.

Nothing prevents the existence of two or more ambients with the same name, either nested or at the same level. Once a name is created, it can be used to name multiple ambients. Moreover, $!n[P]$ generates multiple ambients with the same name. This way, for example, one can easily model the replication of services.

Actions and Capabilities

Operations that change the hierarchical structure of ambients are sensitive. In particular such operations can be interpreted as the crossing of firewalls or the decoding of ciphertexts. Hence these operations are restricted by *capabilities*. Thanks to capabilities, an ambient can allow other ambients to perform certain operations without having to reveal its true name. With the communication primitives of Section 3, capabilities can be transmitted as values.

The process $M.\,P$ executes an action regulated by the capability M, and then continues as the process P. The process P does not start running until the action is executed. The reduction rules for $M.\,P$ depend on the capability M, and are described below case by case.

We consider three kinds of capabilities: one for entering an ambient, one for exiting an ambient and one for opening up an ambient. Capabilities are obtained from names; given a name n, the capability *in n* allows entry into n, the capability *out n* allows exit out of n and the capability *open n* allows the opening of n. Implicitly, the possession of one or all of these capabilities for n is insufficient to reconstruct the original name n.

An entry capability, *in m*, can be used in the action *in m. P*, which instructs the ambient surrounding *in m. P* to enter a sibling ambient named m. If no sibling m can be found, the operation blocks until a time when such a sibling exists. If more than one m sibling exists, any one of them can be chosen. The reduction rule is:

$$n[in\ m.\,P \mid Q] \mid m[R] \longrightarrow m[n[P \mid Q] \mid R]$$

If successful, this reduction transforms a sibling n of an ambient m into a child of m. After the execution, the process *in m. P* continues with P, and both P and Q find themselves at a lower level in the tree of ambients.

An exit capability, *out m*, can be used in the action *out m. P*, which instructs the ambient surrounding *out m. P* to exit its parent ambient named *m*. If the parent is not named *m*, the operation blocks until a time when such a parent exists. The reduction rule is:

$$m[n[out\ m.\ P \mid Q] \mid R] \longrightarrow n[P \mid Q] \mid m[R]$$

If successful, this reduction transforms a child *n* of an ambient *m* into a sibling of *m*. After the execution, the process *in m. P* continues with *P*, and both *P* and *Q* find themselves at a higher level in the tree of ambients.

An opening capability, *open n*, can be used in the action *open n. P*. This action provides a way of dissolving the boundary of an ambient named *n* located at the same level as *open*, according to the rule:

$$open\ n.\ P \mid n[Q] \longrightarrow P \mid Q$$

If no ambient *n* can be found, the operation blocks until a time when such an ambient exists. If more than one ambient *n* exists, any one of them can be chosen.

An *open* operation may be upsetting to both *P* and *Q* above. From the point of view of *P*, there is no telling in general what *Q* might do when unleashed. From the point of view of *Q*, its environment is being ripped open. Still, this operation is relatively well-behaved because: (1) the dissolution is initiated by the agent *open n. P*, so that the appearance of *Q* at the same level as *P* is not totally unexpected; (2) *open n* is a capability that is given out by *n*, so *n*[*Q*] cannot be dissolved if it does not wish to be.

Movement from the Inside or the Outside: Subjective vs. Objective

There are two natural kinds of movement primitives for ambients. The distinction is between "I make you move" from the outside (*objective move*) or "I move" from the inside (*subjective move*). Subjective moves have been described above. Objective moves (indicated by an *mv* prefix), obey the rules:

$$mv\ in\ m.\ P \mid m[R] \longrightarrow m[P \mid R] \qquad\qquad m[mv\ out\ m.\ P \mid R] \longrightarrow P \mid m[R]$$

These two kinds of move operations are not trivially interdefinable. The objective moves have simpler rules. However, they operate only on ambients that are not active; they provide no way of moving an existing running ambient. The subjective moves, in contrast, cause active ambients to move and, together with *open*, can approximate the effect of objective moves (as we discuss later).

In evaluating these alternative operations, one should consider who has the authority to move whom. In general, the authority to move rests in the top-level agents of an ambient, which naturally act as *control agents*. Control agents cannot be injected purely by subjective moves, since these moves handle whole ambients. With objective moves, instead, a control agent can be injected into an ambient simply by possessing an entry capability for it. As a consequence, objective moves and entry capabilities together provide the unexpected power of entrapping an ambient into a location it can never exit:

$$\begin{aligned} &entrap\ m \ \triangleq\ (\nu\ k)\ (k[] \mid mv\ in\ m.\ in\ k.\ \mathbf{0}) \\ &entrap\ m \mid m[P] \longrightarrow^* (\nu k)\ k[m[P]] \end{aligned}$$

The *open* capability confers the right to dissolve an ambient from the outside and reveal its contents. It is interesting to consider an operation that dissolves an ambient form the inside, called *acid*:

$$m[acid.\, P \mid Q] \longrightarrow P \mid Q$$

Acid gives a simple encoding of objective moves:

$$mv\ in\ n.P \triangleq (\nu q)\ q[in\ n.\ acid.\ P]$$
$$mv\ out\ n.P \triangleq (\nu q)\ q[out\ n.\ acid.\ P]]$$

Therefore, *acid* is as dangerous as objective moves, providing the power to entrap ambients. We shall see that *open* can be used to define a capability-restricted version of *acid* that does not lead to entrapment.

2.3 Operational Semantics

We now give an operational semantics of the calculus of section 2.1, based on a structural congruence between processes, ≡, and a reduction relation ⟶. This is a semantics in the style of Milner's reaction relation [14] for the π-calculus, which was itself inspired by the Chemical Abstract Machine of Berry and Boudol [3].

Structural Congruence

$P \equiv P$	$P \mid Q \equiv Q \mid P$
$P \equiv Q \Rightarrow Q \equiv P$	$(P \mid Q) \mid R \equiv P \mid (Q \mid R)$
$P \equiv Q, Q \equiv R \Rightarrow P \equiv R$	$!P \equiv P \mid !P$
$P \equiv Q \Rightarrow (\nu n)P \equiv (\nu n)Q$	$(\nu n)(\nu m)P \equiv (\nu m)(\nu n)P$
$P \equiv Q \Rightarrow P \mid R \equiv Q \mid R$	$(\nu n)(P \mid Q) \equiv P \mid (\nu n)Q$ if $n \notin fn(P)$
$P \equiv Q \Rightarrow !P \equiv !Q$	$(\nu n)(m[P]) \equiv m[(\nu n)P]$ if $n \neq m$
$P \equiv Q \Rightarrow n[P] \equiv n[Q]$	$P \mid \mathbf{0} \equiv P$
$P \equiv Q \Rightarrow M.P \equiv M.Q$	$(\nu n)\mathbf{0} \equiv \mathbf{0}$
	$!\mathbf{0} \equiv \mathbf{0}$

Processes of the calculus are grouped into equivalence classes by the relation ≡, which denotes structural congruence (that is, equivalence up to trivial syntactic restructuring). In addition, we identify processes up to renaming of bound names: $(\nu n)P = (\nu m)P\{n \leftarrow m\}$ if $m \notin fn(P)$. By this we mean that these processes are understood to be identical (for example, by choosing an appropriate representation), as opposed to structurally equivalent.

Note that the following terms are in general distinct:

$!(\nu n)P \not\equiv (\nu n)!P$	replication creates new names
$n[P] \mid n[Q] \not\equiv n[P \mid Q]$	multiple *n* ambients have separate identity

The behavior of processes is given by the following reduction relations. The first three rules are the one-step reductions for *in*, *out* and *open*. The next three rules propagate reductions across scopes, ambient nesting and parallel composition. The final rule allows the use of equivalence during reduction. Finally, $\longrightarrow^*$ is the reflexive and transitive closure of ⟶.

Reduction

$$n[in\ m.\ P \mid Q] \mid m[R] \rightarrow m[n[P \mid Q] \mid R] \qquad P \rightarrow Q \Rightarrow (\nu n)P \rightarrow (\nu n)Q$$
$$m[n[out\ m.\ P \mid Q] \mid R] \rightarrow n[P \mid Q] \mid m[R] \qquad P \rightarrow Q \Rightarrow n[P] \rightarrow n[Q]$$
$$open\ n.\ P \mid n[Q] \rightarrow P \mid Q \qquad P \rightarrow Q \Rightarrow P \mid R \rightarrow Q \mid R$$
$$P' \equiv P,\ P \rightarrow Q,\ Q \equiv Q' \Rightarrow P' \rightarrow Q'$$

2.4 Example: Locks

We can use *open* to encode locks that are released and acquired:

$$acquire\ n.\ P \triangleq open\ n.\ P \qquad release\ n.\ P \triangleq n[] \mid P$$

This way, two agents can "shake hands" before proceeding with their execution:

$$acquire\ n.\ release\ m.\ P \mid release\ n.\ acquire\ m.\ Q$$

2.5 Example: Firewall Access

In this example, an agent crosses a firewall by means of previously arranged passwords k, k', and k''. The agent exhibits the password k' by using a wrapper ambient that has k' as its name. The firewall, which has a secret name w, sends out a pilot ambient, $k[out\ w.\ in\ k'.\ in\ w]$, to guide the agent inside. The pilot ambient enters an agent by performing $in\ k'$ (therefore verifying that the agent knows the password), and is given control by being opened. Then, $in\ w$ transports the agent inside the firewall, where the password wrapper is discarded. The third name, k'', is needed to confine the contents Q of the agent and to prevent Q from interfering with the protocol.

The final effect is that the agent physically crosses into the firewall; this can be seen below by the fact that Q is finally placed inside w. (For simplicity, this example is written to allow a single agent to enter.) Assume $(fn(P) \cup fn(Q)) \cap \{k, k', k''\} = \emptyset$ and $w \notin fn(Q)$:

$$Firewall \triangleq (\nu w)\ w[k[out\ w.\ in\ k'.\ in\ w] \mid open\ k'.\ open\ k''.\ P]$$
$$Agent \triangleq k'[open\ k.\ k''[Q]]$$

There is no guarantee here that any particular agent will make it inside the firewall. Rather, the intended guarantee is that if any agent crosses the firewall, it must be one that knows the passwords.

To express the security property of the firewall we introduce a notion of contextual equivalence, $\simeq$. Let a context $C[]$ be a process containing zero or more holes, and for any process P, let $C[P]$ be the process obtained by filling each hole in C with a copy of P (names free in P may become bound). Then define:

$$P{\downarrow}n \triangleq P \equiv (\nu\, m_1 ... m_i)\,(n[P'] \mid P'') \qquad \text{where } n \notin \{m_1 ... m_i\}$$
$$P{\Downarrow}n \triangleq P \rightarrow^* Q \text{ and } Q{\downarrow}n$$
$$P \simeq Q \triangleq \text{for all } n \text{ and } C[],\ C[P]{\Downarrow}n \Leftrightarrow C[Q]{\Downarrow}n$$

If $(fn(P) \cup fn(Q)) \cap \{k, k', k''\} = \emptyset$ and $w \notin fn(Q)$, then we can show that the interaction of the agent with the firewall produces the desired result up to contextual equivalence.

$$(\nu\, k\, k'\, k'')\,(Agent \mid Firewall) \;\simeq\; (\nu w)\, w[Q \mid P]$$

Since contextual equivalence takes into account all possible contexts, the equation above states that the firewall crossing protocol works correctly in the presence of any possible attacker (that does not know the passwords) that may try to disrupt it.

2.6 Example: Objective Moves and Dissolution

Objective moves are not directly encodable. However, specific ambients can explicitly allow objective moves by using *open*:

$$\begin{array}{lll}
allow\ n & \triangleq & !open\ n \\
mv\ in\ n.P & \triangleq & (\nu k)\ k[in\ n.\ in[out\ k.\ open\ k.\ P]] \\
mv\ out\ n.P & \triangleq & (\nu k)\ k[out\ n.\ out[out\ k.\ open\ k.\ P] \\
n^{\downarrow}[P] & \triangleq & n[P \mid allow\ in] \qquad (n^{\downarrow} \text{ allows } mv\ in) \\
n^{\uparrow}[P] & \triangleq & n[P] \mid allow\ out \qquad (n^{\uparrow} \text{ allows } mv\ out) \\
n^{\downarrow\uparrow}[P] & \triangleq & n[P \mid allow\ in] \mid allow\ out \qquad (n^{\downarrow\uparrow} \text{ allows both } mv\ in \text{ and } mv\ out)
\end{array}$$

These definitions are to be used, for example, as follows:

$$\begin{array}{lll}
mv\ in\ n.P \mid n^{\downarrow\uparrow}[Q\,] & \rightarrow^* & n^{\downarrow\uparrow}[P \mid Q] \\
n^{\downarrow\uparrow}[mv\ out\ n.P \mid Q] & \rightarrow^* & P \mid n^{\downarrow\uparrow}[Q]
\end{array}$$

Similarly, the *acid* primitive discussed previously is not encodable via *open*. However, we can code a form of planned dissolution:

$$acid\ n.\ P \;\triangleq\; acid[out\ n.\ open\ n.\ P]$$

to be used with a helper process *open acid* as follows:

$$n[acid\ n.\ P \mid Q] \mid open\ acid \;\rightarrow^*\; P \mid Q$$

This form of *acid* is sufficient for uses in many encodings where it is necessary to dissolve ambients. Encodings are carefully planned, so it is easy to add the necessary *open* instructions. The main difference with the liberal form of *acid* is that *acid n* must name the ambient it is dissolving. More precisely, the encoding of *acid n* requires both an exit and an open capability for *n*.

2.7 Example: External Choice

A major feature of CCS [13] is the presence of a non-deterministic choice operator (+). We do not take + as a primitive, in the spirit of the asynchronous π-calculus, but we can approximate some aspects of it by the following definitions. The intent is that $n{\Rightarrow}P + m{\Rightarrow}Q$ reduces to P in the presence of an n ambient, and reduces to Q in the presence of an m ambient.

$$\begin{array}{lll}
n{\Rightarrow}P + m{\Rightarrow}Q & \triangleq & (\nu\, p\, q\, r)\,(\\
& & \quad p[in\ n.\ out\ n.\ q[out\ p.\ open\ r.\ P]] \mid \\
& & \quad p[in\ m.\ out\ m.\ q[out\ p.\ open\ r.\ Q]] \mid \\
& & \quad open\ q \mid r[\,])
\end{array}$$

For example, assuming $\{p, q, r\} \cap fn(R) = \emptyset$, we have:

$$(n \Rightarrow P + m \Rightarrow Q) \mid n[R] \quad \longrightarrow^{*}\simeq \quad P \mid n[R]$$

where the relation $\longrightarrow^{*}\simeq$ is the relational composition of $\longrightarrow^{*}$ and $\simeq$.

2.8 Example: Numerals

We represent the number i by a stack of nested ambients of depth i. For any natural number i, let $\underline{i}$ be the numeral for i:

$$\underline{0} \triangleq zero[] \qquad\qquad \underline{i{+}1} \triangleq succ[open\ op \mid \underline{i}]$$

The *open op* process is needed to allow ambients named *op* to enter the stack of ambients to operate on it. To show that arithmetic may be programmed on these numerals, we begin with an *ifzero* operation to tell whether a numeral represents 0 or not.

$$\begin{aligned} &ifzero\ P\ Q \triangleq zero \Rightarrow P + succ \Rightarrow Q \\ &\underline{0} \mid ifzero\ P\ Q \longrightarrow^{*}\simeq \underline{0} \mid P \\ &\underline{i{+}1} \mid ifzero\ P\ Q \longrightarrow^{*}\simeq \underline{i{+}1} \mid Q \end{aligned}$$

Next, we can encode increment and decrement operations.

$$\begin{aligned} &inc.P \triangleq ifzero\ (inczero.P)\ (incsucc.P) \\ &inczero.P \triangleq open\ zero.\ (\underline{1} \mid P) \\ &incsucc.P \triangleq (\nu\ p\ q)\ (p[succ[open\ op]] \mid open\ q.\ open\ p.\ P \mid \\ &\qquad\qquad op[in\ succ.\ in\ p.\ in\ succ.\ (q[out\ succ.\ out\ succ.\ out\ p] \mid \\ &\qquad\qquad open\ op)]) \\ &dec.P \triangleq (\nu\ p)\ (op[in\ succ.\ p[out\ succ]] \mid open\ p.\ open\ succ.\ P) \end{aligned}$$

These definitions satisfy:

$$\underline{i} \mid inc.P \longrightarrow^{*}\simeq \underline{i{+}1} \mid P \qquad\qquad \underline{i{+}1} \mid dec.P \longrightarrow^{*}\simeq \underline{i} \mid P$$

Given that iterative computations can be programmed with replication, any arithmetic operation can be programmed with *inc*, *dec* and *iszero*.

2.9 Example: Turing Machines

We emulate Turing machines in a "mechanical" style. A tape consists of a nested sequence of squares, each initially containing the flag *ff*[]. The first square has a distinguished name to indicate the end of the tape to the left:

$$end^{\downharpoonleft\upharpoonright}[ff[] \mid sq^{\downharpoonleft\upharpoonright}[ff[] \mid sq^{\downharpoonleft\upharpoonright}[ff[] \mid sq^{\downharpoonleft\upharpoonright}[ff[] \mid \ldots]]]]$$

The head of the machine is an ambient that inhabits a square. The head moves right by entering the next nested square and moves left by exiting the current square. The head contains the program of the machine and it can read and write the flag in the current square. The trickiest part of the definition concerns extending the tape. Two tape-stretchers are placed at the beginning and end of the tape and continuously add squares.

$$if\ tt\ P, if\ ff\ Q \triangleq tt \Rightarrow open\ tt.\ P + ff \Rightarrow open\ ff.\ Q$$

$head \triangleq$

$head[!open\ S_1.$ state #1 (example)

mv out head.	jump out to read flag
if tt (*ff*[] | *mv in head. in sq.* S_2[]),	head right, state #2
if ff (*tt*[] | *mv in head. out sq.* S_3[]) |	head left, state #3
... |	more state transitions
S_1[]]	initial state
stretchRht ≜	stretch tape right
(ν*r*) *r*[!*open it. mv out r.* ($sq^{\downarrow\uparrow}$[*ff*[]] | *mv in r. in sq. it*[]) | *it*[]]	
stretchLft ≜	stretch tape left
!*open it. mv in end.*	
(*mv out end.* $end^{\downarrow\uparrow}$[$sq^{\downarrow\uparrow}$[] | *ff*[]] |	
in end. in sq. mv out end. open end. mv out sq. mv out end. it[])	
| *it*[]	
machine ≜ *stretchLft* | $end^{\downarrow\uparrow}$[*ff*[] | *head* | *stretchRht*]	

3 Communication

Although the pure mobility calculus is powerful enough to be Turing-complete, it has no communication or variable-binding operators. Such operators seem necessary, for example, to comfortably encode other formalisms such as the π-calculus.

Therefore, we now have to choose a communication mechanism to be used to exchange messages between ambients. The choice of a particular mechanism is somewhat orthogonal to the mobility primitives. However, we should try not to defeat with communication the restrictions imposed by capabilities. This suggests that a primitive form of communication should be purely local, and that the transmission of non-local messages should be restricted by capabilities.

3.1 Communication Primitives

To focus our attention, we pose as a goal the ability to encode the asynchronous π-calculus. For this it is sufficient to introduce a simple asynchronous communication mechanism that works locally within a single ambient.

Mobility and Communication Primitives

P,Q ::=	processes	*M* ::=	capabilities
(ν*n*)*P*	restriction	*x*	variable
0	inactivity	*n*	name
P | *Q*	composition	*in M*	can enter into *M*
!*P*	replication	*out M*	can exit out of *M*
M[*P*]	ambient	*open M*	can open *M*
M.P	capability action	ε	null
(*x*).*P*	input action	*M.M'*	path
⟨*M*⟩	async output action		

We again start by displaying the syntax of a whole calculus. The mobility primitives are essentially those of section 2, but the addition of communication variables changes some of the details. More interestingly, we add input ($(x).P$) and output ($\langle M\rangle$) primitives and we enrich the capabilities to include paths. We identify capabilities up to the following equations: $L.(M.N) = (L.M).N$ and $M.\varepsilon = M = \varepsilon.M$. As a new syntactic convention, we have that $(x).P \mid Q = ((x).P) \mid Q$.

3.2 Explanations

Communicable Values

The entities that can be communicated are either names or capabilities. In realistic situations, communication of names should be rather rare, since knowing the name of an ambient gives a lot of control over it. Instead, it should be common to communicate restricted capabilities to allow controlled interactions between ambients.

It now becomes useful to combine multiple capabilities into *paths*, especially when one or more of those capabilities are represented by input variables. To this end we introduce a path-formation operation on capabilities ($M.\ M'$). For example, (*in n. in m*). *P* is interpreted as *in n. in m. P*.

We distinguish between ν-bound names and input-bound variables. Variables can be instantiated with names or capabilities. In practice, we do not need to distinguish these two sorts lexically, but we often use *n, m, p, q* for names and *w, x, y, z* for variables.

Ambient I/O

The simplest communication mechanism that we can imagine is local anonymous communication within an ambient (ambient I/O, for short):

$(x).P$	input action	$\langle M\rangle$	async output action

An output action releases a capability (possibly a name) into the local ether of the surrounding ambient. An input action captures a capability from the local ether and binds it to a variable within a scope. We have the reduction:

$$(x).P \mid \langle M\rangle \longrightarrow P\{x\leftarrow M\}$$

This local communication mechanism fits well with the ambient intuitions. In particular, long-range communication, like long-range movement, should not happen automatically because messages may have to cross firewalls. Still, this simple mechanism is sufficient, as we shall see, to emulate communication over named channels, and more generally to provide an encoding of the asynchronous π-calculus.

Remark

To allow both names and capabilities to be output and input, there is a single syntactic sort that includes both. Then, a meaningless term of the form *n. P* can then arise, for instance, from the process $((x).\ x.\ P) \mid \langle n\rangle$. This anomaly is caused by the desire to denote movement capabilities by variables, as in $(x).\ x.\ P$, and from the desire to denote names by variables, as in $(x).\ x[P]$. We permit *n. P* to be formed, syntactically, in order to make substitution always well defined. A simple type system distinguishing names from movement capabilities would avoid this anomaly.

3.3 Operational Semantics

The structural congruence relation is defined as in section 2.3, with the understanding that P and M range now over larger classes, and with the addition of the following equivalences:

Structural Congruence

$P \equiv Q \;\Rightarrow\; M[P] \equiv M[Q]$	$\varepsilon.P \equiv P$
$P \equiv Q \;\Rightarrow\; (x).P \equiv (x).Q$	$(M.M').P \equiv M.M'.P$

We now identify processes up to renaming of bound variables: $(x).P = (y).P\{x{\leftarrow}y\}$ if $y \notin fv(P)$. Finally, we have a new reduction rule:

Reduction

$$(x).P \mid \langle M \rangle \longrightarrow P\{x{\leftarrow}M\}$$

3.4 Example: Cells

A cell *cell c w* stores a value *w* at a location *c*, where a value is a capability. The cell is set to output its current contents destructively, and is set to be "refreshed" with either the old contents (by *get*) or a new contents (by *set*). Note that *set* is essentially an output operation, but it is a synchronous one: its sequel *P* runs only after the cell has been set. Parallel *get* and *set* operations do not interfere.

$$\begin{aligned}
&\mathit{cell}\ c\ w \triangleq c^{\Downarrow}[\langle w \rangle] \\
&\mathit{get}\ c\ (x).\ P \triangleq \mathit{mv\ in}\ c.\ (x).\ (\langle x \rangle \mid \mathit{mv\ out}\ c.\ P) \\
&\mathit{set}\ c\ \langle w \rangle.\ P \triangleq \mathit{mv\ in}\ c.\ (x).\ (\langle w \rangle \mid \mathit{mv\ out}\ c.\ P)
\end{aligned}$$

It is possible to code an atomic *get-and-set* primitive:

$$\mathit{get\text{-}and\text{-}set}\ c\ (x)\ \langle w \rangle.\ P \triangleq \mathit{mv\ in}\ c.\ (x).\ (\langle w \rangle \mid \mathit{mv\ out}\ c.\ P)$$

Named cells can be assembled into ambients that act as record data structures.

3.5 Example: Routable Packets and Active Networks

We define *packet pkt* as an empty packet of name *pkt* that can be routed repeatedly to various destinations. We also define *route pkt with P to M* as the act of placing *P* inside the packet *pkt* and sending the packet to *M*; this is to be used in parallel with *packet pkt*. Note that *M* can be a compound capability, representing a path to follow. Finally, *forward pkt to M* is an abbreviation that forwards any packet named *pkt* that passes by to *M*. Here we assume that *P* does not interfere with routing.

$$\begin{aligned}
&\mathit{packet}\ pkt \triangleq pkt[!(x).x \mid !\mathit{open}\ route] \\
&\mathit{route}\ pkt\ \mathit{with}\ P\ \mathit{to}\ M \triangleq route[\mathit{in}\ pkt.\ \langle M \rangle \mid P] \\
&\mathit{forward}\ pkt\ \mathit{to}\ M \triangleq \mathit{route}\ pkt\ \mathit{with}\ \mathbf{0}\ \mathit{to}\ M
\end{aligned}$$

Since our packets are ambients, they may contain behavior that becomes active within the intermediate routers. Therefore we can naturally model *active networks*, which are characterized by routers that execute code carried by packets.

3.6 Communication Between Ambients

Our basic communication primitives operate only within a given ambient. We now discuss one example of communication across ambients. In addition, in section 3.7 we treat the specific case of channel-based communication across ambients.

It is not realistic to assume direct long-range communication. Communication, like movement, is subject to access restrictions due to the existence of administrative domains. Therefore, it is convenient to model long-range communication as the movement of "messenger" agents that must cross administrative boundaries. Assume, for simplicity, that the location M allows I/O by $!open\ io$. By M^{-1} we indicate a given return path from M.

$@M\langle a\rangle$	$\triangleq$	$io[M.\ \langle a\rangle]$	remote output at M
$@M(x)M^{-1}.\ P$	$\triangleq$	$(\nu n)\ (io[M.\ (x).\ n[M^{-1}.\ P]]\ \vert\ open\ n)$	remote input at M

To avoid transmitting P all the way there and back, we can write input as:

$$@M(x)M^{-1}.\ P \triangleq (\nu n)\ (io[M.\ (x).\ n[M^{-1}.\ \langle x\rangle]]\ |\ open\ n)\ |\ (x).\ P$$

To emulate Remote Procedure Call we write (assuming res contains the result):

$$@M\ arg\langle a\rangle\ res(x)\ M^{-1}.\ P \triangleq$$
$$(\nu n)\ (io[M.\ (\langle a\rangle\ |\ open\ res.\ (x).\ n[M^{-1}.\ \langle x\rangle])]\ |\ open\ n)\ |\ (x).\ P$$

This is essentially an implementation of a synchronous communication (RPC) by two asynchronous communications ($\langle a\rangle$ and $\langle x\rangle$).

3.7 Encoding the π-calculus

The encoding of the asynchronous π-calculus is moderately easy, given our I/O primitives. A channel is simply represented by an ambient: the name of the channel is the name of the ambient. This is very similar in spirit to the join-calculus [9] where channels are rooted at a location. Communication on a channel is represented by local communication inside an ambient. The basic technique is a variation on objective moves. A conventional name, io, is used to transport input and output requests into the channel. The channel opens all such requests and lets them interact.

$ch\ n$	$\triangleq$	$n[!open\ io]$	a channel
$(ch\ n)P$	$\triangleq$	$(\nu n)\ (ch\ n\ \vert\ P)$	a new channel
$n(x).P$	$\triangleq$	$(\nu p)\ (io[in\ n.\ (x).\ p[out\ n.\ P]]\ \vert\ open\ p)$	channel input
$n\langle M\rangle$	$\triangleq$	$io[in\ n.\ \langle M\rangle]$	async channel output

These definitions satisfy the expected reduction $n(x).P\ |\ n\langle M\rangle \longrightarrow^* P\{x\leftarrow M\}$ in the presence of a channel $ch\ n$. Therefore, we can write the following encoding of the π-calculus:

Encoding of the Asynchronous π-calculus

$⟪(\nu n)P⟫ \triangleq (\nu n)\ (n[!open\ io]\ \vert\ ⟪P⟫)$		$⟪P\ \vert\ Q⟫$	$\triangleq$	$⟪P⟫\ \vert\ ⟪Q⟫$
$⟪n(x).P⟫ \triangleq (\nu p)\ (io[in\ n.\ (x).\ p[out\ n.\ ⟪P⟫]]\ \vert\ open\ p)$		$⟪!P⟫$	$\triangleq$	$!⟪P⟫$
$⟪n\langle m\rangle⟫ \triangleq io[in\ n.\ \langle m\rangle]$				

This encoding includes the choice-free synchronous π-calculus, since it can itself be encoded within the asynchronous π-calculus [4, 12].

We can fairly conveniently use these definitions to embed communication on named channels within the ambient calculus (provided the name *io* is not used for other purposes). Communication on these named channels, though, only works within a single ambient. In other words, from our point of view, a π-calculus process always inhabits a single ambient. Therefore, the notion of mobility in the π-calculus (communication of names over named channels) is different from our notion of mobility.

4 Conclusions and Future Work

We have introduced the informal notion of mobile ambients, and we have discussed how this notion captures the structure of complex networks and the behavior of mobile computation. We have then investigated an ambient calculus that formalizes this notion simply and powerfully. Our calculus is no more complex than common process calculi, but supports reasoning about mobility and, at least to some degree, security.

This paper concentrates mostly on examples and intuition. In ongoing work we are developing theories of equivalences for the ambient calculus, drawing on earlier work on the π-calculus. These equivalences will allow us to reason about mobile computation, as briefly illustrated in the firewall crossing example.

On this foundation, we can envision new programming methodologies, programming libraries and programming languages for global computation.

Acknowledgments

Thanks to Cédric Fournet, Paul McJones and Jan Vitek for comments on early drafts. Stuart Wray suggested an improved definition of external choice.

Gordon held a Royal Society University Research Fellowship for most of the time we worked on this paper.

References

[1] Abadi, M. and A.D. Gordon, **A calculus for cryptographic protocols: the spi calculus**. *Proc. Fourth ACM Conference on Computer and Communications Security*, 36-47, 1997.

[2] Amadio, R.M., **An asynchronous model of locality, failure, and process mobility**. *Proc. COORDINATION 97*, Berlin, 1997.

[3] Berry, G. and G. Boudol, **The chemical abstract machine**. *Theoretical Computer Science* **96**(1), 217-248, 1992.

[4] Boudol, G., **Asynchrony and the π-calculus.** *TR 1702, INRIA, Sophia-Antipolis,* 1992.

[5] Cardelli, L., **A language with distributed scope**. *Computing Systems,* **8**(1), 27-59. MIT Press. 1995.

[6] Carriero, N. and D. Gelernter, **Linda in context**. *CACM*, **32**(4), 444-458, 1989.

[7] Carriero, N., D. Gelernter, and L. Zuck, **Bauhaus Linda,** in LNCS 924, 66-76, Springer-Verlag, 1995.

[8] De Nicola, R., G.-L. Ferrari and R. Pugliese, **Locality based Linda: programming with explicit localities**. *Proc. TAPSOFT'97*. 1997.

[9] Fournet, C. and G. Gonthier, **The reflexive CHAM and the join-calculus.** *Proc. 23rd Annual ACM Symposium on Principles of Programming Languages*, 372-385. 1996.

[10] Fournet, C., G. Gonthier, J.-J. Lévy, L. Maranget, D. Rémy, **A calculus of mobile agents.** *Proc. CONCUR'96*, 406-421. 1996.

[11] Gosling, J., B. Joy and G. Steele, **The Java language specification.** Addison-Wesley. 1996.

[12] Honda., K. and M. Tokoro, **An object calculus for asynchronous communication.** *Proc. ECOOP'91*, LNCS 521, 133-147, Springer Verlag, 1991.

[13] Milner, R., **A calculus of communicating systems.** LNCS 92. Springer-Verlag. 1980.

[14] Milner, R., **Functions as processes.** *Mathematical Structures in Computer Science* **2**, 119-141. 1992.

[15] Milner, R., J. Parrow and D. Walker, **A calculus of mobile processes, Parts 1-2.** *Information and Computation*, **100**(1), 1-77. 1992

[16] White, J.E., **Mobile agents.** In *Software Agents*, J. Bradshaw, ed. AAAI Press / The MIT Press. 1996.

Rational Term Rewriting*

A. Corradini[1] and F. Gadducci[2]

[1] Università di Pisa, Dipartimento di Informatica, Corso Italia 40, I-56214 Pisa, Italy (andrea@di.unipi.it).

[2] TUB, Fachbereich 13 Informatik, Franklinstraße 28/29, D-10587 Berlin, Germany (gfabio@cs.tu-berlin.de).

Abstract. Rational terms (possibly infinite terms with finitely many subterms) can be represented in a finite way via μ-terms, that is, terms over a signature extended with self-instantiation operators. For example, $f^\omega = f(f(f(\ldots)))$ can be represented as $\mu_x.f(x)$ (or also as $\mu_x.f(f(x))$, $f(\mu_x.f(x))$, $\ldots$). Now, if we reduce a μ-term t to s via a rewriting rule using standard notions of the theory of Term Rewriting Systems, how are the rational terms corresponding to t and to s related?

We answer to this question in a satisfactory way, resorting to the definition of infinite parallel rewriting proposed in [7]. We also provide a simple, algebraic description of μ-term rewriting through a variation of Meseguer's Rewriting Logic formalism.

1 Introduction

Rational terms are possibly infinite terms with a finite set of subterms. They show up in a natural way in Theoretical Computer Science whenever some finite cyclic structures are of concern (for example data flow diagrams, cyclic term graphs, or process algebras with recursion), and one desires to abstract out from the "degree of folding" of such structures, intuitively identifying those that denote the same infinitary behaviour.

For example, the μ-term $t_1 = \mu_x.ite(B, seq(C_1, x), C_2)$ can be used as a linear representation of a flow chart intended to model the structure of a *while* loop using the *if-then-else (ite)* and the *sequentialization (seq)* statements, where the boolean condition B and the statements C_1 and C_2 are left unspecified. As stressed in [20], the intended meaning of the operator μ_x, when applied to a term $t[x]$ with x free, is of constraining the instantiation of x in t to $\mu_x.t$ only; thus μ_x can be considered as a self-instantiation operator. By performing this self-instantiation once in t_1, we get $t_2 = ite(B, seq(C_1, \mu_x.ite(B, seq(C_1, x), C_2)), C_2)$. Now, both t_1 and t_2 can be seen as a finite representation of the same infinite, rational term $ite(B, seq(C_1, ite(B, seq(C_1, ite(B, seq(C_1, \ldots), C_2)), C_2)), C_2)$, which, in turn, can be regarded as a representative of the equivalence class of μ-terms containing t_1 and t_2. ¿From a computational viewpoint, rational terms are clearly

* Research partly supported by the EC TMR Network GETGRATS (General Theory of Graph Transformation Systems) through the Dipartimento di Informatica of Pisa and the Technical University of Berlin.

a very interesting subclass of infinite terms, because they have a finitary representation; usually, however, this is not unique.

Infinitary extensions of Term Rewriting have been considered by various authors during the last decade [12, 11, 15, 16, 7, 20, 21, 22, 9, 8]. Most of those contributions are concerned with the study of the rewriting relation induced by a set of finite term rules on infinite terms, presenting results about the existence of normal forms (possibly reachable after ω steps), confluence and so on. Only a few of them, namely [20, 21, 8], focus on the subclass of rational terms, regarded essentially as the semantics of some finite but possibly cyclic structures (term graphs or μ-terms).

The goal of this paper is to provide a solid mathematical basis for the theory of rational term rewriting. One main requisite for us is that such a theory must provide a "clean" semantics for the rewriting of the finitary representations of rational terms. This is a not completely trivial task, as shown by the following two simple examples which make use of μ-terms, the finitary representation of rational terms that we shall use along the paper.

Let t be the μ-term $t = \mu_x.f(x)$, representing the rational term $f^\omega \stackrel{def}{=} f(f(f(\ldots)))$, and let $R : f(y) \to g(y)$ be a term rewriting rule. Unlike for example [20], we insist that in our theory it should be possible to apply R to t, obtaining, quite obviously, the reduction $\mu_x.f(x) \to_R \mu_x.g(x)$. If we consider the associated rational terms, this apparently innocuous rewriting step requires some infinitary extension of the theory of term rewriting, because there are infinitely many occurrences of f in f^ω, and all of them have to be changed to g: in fact, the μ-term $\mu_x.g(x)$ represents g^ω.

There are two possible infinitary extensions of term rewriting that allow to formalize such a phenomenon. Using the theory of ***transfinite rewriting*** of [22] (and adopted by most of the papers mentioned above), one obtains g^ω as the limit (in the standard complete metric space of infinite terms [1]) of the infinite (Cauchy) sequence of reductions $f^\omega \to_R g(f^\omega) \to_R g(g(f^\omega)) \leadsto g^\omega$. Using instead the ***infinite parallel rewriting*** of [7], g^ω is obtained in a single reduction step by replacing in parallel all the occurrences of f in f^ω by g: this kind of reduction is defined using standard completion techniques that exploit the CPO structure of possibly partial, possibly infinite terms [19].

And what about the application of the "collapsing" rule $R' : g(y) \to y$ to $\mu_x.g(x)$? There is no apparent reason to forbid it, and one would expect to obtain the reduction $\mu_x.g(x) \to_{R'} \mu_x.x$. Considering the corresponding rational terms, by applying the theory of [22] we have that since $g^\omega \to_{R'} g^\omega$, the limit of infinitely many such reductions cannot be different from g^ω,[3] which is not related at all to $\mu_x.x$. Using the infinite parallel rewriting of [7], instead, we have that g^ω rewrites to $\bot$, the bottom element of the CPO of terms, and $\bot$ is indeed the canonical interpretation of the μ-term $\mu_x.x$, according to the Iteration Algebras framework [3]. An infinite term made of infinitely many nested redexes of collapsing rules (as g^ω in this example) will be called a "hypercollapsing

[3] Actually such a derivation is not ***strongly convergent***, and thus it is not considered admissible in [22].

tower", using the terminology of [22].

This discussion motivates our presentation of rational term rewriting in Section 3, which is an adaptation to the rational case of the definitions and results in [7]. In the same section we also introduce the rewriting of μ-terms, which is as straightforward as possible. The main result of the paper will show the soundness of the (parallel) rewriting of μ-terms with respect to the reduction of possibly infinite, rational set of redexes in their unfolded rational term.

In Section 4 we provide a logical presentation of μ-term rewriting and of rational rewriting. For the logical viewpoint, our starting point is the seminal work of José Meseguer about *Rewriting Logic* [25]. The basic idea is to consider a rewriting system $\mathcal{R}$ as a logical theory, and any rewriting as a sequent entailed by that theory. The entailment relation is defined inductively by suitable deduction rules, showing how sequents can be derived from other sequents. Sequents themselves are triples $\langle \alpha, t, s \rangle$, where α is an element of a so-called *algebra of proof terms*, encoding a justification of the rewriting of t into s.

The original presentation of rewriting logic dealt with the finitary case. We consider here a variation of it, called *(one-step) Preiteration Rewriting Logic*, by introducing suitable rules for μ-terms. The faithfulness of this presentation of μ-term rewriting with respect to the original formulation is expressed by a result stating that there is bijection between sequents relating two terms and parallel reductions between them. The advantage of this logical approach is that not only the terms, but also the reductions are now endowed with an algebraic structure (the structure of proof terms), and this allows us to obtain a more precise relationship between μ-term and rational rewriting with respect to the results in Section 3. In fact, we obtain a faithful (in the above sense) logical presentation of rational rewriting by considering *rational* sequents, i.e., equivalence classes of sequents with respect to suitable axioms.

Finally, in the concluding section we discuss the relationship with related papers, and we hint at some topics for future work.

2 Rational Terms and μ-terms

The study of infinite terms is one of the most relevant contribution of computer science to the field of Universal Algebra. The starting point was the mid-Seventies work of the ADJ group (see e.g. [19, 18]) on continuous algebras, which put the basis for the studies on varieties of *ordered algebras*, that is, algebras where the carrier is a partial order (see also [2]).

We assume the reader to be familiar with the usual notion of *algebra* over a signature Σ (that is, a ranked alphabet of operator symbols $\Sigma = \bigcup_{n \in \mathbb{N}} \Sigma_n$, saying that f is of *arity* n for $f \in \Sigma_n$). We denote by **Σ-Alg** the category of algebras over Σ, and of *Σ-homomorphisms*. *Continuous algebras* are simply algebras where the carrier is not just a set, but rather a complete partial order, and the operators are continuous functions. Correspondingly, since homomorphisms must preserve the algebraic structure, they are required to be strict continuous functions.

Definition 1 (complete partial orders). A partial order $\langle D, \leq \rangle$ is *complete* (is a CPO) if it has an element $\bot$ (called *bottom*) such that $\bot \leq d$ for all $d \in D$, and it has *least upper bounds* (LUB's) for all ω-chains of elements. If $\{d_i\}_{i<\omega}$ is an ω-chain (i.e., $d_i \leq d_{i+1}$ for all $i < \omega$), we denote its LUB by $\bigsqcup_{i<\omega}\{d_i\}$. A *continuous function* $f : \langle D, \leq_D \rangle \to \langle D', \leq_{D'} \rangle$ between CPO's is a function $f : D \to D'$ which preserves LUB's of ω-chains, i.e., $f(\bigsqcup_{i<\omega})\{d_i\} = \bigsqcup_{i<\omega}\{f(d_i)\}$; it is *strict* if $f(\bot_D) = \bot_{D'}$. **CPO** denotes the category of CPO's and continuous functions. □

We denote with **Σ-CAlg** the category of continuous algebras and strict continuous homomorphisms. We recall now the basic definitions and the main results on initial algebras and rational terms that will be used along the paper; these are borrowed from [3, 19, 17], to which we refer the interested reader.

It is well-known that, for each signature Σ, the category **Σ-Alg** has an initial object, often called the *word algebra* and denoted by T_Σ. Its elements are all the terms freely generated from the constants and the operators of Σ, and can be regarded as finite trees whose nodes are labeled by operator symbols. As shown in [19], also the category **Σ-CAlg** has an initial object, denoted CT_Σ. Its elements are possibly infinite, possibly partial terms freely generated from Σ, and they form a CPO where the ordering relation is given by $t \leq t'$ iff t' is "more defined" than t. We introduce directly CT_Σ, since T_Σ can be recovered as a suitable sub-algebra: definitions are borrowed from [19], with minor changes.

Definition 2 (terms as functions). Let ω^* be the set of all finite strings of positive natural numbers; its elements are called *occurrences*, and the empty string is denoted by λ. Furthermore, let Σ be a signature and X be a set of variables such that $\Sigma \cap X = \emptyset$. A *term* over (Σ, X) is a partial function $t : \omega^* \to \Sigma \cup X$ such that the domain of definition of t, $\mathcal{O}(t)$, satisfies (for $w \in \omega^*$ and $i \in \omega$)

- $wi \in \mathcal{O}(t) \Rightarrow w \in \mathcal{O}(t)$;
- $wi \in \mathcal{O}(t) \Rightarrow t(w) \in \Sigma_n$ for some $n \geq i$.

$\mathcal{O}(t)$ is called the *set of occurrences* of t. A term t is *total* if $t(w) \in \Sigma_n \Rightarrow wi \in \mathcal{O}(t)$ for all $0 < i \leq n$; t is *finite* if so is $\mathcal{O}(t)$; and t is *linear* if no variable occurs more than once in it.

Given an occurrence $w \in \omega^*$ and a term $t \in CT_\Sigma(X)$, the *subterm* of t at (occurrence) w is the term t/w defined as $t/w(u) = t(wu)$ for all $u \in \omega^*$. □

The set of terms over (Σ, X) is denoted by $CT_\Sigma(X)$, and CT_Σ stays for $CT_\Sigma(\emptyset)$. For finite, total terms, this description is equivalent to the usual representation of terms as operators applied to other terms. Partial terms are made total in this representation by introducing the undefined term $\bot$, which represents the empty function $\bot : \emptyset \to \Sigma \cup X$, always undefined. Thus, for example, if $x \in X$, $t = f(\bot, g(x))$ is the term such that $\mathcal{O}(t) = \{\lambda, 2, 2 \cdot 1\}$, $t(\lambda) = f \in \Sigma_2$, $t(2) = g \in \Sigma_1$, and $t(2 \cdot 1) = x \in X$.

$CT_\Sigma(X)$ forms a CPO with respect to the "approximation" relation. We say that t *approximates* t' (written $t \leq t'$) iff t is less defined than t' as partial function. The least element of $CT_\Sigma(X)$ with respect to $\leq$ is clearly $\perp$. An ω-chain $\{t_i\}_{i<\omega}$ is an infinite sequence of terms $t_0 \leq t_1 \leq \ldots$. Every ω-chain $\{t_i\}_{i<\omega}$ in $CT_\Sigma(X)$ has a LUB $\bigsqcup_{i<\omega}\{t_i\}$ characterized as follows:

$$t = \bigsqcup_{i<\omega}\{t_i\} \quad \Leftrightarrow \quad \forall w \in \omega^* . \exists i < \omega . \forall j \geq i . t_j(w) = t(w).$$

¿From CT_Σ, T_Σ can be recovered as the subalgebra of finite, total terms. In the paper our main interest is in *rational terms*.

Definition 3 (rational terms). A term t over (Σ, X) is *rational* if the associated set of prefixes $\mathcal{P}(t) = \{\langle w, t(w)\rangle \mid w \in \mathcal{O}(t)\}$ is regular, that is, if it is recognizable from a finite automata. Equivalently, t is rational if the set of all its subterms $\{t/u \mid u \in \mathcal{O}(t)\}$ is finite.

The collection of all rational terms over (Σ, X) is denoted by $RT_\Sigma(X)$, and it is easily shown to be a subalgebra of $CT_\Sigma(X)$, but not a continuous one. □

A different approach to the study of infinite terms, and in particular to the characterization of rational terms, focussed instead on the extension of the notion of signature by means of suitable *recursion operators*, and on an axiomatic characterization of unique fixed-points. A seminal stream (with tight links to the categorical notion of *algebraic theories* [24]) started with the paper on *algebraic iterative theories* by Elgot [13]. Here we recall just a few basic results, for which we refer the reader to [4].

Definition 4 (μ-terms). Let Σ be a signature and X be a (countably infinite) set of variables such that $\Sigma \cap X = \emptyset$. The set $\mu T_\Sigma(X)$ of *μ-terms* over (Σ, X) is defined as the smallest set of expressions satisfying the following clauses:

- $x \in \mu T_\Sigma(X)$ if $x \in X$;
- $f(t_1, \ldots, t_n) \in \mu T_\Sigma(X)$ if $f \in \Sigma_n, t_i \in \mu T_\Sigma(X)$;
- $\mu_x.t \in \mu T_\Sigma(X)$ if $x \in X, t \in \mu T_\Sigma(X)$.

Equivalently, let $\Sigma^\mu_X = \Sigma \uplus \{\mu_x \mid x \in X\}$ be a signature that extends Σ with one unary operator for each variable in X. Then μ-terms over (Σ, X) can also be defined as finite terms over Σ^μ_X, i.e., elements of the word algebra $T_{\Sigma^\mu_X}(X)$. □

Consistently with the interpretation described in the Introduction, operator μ_x is a binding operator for variable x. Thus we define the set of *free variables* $FV(t)$ for a term t in the usual way, we call *closed* any term with no free variables, and we identify terms up to α-conversion.

Substitutions are functions from variables to terms that, by freeness, can be extended in a unique way to operator preserving functions from terms to terms. Since we are dealing with two different kind of terms, we introduce now two types of substitutions which will be used in the sequel.

Definition 5 (continuous and parameter substitutions). Let Σ be a signature and X, Y be two (countably infinite) sets of variables such that $\Sigma \cap X = \Sigma \cap Y = \emptyset$. A *(continuous) substitution* from X to Y is a function $\sigma : X \to CT_\Sigma(Y)$ (used in postfix notation). It uniquely determines a strict continuous Σ-homomorphism (also denoted by σ) from $CT_\Sigma(X)$ to $CT_\Sigma(Y)$, which extends σ as follows:

- $\bot\sigma = \bot$;
- $f(t_1, \ldots, t_n)\sigma = f(t_1\sigma, \ldots, t_n\sigma)$;
- $\left(\bigcup_{i<\omega}\{t_i\}\right)\sigma = \bigcup_{i<\omega}\{t_i\sigma\}$.

A *parameter substitution* is a function $\sigma : X \to \mu T_\Sigma(X \cup Y)$. It uniquely determines an operator preserving function from $\mu T_\Sigma(X)$ to $\mu T_\Sigma(X \cup Y)$, as follows

- $x\sigma = \sigma(x)$;
- $f(t_1, \ldots, t_n)\sigma = f(t_1\sigma, \ldots, t_n\sigma)$;
- $(\mu_x.t)\sigma = \mu_x.(t\sigma_x)$,

where $\sigma_x(y) = x$ if $x = y$, and $\sigma_x(y) = \sigma(y)$ otherwise.

A substitution is *finite* if there is only a finite number of variables x such that $\sigma(x) \neq x$: it will be described as a finite set $\{x_1/t_1, \ldots, x_n/t_n\}$ with $t_i = \sigma(x_i)$ for all $1 \leq i \leq n$. □

As for classical algebras, exploiting the syntactical nature of μ-terms one can define suitable structures where operators can be interpreted, called *preiteration algebras* [4]. For our purposes, it is enough to know that the set $\mu T_\Sigma(X)$ forms the *free* preiteration algebra over X in the category **Σ-PIAlg**, where objects are preiteration algebras and arrows are *preiteration homomorphisms*, that is, homomorphisms preserving also the μ's.

In this framework an *equation* is a pair $\langle t, s\rangle$ of μ-terms, and the class of preiteration algebras satisfying an equational specification forms a suitable *variety*, *à la* Birkhoff. In particular, we are interested in the variety of *iteration algebras*, and more specifically in the *free iteration algebra*. Among the many equivalent axiomatizations of this free algebra, we prefer the following one (based actually on *conditional* equations) for its clarity and conciseness. Other presentations are described in [4], which also presents informal explanations for the rules below.

Definition 6 (free iteration algebra). Given a signature Σ and a (countably infinite) set X of variables, let $\cong$ be the least congruence relation over $\mu T_\Sigma(X)$, closed with respect to parameter substitutions, induced by the following rules

- *(composition)*

$$\frac{}{\mu_x.(t\{x/s\}) = t\{x/\mu_x.(s\{x/t\})\}};$$

- *(left zero)*

$$\frac{x \notin FV(t)}{\mu_x.t = t};$$

– *(regularity)*

$$\frac{u \notin FV(t), \quad \mu_u.(t\{x/u, y/u\}) = \mu_u.(s\{x/u, y/u\})}{\mu_u.(t\{x/u, y/u\}) = \mu_y.(s\{x/\mu_x.t\})}.$$

We define the *free iteration algebra* over (Σ, X) as the set $\mu T_\Sigma(X)_{/\cong}$, obtained by quotienting the free preiteration algebra $\mu T_\Sigma(X)$ by the congruence $\cong$. □

As far as we know, Ginali in her Ph.D. thesis (see [17]) and independently Elgot, Bloom and Tindell [14] were the first to prove a correspondence result between the class of regular trees and Elgot's free iterative theories. Building on that result, Bloom and Ésik proved in [3] the following theorem.

Theorem 7 (rational terms and free iteration algebras). *For any signature Σ and set X of variables, there is a preiteration isomorphism between the class $RT_\Sigma(X)$ of rational trees over (Σ, X) and the class of elements of the free iteration algebra $\mu T_\Sigma(X))_{/\cong}$.* □

In the rest of the paper for a μ-term t we will denote by $[t]$ the rational term corresponding (via the isomorphism mentioned in the last result) to the equivalence class of t modulo the axioms of Definition 6. Intuitively, $[t]$ is obtained as the limit of a chain of μ-terms starting from t and where at each step a suitable self-instantiation (via a parameter substitution) is applied. The only μ-term to which this intuition is not immediately applicable is $\mu_x.x$: the reader can safely assume that $[\mu_x.x] = \bot$ by definition.

3 Rewriting of Rational Terms and of μ-Terms

The standard definition of term rewriting will be extended in this section to the rewriting of μ-terms (i.e., closed elements of $\mu T_\Sigma(X)$) and of infinite terms (elements of CT_Σ) via finite rules. Borrowing from [7], besides the standard sequential derivations we will introduce an infinitary extension called ***infinite parallel rewriting*** which allows one to reduce infinitely many redexes of an infinite term in a single reduction step. In particular, we will focus on the subcase of *rational* rewriting, i.e., the parallel reduction of rational sets of redexes. The main result of the section will show the soundness of μ-term rewriting with respect to rational term rewriting. Definitions and results are presented here for the class of *orthogonal* term rewriting systems only.

Definition 8 (term rewriting systems (TRS)). Let X be a countably infinite set of variables. A *term rewriting system* $\mathcal{R}$ (over X) is a tuple (Σ, L, R), where Σ is a signature,[4] L is a set of labels, and R is a function $R : L \to T_\Sigma(X) \times T_\Sigma(X)$, such that for all $d \in L$, if $R(d) = \langle l, r\rangle$ then $var(r) \subseteq var(l) \subseteq X$ and l is not a variable.

A TRS $\mathcal{R}$ is *orthogonal* if all its rules are left-linear and *non-overlapping*, that is, the left-hand side of each rule does not unify with a non-variable subterm of any other rule in $\mathcal{R}$, or with a proper, non-variable subterm of itself. □

[4] Often the signature will be understood.

Given a term rewriting system (also TRS) $\mathcal{R}$, we usually write $d : l \to r \in R$ if $d \in L$ and $R(d) = \langle l, r \rangle$; to make explicit the variables contained in a rule, we write $d(x_1, \ldots, x_n) : l(x_1, \ldots, x_n) \to r(x_1, \ldots, x_n) \in R$ where $\{x_1, \ldots, x_n\} = var(l)$. For example, the TRS $\mathcal{Z} = \{d : f(x,x) \to a, d_1 : f(x, f(y,z)) \to a\}$ is not orthogonal: d is not left-linear, while $f(x, f(y,z))$ can unify with its subterm $f(y,z)$.

The definitions below introduce the rewriting of infinite terms and of μ-terms.

Definition 9 (subterm replacement). Given terms $t, s \in CT_\Sigma(X)$ and an occurrence $w \in \omega^*$, the *replacement* of s in t at (occurrence) w, denoted $t[w \leftarrow s]$, is the term defined as $t[w \leftarrow s](u) = t(u)$ if $w \not\leq u$ or $t/w = \bot$, and $t[w \leftarrow s](wu) = s(u)$ otherwise.

The definition of subterm replacement applies as it is to μ-terms in $\mu T_\Sigma(X)$, simply considering them as finite terms over the extended signature Σ^μ_X. □

Definition 10 ((plain) redexes and μ-redexes). Let $\mathcal{R} = \langle \Sigma, L, R \rangle$ be a TRS over X. A *(plain) redex* Δ of a term $t \in CT_\Sigma$ is a pair $\Delta = (w, d)$ where $w \in \omega^*$ is an occurrence, $d : l \to r \in R$ is a rule, and there exists a *continuous* substitution $\sigma : var(l) \to CT_\Sigma$ such that $t/w = l\sigma$.

A *μ-redex* Δ of a closed μ-term $t \in \mu T_\Sigma(X)$ is a pair $\Delta = (w, d)$ where $w \in \omega^*$ is an occurrence, $d : l \to r \in R$ is a rule, and there exists a *parameter* substitution $\sigma : var(l) \to \mu T_\Sigma(X)$ such that $t/w = l\sigma$. □

Definition 11 (reduction and derivation). Let $d : l \to r \in R$ be a rule and $\Delta = (w, d)$ be a redex of t. The result of its *application* is $s = t[w \leftarrow r\sigma]$. We also write $t \to_\Delta s$, and we say that t *reduces to* s (via Δ). We say that there is a *derivation* from t to t' if there are redexes $\Delta_1, \ldots, \Delta_n$ such that $t \to_{\Delta_1} t_1 \to_{\Delta_2} \ldots \to_{\Delta_n} t_n = t'$. □

The last definition applies both to plain and to μ-redexes: simply, if Δ is a μ-redex of t, bound variables in t are not affected in some undesirable way thanks to the fact that the matching substitution is required to be a *parameter* substitution. In this case, sometimes we will denote the corresponding reduction by $t \stackrel{\mu}{\to}_\Delta s$.

Sequential term rewriting, as just defined, can be generalized to parallel term rewriting by allowing for the simultaneous application of two or more redexes to a term. The definitions below summarize those in [6] (see also [23, 7]), and are valid for orthogonal TRS's only: as for subterm replacement, all definitions and results lift smoothly to μ-terms.

Definition 12 (residuals). Let $\Delta = (w, d)$ and $\Delta' = (w', d' : l' \to r')$ be two redexes in a term t. The *set of residuals of Δ by Δ'*, denoted by $\Delta \backslash \Delta'$, is defined as:

$$\Delta \backslash \Delta' = \begin{cases} \emptyset & \text{if } \Delta = \Delta'; \\ \{\Delta\} & \text{if } w \not\geq w'; \\ \{(w'w_x u, d) \mid r'/w_x = l'/v_x\} & \text{if } w = w'v_x u \text{ and } l'/v_x \text{ is a variable.} \end{cases}$$

□

Note that $\Delta\backslash\Delta'$ can contain more than one redex, whenever the right-hand side of the rule d' is not linear. As an example, consider the TRS $\mathcal{W} = \{d : f(x) \to g(x,x), d' : a \to b\}$ and the redexes $\Delta = (1, d')$, $\Delta' = (\lambda, d)$ in the term $f(a)$: then $\Delta/\Delta' = \{(1, d'), (2, d')\}$.

Proposition 13 (residual of a reduction). *Let $\Phi \cup \{\Delta\}$ be a finite set of redexes of t, such that $t \to_\Delta s$. Then the set $\Phi\backslash\Delta$ of residuals of Φ by Δ, defined as the union of $\Delta'\backslash\Delta$ for all $\Delta' \in \Phi$, is a set of redexes in s.* □

The well-definedness of the notions below is based on the previous result.

Definition 14 (residual of a sequence, complete development). Let Φ be a finite set of redexes of t and $\rho = (t \to_{\Delta_1} t_1 \ldots \to_{\Delta_n} t_n)$ be a reduction sequence. Then $\Phi\backslash\rho$ is defined as Φ if $n = 0$, and as $(\Phi\backslash\Delta_1)\backslash\rho'$, where $\rho' = (t_1 \to_{\Delta_2} t_2 \ldots \to_{\Delta_n} t_n)$, otherwise.

A *development of* Φ is a reduction sequence such that after each initial segment ρ, the next reduced redex is an element of $\Phi\backslash\rho$. A *complete development of* Φ is a development ρ such that $\Phi\backslash\rho = \emptyset$. □

Proposition 15 (uniqueness of complete developments). *All complete developments ρ and ρ' of a finite set of redexes Φ in a term t are finite, and end with the same term. Moreover, for each redex Δ of t, it holds $\Delta\backslash\rho = \Delta\backslash\rho'$. Therefore we can safely denote by $\Delta\backslash\Phi$ the residuals of Δ by any complete development of Φ (and similarly replacing Δ with a finite set of redexes Φ' of t).* □

Exploiting this result (whose proof can be found in [6]), we define the parallel reduction of a finite set of redexes as any complete development of them.

Definition 16 (parallel reduction). Given a finite set Φ of redexes in a term t, we write $t \to_\Phi t'$ and say that there is a *parallel reduction* from t to t' if there exists a complete development $t \to_{\Delta_1} t_1 \ldots \to_{\Delta_n} t'$ of Φ. □

Thus parallel rewriting allows to reduce a finite set of redexes of a term in a single, parallel step. If we consider an infinite term, there might be infinitely many distinct redexes in it: since the simultaneous rewriting of any finite subset of those redexes is well-defined, by a continuity argument one would expect that also the simultaneous rewriting of infinitely many redexes in an infinite term can be properly defined. We present here a definition which makes use of a suitable limit construction: for details we refer to [7]. It is however worth noticing that since μ-terms are finite by Definition 4, this infinitary extension is meaningful for plain redexes only.

Definition 17 (infinite parallel reduction). Given an infinite set Φ of redexes in a term t, let $t_0 \leq t_1 \leq t_2 \ldots$ be any chain of finite terms such that its LUB is t, and for each $i < \omega$, every redex $(w, d) \in \Phi$ is either a redex of t_i or $t_i(w) = \bot$ (that is, the image of the left-hand side of every redex in Φ is either all in t_i, or it is outside, but does not "cross the boundary"). Let Φ_i be the subset of all redexes in Φ which are also redexes of t_i, and let s_i be the result of the (finite) parallel reduction of t_i via Φ_i (i.e., $t_i \to_{\Phi_i} s_i$). Then we say that there is an *(infinite) parallel reduction* from t to $s \stackrel{def}{=} \bigcup_{i<\omega}\{s_i\}$ via Φ, and we write $t \to_\Phi s$. □

Let us consider the TRS $\mathcal{V} = \{d : f(x) \to g(x), d' : g(x) \to x\}$. Then the infinite set of redexes $\Phi = 1^* \times \{d\} = \{(\lambda, d), (1, d), \ldots\}$ can be applied to the infinite term $t = f^\omega = \bigcup_{i<\omega}\{f^i(\bot)\}$: a suitable chain of finite approximations is given by $t_i = f^i(\bot)$, and the associated subset Φ_i is $\{(1^j, d) \mid j \leq i\}$. Then $t_i \to_{\Phi_i} g^i(\bot)$, and thus $t \to_\Phi g^\omega$ by definition. Next, the infinite set of redexes $\Phi' = 1^* \times \{d'\} = \{(\lambda, d'), (1, d'), \ldots\}$ can be applied to $t' = g^\omega$. Now a suitable chain approximating g^ω is $t'_i = g^i(\bot)$, the associated subsets Φ'_i are $\{(1^j, d') \mid j \leq i\}$, and clearly $t'_i \to_{\Phi'_i} \bot$. Therefore $g^\omega \to_{\Phi'} \bigcup_{i<\omega} \bot = \bot$, which explains formally the reduction of the hypercollapsing tower described in the introduction.

The next result states that the reduction of an infinite set of redexes is a well-given definition.

Proposition 18 (infinite parallel reduction is well-defined). *In the hypotheses of Definition 17:*

1. *For each $i < \omega$, $s_i \leq s_{i+1}$; i.e., $\{s_i\}_{i<\omega}$ is a chain.*
2. *Definition 17 is well-given; i.e., the result of the infinite parallel reduction of t via Φ does not depend on the choice of the chain approximating t, provided that it satisfies the required conditions.*
3. *If the set Φ of redexes is finite, then the infinite parallel reduction of Definition 17 yields the same result as the parallel reduction of Definition 16.* □

¿From infinite parallel rewriting, rational rewriting can be easily recovered by suitably restricting the class of infinite sets of redexes which can be applied to a given rational term.

Definition 19 (rational term rewriting). Let $\mathcal{R} = \langle \Sigma, L, R \rangle$ be an orthogonal TRS over X, and let $\Sigma^* = \Sigma \uplus \{f^* \mid f \in \Sigma\}$ be an auxiliary signature. For a set of redexes Φ in a term t, the associated *marked term* t_Φ is a term over (Σ^*, X) defined by the following clauses:

$$t_\Phi(w) = \begin{cases} f^* & \text{if } (w, d) \in \Phi \text{ and } t(w) = f; \\ t(w) & \text{otherwise.} \end{cases}$$

A set of redexes Φ of a rational term t is *rational* if the associated marked term t_Φ is rational [21]. A parallel reduction $t \to_\Phi s$ is *rational* if so is Φ. □

Thus t_Φ is obtained by marking in t all the operators which are root of a redex in Φ. It is rather easy to prove that if Φ is a rational set of redexes of a term t and $t \to_\Phi s$, then also s is rational.

The main result of this section shows that the rewriting of μ-terms is sound with respect to the *rational* rewriting of rational terms.

Theorem 20 (soundness of μ-rewriting w.r.t. rational rewriting). *Let $\mathcal{R}$ be an orthogonal* TRS.

(1) If Φ is a finite set of μ-redexes of a μ-term t and $t \overset{\mu}{\rightarrow}_{\Phi} s$, then there is a rational set of redexes $\mathcal{U}(\Phi)$ such that $[t] \rightarrow_{\mathcal{U}(\Phi)} [s]$.

(2) If Φ is a rational set of redexes of a term t, then there is a μ-term $\mathcal{F}(t, \Phi)$ and a finite set of μ-redexes $\mathcal{M}(t, \Phi)$ such that $[\mathcal{F}(t, \Phi)] = t$, $\mathcal{F}(t, \Phi) \overset{\mu}{\rightarrow}_{\mathcal{M}(t,\Phi)} s'$, and $[s'] = s$.

Proof outline. (1) The rational set of redexes $\mathcal{U}(\Phi)$ is determined by taking the *marked* μ-term t_{Φ} (in the sense of Definition 19), by unfolding it obtaining the marked rational term $[t_{\Phi}]$, and by considering all redexes of $[t]$ whose root are in correspondence with the marked nodes of $[t_{\Phi}]$.

Next suppose that $[t] \rightarrow_{\mathcal{U}(\Phi)} s'$, i.e., according to Definition 17, that there is a chain of finite terms $t_0 \leq t_1 \leq t_2 \ldots$ having $[t]$ as LUB and satisfying suitable conditions with respect to Φ, such that $t_i \rightarrow_{\Phi_i} s_i$ for all $i < \omega$, and $s' = \bigcup_{i<\omega}\{s_i\}$. Then it can be shown by induction that $s_i \leq [s]$ for all $i < \omega$, which implies $s' \leq [s]$. For the converse, it must be shown (by the way in which the approximation ordering is defined) that for every occurrence w such that $s'(w) = \perp$, also $[s](w) = \perp$ holds. The only not obvious case here is when a $\perp$ is generated in s' by the reduction of a hypercollapsing tower, but this is shown to be possible only if a μ-term equivalent to $\mu_x.x$ is generated in s by the reduction of Φ, which unfolds to $\perp$ in $[s]$.

(2) Since set Φ is rational, so is the marked term t_{Φ}. A marked μ-term t' is shown to exist, such that $[t'] = t_{\Phi}$, and such that for each marked node there is a redex for its unmarked version, $\mathcal{F}(t, \Phi)$, having that node as root.[5] Let then $\mathcal{M}(t, \Phi)$ be the set of such μ-redexes of $\mathcal{F}(t, \Phi)$: it is a rational set of redexes, and the rest of the statement holds by point (1). □

Corollary 21. *For an orthogonal* TRS *$\mathcal{R}$, the rewrite relation induced on rational terms by rational term rewriting of Definition 19 coincides with the rewrite relation induced by μ-term rewriting, modulo the axioms of Definition 6.* □

In our opinion, this result provides a completely satisfactory interpretation (or "semantics") of the rewriting of μ-terms expressed via a suitable notion of rewriting of the corresponding unfoldings.

4 Rational Rewriting, Algebraically

In this section we introduce (one-step) *preiteration* and *rational rewriting logic*, exploiting the rewriting logic formalism proposed in [25] for reasoning in logical terms about rewriting. Such logics will be presented in the form of sequent calculi,

[5] For example, if $t = f^{\omega}$, $d : f(f(y)) \rightarrow g(y)$, and $\Phi = \{(1 \cdot (1 \cdot 1)^i, d) \mid i < \omega\}$, then $t_{\Phi} = f(f^*(f(f^*(\ldots))))$. In this case we cannot take $t' = \mu_x.f(f^*(x))$ (even if $[t'] = t_{\Phi}$), because there is no redex rooted at f^* (indeed, the redex would "cross" the μ operator), but we can take instead $t' = f(\mu_x.f^*(f(x)))$.

via deduction rules which allow to generate sequents. The one-step preiteration and rational rewriting logics are shown to specify sequents which are in one-to-one correspondence with μ-terms and rational reductions, respectively. The added value of this approach is that not only the terms, but also the reductions are now endowed with an algebraic structure (using suitable *proof terms*), and this allows us to obtain a more precise relationship between μ-term and rational rewriting with respect to Corollary 21. Intuitively, using the notation of point (1) of Theorem 20, one would like to identify two sets of μ-redexes Φ and Φ' in equivalent (but distinct) μ-terms t and t' if the induced rational set of redexes coincide, i.e., if $\mathcal{U}(\Phi) = \mathcal{U}(\Phi')$. Interestingly, this can be obtained in the rewriting logic framework by providing the proof terms denoting μ-term reductions with a pre-iteration structure, and by imposing on them exactly the same axioms of Definition 6.

Space constraints forbid us to introduce the deduction rules for sequential composition, which allow to derive sequents which model many-step reductions (as done for example in [25, 9]). This will be included in the full version of the paper: we just discuss in the concluding section the relevance of this extension.

Definition 22 (rewriting sequents). Let $\mathcal{R} = \langle \Sigma, L, R \rangle$ be an orthogonal TRS over X. Let $\Lambda = \cup_n \Lambda_n$ be the signature containing all the rules $d : l \to r \in R$ with the corresponding arity given by the number of variables in d: more precisely, for each n, $\Lambda_n = \{d \mid d(x_1, \ldots, x_n) : l(x_1, \ldots, x_n) \to r(x_1, \ldots, x_n) \in R\}$. A *proof term* α is a μ-term of the preiteration algebra $\mu T_{\mathcal{R}}(X) = \mu T_{\Sigma \cup \Lambda}(X)$ (we assume that there are no clashes of names between the two sets of operators). A *(rewriting) sequent* is a triple $\langle \alpha, t, s \rangle$ (usually written as $\alpha : t \to s$) where α is a proof term and $t, s \in \mu T_\Sigma(X)$. □

A sequent is *closed* if the associated proof term is so. For a given term t and a finite substitution $\{x_1/t_1, \ldots, x_n/t_n\}$, we usually write $t(t_1, \ldots, t_n)$ for $t\sigma$.

Definition 23 (one-step preiteration rewriting logic). Let $\mathcal{R} = \langle \Sigma, L, R \rangle$ be a TRS over X. We say that $\mathcal{R}$ *entails* the *sequent* $\alpha : t \to s$ if it can be obtained by a finite number of applications of the following rules of deduction:

- *(reflexivity)*

$$\frac{x \in X}{x : x \to x};$$

- *(instantiation)*

$$\frac{d : l \to r \in R, \quad d \in \Lambda_n, \quad \alpha_i : t_i \to s_i \text{ for } i = 1, \ldots, n}{d(\alpha_1, \ldots, \alpha_n) : l(t_1, \ldots, t_n) \to r(s_1, \ldots, s_n)};$$

- *(congruence)*

$$\frac{f \in \Sigma_n, \quad \alpha_i : t_i \to s_i \text{ for } i = 1, \ldots, n}{f(\alpha_1, \ldots, \alpha_n) : f(t_1, \ldots, t_n) \to f(s_1, \ldots, s_n)};$$

– *(recursion)*

$$\frac{\alpha : t \rightarrow s, \quad x \in X}{\mu_x.\alpha : \mu_x.t \rightarrow \mu_x.s}.$$

□

The class of sequents entailed by $\mathcal{R}$ induces a set-theoretical rewrite relation over terms, simply obtained by dropping the proof term of a sequent. Rule *reflexivity* is self-explaining: it allows any variable to be rewritten into itself, that is, to play an idle rôle during a rewriting step. Both *recursion* and *congruence* state that the rewrite relation is also *compatible* with respect to the algebraic structure, since it is closed under contexts. Maybe, the most interesting rule is *instantiation*: first, it implies that the transition relation is *stable*, that is, it is closed under substitutions. But the associated sequent describes also the *simultaneous* execution of *nested* rewrites: two subterms matching the left-hand sides of two rules can be rewritten simultaneously, *in parallel*, provided they do not overlap (and this is always the case for orthogonal systems).

Proposition 24 (sequents and parallel μ-term rewriting). *Let $\mathcal{R}$ be an orthogonal* TRS. (1) *If $\mathcal{R}$ entails a closed sequent $\alpha : t \rightarrow s$, then there is a set of μ-redexes $\hat{\Phi}(\alpha)$ such that $t \rightarrow_{\hat{\Phi}(\alpha)} s$ (according to the parallel rewriting of Definition 16).*
(2) *Viceversa, if Φ is a set of μ-redexes of t and $t \rightarrow_\Phi s$, then there is a closed proof term $\hat{\alpha}(\Phi)$ such that $\mathcal{R}$ entails the sequent $\hat{\alpha}(\Phi) : t \rightarrow s$.*
(3) *Functions $\hat{\Phi}$ and $\hat{\alpha}$ are inverse to each other.* □

Exploiting Theorem 7, we could easily obtain a description of the rewriting of rational terms by considering "abstract" sequents of the form $\alpha : [t] \rightarrow [s]$ for each sequent $\alpha : t \rightarrow s$ entailed by a TRS $\mathcal{R}$. However, using Theorem 20 we could obtain a result relating such sequents with the reduction of rational sets of redexes that is weaker than the last proposition, because the bijective correspondence would not hold. To ensure such a bijection we need to consider proof terms as well modulo the axioms of iteration algebras.

Definition 25 (one-step rational rewriting logic). A *rational sequent* has the form $\alpha : t \rightarrow s$, where α is a *rational* proof term (i.e., a rational term in $RT_{\Sigma \cup \Lambda}(X)$), and $t, s \in RT_\Sigma(X)$. A TRS $\mathcal{R}$ *entails* the *rational sequent* $\alpha : t \rightarrow s$ if it entails a sequent $\alpha' : t' \rightarrow s'$ (according to Definition 23) such that $\alpha = [\alpha']$, $t = [t']$, and $s = [s']$. A sequent is *closed* if so is its proof term. □

This definition of rational sequent allows us to lift the result of Proposition 24 to rational rewriting.

Proposition 26 (rational sequents and rational rewriting). *Let $\mathcal{R}$ be an orthogonal* TRS. (1) *If $\mathcal{R}$ entails a closed rational sequent $\alpha : t \rightarrow s$, then there is a rational set of redexes $\hat{\Phi}(\alpha)$ such that $t \rightarrow_{\hat{\Phi}(\alpha)} s$ (according to the rational rewriting of Definition 19).*

(2) *Viceversa, if Φ is a rational set of redexes of t and $t \to_\Phi s$, then there is a closed rational proof term $\hat{\alpha}(\Phi)$ such that $\mathcal{R}$ entails the rational sequent $\hat{\alpha}(\Phi) : t \to s$.*
(3) *Functions $\hat{\Phi}$ and $\hat{\alpha}$ are inverse to each other.* □

5 Discussion and Future Work

The main result presented in this paper is the fact that the parallel rewriting of μ-terms (defined in a very natural way) provides a faithful implementation for rational term rewriting, i.e., for the parallel reduction of a possibly infinite (but rational) set of redexes in a rational term.

Some notions introduced here should be compared with the corresponding ones in [20], even if the focus of the papers is different. The notion of μ-term rewriting of [20] is quite different from ours, firstly because rewriting is defined essentially modulo $\cong$-equivalence, and secondly, and more importantly, because it is not allowed to rewrite a subterm t' of a μ-term t if t' contains a free variable which is bound in t. For example, rule $f(y) \to g(y)$ cannot be applied to the subterm $f(x)$ of $\mu_x.f(x)$. Furthermore, $\mu_x.x$ is not considered as a legal μ-term. Such restrictions are motivated by the authors by potential problems that collapsing rules could cause. Recalling the discussion in the Introduction about the collapsing rule $g(y) \to y$, we can safely claim that such problems are due to the (implicit) use of the infinitary extension of term rewriting proposed in [22] as reference model for theory of μ-term rewriting of the mentioned paper. In fact, such problems simply disappear using the theory of infinite parallel rewriting presented in [7], which provides a satisfactory interpretation for the μ-term $\mu_x.x$, as well as for the reduction of hypercollapsing towers.

Closer to the soundness result of Section 3 are the adequacy results relating term graph rewriting and rational term rewriting proposed in [21] and [8]. In fact, possibly cyclic finite term graphs can be considered as an alternative finite representation of rational terms, where also "horizontal sharing" is allowed. In [21], the notion of *adequacy* between rewriting systems is introduced, which is essentially equivalent to soundness plus a form of partial completeness.[6] In the same paper, it is presented an adequacy result between term graph rewriting and rational term rewriting defined using [22]; however, the result is restricted to the case of systems with at most one collapsing rules, or modulo hypercollapsing towers. In [8] instead, rational rewriting is defined exactly as in this paper, and it is shown that cyclic term graph rewriting using the algebraic approach is adequate for it, even in the presence of collapsing rules.

In the last section we showed essentially that the main result of the paper can be rephrased in a very elegant way by making explicit the algebraic structure of the one-step reductions (using proof terms). Recall that, by Theorem 7, rational

[6] As a concrete example, the result presented in Theorem 20, which is actually stronger than a soundness result by point (2), could be rephrased as "parallel μ-term rewriting is adequate for rational term rewriting".

terms are $\cong$-equivalence classes of μ-terms. Giving to one-step reductions of μ-terms in an obvious way a μ-term structure over a suitable signature, we are able to recover rational rewriting by imposing the congruence $\cong$ ***on proofs terms as well.*** In other words, the relationship between μ-term and rational one-step rewriting is obtained simply by ***lifting*** the relationship between the corresponding class of terms to the level of reductions.

And one can go further, by lifting the same relationship to the level of rewriting sequences; due to space limitation the results we sketch here will appear in the full paper only. ***Full*** rewriting logic introduces a binary operator modeling sequential composition, and lifts the same algebraic structure of one-step reductions to whole derivations as well. The resulting structure provides a bridge between the standard presentation of rewriting and categorical models based on 2-categories as proposed for example in [26, 27], where arrows represent terms and cells represent rewriting sequences. As in the case of the "one-step" variants, we can consider both (full) ***preiteration*** and ***rational*** rewriting logic, and the corresponding categorical presentations based on ***preiteration*** and ***iteration*** 2-categories, respectively [5]. Furhtermore, it can be shown that they can be generated via a free construction from a suitable representation of a term rewriting systems as a suitable ***computad***.

Finally, we mention that the formal framework just described, consisting in lifting the algebraic structure of terms to the level of reductions and of rewriting sequences and obtaining in this way categorical models, provides one interesting application of the general methodology for the semantics of structured transition systems proposed in [10].

References

1. A. Arnold and M. Nivat. The metric space of infinite trees. algebraic and topological properties. *Fundamenta Informaticae*, 4:445–476, 1980.
2. S. Bloom. Varieties of ordered algebras. *Journal of Computer and System Science*, 13:200–210, 1976.
3. S. Bloom and Z. Ésik. *Iteration Theories.* EATCS Monographs on Theoretical Computer Science. Springer Verlag, 1993.
4. S. Bloom and Z. Ésik. Solving polinomials fixed point equations. In *Mathematical Foundations of Computer Science*, volume 841 of *LNCS*, pages 52–67. Springer Verlag, 1994.
5. S.L. Bloom, Z. Ésik, A. Labella, and E.G. Manes. Iteration 2-theories. In *Proceedings AMAST'97*, 1997. To appear.
6. G. Boudol. Computational semantics of term rewriting systems. In M. Nivat and J. Reynolds, editors, *Algebraic Methods in Semantics*, pages 170–235. Cambridge University Press, 1985.
7. A. Corradini. Term rewriting in CT_Σ. In *Proceedings CAAP '93*, volume 668 of *LNCS*, pages 468–484. Springer Verlag, 1993.
8. A. Corradini and F. Drewes. (Cyclic) term graph rewriting is adequate for rational parallel term rewriting. Technical Report TR-97-14, Dipartimento di Informatica, Pisa, 1997.

9. A. Corradini and F. Gadducci. CPO Models for infinite term rewriting. In *Algebraic Methodology and Software Technology*, volume 936 of *LNCS*, pages 368–384. Springer Verlag, 1995.
10. A. Corradini and U. Montanari. An algebraic semantics for structured transition systems and its application to logic programs. *Theoret. Comput. Sci.*, 103:51–106, 1992.
11. N. Dershowitz and S. Kaplan. Rewrite, rewrite, rewrite, rewrite, rewrite.... In *Proc. POPL'89, Austin*, pages 250–259, 1989.
12. N. Dershowitz, S. Kaplan, and D.A. Plaisted. Infinite normal forms (plus corrigendum). In *Proc. ICALP'89*, pages 249–262, 1989.
13. C. C. Elgot. Monadic computations and iterative algebraic theories. In *Logic Colloquium 1973*, volume 80 of *Studies in Logic*, pages 153–169. North Holland, 1975.
14. C.C. Elgot, C.C. Bloom, and R. Tindell. The algebraic structure of rooted trees. *Journal of Computer and System Science*, 16:362–339, 1978.
15. W.M. Farmer, J.D. Ramsdell, and R.J. Watro. A correctness proof for combinator reduction with cycles. *ACM Trans. Program. Lang. Syst.*, 12:123–134, 1990.
16. W.M. Farmer and R.J. Watro. Redex capturing in term graph rewriting. In R.V. Book, editor, *Proceedings of the 4th International Conference on Rewriting Techniques and Applications (RTA'91)*, volume 488 of *LNCS*, pages 13–24. Springer Verlag, 1991.
17. S Ginali. Regular trees and the free iterative theory. *Journal of Computer and System Science*, 18:222–242, 1979.
18. J.A. Goguen, J.W. Tatcher, E.G. Wagner, and J.R Wright. Some fundamentals of order-algebraic semantics. In *Mathematical Foundations of Computer Science*, volume 45 of *LNCS*, pages 153–168. Springer Verlag, 1976.
19. J.A. Goguen, J.W. Tatcher, E.G. Wagner, and J.R Wright. Initial algebra semantics and continuous algebras. *Journal of the ACM*, 24:68–95, 1977.
20. P. Inverardi and M. Venturini-Zilli. Rational rewriting. In *Mathematical Foundations of Computer Science*, volume 841 of *LNCS*, pages 433–442. Springer Verlag, 1994.
21. J.R. Kennaway, J.W. Klop, M.R. Sleep, and F.J. de Vries. On the adequacy of graph rewriting for simulating term rewriting. *ACM Trans. Program. Lang. Syst.*, 16:493–523, 1994.
22. J.R. Kennaway, J.W. Klop, M.R. Sleep, and F.J. de Vries. Transfinite reductions in orthogonal term rewriting system. *Information and Computation*, 119:18–38, 1995.
23. C. Laneve and U. Montanari. Axiomatizing permutation equivalence in the λ-calculus. *Mathematical Structures in Computer Science*, 6:219–249, 1996.
24. F.W. Lawvere. Functorial semantics of algebraic theories. *Proc. National Academy of Science*, 50:869–872, 1963.
25. J. Meseguer. Conditional rewriting logic as a unified model of concurrency. *Theoret. Comput. Sci.*, 96:73–155, 1992.
26. A.J. Power. An abstract formulation for rewrite systems. In *Proceedings Category Theory in Computer Science*, volume 389 of *LNCS*, pages 300–312. Springer Verlag, 1989.
27. D.E. Rydehard and E.G. Stell. Foundations of equational deductions: A categorical treatment of equational proofs and unification algorithms. In *Proceedings Category Theory in Computer Science*, volume 283 of *LNCS*, pages 114–139. Springer Verlag, 1987.

The Appearance of Big Integers in Exact Real Arithmetic Based on Linear Fractional Transformations*

Reinhold Heckmann

FB 14 – Informatik, Universität des Saarlandes
Postfach 151150, D-66041 Saarbrücken, Germany
e-mail: heckmann@cs.uni-sb.de

Abstract. One possible approach to exact real arithmetic is to use linear fractional transformations to represent real numbers and computations on real numbers. In this paper, we show that the bit sizes of the (integer) parameters of nearly all transformations used in computations are proportional to the number of basic computational steps executed so far. Here, a basic step means consuming one digit of the argument(s) or producing one digit of the result.

1 Introduction

Linear Fractional Transformations (LFT's) provide an elegant approach to real number arithmetic [8, 16, 11, 14, 12, 6]. One-dimensional LFT's $x \mapsto \frac{ax+c}{bx+d}$ are used as digits and to implement basic functions, while two-dimensional LFT's $(x, y) \mapsto \frac{axy+cx+ey+g}{bxy+dx+fy+h}$ provide binary operations such as addition and multiplication, and can be combined to infinite expression trees denoting transcendental functions. In Section 2, we present the details of the LFT approach. This provides the background for understanding the results in the remainder of this paper.

LFT's can be modelled within linear algebra. If the four parameters of a one-dimensional LFT are written as a (2,2)-matrix (shortly called *matrix*), functional composition becomes matrix multiplication. Likewise, the eight parameters of a two-dimensional LFT can be written as a (2,4)-matrix (called *tensor*). We refer to matrices and tensors collectively as *transforms*. Basic computational steps such as consuming one digit of the argument(s) (*absorption*) or producing one digit of the result (*emission*) can be realised as variants of matrix multiplication applied to a transform and a digit matrix.

Usually, all the transforms used in real number arithmetic have integer components. Naively, one may think that these components become bigger by absorptions, and become smaller again by emissions. Technically, the components may decrease by *reduction*, i.e., division of all components of the transform by

* Most of the results in this paper were found during a visiting fellowship of the author at Imperial College, London. This visit was organised by Abbas Edalat and funded by EPSRC.

a common factor; as transforms denote rational functions, reduction does not affect their semantics.

Practical experiments have shown, however, that in most cases, the potential for reduction is negligible. The greatest common factor of the components of a transform is usually 1, and in nearly all of the remaining cases, it is just 2. In Sections 3 and 4, we show some upper and lower bounds for common factors. The full proof of the practically observed behaviour is obtained later (Corollary 12 in Section 6.4).

Practical experiments have also shown that in most cases, the bit size of the entries of a transform is roughly equal to the number of emitted digits. The main contribution of this paper is the formalisation (and of course proof) of these practical observations. First, we derive upper bounds for the sizes of the entries of a transform in Section 5. In Section 6, lower bounds for the determinant and the size of the biggest entry are obtained in the case of matrices. Tensors are handled in Section 7. Finally, we discuss these results and their impact on the complexity of real number computation.

2 Exact Real Arithmetic by Linear Fractional Transformations

In this section, we present the framework of exact real arithmetic by LFT's [8, 16, 11]. After a general introduction, we specialise to the version used by the group of Edalat and Potts at Imperial College [14, 12, 13, 15, 6].

2.1 From Digit Streams to Linear Fractional Transformations

There are many ways to represent real numbers as infinite objects [3, 2, 4, 5]. Here, we are only concerned with representations as infinite streams of "digits". These streams are evaluated incrementally; at any given time, only a finite prefix of the stream is known.

There are several different stream representations which can be grouped into two large families: variations of the familiar decimal representation [1, 3, 2, 5, 7, 11, 10], and continued fraction expansions [8, 16, 9].

For the first family, consider the usual decimal representation.[1] A number such as $0.142\cdots$ can be unravelled from left to right as follows:

$$0.142\cdots = \tfrac{1}{10}(1 + 0.42\cdots);\ 0.42\cdots = \tfrac{1}{10}(4 + 0.2\cdots);\ 0.2\cdots = \tfrac{1}{10}(2 + 0.\cdots)$$

Thus, every digit d corresponds to an affine map α_d with $\alpha_d(x) = \frac{1}{10}(d + x) = \frac{x+d}{10}$. A number of the form $0.\cdots$ can be any element of the closed interval $[0, 1]$, and so, a number of the form $0.142\cdots$ can be any element of the interval

[1] This representation is not suitable for practical purposes, as it lacks redundancy, and thus, most arithmetic functions are not computable. However, it provides a familiar example.

$(\alpha_1 \circ \alpha_4 \circ \alpha_2)[0,1] = [0.142, 0.143]$. In general, the infinite stream $0.d_1d_2d_3\cdots$ represents the unique real number in the intersection $\bigcap_{n=1}^{\infty}(\alpha_{d_1} \circ \cdots \circ \alpha_{d_n})[0,1]$.

In the classical continued fraction expansion, irrational numbers in the interval $[0,\infty]$ can be written as $a_0 + \frac{b_0}{a_1 + \frac{b_1}{a_2 + \cdots}}$ with natural numbers a_n and b_n. Every pair $p = (a, b)$ corresponds to the rational function ρ_p with $\rho_p(x) = a + \frac{b}{x} = \frac{ax+b}{x}$. Similar to the case above, an infinite continued fraction corresponds to the intersection $\bigcap_{n=1}^{\infty}(\rho_{p_1} \circ \cdots \circ \rho_{p_n})[0,\infty]$.

The formal similarity between the two approaches presented above leads to the following generalisation [8, 16, 14, 12, 13, 15, 6]: Real numbers in some *base interval* I are represented by infinite streams of digits. Digits are certain *Linear Fractional Transformations* (LFT's) $x \mapsto \frac{ax+c}{bx+d}$, parameterised by numbers a, b, c, d (in practical cases usually integers). The meaning of an infinite stream $\tau_1, \tau_2, \ldots$ of LFT's is the intersection $\bigcap_{n=1}^{\infty}(\tau_1 \circ \cdots \circ \tau_n)(I)$. This intersection is filtered (decreasing) if $\tau_n(I) \subseteq I$ holds for all digits τ_n.

2.2 LFT's and Matrices

Every 2-2-matrix $A = \begin{pmatrix} a & c \\ b & d \end{pmatrix}$ of real numbers denotes an LFT $\langle A \rangle$, which is given by $\langle A \rangle(x) = \frac{ax+c}{bx+d}$. LFT's described by non-singular matrices, i.e., matrices A with determinant $\det A = ad - bc \neq 0$, are considered as endofunctions of $\mathbb{R}^* = \mathbb{R} \cup \{\infty\}$, the one-point compactification of the real line. The value ∞ arises as $r/0$ with $r \neq 0$, and on the other hand, $\langle A \rangle(\infty)$ is defined to be a/b. For LFT's described by singular matrices, an additional 'number' $\perp$ (undefined) is needed which arises as $0/0$. The value of $\langle A \rangle(\perp)$ is defined to be $\perp$.

The mapping $A \mapsto \langle A \rangle$ is not one-to-one; for, $\langle A \rangle = \langle rA \rangle$ holds for all $r \neq 0$. We shall write $A \cong B$ if $\langle A \rangle = \langle B \rangle$, or equivalently $B = rA$ for some $r \neq 0$. Composition of LFT's can be expressed by matrix multiplication: $\langle A \rangle \circ \langle B \rangle = \langle A \cdot B \rangle$. The equivalence relation '$\cong$' is a congruence w.r.t. multiplication. The determinant $\det A$ is a well-known property of a matrix A.

$$\det \begin{pmatrix} a & c \\ b & d \end{pmatrix} = ad - bc \qquad \det(A \cdot B) = \det A \cdot \det B \qquad \det(rA) = r^2 \det A \tag{1}$$

By the last equation, the determinant of a matrix is not invariant under equivalence '$\cong$', but its sign (1, 0, or -1) is, i.e., the sign of the determinant of A is a well-defined property of the LFT $\langle A \rangle$. LFT's with non-zero determinant (non-singular LFT's) are invertible; $\langle A \rangle^{-1}$ is given by $\langle A^{-1} \rangle$. Thus, non-singular LFT's form a group under composition.

A *rational LFT* is an LFT which can be represented by a matrix with rational entries, and therefore even by an integer matrix. As $\langle A \rangle = \langle kA \rangle$ for $k \neq 0$, there are infinitely many integer matrices denoting the same rational LFT. An integer matrix is called *k-reducible* if k is a common factor of its four components. Division of a k-reducible matrix by k is called *reduction by k*. A matrix is *in lowest terms* if there is no common factor other than 1 and -1. All integer matrices different from $\begin{pmatrix} 0 & 0 \\ 0 & 0 \end{pmatrix}$ are equivalent to an integer matrix in lowest terms.

To obtain an integer representation of $\langle A\rangle^{-1}$ for a non-singular integer matrix A, the *pseudo-inverse* A^* can be used. It is defined by

$$\begin{pmatrix} a & c \\ b & d \end{pmatrix}^* = \begin{pmatrix} d & -c \\ -b & a \end{pmatrix} \tag{2}$$

Clearly, $\det(A^*) = \det A$ holds. The main property of the pseudo-inverse operation is

$$A \cdot A^* = A^* \cdot A = \det A \cdot \mathrm{E} \tag{3}$$

where $\mathrm{E} = \left(\begin{smallmatrix} 1 & 0 \\ 0 & 1 \end{smallmatrix}\right)$ is the identity matrix, and so, $A \cdot A^* = A^* \cdot A \cong \mathrm{E}$ if $\det A \neq 0$, whence $\langle A\rangle^{-1} = \langle A^*\rangle$.

2.3 The Signed Digit Approach

The group of Edalat and Potts at Imperial College [13, 6] represents the elements of $\mathbb{R}^\star = \mathbb{R} \cup \{\infty\}$ as infinite streams of matrices $S, D_1, D_2, \ldots$, standing for LFT's. The first matrix is a *sign matrix*, while the remaining ones are *digit matrices*. The base interval is $[0, \infty]$, and so, the meaning of the stream is

$$\bigcap_{n=1}^{\infty} \langle S \cdot D_1 \cdot \ldots \cdot D_n\rangle [0, \infty] \ . \tag{4}$$

The base interval $[0, \infty]$ was chosen because there is a simple check for the inclusion property [14]: for a non-singular matrix A, $\langle A\rangle([0, \infty]) \subseteq [0, \infty]$ holds iff all four entries of A are ≥ 0, or all are ≤ 0. Matrices with entries ≥ 0 are called *positive*. Digit matrices are positive, and so, the intersection (4) is filtered (decreasing).

The number set $\mathbb{R}^\star$ can be visualised as a circle. Intervals $[u, v]$ are counter-clockwise arcs from u to v, e.g., $[0, 1] = \{x \in \mathbb{R} \mid 0 \leq x \leq 1\}$, and $[1, 0] = \{x \in \mathbb{R} \mid 1 \leq x \text{ or } x \leq 0\} \cup \{\infty\}$.

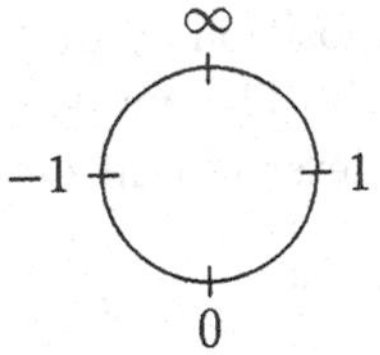

There are four possible sign matrices, corresponding to rotations by 0°, 90°, 180°, and 270°. They can be explicitly described as follows:

$$\begin{aligned} S_+ &= \left(\begin{smallmatrix} 1 & 0 \\ 0 & 1 \end{smallmatrix}\right) & \langle S_+\rangle\,[0, \infty] &= [0, \infty] \\ S_\infty &= \left(\begin{smallmatrix} 1 & 1 \\ -1 & 1 \end{smallmatrix}\right) & \langle S_\infty\rangle[0, \infty] &= [1, -1] \\ S_- &= \left(\begin{smallmatrix} 0 & -1 \\ 1 & 0 \end{smallmatrix}\right) & \langle S_-\rangle\,[0, \infty] &= [\infty, 0] \\ S_0 &= \left(\begin{smallmatrix} 1 & -1 \\ 1 & 1 \end{smallmatrix}\right) & \langle S_0\rangle\,[0, \infty] &= [-1, 1] \end{aligned}$$

S_0 and S_∞ are pseudo-inverse to each other; $S_0 \cdot S_\infty = S_\infty \cdot S_0 = 2\mathrm{E}$ holds.

There are many possible sets of digit matrices, one for every base $r > 1$. Edalat and Potts [6] discuss non-integer bases, but their implementation uses base $r = 2$. In this paper, we consider integer bases $r > 1$.

Fix an integer $r > 1$. Every real number in the interval $[-1, 1]$ has a representation as $\sum_{n=1}^{\infty} k_n r^{-n}$ with integer digits k_n satisfying $|k_n| < r$. (Digits may be negative [1].) As in Section 2.1, these digits correspond to affine maps $\alpha_k^r = \langle A_k^r \rangle$ with $A_k^r = \left(\begin{smallmatrix} 1 & k \\ 0 & r \end{smallmatrix}\right)$.

Since the base interval is not $[-1, 1]$, but $[0, \infty]$, the maps α_k^r have to be transformed into that interval. This can be done by composition with the maps $\langle S_\infty \rangle$ and $\langle S_0 \rangle$, which are mutually inverse bijections between $[-1, 1]$ and $[0, \infty]$. Thus, the actual digit matrices are

$$D_k^r = S_\infty \cdot A_k^r \cdot S_0 = \begin{pmatrix} r+k+1 & r+k-1 \\ r-k-1 & r-k+1 \end{pmatrix} . \tag{5}$$

Since the two entries in the top row differ by 2, these matrices are either in lowest terms or 2-reducible. The latter case occurs iff the parities of r and k are different. In this case, reduction by 2 may be performed. Hence, we distinguish between *unreduced digits* D_k^r and *reduced digits* $\tilde{D}_k^r = \frac{1}{2} D_k^r$. Table 1 illustrates the case $r = 2$. In the column "lowest terms", the first and third matrix ($k \neq 0$) are reduced, while the second matrix ($k = 0$) is unreduced.

Table 1. Digit matrices for base 2

k	A_k^2	D_k^2	lowest terms	$\langle D_k^2 \rangle([0, \infty])$
-1	$\left(\begin{smallmatrix} 1 & -1 \\ 0 & 2 \end{smallmatrix}\right)$	$\left(\begin{smallmatrix} 2 & 0 \\ 2 & 4 \end{smallmatrix}\right)$	$\left(\begin{smallmatrix} 1 & 0 \\ 1 & 2 \end{smallmatrix}\right)$	$[0, 1]$
0	$\left(\begin{smallmatrix} 1 & 0 \\ 0 & 2 \end{smallmatrix}\right)$	$\left(\begin{smallmatrix} 3 & 1 \\ 1 & 3 \end{smallmatrix}\right)$	$\left(\begin{smallmatrix} 3 & 1 \\ 1 & 3 \end{smallmatrix}\right)$	$[\frac{1}{3}, 3]$
1	$\left(\begin{smallmatrix} 1 & 1 \\ 0 & 2 \end{smallmatrix}\right)$	$\left(\begin{smallmatrix} 4 & 2 \\ 0 & 2 \end{smallmatrix}\right)$	$\left(\begin{smallmatrix} 2 & 1 \\ 0 & 1 \end{smallmatrix}\right)$	$[1, \infty]$

2.4 Computation by LFT's

LFT's can not only be used to represent real numbers, but also to perform computations with real numbers. For the sake of simplicity, we only present computations within the interval $[0, \infty]$ where real numbers can be represented by a stream of digit matrices without a leading sign matrix.

Using suitable LFT's $x \mapsto \frac{ax+c}{bx+d}$, basic functions such as $x \mapsto x + 1$, $x \mapsto 2x$, and $x \mapsto \frac{1}{x}$ can be easily expressed. Recall that an LFT maps $[0, \infty]$ into itself iff it can be represented by a positive matrix (all components ≥ 0).

Given a positive matrix M, the actual computation of $\langle M \rangle(x)$ is performed by a sequence of *absorptions* and *emissions*. Absorption means that M consumes the first digit D of x, thereby becoming $M \cdot D$, which is positive again. It corresponds to the equality

$$M \cdot (D_1 \cdot D_2 \cdot \ldots) = (M \cdot D_1) \cdot (D_2 \cdot \ldots) . \tag{6}$$

Emission means that M produces one further digit D of the result, thereby becoming $D^* \cdot M$. It corresponds to the equivalence

$$(D_1 \cdot \ldots \cdot D_n) \cdot M \cong (D_1 \cdot \ldots \cdot D_n \cdot D) \cdot (D^* \cdot M) \,. \tag{7}$$

Emission of a digit D is allowed only if $D^* \cdot M$ is positive. Therefore, a possible strategy for the computation of $\langle M \rangle(x)$ is as follows: emit digits until no further emission is possible, then absorb one digit of x, again emit digits until no longer possible, etc.

2.5 Tensors

To compute sums, products, etc., *two-dimensional LFT's* are employed. They are characterised by 8 parameters, and thus can be represented by 2-4-matrices, so called *tensors*. A tensor $T = \begin{pmatrix} a & c & e & g \\ b & d & f & h \end{pmatrix}$ denotes the function $\langle T \rangle : \mathbb{R}^\star{}_\perp \times \mathbb{R}^\star{}_\perp \to \mathbb{R}^\star{}_\perp$ given by $\langle T \rangle(x, y) = \frac{axy+cx+ey+g}{bxy+dx+fy+h}$. For integer tensors, the notions of reducible, reduction, and lowest terms can be defined analogous to the case of matrices. Likewise for positivity: a two-dimensional LFT maps $[0, \infty]^2$ to $[0, \infty]_\perp$ iff it can be represented by a positive tensor, i.e., a tensor with components ≥ 0. Because of these analogies, we refer to matrices and tensors collectively as *transforms*.

It is easy to represent addition, subtraction, multiplication, and division by suitable integer tensors [8, 16, 14, 12, 13]. Tensors may also be used to represent transcendental functions, e.g., $\arctan x = \langle T_0 \rangle(x, \langle T_1 \rangle(x, \langle T_2 \rangle(x, \ldots)))$ where $T_n = \begin{pmatrix} 0 & 1 & 0 & 0 \\ (n+1)^2 & 0 & 0 & 2n+1 \end{pmatrix}$. It remains to show how to actually compute $\langle T \rangle(x, y)$ for a given positive integer tensor T [12, 13].

Emissions can be done as in the one-dimensional case: in emitting a digit D, tensor T is replaced by $D^* \cdot T$, which is a tensor again. Emission of D is only allowed if $D^* \cdot T$ is positive.

Since digits can be absorbed from both arguments, there are two kinds of *absorptions*: absorption of a digit D from the left argument transforms T into $T \cdot L(D)$, while absorption from the right argument yields $T \cdot R(D)$. Here, $L(D)$ means $D \otimes \mathrm{E}$, and $R(D)$ means $\mathrm{E} \otimes D$. An explicit definition of these operations looks as follows:

$$L\begin{pmatrix} a & c \\ b & d \end{pmatrix} = \begin{pmatrix} a & 0 & c & 0 \\ 0 & a & 0 & c \\ b & 0 & d & 0 \\ 0 & b & 0 & d \end{pmatrix} \qquad R\begin{pmatrix} a & c \\ b & d \end{pmatrix} = \begin{pmatrix} a & c & 0 & 0 \\ b & d & 0 & 0 \\ 0 & 0 & a & c \\ 0 & 0 & b & d \end{pmatrix} \tag{8}$$

They satisfy the following equations:

$$L(A \cdot B) = L(A) \cdot L(B) \qquad R(A \cdot B) = R(A) \cdot R(B) \tag{9}$$

$$L(\mathrm{E}) = R(\mathrm{E}) = \mathrm{E}_4 \qquad L(A) \cdot R(B) = R(B) \cdot L(A) \tag{10}$$

where E_4 denotes the identity 4-4-matrix.

Right absorption can be easily expressed with block matrices. Observe $R(A) = \begin{pmatrix} A & 0 \\ 0 & A \end{pmatrix}$ where the four entries are matrices. Likewise, a tensor can be written as a row $(T^{\mathrm{L}}, T^{\mathrm{R}})$ of two matrices, and so

$$(T^{\mathrm{L}}, T^{\mathrm{R}}) \cdot R(A) = (T^{\mathrm{L}}A, T^{\mathrm{R}}A) . \tag{11}$$

Left and right absorption are closely connected. Let $T^{\times}$ be T with the two middle columns exchanged. Then

$$(T \cdot L(D))^{\times} = T^{\times} \cdot R(D) \qquad (T \cdot R(D))^{\times} = T^{\times} \cdot L(D) . \tag{12}$$

Later, we shall see that D-emissions and D-absorptions have many properties in common. Thus, we introduce a common name: a *D-transaction* at a transform is either a D-emission or a D-absorption.

3 Small Factors

After a transaction at a transform in lowest terms, the entries of the result may have a non-trivial common factor. The most drastic example is $D^* \cdot D = \det D \cdot \mathrm{E}$ for a digit matrix D. Yet apart from this, practical experience shows that common factors are usually quite small. The goal of this section is to find bounds for such factors. We start off with a property involving determinants.

Proposition 1. *Let A be a matrix, and let B be a transform in lowest terms. Then every common factor of the entries of $A \cdot B$ divides* $\det A$.

Proof. Let g be a common factor of $A \cdot B$, i.e., $A \cdot B = gC$ for some transform C. We may compute:

$$g \cdot (A^* \cdot C) = A^* \cdot gC = A^* \cdot A \cdot B \overset{(3)}{=} (\det A \cdot \mathrm{E}) \cdot B = (\det A) \cdot B .$$

Hence, g divides $(\det A) \cdot B$. Since B is in lowest terms, g must divide $\det A$. □

For matrices, there is a dual statement with an analogous proof so that we obtain:

Theorem 2. *Let A and B be matrices in lowest terms. Then every common factor of $A \cdot B$ divides both* $\det A$ *and* $\det B$.

There is a similar statement for the two versions of multiplying a tensor and a matrix:

Proposition 3. *Let T be a tensor in lowest terms, and M an arbitrary matrix. Then every common factor of $T \cdot L(M)$ or $T \cdot R(M)$ divides* $\det M$.

Proof. We consider the L case; the other one is analogous. If $T \cdot L(M) = gC$ for some tensor C, then

$$g \cdot (C \cdot L(M^*)) = T \cdot L(M) \cdot L(M^*) \overset{(9)}{=} T \cdot L(M \cdot M^*)$$
$$\overset{(3)}{=} T \cdot L(\det M \cdot \mathrm{E}) \overset{(10)}{=} T \cdot (\det M \cdot \mathrm{E}_4) = (\det M) \cdot T$$

Since T is in lowest terms, g divides $\det M$. □

Now, consider a transform T in lowest terms. Let T' be the result of a D-absorption at T, i.e., $T' = T \cdot D$ if T is a matrix, or $T' \in \{T \cdot L(D), T \cdot R(D)\}$ if T is a tensor. By Theorem 2 and Proposition 3, any common factor of T' divides $\det D$. If T' is the result of a D-emission at T, i.e., $T' = D^* \cdot T$, then by Prop. 1 any common factor of T' divides $\det D^* = \det D$. Summarising, we obtain:

Theorem 4. *Let T be a transform in lowest terms, and D a digit matrix. After a D-transaction at T, any common factor of the result divides* $\det D$.

How big is $\det D$? Recall the definition of the digit matrices for base r from Section 2.3. As $A^r_k = \left(\begin{smallmatrix} 1 & k \\ 0 & r \end{smallmatrix}\right)$, $\det A^r_k$ is r. Since $\det S_0 = \det S_\infty = 2$, we have $\det D^r_k = \det(S_\infty A^r_k S_0) = 4r$. Therefore, we obtain $\det \tilde{D}^r_k = r$ for reduced digits $\tilde{D}^r_k = \frac{1}{2} D^r_k$.

Corollary 5. *Let T be a transform in lowest terms, and D a digit matrix for base r. After a D-transaction at T, any common factor of the result divides $4r$ if D is unreduced, and even divides r if D is reduced.*

Specialising to the case $r = 2$, we see that any common factor of the result divides 2 in case of a transaction with a non-zero digit ($k \neq 0$), and divides 8 in case of $k = 0$.

Corollary 12 in Section 6.4 shows that in many cases, the result of Corollary 5 can be strengthened from $4r$ (r) to 2 (1), ruling out most reductions.

4 Possibilities for Reductions

In the last section, we have seen that there is not much potential for reductions. Here, we show a result of opposite flavour: certain reductions are always possible.

Consider unreduced digit matrices $D^r_k = S_\infty A^r_k S_0$. We have already mentioned that some of them are in lowest terms, while others are 2-reducible; higher reducibilities do not occur. Multiplying two digit matrices yields:

$$D^r_k D^{r'}_{k'} = S_\infty A^r_k S_0 S_\infty A^{r'}_{k'} S_0 = 2 S_\infty A^r_k A^{r'}_{k'} S_0 = 2 D^{rr'}_{kr'+k'} \tag{13}$$

Here, the second equality is due to $S_0 S_\infty = 2\mathrm{E}$, and the third due to

$$A^r_k \cdot A^{r'}_{k'} = \begin{pmatrix} 1 & k \\ 0 & r \end{pmatrix} \cdot \begin{pmatrix} 1 & k' \\ 0 & r' \end{pmatrix} = \begin{pmatrix} 1 & k' + kr' \\ 0 & rr' \end{pmatrix} \tag{14}$$

together with the estimation $|kr' + k'| \leq (r-1)r' + (r'-1) = rr' - 1$. Iterating (13) leads to

$$D^r_{k_1} \cdot \ldots \cdot D^r_{k_n} = 2^{n-1} D^{r^n}_k \text{ where } k = \sum_{i=1}^{n} k_i r^{n-i} . \tag{15}$$

Hence, we obtain:

1. The product of n digit matrices is always 2^{n-1}-reducible.
2. After 2^{n-1}-reduction, the result is again a digit matrix, and so it is either in lowest terms or 2-reducible.

The result of applying n_1 absorptions and n_2 emissions of unreduced digits to a matrix M has form $A_2^* \cdot M \cdot A_1$ where A_i is a product of n_i digit matrices. Thus, the result has a common factor of $2^{n_1-1} \cdot 2^{n_2-1} = 2^{n_1+n_2-2}$. For a tensor T, we obtain a result of the form $A_3^* \cdot T \cdot L(A_2) \cdot R(A_1)$, and thus a common factor of $2^{n_1+n_2+n_3-3}$.

Theorem 6. *Let T_0 be some initial transform, and T_n the result of applying n transactions with unreduced digits to T_0. Then T_n is at least 2^{n-2}-reducible in case of matrices, and at least 2^{n-3}-reducible in case of tensors.*

5 An Upper Bound for the Entries

Next, we derive an exponential upper bound for the entries of a transform after n transactions. An estimate for the entries is the maximum of their absolute values: $\|\left(\begin{smallmatrix} a & c \\ b & d \end{smallmatrix}\right)\| = \max(|a|,|b|,|c|,|d|)$ for matrices, and analogously for tensors, and vectors $\left(\begin{smallmatrix} a \\ b \end{smallmatrix}\right)$. Let us consider how this norm is affected by emissions.

Recall the definition of the digit matrices for base r (Equation (5) in Section 2.3):

$$D^r_k = \begin{pmatrix} r+k+1 & r+k-1 \\ r-k-1 & r-k+1 \end{pmatrix} . \tag{16}$$

Consider the product of $(D^r_k)^*$ with a vector $\left(\begin{smallmatrix} u \\ v \end{smallmatrix}\right)$:

$$(D^r_k)^* \begin{pmatrix} u \\ v \end{pmatrix} = \begin{pmatrix} 1-k+r & 1-k-r \\ 1+k-r & 1+k+r \end{pmatrix} \begin{pmatrix} u \\ v \end{pmatrix} = \begin{pmatrix} (1-k)(u+v) + r(u-v) \\ (1+k)(u+v) - r(u-v) \end{pmatrix} \tag{17}$$

Using $|k| < r$, we obtain

$$\left\| (D^r_k)^* \begin{pmatrix} u \\ v \end{pmatrix} \right\| \leq (1+|k|+r)(|u|+|v|) \leq 2r \left\| \begin{pmatrix} u \\ v \end{pmatrix} \right\| \tag{18}$$

Since the norm of a transform is the maximum of the norms of its column vectors, we obtain $\|(D^r_k)^* \cdot T\| \leq 2r\|T\|$ — for unreduced digits. For reduced digits, the right hand side is $r\|T\|$.

Now, let us study absorption. For the absorption of a digit into a matrix, it suffices to consider products $(u, v) \cdot D^r_k$ of a row vector and a digit matrix.

$$(u, v) \begin{pmatrix} r+k+1 & r+k-1 \\ r-k-1 & r-k+1 \end{pmatrix} = (r(u+v)+(k+1)(u-v),\ r(u+v)+(k-1)(u-v))$$

By an estimation as above, we obtain $||M \cdot D^r_k|| \leq 2r||M||$ for matrices M. By (11), the block formula for right absorption into a tensor, an analogous result holds for $||T \cdot R(D^r_k)||$, and by (12), the formula connecting left and right absorption, the same holds for $||T \cdot L(D^r_k)||$. Summarising, we obtain:

Proposition 7. *Let T be a transform, D a digit matrix for base r, and T' the result of a D-transaction at T. Then $||T'|| \leq 2r||T||$ if D is unreduced, and $||T'|| \leq r||T||$ if D is reduced.*

By induction, we see that after n transactions, $||T'|| \leq (2r)^n||T||$ holds if unreduced digits are used. Applying all the reductions that are possible by Theorem 6, we obtain:

Theorem 8. *Let T_0 be some initial transform, and T_n the result of applying n transactions in base r to T_0, and all possible reductions. Then $||T_n|| \leq 4r^n||T_0||$ in case of matrices, and $||T_n|| \leq 8r^n||T_0||$ in case of tensors.*

In the moment, there is some hope that further reductions may lead to a much smaller increase. Unfortunately, we shall soon see that this does not work; in most cases, an exponential increase is guaranteed.

6 Big Numbers in Matrices

In this section, we derive lower bounds for the entries of a matrix after n transactions and all possible reductions. This is done by observing how the determinant and another quantity, the column difference, are changed by transactions and reductions, and by deriving a reduction invariant from this.

6.1 Determinant

Determinants are easy because of $\det(A \cdot B) = \det A \cdot \det B$. The determinants of the digit matrices and their pseudo-inverses are calculated in Section 3 just before Corollary 5. In the following list, let M be a matrix, and let M' be the result of applying a transaction to M.

- Transaction with an unreduced digit: $\det M' = 4r \det M$,
- Transaction with a reduced digit: $\det M' = r \det M$,
- Reduction by k: $\det M' = \frac{1}{k^2} \det M$.

These facts allow the derivation of an upper bound for the determinant after n transactions. Working with unreduced digits gives a factor of $(4r)^n$, and performing all reductions admitted by Theorem 6 gives a factor of $2^{-2(n-2)}$. Together, we get the following:

Theorem 9. *Let M_0 be some initial matrix, and M_n the result of applying n transactions in base r to M_0, and all possible reductions. Then* $|\det M_n| \leq 16r^n |\det M_0|$.

6.2 Column Difference

Consider again the explicit formulae for digit matrices of base r and their inverses (Equation (5) in Section 2.3):

$$D_k^r = \begin{pmatrix} r+k+1 & r+k-1 \\ r-k-1 & r-k+1 \end{pmatrix} \qquad (D_k^r)^* = \begin{pmatrix} 1-k+r & 1-k-r \\ 1+k-r & 1+k+r \end{pmatrix} \qquad (19)$$

It is easy to see that in both cases the difference of the two column sums is 0. This motivates the definition of the *column difference* $\operatorname{cd}\left(\begin{smallmatrix} a & c \\ b & d \end{smallmatrix}\right) = (a+b)-(c+d)$ of a matrix. Thus, $\operatorname{cd} D_k^r = \operatorname{cd}(D_k^r)^* = 0$. In general, $\operatorname{cd} A^* = -\operatorname{cd} A$ holds.

Let us compute the column difference of the product of $A = \left(\begin{smallmatrix} a & c \\ b & d \end{smallmatrix}\right)$ and $B = \left(\begin{smallmatrix} a' & c' \\ b' & d' \end{smallmatrix}\right)$:

$$\begin{aligned} \operatorname{cd}(A \cdot B) &= \operatorname{cd} \begin{pmatrix} aa' + cb' & ac' + cd' \\ ba' + db' & bc' + dd' \end{pmatrix} \\ &= (a+b)a' + (c+d)b' - (a+b)c' - (c+d)d' \\ &= (a+b)(a'-c') - (c+d)(d'-b') \end{aligned}$$

If $B = D_k^r$, then $a' - c' = d' - b' = 2$, and so, $\operatorname{cd}(A \cdot D_k^r) = 2 \operatorname{cd} A$. If $A = (D_k^r)^*$, then $a + b = c + d = 2$, and so, $\operatorname{cd}((D_k^r)^* \cdot B) = 2 \operatorname{cd} B$. If reduced digits are used instead, the factor 2 disappears. Thus, we obtain:

- Transaction with an unreduced digit: $\operatorname{cd} M' = 2 \operatorname{cd} M$,
- Transaction with a reduced digit: $\operatorname{cd} M' = \operatorname{cd} M$,
- Reduction by k: $\operatorname{cd} M' = \frac{1}{k} \operatorname{cd} M$.

Hence, the properties of having zero or non-zero column difference are transaction invariants.

6.3 The Quotient

Let M be a matrix with $\operatorname{cd} M \neq 0$. For such a matrix, the quotient $\operatorname{qcd} M = \frac{\det M}{(\operatorname{cd} M)^2}$ is a well-defined rational number. By a transaction with an unreduced digit, this quotient is multiplied by $\frac{4r}{2^2} = r$; by a transaction with a reduced digit, the factor is $\frac{r}{1^2} = r$; and a k-reduction yields a factor of $\frac{1/k^2}{(1/k)^2} = 1$. Thus, the quotient qcd is invariant under reductions, and is multiplied by r in every transaction.

Lemma 10. *Let M_0 be some initial matrix with $\operatorname{cd} M_0 \neq 0$, and M_n the result of applying n transactions in base r to M_0, and all possible reductions. Then* $\operatorname{qcd} M_n = r^n \operatorname{qcd} M_0$.

6.4 Big Determinant

The equation in Lemma 10 can be turned into an integer equation by multiplying with the denominators:

$$\det M_n \cdot (\operatorname{cd} M_0)^2 = r^n \cdot \det M_0 \cdot (\operatorname{cd} M_n)^2 \tag{20}$$

If $\operatorname{cd} M_0 \neq 0$, then $\operatorname{cd} M_n \neq 0$, too. As an integer, $(\operatorname{cd} M_n)^2$ is at least 1. Hence, we obtain:

$$|\det M_n| \cdot (\operatorname{cd} M_0)^2 \geq r^n \cdot |\det M_0| \tag{21}$$

This gives a lower bound for the determinant; an upper bound was provided by Theorem 9.

Theorem 11. *Let M_0 be some initial matrix with* $\operatorname{cd} M_0 \neq 0$, *and M_n the result of applying n transactions in base r to M_0, and all possible reductions. Then*

$$\frac{|\det M_0|}{(\operatorname{cd} M_0)^2} \cdot r^n \leq |\det M_n| \leq 16|\det M_0| \cdot r^n .$$

The upper bound was obtained by working with unreduced digits and performing the 2^{n-1}-reduction guaranteed by Theorem 6. In case of $\det M_0 \neq 0$, the quotient of upper bound over lower bound shows that only a constant number of further reductions is possible; they combine to a factor of at most $4 \operatorname{cd} M_0$. This implies the promised strengthening of Corollary 5:

Corollary 12. *When working with a matrix with non-zero determinant and column difference, the average maximal reducibility is 2 after a transaction with an unreduced digit, and 1 after a transaction with a reduced digit.*

6.5 Law of Big Numbers for Matrices

A lower bound for the determinant of a matrix M can be turned into a lower bound for the norm $||M||$ using the inequality $||M|| \geq \sqrt{\frac{1}{2}|\det M|}$, which follows from the definition of the determinant as $\det \left(\begin{smallmatrix} a & c \\ b & d \end{smallmatrix}\right) = ad - bc$. Thus, we obtain together with Theorem 8:

Theorem 13. *Let M_0 be some initial matrix with* $\operatorname{cd} M_0 \neq 0$, *and M_n the result of applying n transactions in base r to M_0, and all possible reductions. Then*

$$\sqrt{\frac{|\det M_0|}{2(\operatorname{cd} M_0)^2}} \cdot (\sqrt{r})^n \leq ||M_n|| \leq 4||M_0|| \cdot r^n .$$

Thus, if in addition $\det M_0 \neq 0$, *even if all possible reductions are performed, the entries of the matrix are bound to grow exponentially in the number of transactions.*

It sounds a bit more optimistically to speak of the bit sizes of the entries instead of the entries themselves. The bit size of a number m is $\log m$.

Theorem 14 (Law of big numbers).
Let M be a matrix with non-zero determinant and non-zero column difference. After n transactions at M, at least one entry of the result has bit size $\Omega(n)$, even if all possible reductions are performed.

The law of big numbers means that the usage of big integers is unavoidable in exact real arithmetic, at least in the signed digit approach of Edalat's group. It applies even in the simplest cases. For instance, doubling of an unsigned real is effected by the matrix $\left(\begin{smallmatrix} 2 & 0 \\ 0 & 1 \end{smallmatrix}\right)$ that has determinant 2 and column difference 1, halfing by $\left(\begin{smallmatrix} 1 & 0 \\ 0 & 2 \end{smallmatrix}\right)$ with determinant 2 and column difference -1, and addition of 1 by the matrix $\left(\begin{smallmatrix} 1 & 1 \\ 0 & 1 \end{smallmatrix}\right)$ with determinant 1 and column difference -1.

The law of big numbers does not apply to matrices with zero column difference. The simplest example is the identity matrix $\mathrm{E} = \left(\begin{smallmatrix} 1 & 0 \\ 0 & 1 \end{smallmatrix}\right)$. According to (3), after a D-absorption, a subsequent D-emission, and a reduction by $\det D$, the identity matrix is recovered. Repeating this cycle, we see that there are arbitrarily long sequences of transactions at the identity matrix which do not lead to entries bigger than $4r$. It is an open problem whether such a fixed bound can be found for any matrix with column difference 0.

7 Big Numbers in Tensors

In this section, we derive analogues of the results of the previous section for tensors. The proceeding is similar, but a major obstacle is that tensors do not have determinants. Fortunately, a suitable substitute can be found.

7.1 Double Column Difference

We start by introducing an analogue to the column difference of a matrix. For a tensor T, the *double column difference* $\operatorname{dcd} T$ is defined by

$$\operatorname{dcd}\begin{pmatrix} a & c & e & g \\ b & d & f & h \end{pmatrix} = (a+b) - (c+d) - (e+f) + (g+h) \ . \qquad (22)$$

Writing a tensor T as a row $(T^{\mathrm{L}}, T^{\mathrm{R}})$ of two matrices, the double column difference can be reduced to the column differences of the two matrices: $\operatorname{dcd}(T^{\mathrm{L}}, T^{\mathrm{R}}) = \operatorname{cd} T^{\mathrm{L}} - \operatorname{cd} T^{\mathrm{R}}$. Hence, by (11) and the properties of cd, we obtain for all digit matrices D

$$\operatorname{dcd}((T^{\mathrm{L}}, T^{\mathrm{R}}) \cdot R(D)) = \operatorname{cd}(T^{\mathrm{L}} \cdot D) - \operatorname{cd}(T^{\mathrm{R}} \cdot D) = 2 \operatorname{dcd}(T^{\mathrm{L}}, T^{\mathrm{R}}) \, .$$

By $(T \cdot R(D))^{\times} = T^{\times} \cdot L(D)$ (12) and $\operatorname{dcd}(T^{\times}) = \operatorname{dcd} T$, we obtain the corresponding formula $\operatorname{dcd}(T \cdot L(D)) = 2 \operatorname{dcd} T$.
We still have to derive a formula for emission. Recall (17)

$$(D_k^r)^* \begin{pmatrix} u \\ v \end{pmatrix} = \begin{pmatrix} (1-k)(u+v) + r(u-v) \\ (1+k)(u+v) - r(u-v) \end{pmatrix} \qquad (23)$$

which implies

$$(D_k^r)^* \begin{pmatrix} u \\ v \end{pmatrix} = \begin{pmatrix} u' \\ v' \end{pmatrix} \implies u' + v' = 2(u + v) . \tag{24}$$

From this, $\operatorname{dcd}(D^* \cdot T) = 2 \operatorname{dcd} T$ follows for all digit matrices D. Therefore, dcd for tensors behaves exactly as cd for matrices:

- Transaction with an unreduced digit: $\operatorname{dcd} T' = 2 \operatorname{dcd} T$,
- Transaction with a reduced digit: $\operatorname{dcd} T' = \operatorname{dcd} T$,
- Reduction by k: $\operatorname{dcd} T' = \frac{1}{k} \operatorname{dcd} T$.

Again, the properties of having zero or non-zero double column difference are transaction invariants.

7.2 Column Determinant

A suitable substitute for the determinant of a matrix is the *column determinant* $\operatorname{cdet} T$ of a tensor T, defined by

$$\operatorname{cdet} \begin{pmatrix} a & c & e & g \\ b & d & f & h \end{pmatrix} = (a + b)(g + h) - (c + d)(e + f) . \tag{25}$$

Because of (24), $\operatorname{cdet}(D^* \cdot T) = 4 \operatorname{cdet} T$ holds for all tensors T and digit matrices D. Note that in contrast to the determinant of matrices, the factor is not $\det D^* = 4r$, but only 4. On the other side, the column determinant is multiplicative w.r.t. absorptions; for any tensor T and matrix M,

$$\operatorname{cdet}(T \cdot L(M)) = \operatorname{cdet}(T \cdot R(M)) = \operatorname{cdet} T \cdot \det M \tag{26}$$

holds. Here, the first equality follows from (12) and $\operatorname{cdet}(T^{\times}) = \operatorname{cdet} T$, while the proof of the second equality is a straightforward, but tedious exercise in algebraic manipulations.

Summarising and specialising to the case of digit matrices, we obtain:

- Emission of an unreduced digit: $\operatorname{cdet} T' = 4 \operatorname{cdet} T$,
- Emission of a reduced digit: $\operatorname{cdet} T' = \operatorname{cdet} T$,
- Absorption of an unreduced digit: $\operatorname{cdet} T' = 4r \operatorname{cdet} T$,
- Absorption of a reduced digit: $\operatorname{cdet} T' = r \operatorname{cdet} T$,
- Reduction by k: $\operatorname{cdet} T' = \frac{1}{k^2} \operatorname{cdet} T$.

In contrast to matrices, emissions and absorptions behave differently.

7.3 The Quotient

For a tensor T with $\operatorname{dcd} T \neq 0$, we consider the quotient $\operatorname{qdcd} T = \frac{\operatorname{cdet} T}{(\operatorname{dcd} T)^2}$. This quotient is invariant under reductions and also invariant under emissions. Every absorption yields a factor of r.

Lemma 15. *Let T_0 be some initial tensor with* $\operatorname{dcd} T_0 \neq 0$, *and T_n the result of applying n absorptions, any number of emissions, and all possible reductions to T_0. Then* $\operatorname{qdcd} T_n = r^n \operatorname{qdcd} T_0$.

As in the case of matrices, a lower bound for the column determinant follows:

Theorem 16. *Let T_0 be some initial tensor with* $\operatorname{dcd} T_0 \neq 0$, *and T_n the result of applying n absorptions, any number of emissions, and all possible reductions to T_0. Then*

$$\operatorname{cdet} T_n \geq \frac{|\operatorname{cdet} T_0|}{(\operatorname{dcd} T_0)^2} \cdot r^n .$$

7.4 Law of Big Numbers for Tensors

For tensors T, $\|T\| \geq \frac{1}{2}\sqrt{\frac{1}{2}|\operatorname{cdet} T|} = \sqrt{\frac{1}{8}|\operatorname{cdet} T|}$ holds. Thus, we obtain together with Theorem 8:

Theorem 17. *Let T_0 be some initial tensor with* $\operatorname{dcd} T_0 \neq 0$, *and T_n the result of applying n absorptions, any number of emissions, and all possible reductions to T_0. Then*

$$\sqrt{\frac{|\operatorname{cdet} T_0|}{8(\operatorname{dcd} T_0)^2}} \cdot \left(\sqrt{r}\right)^n \leq \|T_n\| \leq 8\|T_0\| \cdot r^n .$$

Theorem 18 (Law of big numbers for tensors).
Let T be a tensor with non-zero column determinant and non-zero double column difference. After n absorptions and any number of emissions at T, at least one entry of the result has bit size $\Omega(n)$, even if all possible reductions are performed.

7.5 Examples

The tensors that realise the four basic arithmetic operations satisfy the hypotheses of the law of big numbers:

Addition:	$\begin{pmatrix} 0 & 1 & 1 & 0 \\ 0 & 0 & 0 & 1 \end{pmatrix}$	$\operatorname{cdet} = -1$	$\operatorname{dcd} = -1$
Subtraction:	$\begin{pmatrix} 0 & 1 & -1 & 0 \\ 0 & 0 & 0 & 1 \end{pmatrix}$	$\operatorname{cdet} = 1$	$\operatorname{dcd} = 1$
Multiplication:	$\begin{pmatrix} 1 & 0 & 0 & 0 \\ 0 & 0 & 0 & 1 \end{pmatrix}$	$\operatorname{cdet} = 1$	$\operatorname{dcd} = 2$
Division:	$\begin{pmatrix} 0 & 1 & 0 & 0 \\ 0 & 0 & 1 & 0 \end{pmatrix}$	$\operatorname{cdet} = -1$	$\operatorname{dcd} = -2$

Yet the tensor for the mean value operation is different:

Mean value:	$\begin{pmatrix} 0 & 1 & 1 & 0 \\ 0 & 0 & 0 & 2 \end{pmatrix}$	$\operatorname{cdet} = -1$	$\operatorname{dcd} = 0$

Does this mean that $\frac{1}{2}x$, which leads to big numbers as shown in Section 6.5, can be computed as $\frac{0+x}{2}$ avoiding big numbers? The answer is no, at least in the case $r = 2$. Let T^{R} be the matrix on the right hand side of the tensor T. The equations $(D^* \cdot T)^{\mathrm{R}} = D^* \cdot T^{\mathrm{R}}$ and $(T \cdot R(D))^{\mathrm{R}} = T^{\mathrm{R}} \cdot D$ hold for all tensors

T and digit matrices D. This means that the right half of $\left(\begin{smallmatrix}0 & 1 & 1 & 0\\ 0 & 0 & 0 & 2\end{smallmatrix}\right)$ behaves exactly as the halfing matrix $\left(\begin{smallmatrix}1 & 0\\ 0 & 2\end{smallmatrix}\right)$ during emissions and absorptions from the right. Since the number 0 is represented by the infinite product $(\tilde{D}^2_{-1})^\omega$, and $\left(T \cdot L(\tilde{D}^2_{-1})\right)^{\mathrm{R}} = 2T^{\mathrm{R}}$, the correspondence is only changed by a common factor during absorptions from the left. Hence, after any number of transactions, the right half of the resulting tensor is a multiple of the matrix resulting from $\left(\begin{smallmatrix}1 & 0\\ 0 & 2\end{smallmatrix}\right)$ by the corresponding sequence of transactions. Thus, it has entries which are at least as big as the entries of the matrix, which are big by Theorem 14.

8 Discussion and Conclusion

The laws of big numbers as derived in this paper apply to unsigned reals only. For instance, halfing in the zero interval $[-1, 1]$ with base $r = 2$ means putting D^2_0 in front of the unsigned part of the argument, an operation possible without employing big integers.

Of course, our results crucially depend on the choice of the digit matrices. All digit matrices for all bases have zero column difference, and this fact is implicitly used in the derivations of the formulae for the cd and dcd values after transactions. A completely different choice of digit matrices, with non-zero column difference, may change everything. Also, the results may look different if irrational bases are used such as the golden ratio. However, we believe that big numbers cannot be avoided even in these cases, although we do not have a proof.

The appearance of big integers affects the complexity of real number arithmetic. Consider an LFT satisfying the hypotheses of the laws of big numbers. If it absorbs and emits digits one by one, then the nth transaction needs time $\Omega(n)$ since it involves integers of bit size $\Omega(n)$. Consequently, the computation of the first n digits of the result of the LFT needs time $\Omega(n^2)$. This time can only be reduced by replacing the one by one treatment of digits by algorithms absorbing and emitting many digits at once. Of course, the price for this reduction in time are much more involved algorithms.

References

1. A. Avizienis. Signed-digit number representations for fast parallel arithmetic. *IRE Transactions on Electronic Computers*, 10:389–400, 1961.
2. H.J. Boehm, R. Cartwright, M. Riggle, and M.J. O'Donell. Exact real arithmetic: A case study in higher order programming. In *ACM Symposium on Lisp and Functional Programming*, 1986.
3. H.J. Boehm and R. Cartwright. Exact real arithmetic: Formulating real numbers as functions. In D. Turner, editor, *Research Topics in Functional Programming*, pages 43–64. Addison-Wesley, 1990.
4. P. Di Gianantonio. *A Functional Approach to Real Number Computation.* PhD thesis, University of Pisa, 1993.

5. P. Di Gianantonio. Real number computability and domain theory. *Information and Computation*, 127(1):11–25, May 1996.
6. A. Edalat and P. Potts. A new representation for exact real numbers. In S. Brookes and M. Mislove, editors, *MFPS '97*, volume 6 of *Electronic Notes in Theoretical Computer Science*, 1997. URL: `http://www.elsevier.nl/locate/entcs/volume6.html`.
7. M. H. Escardó. PCF extended with real numbers. *Theoretical Computer Science*, 162(1):79–115, August 1996.
8. W. Gosper. Continued fraction arithmetic. Technical Report HAKMEM Item 101B, MIT Artificial Intelligence Memo 239, MIT, 1972.
9. P. Kornerup and D. W. Matula. Finite precision lexicographic continued fraction number systems. In *Proc. 7th IEEE Symposium on Computer Arithmetic*, pages 207–214. IEEE Computer Society Press, 1985.
10. V. Menissier-Morain. Arbitrary precision real arithmetic: Design and algorithms. *submitted to J. Symbolic Computation*, 1996.
11. A. Nielsen and P. Kornerup. MSB-first digit serial arithmetic. *J. of Univ. Comp. Scien.*, 1(7), 1995.
12. P. J. Potts and A. Edalat. Exact real arithmetic based on linear fractional transformations. Draft, Imperial College, available from `http://www-tfm.doc.ic.ac.uk/~pjp`, December 1996.
13. P. J. Potts and A. Edalat. Exact real computer arithmetic. Draft, Imperial College, available from `http://www-tfm.doc.ic.ac.uk/~pjp`, March 1997.
14. P. J. Potts. Computable real arithmetic using linear fractional transformations. Draft PhD Thesis, Imperial College, available from `http://www-tfm.doc.ic.ac.uk/~pjp`, June 1996.
15. P. Potts, A. Edalat, and M. Escardó. Semantics of exact real arithmetic. In *Twelfth Annual IEEE Symposium on Logic in Computer Science*. IEEE, 1997.
16. J. E. Vuillemin. Exact real computer arithmetic with continued fractions. *IEEE Transactions on Computers*, 39(8):1087–1105, 1990.

Net Refinement by Pullback Rewriting*

Renate Klempien-Hinrichs

Universität Bremen, Fachbereich 3, Postfach 33 04 40, D–28334 Bremen
email: rena@informatik.uni-bremen.de

Abstract. The theory of graph grammars is concerned with the rule-based transformation of graphs and graph-like structures. As the formalism of Petri nets is founded on a particular type of graphs, the various net refinement methods proposed for their structured design are in particular graph transformations. This paper aims at applying a recently developed technique for graph rewriting, the so-called pullback approach, to describe net refinement. The translation of this technique, which is based on (hyper)graph morphisms, into terms of net morphisms yields a well-defined mechanism closely related to pullback rewriting in hypergraphs. A variant allows to elegantly characterize a particular net refinement operation which modifies the context of the refined transition.

1 Introduction

Graph grammars have been developed as a concept to study the rule-based transformation of graphs and graph-like structures (see [Roz97] for a comprehensive overview). One can distinguish between approaches in which arbitrary subgraphs may be replaced, and approaches to rewrite elementary subgraphs, i.e. vertices, (hyper)edges, or handles. (Hyper)edge rewriting [HK87a, Hab92] is a special case of the double-pushout approach to graph rewriting [Ehr79]; it has been generalized to handle rewriting in [CER93]. With the pullback approach introduced in [Bau95a], a category theoretical framework for vertex rewriting is being developed. It is based on graph morphisms and can deal with both graphs and hypergraphs [BJ97].

A Petri net is usually defined as a bipartite graph (the underlying net structure) where a vertex is either a place or a transition, plus a marking of the places (see e.g. [Rei85]). The marking may change by the firing of transitions, thus leading to a notion of behaviour. A number of methods to refine a place or a transition – i.e. to manipulate the underlying net structure – such that the behaviour of the refined net can be inferred from the behaviour of the original and the refinement net in a compositional way may be found in the literature (for a survey see [BGV91]).

By viewing the underlying net structure of a Petri net as a hypergraph, place or transition refinement becomes the replacement of an elementary item in

* Supported by the EC TMR Network GETGRATS (General Theory of Graph Transformation Systems) through the University of Bordeaux I.

a hypergraph. In [HK87b] and [Vog87], it has been pointed out that hyperedge rewriting describes some types of net refinement. The operation in [GG90] modifies the context of the refined transition by multiplying the places in its pre- and postset and is thus too complex to be described by hyperedge rewriting. However, it can be seen as a special case of the vertex rewriting technique of [Kle96]. Handle rewriting has not yet been evaluated under this aspect.

Another line of research investigates rule-based refinement in the general setting of algebraic high-level nets [PER95, PGE98]. The rules which are used there have been developed from the double-pushout approach to graph rewriting of [Ehr79].

In this paper, the technique of pullback rewriting is translated into terms of net morphisms. The resulting mechanism yields a well-defined notion of net refinement and is closely related to the original pullback rewriting in hypergraphs. Furthermore, it also allows an elegant characterization of the refinement operation in [GG90]. The paper is organized as follows. Section 2 introduces the basic notions of hypergraphs and net structures. The respective categories are studied in Section 3. In Section 4, pullback rewriting in net structures is defined and compared to pullback rewriting in hypergraphs. Section 5 characterizes the net refinement technique of [GG90] in terms of pullback rewriting, and Section 6 contains some concluding remarks.

2 Hypergraphs and net structures

The basic objects considered in this paper, hypergraphs and net structures, are introduced together with the usual notions of the respective morphisms.

Definition 2.1. (Hypergraph.) A *hypergraph* $H = (V, E, src, trg)$ consists of a set V of *nodes*, a set E of *hyperedges* such that $V \cap E = \emptyset$, and two mappings $src, trg\colon E \to \mathcal{P}(V)$ assigning to every hyperedge $e \in E$ a set $src(e) \subseteq V$ of *source nodes* and a set $trg(e) \subseteq V$ of *target nodes*. Subscripts and superscripts carry over to the components of a hypergraph; for example, $H'_n = (V'_n, E'_n, src'_n, trg'_n)$.

Let H and H' be two hypergraphs. A *hypergraph morphism* $f\colon H \to H'$ is a pair of mappings $f = (f_V, f_E)$ with $f_V\colon V \to V'$, $f_E\colon E \to E'$ such that $f_V(src(e)) \subseteq src'(f_E(e))$ and $f_V(trg(e)) \subseteq trg'(f_E(e))$ for all $e \in E$. As usual, the subscripts V and E will be omitted in the sequel. If f is bijective and both f and f^{-1} are hypergraph morphisms, then f is a *hypergraph isomorphism*. In this case, H and H' are *isomorphic*.

Hypergraphs and hypergraph morphisms form a category which is denoted by $\mathcal{H}$.

In a drawing of a hypergraph H, a node v is represented by a circle and a hyperedge e by a square. There is an arrow from v to e if $v \in s(e)$ and an arrow from e to v if $v \in t(e)$. Thus, Fig. 1 shows a hypergraph.

A Petri net consists of a net structure plus a marking. As this paper concentrates on structural aspects, only the former notion is formally defined here; for other notions from net theory see e.g. [Rei85].

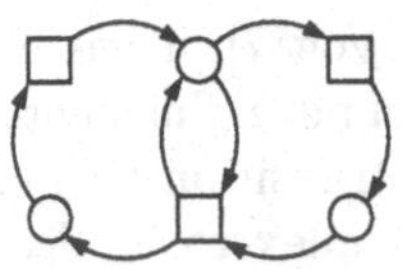

Figure 1. Drawing a hypergraph (or a net structure)

Definition 2.2. (Net structure.) A *net structure* $N = (P, T, F)$ consists of a set P of *places*, a set T of *transitions* such that $P \cap T = \emptyset$, and a *flow relation* $F \subseteq (P \times T) \cup (T \times P)$ the elements of which are called *arcs*. As for graphs, subscripts and superscripts carry over to the components of a net structure.

For an item $x \in P \cup T$, ${}^\bullet x = \{y \in P \cup T \mid (y, x) \in F\}$ denotes the *preset* of x, and $x^\bullet = \{y \in P \cup T \mid (x, y) \in F\}$ its *postset*.

Let N and N' be two net structures. A *net morphism* $f: N \to N'$ is a mapping $f: P \cup T \to P' \cup T'$ satisfying $(f(x), f(y)) \in F'$ and $x \in P \Leftrightarrow f(x) \in P'$ for all $x, y \in P \cup T$ with $f(x) \neq f(y)$ and $(x, y) \in F$. If f is bijective and both f and f^{-1} are net morphisms, then f is a *net isomorphism* and N, N' are *isomorphic*.

Net structures and net morphisms form a category which is denoted by $\mathcal{N}$.

In a drawing of a net structure N, a place p is represented by a circle, a transition t by a square, and an arc (x, y) by an arrow. Thus, Fig. 1 shows a net structure.

The similar representation of hypergraphs and net structures evokes a one-to-one encoding: The hypergraph H is *associated* with the net structure N if $V = P$, $E = T$, $src(e) = {}^\bullet e$ and $trg(e) = e^\bullet$ for all $e \in E$. With respect to this encoding, every hypergraph morphism is associated with a net morphism. The opposite is not true: a net morphism may map a transition on a place (or vice versa). But if a substructure is mapped on one item, then its border has to be of the same type as the item (cf. Figs. 2 and 3, where a dashed line encircles the items the respective mapping identifies).

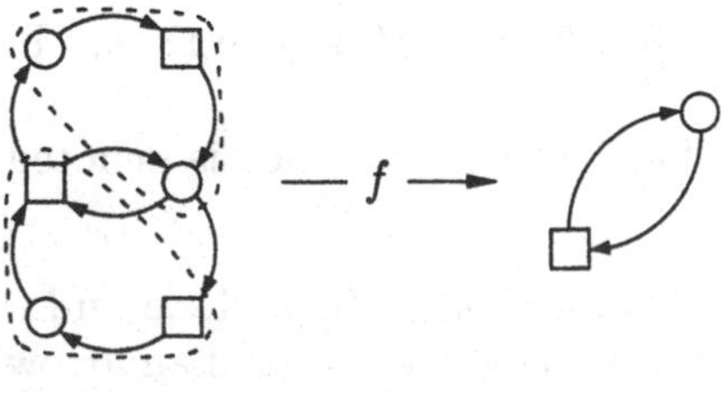

Figure 2. A net morphism without associated hypergraph morphism

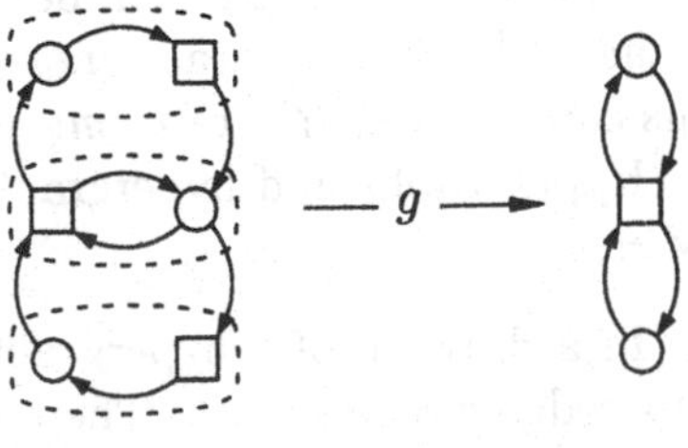

Figure 3. Neither a net morphism nor a hypergraph morphism

3 The categories of hypergraphs and net structures

In this section, the pullback construction for hypergraph morphisms is recalled. The category of hypergraphs is complete and therefore has all pullbacks. The category of net structures does not have all pullbacks, but the pairs of net morphisms for which the pullback exists are characterized, and the pullback construction is given for these cases.

As the notion of a pullback is central for pullback rewriting, the section starts with its general definition. For other concepts from category theory see e.g. [HS79].

Definition 3.1. (Pullback.) Let $\mathcal{C}$ be a category and $(f_i: Y_i \to Z)_{i=1,2}$ a pair of morphisms in $\mathcal{C}$. The *pullback* of $(f_i: Y_i \to Z)_{i=1,2}$ is another pair of morphisms $(g_i: X \to Y_i)_{i=1,2}$ such that $f_1 \circ g_1 = f_2 \circ g_2$, and for every pair of morphisms $(g'_i: X' \to Y_i)_{i=1,2}$ with $f_1 \circ g'_1 = f_2 \circ g'_2$ there is a unique morphism $h: X' \to X$ with $g_i \circ h = g'_i$ for $i = 1, 2$.

Using a definition of hypergraphs as graphs structured by the smallest complete bipartite graph  (i.e. as objects in the comma category of graphs over ) which is equivalent to the one given here, the following fact can be shown analogously to [BJ97].

Fact 3.2. *The category $\mathcal{H}$ is finitely complete and has, in particular, pullbacks. The pullback of a pair of hypergraph morphisms $(f_i: H_i \to H)_{i=1,2}$ consists of the projections $g_i: H_{pb} \to H_i$ with $g_i((x_1, x_2)) = x_i$ $(i = 1, 2)$, where H_{pb} is constructed as follows:*

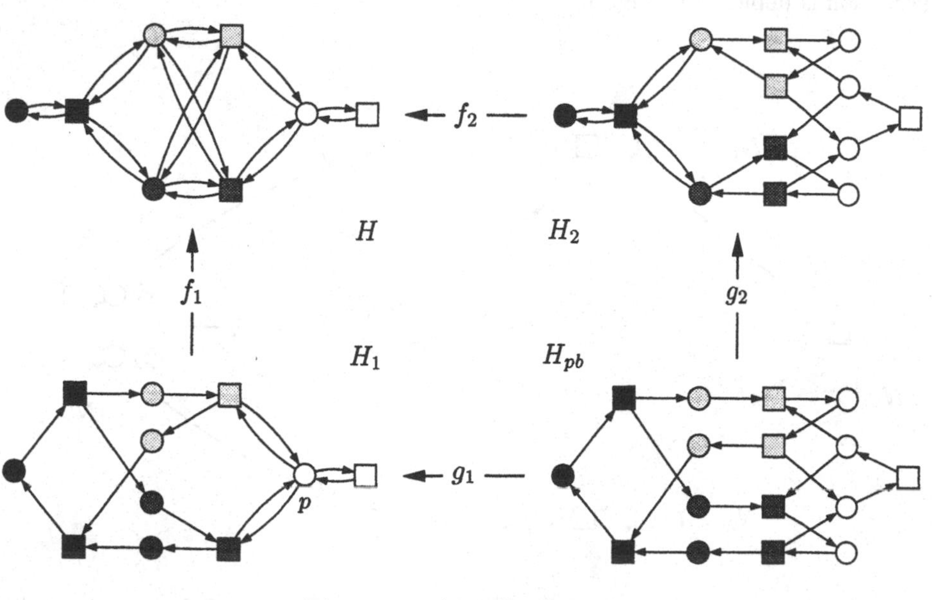

Figure 4. A pullback in $\mathcal{H}$

- $V_{pb} = \{(v_1, v_2) \in V_1 \times V_2 \mid f_1(v_1) = f_2(v_2)\}$,
- $E_{pb} = \{(e_1, e_2) \in E_1 \times E_2 \mid f_1(e_1) = f_2(e_2)\}$,
- $src_{pb}((e_1, e_2)) = \{(v_1, v_2) \in V_{pb} \mid v_1 \in src_1(e_1),\ v_2 \in src_2(e_2)\}$ *and*
- $trg_{pb}((e_1, e_2)) = \{(v_1, v_2) \in V_{pb} \mid v_1 \in trg_1(e_1),\ v_2 \in trg_2(e_2)\}$ *for all* $(e_1, e_2) \in E_{pb}$. ◇

An example for a pullback of hypergraph morphisms f_1, f_2 is given in Fig. 4. The morphisms are indicated by the relative arrangement of the items and their shading. As explained in the next section, this pullback can be interpreted as deriving H_2 from H_1 by rewriting the node p.

Unlike $\mathcal{H}$, the category of net structures is not finitely complete, but the characterization of Theorem 3.3 allows to easily verify that pullbacks do exist in the cases which will be interpreted as net rewriting in the following section.

Theorem 3.3. *For $i = 1, 2$, let N_i and N be net structures and $f_i: N_i \to N$ net morphisms. The pullback of (f_1, f_2) exists if and only if for every item $z \in P \cup T$ of N, at most one of the sets $f_1^{-1}(z)$, $f_2^{-1}(z)$ contains distinct items x and y such that (x, y) belongs to the flow relation of the corresponding net structure.*

Proof. "⇒": Let $z \in P \cup T$ and $p_i, t_i \in f_i^{-1}(z)$ with $(p_i, t_i) \in F_i$ or $(t_i, p_i) \in F_i$, for $i = 1, 2$. Moreover, let $N^\star$ be a net structure and $g_1: N^\star \to N_1$, $g_2: N^\star \to N_2$ net morphisms with $g_1 \circ f_1 = g_2 \circ f_2$.

Now let N' be the net structure with places p_1', p_2', transitions t_1', t_2', and an arc between p_i' and t_i' mirroring (one of) the arc(s) between p_i and t_i $(i = 1, 2)$. Consider the two net morphisms $g_1': N' \to N_1$, $g_2': N' \to N_2$ with $g_1'(p_1') = p_1$, $g_1'(\{t_1', p_2', t_2'\}) = \{t_1\}$, $g_2'(\{p_1', t_1', p_2'\}) = \{p_2\}$, and $g_2'(t_2') = t_2$; clearly, $g_1' \circ f_1 = g_2' \circ f_2$. Finally, let $h: N' \to N^\star$ be a net morphism such that $g_i \circ h = g_i'$. The situation is depicted in Fig. 5.

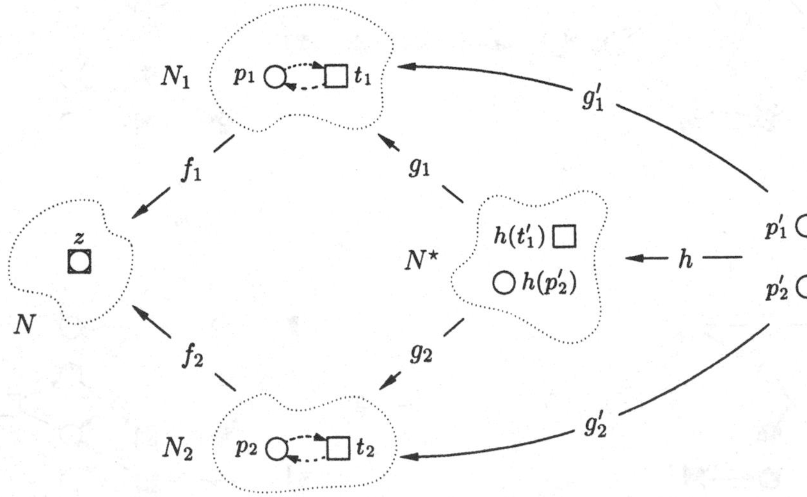

Figure 5. Illustrating the proof of Theorem 3.3

As $g_i \circ h = g'_i$ maps p'_i to p_i and t'_i to t_i, h does not identify p'_i and t'_i ($i = 1, 2$). Therefore, the arc between p'_1 and t'_1 resp. p'_2 and t'_2 implies that $h(t'_1)$ is a transition and $h(p'_2)$ a place. Moreover, $g_i \circ h = g'_i$ identifying t'_1 and p'_2 means that g_i identifies $h(t'_1)$ and $h(p'_2)$ ($i = 1, 2$). Hence, for net morphisms $g''_i: N' \to N_i$ with $g''_1(P' \cup T') = \{t_1\}$ and $g''_2(P' \cup T') = \{p_2\}$, the two distinct net morphisms $h_1, h_2: N' \to N^*$ with $h_1(P' \cup T') = h(t'_1)$ and $h_2(P' \cup T') = h(p'_2)$ fulfil $g_i \circ h_j = g''_i$ ($i, j \in \{1, 2\}$). Thus, (g_1, g_2) cannot be the pullback of (f_1, f_2).

"$\Leftarrow$" (Outline): Let $Z_i := \{z \in P \cup T \mid \exists x, y \in f_i^{-1}(z) \text{ with } (x, y) \in F_i\}$ for $i = 1, 2$. By assumption, Z_1 and Z_2 are disjoint. Let N_{pb} be as follows:

- $P_{pb} = \{(x_1, x_2) \in f_1^{-1}(z) \times f_2^{-1}(z) \mid$
  $(z \in P \setminus (Z_1 \cup Z_2))$ or $(z \in Z_1$ and $x_1 \in P_1)$ or $(z \in Z_2$ and $x_2 \in P_2)\}$,
- $T_{pb} = \{(x_1, x_2) \in f_1^{-1}(z) \times f_2^{-1}(z) \mid$
  $(z \in T \setminus (Z_1 \cup Z_2))$ or $(z \in Z_1$ and $x_1 \in T_1)$ or $(z \in Z_2$ and $x_2 \in T_2)\}$,
- $F_{pb} = \{((x_1, x_2), (y_1, y_2)) \in (P_{pb} \times T_{pb}) \cup (T_{pb} \times P_{pb}) \mid$
  $(x_i, y_i) \in F_i$ and $(x_j = y_j$ or $(x_j, y_j) \in F_j)$ for $i, j \in \{1, 2\}, i \neq j\}$.

Clearly, N_{pb} is a net structure, and it is not difficult to verify that the projections $g_i: N_{pb} \to N_i$ with $g_i((x_1, x_2)) = x_i$ form the pullback of (f_1, f_2) in $\mathcal{N}$. □

4 Net rewriting by pullbacks

In this section, pullback rewriting is defined directly in the category $\mathcal{N}$ of net structures. The basic idea is to achieve the partition of a net structure into three parts – the item to be rewritten, its immediate neighbourhood, and the context of the item – by a net morphism (an *unknown*) to a special net structure (the *alphabet*). Another kind of net morphism to the alphabet (a *rule*) specifies the net structure replacing the item, and its *application* is modelled by the pullback of the two net morphisms. Thus, pullback rewriting yields a notion of net refinement where items in the pre- and postsets of the refined item can be multiplied. Example 4.1, a place refinement, illustrates the usefulness of such an operation and will be formalized as both net and hypergraph rewriting in this section.

The close relationship between pullback rewriting in net structures and in hypergraphs allows to transfer the formalism presented in [BJ97] for an arbitrary number of items to be rewritten – possibly of different types – to net structures, too. The same holds for the notion of parallel rewriting as proposed in [Bau95b].

Example 4.1. (Cf. the reduction example of [GF95].) The (marked) Petri net PN in Fig. 6 models a situation of mutual exclusion, with p as a semaphore. Its refinement to PN' explicitly represents the critical sections and the initialization of their common resources. Moreover, each transition connected with p is split in two to express the entrance into and exit from its associated critical section. ◇

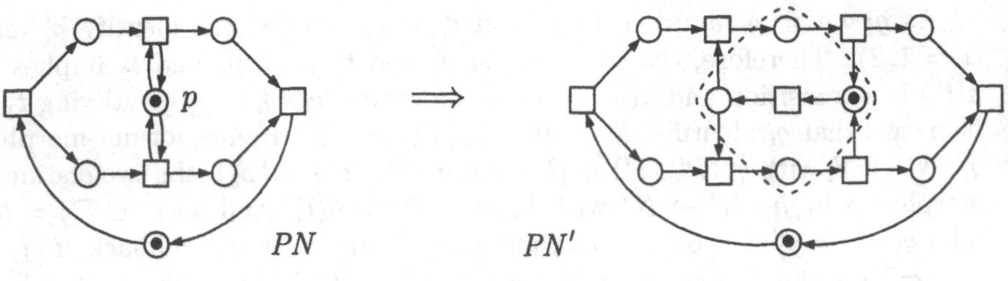

Figure 6. Refining a Petri net

Notation 4.2. For a relation $X \subseteq S \times S$ on a set S, $X^\sigma = X \cup \{(y,x) \mid (x,y) \in X\}$ denotes the symmetric hull. The set of all positive integers is denoted by $\mathbb{N}_+$.

The first mechanism to be presented is place rewriting in net structures. The place rewriting alphabet contains a place p_{-1} (for the place to be rewritten), transitions t_j linking it to neighbour places p_i, and a farther context t_0.

Definition 4.3. (Alphabet.) The *place rewriting alphabet* is the net structure N_A with $P_A = \{p_{-1}\} \cup \{p_i \mid i \in \mathbb{N}_+\}$, $T_A = \{t_0\} \cup \{t_j \mid j \in \mathbb{N}_+\}$, and

$$F_A = \bigcup_{i,j \in \mathbb{N}_+} \{(t_0, p_i), (p_i, t_j), (t_j, p_{-1})\}^\sigma .$$

A substructure $N_{A(m,n)}$ of N_A with $m+1$ places and $n+1$ transitions with $m, n \in \mathbb{N}_+$ "as required" will be used for finite examples; cf. Fig. 7 for $N_{A(2,3)}$.

A place rewriting unknown maps the place to be rewritten on p_{-1} and identifies those linking transitions resp. neighbour places which will be treated equally during a rewriting step.

Definition 4.4. (Unknown.) Let N be a net structure and $p \in P$. A *place rewriting unknown* on p is a net morphism $u_p\colon N \to N_A$ such that

- $u_p^{-1}(p_{-1}) = \{p\}$,
- for every $j \in \mathbb{N}_+$, $x \in u_p^{-1}(t_j)$ implies $\{(x,p)\}^\sigma \cap F \neq \emptyset$, and
- for every $i \in \mathbb{N}_+$, $y \in u_p^{-1}(p_i)$ implies that $j \in \mathbb{N}_+$ and $t \in u_p^{-1}(t_j)$ exist with $\{(y,t)\}^\sigma \cap F \neq \emptyset$.

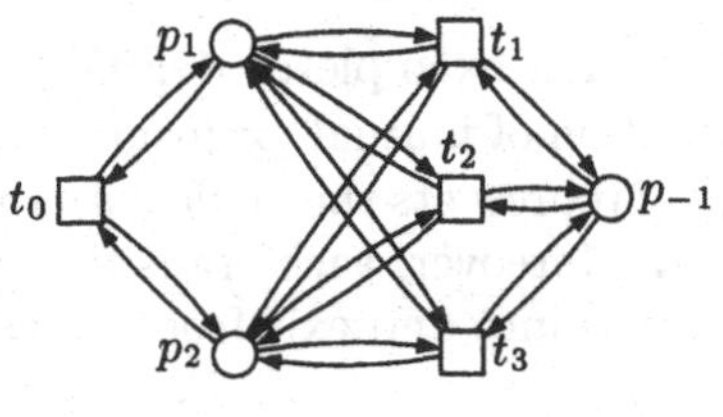

Figure 7. The place rewriting alphabet $N_{A(2,3)}$

A place rewriting rule maps what would classically be called the right-hand side of a production on p_{-1} and fixes its possible connexions to a context through the inverse images of the t_j.

Definition 4.5. (Rule.) A net morphism $r: N_R \to N_A$ is a *place rewriting rule* if

- for every item $x \in \{t_0\} \cup \{p_i \mid i \in \mathbb{N}_+\}$, $r^{-1}(x)$ contains exactly one element,
- $\{(r^{-1}(t_0), r^{-1}(p_i)) \mid i \in \mathbb{N}_+\}^\sigma \subseteq F_R$, and
- for every $j \in \mathbb{N}_+$, $r^{-1}(t_j)$ contains only transitions.

The notions of a rule application and a rewriting step are defined uniformly for all the concrete rewriting mechanisms studied in this and the next section.

Definition 4.6. (Rule application, rewriting step.) Let $\mathcal{C}$ be a category with an alphabet object A, an unknown morphism $u_x: Y \to A$, and a rule morphism $r: R \to A$ such that A, u_x, and r belong to the same rewriting mechanism (e.g. place rewriting in $\mathcal{N}$). The *application* of r at u_x is the pullback of (u_x, r) in $\mathcal{C}$. If Y' is the object constructed by the application of r at u_x (the *derived* object), then $Y \Longrightarrow_{(u_x,r)} Y'$ denotes a *rewriting step.*

Figure 8 formalizes the refinement $PN \Longrightarrow PN'$ of Example 4.1 as the place rewriting step $N \Longrightarrow_{(u_p,r)} N'$. The unknown u_p distinguishes the "upper" from the "lower" context of p, and the rule r specifies the net structure replacing p as well as the splitting of the transitions connected with p. Note that there are alternative choices for u_p and r to derive N' from N.

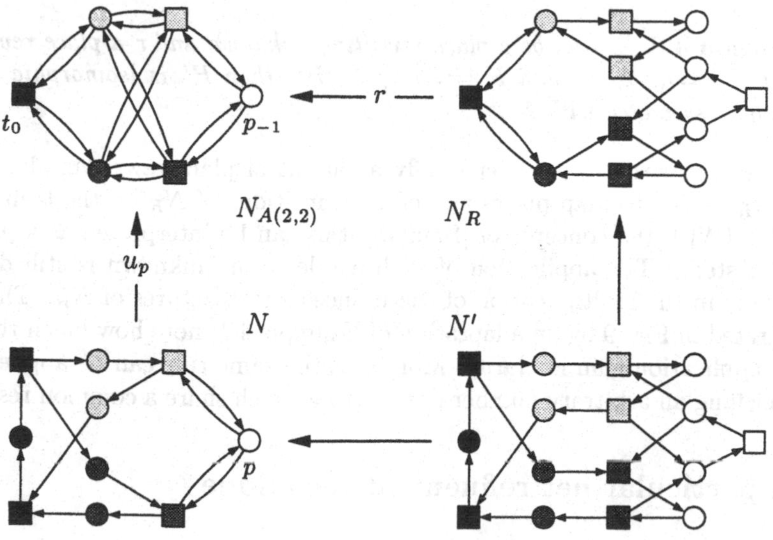

Figure 8. Formalizing Example 4.1 as pullback rewriting

In general, the application of a place rewriting rule r at a place rewriting unknown u_p produces in the derived net structure exactly one copy of the context $u_p^{-1}(t_0)$ of p. Similarly, the $u_p^{-1}(p_i)$ are reproduced, as is the right-hand side of the rule. Only the linking transitions may be multiplied (the factors being the size of the respective inverse images) and have their arcs of the flow relation altered.

Corollary 4.7. *For every place rewriting rule r and unknown u_p, the application of r at u_p is defined.* ◇

Proof. Of N_A, only the item t_0 (resp. p_{-1}) may contain an arc in its inverse image under u_p (resp. r). As $t_0 \neq p_{-1}$, Theorem 3.3 implies the assertion. □

There is a close relationship between place rewriting in $\mathcal{N}$ and node rewriting in $\mathcal{H}$, which differs from that introduced in [BJ97] only in that it deals with directed instead of undirected hypergraphs. Thus, the notions of an alphabet, an unknown, and a rule can be gained from those for place rewriting in $\mathcal{N}$ by changing the (terminal) substructures t_0, p_{-1} of N_A and their inverse images $r^{-1}(t_0), u_p^{-1}(p_{-1})$ into copies of the (terminal) hypergraph , and adjusting the involved net morphisms u_p and r accordingly to hypergraph morphisms $\langle u_p \rangle$ and $\langle r \rangle$. Figure 4 shows how the place rewriting step $N \Longrightarrow_{(u_p,r)} N'$ of Fig. 8 is transformed into the node rewriting step $H \Longrightarrow_{(\langle u_p \rangle, \langle r \rangle)} H'$, where $H = H_1$, $H' = H_{pb}$, $\langle u_p \rangle = f_1$, and $\langle r \rangle = f_2$. The example may be explicit enough so that the formal definitions can be omitted. It also illustrates that for the formalization of net refinement, pullback rewriting in net structures is more adequate than pullback rewriting in hypergraphs: In the latter case, one cannot directly take the hypergraph associated with the net to be refined, but has to alter it in order to get the desired result.

Proposition 4.8. *Let u_p be a place rewriting unknown and r a place rewriting rule. If $N \Longrightarrow_{(u_p,r)} N'$ and $H \Longrightarrow_{(\langle u_p \rangle, \langle r \rangle)} H'$, then H' is isomorphic to the hypergraph associated with N'.*

To end this section, consider briefly a variant of place rewriting allowing a rule $r: N_R \to N_A$ to map places as well as transitions of N_R on the transitions t_i of N_A. (With the concepts of [Bau95b], this can be interpreted as a parallel rewriting step.) The application of such a rule to an unknown is still defined and results in the multiplication of the induced substructures of N_R. The idea is illustrated in Fig. 9 by an adaptation of Example 4.1; note how much the rule and its application gain in clarity. Moreover, the same rule can be applied to a net modelling an arbitrary number of processes which share a common resource.

5 A particular net refinement technique

By the symmetry of net structures, pullback rewriting of places immediately implies a notion of transition rewriting. In this section, a slightly different instance

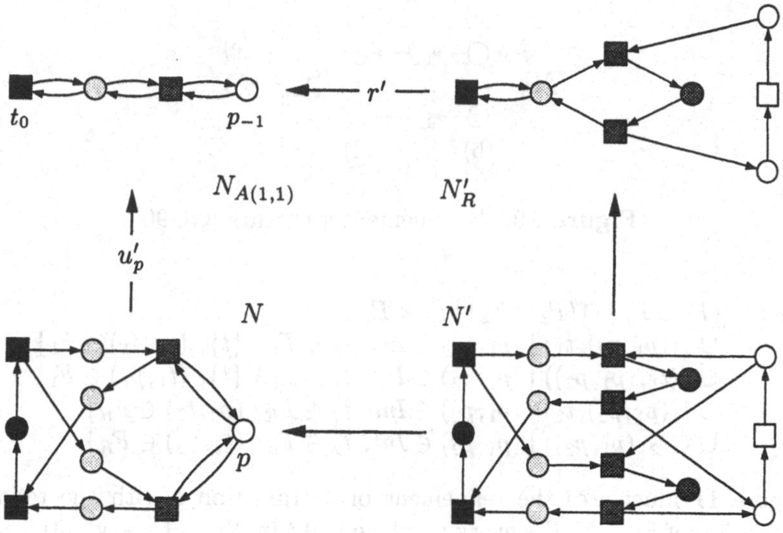

Figure 9. Application of a more general rewriting rule

of pullback rewriting is used to characterize the transition refinement operation introduced in [GG90] for one-safe nets. Their operation allows to infer the behaviour (in particular liveness properties) of a refined net compositionally from the behaviours of the original and the refinement net, and in contrast to previous studies their refinement nets may display initial or terminal concurrency.

Markings and behavioural aspects are not formally considered here; this concerns in particular some additional restrictions for refinement structures.

Notation 5.1. Let N be a net structure. The set ${}^\circ N = \{x \in P \mid {}^\bullet x = \emptyset\}$ contains the *initial places* of N, and $N^\circ = \{x \in P \mid x^\bullet = \emptyset\}$ its *terminal places.*

General assumption [GG90]. In this section, all net structures N are assumed to have arcs $(p,t),(t,p') \in F$ and ${}^\bullet t \cap t^\bullet = \emptyset$ for every $t \in T$.

Definition 5.2. (Refinement structure, cf. [GG90].) A net structure N_R is a *refinement structure* if ${}^\circ N_R \neq \emptyset \neq N_R{}^\circ$ and ${}^\circ N_R \cap N_R{}^\circ = \emptyset$.

Figure 10 shows a refinement structure N_R with initial places $(a),(b)$ and terminal place (e).

Definition 5.3. (Net refinement [GG90].) Let N_1 be a net structure and $t \in T_1$. Moreover, let N_R be a refinement structure (disjoint from N_1). Then the refined net structure $N_2 = N_1[N_R/t]$ is defined by

- $P_2 := (P_1 \setminus ({}^\bullet t \cup t^\bullet)) \cup (P_R \setminus ({}^\circ N_R \cup N_R{}^\circ)) \cup Int$,
  where $Int := ({}^\bullet t \times {}^\circ N_R) \cup (t^\bullet \times N_R{}^\circ)$,
- $T_2 := (T_1 \setminus \{t\}) \cup T_R$, and

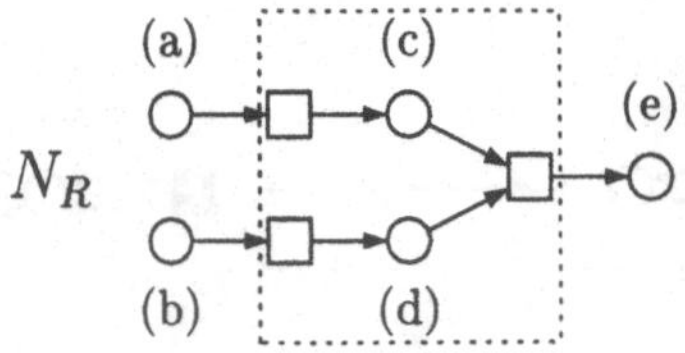

Figure 10. A refinement structure [GG90]

– $F_2 := ((F_1 \cup F_R) \cap (P_2 \times T_2 \cup T_2 \times P_2))$
$\cup \{((p_1,p_2),t_1) \mid (p_1,p_2) \in Int,\ t_1 \in T_1 \setminus \{t\},\ (p_1,t_1) \in F_1\}$
$\cup \{(t_1,(p_1,p_2)) \mid (p_1,p_2) \in Int,\ t_1 \in T_1 \setminus \{t\},\ (t_1,p_1) \in F_1\}$
$\cup \{((p_1,p_2),t_2) \mid (p_1,p_2) \in Int,\ t_2 \in T_R,\ (p_2,t_2) \in F_R\}$
$\cup \{(t_2,(p_1,p_2)) \mid (p_1,p_2) \in Int,\ t_2 \in T_R,\ (t_2,p_2) \in F_R\}$.

Figure 11 illustrates the refinement of a transition t with the refinement structure N_R of Fig. 10: For every preplace p of t in N_1 and every initial place p' in N_R, there is a new place (p,p') in N_2 with ingoing arcs from each transition in the preset of p and outgoing arcs to each transition in the postsets of p and p', and analogously for the postplaces of t and the terminal places in N_R.

This refinement technique can be characterized by pullback rewriting as follows.

Definition 5.4. (Refinement alphabet, unknown, and rule.) The *refinement alphabet* is the net structure N_α with $P_\alpha = \{p_1,p_2\}$, $T_\alpha = \{t_0,t_{-1}\}$, and $F_\alpha = \{(t_0,p_1),(t_0,p_2)\}^\sigma \cup \{(p_1,t_{-1}),(t_{-1},p_2)\}$.

Let N_1 be a net structure and $t \in T_1$. The *refinement unknown* on t is the net morphism $u_t\colon N_1 \to N_\alpha$ with $u_t^{-1}(t_{-1}) = \{t\}$, $u_t^{-1}(p_1) = {}^\bullet t$, and $u_t^{-1}(p_2) = t^\bullet$.

Let N_R be a refinement structure and N'_R a net structure with $P'_R = P_R$, $T'_R = T_R \dot\cup \{t'\}$, and $F'_R = F_R \cup \{(p,t') \mid p \in {}^\circ N_R \cup N_R{}^\circ\}^\sigma$. The *refinement rule* induced by N_R is the net morphism $r\colon N'_R \to N_\alpha$ with $r^{-1}(t_0) = \{t'\}$, $r^{-1}(p_1) = {}^\circ N_R$, and $r^{-1}(p_2) = N_R{}^\circ$.

The conversion of the example above into terms of pullback rewriting is depicted in Fig. 12. Note that the flow relation of N_α is not symmetric. Moreover,

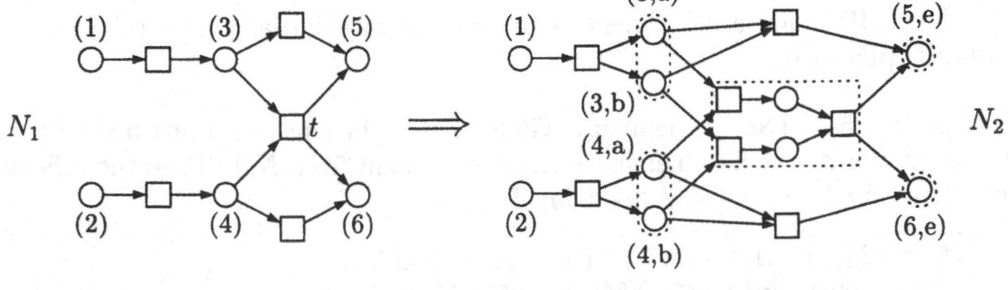

Figure 11. Transition refinement [GG90]

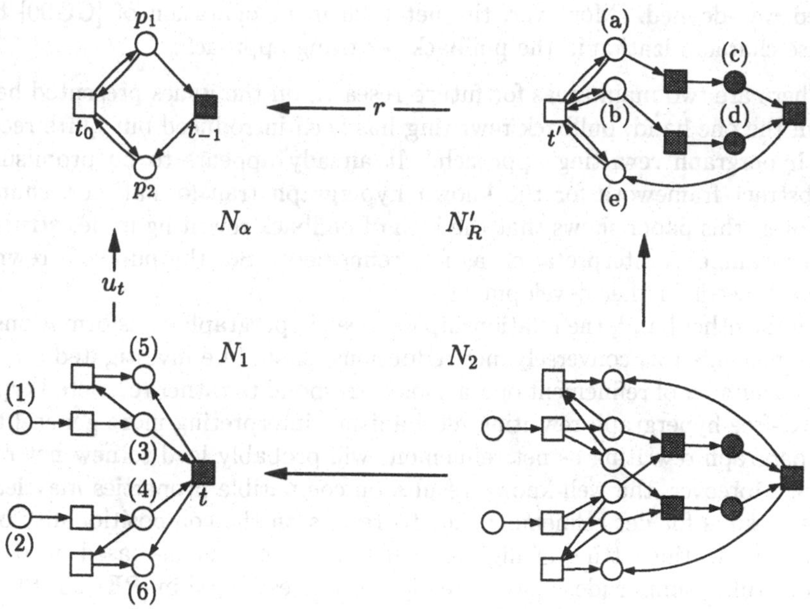

Figure 12. Transition refinement as pullback rewriting

the refinement unknown u_t is a mapping (by the assumption above), and unique for every transition t of a net structure N_1.

Theorem 5.5. *Let N_R be a refinement structure, r the induced refinement rule, N_1 a net structure with $t \in T_1$, and $u_t \colon N_1 \to N_\alpha$ the refinement unknown on t. If $N_1 \Rightarrow_{(u_t,r)} N_2$, then N_2 and $N_1[N_R/t]$ are isomorphic.*

Proof. By construction, N_2 and $N_1[N_R/t]$ only differ in that N_2 contains an item (x, t') for each $x \in (P_1 \cup T_1) \setminus ({}^\bullet t \cup \{t\} \cup t^\bullet)$ and an item (t, y) for each $y \in (P_R \setminus ({}^\circ N_R \cup N_R{}^\circ)) \cup T_R$. □

Note that the canonical vicinity respecting morphism $f \colon N_1[N_R/t] \to N_1$ of [GG90] is (modulo isomorphism) exactly the morphism $f \colon N_2 \to N_1$ generated by the pullback construction.

6 Conclusion

The aim of this work was to investigate an application of the pullback approach to hypergraph transformation by translating the notion of pullback rewriting from terms of hypergraph morphisms into terms of net morphisms. It turned out that unlike the category of hypergraphs, the category of net structures is not complete; in particular, it does not have all pullbacks. Nevertheless, there is an easily verified criterion to determine whether the pullback of two given net morphisms exists. This criterion ensures that net rewriting by pullbacks is indeed well-defined. Moreover, the net refinement operation of [GG90] has a concise characterization in the pullback rewriting approach.

There are two main areas for future research on the issues presented here.

On the one hand, pullback rewriting has been introduced but quite recently as a hypergraph rewriting approach. It already appears to be promising as an abstract framework for the known hypergraph transformation techniques. Moreover, this paper shows that the idea of pullback rewriting in net structures has a meaningful interpretation as net refinement. So, the pullback rewriting approach needs further development.

On the other hand, the relationship between hypergraph transformations and net refinements (or, conversely, net reductions) should be investigated:

As a number of refinement operations correspond to rather restricted types of context-free hypergraph rewriting mechanisms, interpreting more general types of hypergraph rewriting as net refinement will probably lead to new net refinements. Moreover, the well-known results on compatible properties may lead to similar results for net refinement, i.e. to results on the compositionality of net properties. In the setting of high-level nets and refinements based on double-pushout rules, similar ideas have already been investigated in [PER95, PGE98]; the link to the work presented here remains to be established.

Vice versa, finding adequate descriptions of particular types of net refinement as hypergraph rewriting may also lead to extensions of the latter.

Acknowledgement. I thank Annegret Habel and two anonymous referees for their valuable comments on previous versions of this paper. The pictures have been concocted with Frank Drewes's $\LaTeX2_\varepsilon$ package for typesetting graphs. Special thanks go to Anne Bottreau for her timely email.

References

Bau95a. Michel Bauderon. A uniform approach to graph rewriting: the pullback approach. In *Graph-Theoretic Concepts in Computer Science*, volume 1017 of *Lecture Notes in Computer Science*, 101–115, 1995.

Bau95b. Michel Bauderon. Parallel rewriting of graphs through the pullback approach. In *Proc. SEGRAGRA'95*, volume 2 of *Electronic Notes in Theoretical Computer Science*, 8 pages, 1995.

BGV91. Wilfried Brauer, Robert Gold, and Walter Vogler. A survey of behaviour and equivalence preserving refinements of Petri nets. In *Advances in Petri Nets*, volume 483 of *Lecture Notes in Computer Science*, 1–46, 1991.

BJ97. Michel Bauderon and Hélène Jacquet. Node rewriting in hypergraphs. In *Graph-Theoretic Concepts in Computer Science*, volume 1197 of *Lecture Notes in Computer Science*, 31–43, 1997.

CER93. Bruno Courcelle, Joost Engelfriet, and Grzegorz Rozenberg. Handle-rewriting hypergraph grammars. *Journal of Computer and System Sciences*, 46:218–270, 1993.

Ehr79. Hartmut Ehrig. Introduction to the algebraic theory of graph grammars. In *Graph-Grammars and Their Application to Computer Science and Biology*, volume 73 of *Lecture Notes in Computer Science*, 1–69, 1979.

GF95. Anja Gronewold and Hans Fleischhack. Computing Petri net languages by reductions. In *Fundamentals of Computation Theory*, volume 965 of *Lecture Notes in Computer Science*, 253–262, 1995.

GG90. Rob van Glabbeek and Ursula Goltz. Refinement of actions in causality based models. In *Stepwise Refinement of Distributed Systems*, volume 430 of *Lecture Notes in Computer Science*, 267–300, 1990.

Hab92. Annegret Habel. Hypergraph grammars: Transformational and algorithmic aspects. *Journal of Information Processing and Cybernetics EIK*, 28:241–277, 1992.

HK87a. Annegret Habel and Hans-Jörg Kreowski. Characteristics of graph languages generated by edge replacement. *Theoretical Computer Science*, 51:81–115, 1987.

HK87b. Annegret Habel and Hans-Jörg Kreowski. May we introduce to you: Hyperedge replacement. In *Graph Grammars and Their Application to Computer Science*, volume 291 of *Lecture Notes in Computer Science*, 15–26, 1987.

HS79. Horst Herrlich and George E. Strecker. *Category Theory*. Sigma Series in Pure Mathematics. Heldermann Verlag, Berlin, 2nd edition, 1979.

Kle96. Renate Klempien-Hinrichs. Node replacement in hypergraphs: Simulation of hyperedge replacement, and decidability of confluence. In *Graph Grammars and Their Application to Computer Science*, volume 1073 of *Lecture Notes in Computer Science*, 397–411, 1996.

PER95. Julia Padberg, Hartmut Ehrig, and Leila Ribeiro. Algebraic high-level net transformation systems. *Math. Struct. in Comp. Science*, 5:217–256, 1995.

PGE98. Julia Padberg, Magdalena Gajewsky, and Claudia Ermel. Rule-based refinement of high-level nets preserving safety properties. To appear in *Proc. FASE*, *Lecture Notes in Computer Science*, 1998.

Rei85. Wolfgang Reisig. *Petri Nets*, volume 4 of *EATCS Monographs on Theoretical Computer Science*. Springer-Verlag, Berlin Heidelberg, 1985.

Roz97. Grzegorz Rozenberg, ed. *Handbook of Graph Transformations*, volume I: Foundations. World Scientific, Singapore, 1997.

Vog87. Walter Vogler. Behaviour preserving refinements of Petri nets. In *Graph-Theoretic Concepts in Computer Science*, volume 246 of *Lecture Notes in Computer Science*, 82–93, 1987.

On Piecewise Testable, Starfree, and Recognizable Picture Languages

Oliver Matz

Institut für Informatik und Praktische Mathematik
Christian-Albrechts-Universität Kiel, 24098 Kiel, Germany
e-mail: oma@informatik.uni-kiel.de

Abstract. We isolate a technique for showing that a picture language (i.e. a "two-dimensional language") is not recognizable. Then we prove the non-recognizability of a picture language that is both starfree (i.e., definable by means of union, concatenation, and complement) and piecewise testable (i.e., definable by means of allowed subpictures), solving an open question in [GR96].
We also define local, locally testable, and locally threshold testable picture languages and summarize known inclusion results for these classes. The classes of piecewise testable, locally testable, and locally threshold testable picture languages can, as in the word case, be characterized by certain (fragments of) first-order logics.

1 Introduction

In [GRST96,GR96], the authors investigated the class of *recognizable* picture language (as a straightforward generalization of recognizable word languages to two dimensions), and compared it to variants of classes of *regular* picture languages, defined by "regular expressions" built up by union, row- and column-concatenation, and, optionally, iterated row-/column- concatenation and/or complement.

It turns out that the class of recognizable picture languages is not closed under complement, and the regular expressions without complement do not capture the class of recognizable picture languages, in contrast to the Kleene Theorem for the one-dimensional case. One question that remained open was whether every language defined by regular expressions with all of the above-mentioned operations is recognizable. We answer this question negatively, even for the case that the iterated concatenations are omitted, i.e. the "starfree" expressions. For this aim, we recapitulate and isolate a technique for showing the non-recognizability of a picture language. This technique has also been used in [MT97].

Besides, we consider some other adaptions of classes of formal languages to the two-dimensional case, namely different versions of first-order definable languages, as well as piecewise testable, locally testable, and locally threshold testable picture languages, and report some known and some simple results about these. For example, it is shown in [Wil97] that there is a first-order definable picture language that is not starfree.

2 Recognizable Picture Languages

Throughout the paper, we consider a fixed alphabet Γ. A *picture* over Γ is a matrix over Γ. By *picture languages* we refer to sets of pictures. The language of all pictures over Γ is denoted by $\Gamma^{+,+}$. The language of all pictures of size $m \times n$ is denoted by $\Gamma^{m,n}$. There are two different, partial concatenations for pictures: the *row concatenation* $\frac{P}{Q}$ (*column concatenation* PQ, respectively) of two pictures P and Q of the same width (height, respectively) is the picture obtained by appending Q to the bottom (right, respectively) of P. These concatenations can be generalized to languages the straightforward way.

Since picture languages are the two-dimensional analogue to word languages, it is somewhat natural to try to transfer definitions of interesting word language classes to these. We will first give a straightforward definition of *recognizability*.

Definition 1. *A picture language L over Γ is* domino-local *iff there are local word languages L_1, L_2 over Γ such that L is the set of pictures whose columns (considered as words) are in L_1 and whose rows are in L_2.*

A picture language is recognizable *if it is the image of a local picture language under some alphabet projection.*

This definition is consistent with other equivalent definitions of recognizability given in [GRST96,GR96]. (Among these, there is the characterization via existential monadic second-order logic over the signature with the two binary relation symbols S_1 and S_2 for vertical and horizontal successors.)

The following fact has recently been proved by Klaus Reinhard.

Example 1. The set of all pictures over $\{a, b\}$ in which the set of b-positions is connected (where two b-positions are meant to be adjacent iff there are horizontally or vertically next to each other) is recognizable.

The complement of the above language is also recognizable, which is much easier to show.

Definition 2. *For a picture language $L \subseteq \Gamma^{+,+}$ and an integer $m \geq 1$, the* fixed-height-m word language of L, *denoted by $L(m)$, is the following word language over $\Gamma^{m,1}$:*

$$L(m) = \left\{ \begin{pmatrix} a_{11} \\ \vdots \\ a_{m1} \end{pmatrix} \cdots \begin{pmatrix} a_{1n} \\ \vdots \\ a_{mn} \end{pmatrix} \middle| \begin{matrix} a_{11} \cdots a_{1n} \\ \vdots \qquad \vdots \\ a_{m1} \cdots a_{mn} \end{matrix} \in L \right\}.$$

The following lemma is formulated and proven in [MT97]. As far as the author knows, all arguments against recognizable languages depend on this lemma.

Lemma 1. *Let $L \subseteq \Gamma^{+,+}$ recognizable. Then there is a $k \geq 1$ such that for all $m \geq 1$ there is an NFA $\mathcal{A}$ with k^m states that recognizes $L(m)$.*

Proof. Assume L_1, L_2, and Γ are as in Definition 1. Let $m \geq 1$. The states of the constructed NFA are those columns of height m that are, considered as words, in L_1, plus an additional initial state. The transitions and final states are chosen in such a way that each string of corresponding components of a run is in L_2. The transition labels are the images of the target states under the alphabet projection.

The following simple fact has been stated for example in [Bir96,GS96].

Lemma 2. *Let $n \geq 1$, $L \subseteq \Gamma^*$ be recognizable by an NFA with n states. Let $M \subseteq \Gamma^* \times \Gamma^*$ such that*

$$\forall (u,v) \in M : uv \in L,$$
$$\forall (u,v),(u',v') \in M : \{uv', u'v\} \not\subseteq L.$$

Then $|M| \leq n$.

The preceding two lemmas give the following result.

Lemma 3. *Let $L \subseteq \Gamma^{+,+}$ be recognizable. Let (M_m) be a sequence with $\forall m$: $M_m \subseteq \Gamma^{m,+} \times \Gamma^{m,+}$ and*

$$\forall (P,Q) \in M_m : PQ \in L,$$
$$\forall (P,Q),(P',Q') \in M_m : \{PQ', P'Q\} \not\subseteq L.$$

Then $|M_m|$ is $2^{O(m)}$.

Intuitively, this lemma says that for a recognizable picture language, there is no more than exponentially much space to pass information from one side of the picture to the other.

We use the above lemma to reformulate the proof of non-recognizability of an example language from [GRST96].

Proposition 1. *Let L be the set of pictures over $\{a,b\}$ of the form PP where P is a square. Then L is not recognizable.*

Proof. For every $m \geq 1$ let $M_m := \{(P,P) \mid P \in \Gamma^{m,m}\}$. We have for all squares P, P' that $PP' \in L \iff P = P'$, so (M_m) has the property of Lemma 3. But $|M_m| = 2^{m^2}$ is not $2^{O(m)}$, therefore L is not recognizable.

In [GRST96] the non-recognizability of the above language has been shown using essentially the same argument. The complement of L is recognizable, so a corollary is that the class of recognizable picture languages is not closed under complement.

In fact, the author does not know any example for a picture language whose non-recognizability can be shown, but not by this lemma.

We consider another example.

Proposition 2. *Let CORNERS be the set of pictures P over $\{a, b\}$ such that whenever $P(i,j) = P(i',j) = P(i,j') = b$ then also $P(i',j') = b$. (Intuitively: Whenever three corners of a rectangle carry a b, then also the fourth one does.) CORNERS is not recognizable.*

Proof. Let $n \geq 1$. For every partition $\mathcal{P}$ of $\{1, \ldots, 2n\}$ into two-element sets we fix a bijection $\alpha_{\mathcal{P}} : \mathcal{P} \to \{1, \ldots, n\}$. (For example, we can choose $\alpha_{\mathcal{P}}(\{i,i'\})$ to be the number of elements $\{j,j'\}$ of $\mathcal{P}$ for which $\min\{j,j'\} \leq \min\{i,i'\}$.)

Now we choose a picture P over $\{a, b\}$ of size $2n \times n$ such that for all $(i,j) \in \{1, \ldots, 2n\} \times \{1, \ldots, n\}$:

$$P(i,j) = b \iff \exists i' : \{i,i'\} \in \mathcal{P} \wedge j = \alpha_{\mathcal{P}}(\{i,i'\}).$$

Let M_n be the set of all pairs $(P_{\mathcal{P}}, P_{\mathcal{P}})$ where $\mathcal{P}$ is a partition of $\{1, \ldots, 2n\}$ into two-element sets.

Then we have for all partitions $\mathcal{P}, \mathcal{P}'$ that $P_{\mathcal{P}} P_{\mathcal{P}'} \in$ *CORNERS* $\iff \mathcal{P} = \mathcal{P}'$, so (M_n) has the property of Lemma 3.

For the number A_n of partitions of $\{1, \ldots, 2n\}$ into two-element sets one easily verifies the recursion formula $A_1 = 1$, $A_{n+1} = (2n+1)A_n$. We have that $|M_n| = A_n \geq n!$ is not $2^{\mathcal{O}(n)}$ and hence Lemma 3 implies that *CORNERS* is not recognizable.

3 Piecewise Testable Picture Languages

Definition 3. *Let $P \in \Gamma^{m,n}$ and $Q \in \Gamma^{+,+}$. Then P is a* subpicture *of Q if there are strictly monotone functions $f : \{1, \ldots, m\} \to \mathbb{N}_{\geq 1}$ and $g : \{1, \ldots, n\} \to \mathbb{N}_{\geq 1}$ such that $Q(f(i), g(j)) = P(i,j)$ for all $(i,j) \in \{1, \ldots, m\} \times \{1, \ldots, n\}$.*

Let $m, n \in \mathbb{N}_{\geq 1}$. Two pictures Q_1, Q_2 are (m,n)-equivalent ($Q_1 \sim_{mn} Q_2$ for short) iff they have the same subpictures of size $m \times n$. A picture language L is piecewise testable *iff there is some (m,n) such that L is a union of $\sim_{mn}$-equivalence classes.*

Example 2. The picture language *CORNERS* from Proposition 2 is piecewise testable.

The proof is immediate since *CORNERS* is the set of pictures such that no 2×2-subpicture of P has exactly 3 b's, and this property holds for every or for none element of a $(2,2)$-equivalence class.

This example shows that, unlike in the theory of formal word languages, not every piecewise testable picture language is recognizable.

Remark 1. The class of piecewise testable picture languages is characterized by Boolean combinations of existential first-order formulas with the two binary predicates $\leq_1$, $\leq_2$.

The proof is similar to the word case.

Example 3. Let *CROSS* be the language of all pictures over $\{a, b\}$ containing

$$\begin{matrix} a & b & a \\ b & b & b \\ a & b & a \end{matrix}$$

as a subpicture. *CROSS* is piecewise testable.

4 Starfree Picture Languages

Definition 4. *The class of* starfree picture languages over Γ *is given by the smallest set that contains all finite picture languages over* Γ *and is closed under row- and column concatenation, finite union, and complement.*

The class of recognizable picture languages is closed under row- and column concatenation and union, but (as mentioned before) not under complement. In [GRST96] the authors asked whether, nevertheless, every starfree picture language is recognizable. We answer this question negatively.

Proposition 3. *The picture language CORNERS from Proposition 2 is starfree.*

Proof. Let $K := \bigcup \begin{pmatrix} (w\,(\sim\emptyset)\,x) \\ (\sim\emptyset) \\ (y\,(\sim\emptyset)\,z) \end{pmatrix}$, where the union ranges over all quadruples $(w, x, y, z) \in \{a, b\}^4$ such that $wxyz \in b^*ab^*$, and $\sim$ denotes complement w.r.t. $\{a, b\}^{+,+}$. Then K is the set of all pictures over $\{a, b\}$ such that exactly one of the corners carries an a.

Clearly, $\begin{pmatrix} (\sim\emptyset) \\ ((\sim\emptyset)\,K\,(\sim\emptyset)) \\ (\sim\emptyset) \end{pmatrix}$ is the complement of L, so L is starfree.

The following is shown in [Wil97]:

Lemma 4. *The language CROSS from Example 3 is not starfree.*

5 Local, Locally Testable, and Locally Threshold Testable Picture Languages

We give straightforward adaptions of definitions of languages classes defined by certain "local" properties. These definitions can also be found, for instance, in [GRST96].

Definition 5. *Let* $P \in \Gamma^{m,n}$ *and* $Q \in \Gamma^{m',n'}$. *Then* P *is a* subblock *of* Q *if there are* $k \leq m' - m$ *and* $l \leq n' - n$ *such that* $Q(i, j) = P(k + i, l + j)$ *for all* $(i, j) \in \{1, \dots, m\} \times \{1, \dots, n\}$.

For a picture P *over* Γ, *we denote by* $\hat{P}$ *the picture over* $\Gamma \cup \{\#\}$ *that results from* P *by surrounding it with the fresh boundary symbol* $\#$.

A picture language L is local *iff there is some set Δ of 2×2-pictures over $\Gamma \cup \{\#\}$ such that L contains exactly those pictures P for which the (2×2)-subblocks of $\hat{P}$ are in Δ.*

Let $m, n \in \mathbb{N}_{\geq 1}$. Two pictures Q_1, Q_2 are (m,n)-block-equivalent *($Q_1 \cong_{mn} Q_2$ for short) iff $\hat{Q_1}$ and $\hat{Q_2}$ have the same set of subblocks of size $m \times n$. A picture language L is* locally testable *iff there is some (m,n) such that L is a union of (m,n)-block-equivalence classes.*

Let $d, t \geq 1$. Two pictures Q_1, Q_2 are (d,t)-block-threshold-equivalent *iff for every square picture P of size $d' \times d'$ (with $d' \leq d$), the numbers of occurrences of P as a subblock in $\hat{Q_1}$ (respectively $\hat{Q_2}$) are equal or both $> t$. A picture language is* locally threshold testable *iff there are d, t such that L is a union of (d,t)-block-threshold-equivalence classes.*

Since every local language is a union of $(2,2)$-block-equivalence classes, and (m,n)-block-equivalence is coarser than $(\max\{m,n\},0)$-block-threshold-equivalence, we have that every domino-local language is local, every local language is locally testable, and every locally testable picture language is locally threshold testable.

In [GR96] it is shown that the class of recognizable picture languages is the class of those picture languages that can be obtained from a local picture language via alphabet projection.

Remark 2. 1. The class of locally threshold testable picture languages is characterized by first-order logic over the signature $\{S_1, S_2\}$ with two binary relation symbols S_1, S_2 for the two successor relations.
2. The class of locally testable picture languages is characterized by Boolean combinations of existential first-order sentences over the signature $\{S_1, S_2,$ *left, right, top, bottom*$\}$, where the latter four predicates are unary and say that a position is at the respective border.

The first statement is shown in [GRST96] and the second can be proved similarly to the case of word languages.

6 An Overview of Language Classes and Open Questions

Let us denote the classes of recognizable, piecewise testable, starfree, local, and first-order definable[1] picture languages by *REC*, *PT*, *SF*, *LOC*, and *FO*($\leq_1, \leq_2$), respectively. We have the inclusion diagram presented in the following figure, where lines indicate proper inclusions and non-connected classes are incomparable for non-trivial alphabets.

[1] in the sense of [Wil97], i.e., over the signature with binary relation symbols $\leq_1$ and $\leq_2$ for vertical and horizontal orderings

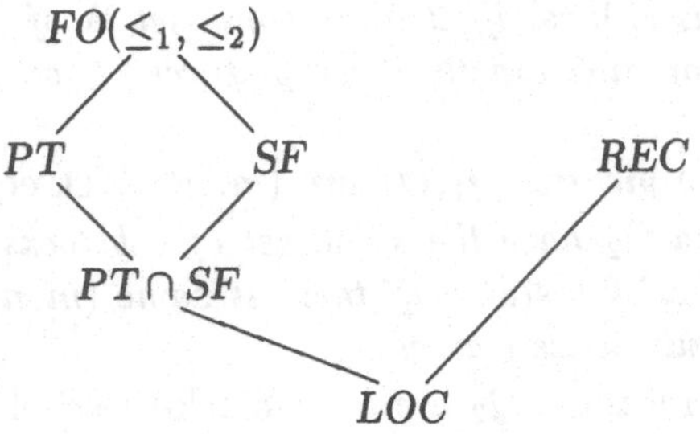

(Simple proofs show that every starfree and every piecewise testable picture language is first-order definable. This infers e.g. $FO(\leq_1, \leq_2) \not\subseteq REC$, correcting a mistake in [Mat95]. The non-inclusion results $REC \not\subseteq FO(\leq_1, \leq_2)$ and $FO(\leq_1, \leq_2) \not\subseteq PT$, and $SF \not\subseteq PT$ carry over from the theory of formal word languages because when restricted to pictures of height one, each of these classes equals the respective class of word languages.)

If we denote the classes of locally testable and locally threshold testable picture languages by *LT* and *LTT*, respectively, we have the following inclusion chain

$$LOC \subsetneq LT \subsetneq LTT \subsetneq FO(\leq_1, \leq_2).$$

Here, the non-inclusions are again witnessed by the well-known examples from word language theory, and the last inclusion is trivially inferred by the logical characterizations of Remark 2.

Since *REC* is not closed under complement (as mentioned after Proposition 1) whereas the classes $FO(\leq_1, \leq_2)$, *PT*, and *SF* are, the class *co-REC* of complements of recognizable picture languages is incomparable to all of these classes, too.

Concluding, one could say that in the world of picture languages, only trivial language class inclusions hold. (Unlike in the theory of word languages, where we have $PT \subsetneq SF = FO \subsetneq REC$.) Another justification for this statement is the fact that also the class of context-free picture languages (as defined in [Mat97]) is incomparable to every other class of picture languages mentioned here (including *LOC*).

One open question is: Is there a natural example for a non-recognizable picture language for which Lemma 3 fails to prove the non-recognizability? One candidate is the language of squares over $\{a, b\}$ that have as many a's as b's. It is easy to see that Lemma 3 cannot be used to show the non-recognizability of this example language, however we conjecture that it is not recognizable.

References

[Bir96] Jean-Camille Birget. The state complexity of $\overline{\Sigma^* \overline{L}}$. *Information Processing Letters*, 58:185–188, 1996.

[GR96] D. Giammarresi and A. Restivo. Two-dimensional languages. In G. Rozenberg and A. Salomaa, editors, *Handbook of Formal Language Theory*, volume III. Springer-Verlag, New York, 1996.

[GRST96] D. Giammarresi, A. Restivo, S. Seibert, and W. Thomas. Monadic second-order logic and recognizability by tiling systems. *Information and Computation*, 125:32–45, 1996.

[GS96] Ian Glaister and Jeffrey Shallit. A lower bound technique for the size of nondeterministic finite automata. *Information Processing Letters*, 125:32–45, 1996.

[Mat95] Oliver Matz. *Klassifizierung von Bildsprachen mit rationalen Ausdrücken, Grammatiken und Logik-Formeln*. Diploma thesis, Christian-Albrechts-Universität Kiel, 1995. (German).

[Mat97] Oliver Matz. Regular expressions and context-free grammars for picture languages. In Rüdiger Reischuk, editor, *STACS'97*, volume 1200 of *Lect. Notes Comput. Sci.*, pages 283–294, Lübeck, Germany, 1997. Springer-Verlag.

[MT97] Oliver Matz and Wolfgang Thomas. The monadic quantifier alternation hierarchy over graphs is infinite. In *Twelfth Annual IEEE Symposium on Logic in Computer Science*, pages 236–244, Warsaw, Poland, 1997. IEEE.

[Wil97] Thomas Wilke. Star-free picture expressions are strictly weaker than first-order logic. In Pierpaolo Degano, Roberto Gorrieri, and Alberto Marchetti-Spaccamela, editors, *Automata, Languages and Programming*, volume 1256 of *Lect. Notes Comput. Sci.*, pages 347–357, Bologna, Italy, 1997. Springer.

Functor Categories and Two-Level Languages

E. Moggi

DISI - Univ. di Genova, via Dodecaneso 35, 16146 Genova, Italy
phone: +39 10 353-6629, fax: +39 10 353-6699, e-mail: moggi@disi.unige.it

Abstract. We propose a denotational semantics for the two-level language of [GJ91, Gom92], and prove its correctness w.r.t. a standard denotational semantics. Other researchers (see [Gom91, GJ91, Gom92, JGS93, HM94]) have claimed correctness for lambda-mix (or extensions of it) based on denotational models, but the proofs of such claims rely on imprecise definitions and are basically flawed. At a technical level there are two important differences between our model and more naive models in **Cpo**: the domain for interpreting dynamic expressions is more abstract (we interpret code as λ-terms modulo α-conversion), the semantics of *newname* is handled differently (we exploit functor categories). The key idea is to interpret a two-level language in a suitable functor category $\mathbf{Cpo}^{\mathcal{D}^{op}}$ rather than **Cpo**. The semantics of *newname* follows the ideas pioneered by Oles and Reynolds for modeling the stack discipline of Algol-like languages. Indeed, we can think of the objects of $\mathcal{D}$ (i.e. the natural numbers) as the states of a name counter, which is incremented when entering the body of a λ-abstraction and decremented when coming out. Correctness is proved using Kripke logical relations (see [MM91, NN92]).

Introduction

Two-level languages are an important tool for analyzing programs. In the context of partial evaluation they are used to identify those parts of the program that can be reduced statically, and those that have to be evaluated dynamically. We take as representative of these two-level languages that described in [GJ91], which we call PCF_2, since it can be considered as the "PCF of two-level languages". The main aims of this paper are: to point out the flaws in the semantics and correctness proof given in [Gom92], and to propose an alternative semantics for which one can prove correctness.

The interpretation of dynamic λ-abstraction given in [GJ91, Gom92] uses a *newname* construct "informally". Indeed, Gomard and Jones warn that "the generation of new variable names relies on a side-effect on a global state (a name counter). In principle this could have been avoided by adding an extra parameter to the semantic function, but for the sake of notational simplicity we use a less formal solution". Because of this informality, [GJ91, Gom92] are able to use a simplified semantic domain for dynamic expressions, but have to hand wave when it comes to the clause for dynamic λ-abstraction. This informality is maintained also in the correctness proof of [Gom92]. It is possible to fix the informal semantics using a name-counter (as suggested by Gomard and Jones), but then it is unclear how to fix the correctness proof. In fact, several experts were unable to propose a patch. Lack of precision in the definition of denotational semantics and consequent flaws in correctness proofs are not confined to [Gom92], indeed

- Chapter 4 of [Gom91] and Chapter 8 of [JGS93] contain the same definitions, results and proofs
- [GJ91] quotes the same definitions and results (but without proofs)
- while [HM94] adapts Gomard's technique to establish correctness for a polymorphic binding-time analysis (and introduces further flaws in the denotational semantics).

The specific model we propose is based on a functor category. In denotational semantics functor categories have been advocated by [Ole85] to model Algol-like languages, and more generally they have been used to model locality and dynamic creation (see [OT92, PS93, FMS96]). For this kind of modeling they outperform the more traditional category **Cpo** of cpos (i.e. posets with lubs of ω-chains and ω-continuous maps). Therefore, they are a natural candidate for modeling the *newname* construct of [GJ91].

In the proposed functor category model the domain of residual programs is a bit more abstract than expected, namely α-convertible programs are identified. This identification is necessary for defining the category $\mathcal{D}$ of dynamic expressions, but it seems also a *desirable abstraction*. Functor categories are definitely more complex than **Cpo**, but one can avoid most of the complexities by working in a metalanguage (with computational types). Indeed, it is only in few critical places, where it is important to know which category (and which monad) is used. The graduate textbook [Ten91] gives the necessary background on functor categories for denotational semantics to understand our functor category model. In **Cpo** models the renaming of bound dynamic variables (used in the interpretation of dynamic λ-abstraction) is modeled via a side-effect monad with a name-counter as state, on the contrary in the functor category model renaming is handled by the functor category itself (while non-termination at specialization-time is modeled by the lifting monad).

The paper is organized as follows: Section 1 recall the two-level language of [GJ91, Gom92] which we call PCF_2; Section 2 describes a general way for interpreting PCF_2 via translation into a metalanguage with computational types, and explains what's wrong with previously proposed semantics of PCF_2; Section 3 describes our functor category model for PCF_2 and proves correctness; Section 4 make a comparison of the semantics.

Acknowledgments. I wish to thank Olivier Danvy and Neil Jones for e-mail discussions, which were very valuable to clarify the intended semantics in [GJ91, Gom92], and to identify the critical problem in the correctness proof. Neil Jones has kindly provided useful bibliographic references and made available relevant internal reports.

1 The two-level language of Gomard and Jones

In this section we recall the main definitions in [GJ91, Gom92], namely: the untyped object language λ_o and its semantics, the two-level language PCF_2 and its *semantics* (including with the problematic clause for $\underline{\lambda}$). Both semantics are given via a translation into a metalanguage with computational type (see [Mog91, Mog97b]). In the case of λ_o the monad corresponds to dynamic computations, while in the case of PCF_2 it corresponds to static computations.

1.1 The untyped object language

The object language λ_o is an untyped λ-calculus with a set of ground constants c (which includes the truth values)

$$M ::= x \mid \lambda x.M \mid M_1@M_2 \mid fix\ M \mid if\ M_1\ M_2\ M_3 \mid c$$

There is a canonical CBN interpretation of λ_o in $D = (const+(D \to D))_\bot$, where *const* is the flat cpo of ground constants (ordered by equality). This interpretation can be described via a CBN translation $\_^n$ into a suitable metalanguage with computational types, s.t. a λ_o-term M is translated into a meta-term M^n of type TV with $V = const + (TV \to TV)$, or more precisely $\overline{x} : TV \vdash_{ML} M^n : TV$ when M is a λ_o-term with free variables included in the sequence $\overline{x}$:

- $x^n = x$
- $c^n = [inl(c)]$
- $(\lambda x.M)^n = [inr(\lambda x : TV.M^n)]$
- $(M_1@M_2)^n = \text{let } u \Leftarrow M_1{}^n \text{ in case } u \text{ of } inr(f) \Rightarrow f(M_2{}^n)$
  $\qquad\qquad\qquad\qquad\qquad\qquad\qquad\qquad\quad \_ \Rightarrow \bot$
  where $\bot : TV$ is the least element of TV
- $(if\ M\ M_1\ M_2)^n = \text{let } u \Leftarrow M^n \text{ in case } u \text{ of } \begin{array}{l} inl(true) \Rightarrow M_1{}^n \\ inl(false) \Rightarrow M_2{}^n \\ \_ \Rightarrow \bot \end{array}$
- $(fix\ M)^n = \text{let } u \Leftarrow M^n \text{ in case } u \text{ of } inr(f) \Rightarrow Y(f)$
  $\qquad\qquad\qquad\qquad\qquad\qquad\qquad\qquad \_ \Rightarrow \bot$
  where $Y : (TV \to TV) \to TV$ is the least fixed-point of TV

Note 1. T can be any strong monad on **Cpo** s.t.: (i) each TX has a bottom element $\bot$; (ii) $\text{let } x \Leftarrow \bot \text{ in } e = \bot$, i.e. $\bot$ is preserved by $f^* : TX \to TY$ for any $f : X \to TY$. With these properties one can interpret recursive definitions of programs and solve domain equations involving T.

The interpretation by Gomard amounts to take $TX = X_\bot$ and $D = TV$.

1.2 The two-level language PCF_2

The two-level language PCF_2 can be described as a simply typed λ-calculus over the base types *base* and *code* with additional operations. The raw syntax of PCF_2 is given by

- types $\tau ::= base \mid code \mid \tau_1 \to \tau_2$
- terms $e ::= x \mid \lambda x : \tau.e \mid e_1 @ e_2 \mid fix_\tau\ e \mid if_\tau\ e_1\ e_2\ e_3 \mid c \mid$
  $lift\ e \mid \underline{\lambda} x.e \mid e_1 \underline{@} e_2 \mid \underline{fix}\ e \mid \underline{if}\ e_1\ e_2\ e_3 \mid \underline{c}$

The well-formed terms of PCF_2 are determined by assigning types to constants:

- $fix_\tau : (\tau \to \tau) \to \tau$
- $if_\tau : base, \tau, \tau \to \tau$
- $c : base$
- $lift : base \to code$
- $\underline{\lambda} : (code \to code) \to code$, following Church we have taken $\underline{\lambda}$ to be a higher order constant rather than a binder (all the binding is done by λ). The two presentations are equivalent: the term $\underline{\lambda} x.e$ of [GJ91] can be replaced by $\underline{\lambda}(\lambda x : code.e)$, while the constant $\underline{\lambda}$ can be defined as $\lambda f : code \to code.\underline{\lambda} x.f @ x$.
- $\underline{@} : code, code \to code$
- $\underline{fix} : code \to code$
- $\underline{if} : code, code, code \to code$
- $\underline{c} : code$

Remark. The language PCF_2 corresponds to the well-annotated expressions of Gomard and Jones. For two-level languages with dynamic type constructors (e.g. that in [HM94]) it is necessary to distinguish between static and dynamic types. In PCF_2 the only dynamic type is *code*, and there is no need to make this explicit.

2 Models of PCF_2 in Cpo

The interpretation of PCF_2 is described by a translation $\_^s$ into a suitable metalanguage with computational types, s.t. $x_1 : \tau_1{}^s, \ldots, x_n : \tau_n{}^s \vdash_{ML} e^s : \tau^s$ when $x_1 : \tau_1, \ldots, x_n : \tau_n \vdash_{PCF_2} e : \tau$. The translation highlights that static computations take place only at ground types (just like in PCF and Algol).

- $base^s = T(const)$, where *const* is the flat cpo of ground constants
- $code^s = T(exp)$, where *exp* is the flat cpo of open λ_o-terms with (free and bound) variables included in $var = \{x_n | n \in N\}$. When translating terms of PCF_2 we make use of the following expression-building operations:
  - $build\_const : const \to exp$ is the inclusion of ground constants into terms
  - $build\_var : var \to exp$ is the inclusion of variables into terms.
  - $build\_@ : exp, exp \to exp$ is the function $M_1, M_2 \mapsto M_1 @ M_2$ which builds an application. There are similar definitions for $build\_fix$ and $build\_if$.

- $build\_\lambda : var, exp \to exp$ is the function $x, M \mapsto \lambda x.M$ which builds a λ-abstraction.

- $(\tau_1 \to \tau_2)^s = {\tau_1}^s \to {\tau_2}^s$
- $x^s = x$
- $c^s = [c]$
- $(\lambda x : \tau.e)^s = \lambda x : \tau^s.e^s$
- $(e_1 @ e_2)^s = {e_1}^s @ {e_2}^s$
- $(if_\tau\ e\ e_1\ e_2)^s = \text{let } u \Leftarrow e^s \text{ in case } u \text{ of } \begin{array}{l} true \Rightarrow {e_1}^s \\ false \Rightarrow {e_2}^s \\ \_ \Rightarrow \bot \end{array}$

  where $\bot$ is the least element of τ^s
- $(fix_\tau\ e)^s = Y(e^s)$, where Y is the least fixed-point of τ^s
- $(\ell ift\ e)^s = \text{let } x \Leftarrow e^s \text{ in } [build\_const(x)]$
- $\underline{c}^s = [build\_const(c)]$
- $(\underline{op}\ \overline{e})^s = \text{let } \overline{M} \Leftarrow \overline{e}^s \text{ in } [build\_op\ \overline{M}]$, where $op \in \{fix, @, if\}$

* $(\underline{\lambda}\ e)^s = \text{let } x \Leftarrow newname \text{ in let } M \Leftarrow e^s([build\_var(x)]) \text{ in } [build\_\lambda(x, M)]$
  where $newname : T(var)$ generates a *fresh variable* of the object language.

The monad T for static computations should satisfy the same additional properties stated in Note 1.

Remark. In the above interpretation/translation the meaning of *newname* (and $\underline{\lambda}$) is not fully defined, indeed one should fix first the interpretation of computational types TX.
The interpretation of [GJ91, Gom92] uses *simplified* semantic domains (which amount to use the lifting monad $TX = X_\bot$), but with these domains there is no way of interpreting *newname* (consistently with the informal description). Therefore, most of the stated results and proofs are inherently faulty.
Gomard and Jones are aware of the problem and say that "the generation of new variables names relies on a side effect on a global state (a name-counter)... but for the sake of notational simplicity we have used a less formal solution". Their proposed solution amounts to use a side-effect monad $TX = (X \times N)_\bot^N$, and to interpret $newname : T(var)$ as $newname = \lambda n : N.up(\langle x_n, n+1 \rangle)$, where $up_X : X \to X_\bot$ is the inclusion of X into its lifting.
A simpler solution, suggested by Olivier Danvy, uses a state-reader monad $TX = X_\bot^N$. In this case one can interpret the operation $newname'_X : (TX)^{var} \to TX$ as $newname'_X(f) = \lambda n : N.fx_n(n+1)$, and use it for translating $\underline{\lambda}$

- $(\underline{\lambda}\ e)^s = newname'_{exp}(\lambda x : var.\text{let } M \Leftarrow e^s([build\_var(x)]) \text{ in } [build\_\lambda(x, M)])$.

The only place where a name-counter is really needed is for generating code, so we could use the simpler translation $base^s = const_\bot$ and $code^s = T(exp)$. This is similar to what happens in Algol, where expressions cannot have side-effects, while commands can.

2.1 Correctness: attempts and failures

Informally speaking, correctness for PCF_2 should say that for any $\emptyset \vdash_{PCF_2} e : code$ if the static evaluation of e terminates and produces a λ_o-term M : exp, then λ_o-terms M and e^ϕ are *equivalent*, where $\_^\phi$ is the translation from PCF_2 to λ_o erasing types and annotations. In fact, this is an over-simplified statement, since one want to consider PCF_2-terms $\overline{x} : code \vdash_{PCF_2} e : code$ with free dynamic variables.

In a denotational setting one could prove correctness by defining a logical relation (see [MW85, Mit96]) between two interpretations of PCF_2

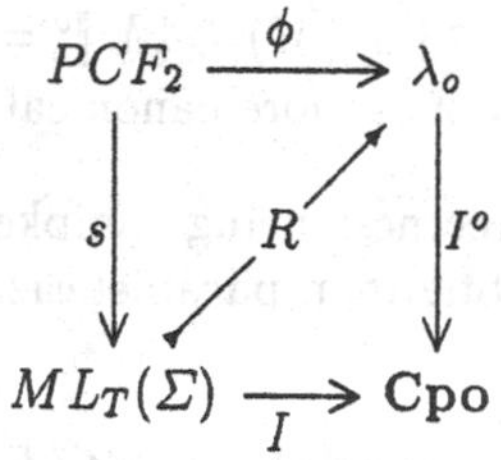

The parameterized logical relation $R^\tau_\rho \subseteq [\![\tau^s]\!] \times D$, where $\rho : var \to D$, proposed by [Gom92] is defined as follows

- $\bot\ R^{base}_\rho\ d$ and $up(b)\ R^{base}_\rho\ d \overset{\Delta}{\Longleftrightarrow} d = up(in_1\ b)$
- $\bot\ R^{code}_\rho\ d$ and $up(M)\ R^{code}_\rho\ d \overset{\Delta}{\Longleftrightarrow} d = [\![M]\!]^o_\rho$
- $f\ R^{\tau_1 \to \tau_2}_\rho\ d \overset{\Delta}{\Longleftrightarrow} x\ R^{\tau_1}_\rho\ y \supset (f@x)\ R^{\tau_2}_\rho\ (d@^o y)$, this is the standard way of defining at higher types a logical relation between typed applicative structures.

Gomard interprets types according to the informal semantics, i.e. $[\![base^s]\!] = const_\bot$ and $[\![code^s]\!] = exp_\bot$. According to the fundamental lemma of logical relations, if the two interpretations of each operation/constant of PCF_2 are logically related, then the two interpretations of each PCF_2-term are logically related. It is easy to do this check for all operations/constants except $\underline{\lambda}$. In the case of $\underline{\lambda}$ one can only hand wave, since the interpretation is informally given. Therefore, Gomard concludes that he has proved correctness.

Remark. Gomard does not mention explicitly logical relations. However, his definition of R is given by induction on the structure of PCF_2-types, while correctness is *proved* by induction of the structure PCF_2-terms $\Gamma \vdash_{PCF_2} e : \tau$. This is typical of logical relations.

In order to patch the proof one would have to change the definition of R^{code}_ρ, since in the intended semantics $[\![code^s]\!] = exp^N_\bot$ or $(exp \times N)^N_\bot$, and check the case of $\underline{\lambda}$ (which now has an interpretation). We doubt that this can be done, for the following reasons (for simplicity we take $[\![code^s]\!] = exp^N_\bot$):

- The interpretation of $\underline{\lambda}$ may capture variables that ought to remain free. For instance, consider the interpretation of $x : code \vdash_{PCF_2} \underline{\lambda} y.x : code$, which is a function $f : exp_\perp^N \to exp_\perp^N$, and the element $[M] = \lambda n.up(M)$ of $exp_\perp^N$, then $f([M]) = \lambda n.up(\lambda x_n.M)$ (here there is some overloading in the use of λ, since λn is a semantic lambda while λx_n is syntactic). Depending on the choice of n we may bind a variable free in M, therefore the semantics of $\underline{\lambda}$ fails to ensure *freshness* of x_n.
- The semantic domain $exp_\perp^N$ has junk elements in comparison to $exp_\perp$, and so there are several ways of defining $u\ R_\rho^{code}\ d$, e.g.
  - $\forall n : N.\forall M : exp.u(n) = up(M) \supset [\![M]\!]_\rho^o = d$
  - $\exists n : N.\forall M : exp.u(n) = up(M) \supset [\![M]\!]_\rho^o = d$
  - $\exists M : exp.\forall n : N.u(n) \equiv_\alpha up(M) \supset [\![M]\!]_\rho^o = d$

  but none of them works (nor is more canonical than the others).

If there is a way to prove correctness using (Kripke) logical relations, it is likely to involve something more subtle than parameterization by $\rho : var \to D$.

3 A functor category model of PCF_2

In this section we define a categorical model of PCF_2 in a **Cpo**-enriched functor category $\widehat{\mathcal{D}} = \mathbf{Cpo}^{\mathcal{D}^{op}}$, where $\mathcal{D}$ is a *syntactic* category corresponding to λ_o, and the objects of $\mathcal{D}$ can be viewed as states of a name-counter. The main property of this model is that the hom-set $\widehat{\mathcal{D}}(exp^n, exp)$ is isomorphic to the set of λ_o-terms modulo α-conversion whose free variables are included in $\{x_0, \ldots, x_{n-1}\}$.

3.1 The dynamic category

We define $\mathcal{D}$ like the category associated to an algebraic theory (as proposed by Lawvere in [Law63]), i.e.:

- an object of $\mathcal{D}$ is a natural number; we identify a natural number n with the set $\{0, \ldots, n-1\}$ of its predecessors;
- an arrow from m to n, which we call **substitution**, is a function $\sigma : n \to \Lambda(m)$, where $\Lambda(m)$ is the set of λ_o-terms modulo α-conversion with free variables included in $\{x_0, \ldots, x_{m-1}\}$; thus $\mathcal{D}(m, n) = \Lambda(m)^n$;
- composition is given by composition of substitutions with renaming of bound variables (which is known to respect α-conversion). Namely, for $\sigma_1 : m \to n$ and $\sigma_2 : n \to p$ the substitution $(\sigma_2 \circ \sigma_1) : m \to p$ is given by $(\sigma_2 \circ \sigma_1)(i) = N_i[\sigma_1]$, where $i \in p$, $N_i = \sigma_2(i) \in \Lambda(n)$, $N_i[\sigma_1] \in \Lambda(m)$ is the result of applying in *parallel* to N_i the substitutions $x_j := M_j$ with $j \in m$.
  Identities are given by identity substitutions $id : n \to \Lambda(n)$.

It is easy to see that $\mathcal{D}$ has finite products: the terminal object is 0, and the product of m with n is $m + n$. Therefore, the object n is the product of n copies of the object 1, moreover $\mathcal{D}(m, 1) = \Lambda(m)$.

Remark. We can provide an informal justification for the choice of $\mathcal{D}$. The objects of $\mathcal{D}$ correspond to the states of a name-counter: state m means that m names, say $x_0, \ldots, x_{m-1}$, have been created so far.
For the choice of morphisms the justification is more technical: it is *almost* forced when one wants $\widehat{\mathcal{D}}(exp^m, exp)$ to be isomorphic to the set of λ_o-terms whose free variables are included in $\{x_0, \ldots, x_{m-1}\}$. In fact, the natural way of interpreting exp in $\widehat{\mathcal{D}}$ is with a functor s.t. $exp(m)$ = the set of λ_o-terms with free names among those available at state m. If we require $F = Y(1)$, i.e. the image of $1 \in \mathcal{D}$ via the Yoneda embedding, and m to be the product in $\mathcal{D}$ of m copies of 1, then we have $\widehat{\mathcal{D}}(exp^m, exp) = \widehat{\mathcal{D}}(Y(1)^m, Y(1)) = \widehat{\mathcal{D}}(Y(m), Y(1)) = \mathcal{D}(m, 1) = exp(m)$. Therefore, we can conclude that $\mathcal{D}(m, n) = exp(m)^n$. Moreover, to define composition in $\mathcal{D}$ we are forced to take λ_o-terms modulo α-conversion.

3.2 The static category

We define $\widehat{\mathcal{D}}$ as the functor category $\mathbf{Cpo}^{\mathcal{D}^{op}}$, which is a variant of the more familiar topos of presheaves $\mathbf{Set}^{\mathcal{D}^{op}}$. Categories of the form $\widehat{\mathcal{W}}$ (where $\mathcal{W}$ is a small category) have been used in [Ole85] for modeling local variables in Algol-like languages. $\widehat{\mathcal{W}}$ enjoys the following properties:

- it has small limits and colimits (computed pointwise), and exponentials;
- it is **Cpo**-enriched, thus one can interpret fix-point combinators and solve recursive domain equations by analogy with **Cpo**;
- there is a full and faithful embedding $Y : \mathcal{W} \to \widehat{\mathcal{W}}$, which preserves limits and exponentials. This is basically the Yoneda embedding $Y(w) = \mathcal{W}(\_, w)$.
- the functor $\Delta : \mathbf{Cpo} \to \widehat{\mathcal{W}}$ s.t. $(\Delta X)(\_) = X$ has left and right adjoints.

Since $\mathcal{D}$ has a terminal object, $\Delta : \mathbf{Cpo} \to \widehat{\mathcal{D}}$ is full and faithful, and its right adjoint is the global section functor $\Gamma : \widehat{\mathcal{D}} \to \mathbf{Cpo}$ s.t. $\Gamma F = \widehat{\mathcal{D}}(1, F) = F(0)$.
A description of several constructions in $\widehat{\mathcal{W}}$ relevant for denotational semantics can be found in [Ten91]. Here we recall only the definition of exponentials.

Definition 2. The exponential object G^F in $\widehat{\mathcal{W}}$ is the functor s.t.

- $G^F(w)$ is the cpo of families $s \in \prod_{f:w' \to w} \mathbf{Cpo}(Fw', Gw')$ ordered pointwise and satisfying the **compatibility condition**

$$\begin{array}{ccc} w & \xleftarrow{f_1} & w_1 \\ & \nwarrow^{f_2} & \uparrow g \\ & & w_2 \end{array} \quad \text{in } \mathcal{W} \text{ implies} \quad \begin{array}{ccc} Fw_1 & \xrightarrow{s_{f_1}} & Gw_1 \\ Fg \downarrow & & \downarrow Gg \\ Fw_2 & \xrightarrow[s_{f_2}]{} & Gw_2 \end{array} \quad \text{in } \mathbf{Cpo}$$

- $(G^F f s)_g = s_{f \circ g}$ for any $w'' \xrightarrow{g} w' \xrightarrow{f} w$ in $\mathcal{W}$.

We recall also the notion of ω-inductive relation in a **Cpo**-enriched functor category $\widehat{\mathcal{W}}$, which is used in the correctness proof.

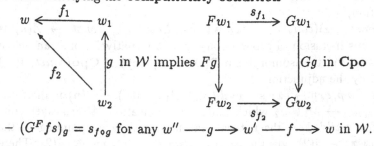

Definition 3. Given an object $X \in \widehat{\mathcal{W}}$, a (unary) ω-inductive relation $R \subseteq X$ in $\widehat{\mathcal{W}}$ consists of a family $\langle R_w \subseteq Xw | w \in \mathcal{W}\rangle$ of ω-inductive relations in **Cpo** satisfying the **monotonicity condition**:

– $f : w' \to w$ in $\mathcal{W}$ and $x \in R_w \subseteq Xw$ implies $Xfx \in R_{w'} \subseteq Xw'$.

3.3 Interpretation of PCF_2

By analogy with Section 1, we parameterize the interpretation of PCF_2 in $\widehat{\mathcal{D}}$ w.r.t. a strong monad T on **Cpo** satisfying the additional properties stated in Note 1. Any such T induces a strong monad $T^{\mathcal{D}^{op}}$ on $\widehat{\mathcal{D}}$ satisfying the same additional properties. With some abuse of language we write T for its *pointwise extension* $(T^{\mathcal{D}^{op}} F)(m) = T(F(m))$.
In the proof of correctness we take $TX = X_\perp$, since the monad has to account only for the possibility of non-termination at specialization-time, while the interpretation of $\underline{\lambda}$ exploits only the functor category structure (and not the monad, as done for the interpretations in **Cpo**).
Also in this case the interpretation of PCF_2 can be described by a *standard* translation $\_^s$ into a suitable metalanguage with computational types (which play only a minor role). The key differences w.r.t. the interpretation/translation of Section 2 are: the interpretation of *exp* (which is not the image of a cpo via the functor Δ), and the expression-building operation *build_*λ (which has type $(exp \to exp) \to exp$, as expected in a higher-order syntax encoding of λ_o).

- $base^s = T(\Delta(const))$, where *const* is the flat cpo of ground constants. Therefore, $base(n) = T(const)$ and so global elements of *base* correspond to elements of the cpo $T(const)$.
- $code^s = T(exp)$, where $exp = Y(1)$, i.e. the image of $1 \in \mathcal{D}$ via the Yoneda embedding $Y : \mathcal{D} \to \widehat{\mathcal{D}}$. Therefore, $exp(n) = \Lambda(n)$ and $code(n) = T(\Lambda(n))$. It is also immediate to show that $\widehat{\mathcal{D}}(exp^n, exp)$ is isomorphic to $\Lambda(n)$:
  - $\widehat{\mathcal{D}}(Y(1)^n, Y(1)) \cong$ because Y preserves finite products
  - $\widehat{\mathcal{D}}(Y(n), Y(1)) \cong$ because Y is full and faithful
  - $\mathcal{D}(n, 1) \cong \Lambda(n)$ by definition of $\mathcal{D}$.

  When translating terms of PCF_2 we make use of the following expression-building operations (which are interpreted by morphisms in $\widehat{\mathcal{D}}$, i.e. natural transformation):
  - *build_const* : $\Delta(const) \to exp$ s.t. $build\_const_n : const \to \Lambda(n)$ is the obvious inclusion of ground constants. Alternatively, one can define *build_const* via the isomorphism $\widehat{\mathcal{D}}(\Delta(const), exp) \cong \mathbf{Cpo}(const, \Lambda(0))$ induced by the adjunction $\Delta \dashv \Gamma$.
  - *build_@* : $exp, exp \to exp$ s.t. $build\_@_n : \Lambda(n), \Lambda(n) \to \Lambda(n)$ is the function $M_1, M_2 \mapsto M_1@M_2$ which builds an application. Alternatively, one can define *build_@* as the natural transformation corresponding to the term $x_0@x_1 \in \Lambda(2)$, via the isomorphism $\widehat{\mathcal{D}}(exp^2, exp) \cong \Lambda(2)$. There are similar definitions for *build_fix* and *build_if*.
  - *build_*λ : $exp^{exp} \to exp$ is the trickiest part and is defined below.

- the interpretation of static operations/constants is obvious, in particular we have least fixed-points because $\widehat{\mathcal{D}}$ is **Cpo**-enriched.
- $(\mathit{lift}\ e)^s = \text{let } x \Leftarrow e^s \text{ in } [\mathit{build\_const}(x)]$
- $\underline{c}^s = [\mathit{build\_const}(c)]$
- $(\underline{op}\ \overline{e})^s = \text{let } \overline{M} \Leftarrow \overline{e}^s \text{ in } [\mathit{build\_op}\ \overline{M}]$, where $op \in \{\mathit{fix}, @, \mathit{if}\}$

* $\underline{\lambda} : \mathit{code}^{\mathit{code}} \to \mathit{code}$ is defined in terms of $\mathit{build\_\lambda} : \mathit{exp}^{\mathit{exp}} \to \mathit{exp}$ as explained below.

To define the components of the natural transformation $\mathit{build\_\lambda} : \mathit{exp}^{\mathit{exp}} \to \mathit{exp}$ we use the following fact, which is an easy consequence of Yoneda's lemma.

Lemma 4. *For any $u \in \mathcal{W}$ and $F \in \widehat{\mathcal{W}}$ there is a natural isomorphism between the functors $F^{Y(u)}$ and $F(\_ \times u)$.*

By Lemma 4, $\mathit{build\_\lambda}$ amounts to a natural transformation from $\mathcal{D}(\_ + 1, 1)$ to $\mathcal{D}(\_, 1)$. We describe $\mathit{build\_\lambda}$ through a diagram:

$$\begin{array}{ccccc}
m & M \in \Lambda(m+1) & \xmapsto{\mathit{build_\lambda}_m} & (\lambda x_m.M) \in \Lambda(m) \\
\uparrow \sigma \in \mathcal{D} & \Big\downarrow _ \circ (\sigma + 1) & \text{in } \mathbf{Cpo} & \Big\downarrow _ \circ \sigma \\
n & M[\sigma + 1] \in \Lambda(n+1) & \xmapsto[\mathit{build_\lambda}_n]{} & (\lambda x_n.M)[\sigma] \in \Lambda(n)
\end{array}$$

Observe that $\mathcal{D}(\_, 1) = \Lambda(\_)$, the substitution $(\sigma + 1) : m + 1 \to \Lambda(n+1)$ is like σ on m and maps m to x_n, while the commutativity of the diagram follows from $(\lambda x_n.M[\sigma + 1]) \equiv_\alpha (\lambda x_m.M)[\sigma]$.
To define $\underline{\lambda} : T(\mathit{exp})^{T(\mathit{exp})} \to T(\mathit{exp})$ we need the following lemma.

Lemma 5. *For any functor $T : \mathbf{Cpo} \to \mathbf{Cpo}$, $u \in \mathcal{W}$ and $F \in \widehat{\mathcal{W}}$ there is a natural isomorphism between the functors $(TF)^{Y(u)}$ and $T(F^{Y(u)})$.*

Proof. For any $v \in \mathcal{W}$ we give an isomorphism between $(TF)^{Y(u)}(v)$ and $T(F^{Y(u)})(v)$:

- $(TF)^{Y(u)}(v) =$ by Lemma 4
- $(TF)(u \times v) =$ since T is extended pointwise to $\widehat{\mathcal{W}}$
- $T(F(u \times v)) =$ by Lemma 4
- $T(F^{Y(u)}(v)) =$ since T is extended pointwise to $\widehat{\mathcal{W}}$
- $T(F^{Y(u)})(v)$

It is immediate to see that this family of isomorphisms is natural in v.

By exploiting the isomorphism $i : T(\mathit{exp})^{\mathit{exp}} \to T(\mathit{exp}^{\mathit{exp}})$ given by Lemma 5, one can define $\underline{\lambda} : T(\mathit{exp})^{T(\mathit{exp})} \to T(\mathit{exp})$ in a metalanguage with computational types as

$$\underline{\lambda}(f) = \text{let } f' \Leftarrow i(\lambda x : \mathit{exp}.f([x])) \text{ in } [\mathit{build\_\lambda}(f')]$$

Remark. The category $\widehat{D}$ has two full sub-categories D and **Cpo**, which have a natural interpretation: D corresponds to dynamic types, while **Cpo** corresponds to pure static types, i.e. those producing no residual code at specialization time (e.g. *base*). A key property of pure static expressions is that they cannot depend on dynamic expressions. Semantically this means that the canonical map $(\Delta X) \to (\Delta X)^{Y(u)}$, i.e. $x \mapsto \lambda y : Y(u).x$, is an isomorphism. In fact, by Lemma 4 $(\Delta X)^{Y(u)}$ is naturally isomorphic to $(\Delta X)(\_ \times u)$, which is (ΔX).

3.4 Correctness and logical relations

The semantics for the two-level language PCF_2 was used in [GJ91, Gom92] to prove a correctness theorem for partial evaluation. The correctness theorem relates the interpretation I^o of the object language λ_o in **Cpo** to the interpretation I^2 of the two-level language PCF_2 in $\widehat{D}$.

The first step is to define a translation $\_^\phi$ from PCF_2 to λ_o, i.e. $\overline{x} : \overline{\tau} \vdash_{PCF_2} e : \tau$ implies $\overline{x} \vdash_{\lambda_o} e^\phi$, which erases types and annotations, so $(\lambda x : \tau.e)^\phi = \lambda x.e^\phi$, $(op_\tau \ \overline{e})^\phi = op \ \overline{e}^\phi$, $(\underline{op} \ \overline{e})^\phi = op \ \overline{e}^\phi$ and $(lift \ e)^\phi = e^\phi$. By composing the translation ϕ with the interpretation I^o we get an interpretation of I^1 of PCF_2 in **Cpo**, where every type is interpreted by the cpo $D = (const + (D \to D))_\perp$.

At this stage we can state two correctness criteria (the first being a special case of the second), which exploit in an essential way the functor category structure:

- Given a closed PCF_2-expression $\emptyset \vdash e : code$, its I^2 interpretation is a global element d of $exp_\perp \in \widehat{D}$, and therefore $d_0 \in \Lambda(0)_\perp$. Correctness for e means: $d_0 = up(M)$ implies $[\![M]\!]^o = [\![e^\phi]\!]^o \in D$, for any $M \in \Lambda(0)$.
- Given an open PCF_2-expression $\overline{x} : code \vdash e : code$ where $\overline{x} = x_0, \ldots, x_{n-1}$, its I^2 interpretation is a morphism $f : exp_\perp^n \to exp_\perp$, and therefore $f_n : \Lambda(n)_\perp^n \to \Lambda(n)_\perp$. Correctness for e means: $f_n(up(x_0), \ldots, up(x_{n-1})) = up(M)$ implies $[\![\overline{x} \vdash M]\!]^o = [\![\overline{x} \vdash e^\phi]\!]^o : D^n \to D$, for any $M \in \Lambda(n)$.

The proof of correctness requires a stronger result, which amounts to prove that the two interpretations of PCF_2 are *logically related*. However they live in different categories. Therefore, before one can relate them via a (Kripke) logical relation R between typed applicative structures (see [MM91]), they have to be moved (via limit preserving functors) to a common category $\widehat{\mathcal{E}}$.

$$
\begin{array}{ccc}
PCF_2 & \xrightarrow{I^1} & \hat{1} = \mathbf{Cpo} \\
\Big\downarrow{\scriptstyle I^2} & {\scriptstyle R} \ \nearrow & \Big\downarrow{\scriptstyle !} = \Delta \\
\widehat{D} & \xrightarrow[\hat{\pi}]{} & \widehat{\mathcal{E}}
\end{array}
$$

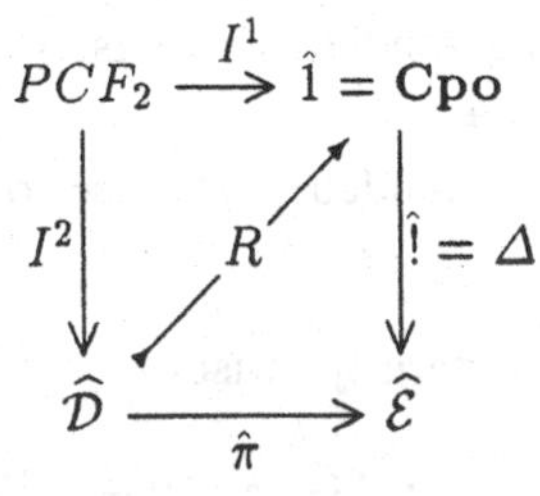

- $\mathcal{E}$ is the category whose objects are pairs $\langle m \in D, \rho \in D^m \rangle$, while morphisms from $\langle m, \rho \rangle \to \langle n, \rho' \rangle$ are those $\sigma : m \to n$ in D s.t. $\rho' = [\![\sigma]\!]_\rho$
- $\pi : \mathcal{E} \to D$ is the obvious projection functor $\langle m, \rho \rangle \mapsto m$.

The Kripke logical relation R is a family of ω-inductive relations (see Definition 3) R^τ in $\widehat{\mathcal{E}}$ defined by induction on the structure of types τ in PCF_2.

base $R^{base}_{\langle m,\rho\rangle} \subset const_\perp \times D$ s.t. $\perp R_{\langle m,\rho\rangle} d$ and $up(c) R_{\langle m,\rho\rangle} d \stackrel{\Delta}{\iff} d = up(inl\ c)$

code $R^{code}_{\langle m,\rho\rangle} \subset \Lambda(m)_\perp \times D$ s.t. $\perp R_{\langle m,\rho\rangle} d$ and $up(M) R_{\langle m,\rho\rangle} d \stackrel{\Delta}{\iff} d = [\![M]\!]_\rho$

We must check that R^{code} satisfies the monotonicity property of a Kripke relation, i.e. $\sigma : \langle m,\rho\rangle \to \langle n,\rho'\rangle$ in $\mathcal{E}$ and $up(M) R^{code}_{\langle n,\rho'\rangle} d$ implies $up(M[\sigma]) R^{code}_{\langle m,\rho\rangle} d$. This follows from $\rho' = [\![\sigma]\!]_\rho$, i.e. from the definition of morphism in $\mathcal{E}$, and $[\![M[\sigma]]\!]_\rho = [\![M]\!]_{[\![\sigma]\!]_\rho}$, i.e. the substitution lemma for the interpretation of λ_o. More diagrammatically this means

$$\begin{array}{cccccc}
\mathcal{D} & \mathcal{E} & & code & R^{code} & D \\
m & \langle m,\rho\rangle & & up(M[\sigma]) R_{\langle m,\rho\rangle} & & [\![M[\sigma]]\!]_\rho \\
\sigma \downarrow & \sigma \downarrow & & \uparrow code(\sigma) & & \| \\
n & \langle n,\rho'\rangle & & up(M)\ R_{\langle n,\rho'\rangle} & & [\![M]\!]_{\rho'} = d
\end{array}$$

The family R on functional types is defined (in the internal language) in the standard way, i.e. $f R^{\tau_1\to\tau_2} g \stackrel{\Delta}{\iff} \forall x,y. x R^{\tau_1} y \supset f @^2 x R^{\tau_2} g @^1 y$, where $@^i$ is the binary application of the applicative structure used for the interpretation I^i. The definition of the Kripke logical relation at types *base* and *code* says that partial evaluation is only partially correct, namely if it terminates it gives the expected result.

By the fundamental lemma of logical relations, to prove that the interpretations I^1 and I^2 of PCF_2 are logically related it suffices to show that the interpretation of all higher-order constants (besides @ and λ) are logically related. This is a fairly straightforward check, therefore we consider only few cases, including the critical one of dynamic λ-abstraction.

$\underline{@}$ Since $\underline{@}^2$ is strict, we need to prove only that $up(M_i) R_{\langle m,\rho\rangle} d_i$ (for $i = 1,2$) implies $up(M_1) \underline{@}^2 up(M_2) \stackrel{\Delta}{=} up(M_1 @ M_2) R_{\langle m,\rho\rangle} d_1 @^1 d_2 \stackrel{\Delta}{=} d_1 \underline{@}^1 d_2$

By definition of R at type *code*, we have to prove that $[\![M_1 @ M_2]\!]_\rho = d_1 @^1 d_2$

- $[\![M_i]\!]_\rho = d_i$, because $up(M_i) R_{\langle m,\rho\rangle} d_i$
- $[\![M_1 @ M_2]\!]_\rho = @^1([\![M_1]\!]_\rho, [\![M_2]\!]_\rho)$, by definition of I^1
- therefore $[\![M_1 @ M_2]\!]_\rho = d_1 @^1 d_2$

fix_τ We need to prove that $f R^{\tau\to\tau} g$ implies $(\sqcup_i x_i) R^\tau (\sqcup_i y_i)$, where $x_0 = y_0 = \perp$ and $x_{i+1} = f @^2 x_i$ and $y_{i+1} = g @^1 y_i$.

This follows immediately from ω-inductivity of R^τ, i.e.

- $\perp R^\tau \perp$ and
- $(\sqcup_i x_i) R^\tau (\sqcup_i y_i)$ when $x_{i\in\omega}$ and $y_{i\in\omega}$ are ω-chains and $\forall i. x_i R^\tau y_i$

ω-inductivity of R^τ can be proved by a straightforward induction on τ.

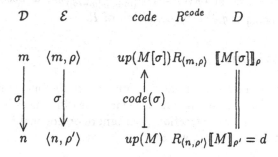

$\underline{\lambda}$ The case of $\underline{\lambda} : (code \to code) \to code$ is the most delicate one. Suppose that $f R^{code \to code}_{\langle m,\rho \rangle} g$, we have to prove that $\underline{\lambda}_m(f) R^{code}_{\langle m,\rho\rangle} up(inr(\lambda d : D.g@^1 d))$.
For this we need an explicit description of $\underline{\lambda}_m(f) \in \Lambda(m)_\perp$

- $\underline{\lambda}_m(f) = \perp$ when $f_{\pi:m+1\to m}(up\ x_m) = \perp$, where $\pi : m+1 \to m$ is the first projection in $\mathcal{D}$ and we exploit the definition of exponentials in $\widehat{\mathcal{D}}$;
- $\underline{\lambda}_m(f) = up(\lambda x_m.M)$ when $up(M) = f_{\pi:m+1\to m}(up\ x_m) \in \Lambda(m+1)_\perp$.

We can ignore the first case, since when $\underline{\lambda}_m(f) = \perp$ there is nothing to prove. In the second case, we have to prove that $[\![\lambda x_m.M]\!]_\rho = up(inr(\lambda d : D.g@^1 d))$, i.e. $[\![M]\!]_{\rho[m\mapsto d]} = g@^1 d$ for any $d \in D$

- $up(x_m) R^{code}_{\langle m+1,\rho[m\mapsto d]\rangle} d$, by definition of R
- $up(M) \stackrel{\Delta}{=} f_{\pi:m+1\to m}(up\ x_m) R^{code}_{\langle m+1,\rho[m\mapsto d]\rangle} g@^1 d$, because $f R^{code\to code}_{\langle m,\rho\rangle} g$
- $[\![M]\!]_{\rho[m\mapsto d]} = g@^1 d$, by definition of R.

4 Comparisons

In this section we make a comparative analysis of the interpretations of PCF_2 in **Cpo** and $\widehat{\mathcal{D}}$. In fact, to highlight more clearly the differences in the interpretations of *code* and dynamic λ-abstraction (and ignore orthogonal issues), it is better to work in a simplified setting, where

- λ_o is the pure untyped λ-calculus;
- PCF_2 is the simply typed λ-calculus with atomic type *code*, and additional operations $\underline{@} : code, code \to code$ and $\underline{\lambda} : (code \to code) \to code$.

With this simplification one can ask for total correctness of the interpretation of PCF_2 w.r.t. an interpretation of λ_o in **Cpo** (say in the standard model $D = (D \to D)_\perp$ for the lazy λ-calculus). Moreover, the interpretation of PCF_2 without fix_τ can be given in **Set** or $\mathbf{Set}^{\mathcal{D}^{op}}$, where the syntactic category $\mathcal{D}$ has to be changed to reflect the simplifications in λ_o.
The following table summarizes the key differences between the original interpretation proposed by Gomard (Gomard's naive), its patching (Gomard's patched) and the interpretation in $\widehat{\mathcal{D}}$ (functor category).

Semantics	Gomard's patched	Gomard's naive	functor category
category	**Set**	**Set**	$\mathbf{Set}^{\mathcal{D}^{op}}$
$[\![code]\!]$	exp^N	exp	$\Lambda(n)$ at stage n
$[\![code \to code]\!]$	$(exp^N)^{(exp^N)}$	exp^{exp}	$\Lambda(n+1)$ at stage n
$[\![\underline{\lambda}]\!]$	use counter	not defined	use functor category
R^{code}	not defined	$R_{\rho:N\to D}$	$R_{n:N,\rho:n\to D}$
correctness proof	not stated	not meaningful	by Kripke log. rel.

Where exp is the set of λ-terms with variables in N, $\Lambda(n)$ is the set of λ-terms modulo α-conversion with free variables in n, and $D \in$ **Cpo** is a domain for interpreting the lazy λ-calculus, i.e. $D = (D \to D)_\perp$. When describing the functor in $\widehat{\mathcal{D}}$ interpreting a certain type of PCF_2, we have given only its action on objects. The comparison shows that:

- The functor category interpretation is very similar to Gomard's naive interpretation, when it comes to the definition of $[\![code]\!]$ and R^{code}, though more care is taken in spelling out what object variables may occur free in an object expression.
- The advantage of working in a functor category becomes apparent in the interpretation $code \rightarrow code$, this explains also why the functor category can handle the interpretation of $\underline{\lambda}$.
- Gomard's patched has strong similarities with the simple-minded semantics in **Cpo** for modeling local variables in Algol-like languages. In fact, Gomard's patched semantics parameterizes the meaning of expressions, but not that of types, w.r.t. the number of names generated used so far.

Conclusions and future work

The first part of the paper recalls the main definitions and results in [Gom92], points out the problems with the published interpretation of the two-level language PCF_2, presents possible ways of fixing the interpretation (these were proposed by Olivier Danvy, Fritz Henglein and Neil Jones during several e-mail exchanges) along the lines hinted by Gomard. After fixing the interpretation of PCF_2, there are however problems in fixing the correctness proof in [Gom92]. In the second part of the paper we propose an alternative semantics, and prove correctness for it. We have also cast doubts on the possibility of giving an interpretation of PCF_2 in **Cpo** and prove its correctness w.r.t. the standard interpretation of λ_o **using a logical relation.**
An alternative approach to correctness is proposed in [Wan93]. This avoids any explicit use of operational or denotational semantics, instead he proves correctness modulo β-conversion. Wand uses logical relations, and represents dynamic expressions using higher-order abstract syntax (while [Gom92] uses concrete syntax, and can distinguish α-convertible expressions).
Similar problems to those pointed out in Section 2 are present in other correctness proofs (e.g. [HM94]), which adapt Gomard's approach to more complex two-level languages. We would like to test whether the functor category approach scales up to these languages.

References

[FMS96] M. Fiore, E. Moggi, and D Sangiorgi. A fully-abstract model for the pi-calculus. In *11th LICS Conference*. IEEE, 1996.

[GJ91] K. Gomard and N. Jones. A partial evaluator for the untyped lambda calculus. *J. of Func. Program.*, 1(1), 1991.

[Gom91] Carsten Krogh Gomard. *Program Analysis Matters*. PhD thesis, DIKU, November 1991. DIKU report 91/17.

[Gom92] K. Gomard. A self-applicable partial evaluator for the lambda calculus. *ACM Trans. on Progr. Lang. and Systems*, 14(2), 1992.

[HM94] F. Henglein and C. Mossin. Polymorphic binding-time analysis. In D. Sanella, editor, *ESOP'94*, volume 788 of *LNCS*. Springer Verlag, 1994.

[JGS93] Neil D. Jones, Carsten K. Gomard, and Peter Sestoft. *Partial Evaluation and Automatic Program Generation*. Prentice Hall International, 1993.

[Law63] F.W. Lawvere. Functorial semantics of algebraic theories. *Proc. Nat. Acad. Sci. U.S.A.*, 50, 1963.

[Mit96] John C. Mitchell. *Foundations of Programming Languages*. The MIT Press, Cambridge, MA, 1996.

[MM91] J. Mitchell and E. Moggi. Kripke-style models for typed lambda calculus. *Journal of Pure and Applied Algebra*, 51, 1991.

[Mog91] E. Moggi. Notions of computation and monads. *Information and Computation*, 93(1), 1991.

[Mog97a] E. Moggi. A categorical account of two-level languages. In *MFPS XIII*, ENTCS. Elsevier, 1997.

[Mog97b] E. Moggi. Metalanguages and applications. In *Semantics and Logics of Computation*, Publications of the Newton Institute. CUP, 1997.

[MW85] A. Meyer and M. Wand. Continuation semantics in typed lambda calculus. In R. Parikh, editor, *Logics of Programs '85*, volume 193 of *LNCS*. Springer Verlag, 1985.

[NN92] F. Nielson and H.R. Nielson. *Two-Level Functional Languages*. Number 34 in Cambridge Tracts in Theoretical Computer Science. CUP, 1992.

[Ole85] F.J. Oles. Type algebras, functor categories and block structure. In M. Nivat and J.C. Reynolds, editors, *Algebraic Methods in Semantics*, 1985.

[OT92] P.W. O'Hearn and R.D. Tennent. Semantics of local variables. In *Applications of Categories in Computer Science*, number 177 in L.M.S. Lecture Notes Series. CUP, 1992.

[PS93] A.M. Pitts and I.D.B. Stark. Observable properties of higher order functions that dynamically create local names, or: What's *new*? In *Math. Found. of Comp. Sci. '93*, volume 711 of *LNCS*. Springer Verlag, 1993.

[Ten91] R.D. Tennent. *Semantics of Programming Languages*. Prentice Hall, 1991.

[Wan93] Mitchell Wand. Specifying the correctness of binding-time analysis. *Journal of Functional Programming*, 3(3):365–387, July 1993.

Deciding Properties for Message Sequence Charts

Anca Muscholl[1], Doron Peled[2] and Zhendong Su[3]

[1] Institut für Informatik, Universität Stuttgart,
Breitwiesenstr. 20-22, 70565 Stuttgart, Germany
[2] Bell Laboratories, Lucent Technologies, 600 Mountain Av., Murray Hill, NJ 07974,
and Carnegie Mellon University, School of Computer Science, Pittsburgh, PA,
15213-3891, USA
[3] EECS Department, University of California, Berkeley, CA 94710-1776, USA

Abstract. Message sequence charts (MSC) are commonly used in designing communication systems. They allow describing the communication skeleton of a system and can be used for finding design errors. First, a specification formalism that is based on MSC graphs, combining finite message sequence charts, is presented. We present then an automatic validation algorithm for systems described using the message sequence charts notation. The validation problem is tightly related to a natural language-theoretic problem over *semi-traces* (a generalization of Mazurkiewicz traces, which represent partially ordered executions). We show that a similar and natural decision problem is undecidable.

1 Introduction

Message sequence charts (MSC) are a notation widely used for the early design of communication protocols. With its graphical representation, it allows to describe the communication skeleton of a protocol by indicating the messages that are sent between its different processes. Using message sequence charts one can document the *features* of a system, and the way its parts interact. Although MSCs often do not contain the full information that is needed for implementing the described protocols, they can be used for various analysis purposes. For example, one can use MSCs to search for missing features or incorrect behaviors. It is possible to detect mistakes in the design, e.g., the existence of *race conditions* [1] or *non-local choice* [2]. Another task that is often done using MSCs is providing 'feature transparence', namely upgrading a communication system in a way that all the previous services are guaranteed to be supported.

In recent years MSCs have gained popularity and interest. An international committee (ITU-Z 120 [7]) has been working on developping standards for MSCs. Some tools for displaying MSCs and performing simple checks were developed [1,8]. We model systems of MSCs, allowing a (possibly infinite) family of (finite or infinite) executions. Each execution consists of a finite or infinite set of *send* and *receive* events, together with a partial (causal) order between them. Such a system is denoted using *MSC graphs*, where individual MSCs are combined to form a branching and possibly looping structure. Thus, an MSC graph describes a way of combining partially ordered executions of events.

We suggest in this paper a specification formalism for MSC properties based on directed graphs: each node of the graph consists of a template, which includes a set of communication events, and the causal order between them. We study three alternative semantics for the specification by MSC graphs:

- Using the same semantics as for an MSC system. Namely, each maximal sequence corresponds exactly to one execution.
- With gaps, i.e., as a template, where only part of the events (and the order between them) is specified. Moreover, choices in the specification graph correspond to different possible ways to continue the execution.
- Again with gaps, but with choices corresponding to conjunctions. Namely an execution matching the specification must include all the events in every possible path of the specification, respecting the associated causal orders.

The main focus of this paper is on developping an algorithm for deciding whether there are executions of the checked system of MSCs that match the specification. Such an execution is considered as a 'bad' execution and if exists it should be reported as a counter-example for the correctness of the system. For the first semantics we show in Section 5 that the matching problem is undecidable. For the last two problems we provide algorithms and we show them to be NP-complete, see Section 4. In the special case of matching two single MSCs we provide a deterministic polynomial time algorithm, improving the result of [8], see Section 3. The complexity of related problems has been studied for pomset languages [6]. In contrast, in [6] only finite pomset languages are studied (however, over a richer structure).

The matching problem can also be represented as a decision problem for *semi-traces* [4]. A semi-trace is a set of words that is obtained from some word by means of (not necessarily symmetric) rewriting rules. These rules allow commuting pairs of adjacent letters. A semi-trace language is a set of words closed under these given rewriting rules. We provide a natural transformation from MSCs to semi-traces. This allows explaining our decidability result as a decision problem on rational languages of semi-traces. One surprising consequence of this translation is that it applies in the same way to two rather different communication semantics for a natural subclass of MSCs: that of asynchronous fifo communication and that of synchronous (handshake) communication.

Work is in progress to add the proposed validation framework to a toolset that was developed for manipulating MSCs [1]. This paper concludes with several open problems and suggested work.

2 Charts and MSC Graphs

In this section, we introduce message sequence charts (MSC) and MSC graphs, as well as the matching problem.

Definition 1 (MSC). A message sequence chart M is a quintuple $\langle E, <, L, T, \mathcal{P} \rangle$ where E is a set of events, $< \subseteq E \times E$ is an acyclic relation, $\mathcal{P}$ is a set of processes, $L : E \to \mathcal{P}$ is a mapping that associates each event with a process, and $T : E \to \{s, r\}$ is a mapping that describes the type of each event (*send* or *receive*).

The order relation $<$ is called the ***visual ordering*** of events and it is obtained from the syntactical representation of the chart (e.g. represented according to the standard syntax ITU-Z 120). It is called 'visual' since it reflects the graphical representation of MSCs. We distinguish between two types of visual ordering as follows. We let $<_c = \{(e, e') \mid T(e) = s, T(e') = r$ and e, e' are the send and receive events of the same message$\}$ denote the message ordering. Furthermore, for $P \in \mathcal{P}$ let $E_P = \{e \mid e \in E \wedge L(e) = P\}$, i.e., E_P is the set of events that belong to process P. We define the relation $<_P = < \cap (E_P \times E_P)$ that represents the ordering between events of P only. Then the visual order $<$ is the union of these orders, i.e., $< = <_c \cup (\bigcup_{P \in \mathcal{P}} <_P)$.

Thus, for two events e and f, we have $e < f$ if and only if one of the following holds:

- e and f are the send and receive event of the same message. In this case, we call e and f a ***message pair***.
- e and f belong to the same process P, with e appearing before f on the process line. This imposes a total order among all events of P, for every process P.

In general, the visual order provides more ordering than intended by the designer. Therefore we associate with every chart a causal structure providing the intended ordering. Causal structures are related to ***pomsets*** [11], ***event structures*** [9], and ***traces*** [5]. A causal structure is obtained from an MSC by means of a given semantics. Formally, the causal structure of an MSC M is a quintuple $\mathrm{tr}(M) = \langle E, \prec, L, T, \mathcal{P} \rangle$, where the only component that differs from the definition of an MSC is the relation $\prec$, called the ***precedence order*** of events. For two events e and f, we have $e \prec f$ if and only if event e must terminate before event f starts. The transitive closure $\prec^*$ of $\prec$ is called the ***causal order***. Events which are not causally ordered can occur independently of each other.

The precedence order of events is defined by a set of semantic rules. As the semantics used throughout the paper, we give below the set of rules for an architecture with fifo queues. This means that every one-directional communication between two processes is done through a fifo channel. For this architecture we have in the visual order for each message pairs $e <_c f$ and $e' <_c f'$ with $e <_P e'$ and $L(f) = L(f') = P'$ also $f <_{P'} f'$. Then, for two events e and f, let $e \prec f$ for the ***fifo semantics*** if one of the following holds:

1. Two sends from the same process:
$$T(e) = T(f) = s \wedge e <_P f \text{ for some process } P.$$
2. A message pair: $T(e) = s \wedge T(f) = r \wedge e <_c f$.

3. Messages ordered by the fifo queue:

$$T(e) = T(f) = r \ \wedge \ e <_P f \text{ for some process } P \ \wedge$$
$$\exists e', f' \ (e' <_c e \ \wedge \ f' <_c f \ \wedge \ e' <_{P'} f' \text{ for some process } P').$$

4. A receive precedes a send on the same process line:

$$T(e) = r \ \wedge \ T(f) = s \ \wedge \ e <_P f \text{ for some process } P.$$

Remark 2. For a causal structure $\mathcal{O} = \langle E, \prec, L, T, \mathcal{P} \rangle$ we use the usual notation $e\downarrow$ for the downward closure of an event $e \in E$ w.r.t. the partial order of $\mathcal{O}$, i.e. $e\downarrow = \{f \in E \mid f \prec^* e\}$. The notion of a minimal element e in $\mathcal{O}$ is also standard, meaning that $e' \prec^* e$ implies $e' = e$. We denote by $\min(\mathcal{O})$ the set of minimal elements of the partial order of $\mathcal{O}$.

Note that the following relation between configurations associated to a message pair holds under the fifo semantics:

Lemma 3. *Let $e <_c f$ be a message pair. Then we have under the fifo semantics:*

$$f\downarrow = e\downarrow \cup \{f_1 \in E \mid T(f_1) = r,\ L(f_1) = L(f) \text{ and}$$
$$e_1 <_c f_1 \text{ for } e_1 \text{ with } e_1 \preceq e,\ T(e_1) = s,\ L(e_1) = L(e)\}.$$

2.1 Templates and the Matching Problem

An MSC M *matches* an MSC N (or is *embedded* in N) if the chart N respects the causal order on the events specified by M. (Clearly, matching is defined with respect to a given semantics.) The MSC M is called a *template MSC* and it represents the specification, whereas the MSC N is called a *system* MSC. For matching M against N it suffices to consider the reduced partial order of M. Moreover, a template is viewed as a possibly partially specified execution of the system. The actual executions may contain additional messages, which may induce additional ordering.

Definition 4 (Matching a template with an MSC). Under a given semantics, a template M with the causal structure $\text{tr}(M) = \langle E_M, \prec_M, L_M, T_M, \mathcal{P}_M \rangle$ matches a chart N with the causal structure $\text{tr}(N) = \langle E_N, \prec_N, L_N, T_N, \mathcal{P}_N \rangle$ if and only if $\mathcal{P}_M \subseteq \mathcal{P}_N$ and there exists an injective mapping (called *embedding*) $h : E_M \to E_N$ such that

- for each $e \in E_M$, we have $L_N(h(e)) = L_M(e)$ and $T_N(h(e)) = T_M(e)$ (preserving processes and types), and
- if $e_1 \prec_M e_2$ then $h(e_1) \prec_N h(e_2)$ (preserving the causal order).

Let $\mathcal{P} = \{P_1, \ldots, P_n\}$ denote the set of processes. For an event $e \in E$ we are often interested in its 'message type' msg(e) and we let $\text{msg}(e) = s_{ij}$, if e is a send event from P_i to P_j, and $\text{msg}(e) = r_{ij}$ if e is a receive event of P_j from P_i, respectively. Let $\text{msg}(M) = \{\text{msg}(e) \mid e \in E_M\}$.

Note that under the fifo semantics the injectivity of the embedding is already implied by the two other properties in the definition above. Moreover, under this semantics we have a simpler characterization of embeddings, which takes into account just message types:

Lemma 5. *Let M, N denote two MSCs and let $h : M \to N$ be a mapping. Then h is an embedding from M to N if and only if the following conditions hold for any two events $e, f \in E_M$:*

1. *If (e, f) is a message pair, then $(h(e), h(f))$ is also a message pair between the same processes.*
2. *Let $e \prec_M f$ such that (e, f) is not a message pair (thus, e, f are on the same process). Then $msg(h(e)) = msg(e)$, $msg(h(f)) = msg(f)$ and $h(e) <_N h(f)$ holds in the visual order $<_N$ of N.*

Let $\mathcal{M}$ denote the class of finite message sequence charts. Let $M_i = \langle E_i, <_i, L_i, T_i, \mathcal{P}_i \rangle$ be two MSCs, $i = 1, 2$. The (syntactic) concatenation of M_1 and M_2, denoted M_1M_2, is defined by letting $M_1M_2 = \langle E_1 \dot{\cup} E_2, <, L, T, \mathcal{P}_1 \cup \mathcal{P}_2 \rangle$ with $L|_{E_i} = L_i, T|_{E_i} = T_i$ and $< = <_1 \cup <_2 \cup \{(e, e') \mid e \in E_1, e' \in E_2, L(e) = L(e')\}$. Here, $E_1 \dot{\cup} E_2$ means the disjoint union of the event sets of M_1 and M_2. The concatenation of an infinite sequence $M_1, M_2, \ldots$ is defined in an analogous way. Message sequence graphs (MSC graphs, sometimes called *high-level MSCs* [7]), are used to compose MSCs to larger systems. Equivalently, one can compose MSCs using rational operations, i.e. union, concatenation and iteration. MSC graphs are finite directed graphs where each node of the graph is associated with a finite MSC [1].

Definition 6 (MSC graph). An MSC graph N is a quadruple $\langle \mathcal{S}, \tau, s_0, c \rangle$ where $\langle \mathcal{S}, \tau, s_0 \rangle$ is a finite, directed graph with states set $\mathcal{S}$, transition relation $\tau \subseteq \mathcal{S} \times \mathcal{S}$ and starting state $s_0 \in \mathcal{S}$. The mapping $c : \mathcal{S} \to \mathcal{M}$ assigns to each node a finite MSC.

Let $\xi = s_1, s_2, \ldots$ be a (possibly infinite) path in N, i.e. $(s_i, s_{i+1}) \in \tau$ for every i. The execution (MSC) defined by ξ is given by $c(\xi) = c(s_1)c(s_2)\ldots$.

In order to distinguish MSC graphs from finite MSCs we denote throughout the paper a finite MSC (not bounded to any MSC graph) as a *single MSC*.

In an MSC graph $N = \langle \mathcal{S}, \tau, s_0, c \rangle$, a path ξ is called *maximal* if it begins with the starting state s_0 and it is not a proper prefix of another path. Notice that a maximal path can be either infinite or finite. Let also $\text{msg}(N) = \cup_{s \in \mathcal{S}} \text{msg}(c(s))$.

Fig. 1 shows an example of an MSC graph where the state in the upper left corner is the starting state. Note that the executions of this system are either finite or infinite. Also note that the events of receiving messages of fail and report are not causally ordered.

Definition 7 (Matching paths). Let ξ_1 and ξ_2 be two finite or infinite paths in some MSC graphs. Then ξ_1 matches ξ_2 if $c(\xi_1)$ matches $c(\xi_2)$.

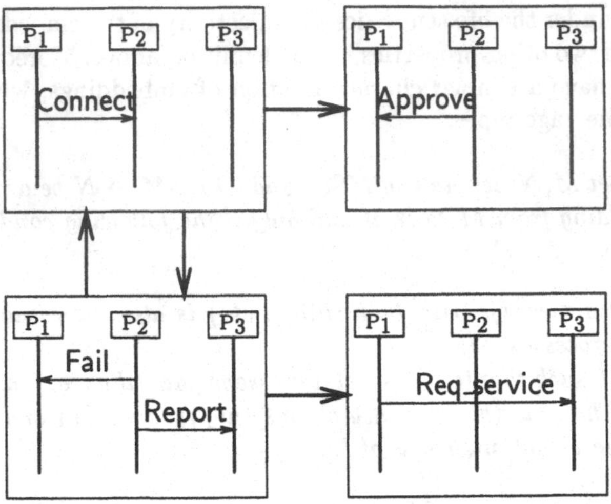

Fig. 1. A system MSC graph.

A *strongly connected component* C of a directed graph $\langle \mathcal{S}, \tau \rangle$ is a subset $C \subseteq \mathcal{S}$ such that for any $u, v \in C$, there is a nonempty path from u to v. A maximal strongly connected component is a strongly connected component which is maximal w.r.t. set inclusion.

3 Matching a Template

In this section, we consider the problem of matching a single template MSC with an MSC graph. As a first result, we show that we can check whether a template can be embedded into a single MSC in polynomial time. (Recall that we assume that the fifo semantics is used.) This algorithm refines the result of [8], where a PSPACE algorithm was exhibited without specifying the semantics. The present matching algorithm is based on the simple observation that it suffices to match a suitable minimal send event and the corresponding receive event with the first occurrence of a message pair of the same type.

Proposition 8. *Let* $M = \langle E_M, <_M, L_M, T_M, \mathcal{P}_M \rangle$, $N = \langle E_N, <_N, L_N, T_N, \mathcal{P}_N \rangle$ *be single MSCs. For each event* $e \in \min(tr(M))$ *which is minimal w.r.t.* $\prec_M^*$ *let* $\mu(e) \in E_N$ *denote the first event in* N *with* $msg(e) = msg(\mu(e))$. *Choose* $e_0 \in \min(tr(M))$ *be such that* $\mu(e_0)$ *is minimal within the set* $\{\mu(e) \mid e \in \min(tr(M))\}$. *Let* f_0, *resp.* f_0', *denote the corresponding receive events of* e_0, *resp.* $\mu(e_0)$. *Let* $M' = M \setminus \{e_0, f_0\}$ *and* $N' = N \setminus \{g' \in E_N \mid g' \prec_N^* f_0'\}$. *Then* M *matches* N *if and only if* e_0 *is well-defined and* M' *matches* N'. *Moreover, if* $h' : M' \to N'$ *is an embedding of* M' *into* N', *then* $h' \cup \{e_0 \mapsto \mu(e_0), f_0 \mapsto f_0'\}$ *is an embedding of* M *into* N.

Proof. Note first that all minimal elements of $\mathrm{tr}(M)$ are send events. Suppose that M matches N via $h : M \to N$, where $h(e_0) \neq \mu(e_0)$ (hence, $h(f_0) \neq f_0'$). Let $e_0' := \mu(e_0)$ and let $\hat{h}$ be given by $\hat{h}(e_0) = e_0'$, $\hat{h}(f_0) = f_0'$ and $\hat{h}(g) = h(g)$ for every $g \notin \{e_0, f_0\}$. Now, if $e_0 \prec_M g$, then $h(e_0) \prec_N h(g)$ and hence also $e_0' \prec_N h(g)$, since $e_0' \prec_N h(e_0)$ and $e_0', h(e_0)$ have the same message type. A similar argument holds for $f_0 \prec_M g$, which shows that $\hat{h}$ is again an embedding from M to N. In order to show that M' matches N' it suffices to show that $\hat{h}(E_M) \cap \{g' \in E_N \mid g' \prec_N^* f_0'\} = \{e_0', f_0'\}$. Assume the contrary, i.e. there exists $g \in E_M$ such that $\hat{h}(g) \prec_N^* f_0'$ and $\hat{h}(g) \notin \{e_0', f_0'\}$. Since every receive event is preceded by its corresponding send event, we may assume that $T_M(g) = s$, i.e. g is a send event. Let $e_1 \in \min(\mathrm{tr}(M))$ be a minimal event with $e_1 \prec_M^* g$, then $\hat{h}(e_1) \prec_N^* \hat{h}(g) \prec_N^* f_0'$. By Lemma 3 we obtain that $\hat{h}(e_1) \prec_N^* e_0'$, since e_1 is a send event. By the definition of μ we have $\mu(e_1) \prec_N^* \hat{h}(e_1)$, hence $\mu(e_1) \prec_N^* e_0'$. Thus, by the choice of e_0 we obtain $\mu(e_1) = e_0'$. Therefore, $e_0' \prec_N^* \hat{h}(g) \prec_N^* f_0'$, which yields $e_0' = \hat{h}(g)$ due to $T_M(g) = s$, contradiction.

Suppose finally that M' matches N' via h' and consider some event g in M'. If $e_0 \prec_M g$, then we also have $e_0' \prec_N h'(g)$, since h' preserves message types and $h'(g) \in E_{N'}$. Similarly, $f_0 \prec_M g$ implies $e_0' \prec_N h'(g)$, which shows that $h' \cup \{e_0 \mapsto e_0', f_0 \mapsto f_0'\}$ is an embedding of M into N.

Remark 9. Proposition 8 yields an embedding algorithm, mapping the events of M in such a way that minimal events are mapped first, to the first event with the same type. This algorithm is of linear complexity if we keep $\min(\mathrm{tr}(M))$, resp. $\{\mu(e) \mid e \in \min(\mathrm{tr}(M))\}$ in two lists. More precisely, note that on each process of M, resp. N, there is at most one event $e \in \min(\mathrm{tr}(M))$, resp. $\mu(e)$. Moreover, we will record for each process of N the event on that process line which is of the form $\mu(e)$ for some $e \in \min(\mathrm{tr}(M))$, if there is one on that process. This additional information is needed in order to update the set of minimal elements of $\{\mu(e) \mid e \in \min(\mathrm{tr}(M))\}$ in constant time. For the complexity of our algorithm note first that $\min(\mathrm{tr}(M'))$ can be updated in constant time, since at most two new minimal events can occur on $L(e_0)$ and $L(f_0)$. Moreover, for $e_1 \in \min(\mathrm{tr}(M')) \setminus \min(\mathrm{tr}(M))$ we can check whether $\mu(e_1)$ is minimal in $\{\mu(e) \mid e \in \min(\mathrm{tr}(M'))\}$ in constant time, using the additional information mentioned above. This suffices, since $\mu(e_1)$ is a send event and every event preceding it in the visual order is a predecessor in the causal order, too. Hence, $\mu(e_1)$ is not minimal within $\{\mu(e) \mid e \in \min(\mathrm{tr}(M'))\}$ if and only if its process contains an event $\mu(e_2)$, $e_2 \in \min(\mathrm{tr}(M'))$, such that $\mu(e_2) <_{N'} \mu(e_1)$.

Note also that the embedding h suggested by Proposition 8 is actually unique. It is not difficult to show that an event $e \in E_M$ is mapped by h to $e' \in E_N$ if and only if e' is the minimal event w.r.t. $\prec_N^*$ such that $e\downarrow$ matches $e'\downarrow$.

In the remaining of this section we consider the exact complexity of matching a template MSC with an MSC graph.

Definition 10 (Matching a template with an MSC graph). A template MSC M matches an MSC graph N if M matches some maximal path of N.

Matching a template against an MSC graph actually requires only paths of bounded length to be checked:

Proposition 11. *Let N be an MSC graph and let M be a single template MSC such that M matches N. Then there is a path in N that embeds M and has length at most md, where m is the number of messages in M and d is the maximal length of a simple path in N (i.e. of a path where no node appears twice).*

Proposition 11 yields a non-deterministic algorithm for matching a template with an MSC graph which guesses a path in N and verifies that the template matches the graph. The algorithm is polynomial in the size of the template and the number of nodes in the graph. The proposition below shows that matching is also NP-hard.

Proposition 12. *Matching a single template MSC with an MSC graph is NP-complete, even if the graph is acyclic.*

Proof. It suffices to show that matching is NP-hard. For this, we reduce the satisfiability problem for formulas in conjunctive normal form (CNF-SAT) to the MSC matching problem.

Consider a formula $\bigwedge_{j=1}^{k} C_j$ with clauses (disjunctions) C_j over the variables $x_1, \ldots, x_l$. For each clause C_j we take two processes, P_j and R_j. Let $m(j)$ denote a message from P_j to R_j. Note that the events of different messages $m(i), m(j)$, $i \neq j$, are not causally ordered. Then the template M is given as $M = m(1) \cdots m(k)$. The system graph $N = \langle \mathcal{S}, \tau, s_0, c \rangle$ contains for each variable x_i three states denoted as o_i, p_i and n_i, i.e. $\mathcal{S} = \{o_i, p_i, n_i \mid 1 \leq i \leq l\}$. Let $s_0 = o_1$. The edge set is given by $\tau = \{(o_i, p_i), (o_i, n_i), (p_j, o_{j+1}), (n_j, o_{j+1}) \mid 1 \leq i \leq l, 1 \leq j < l\}$. The assignment of MSC to states is as follows: for every i, $c(o_i) = \emptyset$, $c(p_i) = \{m(j) \mid x_i \text{ occurs in } C_j\}$ and $c(n_i) = \{m(j) \mid \bar{x}_i \text{ occurs in } C_j\}$. That is, $c(p_i)$ contains messages associated to all clauses satisfied by $x_i :=$ true, whereas $c(n_i)$ contains messages associated to all clauses satisfied by $x_i :=$ false. Thus, a maximal path in the MSC graph N corresponds exactly to an assignment of the variables. The single MSC M matches a maximal path of N if and only if the assignment given by the path satisfies all clauses.

4 Matching MSC Graphs

In this section, we discuss our extension of the matching algorithm to deal with MSC graphs. Adopting the same convention for matching two single MSCs, we call one of the MSC graphs the *template* (MSC) graph. The other graph is called the *system* (MSC) graph.

The template graph represents a collection of properties (behaviors), each defined by one of its maximal paths. Then for the or-semantics as defined below, the template corresponds to a non-deterministic choice among these behaviors, so an execution of the system needs to contain at least one of the executions

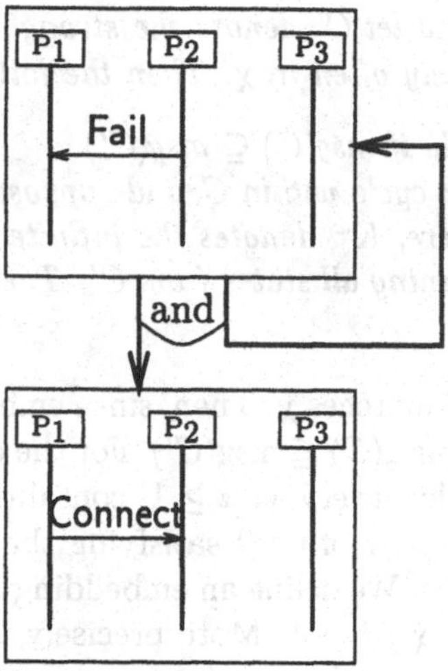

Fig. 2. A template MSC graph.

described by the template. For the and-semantics an execution of the system matches the template if it contains all the executions of the template MSC graph.

Definition 13 (Matching a template graph with a system graph). Let M and N be two MSC graphs.

1. M *or-matches* N if there exists a maximal path ξ' of N and a maximal path ξ of M which matches ξ'.
2. M *and-matches* N if there exists a maximal path ξ' of N such that all maximal paths ξ of M match ξ'.

Consider the and-graph template in Fig. 2. This template matches the system of Fig. 1, since the system may alternate infinitely often between Connect and Fail.

The next lemmas present some fundamental properties of matching paths of MSC graphs. A *subpath* ξ' of a path $\xi = s_0, s_1, \ldots$ in some graph G is a path of G of the form $\xi' = s_{i_0}, s_{i_1}, s_{i_2}, \ldots$ with $i_0 < i_1 < \ldots$. In this case, we denote ξ a *superpath* of ξ'.

Lemma 14. *Let M, N be two MSC graphs and let ξ_1, ξ_2 denote paths in M, N, resp. Let ξ_1 match ξ_2. Then for every subpath ξ_1' of ξ_1 and every superpath ξ_2' of ξ_2, ξ_1' matches ξ_2'.*

Proposition 15. *Let M, N be two MSC graphs and consider an infinite path ξ in M such that every state from ξ occurs infinitely often in ξ. Let C be the strongly connected component of M induced by the states from ξ. Consider also* *an infinite path χ in N and let C' denote the strongly connected component of the states occurring infinitely often in χ. Then the following holds:*

1. *ξ matches χ if and only if $msg(C) \subseteq msg(C')$.*
2. *Let K denote a simple cycle within C and suppose that ξ matches χ. Then K^ω matches χ, too (here, K^ω denotes the infinite path $KK\ldots$).*
3. *Let $\hat{K}$ be a cycle containing all states from C'. Then ξ matches χ if and only if ξ matches $\hat{K}^\omega$.*

Proof. Suppose first that ξ matches χ. Then, since embeddings preserve message types, it is easily seen that $\text{msg}(C) \subseteq \text{msg}(C')$. For the converse let $\chi = \chi_0\chi_1\cdots$, with χ_i finite paths such that every χ_i, $i \geq 1$, contains all states from C'. Also, consider a linearization $e_1e_2\ldots$ of $\text{tr}(\xi)$ satisfying the property that for each i, (e_{2i-1}, e_{2i}) is a message pair. We define an embedding h inductively by mapping (e_{2i-1}, e_{2i}) to events from χ_i, $i \geq 1$. More precisely, h maps e_{2i-1} to the first event e' occurring in $c(\chi_i)$ satisfying $\text{msg}(e_{2i-1}) = \text{msg}(e')$. Then, e_{2i} is mapped by h to the corresponding receive event of e'. By Lemma 5 it is easy to check that h preserves the causal order.

The second assertion of the proposition is obtained directly from Lemma 14, whereas the last assertion is a consequence of the first one.

4.1 The Complexity of OR-Matching

The next theorem shows that for or-matching two MSC graphs only finite paths have to be considered for an embedding. More precisely, for the recurrent part of a path only the message types of events are relevant. For a strongly connected component C and a state s we denote below a path from s to some node in C as a path from s to C.

Theorem 16. *Let $M = \langle S, \tau, s_0, c\rangle$ be a template graph and $N = \langle S', \tau', s_0', c'\rangle$ be a system graph. Then M or-matches N if and only if either there exists a finite maximal path of M which matches N, or there exist*

- *a simple cycle K in M and a simple path ξ from s_0 to K,*
- *a strongly connected component C' of N and a path χ from s_0' to C',*

such that ξ matches χ and $msg(K) \subseteq msg(C')$.

Proof. Suppose that M or-matches N via an infinite maximal path. Then, by Lemma 14 and Proposition 15(2) we also obtain a path of M of the form $\xi KK\ldots$ which matches N, where K is a simple cycle and ξ is a simple path from s_0 to K. Let ρ denote a path in N such that ξK^ω matches ρ. Moreover, let χ be a minimal prefix of ρ such that ξ matches χ and the corresponding suffix is a strongly connected component of N. Then, by applying Proposition 15(1), we obtain the result.

For the converse we may use again Proposition 15(1) in order to extend the embedding of ξ into χ to an embedding of ξK^ω into a path in N starting with χ.

First note that in Theorem 16 the path χ is in general not simple. But by Proposition 11 its length is bounded by size(ξ) $\cdot$ n, with size(ξ) denoting the number of messages in ξ, and n denoting the number of states in N. Note also that we can require above that C' is a maximal strongly connected component, due to Lemma 14. Hence, an algorithm based on Theorem 16 would first compute in linear time all maximal strongly connected components of N. Then, for each maximal strongly connected component C' consider the states s of M with $\text{msg}(c(s)) \subseteq \text{msg}(C')$ and the subgraph $M_{C'}$ induced by these states. The algorithm checks whether there is some simple path ξ from s_0 to some strongly connected component of $M_{C'}$ which matches a path χ from s'_0 to C'. (The length of χ is bounded by a polynomial in the size of ξ and the size of N.)

The complexity of the above algorithm basically derives from two problems: one consists of finding all simple paths from the initial node to a given subgraph, and the second one is the problem of matching a single template MSC with an MSC graph. Clearly, Theorem 16 directly yields an NP-algorithm for or-matching. Moreover, by Proposition 12 already the case where the template graph is a single node is NP-hard. Hence, we obtain:

Corollary 17. *The or-matching problem for MSC graphs is NP-complete.*

4.2 The Complexity of AND-Matching

For the and-matching problem we need to deal not only with strongly connected components, but also with states reachable from some strongly connected component. The reason is that some of the events in such states have to be mapped to events belonging to recurrent states in the system graph.

For an MSC graph $M = \langle S, \tau, s_0, c\rangle$ let $\mathcal{S}_c \subseteq \mathcal{S}$ denote the set of nodes belonging to some strongly connected component of M. For each state $s \in \mathcal{S}$ let us partition the events belonging to the single MSC $c(s)$ associated with s in two sets $c_f(s), c_\omega(s)$ as follows. For each event $e \in c(s)$ let $e \in c_\omega(s)$ if and only if there exist some state $s' \in \mathcal{S}_c$, some event e' in $c(s')$ and a path ξ from s' to s with $e' \prec^*_\xi e$ for the causal order $\prec^*_\xi$ associated to the execution of ξ. We denote by E_ω the set of events $\{e \mid e \in c_\omega(s), s \in \mathcal{S}\}$. The set E_ω can be computed in polynomial time as follows: let $E_\omega := \{e' \mid e' \in c(s'), s' \in \mathcal{S}_c\}$. Then for every $e \notin E_\omega, e \in c(s)$, test whether there is some event $e' \in E_\omega$, $e' \in c(s')$, such that s is reachable from s' through a path ξ and $e' \prec_\xi e$ for the execution of that path. Note that $e' \prec_\xi e$ holds if and only if $e' \prec_\chi e$ holds for any other path χ from s' to s. Moreover, by Lemma 3 the condition $e' \prec_\xi e$ can be checked by examining the message types of e, e'. If the test is positive, then let $E_\omega = E_\omega \cup \{e\}$. This step is repeated until no more events can be added. Note also that for every $e \in c_\omega(s)$ and $e' \in c(s)$ with $e \prec^*_{c(s)} e'$, also $e' \in c_\omega(s)$ holds. Moreover, for every message pair $e_1 <_c e_2$ in $c(s)$ we have $e_1 \in c_f(s)$ if and only if $e_2 \in c_f(s)$ (this is easily checked using Lemma 3.) The set $c_f(s)$ together with the visual order inherited from $c(s)$ is thus a single MSC which we also denote by $c_f(s)$ (analogously for $c_\omega(s)$). By the previous remarks we have that the causal order of $c(s)$ is the same as the causal order of $c_f(s)c_\omega(s)$. Finally, for $s \in \mathcal{S}_c$ we have $c(s) = c_\omega(s)$.

Theorem 18. *Let $M = \langle \mathcal{S}, \tau, s_0, c \rangle$ be a template graph and $N = \langle \mathcal{S}', \tau', s_0', c' \rangle$ be a system graph. Define a mapping $\hat{c} : \mathcal{S} \to \mathcal{M}$ by letting $\hat{c}(s) = c_f(s)$. Let $\hat{M} = \langle \hat{\mathcal{S}}, \hat{\tau}, s_0, \hat{c} \rangle$ denote the MSC graph with states set $\hat{\mathcal{S}} = \{s \in \mathcal{S} \mid \hat{c}(s) \neq \emptyset\} \cup \{s_0\}$ and $(s, s') \in \hat{\tau}$ if and only if $s, s' \in \hat{\mathcal{S}}$ such that $\neg(s = s' = s_0)$ and there is a path $s = s_1, \ldots, s_k = s'$ in M satisfying $\hat{c}(s_i) = \emptyset$ for all $1 < i < k$. Then M and-matches N if and only if there exists a subgraph C' of N and a path χ from s_0' to C' such that*

1. *All paths in $\hat{M}$ match χ.*
2. *If M contains cycles then $msg(E_\omega) \subseteq msg(C')$ and C' is a strongly connected component of N.*

Proof. First, note that the MSC graph $\hat{M}$ is acyclic (since the only possible loop would be a self-loop of s_0, which has been excluded by definition).

Suppose that M and-matches N and consider a path ρ in N such that all maximal paths in M match ρ. If M is acyclic, hence $M = \hat{M}$, then we are done by choosing an appropriate finite prefix χ of ρ. So suppose that $\mathcal{S}_c \neq \emptyset$, then ρ must be infinite. Let C' be the strongly connected component containing exactly the states occurring infinitely often in ρ. Let ξ be a (finite) path from $\hat{M}$. Then it is easy to verify that there exists a path σ in M such that the causal order of the execution of ξ is a prefix of the causal order of the execution of σ. Hence, ξ matches ρ, too. Let χ be a finite prefix of ρ such that all (finite) paths from $\hat{M}$ match χ and the corresponding suffix is a strongly connected component of N. Finally, consider an event e in some $c_\omega(s)$, for some state s. Then there exists for each $n \geq 0$ a path ξ from s_0 to s such that the configuration $e \downarrow$ of the occurrence of e in the last node of ξ contains at least n events. Hence, there is some state s' occurring in ρ infinitely often, such that msg(e) = msg(e') holds for some event e' in s'. This concludes one direction of the proof.

Conversely, suppose that M has cycles. Let $\xi = s_0, s_1, \ldots$ be a maximal (finite or infinite) path in M. Note that the causal order associated to the execution $c(\xi)$ of ξ is identical to the causal order of $c_f(\xi)c_\omega(\xi)$, where $c_f(\xi) = c_f(s_0)c_f(s_1)\ldots$ and $c_\omega(\xi) = c_\omega(s_0)c_\omega(s_1)\ldots$. Moreover, $c_f(s_0)c_f(s_1)\ldots$ is a finite MSC since there can be only a finite number of nodes s_i with $c_f(s_i) \neq \emptyset$. Also, $c_f(s_0)c_f(s_1)\ldots$ is the execution of a finite path in $\hat{M}$, thus it matches χ. Since msg(E_ω) $\subseteq$ msg(C') we obtain similarly to Proposition 15 that the MSC $c_\omega(s_0)c_\omega(s_1)\ldots$ matches $\hat{K}^\omega$, for some fixed cycle $\hat{K}$ containing all the states from C'. Thus, ξ matches $\chi\hat{K}^\omega$, which shows the claim.

By the previous theorem we have to consider the problem of and-matching a single MSC against an *acyclic* MSC graph. The next proposition shows that for and-matching an acyclic graph it suffices to look for a mapping which is an embedding for *all* the paths (instead of embedding each path separately).

Proposition 19. *Let M be an acyclic MSC graph and let N be a single MSC. Then M and-matches N if and only if there exists a mapping $g : M \to N$ which is an embedding for* all *paths in M.*

Proof. Suppose that M and-matches N and let g_ξ denote an embedding of a maximal path ξ of M in N. Let Ξ denote the set of all maximal paths of M. Define a mapping $g : M \to N$ by letting $g(e) = \max\{g_\xi(e) \mid \xi \in \Xi, e \text{ occurs on } \xi\}$. Note that for a fixed event e the set $\{g_\xi(e) \mid \xi \in \Xi, e \text{ occurs on } \xi\}$ is totally ordered w.r.t. $\prec_N^*$. This is due to the fifo semantics, since for each e, e' with $\text{msg}(e) = \text{msg}(e')$ we have either $e \preceq e'$ or $e' \preceq e$.

We show that g is an embedding for every path $\xi \in \Xi$. If $e <_c f$ is a message pair in M, then $g(e) <_c g(f)$ holds, due to the fifo semantics. Thus, suppose that $e \prec_\xi f$ and $e \not<_c f$ both hold, where $\prec_\xi$ denotes the causal order associated to the execution of ξ. Let $\chi \in \Xi$ be a path also containing e, f. Note that we have $e \prec_\chi f$ due to M being acyclic. Hence, $g_\chi(e) \prec_N g_\chi(f)$. By the definition of g we finally obtain $g(e) \prec_N g(f)$.

The previous proposition shows that there exists a mapping g for matching all paths in M with N. This yields an NP-algorithm for matching an acyclic MSC graph M with a single MSC (note that after guessing the mapping g we test the embedding property for every pair of events e, f with $e \prec_\xi f$ for some path ξ). We now show that we can even find a canonical mapping deterministically in polynomial time (similar to Proposition 8).

Proposition 20. *Let $M = \langle S, \tau, s_0, c\rangle$ be an acyclic MSC graph and let $s \in S$ be a source node, i.e. a node without predecessors. Let $N = \langle E_N, <_N, L_N, T_N, \mathcal{P}_N\rangle$ be a single MSC. Assume that M and-matches N and let $h : c(s) \to N$ be defined by*

$$h(e) = e' \textit{ if } e' \textit{ is minimal w.r.t. } \prec_N^* \textit{ such that } e\downarrow \textit{ matches } e'\downarrow$$

Let $g : M \to N$ be a mapping which is an embedding for all paths from M in N. We define a mapping $g' : M \to N$ by letting $g'|_{c(s)} = h$ and $g'(e) = g(e)$ for every $e \notin c(s)$. Then g' is also a mapping which embeds all paths of M into N.

Proof. It can be easily verified that for every event $e \in c(s)$ and every mapping $g : M \to N$ which is an embedding for all paths in M (in particular for $c(s)$) one has $h(e) \prec_N g(e)$. Therefore, if $e \prec_\xi^* f$ holds for the execution of a nonempty path ξ from s to s' for two events e, f with $e \in s$ and $f \in s'$, then also $h(e) \prec_N g(f)$ holds.

Proposition 20 yields a polynomial-time algorithm for matching an acyclic and-graph with an MSC defined by a path. We first determine for each node s and for each event $e \in c(s)$ the immediate predecessor events of e (w.r.t. the causal order) located in s and in the nodes preceding s. Then we embed a source node s of M and iterate this procedure with $M \setminus \{s\}$. When processing the current node s events in $c(s)$ are mapped according to the partial order (starting with minimal elements) as suggested by Proposition 8. That is, a suitable event $e \in \min(\mathrm{tr}(M))$ is mapped to the minimal event e' of the same type in N, such that $e' \downarrow$ contains all events to which the immediate predecessor events of e were mapped to.

Together with Theorem 18 we obtain an NP-algorithm for the and-matching problem by first guessing a subgraph C' of the system graph N and a path χ from the starting node of N to some node in C'. Then we verify deterministically that the acyclic MSC graph $\hat{M}$ defined in Theorem 18 and-matches the single MSC corresponding to χ. Note that due to Proposition 19 we can bound the length of χ by a polynomial in the number of messages in $\hat{M}$ and the number of nodes in N. Together with Proposition 12 we obtain:

Corollary 21. *The and-matching problem for MSC graphs is NP-complete.*

5 An Undecidable Problem

The matching problems considered previously were based on the paradigm that templates represent partial specifications of system behaviors. We show below that if we require that templates represent exact behaviors, then the or-matching problem is undecidable.

For the fifo semantics considered in this paper we show first that considering a message pair as a single letter we obtain an isomorphism between the causal orders of a natural subclass of message sequence charts and partial orders of *semi-traces*. Semi-traces are objects known from the algebraic study of concurrency (for a survey on semi-traces see Chapter 12 in [5]).

Formally, assume that $\mathcal{P} = \{P_1, \ldots, P_m\}$ is the set of processes. We associate an alphabet $\Sigma = \{m_{ij} \mid 1 \leq i \neq j \leq m\}$ and a *non-commutation relation* $\mathrm{SD} \subseteq \Sigma \times \Sigma$, $\mathrm{SD} = \{(m_{ij}, m_{ik}) \mid j \neq i \neq k\} \cup \{(m_{ij}, m_{jk}) \mid i \neq j \neq k\}$. The idea underlying SD is to consider in the precedence order the order between sends on the same process and receives ordered by the fifo condition (m_{ij}, m_{ik}), and receives followed by sends on the same process line (m_{ij}, m_{jk}). The complementary relation, $\mathrm{SI} = (\Sigma \times \Sigma) \setminus \mathrm{SD}$, called *semi-commutation relation*, yields a rewriting system $\{ab \to ba \mid (a,b) \in \mathrm{SI}\}$, which will be also denoted by SI. A semi-trace $[w]$ is a set of words, $[w] = \{v \in \Sigma^* \mid w \xrightarrow{*}_{\mathrm{SI}} v\}$. The concatenation of two semi-traces $[u], [v]$ is defined as $[u][v] = [uv]$. It is an associative operation and the set of all semi-traces over (Σ, SI) together with the concatenation is a monoid with identity $1 = [\epsilon]$, which is denoted $(\mathbb{M}(\Sigma, \mathrm{SI}), \cdot, 1)$. Note also that the relation SD is reflexive. Moreover, $[w] = [w']$ holds if and only if w can be rewritten into w' by using symmetric rules only.

In the next proposition we show that a naturally arising subclass of MSCs can be identified with semi-traces. We restrict our consideration to MSCs satisfying the condition that in the visual representation no two message lines intersect. We denote this subclass as *ordered* MSCs. Clearly, ordered MSCs satisfy the fifo condition on the visual order. Note also that the syntactic concatenation of

MSCs induces a concatenation operation for the associated causal orders, which is associative.

Proposition 22. *Let $\mathcal{M}_o$ denote the set of ordered MSCs over the set of processes $\mathcal{P} = \{P_1, \dots, P_m\}$ and let (Σ, SI) be defined as above. Then the monoid of causal orders over $\mathcal{M}$ is isomorphic to $(\mathbb{M}(\Sigma, SI), \cdot, 1)$.*

Proof. Let $M = \langle E, <, L, T, \mathcal{P}\rangle$ and define a homomorphism $h : E_M^* \to \Sigma^*$ by letting $h(e) = m_{ij}$, if e is a send event from P_i to P_j, and $h(e) = \lambda$ if e is a receive event. To M we associate a language t_M over Σ^*:

$$t_M = \{h(z) \mid z \in E_M^* \text{ is a linearization of } \prec_M^*\}$$

Then we can show that t_M is a semi-trace over (Σ, SI). For this, we first define a linearization $z_0 \in E_M^*$ of M inductively by choosing some message pair (e, f) of M satisfying

- e is minimal w.r.t. the visual order $<$ in M
- for every $g \in E_M$: $g < f \Leftrightarrow g = e$

and letting $z_0 = efz_0'$, where z_0' is defined accordingly for $M' := M \setminus \{e, f\}$. (Note that the existence of e, f as above is due to M being an ordered MSC.) Then we claim that $t_M = [h(z_0)]$, i.e. t_M is the semi-trace associated to $h(z_0)$. We show this by induction on the length of t_M. For lack of space, the details are left to the full version of the paper.

Traces [5] result from in symmetric rewriting rules, i.e. both SI and SD are symmetric relations. For the trace monoid given by the rules $ab = ba$, $cd = dc$ it is known that one cannot decide for given regular languages $L_1, L_2 \subseteq \{a, b, c, d\}^*$ whether $[L_1] \cap [L_2]$ is empty [3], where $[L] = \cup_{u \in L}[u]$ denotes the closure of L under $\stackrel{*}{\to}_{\mathrm{SI}}$.

Proposition 23. *Let M, N be two MSC graphs. Then it is undecidable whether there exist two maximal paths ξ_1 in M, ξ_2 in N such that the associated MSCs m_1, m_2 have the same causal order under the fifo semantics.*

Proof. We consider four processes, $\mathcal{P} = \{P_1, P_2, P_3, P_4\}$ and we denote by s_a, r_a a message pair from P_1 to P_2, resp. by s_b, r_b a message pair from P_2 to P_1. Dually, s_c, r_c denotes a message pair from P_3 to P_4, whereas s_d, r_d is a message pair from P_4 to P_3. Then we associate to each letter a, b, c, d an MSC as given by the mapping h, with $h(x) = s_x r_x$, for $x \in \{a, b, c, d\}$. Moreover, h induces a homomorphism from $\{a, b, c, d\}^*$ to $\mathcal{M}$.

Note that for any word u over $\{a, b, c, d\}$ the partial order $\mathrm{tr}(h(u))$ consists of two totally ordered sequences, one over events between processes P_1 and P_2, the other over events between P_3 and P_4. Moreover, these total orders are completely independent. Viewed as a mapping from $\mathbb{M}(\Sigma, \mathrm{SI})$ to $\mathrm{tr}(\mathcal{M})$, h is injective. This, together with [3], concludes our proof.

Let us comment our results in the context of semi-trace languages. One cannot decide the emptiness of the intersection of two MSC graphs since given two regular languages $L, K \subseteq \Sigma^\omega$ and a semi-commutation relation SI over Σ, the question whether the intersection $[L] \cap [K]$ is nonempty is undecidable. In contrast, the or-matching problem of Section 4.1 can be expressed as a very particular instance of the above problem. Before going into some details, let us fix notations. For a language $L \subseteq \Sigma^*$, we denote by $L \sqcup\!\sqcup \Sigma^*$ the shuffle of L and Σ^*, i.e. the language $\{u_1 v_1 u_2 v_2 \cdots u_n v_n \mid u_1 u_2 \cdots u_n \in L, v_i \in \Sigma^*\}$. The shuffle $L \sqcup\!\sqcup \Sigma^\omega$ for $L \subseteq \Sigma^* \cup \Sigma^\omega$ is defined analogously.

Formally, the or-matching problem for the semantics with gaps is equivalent to the question whether the intersection $[L \sqcup\!\sqcup \Sigma^\omega] \cap [K]$ is empty or not, for regular languages $L, K \subseteq \Sigma^\omega$. The crucial point now is that $[L \sqcup\!\sqcup \Sigma^\omega]$ has a very particular form. Suppose without loss of generality that $L = UV^\omega$, with $U, V \subseteq \Sigma^*$ regular languages such that every element of V has the same alphabet $A \subseteq \Sigma$. Then $UV^\omega \sqcup\!\sqcup \Sigma^\omega = (U \sqcup\!\sqcup \Sigma^*)\ \mathrm{Inf}(A)$, with $\mathrm{Inf}(A) = \{u \in \Sigma^\omega \mid |u|_a = \infty, \forall a \in A\}$. Moreover, $[UV^\omega \sqcup\!\sqcup \Sigma^\omega] = [(U \sqcup\!\sqcup \Sigma^*)]\ \mathrm{Inf}(A)$. But it is easy to check that $U \sqcup\!\sqcup \Sigma^*$ is a very simple regular language, a finite union of languages of the form $\Sigma^* a_1 \Sigma^* a_2 \Sigma^* \cdots a_k \Sigma^*$ for some letters $a_i \in \Sigma$. (This family of languages corresponds exactly to level '1/2' in the concatenation hierarchy of Straubing-Thérien [10]). Finally, $[\Sigma^* a_1 \Sigma^* a_2 \Sigma^* \cdots a_k \Sigma^*] = \bigcup_{a_{i_1} \cdots a_{i_k} \in [a_1 \cdots a_k]} \Sigma^* a_{i_1} \Sigma^* \cdots a_{i_k} \Sigma^*$.

6 Conclusion

In this paper we presented specification and verification methods for MSCs, which employ languages of *partially ordered executions*. We were interested in the problem of deciding whether there is an execution of the given MSC system that matches the specification. We considered three alternative semantics and showed that the matching problem under both the or-semantics and the and-semantics is NP-complete. Under a semantics which allows no gaps in the specification the matching problem becomes the intersection of two MSC graphs. We showed that this problem is undecidable. Some open directions for further research include extending the framework by allowing and/or-graphs and negation, expressing the finite occurrence of certain events, and obtaining complementable specification formalisms.

References

1. R. Alur, G. Holzmann, and D. Peled. An analyzer for message sequence charts. *Software Concepts and Tools*, 17(2):70–77, 1996.
2. H. Ben-Abdallah and S. Leue. Syntactic detection of process divergence and non-local choice in message sequence charts. In E. Brinksma, editor, *Proceedings of theTools and Algorithms for the Construction and Analysis of Systems, Third International Workshop, TACAS'97*, number 1217 in Lecture Notes in Computer Science, pages 259–274, Enschede, The Netherlands, 1997. Springer.
3. J. Berstel. *Transductions and context-free languages.* Teubner Studienbücher, Stuttgart, 1979.

4. M. Clerbout and M. Latteux. Partial commutations and faithful rational transductions. *Theoretical Computer Science*, 34:241–254, 1984.
5. V. Diekert and G. Rozenberg, editors. *The Book of Traces.* World Scientific, Singapore, 1995.
6. J. Feigenbaum, J. Kahn, and C. Lund. Complexity results for pomset languages. *SIAM Journal Disc. Math.*, 6(3):432–442, 1993.
7. ITU-T Recommendation Z.120, Message Sequence Chart (MSC), March 1993.
8. V. Levin and D. Peled. Verification of message sequence charts via template matching. In *TAPSOFT (FASE)'97, Theory and Practice of Software Development*, volume 1214 of *Lecture Notes in Computer Science*, pages 652–666, Lille, France, 1997. Springer.
9. M. Nielsen, G. Plotkin, and G. Winskel. Petri nets, event structures and domains, part 1. *Theoretical Computer Science*, 13:85–108, 1981.
10. J.-E. Pin. Syntactic semigroups. In G. Rozenberg and A. Salomaa, editors, *Handbook of Formal Languages*, volume 1, pages 679–738. Springer, Berlin-Heidelberg-New York, 1997.
11. V. R. Pratt. Modelling concurrency with partial orders. *International Journal of Parallel Programming*, 15(1):33–71, 1986.

The Church-Rosser Languages Are the Deterministic Variants of the Growing Context-Sensitive Languages

Gundula Niemann and **Friedrich Otto**

Fachbereich Mathematik/Informatik, Universität Kassel, D–34109 Kassel
e-mail: `<niemann,otto>@theory.informatik.uni-kassel.de`

Abstract. The growing context-sensitive languages have been classified through the shrinking two-pushdown automaton, the deterministic version of which characterizes the class of generalized Church-Rosser languages (Buntrock and Otto 1995). Exploiting this characterization we prove that this latter class coincides with the class of Church-Rosser languages that was introduced by McNaughton, Narendran, and Otto (1988). Based on this result several open problems of McNaughton et al can be answered.

1 Introduction

If R is a finite and length-reducing string-rewriting system on some finite alphabet Σ, then there exists a linear-time algorithm that, given a string $w \in \Sigma^*$ as input, computes an irreducible descendant w_0 of w with respect to the reduction relation $\rightarrow_R^*$ that is induced by R [2,3]. If, in addition, the system R is *confluent*, then the irreducible descendant w_0 is uniquely determined by w. Hence, in this situation two strings u and v are congruent modulo the Thue congruence $\leftrightarrow_R^*$ induced by R if and only if their respective irreducible descendants u_0 and v_0 coincide. Thus, the word problem for a finite, length-reducing, and confluent string-rewriting system is decidable in linear time.

Motivated by this result McNaughton, Narendran, and Otto [11] introduced the notion of a *Church-Rosser language.* A Church-Rosser language $L \subseteq \Sigma^*$ is given through a finite, length-reducing, and confluent string-rewriting system R on some alphabet Γ properly containing Σ, two irreducible strings $t_1, t_2 \in (\Gamma \setminus \Sigma)^*$, and an irreducible letter $Y \in \Gamma \setminus \Sigma$ satisfying the following condition for all strings $w \in \Sigma^*$: $w \in L$ if and only if $t_1 w t_2 \rightarrow_R^* Y$. Hence, the membership problem for a Church-Rosser language is decidable in linear time, and so the class CRL of Church-Rosser languages is contained in the class CSL of context-sensitive languages.

On the other hand, the class CRL contains the class DCFL of deterministic context-free languages, and it contains some languages that are not even context-free [11]. Hence, the class CRL can be seen as an extension of the class DCFL that preserves the linear-time decidability of the membership problem. As such it is certainly an interesting language class.

Accordingly, McNaughton et al established some closure properties for the class CRL, but it remained open whether the class CRL is closed under the operation of complementation. Accordingly, they introduced the class of *Church-Rosser decidable languages* CRDL, which still contains the class DCFL and which is closed under complementation. Also it remained open at the time whether or not every context-free language is a Church-Rosser language, although it was conjectured that the linear language $L_0 := \{ww^{\sim} | w \in \{a,b\}^*\}$ is not a Church-Rosser language. Here $w^{\sim}$ denotes the reversal of the string w.

After their introduction the Church-Rosser languages did not receive much attention until another, seemingly unrelated development had taken place. Dahlhaus and Warmuth [8] considered the class GCSL of *growing context-sensitive languages*. These languages are generated by context-sensitive grammars each production rule of which is strictly length-increasing. They proved that these languages have membership problems that are decidable in polynomial time. Although it might appear from the definition that GCSL is not an interesting class of languages, Buntrock and Loryś showed that GCSL is an *abstract family of languages* [5], that is, this class of languages is closed under union, concatenation, iteration, intersection with regular languages, ε-free homomorphisms, and inverse homomorphisms. Exploiting these closure properties Buntrock and Loryś characterized the class GCSL through various other classes of grammars that are less restricted [5,6].

Using these grammars Buntrock and Otto [7] obtained a characterization of the class GCSL by a nondeterministic machine model, the so-called *shrinking pushdown automaton with two pushdown stores* (sTPDA). The input for such a machine is provided as the initial contents of one of the pushdown stores, and it accepts either by final state or (equivalently) by empty pushdown stores. A positive weight is assigned to each tape symbol and each internal state symbol of the machine. By adding up the weights this gives a weight for each configuration. Now it is required that the weight of the actual configuration decreases with each step of the machine. It is with respect to these weights that the two-pushdown automaton is called *shrinking*.

Since the sTPDA is a nondeterministic device, it was only natural to consider the class of languages that are accepted by the deterministic variant of it. As it turned out the deterministic sTPDA accept exactly the so-called *generalized Church-Rosser languages*, which are obtained from the Church-Rosser languages by admitting finite, *weight-reducing*, and confluent string-rewriting systems in the definition [7]. Thus, the class GCRL of generalized Church-Rosser languages coincides with the class of 'deterministic growing context-sensitive languages.' In particular, it follows that this class is closed under complementation. Further, Buntrock and Otto concluded from this result that the language classes CFL and GCRL, and therewith the classes CFL and CRL, are indeed incomparable under set inclusion. Since CFL is contained in GCSL, it follows that GCRL is properly contained in the class GCSL, that is, we obtain the following chain of (proper) inclusions:

$$\mathsf{DCFL} \subset \mathsf{CRDL} \subseteq \mathsf{CRL} \subseteq \mathsf{GCRL} \subset \mathsf{GCSL} \subset \mathsf{CSL},$$

where it was left open whether or not the two inclusions CRDL $\subseteq$ CRL $\subseteq$ GCRL are proper.

Here we show that the three language classes CRDL, CRL, and GCRL coincide. Our proof makes use of the above-mentioned characterization of the generalized Church-Rosser languages through the deterministic sTPDA. We will prove that each language that is accepted by some deterministic sTPDA is actually a Church-Rosser decidable language. Hence, GCRL $\subseteq$ CRDL implying that the three classes above actually coincide. Hence, the class of Church-Rosser languages can be characterized as the class of deterministic growing context-sensitive languages.

It remains to determine the closure properties of this class of languages. The closure under the operation of taking the complement follows from the above characterization. Recently, Otto, Katsura, and Kobayashi [12] proved that the class of Church-Rosser languages is a basis for the recursively enumerable (r.e.) languages. Here, a class of languages $\mathbb{C}$ is called a *basis* for the r.e. languages, if, for each r.e. language $L \subseteq \Sigma^*$, there exists a language $C \in \mathbb{C}$ on some alphabet Γ strictly containing Σ such that $L = \pi_\Sigma(C)$, where π_Σ denotes the canonical projection from Γ^* onto Σ^*. It follows that the class CRL is not closed under morphisms.

This paper is organized as follows. In Section 2 we introduce the necessary notation regarding string-rewriting systems and restate the definitions of the various classes of Church-Rosser languages. In the next section we introduce the shrinking two-pushdown automaton and restate some results from Buntrock and Otto [7]. In addition we prove a technical result for this type of automaton. Then in Section 4 we prove the announced main result, and in the next section we summarize the known closure and non-closure properties of the class CRL. In the final section we review our results and draw some easy consequences.

2 The Church-Rosser Languages

Here we restate the main definitions and establish notation regarding the various classes of Church-Rosser languages. For additional information concerning the notions introduced the reader is asked to consult the literature, where [3] serves as our main reference concerning the theory of string-rewriting systems, and [10] is our main reference for formal language and automata theory.

Let Σ be a finite alphabet. Then Σ^* denotes the set of strings over Σ including the empty string ε, and $\Sigma^+ := \Sigma^* \setminus \{\varepsilon\}$. A function $\varphi\colon \Sigma \to \mathbb{N}_+$ is called a *weight-function*. Its extension to Σ^*, which we will also denote by φ, is defined inductively through $\varphi(\varepsilon) := 0$ and $\varphi(wa) := \varphi(w) + \varphi(a)$ for all $w \in \Sigma^*$ and $a \in \Sigma$. A particular weight-function is the *length-function* $|.|\colon \Sigma \to \mathbb{N}_+$, which assigns each letter the weight (length) 1.

A *string-rewriting system* R on Σ is a subset of $\Sigma^* \times \Sigma^*$. An element $(\ell, r) \in R$ is called a *rewrite rule* or simply a *rule*, and it will usually be written as $(\ell \to r)$. A string-rewriting system R induces several binary relations on Σ^*, the simplest of which is the *single-step reduction relation*

$$\rightarrow_R := \{(u\ell v, urv) \mid u, v \in \Sigma^*, (\ell \rightarrow r) \in R\}.$$

Its reflexive and transitive closure is the *reduction relation* $\rightarrow_R^*$ induced by R, and its reflexive, symmetric, and transitive closure $\leftrightarrow_R^*$ is the *Thue congruence* generated by R.

If $u \rightarrow_R^* v$, then u is an *ancestor* of v, and v is a *descendant* of u. If there is no $v \in \Sigma^*$ such that $u \rightarrow_R v$ holds, then the string u is called *irreducible* (mod R). By IRR(R) we denote the set of all irreducible strings. If R is finite, then IRR(R) is obviously a regular language.

The string-rewriting system R is called

- *length-reducing* if $|\ell| > |r|$ holds for each rule $(\ell \rightarrow r) \in R$,
- *weight-reducing* if there exists a weight-function φ such that $\varphi(\ell) > \varphi(r)$ holds for each rule $(\ell \rightarrow r) \in R$,
- *confluent* if, for all $u, v, w \in \Sigma^*$, $u \rightarrow_R^* v$ and $u \rightarrow_R^* w$ imply that v and w have a common descendant.

If a string-rewriting system R is weight-reducing, then it allows no infinite reduction sequence of the form $w_0 \rightarrow_R w_1 \rightarrow_R \ldots$; indeed, if $w_0 \rightarrow_R w_1 \rightarrow_R \ldots \rightarrow_R w_m$, then $m \leq \varphi(w_0)$. If, in addition, R is confluent, then each string $w \in \Sigma^*$ has a unique irreducible descendant $w_0 \in$ IRR(R). Actually, in this situation $u \leftrightarrow_R^* v$ if and only if $u_0 = v_0$. Since u_0 can be determined from u in linear time, this shows that the Thue congruence $\leftrightarrow_R^*$ is decidable in linear time for each finite, weight-reducing, and confluent string-rewriting system.

Definition 1.

(a) A language $L \subseteq \Sigma^*$ is a Church-Rosser language (CRL) *if there exist an alphabet $\Gamma \supsetneq \Sigma$, a finite, length-reducing, confluent string-rewriting system R on Γ, two strings $t_1, t_2 \in (\Gamma \setminus \Sigma)^* \cap$ IRR(R), and a letter $Y \in (\Gamma \setminus \Sigma) \cap$ IRR(R) such that, for all $w \in \Sigma^*$, $t_1 w t_2 \rightarrow_R^* Y$ if and only if $w \in L$.*
(b) A language $L \subseteq \Sigma^*$ is a Church-Rosser decidable language (CRDL) *if it is a Church-Rosser language, and there exists a letter $N \in (\Gamma \setminus \Sigma) \cap$ IRR(R) such that, for all $w \in \Sigma^*$, $t_1 w t_2 \rightarrow_R^* N$ if and only if $w \notin L$.*
(c) A language $L \subseteq \Sigma^*$ is a generalized Church-Rosser language (GCRL) *if there exist an alphabet $\Gamma \supsetneq \Sigma$, a finite, weight-reducing, confluent string-rewriting system R on Γ, two strings $t_1, t_2 \in (\Gamma \setminus \Sigma)^* \cap$ IRR(R) and a letter $Y \in (\Gamma \setminus \Sigma) \cap$ IRR(R) such that, for all $w \in \Sigma^*$, $t_1 w t_2 \rightarrow_R^* Y$ if and only if $w \in L$.*

Analogously to (b) the class of *generalized Church-Rosser decidable languages* could be defined, but the results of Buntrock and Otto [7] imply that this class coincides with the class GCRL of generalized Church-Rosser languages.

3 Shrinking Two-Pushdown Automata

In [7] Buntrock and Otto introduce the following type of automaton in order to characterize the class GCSL of growing context-sensitive languages.

Definition 2.

(a) *A* two-pushdown automaton (TPDA) *is a nondeterministic automaton with two pushdown stores. It is defined as a 7-tuple* $M = (Q, \Sigma, \Gamma, \delta, q_0, \bot, F)$, *where*
- Q *is the finite set of states,*
- Σ *is the finite input alphabet,*
- Γ *is the finite tape alphabet with* $\Gamma \supsetneq \Sigma$ *and* $\Gamma \cap Q = \emptyset$,
- $q_0 \in Q$ *is the initial state,*
- $\bot \in \Gamma \setminus \Sigma$ *is the bottom marker of pushdown stores,*
- $F \subseteq Q$ *is the set of final (or accepting) states, and*
- $\delta : Q \times \Gamma \times \Gamma \to 2^{Q \times \Gamma^* \times \Gamma^*}$ *is the transition relation, where* $\delta(q, a, b)$ *is a finite set for each triple* $(q, a, b) \in Q \times \Gamma \times \Gamma$.

M *is a* deterministic two-pushdown automaton (DTPDA), *if* δ *is a (partial) function from* $Q \times \Gamma \times \Gamma$ *into* $Q \times \Gamma^* \times \Gamma^*$.

(b) *A* configuration *of a* (D)TPDA M *is described as* uqv *with* $q \in Q$ *and* $u, v \in \Gamma^*$, *where* u *is the contents of the first pushdown store with the first letter of* u *at the bottom and the last letter of* u *at the top,* q *is the current state, and* v *is the contents of the second pushdown store with the last letter of* v *at the bottom and the first letter of* v *at the top.* M *induces a* computation relation $\vdash_M^*$ *on the set of configurations, which is the reflexive, transitive closure of the* single-step computation relation $\vdash_M$ *(see,e.g., [10]). For an input string* $w \in \Sigma^*$, *the corresponding* initial configuration *is* $\bot q_0 w \bot$. M *accepts by empty pushdown stores:*

$$N(M) := \{w \in \Sigma^* \mid \exists q \in Q : \bot q_0 w \bot \vdash_M^* q\}.$$

(c) *A* (D)TPDA M *is called* shrinking *if there exists a weight function* $\varphi : Q \cup \Gamma \to \mathbb{N}_+$ *such that, for all* $q \in Q$ *and* $a, b \in \Gamma$, *if* $(p, u, v) \in \delta(q, a, b)$, *then* $\varphi(upv) < \varphi(aqb)$. *By* sTPDA *and* sDTPDA *we denote the corresponding classes of shrinking automata.*

Thus, if M is a shrinking TPDA with weight-function φ, then $\varphi(u_1q_1v_1) > \varphi(u_2q_2v_2)$ holds for all configurations $u_1q_1v_1$ and $u_2q_2v_2$ of M that satisfiy $u_1q_1v_1 \vdash_M u_2q_2v_2$. Observe that the input is provided to a TPDA as the initial contents of its second pushdown store, and that in order to accept a TPDA is required to empty its pushdown stores. Thus, it is forced to consume the input completely. Using standard techniques from automata theory it can be shown that, for a (shrinking) (D)TPDA $M = (Q, \Sigma, \Gamma, \delta, q_0, \bot, F)$, we may require that the special symbol $\bot$ can only occur at the bottom of a pushdown store, and that no other symbol can occur at that place.

From the definition of the transition relation δ we see that M halts immediately whenever one of its pushdown stores is emptied. Because of the above property this happens if and only if a transition of the form $(q, a, \bot) \mapsto (q', \alpha, \varepsilon)$ or $(q, \bot, b) \mapsto (q', \varepsilon, \beta)$ is performed. Thus, we can assume without loss of generality that, if M does accept on input $w \in \Sigma^*$, then $\bot q_0 w \bot \vdash_M^* q$ for some $q \in F$, and if M does not accept on input $w \in \Sigma^*$, then $\bot q_0 w \bot \vdash_M^* \bot q$ for some $q \in F$, that is, even in this situation M empties its second pushdown store completely and only leaves the bottom marker on its first pushdown store before it halts. Hence, all the halting and accepting configurations of M are of the form q, where $q \in F$, and all the halting and rejecting configurations of M are of the form $\bot q$, where $q \in F$. In addition, we can assume that M only has a single halting state.

Buntrock and Otto established the following characterization for the classes of languages that are accepted by nondeterministic or deterministic shrinking TPDAs, respectively.

Proposition 3. [7]

(a) A language is accepted by some shrinking TPDA *if and only if it is growing context-sensitive.*

(b) A language is accepted by some shrinking DTPDA *if and only if it is a generalized Church-Rosser language.*

A detailed presentation of the class GCSL of growing context-sensitive languages can be found in Buntrock's Habilitationsschrift [4]. The above proposition shows that the generalized Church-Rosser languages can be interpreted as the deterministic variants of the growing context-sensitive languages.

We close this section with a technical lemma on shrinking TPDA that we will need in the next section to prove our main result.

Lemma 4. *Let M be a* TPDA *that is shrinking with respect to the weight-function φ. Then there exists a* TPDA *M' accepting the same language as M such that M' is deterministic, if M is, and M' is shrinking with respect to a weight-function ψ that satisfies the following condition:*

(*) Whenever $u_1q_1v_1$ and $u_2q_2v_2$ are configurations of M' such that $u_1q_1v_1 \vdash_{M'} u_2q_2v_2$, then $\psi(u_1q_1v_1) - \psi(u_2q_2v_2) = 1$.

Proof. Let $M = (Q, \Sigma, \Gamma, \delta, q_0, \bot, F)$ be a TPDA that is shrinking with respect to the weight-function $\varphi : Q \cup \Gamma \to \mathbb{N}_+$, that is, $\varphi(aqb) - \varphi(upv) > 0$ for all $q \in Q$, $a, b \in \Gamma$, and $(p, u, v) \in \delta(q, a, b)$. We construct a TPDA $M' := (Q', \Sigma, \Gamma, \delta', q_0, \bot, F)$ and a weight-function $\psi : Q' \cup \Gamma \to \mathbb{N}_+$ as follows.

First we number the instructions of M, that is, the lines in the table describing the transition relation δ, from 1 to m. For each $i \in \{1, \ldots, m\}$, let the i-th instruction of M be denoted as $(p_i, u_i, v_i) \in \delta(q_i, a_i, b_i)$, and let $\gamma_i := \varphi(a_iq_ib_i) - \varphi(u_ip_iv_i)$.

If $\gamma_i = 1$, then take $Q'_i := \emptyset$ and add the transition $(q_i, a_i, b_i) \rightarrow (p_i, u_i, v_i)$ to δ'. If $\gamma_i > 1$, then take $Q'_i := \{q_{i,1}, \ldots, q_{i,\gamma_i-1}\}$, where $q_{i,1}, \ldots, q_{i,\gamma_i-1}$ are $\gamma_i - 1$ new states, and add the following transitions to δ':

$$\begin{aligned}(q_i, a_i, b_i) &\rightarrow (q_{i,1}, a_i, b_i),\\ (q_{i,j}, a_i, b_i) &\rightarrow (q_{i,j+1}, a_i, b_i),\ j = 1, \ldots, \gamma_i - 2,\\ (q_{i,\gamma_i-1}, a_i, b_i) &\rightarrow (p_i, u_i, v_i).\end{aligned}$$

Finally, let $Q' := Q \cup \bigcup_{i=1}^{m} Q'_i$, let δ' consist of all the transitions introduced so far, and define a preliminary weight-function $\psi' : Q' \cup \Gamma \rightarrow \mathbb{Z}$ as follows:

$$\begin{aligned}\psi'(a) &:= \varphi(a) && \text{for all } a \in \Gamma,\\ \psi'(q_i) &:= \varphi(q_i) && \text{for all } q_i \in Q,\\ \psi'(q_{i,j}) &:= \varphi(q_i) - j && \text{for all } i \in \{1, \ldots, m\} \text{ and } j \in \{1, \ldots, \gamma_i - 1\}.\end{aligned}$$

It is easily verified that $\psi'(u_1q_1v_1) - \psi'(u_2q_2v_2) = 1$ holds for all configurations $u_1q_1v_1$ and $u_2q_2v_2$ of M' that satisfy $u_1q_1v_1 \vdash_{M'} u_2q_2v_2$. Unfortunately, ψ' may not be an acceptable weight-function, since $\psi'(q_{i,j})$ could be a negative number for some choices of i and j.

To correct this problem let $\mu := \min\{\psi'(p') \mid p' \in Q'\}$. If $\mu < 0$, then choose $\psi(q') := \psi'(q') + |\mu| + 1$ for all $q' \in Q'$, otherwise, let $\psi(q') := \psi'(q')$ for all $q' \in Q'$. Also choose $\psi(a) := \psi'(a)$ for all $a \in \Gamma$. Then $\psi : Q' \cup \Gamma \rightarrow \mathbb{N}_+$ is a weight-function such that $\psi(u_1q_1v_1) - \psi(u_2q_2v_2) = 1$ holds for all configurations $u_1q_1v_1$ and $u_2q_2v_2$ of M' that satisfy $u_1q_1v_1 \vdash_{M'} u_2q_2v_2$.

It is easily seen that $N(M') = N(M)$ and that M' is deterministic, if M is deterministic. □

Thus, in the following we can always assume that in each step of a sTPDA the weight of the actual configuration decreases by 1. Hence, if $u_1q_1v_1$ and $u_2q_2v_2$ are configurations of an sTPDA M with weight-function φ such that $u_1q_1v_1 \vdash_M^k u_2q_2v_2$ for some $k \in \mathbb{N}$, then $\varphi(u_1q_1v_1) - \varphi(u_2q_2v_2) = k$.

4 The Main Result

From the definitions we know that CRDL $\subseteq$ CRL $\subseteq$ GCRL holds. Here we prove that also GCRL $\subseteq$ CRDL holds, thus showing that the three classes actually coincide.

Theorem 5. GCRL $\subseteq$ CRDL.

Proof. Let $L \subseteq \Sigma^*$ be a generalized Church-Rosser language. By Proposition 3(b) there exist a DTPDA $M = (Q, \Sigma, \Gamma, \delta, q_0, \perp, F)$ and a weight-function φ such that $N(M) = L$, where M is shrinking with respect to φ. As observed in the previous section we can assume the following:

(i) Each non-halting configuration of M is of the form $\bot uqv\bot$ for some $u, v \in (\Gamma \setminus \{\bot\})^*$ and $q \in (Q \setminus F)$.
(ii) $F = \{q_f\}$, that is, M has a single halting state only.
(iii) The only accepting and halting configuration of M that is reachable from an initial configuration is the configuration q_f.
(iv) The only non-accepting and halting configuration of M that is reachable from an initial configuration is the configuration $\bot q_f$.
(v) If $u_1q_1v_1 \vdash_M u_2q_2v_2$, then $\varphi(u_1q_1v_1) - \varphi(u_2q_2v_2) = 1$ (Lemma 4).

Let # be a new symbol. We define a morphism $h : (\Gamma \cup Q)^* \to (\Gamma \cup Q \cup \{\#\})^*$ by taking $h(a) := a\#^{\varphi(a)-1}$ for all $a \in \Gamma \cup Q$. Then $|h(w)| = \varphi(w)$ for all $w \in (\Gamma \cup Q)^*$, and $h(\Gamma \cup Q) \subseteq (\Gamma \cup Q \cup \{\#\})^+$ is a prefix code. Thus, the morphism $h : (\Gamma \cup Q)^* \to (\Gamma \cup Q \cup \{\#\})^*$ is an injective mapping. Further, let $\mu := \max\{\varphi(a) \mid a \in \Gamma \cup Q\}$ denote the maximal weight of any letter from $\Gamma \cup Q$.

In order to show that the language L is actually Church-Rosser decidable, we now construct a finite, length-reducing, and confluent string-rewriting system R on some finite alphabet $\Delta \supsetneq \Sigma$ that will witness this fact. Essentially R will simulate the computations of the sDTPDA M. However, this cannot be a straightforward simulation, since R is length-reducing, while M is shrinking only with respect to the weight-function φ. Therefore we would like to replace a configuration $\bot uqv\bot$ of M by the string $h(\bot uqv\bot)$. Since this replacement increases the length of the string considered, we need to compress the resulting string by combining several letters into a single new letter. This, however, creates another problem. If $\bot u_1q_1v_1\bot \vdash_M \bot u_2q_2v_2\bot$, then by (v) $|h(\bot u_1q_1v_1\bot)| - 1 = |h(\bot u_2q_2v_2)|$, but for the compressed forms of the strings $h(\bot u_1q_1v_1\bot)$ and $h(\bot u_2q_2v_2\bot)$ the length might be the same. To overcome this problem we choose the fixed rate of compression 2μ, and simulate 2μ steps of M through a single application of a rule of R. If $\bot u_1q_1v_1\bot \vdash_M^{2\mu} \bot u_2q_2v_2\bot$, then $|h(\bot u_1q_1v_1\bot)| - 2\mu = |h(\bot u_2q_2v_2\bot)|$, and hence, if γ_1 and γ_2 are the compressed forms of $h(\bot u_1q_1u_1\bot)$ and $h(\bot u_2q_2v_2\bot)$, respectively, then $|\gamma_1| - 1 = \frac{|h(\bot u_1q_1v_1\bot)|-2\mu}{2\mu} = \frac{|h(\bot u_2q_2v_2\bot)|}{2\mu} = |\gamma_2|$.

To perform this construction we first determine the alphabet Δ. Let $\overline{\Gamma} \cup \{\overline{\#}\}$ be a new alphabet that is in 1-to-1 correspondence to $\Gamma \cup \{\#\}$, and let $\overline{} : \Gamma \cup \{\#\} \to \overline{\Gamma} \cup \{\overline{\#}\}$ denote this correspondence. Further, define four new alphabets as follows:

$$\begin{aligned}
A_{\leq} &:= \{a_w \mid w \in (\Gamma \cup \{\#\})^* \text{ and } 1 \leq |w| \leq \mu\},\\
A &:= \{a_w \mid w \in (\Gamma \cup \{\#\})^* \text{ and } |w| = 2\mu\},\\
\overline{A} &:= \{a_{\overline{w}} \mid \overline{w} \in (\overline{\Gamma} \cup \{\overline{\#}\})^* \text{ and } |\overline{w}| = 2\mu\}, \text{ and}\\
A_Q &:= \{a_{\overline{u}qv} \mid \overline{u} \in (\overline{\Gamma} \cup \{\overline{\#}\})^*, q \in Q,\ v \in (\Gamma \cup \{\#\})^* \text{ and } |\overline{u}qv| = 2\mu\}.
\end{aligned}$$

Thus, each letter $a_w \in A_{\leq} \cup A \cup \overline{A} \cup A_Q$ represents a string w of length at most 2μ. Finally, we take $\Delta := \Sigma \cup \{q_0, \overline{\bot}, \bot, Y, N\} \cup A_{\leq} \cup A \cup \overline{A} \cup A_Q$, where we assume that all the subalphabets displayed are pairwise disjoint.

To simplify the following considerations we define a morphism

$$\pi : (A_{\leq} \cup A \cup \overline{A} \cup A_Q)^* \to (\Gamma \cup Q \cup \{\#\})^*$$

through the following mapping:

$$a \mapsto \begin{cases} w, & \text{if } a = a_w \quad \in A_{\leq} \cup A, \\ w, & \text{if } a = a_{\overline{w}} \quad \in \overline{A}, \\ uqv, & \text{if } a = a_{\overline{u}qv} \in A_Q. \end{cases}$$

Thus, π replaces each letter $a \in A_{\leq} \cup A \cup \overline{A} \cup A_Q$ by the string it represents, where in addition each factor $\overline{u} \in (\overline{\Gamma} \cup \{\overline{\#}\})^+$ is replaced by the corresponding string $u \in (\Gamma \cup \{\#\})^+$.

The string-rewriting system R will consist of four subsystems R_0, R_1, R_2, and R_3.

(0) The subsystem R_0 is used to take care of those inputs $w \in \Sigma^*$ for the sDTPDA M that are short:

$$\begin{aligned} R_0 := & \{\overline{\bot}q_0 w\bot \to Y \mid w \in \Sigma^*,\ \varphi(w\bot) \leq 4\mu, \text{ and } w \in L\} \\ & \cup \{\overline{\bot}q_0 w\bot \to N \mid w \in \Sigma^*,\ \varphi(w\bot) \leq 4\mu, \text{ and } w \notin L\}. \end{aligned}$$

Obviously, R_0 is a finite system containing only length-reducing rules, and there are no non-trivial overlaps between the left-hand sides of the rules of R_0.

(1) The subsystem R_1 transforms the description $\overline{\bot}q_0 w\bot$ of an initial configuration $\bot q_0 w\bot$ of M into a compressed form $c \in \overline{A}^* \cdot A_Q \cdot A^*$, if w is sufficiently long. It consists of three parts.

(1.1) $R_{1,1} := \{w\bot \to \alpha'\alpha_1\alpha_2 \mid w = av \in \Sigma^*$ for some $a \in \Sigma$ such that $\varphi(v\bot) \leq 4\mu < \varphi(w\bot) \leq 5\mu$, $\alpha' \in A_{\leq}$, and $\alpha_1, \alpha_2 \in A$ satisfying $\pi(\alpha'\alpha_1\alpha_2) = h(w\bot)\}$.

Since $4\mu < \varphi(w\bot) \leq (|w| + 1) \cdot \mu$, we see that $|w| > 3$. Hence, $R_{1,1}$ is a finite system of length-reducing rules. The given weight restrictions for $w\bot$ imply that the left-hand side of no rule of $R_{1,1}$ is a proper suffix of the left-hand side of any other rule of $R_{1,1}$. Further, the right-hand side $\alpha'\alpha_1\alpha_2$ of a rule of $R_{1,1}$ is uniquely determined by the left-hand side, since the morphism h is injective. Hence, there are no non-trivial overlaps between the left-hand sides of the rules of $R_{1,1}$.

(1.2) $R_{1,2} := \{w\alpha'_1 \to \alpha'_2\alpha \mid w = av \in \Sigma^*$ for some $a \in \Sigma, \alpha'_1, \alpha'_2 \in A_{\leq}$, and $\alpha \in A$ such that $|h(v)\pi(\alpha'_1)| \leq 2\mu < |h(w)\pi(\alpha'_1)| \leq 3\mu$ and $\pi(\alpha'_2\alpha) = h(w)\pi(\alpha'_1)\}$.

Since $|\pi(\alpha'_1)| \leq \mu$, $2\mu < |h(w)\pi(\alpha'_1)| = \varphi(w) + |\pi(\alpha'_1)|$ implies that $\varphi(w) > \mu$, which in turn yields $|w| \geq 2$. Hence, $R_{1,2}$ is a finite system containing only length-reducing rules. As above it follows that there are no non-trivial overlaps between the left-hand sides of the rules of $R_{1,2}$.

(1.3) Working from right to left the rules of the subsystems $R_{1,1}$ and $R_{1,2}$ replace suffixes $v\bot$ of $\overline{\bot}q_0 w\bot$ by the compressed form $c \in A_{\leq} \cdot A^*$ of $h(v\bot)$. The subsystem $R_{1,3}$ will be used to replace the remaining prefix $\overline{\bot}q_0 u$ such that the resulting string belongs to $\overline{A}^* \cdot A_Q \cdot A^*$, that is, it is the compressed form of a string $x \in (\Gamma \cup Q)^*$ satisfying $|h(x)| \equiv 0 \bmod 2\mu$. Unfortunately, the initial configuration $\bot q_0 w \bot$ may not satisfy this requirement. Therefore, if $|h(\bot q_0 w \bot)| \equiv r \bmod 2\mu$ for some $r \in \{1, \ldots, 2\mu - 1\}$, then instead of compressing this initial configuration, we compress the configuration $\bot uqv\bot$ that is obtained from $\bot q_0 w \bot$ after r steps of M. Then $|h(\bot uqv\bot)| = |h(\bot q_0 w\bot)| - r \equiv 0 \bmod 2\mu$, and hence, $h(\bot uqv\bot)$ can be encoded through a string $c \in \overline{A}^* \cdot A_Q \cdot A^*$ such that $\pi(c) = h(\bot uqv\bot)$.

In each step the sDTPDA M can remove at most one symbol from the top of its second pushdown store. Thus, the first $2\mu - 1$ steps of the computation of M on input w depend only on the prefix u of w of length $2\mu - 1$. Hence, the rules of $R_{1,3}$ will encode all computations of M of this form.

$$
\begin{aligned}
R_{1,3} := \{ & \overline{\bot} q_0 w \alpha' \alpha_1 \cdots \alpha_n \to \beta_1 \cdots \beta_m \mid w \in \Sigma^*, \alpha' \in A_{\leq}, \alpha_1, \ldots, \alpha_n \in A \\
& \text{such that } |h(w)\pi(\alpha')| \leq 2\mu, 2 \leq n \leq \mu, \text{ where } n < \mu \\
& \text{implies that } \pi(\alpha'\alpha_1 \cdots \alpha_n) \in ((\Gamma \setminus \{\bot\}) \cup \{\#\})^* \cdot h(\bot), \\
& \text{and } \beta_1, \ldots, \beta_m \in \overline{A} \cup A_Q \cup A \text{ satisfy the following conditions:} \\
& \text{(i) } \beta_1 \cdots \beta_m \in \overline{A}^* \cdot A_Q \cdot A^*, \\
& \text{(ii) } h(w)\pi(\alpha'\alpha_1 \cdots \alpha_n) = h(v)x \text{ for some } v \in (\Gamma \setminus \{\bot\})^* \cdot \{\bot, \varepsilon\} \\
& \quad \text{and } x \in (\Gamma \cup \{\#\})^* \text{ satisfying } |x| < \mu, \text{ and} \\
& \text{(iii) } \pi(\beta_1 \cdots \beta_m) = h(u_1 q_1 v_1)x \text{ for some } u_1, v_1 \in \Gamma^* \text{ and } q_1 \in Q \\
& \quad \text{such that } \bot q_0 v \vdash_M^r u_1 q_1 v_1, \text{ where } r \in \{0, 1, \ldots, 2\mu - 1\} \\
& \quad \text{satisfies } |h(\bot q_0 w)\pi(\alpha')| \equiv r \bmod 2\mu \}.
\end{aligned}
$$

If $(\overline{\bot} q_0 w \alpha' \alpha_1 \cdots \alpha_n \to \beta_1 \cdots \beta_m) \in R_{1,3}$, then $m \in \{n, n+1, n+2\}$. Hence, $R_{1,3}$ is a finite system of length-reducing rules. It can easily be checked that there are no non-trivial overlaps between the left-hand sides of the rules of $R_{1,3}$.

The subsystem R_1 is now taken as $R_1 := R_{1,1} \cup R_{1,2} \cup R_{1,3}$. From the definitions given it follows immediately that there are no non-trivial overlaps between the left-hand sides of the rules of R_1.

(2) The subsystem R_2 simulates the computations of the sDTPDA M on strings that represent compressed forms of configurations. Each application of a rule of R_2 simulates 2μ steps of M.

$$
\begin{aligned}
R_2 := \{ & \alpha_1 \cdots \alpha_n \gamma \alpha_{n+1} \cdots \alpha_{n+m} \to \beta_1 \cdots \beta_{n+m} \mid \alpha_1, \ldots, \alpha_n \in \overline{A}, \gamma \in A_Q, \\
& \alpha_{n+1}, \ldots, \alpha_{n+m} \in A \text{ such that } n, m \leq \mu + 1, \text{ where} \\
& 1 \leq n \leq \mu \text{ implies that } \pi(\alpha_1) \text{ has prefix } h(\bot), \\
& n = 0 \qquad \text{implies that } \pi(\gamma) \text{ has prefix } h(\bot) \text{ and } m \geq 2, \\
& 1 \leq m \leq \mu \text{ implies that } \pi(\alpha_{n+m}) \text{ has suffix } h(\bot), \text{ and} \\
& m = 0 \qquad \text{implies that } \pi(\gamma) \text{ has suffix } h(\bot) \text{ and } n \geq 2, \\
& \beta_1, \ldots, \beta_{n+m} \in \overline{A} \cup A_Q \cup A \text{ such that } \beta_1 \cdots \beta_{n+m} \in \overline{A}^* \cdot A_Q \cdot A^*, \\
& \pi(\alpha_1 \cdots \alpha_n \gamma \alpha_{n+1} \cdots \alpha_{n+m}) = x_1 h(uqv) x_2 \text{ for some } u, v \in \Gamma^*, q \in Q, \\
& x_1 \in \{\#\}^*, x_2 \in \Gamma \cdot \{\#\}^*, |x_1|, |x_2| < \mu, x_2 \notin h(\Gamma), \\
& \text{and } \pi(\beta_1 \cdots \beta_{n+m}) = x_1 h(u_1 q_1 v_1) x_2 \text{ for some } u_1, v_1 \in \Gamma^*, q_1 \in Q, \\
& \text{such that } uqv \text{ and } u_1 q_1 v_1 \text{ are valid subconfigurations of } M \\
& \text{satisfying } uqv \vdash_M^{2\mu} u_1 q_1 v_1 \}.
\end{aligned}
$$

The conditions on the integers n and m imply that $n+m \geq 2$. Further, all rules of R_2 are obviously length-reducing. Since uqv and $u_1q_1v_1$ must be valid subconfigurations of M, $\perp$ can occur at most as the first and/or the last letter. Hence, the left-hand side of no rule of R_2 is contained in the left-hand side of another rule of R_2. Finally, the right-hand side of a rule of R_2 is uniquely determined by its left-hand side. Thus, there are no non-trivial overlaps between the left-hand side of the rules of R_2.

(3) The subsystem R_3 ends the simulation of computations of M.

$$\begin{aligned} R_3 := & \{\alpha_1\alpha_2 \to Y \mid \alpha_1,\alpha_2 \in \overline{A} \cup A_Q \cup A,\ \alpha_1\alpha_2 \in \overline{A}^* \cdot A_Q \cdot A^*,\ \pi(\alpha_1\alpha_2) = \\ & \quad h(\perp uqv\perp) \text{ for some } u,v \in \Gamma^* \text{ and } q \in Q, \text{ and } \perp uqv\perp \vdash_M^* q_f\} \\ \cup & \{\alpha_1\alpha_2 \to N \mid \alpha_1,\alpha_2 \in \overline{A} \cup A_Q \cup A,\ \alpha_1\alpha_2 \in \overline{A}^* \cdot A_Q \cdot A^*,\ \pi(\alpha_1\alpha_2) = \\ & \quad h(\perp uqv\perp) \text{ for some } u,v \in \Gamma^* \text{ and } q \in Q, \text{ and } \perp uqv\perp \vdash_M^* \perp q_f\}. \end{aligned}$$

Obviously, R_3 is a finite length-reducing system, and there are no non-trivial overlaps between the left-hand side of the rules of R_3.

Finally, we take $R := R_0 \cup R_1 \cup R_2 \cup R_3$. Then R is indeed a finite string-rewriting system that contains length-reducing rules only. It is easily verified that there are no non-trivial overlaps between the left-hand sides of the rules of R. Hence, we see that R is also confluent.

It remains to prove the following statements for all $w \in \Sigma^*$:

(i) If $w \in L$, then $\overline{\perp}q_0w\perp \to_R^* Y$.
(ii) If $w \notin L$, then $\overline{\perp}q_0w\perp \to_R^* N$.

These statements show that the system R, together with the strings $t_1 := \overline{\perp}q_0$ and $t_2 := \perp$ and the letters Y and N, witnesses the fact that L is a Church-Rosser decidable language. The proof of the statements above will be divided into several claims and their proofs. The first one follows immediately from the choice of the subsystem R_0.

Claim 1. For all $w \in \Sigma^*$ satisfying $\varphi(w) \leq 4\mu - \varphi(\perp)$ the statements (i) and (ii) hold.

Hence, for the following considerations we can assume that the string $w \in \Sigma^*$ satisfies $\varphi(w) > 4\mu - \varphi(\perp)$, that is, $\varphi(w\perp) > 4\mu$.

Claim 2. Let $w \in \Sigma^*$ such that $\varphi(w\perp) > 4\mu$, and let $r \in \{0,1,\ldots,2\mu-1\}$ such that $\varphi(\perp q_0w\perp) = k \cdot 2\mu + r$ for some $k \in \mathbb{N}$. Then there exist $\alpha_1,\ldots,\alpha_k \in \overline{A} \cup A_Q \cup A$ satisfying the following conditions:

(i) $\alpha_1\alpha_2\cdots\alpha_k \in \overline{A}^* \cdot A_Q \cdot A^*$,
(ii) $\pi(\alpha_1\cdots\alpha_k) = h(\perp uqv\perp)$ for some configuration $\perp uqv\perp$ of M, where $\perp q_0w\perp \vdash_M^\tau \perp uqv\perp$, and
(iii) $\overline{\perp}q_0w\perp \to_{R_1}^* \alpha_1\cdots\alpha_k$.

Proof. Let $w \in \Sigma^*$ satisfy $\varphi(w\perp) > 4\mu$, and let $k \in \mathbb{N}$ and $r \in \{0,1,\ldots,2\mu-1\}$ such that $\varphi(\perp q_0w\perp) = k \cdot 2\mu + r > 4\mu$. The computation of M starting from the initial configuration $\bot q_0 w \bot$ either ends with the accepting configuration q_f of weight $\varphi(q_f) \leq \mu$ or with the non-accepting configuration $\bot q_f$ of weight $\varphi(\bot q_f) \leq 2\mu$. Hence, this computation consists of more than 2μ steps. Thus, there is a (uniquely determined) configuration $\bot uqv\bot$ of M such that $\bot q_0 w\bot \vdash_M^r \bot uqv\bot$. Since $\varphi(\bot uqv\bot) = \varphi(\bot q_0 w\bot) - r = k \cdot 2\mu$, there exist $\alpha_1, \ldots, \alpha_k \in \overline{A} \cup A_Q \cup A$ such that $\alpha_1\alpha_2 \cdots \alpha_k \in \overline{A}^* \cdot A_Q \cdot A^*$ and $\pi(\alpha_1 \cdots \alpha_k) = h(\bot uqv\bot)$. It follows easily from the definition of the rules of the system R_1 that $\overline{\bot} q_0 w \bot \rightarrow_{R_{1,1}} w_1 \rightarrow^*_{R_{1,2}} w_2 \rightarrow_{R_{1,3}} \alpha_1\alpha_2 \cdots \alpha_k$ holds for some strings w_1 and w_2. □

Claim 3. Let $\bot uqv\bot$ be a configuration of M such that $\varphi(\bot uqv\bot) = s \cdot 2\mu$ for some $s \geq 3$, and let $\alpha_1, \ldots, \alpha_s \in \overline{A} \cup A_Q \cup A$ such that $\alpha_1 \cdots \alpha_s \in \overline{A}^* \cdot A_Q \cdot A^*$ and $\pi(\alpha_1 \cdots \alpha_s) = h(\bot uqv\bot)$. If $\bot uqv\bot$ is reachable from an initial configuration, then there exist a configuration $\bot u_1 q_1 v_1 \bot$ of M and letters $\beta_1, \ldots, \beta_{s-1} \in \overline{A} \cup A_Q \cup A$ such that the following conditions are satisfied:

(i) $\beta_1\beta_2 \cdots \beta_{s-1} \in \overline{A}^* \cdot A_Q \cdot A^*$,
(ii) $\pi(\beta_1\beta_2 \cdots \beta_{s-1}) = h(\bot u_1 q_1 v_1 \bot)$,
(iii) $\bot uqv\bot \vdash_M^{2\mu} \bot u_1 q_1 v_1 \bot$, and
(iv) $\alpha_1\alpha_2 \cdots \alpha_s \rightarrow_{R_2} \beta_1\beta_2 \cdots \beta_{s-1}$.

Proof. Let $\bot uqv\bot$ be a configuration of M such that $\varphi(\bot uqv\bot) = s \cdot 2\mu$ for some $s \geq 3$. If $\bot uqv\bot$ is reachable from some initial configuration, that is, $\bot q_0 w\bot \vdash_M^* \bot uqv\bot$ for some $w \in \Sigma^*$, then $\bot uqv\bot \vdash_M^* q_f$ or $\bot uqv\bot \vdash_M^* \bot q_f$, depending on whether $w \in L$ or $w \notin L$, respectively. Since the weight of the actual configuration decreases by 1 in each step, we see that there exists a unique configuration $\bot u_1 q_1 v_1 \bot$ such that $\bot uqv\bot \vdash_M^{2\mu} \bot u_1 q_1 v_1 \bot$ and $\varphi(\bot u_1 q_1 v_1 \bot) = \varphi(\bot uqv\bot) - 2\mu = (s-1) \cdot 2\mu$. Hence, there exist (uniquely determined) $\beta_1, \beta_2, \ldots, \beta_{s-1} \in \overline{A} \cup A_Q \cup A$ satisfying $\beta_1\beta_2 \cdots \beta_{s-1} \in \overline{A}^* \cdot A_Q \cdot A^*$ and $\pi(\beta_1\beta_2 \cdots \beta_{s-1}) = h(\bot u_1 q_1 v_1 \bot)$.

During the computation $\bot uqv\bot \vdash_M^{2\mu} \bot u_1 q_1 v_1 \bot$ a suffix u' of u and a prefix v' of v are involved that satisfy $|u'|, |v'| \leq 2\mu$. Hence, this computation can be described completely by using a window of length $2\mu + 1 + 2\mu = 4\mu + 1$ that is placed on $\bot uqv\bot$ in such a way that the state symbol q appears in the middle. The corresponding section of $h(\bot uqv\bot)$ is contained in a substring $\alpha'_1 \cdots \alpha'_n \gamma' \alpha'_{n+1} \cdots \alpha'_{n+m} \in \overline{A}^* \cdot A_Q \cdot A^*$ of $\alpha_1\alpha_2 \cdots \alpha_s$ satisfying $n, m \leq \mu + 1$. From the definition of the subsystem R_2 we see that each rule of R_2 just simulates 2μ steps of M on a substring of this form. Hence, it follows that $\alpha_1\alpha_2 \cdots \alpha_s \rightarrow_{R_2} \beta_1\beta_2 \cdots \beta_{s-1}$ holds. □

Claim 4. Let $\bot uqv\bot$ be a configuration of M such that $\varphi(\bot uqv\bot) = 4\mu$, and let $\alpha_1, \alpha_2 \in \overline{A} \cup A_Q \cup A$ such that $\alpha_1\alpha_2 \in \overline{A}^* \cdot A_Q \cdot A^*$ and $\pi(\alpha_1\alpha_2) = h(\bot uqv\bot)$. If $\bot uqv\bot$ is reachable from an initial configuration, then either $\alpha_1\alpha_2 \rightarrow_{R_3} Y$ or $\alpha_1\alpha_2 \rightarrow_{R_3} N$.

Proof. Let $\bot uqv\bot$ be a configuration of M such that $\varphi(\bot uqv\bot) = 4\mu$, and let $\alpha_1, \alpha_2 \in \overline{A} \cup A_Q \cup A$ such that $\alpha_1\alpha_2 \in \overline{A}^* \cdot A_Q \cdot A^*$ and $\pi(\alpha_1\alpha_2) = h(\bot uqv\bot)$. If $\bot uqv\bot$ is reachable from some initial configuration, then $\bot q_0 w\bot \vdash_M^* \bot uqv\bot$ for some $w \in \Sigma^*$. If $w \in L$, then $\bot uqv\bot \vdash_M^* q_f$, and if $w \notin L$, then $\bot uqv\bot \vdash_M^* \bot q_f$. Thus, either $(\alpha_1\alpha_2 \to Y) \in R_3$ or $(\alpha_1\alpha_2 \to N) \in R_3$. □

We now verify that R does indeed witness the fact that L is a Church-Rosser decidable language. Let $w \in \Sigma^*$. If $\varphi(w) \leq 4\mu - \varphi(\bot)$, then we see from Claim 1 that $\overline{\bot} q_0 w\bot \to_R Y$ if $w \in L$, and $\overline{\bot} q_0 w\bot \to_R N$, if $w \notin L$. Assume therefore that $\varphi(w) > 4\mu - \varphi(\bot)$. Then by Claim 2 there exist a configuration $\bot u_1 q_1 v_1 \bot$ of M and $\alpha_1, \alpha_2, \ldots, \alpha_k \in \overline{A} \cup A_Q \cup A$ such that

(i) $\alpha_1\alpha_2 \cdots \alpha_k \in \overline{A}^* \cdot A_Q \cdot A^*$,
(ii) $\pi(\alpha_1\alpha_2 \cdots \alpha_k) = h(\bot u_1 q_1 v_1 \bot)$,
(iii) $\bot q_0 w\bot \vdash_M^* \bot u_1 q_1 v_1 \bot$, and
(iv) $\overline{\bot} q_0 w\bot \to_R^* \alpha_1 \cdots \alpha_k$.

If $k > 2$, then Claim 3 applies. Hence, there are configurations $\bot u_i q_i v_i \bot$ of M and strings $\delta_i \in \overline{A}^* \cdot A_Q \cdot A^*$, $i = 2, \ldots, k-1$, such that $\bot u_{i-1} q_{i-1} v_{i-1} \bot \vdash_M^{2\mu} \bot u_i q_i v_i \bot$, $\pi(\delta_i) = h(\bot u_i q_i v_i \bot)$, $\alpha_1 \cdots \alpha_k \to_R \delta_2 \to_R \ldots \to_R \delta_{k-1}$, and $|\delta_i| = k - i + 1$ for all $i = 2, \ldots, k-1$. Finally, $|\delta_{k-1}| = 2$ implies that $\delta_{k-1} \to_R Y$ or $\delta_{k-1} \to_R N$ by Claim 4. From the definition of R_3 we see that the former is the case if and only if $w \in L$. Thus, for $w \in L$, we have $\overline{\bot} q_0 w\bot \to_R^* \alpha_1 \cdots \alpha_k \to_R \ldots \to_R \delta_{k-1} \to_R Y$, and for $w \notin L$, we have $\overline{\bot} q_0 w\bot \to_R^* \alpha_1 \cdots \alpha_k \to_R \ldots \to_R \delta_{k-1} \to_R N$. This completes the proof of Theorem 5. □

From Theorem 5 we obtain our main result.

Corollary 6. *The three language classes* CRDL, CRL, *and* GCRL *coincide.*

Thus, the Church-Rosser languages are indeed the deterministic variants of the growing context-sensitive languages.

5 Closure Properties

In this section we summarize the known closure and non-closure properties of the class CRL and we prove two new non-closure properties, which, however, were already announced by Buntrock and Otto [7].

From the definition of the class CRDL we immediately obtain the following result.

Proposition 7. *The class of Church-Rosser languages is closed under complementation, that is, if $L \subseteq \Sigma^*$ is a Church-Rosser language, then so is the language $\overline{L} := \Sigma^* \setminus L$.*

From the characterization of the class GCRL through the shrinking DTPDA we can conclude the following closure properties.

Proposition 8.

(a) The class CRL *is closed under intersection with regular languages, that is, if* $L \in \mathsf{CRL}$ *and* L_1 *is a regular language, then* $L \cap L_1 \in \mathsf{CRL}$.
(b) The class CRL *is closed under inverse morphisms, that is, if* $L \subseteq \Sigma^*$ *is in* CRL *and* $h : \Delta^* \to \Sigma^*$ *is a morphism, then* $h^{-1}(L) \in \mathsf{CRL}$.

Finally, from [11] we recall the following closure properties.

Proposition 9.

(a) CRL *is closed under reversal, that is, if* L *is a Church-Rosser language, then so is the language* $L^{\sim} := \{w^{\sim} \mid w \in L\}$.
(b) CRL *is closed under left quotient and right quotient with a single string, that is, if* $L \subseteq \Sigma^*$ *is a Church-Rosser language and* $z \in \Sigma^*$, *then* $L/\{z\} = \{w \in \Sigma^* \mid wz \in L\}$ *and* $\{z\} \setminus L := \{w \in \Sigma^* \mid zw \in L\}$ *are Church-Rosser languages, too.*

In [12] it is shown that the class CRL is a basis for the recursively enumerable languages. Further, it is shown by Buntrock in [4] that the closure of the class GCRL (= CRL) under ε-free morphisms yields the class GCSL. Hence, we obtain the following non-closure properties.

Proposition 10. *The class* CRL *is neither closed under projections nor under* ε*-free morphisms.*

The Gladkij language $L_{\mathrm{Gl}} := \{w¢w^{\sim}¢w \mid w \in \{a,b\}^*\}$ is a context-sensitive language that is not growing context-sensitive [9,1,7]. Now L_{Gl} can be written as $L_{\mathrm{Gl}} = L_1 \cap L_2$, where $L_1 := \{w¢w^{\sim}¢z \mid w,z \in \{a,b\}^*\}$ and $L_2 := \{w¢z¢z^{\sim} \mid w,z \in \{a,b\}^*\}$. Obviously, L_1 and L_2 are both deterministic context-free, and hence, they are both Church-Rosser languages. Since $L_1 \cap L_2 \notin \mathsf{GCSL}$, we have $L_1 \cap L_2 \notin \mathsf{CRL}$. This shows the following.

Proposition 11. *The class* CRL *is neither closed under intersection nor under union.*

6 Conclusion

We have shown that the three language classes CRDL and CRL of [11] and GCRL of [7] coincide. Because of the characterization of the latter class through the deterministic variant of the shrinking TPDA [7] this class of languages can be considered as the class of 'deterministic growing context-sensitive languages'. Based on these characterizations we have obtained some closure properties and some non-closure properties for the class of Church-Rosser languages. However, many questions regarding closure and non-closure properties remain open. Also it remains the question of whether or not the language $L_0 := \{ww^{\sim} \mid w \in \{a,b\}^*\}$ is a Church-Rosser language.

Finally, based on the fact that the classes CFL and CRL are incomparable under set inclusion, we obtain the following undecidability result from McNaughton et al [11].

Proposition 12.

(a) The emptiness and the finiteness problems for Church-Rosser languages are undecidable in general.
(b) It is undecidable in general whether a given context-free language is a Church-Rosser language.
(c) It is undecidable in general whether a given Church-Rosser language is context-free.

References

1. R.V. Book. *Grammars with Time Functions.* PhD thesis, Harvard University, Cambridge, Massachusetts, February 1969.
2. R.V. Book. Confluent and other types of Thue systems. *J. Association Computing Machinery*, 29:171–182, 1982.
3. R.V. Book and F. Otto. *String-Rewriting Systems.* Springer-Verlag, New York, 1993.
4. G. Buntrock. *Wachsende kontext-sensitive Sprachen.* Habilitationsschrift, Fakultät für Mathematik und Informatik, Universität Würzburg, July 1996.
5. G. Buntrock and K. Loryś. On growing context-sensitive languages. In W. Kuich, editor, *Proc. of 19th ICALP*, Lecture Notes in Computer Science 623, pages 77–88. Springer-Verlag, Berlin, 1992.
6. G. Buntrock and K. Loryś. The variable membership problem: Succinctness versus complexity. In P. Enjalbert, E.W. Mayr, and K.W. Wagner, editors, *Proc. of 11th STACS*, Lecture Notes in Computer Science 775, pages 595–606. Springer-Verlag, Berlin, 1994.
7. G. Buntrock and F. Otto. Growing context-sensitive languages and Church-Rosser languages. In E.W. Mayr and C. Puech, editors, *Proc. of 12th STACS*, Lecture Notes in Computer Science 900, pages 313–324. Springer-Verlag, Berlin, 1995.
8. E. Dahlhaus and M. Warmuth. Membership for growing context-sensitive grammars is polynomial. *J. Computer System Sciences*, 33:456–472, 1986.
9. A.W. Gladkij. On the complexity of derivations for context-sensitive grammars. *Algebri i Logika Sem.*, 3:29–44, 1964. In Russian.
10. J.E. Hopcroft and J.D. Ullman. *Introduction to Automata Theory, Languages, and Computation.* Addison-Wesley, Reading, M.A., 1979.
11. R. McNaughton, P. Narendran, and F. Otto. Church-Rosser Thue systems and formal languages. *J. Association Computing Machinery*, 35:324–344, 1988.
12. F. Otto, M. Katsura, and Y. Kobayashi. Cross-sections for finitely presented monoids with decidable word problems. In H. Comon, editor, *Rewriting Techniques and Applications*, Lecture Notes in Computer Science 1232, pages 53–67. Springer-Verlag, Berlin, 1997.

Deterministic Rational Transducers and Random Sequences

Sylvain Porrot[1], Max Dauchet[2], Bruno Durand[3], Nikolai K. Vereshchagin[3,4]
[1]LAIL, URA CNRS 1440
Bâtiment P2, Université des Sciences et Technologies de Lille
59655 Villeneuve d'Ascq CEDEX, France
Tel & Fax : (33) 03 20 43 47 43 - email : porrot@lifl.fr
[2]LIFL, URA CNRS 369
Bâtiment M3, Université des Sciences et Technologies de Lille
59655 Villeneuve d'Ascq CEDEX, France
Tel : (33) 03 20 43 45 88 - email : dauchet@lifl.fr
[3]LIP, ENS-Lyon CNRS
46 Allée d'Italie
69634 Lyon CEDEX 07, France
e-mail : Bruno.Durand@ens-lyon.fr
[4]Dept. of Mathematical Logic and Theory of Algorithms
Moscow State University
Vorobjevy Gory, Moscow, Russia
e-mail : ver@mech.math.msu.su

Abstract

This paper presents some results about transformations of infinite random sequences by letter to letter rational transducers. We show that it is possible by observing initial segments of a given random sequence to decide whether two given letter to letter rational transducers have the same output on that sequence. We use the characterization of random sequences by *Kolmogorov Complexity.* We also prove that the image of a random sequence is either random, or non-random and non-recursive, or periodic, depending on some transducer's structural properties that we give.

Introduction

This paper starts the study of the deterministic rational transducers behaviour on infinite random sequences. Firstly, we show that it is possible by observing initial segments of a given random sequence to decide whether two given letter to letter rational transducers have the same output on that sequence (we call this problem *equality problem*). The analogous problem is undecidable on the class of all input sequences. Secondly, we prove that the image of a random sequence is either random or non-random and non-recursive or periodic, depending on the transducer's structural properties. Finally, we derive an arithmetical theorem from the previous result : the image of a 'random real' by a letter to letter rational transducer is either rational or transcendental.

This work is a part of a larger study on transformations processes of discrete curves. These processes are 'real time' transformations on random sequences. For us, 'real time' means that the computation time as well as the memory of the processes are bounded. Consequently, these processes are rational transducers [PD97].

The concept of random sequence has been well defined for the first time by Martin-Löf in 1966 [ML66]. A sequence is random if and only if it does not belong to any constructive null set. Theory of *Kolmogorov Complexity* provides a characterization of such sequences in terms of compressibility. Levin and Schnorr have shown that the notions of random sequences and incompressible sequences are equivalent [Lev73] [Sch73]. This theory has enabled to obtain results on regular languages [Sei86] [CL88] [LV93], but our aim is different. The originality of this paper lies in the study of the effect of algebraic objects (rational transducers) on random sequences. This is another approach to Markov chains, which are probabilistic finite automata : here we consider deterministic automata and it is the input sequence that chooses the transitions. This choice is 'typically random' when the sequence is random.

We briefly present in section 1.1 the definition of random sequences due to Martin-Löf, and an equivalent definition in terms of *Kolmogorov Complexity*. There are several variants of this theory (see the foreword of Chaitin in [Cal94]), but here we consider only the *Prefix Complexity*. This variant is more convenient for the study of infinite sequences.

We consider classical rational transducers [MS97], introduced by M. Nivat [Niv68], reading infinite binary sequences in input and, unlike Büchi automata e.g. [Tho90], without any particular acceptance conditions. We do not require that for each state and each input letter there exists the corresponding transition. We say that a transducer accepts a sequence if it can read all its letters. In section 1.2, we introduce a classification of transducers' states. This classification is drawn from the theory of Markov chains [MT96]. The main aim of this classification is Lemma 5. It gives a necessary and sufficient condition of the acceptance of a random sequence.

In part 2, we show that the equality problem of two transducers is decidable on the class of random sequence, when it is undecidable on the class of all sequences. In order to accepts an infinite sequence if and only if both initial transducers accept this sequence and have the same output.

In part 3, Theorem 2 establishes a classification of the images of random sequences. This classification depends on the transducer's structural properties. On the one hand, the image of a random sequence is random if and only if there are not two paths with the same output linking two recurrent states. On the other hand, the image of a random sequence has finite complexity if and only if all paths starting from a recurrent state have the same output. Moreover, in this case, the image sequence is periodic.

Section 3.2 presents an application of the previous result within the frame of arithmetic. We call *random real* a real number of which the binary expansion is a random sequence. Theorem 3 claims that the image of any random real by a letter to letter rational transducer is either rational or transcendental.

1 Preliminaries

1.1 Random sequences and Kolmogorov Complexity

In this part we briefly present the definition of random sequences from Martin-Löf and the theory of *Kolmogorov Complexity*. In the following we call *word* (respectively *sequence*) any finite (respectively any infinite) string over the binary alphabet $\{0, 1\}$.

1.1.1 Random sequences

The first satisfactory definition of a random sequence has been given by Martin-Löf in [ML66]. A sequence is random if and only if it does not belong to any constructive null set. More precisely, a sequence s is *non random* if and only if there is a recursive function $u(i, j)$, mapping pairs of integers to words, satisfying the following properties :

1. $\forall\, i\ \mu(\Omega_i) \leq 2^{-i}$;
2. $\forall\, i\ s \in \Omega_i$.

where $\Omega_i = \bigcup_j \Gamma_{u(i,j)}$, $\Gamma_{u(i,j)}$ being the set of all the sequences having the prefix $u(i, j)$, and μ denotes uniform measure on the set of all sequences.

1.1.2 Kolmogorov Complexity

Theory of *Kolmogorov Complexity* [LV97], also called *Algorithmic Information Theory*, gives rigorous mathematical foundations to the notion of information quantity contained in an object x. This quantity $K(x)$ is the length of a smallest program computing x without any input. The programming language must satisfy the following property : for any computable partial function ϕ mapping words to words there exists a constant C such that for any p in the domain of ϕ there exists a program computing $\phi(p)$ of length at most length$(p)+C$. We will use the variant of *Kolmogorov Complexity* called *Prefix Complexity*, in which the set of programs must be a *prefix set* : none of the programs is the prefix of another program. The complexity varies no more than by an additive constant when we change the programming language. Indeed,

$$\exists\, C\ \forall\, x\ |K_1(x) - K_2(x)| < C$$

where $K_1(x)$ and $K_2(x)$ are Kolmogorov complexities defined for two different programming languages.

1.1.3 Randomness and incompressibility

Theory of *Kolmogorov Complexity* provides a characterization of randomness using incompressibility properties. Actually Levin and Schnorr [Lev73] [Sch73] have shown that random sequences are exactly those incompressible for some variants of *Kolmogorov Complexity*. Their proof can be easily translated in the frame of *Prefix Complexity* that we use here. More specifically, all prefixes of a random sequence are compressible for less than a constant. Formally, if $a_{1:n}$ is the prefix of length n of a sequence a, then this sequence is random if and only if :

$$\exists\, c\ \forall\, n\ K(a_{1:n}) \geq n - c$$

A random sequence is non-recursive, but non-random ones may be either recursive or non-recursive.

- Assume for example that the sequence 010011010110... is random. Then the sequence 001100001111..., where each letter of the previous sequence appears twice, is non-random and non-recursive.
- The sequence 010101010101... is non-random and recursive.

In several proofs we show that a sequence a is non-random building a program that computes a using another sequence a' as an input. This program uses at most the λn first letters of a' to compute the n first letters of a, with $\lambda < 1$. The following lemma expresses this idea.

Lemma 1 *Let a and a' be two sequences. If there exists a program P such that :*

$$\exists\ (u_n)_{n\in\mathbf{N}}\ \exists\ (v_n)_{n\in\mathbf{N}}\ \exists\ \lambda < 1 \text{ such that } \forall\ n\ P(a'_{1:u_n}) = a_{1:v_n} \text{ and } u_n \leq \lambda v_n$$

then a is non-random.

Proof We will give an upper bound of the complexity of the prefix words $a_{1:v_n}$ of a. The program $< P, a'_{1:u_n} >$ computes $a_{1:v_n}$, but the set of these programs is not a prefix set. In order to obtain such a set we have to use the prefix coding of $a'_{1:u_n}$, denoted by $\overline{a'_{1:u_n}}$. For all n we have $K(a_{1:v_n}) \leq |\overline{a'_{1:u_n}}| + |P| + O(1)$. A classical upper bound for the prefix coding of a word w is $|w| + 2\log(|w|) + O(1)$. Hence we have :

$$\begin{aligned} \forall\, n\; K(a_{1:v_n}) &\leq |a'_{1:u_n}| + 2\log(|a'_{1:u_n}|) + O(1) \\ &\leq \lambda |a_{1:v_n}| + 2\log(|a_{1:v_n}|) + O(1) \end{aligned}$$

Let $c > 0$ be fixed. There exists n_c such that :

$$\forall\, n \geq n_c\; \lambda|a_{1:v_n}| + 2\log(|a_{1:v_n}|) + O(1) \leq |a_{1:v_n}| - c$$

Eventually we have :

$$\forall\, c\, \exists\, n_c\, \forall\, n \geq n_c\; K(a_{1:v_n}) \leq |a_{1:v_n}| - c$$

Therefore a is non-random.

□

1.2 Transducers

We consider classical transducers without final states since inputs are only infinite sequences. In this first approach we consider only letter to letter transducers : the output is a letter at each letter read in input. When the transducer reaches a state where there is no transition labelled by the input letter, it halts and we say that it rejects the input sequence. Otherwise it accepts the input sequence.
We give now some definitions and preliminary results considering only inputs on transitions.

Definition 1 *Let T be a transducer and a be a sequence accepted by T. A state of T is* recurrent *for a if it is reached an infinity of times with a as an input. T_a denotes the set of recurrent states for a.*

Definition 2 *Let q be a state of T. Let $occ^a_n(q)$ denote the number of occurences of the state q during the reading of $a_{1:n}$. The frequency $f^a(q)$ of q is defined by :*

$$f^a(q) = \limsup_{n\to\infty} \frac{occ^a_n(q)}{n}$$

A state q is frequent *if $f^a(q) > 0$.*

Definition 3 *Let q be a state of T and t be a transition from q. Let $occ^a_n(t)$ denote the number of occurences of the transition t during the n first occurences of the state q with a as an input. The frequence $f^a(t)$ of t is defined by :*

$$f^a(t) = \limsup_{n\to\infty} \frac{occ^a_n(t)}{n}$$

Lemma 2 *Let a be a sequence accepted by T. T contains at least one frequent state.*

Proof Suppose that for each state q_i of T_a we have $f(q_i) = 0$. Let $\epsilon = \frac{1}{2Q}$ where Q is the number of states of T. Therefore we have :

$$\begin{aligned} \exists\, n\, \forall\, q_i \in T \quad \frac{occ_n^a(q_i)}{n} &\leq \epsilon \\ \sum_{i=1}^{Q} \frac{occ_n^a(q_i)}{n} &\leq \epsilon Q \\ 1 &\leq \frac{1}{2} \end{aligned}$$

□

Definition 4 *A* complete *state is a state out of which get two transitions labelled by 0 and 1. We say that a set of states is* complete *if each state of this set is complete.*

Claim 1 *Consider the preorder on the set of the states of a transducer defined by :*

$$q < q' \Leftrightarrow \text{we can reach } q' \text{ from } q$$

and the equivalence classes of states. We say that maximal classes are absorbing. *There is an algorithm that splits a transducer in sub-automata $T_1, \ldots, T_N$ and T_P (See Figure 1. $T_1, \ldots, T_N$ are the complete absorbing classes and T_P is the union of the remaining classes.*

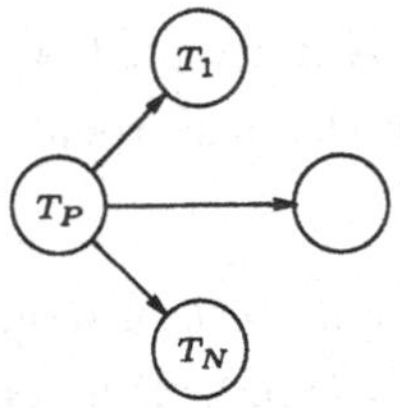

Figure 1: Complete absorbing classes

Lemma 3 *Let a be a random sequence accepted by T. Any frequent state of T is complete.*

Proof Let q be a frequent state. Suppose that q is not complete. Thus, there is only one transition from this state, say the transition labelled by input letter 0 and leading to the state q'. We show this implies that a is non-random. Consider the sequence a' obtained as follows : in the sequence a we delete letters read at each occurence of q. The following program computes a using T and a'.

```
Program P(a')
    Repeat
        If T is in state q do
            Output 0 ; Place T in state q'
        Else
            Read a letter b of a' and output b
            Simulate T on input b
        End if
    End repeat
End
```

Since q is frequent we have $\limsup_{n\to\infty} \frac{occ_n^a(q)}{n} = \alpha$ with $\alpha > 0$. Thus there is a series $(v_n)_{n\in\mathbf{N}}$ and n_0 such that for all $n > n_0$ we have $\frac{occ_{v_n}^a(q)}{v_n} \geq \frac{\alpha}{2}$. Let $u_n = v_n - occ_{v_n}^a(q)$. For all $n > n_0$ we have $u_n \leq \lambda v_n$ with $\lambda = 1 - \frac{\alpha}{2} < 1$. The program P is such that for all n we have $P(a'_{1:u_n}) = a_{1:v_n}$. Thus hypothesis of Lemma 1 are satisfied, what enables us to conclude that a is non-random.

□

Lemma 4 *Let a be a random sequence accepted by T. Then all states of T_a are frequent and T_a is a complete absorbing class.*

Proof According to Lemma 2, T contains at least one frequent state q. This state belongs to T_a and, according to lemma 3, is complete. Let t_0 (respectively t_1) be the transition accepting 0 (respectively 1) and leading to q_0 (respectively q_1) from q (q_0 and q_1 can be the same).

Step 1 : We show that both transitions t_0 and t_1 are frequent. Suppose for example that t_0 is not frequent, i.e. $f^a(t_0) = 0$. Obviously we have $f^a(t_1) = 1$. Consider the sequence a' defined as follows : in the sequence a we delete each 1 read at each occurence of t_1 and we replace each 0 read at each occurence of t_0 with a prefix code of the number of occurences of t_1 before the next occurence of t_0. The following program computes a using a'.

```
Program P(a')
    Let n be the number of occurences of t1 before next occurence of t0
    Repeat
        If T is in state q then
            If n = 0 then
                Output 0 ; Let n be the prefix coded number appearing
                from current position in a'
                Place T in state q0
            Else
                Output 1 ; Let n = n - 1
                Place T in state q1
            End if
        Else
            Read a letter b of a' and output b
            Simulate T on input b
        End if
    End repeat
End
```

The same arguments as in the proof of Lemma 3 enable us to conclude that a is non-random.

Conclusion : Since $f^a(q) > 0$, $f^a(t_0) > 0$ and $f^a(t_1) > 0$ both states q_0 and q_2 are frequent.

Step by step we show that any state reachable from q is frequent and thus, according to Lemma 3, is complete. Such a state is recurrent. Therefore, the class of q is absorbing and complete.

□

The following lemma is an immediate corollary of Lemma 4 and of the fact that a complete absorbing class accepts any sequence.

Lemma 5 *For all random sequence a, T accepts a if and only if T reaches on a one of its complete absorbing classes.*

2 Decidability of the equality of letter to letter rational transducers on random sequences

We say that two transducers T_1 and T_2 are equal on a sequence s if $T_1(s) = T_2(s)$. Note the difference between this definition and the definition of the equivalence of transducers : T_1 and T_2 are equivalent if $T_1(w) = T_2(w)$ for all word w. The equality of a class Θ of rational transducers on a class S of sequences is decidable if there is an algorithm that decides, for any transducers T_1 and T_2 in Θ, and any sequence s in S spelled letter by letter, whether $T_1(s) = T_2(s)$, using a finite prefix (of unknown length) of s.

$$\exists\ A\ \forall\ (T_1, T_2) \in \Theta^2\ \forall\ s \in S\ \begin{cases} A(T_1, T_2, s) = yes & \text{if } T_1(s) = T_2(s) \\ A(T_1, T_2, s) = no & \text{otherwise} \end{cases}$$

If Θ is the set of letter to letter rational transducers and S is the set of all sequences, the equality is not decidable. Consider transducers T_1 and T_2 defined in Figure 2. Suppose

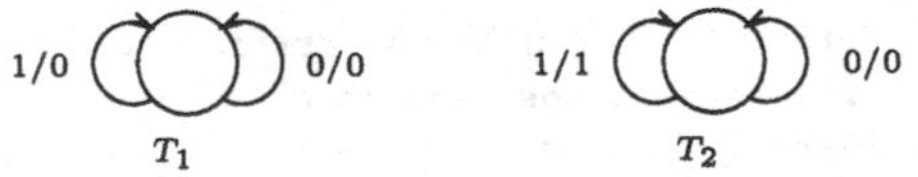

Figure 2: Two transducers equal on 0^∞ and not equal on 0^n10^∞

there is an algorithm A deciding, for any sequence s, whether both transducers T_1 and T_2 are equal on s. Let $s_1 = 0^\infty$. Since $T_1(s_1) = T_2(s_1)$, $A(T_1, T_2, s_1)$ halts having read a prefix of length n of s_1 and outputs *yes*. Now, let $s_2 = 0^n10^\infty$. Since the n

first letters of s_1 and s_2 are the same, $A(T_1, T_2, s_2)$ halts and outputs *yes*, although we obviously have $T_1(s_2) \neq T_2(s_2)$.

However, the equality becomes decidable if we restrict ourselves to random sequences. In order to show this result, we need to define the notion of product transducer.

Definition 5 *Let T_1 and T_2 be two transducers. Their product transducer $T = T_1 \times T_2$ is defined as follows : if we can reach q_1' from q_1 in the transducer T_1 and q_2' from q_2 in the transducer T_2, with the same letter b_{in} in input and the same letter b_{out} in output, then T contains a transition between (q_1, q_2) and (q_1', q_2') reading b_{in} and outputting b_{out}.*

The product transducer $T = T_1 \times T_2$ accepts a sequence a if and only if T_1 and T_2 accept a and output the same sequence.

Theorem 1 *The equality of letter to letter rational transducers on random sequences is decidable.*

Proof Let a be a random sequence. T_1 and T_2 accept a and output the same sequence if and only if their product transducer T accepts a or, according to Lemma 5, if and only if T reaches on a one of its complete absorbing classes. If T halts, we distinguish there are different cases :

- T_1 and T_2 accept a and output different sequences and thus T_1 and T_2 are not equal on a ;
- one transducer accepts a and the other rejects a : T_1 and T_2 are not equal on a ;
- T_1 and T_2 rejects a : if the output words are the same T_1 and T_2 are equal on a, otherwise they are not.

Finally, T_1 and T_2 are equal on a if and only if either T reaches on a one of its complete absorbing classes or T, T_1, T_2 halt simultaneously with the same output words. These observations lead to the following decision algorithm :

```
Program A(T1,T2,a)
    Build product transducer T = T1 × T2
    Split T in complete absorbing classes as in claim 1
    For each letter of a repeat
        If T reaches one of its complete absorbing classes then
            Output yes ; Halt
        Elseif T halts then
            If T1 and T2 halt at same place and output same word then
                Output yes ; Halt
            Else
                Output no ; Halt
            End if
        End if
    End for
End
```

□

3 Classification of images of random sequences

In this part we are interested in the images of random sequences by letter to letter rational transducers. Theorem 2 shows the influence of the transducer's structure on the sequence we obtain.

Definition 6 *A state q is* partially indifferent *if there are two different input words having the same length, leading to a same state from q and having the same image.*

Definition 7 *A state q is* discriminating *if there exists $l > 0$ satisfying the following property : from q, the images of two words w_1 and w_2 of length l end with same letter if and only if w_1 and w_2 start with same letter.*

Theorem 2 *Let T be a letter to letter rational transducer, let a be a random sequence accepted by T and let s denote $T(a)$.*

1. *if T_a does not contain any partially indifferent state then s is random ;*
2. *(a) if T_a contains at least one partially indifferent state then s is non-random. Moreover :*
   (b) if T_a contains a discriminating state then s is non-recursive ;
   (c) if T_a does not contain any discriminating state, then s is recursive and periodic : $s = uv^*$.

Remark 1 Let Q denote the number of states of a transducer T. We can show that the existence of a partially indifferent state in T is decidable in a time $\mathcal{O}(Q^2)$ and the existence of a discriminating state in T is decidable in a time $\mathcal{O}(2^{2Q})$.

Example 1 Call a transducer one-to-one if it defines an injective mapping on (infinite) sequences. A one-to-one transducer does not contain any partially indifferent state. The transducer of Figure 3 is a non-trivial example of a one-to-one transducer, that transforms a sequence a in $0a$. It is non-trivial because it is not just a injective morphism of words.

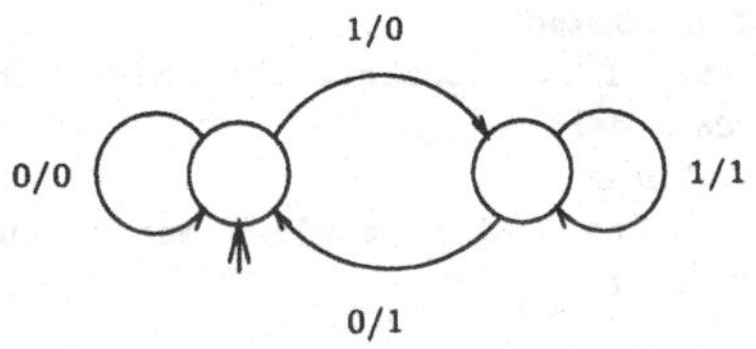

Figure 3: A non trivial one-to-one transducer

Example 2 Injectivity is not a necessary condition to map random sequences on random sequences. Consider the transducer T of Figure 4. Since sequences 0^∞ and 10^∞ have the same image 01^∞, T is not a one-to-one transducer. However, T does not contain any partially indifferent state since there is no state reachable from two transitions having same output letter.

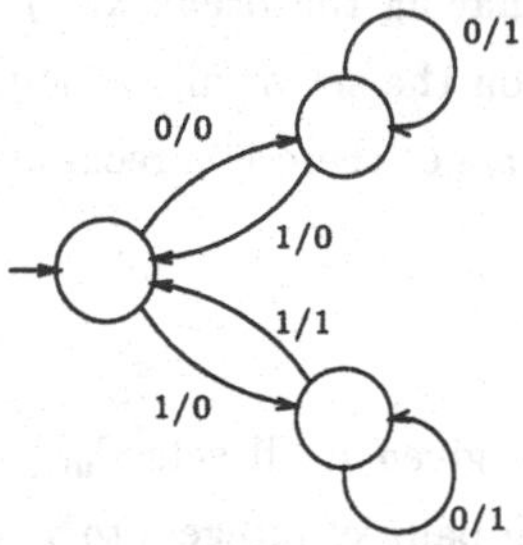

Figure 4: A many-to-one transducer without partially indifferent states

3.1 Proof

Proof of ***1.*** **and** ***2.(a)*** We have to show that s is random if and only if T_a does not contain any partially indifferent state.

Only if : We prove that if T_a contains at least one partially indifferent state q then s is non-random.

Since q is a partially indifferent state, there are two words w_1 and w_2 leading to the same state q' from q and outputting the same word u. Let l be the length of w_1 and w_2. Let f be a coding function from $\{0,1\}^l$ to $\{0,1\}^l$ such that $f(w_1)$ and $f(w_2)$ differ only in their last letter. For example let $f(w_1) = v0$ and $f(w_2) = v1$, where v is a word of length $l-1$. Let a' be defined as follows : in the sequence a we replace each word w of length l read from state q with v if $w = w_1$ or $w = w_2$, with $f(w)$ otherwise. The following program computes s with a' as an input.

```
Program P(a') Simulate T on input sequence a'
    Each time T reaches state q do
        Let w be word of length l − 1 from current position in a'
        If w = v then
            Output u
            Place T in state q'
        Else
            Let w be word of length l from current position in a'
            Let w' be the word such that f(w') = w
            Replace w with w' in a'
            Resume simulation of T
        End if
    End do
End
```

The same arguments as in the proof of Lemma 3 enable us to conclude that s is non-random.

If : We prove that if T_a does not have any partially indifferent state then s is random. Suppose that s is non-random. We show that this implies that a is non-random too. Let $u(i,j)$ denote a recursive function mapping pairs of integers to words. Let $\Gamma_{u(i,j)}$ denote the set of all sequences having the prefix $u(i,j)$, let Ω_i denote $\bigcup_j \Gamma_{u(i,j)}$ and let μ denotes uniform measure on the set of all sequences. Since s is non-random, s belongs to a constructive null set, i.e. there is a recursive function $u(i,j)$ such that :

1. $\forall\ i\ \mu(\Omega_i) \leq 2^{-i}$
2. $\forall\ i\ s \in \Omega_i$

Note that we can suppose that, given i, all sets $\Gamma_{u(i,j)}, j \in \mathbb{N}$ are disjoint. We will define a function $\hat{u}(i,j)$ mapping pairs of integers to words such that for all i we have $\{T(\hat{u}(i,j)) \mid j \in \mathbb{N}\} = \{u(i,j) \mid j \in \mathbb{N}\}$. The following program $P(i,j)$ computes $\hat{u}(i,j)$ using the recursive function $u(i,j)$ and the transducer T.

```
Program P(i,j)
    count = 0 ; k = 0
    Repeat
        k = k + 1 ; w = u(i,k)
        For all words ŵ of length |w| do
            If T(ŵ) = w then
                count = count + 1
                If count = j then
                    Output ŵ ; Halt
                End if
            End if
        End for
    End repeat
End
```

Since $u(i,j)$ is recursive, $\hat{u}(i,j)$ is recursive too. Let $\hat{\Omega}_i = \bigcup_j \Gamma_{\hat{u}(i,j)}$. Since $\hat{u}(i,j)$ is the preimage of a $u(i,k)$, a belongs to $\hat{\Omega}_i$ for all i. Moreover we have :

$$\forall\ i\ \mu(\hat{\Omega}_i) \leq \sum_j \mu(\Gamma_{\hat{u}(i,j)})$$

Let Q be the number of states of T. Since T_a does not contain any partially indifferent state there are at most Q different words having the same image. Thus we have :

$$\begin{aligned}\forall\ i\ \mu(\hat{\Omega}_i) &\leq \sum_j Q\mu(\Gamma_{u(i,j)}) \\ &= Q\mu(\Omega_i) \\ &\leq Q2^{-i}\end{aligned}$$

Hence a belongs to a constructive null set defined by $\hat{u}(i,j)$: a is non-random.

□

Proof of *2.(b)* Let q be a discriminating state. There exists $l > 0$ such that, observing the last letter of the image of an input word of length l from q, we can retrieve the first letter of this input word. Assume for example that all words of length l starting with 0 (respectively with 1) have their images ending with 0 (respectively with 1).
Suppose s is recursive. Let P be a program that computes s. Consider the sequence a' defined as follows : in the sequence a we delete letters read at each occurence of q. The following program computes a using P, T and a'. Let q_0 (respectively q_1) denote the state reached when 0 (respectively 1) is read at state q.

```
Program P(a')
    Repeat
        If T is in state q then
            Compute next n-th letter of s using program P
            If this letter is 0 then
                Output 0 ; Place T in state q0
            Else
                Output 1 ; Place T in state q1
            End if
        Else
            Read a letter b of a' and output b
            Simulate T on input b
        End if
    End repeat
End
```

The same arguments as in the proof of Lemma 3 enable us to conclude that a is non-random.

□

Proof of *2.(c)* Firstly we prove the following property : for all state q of T_a, for all l, for all words w_1 and w_2 of length l, the images of w_1 and w_2 from q are the same. We use a recurrent reasoning on l to show this. $W(q, l)$ denotes the set of image words of length l from q.
Step 1 : The property is true for $l = 1$. Indeed each state outputs the same letter whatever the input letter is, since each state of T_a is not discriminating.
Step 2 : Let q be a state of T_a. Let q_0 (respectively q_1) be the state reached from q when 0 (respectively 1) is read. Suppose the property is true for all $l \leq L$. Thus all words of $W(q_0, L)$ (respectively $W(q_1, L)$) end with the same letter b_0 (respectively b_1). Since q is not discriminating, we necessarily have $b_0 = b_1$. Thus all input words of length $L + 1$ have images ending with same letter from q.
We prove now that s is periodic, i.e. there are two words u and v such that $s = uv^*$. Let a' be the suffix sequence of a read from the first occurence of a recurrent state q. According to the previous property, we have $q(a') = q(0^*)$. Since the automaton is finite and deterministic, there is necessary a loop.

□

3.2 From an arithmetical point of view

The following theorem is an application of Theorem 2 within the frame of arithmetic. We call 'random real' a real of which the binary expansion is a random sequence. We remind of the reader that a real is *algebraic* if it is the root of a polynomial equation having integer coefficients. A real is *transcendental* if it is not algebraic.

Theorem 3 *The image of a random real by a letter to letter rational transducer is either rational or transcendental.*

Proof Let a be the binary expansion of the image of a random real. If a has a finite complexity then it is periodic and then the real number is rational. If a has an infinite complexity then the real number is transcendental. Indeed, since an algebraic number is a root of a polynomial equation with integer coefficients, it has a finite complexity : we can give more and more accurate approximations of this root using an algorithm.

□

Open problems

In this first approach we have only considered letter to letter rational transducers. We should study whether the results we have obtained remain true in the general case. Moreover we think that links between simple and 'pure' algebraic objects (rational transducers) and 'pure' complex objects (random sequences), and also the links with Markov chains, should be study thoroughly.

References

[Cal94] C. Calude. *Information and Randomness, an Algorithmic Perspective.* Springer-Verlag, 1994.

[CL88] M. Chrobak and M. Li. $k+1$ heads are better than k for PDAs. *J. Comput. Syst. Sci.*, 37 :144–155, 1988.

[Lev73] L.A. Levin. On the notion of random sequence. *Soviet Math. Dokl.*, 14 :1413–1416, 1973.

[LV93] M. Li and P. Vitányi. A new approach to formal language theory by Kolmogorov's complexity. *SIAM J. Comput.*, 24 :398–410, 1993.

[LV97] M. Li and P. Vitányi. *An Introduction to Kolmogorov Complexity and its Applications.* Springer-Verlag, 1997.

[ML66] P. Martin-Löf. The definition of random sequences. *Inform. Contrib.*, 9 :602–619, 1966.

[MS97] A. Mateescu and A. Salomaa. Aspect of classical language theory. In *Handbook of Formal Languages*, volume 1, pages 175–251. Springer-Verlag, 1997.

[MT96] S.P. Meyn and R.L. Tweedie. *Markov Chains and Stochastic Stability*. Springer-Verlag, 1996.

[Niv68] M. Nivat. Transductions de langages de chomsky. *Annales de l'Institut Fourier*, 18 :339–455, 1968.

[PD97] S. Porrot and M. Dauchet. Discrete curves complexity. Rapport interne, LAIL, 1997.

[Sch73] C.P. Schnorr. Process complexity and effective random tests. *J. Comput. System Sci.*, 7 :376–388, 1973.

[Sei86] J. Seiferas. A simplified lower bound for context-free-language recognition. *Inform. Contrib.*, 69 :255–260, 1986.

[Tho90] W. Thomas. Automata on infinite objects. In *Handbook of Theoretical Computer Science*, volume B, pages 133–191. Elsevier, 1990.

Resource Based Models for Asynchrony*

J. Rathke
Dipartimento di Informatica e Scienze dell'Informazione
Università degli Studi di Genova
via Dodecaneso 35, 16146 Genova, Italy
julianr@cogs.susx.ac.uk

Abstract

We propose a new graph-based approach to modelling asynchronous languages and show how the new model can be viewed as a collapse of the standard transition system model for asynchronous behaviour by utilising the commuting properties of asynchronous transitions.

The motivation behind these new models stems from the issue of regularity for asynchronous processes. We note that the class of regular processes fails to contain many useful asynchronous processes and we identify a larger subclass of BPP accordingly. We call this new class *asynchronously regular processes.*

Using the new models we provide two appealing abstract characterisations of asynchronous bisimulation equivalence, namely, as spans of open maps and as a winning strategies for a bisimulation game. Also, by exploiting the coincidence of finite graphs with regular processes we see that bisimulation is polynomial time decidable over our class of asynchronously regular processes.

1 Introduction

It is becoming increasingly clear that the nature of output messages in languages such as the asynchronous π-calculus, [2, 6], Pict [13] and the Join-calculus, [4] is one of persistent resources. Recently, this persistence of output was exposed at the level of transition systems by identifying certain commuting properties guaranteed of asynchronous systems [14]. Given such a situation, it would seem reasonable to question whether transition systems afford a good representation of asynchronous processes. After all, the ordering of transitions in a graph is used merely to reflect the precedence of actions which can be performed by the process. The distinguishing feature of output actions is that they cannot preclude other actions; so why model them as transitions?

Our approach is to view output messages purely in terms of resources. Our models, resource graphs, have no output transitions but instead record the availability of output resources as computation progresses. This might be achieved by allowing each node to be a pair containing some 'state' of the system along with the multiset of resources which are currently available. In fact, we see in Section 3.1 that this is pretty much how the transition system model behaves so little is to be gained from this solution. A much more compact representation is possible if we don't explicitly record the current resources available but simply see how resources *become* available. We augment each input and τ transition with the multiset of outputs which become available as a result of performing this transition. It should be clear that we will also need to store the information of which resources are initially available in a system. For example, the process

$$P = c! \parallel a?(b! \parallel b! \parallel Q) + \tau.(d! \parallel R)$$

has an initial resource $\{c!\}$ and two immediate transitions $P \xrightarrow{a?}$ and $P \xrightarrow{\tau}$ which release the resources $\{b!, b!\}$ and $\{d!\}$ respectively. We represent these two transitions as

$$P \overset{a,\{b,b\}}{\rightsquigarrow} Q \text{ and } P \overset{\tau,\{d\}}{\rightsquigarrow} R,$$

where the input/output sense of actions is now implicit. This move to recording resources on edges rather than at nodes allows many more *infinite state* processes to be modelled by finite resource graphs.

*On leave from the University of Sussex. Supported by the EU-HCM Express network.

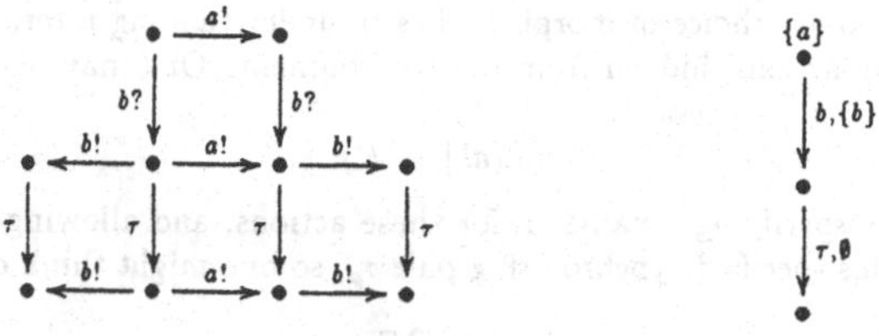

Figure 1: Transition system and resource graph for $a! \parallel (b?(b! \parallel \tau.\,\mathbf{nil}\,))$

To contrast the standard transition system models with the resource graph interpretation of a process consider the example process in Figure 1. The redundancy in the transition system model is highlighted well by the uniform shape of asynchronous transition systems imposed by Selinger's axioms [14]. We know, owing to the asynchronous nature of the language, that the $a!$ is possible at the initial node and, until it is used, will continue to be available, thus in the resource graph model this information is utilised to create a more compact graph.

The models for the process

$$P = a?(b! \parallel P)$$

are more illuminating. This process will in fact be modelled by an infinite transition system,

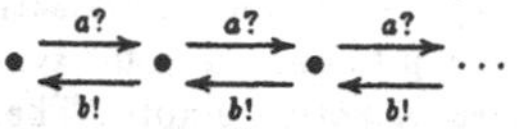

yet the structure of the process is very simple — at all times there is an $a?$ action possible and for each $a?$ action performed an additional $b!$ resource becomes available. Initially there are no $b!$ resources available. In fact, this gives us a resource graph with a single node, initial resource set is empty and there is a single looping transition

So far we have shown how we could tailor transition systems to be more suited to modelling asynchronous processes. But we must consider how this would actually benefit us. The examples show us that we immediately have a more compact representation of systems, so this could clearly be useful when it comes to checking equivalence of processes. Ideally we could check bisimulation between processes by building their resource graphs and checking some kind of bisimulation on these. This would necessitate defining the appropriate notion of bisimulation for resource graphs. Given such a situation, we would easily obtain a decision procedure for checking bisimilarity for the class of processes which receive finite resource graph models.

It is well known that finite state transition systems correspond (up to strong bisimulation) to *regular* processes in CCS, that is processes which make no use of the static operators, parallel composition and restriction underneath recursion [9, 10]. If we forbid the use of parallel composition and restriction under recursion from asynchronous CCS we lose a great deal of expressive power, in fact, we lose the ability to perform more than a finite number of output actions. This sorry state of affairs would mean that even the paradigmatic asynchronous buffer process

$$\mathbf{rec}\, X.a?(a! \parallel X)$$

is not expressible. This restricted use of parallelism is certainly too strong for asynchronous languages and we must consider a weaker notion of regularity. We propose that a parallel composition $p \parallel q$ in the scope of recursion binders be allowed providing that either p or q is merely an output message – we call such processes asynchronously regular. The class of asynchronously regular processes would now include the asynchronous buffer process shown above as well as many other *infinite state* processes. Moreover, all such processes will be modelled by finite resource graphs.

In order to define bisimulation on resource graphs we appeal to the abstract definition proposed by Joyal, Nielsen, Winskel [7]. This definition simply requires us to choose a suitable category in which to observe basic computation paths. Using intuition gleaned from [1] to choose our notion of morphism of resource graphs, we see that the notion of asynchronous bisimulation proposed by [1] exists in an abstract form. The key to our choice of morphism lies in understanding internal τ actions as a pair of unspecified synchronising actions, hidden from the environment. One may like to think of τ prefixing as syntactic sugar for

$$\nu a.(a! \parallel a?P).$$

We consider what effects specifying a name, a, for these actions, and allowing them to be seen by the environment, has; call this specified synchronising pair τ_a, so one might think of τ_a prefixing as

$$a! \parallel a?P.$$

To define our notion of morphism on resource graphs we discuss general considerations about morphisms of labelled graphs. We think of a morphism

$$f : G \longrightarrow G'$$

between two labelled graphs as representing that G' is a refinement of G. That is to say that G is more specified than G'. A morphism should refine transitions of the graph in some way. We will outline what we understand by refinement.

Transitions represent both local communication, τ moves, and capacity for interacting in a more global sense, $a?$ and $a!$ moves. Given a process p, we can observe the global computations it can engage in by inducing them using an environment process e situated in parallel with p. We say that e *offers* an action $a!$, say, if $e \xrightarrow{a!}$, and that p *accepts* this offer if it synchronises with e to perform an internal reduction or computation. A transition $p \xrightarrow{\alpha} p'$ of some transition system can be understood then as saying that the least offer one need make p to observe some synchronisation and reduction to p' is $\hat{\alpha}$, where $\hat{a}! = a?$, $\hat{a}? = a!$, and $\hat{\tau}$, specified or not, is empty. The ordering on offers is simply that the empty offer is less than all other offers, which are incomparable. We will expect that any τ_a transition can be refined by a τ transition because we have information about the computation yielded by τ_a, the name of the channel on which synchronisation occurs, that we do not have of the computation given by the τ action. We say that a computation is *covert* if we do not know the name of the synchronising channel. All computations induced by τ prefixes are covert. Using this definition we say that

$$p \xrightarrow{\alpha} p' \ f\text{-refines } q \xrightarrow{\beta} q'$$

if p maps to q and q maps to q' under the morphism f, such that the least offer $\hat{\alpha}$ made to p can also be accepted by q to induce a reduction to q'. If the induced computation of p is covert then the corresponding induced computation of q must also be covert. More precisely we ask that

$$\hat{\alpha} \parallel p \longrightarrow p' \text{ implies } \hat{\alpha} \parallel q \longrightarrow q'$$

such that if we don't know the name on which p synchronises then we cannot know the name on which q synchronises. We can see that following refinements hold for transition systems,

$$\begin{array}{lll} p \xrightarrow{\alpha} p' & f\text{-refines} & f(p) \xrightarrow{\alpha} f(p') \\ p \xrightarrow{\tau_a} p' & f\text{-refines} & f(p) \xrightarrow{\tau} f(p'), \end{array}$$

and these give rise to a fairly unsurprising definition [16] of morphism for asynchronous transition systems. However, we observe a peculiarity in the category of resource graphs. Edges of resource graphs are labelled with pairs, $m \overset{\alpha,S}{\leadsto} m'$. Refinement of these edges will have to take into account the resources which are collected. To spell this out we say

$$m \overset{\alpha,S}{\leadsto} m' \ f\text{-refines } n \overset{\beta,S'}{\leadsto} n'$$

if m maps to m', and n maps to n' such that the least offer $\hat{\alpha}$ which (covertly) reduces m to state m' with S extra resources can also be accepted by n so that the (covert) reduction induced takes us to state n' with the same extra resources. Under this definition we have the following refinements

$$\begin{array}{lll} m \overset{\alpha,S}{\leadsto} m' & f\text{-refines} & f(m) \overset{\alpha,S}{\leadsto} f(m') \\ m \overset{a,S+\{a\}}{\leadsto} m' & f\text{-refines} & f(m) \overset{\tau_a,S}{\leadsto} f(m') \\ m \overset{\tau_a,S}{\leadsto} m & f\text{-refines} & f(m) \overset{\tau,S}{\leadsto} f(m'). \end{array}$$

The second refinement holds because the least offer $a!$ made to m can be accepted by $f(m)$ to reduce to $f(m')$ with S extra resources, along with the extra a resource which was unused by the τ_a.

By considering refinement to be transitive we can dispense with the idea of $m \overset{\tau_a, S}{\rightsquigarrow}$ transitions for resource graphs altogether and simply use $m \overset{a, S+\{a\}}{\rightsquigarrow} m'$ instead. The chief feature of our resource graphs morphisms then is that a morphism from R to R' allows us to specify in R, a name for an internal synchronisation in R'. We reinforce these intuitions by exploiting the game theoretic characterisation of bisimulation to highlight the rôle of τ synchronisations as specified and unspecified pairs of actions.

We briefly outline the structure of the remainder. The following short section recalls the category of transition systems and describes the asynchrony axioms. In Section 3 we define our category of resource graphs and relate them to transition systems. Bisimulation equivalence is defined as the span of open maps in this category and we characterise it using bisimulation like relations. The game theoretic description of this equivalence is spelled out in Section 4. We demonstrate the usefulness of our models in Section 5 by giving an enhanced notion of regularity for asynchronous systems and prove that bisimulation equivalence is polynomial time decidable over this class. Section 6 contains our conclusions.

Acknowledgments: The author(s) would like to thank Catuscia Palamidessi and Guy McCusker for carefully reading a draft of this paper and suggesting many improvements. Thanks also to Colin Stirling for providing some useful pointers in the literature. This work was carried out during research visits at INRIA, Sophia-Antipolis and the University of Genova, which were funded by the EU-HCM Express network. I would sincerely like to thank Catuscia Palamidessi and Ilaria Castellani and their respective institutions for their extreme generosity and for directing me in my research.

2 Asynchronous systems

We recall, from [16], the definition of the category of transition systems, $\mathcal{TS}$ and describe the sub-category, $\mathcal{ATS}$, of asynchronous transition systems, as characterised by Selinger.

Firstly, objects of $\mathcal{TS}$ are transition systems, $(\mathcal{N}, n_0, L, \longrightarrow)$ where n_0 is a specified initial node. Morphisms in $\mathcal{TS}$ are pairs of morphisms

$$(\sigma, \lambda) : (\mathcal{N}, n_0, L, \longrightarrow) \rightarrow (\mathcal{N}', n_0', L', \longrightarrow)$$

such that $\sigma : \mathcal{N} \rightarrow \mathcal{N}'$ and $\lambda : L \rightharpoonup L'$ is a partial function with the property that

$$n \xrightarrow{a} n' \text{ implies } \begin{cases} \sigma n \xrightarrow{\lambda a} \sigma n' & \text{if } \lambda a \downarrow \\ \sigma n = \sigma n' & \text{otherwise.} \end{cases}$$

Composition of morphisms is given by pairwise (partial) function composition and the identity morphisms are simply pairs of identity functions on the respective sets.

A morphism $(\sigma, \lambda) : T \rightarrow T'$ indicates that T' is a refinement of T in the sense that T is more specified than T'. Observe that T may have more atomic actions than T' with extra transitions pertaining to these actions. Also, T may have a more specific structure than T', with less non-determinism and fewer transitions. Indeed, when the λ component of a morphism is the identity then this morphism is simply an inclusion of T in T'. This idea of a morphism being a refinement is examined again in the category of resource graphs.

The particular sub-category $\mathcal{ATS}$ of $\mathcal{TS}$ in which we are interested is described as follows. Objects of the category are transition systems whose label set L is typed, that is

$$L \subseteq \mathcal{A} \times \{!, ?, \tau\} \cup \{\tau\}$$

where $\mathcal{A}$ is some set of channel names. That is, each action is either an output, $a!$, an input $a?$, the result of a synchronisation of these τ_a, or an internal, hidden, synchronisation, τ. These transition systems are subject to certain axioms, presented in Figure 2 which characterise their asynchronous behaviour [14].

Morphisms of $\mathcal{ATS}$ are similar to morphisms in $\mathcal{TS}$ except that the relabelling component λ is now a partial function on $\mathcal{A}$. We write τ_a° to mean either τ_a or τ and define $\lambda a! = (\lambda a)!$, $\lambda a? = (\lambda a)?$, $\lambda \tau = \tau$, and $\lambda \tau_a = \tau_{\lambda a}^\circ$. Composition and identities are defined as in $\mathcal{TS}$.

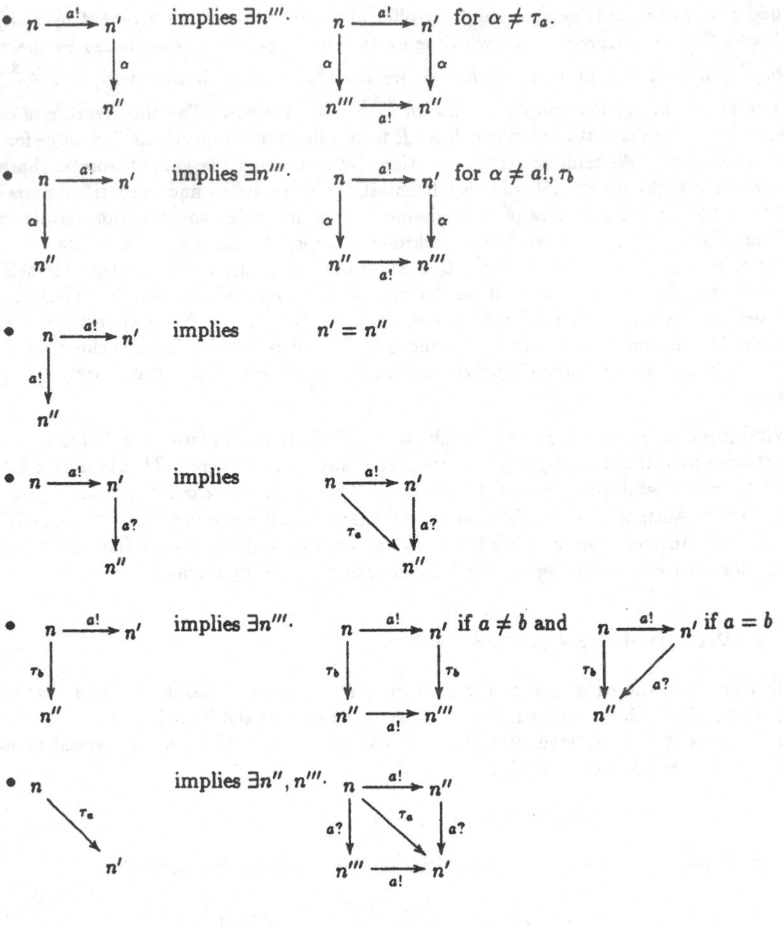

Figure 2: Axioms for asynchronous transition systems

3 Resource graphs

A ***resource graph*** is a graph based model for systems in which there is some notion of resource, that is, some action which is persistent and not subject to reactive behaviour. A resource's use is never precluded. The particular application we have in mind is for modelling asynchronous systems wherein the ! actions of the systems are considered as resources.

Formally, a resource graph is a quintuple

$$(\mathcal{M}, \mathcal{A}, m_0, S_0, \rightsquigarrow)$$

where $\mathcal{M}$ is a set of nodes, $\mathcal{A}$ is some set of names, m_0 is a specified initial node in $\mathcal{M}$ and S_0 is a multiset of resources which are initially available. We write $\mathcal{A}^{**}$ for the set of all multisets over the set $\mathcal{A}$. So we see that $S_0 \in \mathcal{A}^{**}$. The edges of the graph are given by

$$\rightsquigarrow \subseteq \mathcal{M} \times (\mathcal{A} \cup \{\tau\}) \times \mathcal{A}^{**} \times \mathcal{M}$$

and we write $m \overset{a,S}{\rightsquigarrow} m'$ if $(m, a, S, m') \in \rightsquigarrow$. We will use $+$ and $-$ to denote union and difference where multiset difference $S - S'$ is a partial operator and is only defined when $S' \subseteq S$. These operators are extended pointwise to multiset valued functions.

We can now describe our category of resource graphs, in fact we describe two. The first, $\mathcal{RG}$, has morphisms similar to the category $\mathcal{ATS}$ in that a morphism represents refinement by introducing extra atomic actions and embedding. We use this category to relate the standard transition system models to resource graph models. The second category we define, $\mathcal{RGA}$, contains morphisms which, following the ideas outlined in the introduction, also allow refinement by specifying on which name a synchronisation takes place. The two categories are such that $\mathcal{RG}$ is a lluf sub-category of $\mathcal{RGA}$.

The objects of $\mathcal{RG}$ are resource graphs. A morphism $(\sigma, \lambda, \varphi)$ from

$$R = (\mathcal{M}, \mathcal{A}, m_0, S_0, \rightsquigarrow)$$

to

$$R' = (\mathcal{M}', \mathcal{A}', m_0', S_0', \rightsquigarrow)$$

is a triple where σ is a function $\mathcal{M} \rightarrow \mathcal{M}'$, λ is a partial function $\mathcal{A} \cup \{\tau\} \rightarrow \mathcal{A}' \cup \{\tau\}$ which preserves τ and φ is a function $\mathcal{M} \rightarrow \mathcal{A}'^{**}$ such that the following conditions are satisfied:

(i) $\sigma m_0 = m_0'$

(ii) $\lambda S_0 + \varphi m_0 = S_0'$

(iii) $m \overset{a,S}{\rightsquigarrow} m'$ implies

$$\begin{cases} \sigma m \overset{\lambda a, S'}{\rightsquigarrow} \sigma m' \text{ where } S' = \lambda S + \varphi m' - \varphi m & \text{if } \lambda a \downarrow \\ \sigma m = \sigma m' \text{ and } \lambda S = \emptyset, \varphi m = \varphi m' & \text{otherwise.} \end{cases}$$

The φ component of a morphism allows for a resource graph to be embedded within a larger resource graph containing additional resources available at each node. Identity morphisms in $\mathcal{RG}$ are of the form $(Id, Id, C_\emptyset)$ where $C_\emptyset$ denotes the constant empty multiset function. Composition is defined by

$$(\sigma, \lambda, \varphi); (\sigma', \lambda', \varphi') = (\sigma; \sigma', \lambda; \lambda', (\varphi; \lambda' + \sigma; \varphi')).$$

It is straightforward enough to check that $\mathcal{RG}$ is indeed a category.

3.1 Relating the transition system and resource graph models

We describe an adjunction $\mathcal{ATS} \underset{ra}{\overset{ar}{\rightleftarrows}} \mathcal{RG}$ (with $ar \dashv ra$) between our category of asynchronous transition systems and our simple category of resource graphs. The counit of this adjunction is in fact an isomorphism so the adjunction is a reflection.

The functor $ra : \mathcal{RG} \rightarrow \mathcal{ATS}$ acts on objects as follows:

$$ra(\mathcal{M}, \mathcal{A}, m_0, S_0, \rightsquigarrow) = (\mathcal{M} \times \mathcal{A}^{**}, \mathcal{A}, (m_0, S_0), \longrightarrow)$$

where $\longrightarrow$ is defined by

$$\begin{array}{lll} (m, S + \{a\}) \xrightarrow{a!} (m, S) & & \\ (m, S) \xrightarrow{a?} (m', S') & \text{if } m \overset{a,S''}{\rightsquigarrow} m' & \text{and } S' = S + S'' \\ (m, S) \xrightarrow{\tau} (m', S') & \text{if } m \overset{\tau,S''}{\rightsquigarrow} m' & \text{and } S' = S + S'' \\ (m, S + \{a\}) \xrightarrow{\tau_a} (m', S') & \text{if } m \overset{a,S''}{\rightsquigarrow} m' & \text{and } S' = S + S''. \end{array}$$

On morphisms we have that $ra(\sigma, \lambda, \varphi) = (\sigma', \lambda)$ where $\sigma'(m, S) = (\sigma m, \lambda S + \varphi m)$.

In the other direction we need a couple of preliminary definitions before we can describe ar. Firstly, given an asynchronous transition system we let $\asymp$ denote the least equivalence on its nodes such that

$$n \xrightarrow{a!} n' \text{ implies } n \asymp n'.$$

Secondly, we write $n \xrightarrow{S!}$ if there exists a (possibly infinite) sequence of transitions

$$n \xrightarrow{a_1!} n_1 \xrightarrow{a_2!} \ldots \xrightarrow{a_k!} n_k \xrightarrow{a_{k+1}!} \ldots$$

such that $\sum_k a_k = S$. Define $Outs(n)$ to be the maximum S such that $n \xrightarrow{S!}$.

We can now describe our functor ar. On objects:

$$ar(\mathcal{N}, n_0, L, \longrightarrow) = (\mathcal{N}/\asymp, \mathcal{A}, [n_0], Outs(n_0), \rightsquigarrow)$$

where $\mathcal{A}$ is the first projection of the label set $L \subseteq \mathcal{A} \times \{!, ?, \tau\}$ and $\rightsquigarrow$ is defined by

$$\begin{array}{l} [n] \overset{a,S}{\rightsquigarrow} [n'] \text{ if } n \xrightarrow{a?} n' \\ [n] \overset{\tau,S}{\rightsquigarrow} [n'] \text{ if } n \xrightarrow{\tau} n' \end{array} \quad \text{and } S = Outs(n') - Outs(n).$$

The reader is invited to check that the asynchrony axioms guarantee that $Outs(n) \subseteq Outs(n')$, thus ensuring that this does define a resource graph.

On morphisms we have that $ar(\sigma, \lambda) = ([\sigma], \lambda, (\sigma; Outs(\_) - Outs(\_); \lambda))$ where $[\sigma][n] = [\sigma n]$ and the third component is applied to any representative of the $\asymp$ equivalence class. This is a well-defined resource graph morphism because of the asynchrony axioms.

Theorem 3.1 *ar is left adjoint to ra, moreover the counit, ra; ar* $\xrightarrow{\varepsilon}$ *Id, of the adjunction is an isomorphism.*

Proof: The counit of the adjunction is $(\varepsilon, Id, C_\bullet)$ where $\varepsilon([(m, S)]) = m$. This is easily seen to be natural and universal and it has an inverse $(Id, \varepsilon^{-1}, C_\bullet)$ where $\varepsilon^{-1}(m) = [(m, \emptyset)]$. Dually, the unit of the adjunction is $(Id, [\_] \times Outs(\_))$. □

We see that the unit of the adjunction does not necessarily have an inverse. This is because in mapping our resource graph to a transition system we consider all configurations of nodes and multisets. This includes many configurations which don't necessarily arise during computation. Thus, if we restrict our attention to those configurations which are *reachable*, in some sense, then we can find an inverse for our unit.

To this end, define the set of *reachable configurations* of a resource graph to be $Reach(m_0, S_0)$ where $Reach$ is defined inductively as follows:

$$\begin{array}{lcl} Reach_0(m, S) & = & \emptyset \\ Reach_{n+1}(m, S) & = & \{(m, S') \mid S' \subseteq S\} \cup \bigcup_{m \overset{a,S''}{\rightsquigarrow} m'} Reach_n(m', S'' + S). \end{array}$$

Let $Reach(m, S) = \bigcup_{n \geq 0} Reach_n(m, S)$.

We immediately note that all reachable configurations of the resource graph $ar(T)$ are of the form $([n], Outs(n))$ for some $n \in T$. Thus, by replacing the set of all configurations $\mathcal{M} \times \mathcal{A}^{**}$ by just the reachable ones, $Reach(m_0, S_0)$, we can obtain an equivalence between the sub-categories of $\mathcal{ATS}$ and $\mathcal{RG}$ whose graphs only contain reachable states.

3.2 A larger category of resource graphs

We now consider a slightly more general category $\mathcal{RGA}$ of which $\mathcal{RG}$ is a lluf sub-category, that is, the objects of $\mathcal{RGA}$ are exactly the objects of $\mathcal{RG}$. The extension lies in the notion of morphism. We relax the definition of morphism of resource graphs in accordance with the motivation outlined in the introduction. The generalisation is tantamount to allowing a τ action of the target graph to be specified as a synchronisation on a particular name. We argued that a synchronisation on channel a is a refinement of the action $a?$ where an extra $a!$ resource is made available. The new notion of morphism utilises this observation.

A morphism of $\mathcal{RGA}$ is a triple $(\sigma, \lambda, \varphi)$ as above, however we ask that the following conditions be satisfied instead:

(i) $\sigma m_0 = m'_0$ as above

(ii) $\lambda S_0 + \varphi m_0 = S'_0$ as above

(iii) $m \overset{\tau,S}{\rightsquigarrow} m'$ implies $\sigma m \overset{\tau,S'}{\rightsquigarrow} \sigma m'$

(iv) $m \overset{a,S}{\rightsquigarrow} m'$ implies

$$\begin{cases} \sigma m \overset{\lambda a,S'}{\rightsquigarrow} \sigma m' \text{ or} \\ \sigma m \overset{\tau,S''}{\rightsquigarrow} \sigma m' \end{cases} \text{if } \lambda a \downarrow$$
$$\sigma m = \sigma m' \text{ and } \lambda S = \emptyset, \varphi m = \varphi m' \quad \text{otherwise}$$

where $S' = \lambda S + \varphi m' - \varphi m$ and $S'' = (\lambda(S - \{a\})) + \varphi m' - \varphi m$. Identities and composition are defined as in $\mathcal{RG}$ and $\mathcal{RGA}$ is also seen to be a category.

3.3 Bisimulation on resource graphs

We propose a definition of bisimulation, suitable for resource graphs, in abstract form. Namely, we use the machinery of open maps, [7], to declare two resource graphs with label the same label set $\mathcal{A}$, bisimilar if there exists a span of open maps between them in the sub-category $\mathcal{RGA}_o$ of $\mathcal{RGA}$. All of this sub-category's objects have label set $\mathcal{A}$ and all morphisms have the identity as the λ component. Furthermore, edges in the graphs of $\mathcal{RGA}_o$ enjoy the following determinacy conditions:

$$m \overset{\alpha,S}{\rightsquigarrow} m' \quad \text{and} \quad m \overset{\alpha,S'}{\rightsquigarrow} m' \quad \text{implies} \quad S = S'$$
$$m \overset{a,S+\{a\}}{\rightsquigarrow} m' \quad \text{and} \quad m \overset{\tau,S'}{\rightsquigarrow} m' \quad \text{implies} \quad S = S'$$

One should note that this determinacy condition is a technical restriction and can easily be enforced in an arbitrary resource graph by simply sending offending pairs of transitions to different targets.

We define *paths* in $\mathcal{RGA}_o$ to be resource graphs of the form

$$m_0 \overset{\alpha_1,S_1}{\rightsquigarrow} m_1 \overset{\alpha_2,S_2}{\rightsquigarrow} \dots \overset{\alpha_k,S_k}{\rightsquigarrow} m_k$$

with initial node m_0 and initial resources S_0.

Recall that we call a morphism $f : R \to R'$ *open* if for all paths P, Q such that the following commutes

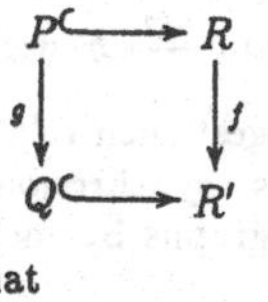

then we have a morphism $h : Q \to R$ such that

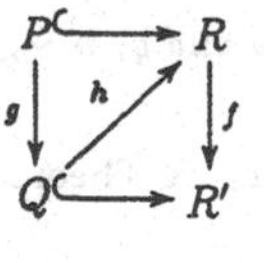

(we use $\hookrightarrow$ to denote inclusion morphisms).

Define bisimulation then as $R \sim_o R'$ iff there exists a

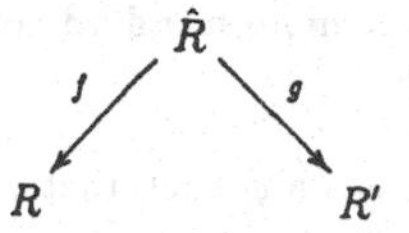

with f, g open. It is easy to see that $\sim_o$ is both reflexive and symmetric, but to prove that it is transitive it is sufficient to check that $\mathcal{RGA}_o$ has pullbacks [7].

Proposition 3.2 *$\mathcal{RGA}_o$ has pullbacks, which makes $\sim_o$ an equivalence relation.*

3.4 Characterising $\sim_o$

The abstract definition of bisimulation using open maps, while being quite general, is not particularly illuminating. For this reason it is natural to seek simpler characterisations of this relation.

To this end we consider the following class of relations. For resource graphs

$$(\mathcal{M}, \mathcal{A}, m_0, S_0, \rightsquigarrow) \text{ and } (\mathcal{M}', \mathcal{A}, m_0', S_0', \rightsquigarrow)$$

such that $S_0 = S_0'$ we call a symmetric relation $\mathcal{B}$ on $\mathcal{M} \times \mathcal{M}'$ a *resource graph bisimulation* if $(m_0, m_0') \in \mathcal{B}$ and whenever $(m_1, m_2) \in \mathcal{B}$ then

- if $m_1 \overset{\tau,S}{\rightsquigarrow} m_1'$ then there exists a m_2' such that $m_2 \overset{\tau,S}{\rightsquigarrow} m_2'$ with $(m_1', m_2') \in \mathcal{B}$
- if $m_1 \overset{a,S}{\rightsquigarrow} m_1'$ then there exists a m_2' such that $m_2 \overset{a,S}{\rightsquigarrow} m_2'$ or $m_2 \overset{\tau,S'}{\rightsquigarrow} m_2'$ with $(m_1', m_2') \in \mathcal{B}$, and $S' + \{a\} = S$.

We write $R \sim_{rg} R'$ if there exists a resource graph bisimulation relating R and R'.

Theorem 3.3 *$\sim_{rg}$ and $\sim_o$ coincide.*

3.5 A model for asynchronous CCS

We recall the notion of asynchronous bisimulation, $\sim_{as}$, as proposed by Amadio, Castellani, Sangiorgi [1] (albeit for the π-calculus and without τ_a actions) and show that the functor ar and the equivalence $\sim_o$ provide a fully abstract interpretation for $\sim_{as}$.

A symmetric relation $\mathcal{B}$ on asynchronous CCS processes is called an asynchronous bisimulation if whenever $(p, q) \in \mathcal{B}$ we have

- if $p \xrightarrow{a!} p'$ then there exists a q' such that $q \xrightarrow{a!} q'$ with $(p', q') \in \mathcal{B}$.
- if $p \xrightarrow{\tau_a} p'$ then there exists a q' such that $q \xrightarrow{\tau_a^\circ} q'$ with $(p', q') \in \mathcal{B}$.
- if $p \xrightarrow{\tau} p'$ then there exists a q' such that $q \xrightarrow{\tau} q'$ with $(p', q') \in \mathcal{B}$.
- if $p \xrightarrow{a?} p'$ then there exists a q' such that $q \xrightarrow{a?} q'$ with $(p', q') \in \mathcal{B}$ or $q \xrightarrow{\tau_a^\circ} q'$ with $(p', a! \parallel q') \in \mathcal{B}$.

Recall that τ_a° means either τ_a or τ. The largest such relation will be denoted $\sim_{as}$.

By considering asynchronous processes as asynchronous transition systems, via operational semantics, we can interpret processes as resource graphs by means of the functor ar. This interpretation is fully abstract for $\sim_{as}$.

Theorem 3.4 *For asynchronous processes p and q, $p \sim_{as} q$ if and only if $ar(p) \sim_o ar(q)$.*

Proof: Show $p \sim_{as} q$ iff $ar(p) \sim_{rg} ar(q)$ and use Theorem 3.3. □

The reader should note that $\sim_{as}$ is an atypical notion of bisimulation for transitions systems and differs from the one in [1] in that τ actions must be matched solely by τ actions, thereby disallowing the possibility of matching with a τ_a action. A more standard notion of equivalence is gained by replacing the third matching condition above with

$$\text{if } p \xrightarrow{\tau} p' \text{ then there exists a } q' \text{ such that } q \xrightarrow{\tau_a^\circ} q' \text{ with } (p', q') \in \mathcal{B}.$$

Let $\sim_{as}^+$ denote the equivalence yielded by this modification. This situation is of course rather unsatisfactory in general, but we can at least console ourselves with the fact that $\sim_{as}$ coincides with the more standard $\sim_{as}^+$ on the class of transition systems for which *Outs* is always finite at each node. In particular $\sim_{as}$ and $\sim_{as}^+$ coincide on our class of regular processes in Section 5.

Proposition 3.5 *$\sim_{as}$ q and $\sim_{as}^+$ coincide on the class of transition systems such that Outs is finite at each node.*

Proof: One inclusion is immediate. For the reverse inclusion we need to show that $\sim_{as}^{+}$ is an asynchronous bisimulation. The only way that $\sim_{as}^{+}$ may fail to be an asynchronous bisimulation is if, given $p \sim_{as}^{+} q$ we have $p \xrightarrow{\tau} p'$ being matched by $q \xrightarrow{\tau_a} q'$ for some q'. We show that there must be a matching τ transition in this case. Now, we know that $Outs(p)$ is finite and that each of these output transitions from p must be matched by q. Therefore there exist p_0, q_0 such that

$$p \xrightarrow{a_1!} \cdots \xrightarrow{a_n!} p_0 \quad \text{and} \quad q \xrightarrow{a_1!} \cdots \xrightarrow{a_n!} q_0,$$

$Outs(p_0) = Outs(q_0) = \emptyset$ and $p_0 \sim_{as}^{+} q_0$. We know that asynchrony ensures $p_0 \xrightarrow{\tau} p_0'$ for some p_0' and that this must be matched by $q_0 \xrightarrow{\tau} q_0'$ because q_0 can no longer perform a τ_a transition as $Outs(q_0) = \emptyset$. Again, by asynchrony we know that $q \xrightarrow{\tau} q''$ for some q''. It is easy to check that $p' \sim_{as}^{+} q''$ follows from $p_0' \sim_{as}^{+} q_0'$. □

4 Game theoretic description of $\sim_o$

We extend our characterisation of asynchronous bisimulation further by showing how the notion can be captured as winning strategies of a suitable game. The use of games to characterise bisimulation has provided a conceptually powerful tool for understanding bisimulation as an equivalence which captures interaction [15]. In our setting the game characterisation helps us understand the rôle of τ as a pair of unspecified, complementary actions.

We give a general definition of what we mean by a *game* and instantiate this definition later to give us our appropriate equivalence. So, a game Γ, is a quadruple $(C, c_0, \triangleright, \lambda)$ where C is a set of configurations with a specified initial configuration c_0. The relation $\triangleright \subseteq C \times C$ comprises the rules of the game. This relation tells us how play may continue from one move to the next. The function $\lambda : C \to \{O, P\}$ labels moves as either Opponent or Player moves according to who is next to play - we require $\lambda c_0 = O$ and $\lambda c \neq \lambda c'$ whenever $c \triangleright c'$. A play of a game is a sequence

$$c_0 \triangleright c_1 \triangleright c_2 \triangleright \cdots \triangleright c_k \triangleright \cdots$$

We write $P(\Gamma)$ for the set of all plays and abuse notation by writing λcs to mean the label of the last move of cs (if it exists). A play, cs, is called maximal if it is infinite or cannot be extended, that is there is no move c such that $cs \triangleright c$.

We say that O wins the finite play cs if $\lambda cs = P$ and cs is maximal. Dually, we say that P wins a (possibly) infinite play if $\lambda cs = O$ and the play is maximal. A strategy for O is a partial function from $Pos(O) = \{cs \mid \lambda cs = O\}$ to $M(P) = \{c \mid \lambda c = P\}$. We can define a strategy for P similarly.

Given an O-strategy π_o, we write $P(\pi_o)$ for

$$\{cs \in P(\Gamma) \mid \forall cs' \sqsubset cs \cdot \lambda cs' = O \text{ implies } (cs' \triangleright \pi_o(cs')) \sqsubset cs\}$$

where $\sqsubset$ is the prefix ordering on plays. We say that the strategy π_o is winning if all maximal plays of $P(\pi_o)$ are finite and labelled P.

Dually, we can define $P(\pi_p)$ for player strategies π_p and say that π_p is winning if all maximal plays of $P(\pi_p)$ are infinite or labelled O.

4.1 The asynchronous bisimulation game

We can now describe the game which characterises asynchronous bisimulation simply by describing the configurations of the game and the rules. Before formally defining these however, we give an intuitive explanation of the game.

Imagine a table containing a pile of cards, labelled with names from some set $\mathcal{A}$, arranged in such a way as to model a resource graph. In addition to this pile of cards there is a hand of cards kept as a reserve. So, if the resource graph has a $m \overset{a,S}{\rightsquigarrow} m'$ transition, this means there will be an a card available for play from the pile. If it is played then the cards in S must be picked up and kept in the reserve hand and the pile of cards will now reflect state m'. If the resource graph has a $m \overset{\tau,S}{\rightsquigarrow} m'$ transition then the player has a blank card available. If she wishes to play this blank card she must pencil in a name, play

Left Rules: If $d \in \{L, E\}$

Table:

$$((m,S),(m',S'),zs,d) \rhd ((m'',S+S''),(m',S'),a?zs,\bar{d})$$
$$\text{if } m \overset{a,S''}{\rightsquigarrow} m'' \text{ and } d = L \text{ implies } hd(zs) = a?$$

Reserve:

$$((m,S),(m',S'),zs,d) \rhd ((m,S-\{a\}),(m',S'),a!zs,\bar{d})$$
$$\text{if } d = L \text{ implies } hd(zs) = a!$$

Blank:

$$((m,S),(m',S'),zs,d) \rhd ((m'',S+S''+\{a\}),(m',S'),a?zs,\bar{d})$$
$$\text{if } m \overset{\tau,S''}{\rightsquigarrow} m'' \text{ and } d = L \text{ implies } hd(zs) = a!$$

Right Rules: If $d \in \{R, E\}$

Table:

$$((m,S),(m',S'),zs,d) \rhd ((m,S),(m'',S'+S''),a?zs,\underline{d})$$
$$\text{if } m' \overset{a,S''}{\rightsquigarrow} m'' \text{ and } d = R \text{ implies } hd(zs) = a?$$

Reserve:

$$((m,S),(m',S'),zs,d) \rhd ((m,S),(m',S'-\{a\}),a!zs,\underline{d})$$
$$\text{if } d = R \text{ implies } hd(zs) = a!$$

Blank:

$$((m,S),(m',S'),zs,d) \rhd ((m,S),(m'',S'+S''+\{a\}),a?zs,\underline{d})$$
$$\text{if } m' \overset{\tau,S''}{\rightsquigarrow} m'' \text{ and } d = R \text{ implies } hd(zs) = a!$$

where $\bar{L} = E$, $\bar{E} = R$ and $\underline{R} = E$, $\underline{E} = L$.

Figure 3: Rules for asynchronous bisimulation game

---

it, pick up the cards in S for the reserve hand and in addition to these must fill in a blank card with the same name and place it in the reserve hand. A card from the reserve hand may be played irrespective of the pile of cards representing the resource graph.

A configuration of our game is a pair of the above tables, that is, two tables with a pile of cards and a separate reserve hand each. At each turn, Opponent can play a card from either table and Player must play the same card from the other table. The only extra condition is that a card from a reserve hand is played by Player if and only if Opponent has played her card from a reserve hand.

Opponent always starts and play continues until one of the players becomes stuck. Opponent wins if Player becomes stuck and Player wins otherwise.

To formalise this, given two resource graphs

$$R = (\mathcal{M}, \mathcal{A}, m_0, S_0, \rightsquigarrow) \text{ and } R' = (\mathcal{M}', \mathcal{A}, m_0', S_0', \rightsquigarrow)$$

we describe the game $\Gamma_A(R, R')$ as the quadruple $(\mathcal{C}, c_0, \rhd, \lambda)$ where $\mathcal{C}$ is the set of all

$$((m,S),(m',S'),zs,d)$$

such that $m \in \mathcal{M}$, $m' \in \mathcal{M}'$, $S, S' \in \mathcal{A}^{**}$, $zs \in (\mathcal{A} \times \{!,?\})^{**}$ and $d \in \{L, R, E\}$. Clearly, the nodes of the resource graphs represents the pile of cards on the tables and the respective multisets represent the reserve hands. We use the list zs to represent the cards that have already been played and d merely to indicate which table must be played from next, the *Left*, *Right* or Either. The cards in zs are tagged with a ! or a ? to indicate whether the card was played from a table or a reserve hand. It should be no surprise then that the initial configuration is

$$c_0 = ((m_0, S_0), (m_0', S_0'), \varepsilon, E).$$

We can label moves by using the last component so that $\lambda c = P$ if $d \in \{L, R\}$ and $\lambda c = O$ if $d = E$. The rules for the game are given in Figure 3 and fall into three pairs of symmetric rules which describe the moves of playing a card from the table, the reserve hand and playing a blank card by penciling in a name.

We write $R \sim_\Gamma R'$ if there exists a winning Player strategy according to the rules of $\Gamma_A(R, R')$. It is simple enough to see that this is indeed an equivalence relation, in fact this is exactly resource graph bisimulation.

Theorem 4.1 *$\sim_{rg}$ coincides with $\sim_\Gamma$.*

Proof: It is easy to see that $\sim_{rg} \subseteq \sim_\Gamma$. For the reverse inclusion, given a winning strategy, it is sufficient to build a bisimulation relation. This is constructed as pairs of nodes which occur in the configurations of plays according to the winning strategy. We take exactly those pairs which occur after Player moves. To see that this will be a resource graph bisimulation we note that τ transitions must be matched by τ transitions — otherwise Opponent could win by choosing a fresh name to pencil in on the blank card given by the τ action. Player couldn't hope to match this unless he had also had a τ move available. To see that the resources being collected by each graph must be identical we note that, otherwise, Opponent could win by simply playing a move from the larger of the two reserve hands. □

5 Regular asynchronous processes

We hinted earlier that our new model would lend itself to providing a notion of *regular* process for asynchronous calculi whereby regular terms have finite graphs. By *finite* graph we mean finitely many nodes, finitely many transitions and each resource multiset is finite. So far we have interpreted asynchronous CCS in $\mathcal{RG}$ indirectly by first giving an $\mathcal{ATS}$ semantics and then applying the functor ar. This approach suffices for modelling our language; indeed, to establish a regular term/finite resource graph relationship one need only show that the equivalence relation used by the functor ar has finite index on transition systems generated by regular terms. However, this method is slightly unsatisfactory as it involves building potentially infinite graphs and collapsing them. What would be more pleasing is a direct interpretation of $aCCS$ in $\mathcal{RGA}$ by which regular terms immediately receive finite graph models. Furthermore, we should require that this interpretation be compositional and coincides (up to equivalence) with the indirect interpretation.

In fact, for our purposes it suffices to interpret what we will refer to as *(asynchronously) regular* terms of $aCCS$. These can be characterised by the following grammar

$$p ::= \mathbf{nil} \mid X \mid a! \parallel p \mid p \parallel a! \mid \sum_I \alpha_i.p_i \mid \mathbf{rec}\, X.p$$

where I is a finite indexing set, X is drawn from some set of variables Var, the α_i are either $a?$ or τ and all recursions are guarded. We adopt the conventional notions of free and bound variables here.

To interpret recursion, we take the approach of [9] and augment resource graphs with an extra component. This new component, $\lhd$ is a relation on nodes of the graph and the ambient set of recursion variables, Var. We say that a variable, X, is *unguarded* at a node m if $m \lhd X$ and we call a resource graph *closed* if $\lhd$ is the empty relation.

We make use of the following operators on resource graphs: firstly, we note that resource graphs have a tensor product structure, $\otimes$, with unit I. Given graphs

$$R = (\mathcal{M}, \mathcal{A}, m_0, S_0, \rightsquigarrow, \lhd)$$

and

$$R' = (\mathcal{M}', \mathcal{A}', m'_0, S'_0, \rightsquigarrow, \lhd')$$

this is defined in the obvious way as

$$R \otimes R' = (\mathcal{M} \times \mathcal{M}', \mathcal{A} + \mathcal{A}', (m_0, m'_0), S_0 + S'_0, \rightsquigarrow_\otimes, \lhd \cup \lhd')$$

where

$$(m,n) \overset{\alpha,S}{\rightsquigarrow}_{\otimes} (m',n) \quad \text{if } m \overset{\alpha,S}{\rightsquigarrow} m'$$
$$(m,n) \overset{\alpha,S}{\rightsquigarrow}_{\otimes} (m,n') \quad \text{if } n \overset{\alpha,S}{\rightsquigarrow} n'.$$

The tensor unit is $I = (\{\bullet\}, \emptyset, \bullet, \emptyset, \emptyset, \emptyset)$. The definition of $\otimes$ easily lifts to morphisms to become a bifunctor on $\mathcal{RGA}$.

We interpret an output action $a!$ as the resource graph

$$(\{\bullet\}, \{a\}, \bullet, \{a\}, \emptyset, \emptyset)$$

and we will refer to this graph simply by $a!$. Similarly, use the name X to refer to the resource graph

$$(\{\bullet\}, \emptyset, \bullet, \emptyset, \emptyset, \{(\bullet, X)\}).$$

Another useful operation is that of the lifted sum of resource graphs. Given an I indexed set of graphs R_i, an I indexed set of actions α_i, and a multiset S, we define

$$\sum(\alpha_i, R_i) = ((\bigcup \mathcal{M}_i) + \{\bullet\}, \bigcup \mathcal{A}_i \cup \{\alpha_i \mid \alpha_i \neq \tau\}, \bullet, \emptyset, \rightsquigarrow_{\perp}, \bigcup \lhd_i)$$

where $\rightsquigarrow_{\perp} = \bigcup_i \rightsquigarrow_i \cup \left\{\bullet \overset{\alpha_i, S_{0i}}{\rightsquigarrow} m_{0i}\right\}$.

Finally, we describe how we interpret recursion over resource graphs. Given a graph R, we define **rec** $X.R$ to be the graph

$$(\mathcal{M}, \mathcal{A}, m_0, S_0, \rightsquigarrow_+, \lhd_+)$$

where $\lhd_+$ is just $\lhd$ with all pairs (m, X) removed. $\rightsquigarrow_+$ is defined in two steps. Firstly, define

$$m \overset{\alpha,S}{\rightsquigarrow}_1 m' \quad \text{if} \quad m \overset{\alpha,S}{\rightsquigarrow} m' \quad \text{and } m' \not\lhd X$$
$$m \overset{\alpha,S+S_0}{\rightsquigarrow}_1 m' \quad \text{if} \quad m \overset{\alpha,S}{\rightsquigarrow} m' \quad \text{and } m' \lhd X.$$

Then, let $m \overset{\alpha,S}{\rightsquigarrow}_+ m'$ if $m_0 \overset{\alpha,S}{\rightsquigarrow}_1 m'$ and $m \lhd X$, or $m \overset{\alpha,S}{\rightsquigarrow}_1 m'$.

The informed reader will notice that this definition of recursion differs slightly from that in [9] and is not sufficient to model general recursion, but we exploit the property that regular terms never have more than one unguarded variable to give a simple definition.

These operators now allow us to interpret regular terms of *aCCS* in the desired manner:

$$\begin{aligned}
[\![\,\mathbf{nil}\,]\!] &= I \\
[\![X]\!] &= X \\
[\![a! \parallel p]\!] &= a! \otimes [\![p]\!] \\
[\![p \parallel a!]\!] &= [\![p]\!] \otimes a! \\
[\![\textstyle\sum \alpha_i.p_i]\!] &= \textstyle\sum(\alpha_i, [\![p_i]\!]) \\
[\![\mathbf{rec}\, X.p]\!] &= \mathbf{rec}\, X.[\![p]\!].
\end{aligned}$$

Let $\hat{p}$ denote the transition system that would model p using the standard SOS semantics of CCS.

Proposition 5.1

(i) The resource graph $[\![p]\!]$ *is finite for any regular term* p.

(ii) If p *is closed then* $[\![p]\!]$ *is a closed graph.*

(iii) Every finite closed graph is $\sim_{rg}$ *equivalent to* $[\![p]\!]$ *for some regular* p.

(iv) $ar(\hat{p}) \sim_{rg} [\![p]\!]$.

This firmly establishes the correspondence between asynchronously regular terms and finite resource graphs.

5.1 Deciding bisimulation equivalence

To see the usefulness of having finite models we need only look at the problem of deciding bisimulation equivalence. It is evident that $\sim_{as}$ will be a decidable equivalence over asynchronously regular terms due to work on infinite state transition systems [3]. Specifically, asynchronously regular terms are a small subclass of BPP and bisimulation equivalence is decidable over this class of processes. What is not clear however is the complexity of this decision procedure. The proofs that bisimulation equivalence is decidable over BPP do not provide any upper bounds for the decision procedure [5, 11]. The class of asynchronously regular processes are much simpler than BPP and therefore allow us to find such bounds. In fact, because our models for this class are finite then standard techniques apply [8, 12].

Theorem 5.2 *Asynchronous bisimulation equivalence, $\sim_{as}$, is decidable in polynomial time for (asynchronously) regular processes.*

Proof: In order to decide $P \sim_{as} Q$, by Proposition 5.1, Proposition 3.5 and Theorem 3.4 it is sufficient to check $[P] \sim_{rg} [Q]$. We know by Proposition 5.1, (i) that these resource graphs are finite. The decision procedure now follows by first checking the initial resource sets of each graphs, and then solving the partition refinement problem of [12] for the finite set of relations

$$\begin{array}{lll} mE_{\tau,S}m' & \text{if} & m \overset{\tau,S}{\rightsquigarrow} m' \\ mE_{a,S}m' & \text{if} & m \overset{a,S}{\rightsquigarrow} m' \\ mE^{+}_{a,S}m' & \text{if} & m \overset{a,S+\{a\}}{\rightsquigarrow} m' \text{ or } m \overset{\tau,S}{\rightsquigarrow} m'. \end{array}$$

These relations are finite in number because we know that only finitely many names are used and only finitely many different S appear on the edges of our graphs. □

We have now provided a notion of regularity for asynchronous processes which allows much more expressivity than the standard notion of regularity for CCS. We have also shown that a suitable notion of bisimulation equivalence is polynomial time decidable over this class of processes. Unfortunately though, this enhanced notion of regularity is not as robust as we would like. In particular, it is the case that one can form parallel compositions and restrictions of CCS regular terms and stay within the class of regular processes [9, 10]. Sadly, this is not the case in the present work. Whilst parallel composition preserves finiteness of the models of regular terms, the restriction of such graphs does not. In fact, using the familiar argument of reducing bisimulation equivalence to the halting problem for two-counter Minsky Machines [11] we can show that allowing restriction of regular terms, unsurprisingly, entails undecidability of our equivalence.

We conclude this section by briefly mentioning that the direct interpretation of asynchronously regular CCS terms as resource graphs can be extended to whole of *aCCS* in such a way as to ensure that Proposition 5.1, (iv) still holds. This extension is non-trivial however and involves defining both the recursion and restriction operators on graphs as the least fixed point of certain functionals so that the resulting resource graphs may become infinite.

6 Conclusion

We have presented a novel approach to modelling asynchronous systems. The chief feature of these new models is the treatment of asynchronous transmission as the use of resources. Resource graphs yield a direct presentation of asynchronous behaviour, without recourse to various commutativity axioms. They also provide a compact representation of many infinite state systems, thereby allowing effective procedures for deciding bisimilarity. We discovered that the somewhat unorthodox notion of asynchronous bisimilarity arises naturally in the category of resource graphs and provided insightful characterisations of this equivalence.

The present work is concerned with synchronising processes rather than communicating processes, that is, no information is transmitted by output actions. Therefore a treatment of asynchrony in the π-calculus is beyond the scope of resource graphs as presented. An issue worth further investigation is a generalisation of the resource graph model which could cater for name passing and dynamic scoping as can be found in the π-calculus.

References

[1] R. Amadio, I. Castellani, and D. Sangiorgi. On bisimulations for the asynchronous π-calculus. In U. Montanari and V.Sassone, editors, *Proceedings CONCUR 96,* Pisa, volume 1119 of *Lecture Notes in Computer Science*, pages 147–162. Springer-Verlag, 1996.

[2] G. Boudol. Asynchrony and the π-calculus. Technical Report 1702, INRIA, Sophia-Antipolis, 1991.

[3] S. Christensen, Y. Hirshfield, and F. Moller. Bisimulation equivalence is decidable for basic parallel processes. In E. Best, editor, *Proceedings CONCUR 93*, Hildesheim, volume 715 of *Lecture Notes in Computer Science*, pages 143–157. Springer-Verlag, 1993.

[4] C. Fournet and G. Gonthier. The reflexive CHAM and the join-calculus. In *Proc. ACM-POPL*, 1996.

[5] Y. Hirshfeld, M. Jerrum, and F. Moller. A polynomial algorithm for deciding bisimulation equivalence of normed basic parallel processes. In *Proc. Mathematical Structures in Computer Science*, 1996.

[6] K. Honda and M. Tokoro. An object calculus for asynchronous communication. In *Proc. ECOOP 91, Geneve*, 1991.

[7] A. Joyal, M. Nielsen, and G. Winskel. Bisimulation and open maps. In *Proceedings* 8th *Annual Symposium on Logic in Computer Science*, pages 418–427. IEEE Computer Society Press, 1993.

[8] P.C. Kanellakis and S.A. Smolka. CCS expressions, finite state processes, and three problems of equivalence. *Information and Computation*, 86:43–68, 1990.

[9] R. Milner. A complete inference system for a class of regular behaviours. *Journal of Computer and System Sciences*, 28:439–466, 1984.

[10] R. Milner. *Communication and Concurrency*. Prentice-Hall International, Englewood Cliffs, 1989.

[11] F. Moller. Infinite results. In U. Montanari and V.Sassone, editors, *Proceedings CONCUR 96*, Pisa, volume 1119 of *Lecture Notes in Computer Science*, pages 195–216. Springer-Verlag, 1996.

[12] R. Paige and R. Tarjan. Three partition refinement algorithms. *SIAM Journal on Computing*, 16(6):973–989, 1987.

[13] B. Pierce and D. Turner. Pict: A programming language based on the π-calculus, 1996. Univeristy of Cambridge.

[14] P. Selinger. First-order axioms for asynchrony. In M. Bednarczyk, editor, *Proceedings CONCUR 97*, Warsaw, volume 1243 of *Lecture Notes in Computer Science*, pages 376–390. Springer-Verlag, 1997.

[15] C. Stirling. Bisimulation, model checking and other games, 1997. Notes for Mathfit Instructional Meeting on Games and Computation, University of Edinburgh.

[16] G. Winskel and M. Nielsen. Models for concurrency. In S. Abramsky, Dov M. Gabbay, and T.S.E. Maibaum, editors, *Handbook of Logic in Computer Science, Volume 4*, pages 1–148. Oxford University Press, 1995.

Author Index

Aceto, L. 20
Albayrak, C. A. 35
Amadio, R. M. 48

Baldan, P. 63
Beauquier, D. 81
Boreale, M. 95
Bottreau, A. 110
Bukatin, M. A. 125

Cardelli, L. 140
Corradini, A. 156
Corradini, A. 63
Coupet-Grimal, S. 48

Dauchet, M. 258
De Nicola, R. 95
Durand, B. 258

Fokkink, W. 20

Gadducci, F. 156
Gordon, A. D. 140

Heckmann, R. 172

Ingólfsdóttir, A. 20

Klempien-Hinrichs, R. 189

Matz, O. 203
Métivier, Y. 110
Mislove, M. 1
Moggi, E. 211
Montanari, U. 63
Muscholl, A. 226

Niemann, G. 243
Noll, T. 35

Otto, F. 243

Peled, D. 226
Porrot, S. 258
Pugliese, R. 95

Rathke, J. 273

Shorina, S. Y. 125
Su, Z. 226

Vereshchagin, N. K. 258

Lecture Notes in Computer Science

For information about Vols. 1–1300

please contact your bookseller or Springer-Verlag

Vol. 1301: M. Jazayeri, H. Schauer (Eds.), Software Engineering - ESEC/FSE'97. Proceedings, 1997. XIII, 532 pages. 1997.

Vol. 1302: P. Van Hentenryck (Ed.), Static Analysis. Proceedings, 1997. X, 413 pages. 1997.

Vol. 1303: G. Brewka, C. Habel, B. Nebel (Eds.), KI-97: Advances in Artificial Intelligence. Proceedings, 1997. XI, 413 pages. 1997. (Subseries LNAI).

Vol. 1304: W. Luk, P.Y.K. Cheung, M. Glesner (Eds.), Field-Programmable Logic and Applications. Proceedings, 1997. XI, 503 pages. 1997.

Vol. 1305: D. Corne, J.L. Shapiro (Eds.), Evolutionary Computing. Proceedings, 1997. X, 307 pages. 1997.

Vol. 1306: C. Leung (Ed.), Visual Information Systems. X, 274 pages. 1997.

Vol. 1307: R. Kompe, Prosody in Speech Understanding Systems. XIX, 357 pages. 1997. (Subseries LNAI).

Vol. 1308: A. Hameurlain, A M. Tjoa (Eds.), Database and Expert Systems Applications. Proceedings, 1997. XVII, 688 pages. 1997.

Vol. 1309: R. Steinmetz, L.C. Wolf (Eds.), Interactive Distributed Multimedia Systems and Telecommunication Services. Proceedings, 1997. XIII, 466 pages. 1997.

Vol. 1310: A. Del Bimbo (Ed.), Image Analysis and Processing. Proceedings, 1997. Volume I. XXII, 722 pages. 1997.

Vol. 1311: A. Del Bimbo (Ed.), Image Analysis and Processing. Proceedings, 1997. Volume II. XXII, 794 pages. 1997.

Vol. 1312: A. Geppert, M. Berndtsson (Eds.), Rules in Database Systems. Proceedings, 1997. VII, 214 pages. 1997.

Vol. 1313: J. Fitzgerald, C.B. Jones, P. Lucas (Eds.), FME '97: Industrial Applications and Strengthened Foundations of Formal Methods. Proceedings, 1997. XIII, 685 pages. 1997.

Vol. 1314: S. Muggleton (Ed.), Inductive Logic Programming. Proceedings, 1996. VIII, 397 pages. 1997. (Subseries LNAI).

Vol. 1315: G. Sommer, J.J. Koenderink (Eds.), Algebraic Frames for the Perception-Action Cycle. Proceedings, 1997. VIII, 395 pages. 1997.

Vol. 1316: M. Li, A. Maruoka (Eds.), Algorithmic Learning Theory. Proceedings, 1997. XI, 461 pages. 1997. (Subseries LNAI).

Vol. 1317: M. Leman (Ed.), Music, Gestalt, and Computing. IX, 524 pages. 1997. (Subseries LNAI).

Vol. 1318: R. Hirschfeld (Ed.), Financial Cryptography. Proceedings, 1997. XI, 409 pages. 1997.

Vol. 1319: E. Plaza, R. Benjamins (Eds.), Knowledge Acquisition, Modeling and Management. Proceedings, 1997. XI, 389 pages. 1997. (Subseries LNAI).

Vol. 1320: M. Mavronicolas, P. Tsigas (Eds.), Distributed Algorithms. Proceedings, 1997. X, 333 pages. 1997.

Vol. 1321: M. Lenzerini (Ed.), AI*IA 97: Advances in Artificial Intelligence. Proceedings, 1997. XII, 459 pages. 1997. (Subseries LNAI).

Vol. 1322: H. Hußmann, Formal Foundations for Software Engineering Methods. X, 286 pages. 1997.

Vol. 1323: E. Costa, A. Cardoso (Eds.), Progress in Artificial Intelligence. Proceedings, 1997. XIV, 393 pages. 1997. (Subseries LNAI).

Vol. 1324: C. Peters, C. Thanos (Eds.), Research and Advanced Technology for Digital Libraries. Proceedings, 1997. X, 423 pages. 1997.

Vol. 1325: Z.W. Raś, A. Skowron (Eds.), Foundations of Intelligent Systems. Proceedings, 1997. XI, 630 pages. 1997. (Subseries LNAI).

Vol. 1326: C. Nicholas, J. Mayfield (Eds.), Intelligent Hypertext. XIV, 182 pages. 1997.

Vol. 1327: W. Gerstner, A. Germond, M. Hasler, J.-D. Nicoud (Eds.), Artificial Neural Networks – ICANN '97. Proceedings, 1997. XIX, 1274 pages. 1997.

Vol. 1328: C. Retoré (Ed.), Logical Aspects of Computational Linguistics. Proceedings, 1996. VIII, 435 pages. 1997. (Subseries LNAI).

Vol. 1329: S.C. Hirtle, A.U. Frank (Eds.), Spatial Information Theory. Proceedings, 1997. XIV, 511 pages. 1997.

Vol. 1330: G. Smolka (Ed.), Principles and Practice of Constraint Programming – CP 97. Proceedings, 1997. XII, 563 pages. 1997.

Vol. 1331: D. W. Embley, R. C. Goldstein (Eds.), Conceptual Modeling – ER '97. Proceedings, 1997. XV, 479 pages. 1997.

Vol. 1332: M. Bubak, J. Dongarra, J. Waśniewski (Eds.), Recent Advances in Parallel Virtual Machine and Message Passing Interface. Proceedings, 1997. XV, 518 pages. 1997.

Vol. 1333: F. Pichler. R.Moreno-Díaz (Eds.), Computer Aided Systems Theory – EUROCAST'97. Proceedings, 1997. XII, 626 pages. 1997.

Vol. 1334: Y. Han, T. Okamoto, S. Qing (Eds.), Information and Communications Security. Proceedings, 1997. X, 484 pages. 1997.

Vol. 1335: R.H. Möhring (Ed.), Graph-Theoretic Concepts in Computer Science. Proceedings, 1997. X, 376 pages. 1997.

Vol. 1336: C. Polychronopoulos, K. Joe, K. Araki, M. Amamiya (Eds.), High Performance Computing. Proceedings, 1997. XII, 416 pages. 1997.

Vol. 1337: C. Freksa, M. Jantzen, R. Valk (Eds.), Foundations of Computer Science. XII, 515 pages. 1997.

Vol. 1338: F. Plášil, K.G. Jeffery (Eds.), SOFSEM'97: Theory and Practice of Informatics. Proceedings, 1997. XIV, 571 pages. 1997.

Vol. 1339: N.A. Murshed, F. Bortolozzi (Eds.), Advances in Document Image Analysis. Proceedings, 1997. IX, 345 pages. 1997.

Vol. 1340: M. van Kreveld, J. Nievergelt, T. Roos, P. Widmayer (Eds.), Algorithmic Foundations of Geographic Information Systems. XIV, 287 pages. 1997.

Vol. 1341: F. Bry, R. Ramakrishnan, K. Ramamohanarao (Eds.), Deductive and Object-Oriented Databases. Proceedings, 1997. XIV, 430 pages. 1997.

Vol. 1342: A. Sattar (Ed.), Advanced Topics in Artificial Intelligence. Proceedings, 1997. XVII, 516 pages. 1997. (Subseries LNAI).

Vol. 1343: Y. Ishikawa, R.R. Oldehoeft, J.V.W. Reynders, M. Tholburn (Eds.), Scientific Computing in Object-Oriented Parallel Environments. Proceedings, 1997. XI, 295 pages. 1997.

Vol. 1344: C. Ausnit-Hood, K.A. Johnson, R.G. Pettit, IV, S.B. Opdahl (Eds.), Ada 95 – Quality and Style. XV, 292 pages. 1997.

Vol. 1345: R.K. Shyamasundar, K. Ueda (Eds.), Advances in Computing Science - ASIAN'97. Proceedings, 1997. XIII, 387 pages. 1997.

Vol. 1346: S. Ramesh, G. Sivakumar (Eds.), Foundations of Software Technology and Theoretical Computer Science. Proceedings, 1997. XI, 343 pages. 1997.

Vol. 1347: E. Ahronovitz, C. Fiorio (Eds.), Discrete Geometry for Computer Imagery. Proceedings, 1997. X, 255 pages. 1997.

Vol. 1348: S. Steel, R. Alami (Eds.), Recent Advances in AI Planning. Proceedings, 1997. IX, 454 pages. 1997. (Subseries LNAI).

Vol. 1349: M. Johnson (Ed.), Algebraic Methodology and Software Technology. Proceedings, 1997. X, 594 pages. 1997.

Vol. 1350: H.W. Leong, H. Imai, S. Jain (Eds.), Algorithms and Computation. Proceedings, 1997. XV, 426 pages. 1997.

Vol. 1351: R. Chin, T.-C. Pong (Eds.), Computer Vision – ACCV'98. Proceedings Vol. I, 1998. XXIV, 761 pages. 1997.

Vol. 1352: R. Chin, T.-C. Pong (Eds.), Computer Vision – ACCV'98. Proceedings Vol. II, 1998. XXIV, 757 pages. 1997.

Vol. 1353: G. BiBattista (Ed.), Graph Drawing. Proceedings, 1997. XII, 448 pages. 1997.

Vol. 1354: O. Burkart, Automatic Verification of Sequential Infinite-State Processes. X, 163 pages. 1997.

Vol. 1355: M. Darnell (Ed.), Cryptography and Coding. Proceedings, 1997. IX, 335 pages. 1997.

Vol. 1356: A. Danthine, Ch. Diot (Eds.), From Multimedia Services to Network Services. Proceedings, 1997. XII, 180 pages. 1997.

Vol. 1357: J. Bosch, S. Mitchell (Eds.), Object-Oriented Technology. Proceedings, 1997. XIV, 555 pages. 1998.

Vol. 1358: B. Thalheim, L. Libkin (Eds.), Semantics in Databases. XI, 265 pages. 1998.

Vol. 1360: D. Wang (Ed.), Automated Deduction in Geometry. Proceedings, 1996. VII, 235 pages. 1998. (Subseries LNAI).

Vol. 1361: B. Christianson, B. Crispo, M. Lomas, M. Roe (Eds.), Security Protocols. Proceedings, 1997. VIII, 217 pages. 1998.

Vol. 1362: D.K. Panda, C.B. Stunkel (Eds.), Network-Based Parallel Computing. Proceedings, 1998. X, 247 pages. 1998.

Vol. 1363: J.-K. Hao, E. Lutton, E. Ronald, M. Schoenauer, D. Snyers (Eds.), Artificial Evolution. XI, 349 pages. 1998.

Vol. 1364: W. Conen, G. Neumann (Eds.), Coordination Technology for Collaborative Applications. VIII, 282 pages. 1998.

Vol. 1365: M.P. Singh, A. Rao, M.J. Wooldridge (Eds.), Intelligent Agents IV. Proceedings, 1997. XII, 351 pages. 1998. (Subseries LNAI).

Vol. 1367: E.W. Mayr, H.J. Prömel, A. Steger (Eds.), Lectures on Proof Verification and Approximation Algorithms. XII, 344 pages. 1998.

Vol. 1368: Y. Masunaga, T. Katayama, M. Tsukamoto (Eds.), Worldwide Computing and Its Applications — WWCA'98. Proceedings, 1998. XIV, 473 pages. 1998.

Vol. 1370: N.A. Streitz, S. Konomi, H.-J. Burkhardt (Eds.), Cooperative Buildings. Proceedings, 1998. XI, 267 pages. 1998.

Vol. 1372: S. Vaudenay (Ed.), Fast Software Encryption. Proceedings, 1998. VIII, 297 pages. 1998.

Vol. 1373: M. Morvan, C. Meinel, D. Krob (Eds.), STACS 98. Proceedings, 1998. XV, 630 pages. 1998.

Vol. 1375: R. D. Hersch, J. André, H. Brown (Eds.), Electronic Publishing, Artistic Imaging, and Digital Typography. Proceedings, 1998. XIII, 575 pages. 1998.

Vol. 1376: F. Parisi Presicce (Ed.), Recent Trends in Algebraic Development Techniques. Proceedings, 1997. VIII, 435 pages. 1998.

Vol. 1377: H.-J. Schek, F. Saltor, I. Ramos, G. Alonso (Eds.), Advances in Database Technology – EDBT'98. Proceedings, 1998. XII, 515 pages. 1998.

Vol. 1378: M. Nivat (Ed.), Foundations of Software Science and Computation Structures. Proceedings, 1998. X, 289 pages. 1998.

Vol. 1379: T. Nipkow (Ed.), Rewriting Techniques and Applications. Proceedings, 1998. X, 343 pages. 1998.

Vol. 1380: C.L. Lucchesi, A.V. Moura (Eds.), LATIN'98: Theoretical Informatics. Proceedings, 1998. XI, 391 pages. 1998.

Vol. 1381: C. Hankin (Ed.), Programming Languages and Systems. Proceedings, 1998. X, 283 pages. 1998.

Vol. 1382: E. Astesiano (Ed.), Fundamental Approaches to Software Engineering. Proceedings, 1998. XII, 331 pages. 1998.

Vol. 1383: K. Koskimies (Ed.), Compiler Construction. Proceedings, 1998. X, 309 pages. 1998.